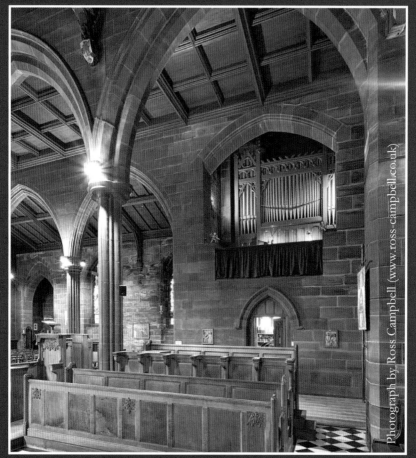

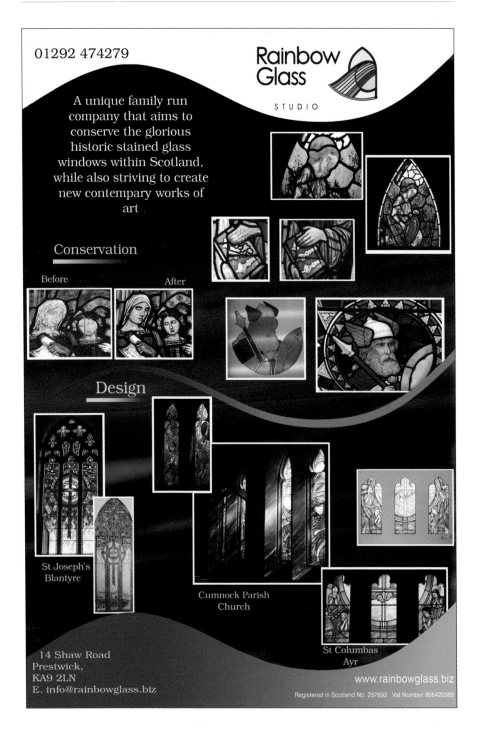

'The Earth is the Lord's and all that is in it; the world, and those who live in it'

Psalm 24:1

Keep in touch with Christian Aid Scotland:

caid.org.uk/Scotland

facebook.com/ ChristianAidScotland

glasgow@christian- aid.org

We believe in life before death

Christian Aid helps communities adapt to the effects of climate change. In this village in Ethiopia, a new solar-powered water system has given women like Ayilu Ayuki much easier access to water.

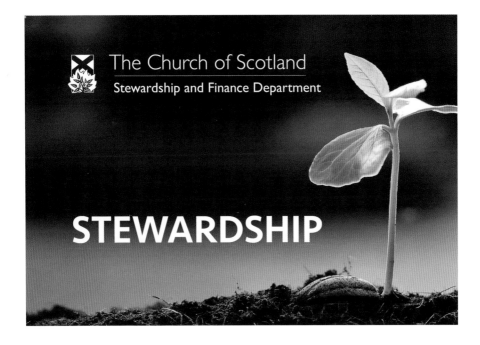

We offer tailored Stewardship programmes for your church.

Inspire and motivate your members with our **money, time and talents** programmes.

Contact us to book your own consultant to work alongside your congregation at **no charge**.

We also assist with:
• Using GRANTfinder to search for potential funders for your project
• Web and text donations, legacies and Gift Aid advice

Email: sfadmin@churchofscotland.org.uk
Tel: 0131 225 5722

Scottish Charity Number: SC011353

www.churchofscotland.org.uk/stewardship

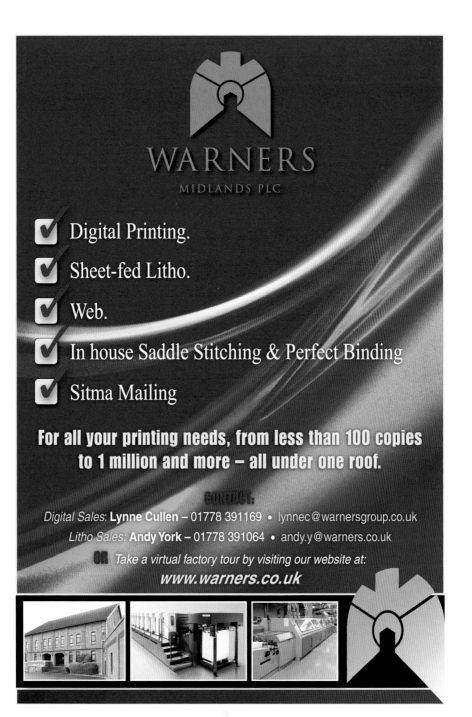

The Right Reverend Derek Browning MA BD DMin

MODERATOR

FROM THE MODERATOR

In a digital age where some wonder about the purpose and point of books, I find that there is something comforting and inclusive in the annual arrival of the Year Book. There has been a move to use more digital means at the General Assembly and particularly with the 'Blue Book' but a decision has been taken that will mean that there will continue to be a print publication, partly because not everyone has access to (or wants to use) electronic equipment, and partly because with the rapid changes in tecŸology, who can prophesy what will be in use ten or twenty years from now? Books, however, go on for centuries!

Our Year Book is part compendium of information, part statistical return, part address book, and part family album. Within its covers it encompasses much of the recorded work of the Church of Scotland. It tells stories of different ministries, situations, initiatives and forms of service. Even the briefest of perusals gives a contemporary context for the Church that we love and serve. It embraces the past, present and future in elegant economy and for those working within the Church is a constant companion and source of useful and accessible information. The Revd Douglas Galbraith, its editor, is to be thanked warmly for the huge effort it takes to produce this volume.

Please take time to enjoy as well as use this marvellous book. I warmly commend the 2017–2018 Year Book to you. It will continue to inform, advise, and link you to the past, present, and future of the Church of Scotland. As the Year Book tells the story of the Church of Scotland, it continues to add to it.

Derek Browning

BHON MHODARÀTAIR

Ann an linn didseatach anns am bi cuid a' ceasnachadh adhbhar agus luach leabhraichean, bidh mi a' faireachdainn gu bheil rudeigin sòlasach agus mòr-chuairteach mun Leabhar BliadŸail a bhidh a' nochdadh gach bliadŸa. Thathas air a bhith a' gluasad a dh' ionnsaigh barrachd cleachdaidh didseatach aig an Àrd Sheanadh agus gu sònraichte leis an 'Leabhar Gorm', ach chaidh co-dhùnadh gun tèid leantainn air foillseachadh ann an clò, gu ìre air sgàth 's nach eil cothrom aig a h-uile duine air uidheam dealanach (no eadhon a bhith ag iarraidh a chleachdadh), agus gu ìre leis mar a tha teicneòlas a' sìor atharrachadh, cò a chanas de bhios sinn a' cleachdadh ann an deich no fichead bliadŸa air adhart? Leanaidh leabhraichean, ge tà, fad linntean.

Tha an Leabhar BliadŸail againn ann am pàirt na ghoireas fiosrachaidh, mar phàirt na aithisg air àireamhan, mar phàirt na leabhar seòlaidhean, agus mar phàirt na leabhar-dhealbh teaghlaich. Na bhroinn tha e a' toirt a-steach mòran de dh'obair chlàraichte Eaglais na h-Alba. Tha sgeulachdan ann mu dhiofar mhinistrealachdan, shuidheachaidhan, iomairtean agus mhodhan seirbhis. Bheir eadhon sùil ghoirid orra co-theacsa co-aimsireil dhuinn mun Eaglais a tha sinn a' gràdhachadh agus do bheil sinn a' toirt seirbhis. Tha e a' toirt a-steach an t-àm a dh'fhalbh, an t-àm anns a bheil sinn beo agus an t-àm ri teachd ann an dòigh a tha grinn is cuimir, agus dhaibhsan a tha ag obair taobh a-staigh na h-eaglaise tha e na chompanach seasmhach agus na stòr de dh'fhiosrachadh feumail is ruigsinneach. Bu chòir dhuinn taing mhòr a thoirt don Urramach Dùbhghlas Mac a' Bhreatannaich, an neach-deasaiche, airson an fhìor oidhirp a tha an cois an leabhar seo a thoirt gu buil.

Tha mi'n dòchas gun còrd an leabhar seo ribh agus gun cleachd sibh e. Tha mi a' sìor mholadh Leabhar BliadŸail 2017–2018 dhuibh. Gheibh sibh fiosrachadh, comhairle agus ceangal ann ris an àm a dh'fhalbh, a tha an làthair agus ri teachd ann an Eaglais na h-Alba.

Mar a tha an Leabhar BliadŸail ag innse sgeulachd Eaglais na h-Alba, tha e cuideachd a' cur tuilleadh ris.

Derek Browning
translation by the Very Revd Dr Angus Morrison

EDITOR'S PREFACE

No fewer than 303 of our users responded to the Survey made to accompany the publication of the previous edition of the Year Book. The questions were designed not just to gauge which parts of the book were most useful, and whether the current distribution between print and pixel was about right, but also to learn if, in your view, the time was ripe to make fuller use of electronic media. But just as helpful as the boxes ticked were the choice words that accompanied them, twice as telling as totalling the ticks!

They ranged from the terse: 'It's essential – don't muck about with it!' right through to: 'I support wholeheartedly the idea of creating an e-version of the book', with the whole gamut in between – including the user who complained that 'you need an Induction to be able to navigate it'. The strongest arguments were for print (bearing in mind that the most heavily used sections are currently in print). A book was portable, you could take it to meetings, grab it while you're on the phone; you could dip into it, make a quick reference; it was accessible (this from someone who worked in an IT profession), it was easier to have to hand than managing multiple windows on screen; you can scribble on it, add notes, corrections. One optimistic respondent declared that 'you can find just about anything in it' – a kind of ecclesiastical Mrs Beeton's perhaps?

Remote readers also reminded us that in Highland and Island areas internet reception can be poor, and downloading on dialup often intermittent and expensive. One or two saw it as an important historical record and asked whether, if it went electronic, there would be a mechanism for preserving details each year. Several regretted that the procedural information (weddings, vacancies etc.) was no longer to be found in the print edition. Even the list of grid references of churches found their champions, although one of these added the qualifier, 'Although I have had no need to use the church grid refs, it's where I would go if I did need to find one!'

But there were also those who agreed that, as an earlier editorial put it, 'the medium that was born in Gutenberg's boast that "with my twenty-six soldiers of lead I shall conquer the world" can no longer exist alone in the digital landscape of today'. These argued that digitalisation was only to be expected given the development of information tecŸology; that the internet was handier and easy to use; that it was potentially more searchable; that paper is saved; that there would be less expense in printing and distributing books.

Of course, there were some reservations: websites, including the Church's own, was (like the Church itself) *semper reformanda*. Some suggested that to obviate the need for searching through different websites or web pages, there should be a one-stop shop where all the Year Book type of information could be found together (one response recalled the searchable CD that came with the 2013 edition).

A telling argument in favour of an online-based resource related to the fact that the book was already out of date on the day it was published. One cannot quarrel with that – in spite of editorial efforts to divine the future. ... Approached for his new address, one minister expostulated: 'Wow! I had no idea that the Department of Dark Arts was on to me so soon! I only retired yesterday lunchtime!' It is hoped, however, to post updates on the Book's web pages at relatively frequent intervals.

Two other small matters. The Year Book is by way of being a 'book of record' in that it contains information, such as degrees, which may not seem to matter from day to day but which might in some circumstance be of use. In the latter, we have in this edition followed academic convention in not specifying whether a degree was taken to honours level or not. A large number where no such distinction is stated in the book have been honours degrees, while there is of course much variation between structures of degree and qualification.

Another matter concerns the seeming invidious distinction between men and women (and between women and women) in that their titles-of-address have for some years been added in brackets. A motion before the last General Assembly attempted to end this seemingly discriminatory practice. However, it failed to win a majority and it is worth explaining here that the practice arose so as to avoid embarrassment when people did not know how to address a woman formally, in writing or in direct speech. The editor has continued what he found in place, that women are asked what they prefer, one of the titles or none at all, and he is happy to abide by what people wish. At least this practice strikes a blow against the use of 'Reverend' as a title, imported from cinematic culture, as in 'Dear Reverend Knox', or 'The Reverend Melville will now say grace', which is not only quite ungrammatical but creates a clerical class which is inimical to our understanding of the ministry.

As always, the Year Book is the creation of several people. Warm thanks to Claire Ruben of FairCopy, our patient and flexible copy editor, and to our contacts at Hymns A&M; to the department of Communication in '121'; to the Presbytery Clerks and the staff at the Church's Offices; to Fiona Tweedie for conducting and interpreting the Survey of users; to those who compiled some of the Sections or items within them, in print or online: Angus Morrison (the Gaelic material), Roy Pinkerton with David Stewart (readjustments, grid references, editorial advice), Sandy Gemmill (statistics), Stephen Blakey (Forces Chaplains), Douglas Aitken and Laurence Wareing (General Assembly report); the Deputy Solicitor Jennifer Hamilton (Legal Names and Scottish Charity Numbers); and with warmest thanks, finally, to the Revd Dr Roddy MacLeod MBE, rightfully fêted by the General Assembly for his 37 years as Gaelic Editor of *Life and Work* and who, up until our previous issue, had been our own Gaelic Editor for many years.

Much of this editorial preface has been about the Survey of users. I've been putting off recording this forthright comment by one respondent who, somewhat crushingly, declared: 'I don't read the Prefaces!' (… if there is anyone still with me …).

Douglas Galbraith
yearbookeditor@churchofscotland.org.uk

SECTION 1

Assembly Councils,
Committees, Departments and Agencies

The symbol > used in website information indicates the headings to be selected as they appear

THE DEPARTMENT OF THE GENERAL ASSEMBLY

The Department of the General Assembly supports the General Assembly and the Moderator, the Council of Assembly and the Ecumenical Relations Committee. In addition, Departmental staff service the following Committees (qv): Assembly Arrangements, Legal Questions, the Committee to Nominate the Moderator, the Nomination Committee, the Committee on Overtures and Cases, and the Committee on Classifying Returns to Overtures. The Clerks of Assembly are available for consultation on matters of Church Law, Practice and Procedure.

Principal Clerk:	Rev. Dr George Whyte
Acting Depute Clerk of the General Assembly:	Ms Christine Paterson LLB DipLP
Personal Assistant to the Principal Clerk and Depute Clerk:	Mrs Linda Jamieson Tel. 0131-240 2240
Senior Administration Officer: (Assembly Arrangements and Moderatorial Support)	Ms Catherine McIntosh MA 0131-225 5722 ext. 2250
Secretary to the Council of Assembly:	Rev. Dr Martin Scott
Executive Officer:	Mrs Catherine Forsyth MA
Audit and Compliance Officer:	Mrs Debra Livingstone MA FCCA
Senior Administration Officer: (Council of Assembly, Central Services Committee and Nomination Committee)	Mrs Pauline Wilson BA Tel: 0131-240 2229
Administrator:	Mrs Valerie Jenkins
Interfaith Programme Officer:	Ms Mirella Yandoli MDiv MSt
Worship Development and Mission Statistics Co-ordinator:	Rev. Dr Fiona Tweedie Tel: 0131-240 3007
Ecumenical Officer:	Rev. Dr JoŸ L. McPake
Senior Administrator: (Ecumenical Relations)	Miss Rosalind Milne Tel: 0131-240 2208

Personnel in this department are also listed with the Councils and Committees that they serve

Contact: Tel: 0131-240 2240
　　　　　Fax: 0131-240 2239
　　　　　E-mail: pcoffice@churchofscotland.org.uk
Further information:
www.churchofscotland.org.uk > About us > Councils, committees > Departments > General Assembly

1. COUNCILS

1.1 THE COUNCIL OF ASSEMBLY

The function of the Council is to co-ordinate, support and evaluate the work of the Councils and Committees of the Church, to assist the General Assembly in determining and implementing policies, and to take necessary administrative decisions in between General Assemblies. The voting members of the Council of Assembly act as the Charity Trustees for the Unincorporated Councils and Committees of the General Assembly: Scottish Charity No. SC011353.

Convener: Dr Sally E. Bonnar MB ChB FRCPsych
Vice-Convener: Miss Catherine Coull LLB
Secretary: Rev. Dr Martin C. Scott

Contact: Mrs. Pauline Wilson BA, Senior Administrative Officer
Tel: 0131-240 2229, E-mail: pwilson@churchofscotland.org.uk
Further information:
www.churchofscotland.org.uk > About us > Councils, committees > Councils > Council of Assembly

1.2 THE CHURCH AND SOCIETY COUNCIL

The Council seeks to engage on behalf of the Church in national, political and social issues through research, theological reflection, resourcing the local church, and by engaging with leaders in civic society, public bodies, professional associations and other networks. The Council seeks to put the wisdom of local congregations and those with lived experience of poverty and injustice at the heart of its work. Its focus for the next decade, after a consultation involving 10,000 respondents: investing in young people, local communities where people flourish, the health and wellbeing of all, caring for creation, global friendships, an economy driven by equality, doing politics differently.

Convener: Rev. Dr Richard E. Frazer
Vice-Conveners: Wendy Young BSc PGCE MLitt
                Pauline Edmiston BD
Secretary: Rev. Dr H. Martin J. JoŸstone
                mjoŸstone@churchofscotland.org.uk

Contact: churchandsociety@churchofscotland.org.uk   Tel: 0131-240 2206
Further information:
www.churchofscotland.org.uk > About us > Councils, committees > Councils > Church and Society
www.churchofscotland.org.uk > speak out

1.3   THE MINISTRIES COUNCIL

The Council's remit is to recruit, train and support ministries in every part of Scotland, to monitor their deployment, working in partnership with ecumenical, inter-faith and statutory agencies, and giving priority to the poorest and most marginalised sections of the community.

Convener:	Rev. Neil M Glover
Vice-Conveners:	Rev. Colin M. Brough BSc BD
	Dr JoŸ Dent MB ChB MMEd
	Rev. Dr Marjory A. MacLean
	Rev. Derek H.N. Pope BD

Council Secretary:	Rev Jayne E. Scott BA MEd MBA
Depute:	Ms Catherine Skinner BA MA
Priority Areas:	Ms Shirley Grieve BA PGCE (0141-248 2905)
Vocation and Support:	Rev. Lezley J Stewart BD ThM MTh
Partnership Development:	Rev. Angus R. Mathieson MA BD
Human Resources:	Mr Daran Golby BA CIPD
Training Development:	Mr David Plews MA MTh
Pastoral Support:	Mrs Gabrielle Dench LLB BA MPC
Go For It:	Vacant

Contact: Tel: 0131-225 5722; Fax: 0131 240 2201; E-mail: ministries@churchofscotland.org.uk

Further information:
www.churchofscotland.org.uk > About us > Councils, committees > Councils > Ministries Council
www.churchofscotland.org.uk > Serve > Ministries Council > Ministries in the Church
Pulpit Supply Fees: www.churchofscotland.org.uk/yearbook > Section 3F

1.4   THE MISSION AND DISCIPLESHIP COUNCIL

The Council's remit is to stimulate and support the Church by the provision of resources nationally, regionally and locally in worship, witness, mission and discipleship. This includes the development of strategies and materials in the areas of adult education, resourcing elders, work with young adults, young people and children (including those with particular needs and disabilities), as well as in liturgy, and church art and architecture.

Convener:	Rev. Norman A. Smith MA BD
Vice-Conveners:	Rev. Daniel J.M. Carmichael MA BD
	Rev. W. Martin Fair BA BD DMin
	Rev. Jamie Milliken BD

Council Secretary:	Rev. Dr Alister W. Bull

Church Without Walls: Mrs Lesley Hamilton-Messer MA
Congregational Learning: Mr Ronald H. Clarke BEng MSc PGCE
Resourcing Worship: Mr Graham Fender-Allison BA

Church Art and Architecture:
Convener: Rev. William T. Hogg MA BD
Contact: gentrustees@churchofscotland.org.uk

Contact: Lynn Hall
        (E-mail: mandd@churchofscotland.org.uk)
Further information:
www.churchofscotland.org.uk > About us > Councils, committees > Mission and Discipleship
www.resourcingmission.org.uk

Church Art and Architecture www.churchofscotland.org.uk > Resources > Subjects > Art and Architecture resources

For The Netherbow: Scottish Storytelling Centre see below 2.23
For Life and Work see below 2.15
For Saint Andrew Press see below 2.21

1.5 THE SOCIAL CARE COUNCIL
(CrossReach)
Charis House, 47 Milton Road East, Edinburgh EH15 2SR
Tel: 0131-657 2000; Fax: 0131-657 5000
E-mail: info@crossreach.org.uk; Website: www.crossreach.org.uk

The Social Care Council, known as CrossReach, provides social-care services as part of the Christian witness of the Church to the people of Scotland, and engages with other bodies in responding to emerging areas of need. CrossReach operates 75 services across the country.

Convener: Mr Bill Steele
Vice-Conveners: Ms Irene McGugan
             Rev. Hugh M Stewart

Chief Executive Officer: Viv Dickenson (viv.dickenson@crossreach.org.uk)

Director of Services to Older People: Allan Logan (allan.logan@crossreach.org.uk)
Director of Adult Care Services: Calum Murray (calum.murray@crossreach.org.uk)
Director of Children and Families: Sheila Gordon (sheila.gordon@crossreach.org.uk)
Director of Finance and Resources: Ian Wauchope (ian.wauchope@crossreach.org.uk)
Director of Human Resources and
   Organisational Development: Mari Rennie (mari.rennie@crossreach.org.uk)

Further information: www.crossreach.org.uk

For sharing local experience and inititatives: www.socialcareforum.scot

1.6   THE WORLD MISSION COUNCIL

The Council's remit is to enable and encourage the Church of Scotland to accompany partner churches around the world and to keep the Church informed about issues and engaged in this endeavour as together we seek to live the Christian life and offer support to each other in our witness to Christ in the world. The Council is also the principal link with Christian Aid.

Convener:	Rev. Iain D. Cunningham MA BD
Vice-Conveners:	Rev. Susan M. Brown BD DipMin
	Mrs Maureen V. Jack MA MEd MSc

Council Secretary:	Rev. Ian W. Alexander BA BD STM
Secretaries:	Mrs Jennie Chinembiri (Africa and Caribbean)
	Ms Carol Finlay (Twinning and Local Development)
	Mr Kenny Roger (Middle East Secretary)
	Mr Sandy Sneddon (Asia)

Contact: Tel: 0131-225 5722
E-mail: world@churchofscotland.org.uk
Further Information:
www.churchofscotland.org.uk > About us > Councils, committees > Councils > World Mission
www.churchofscotland.org.uk > Serve > World Mission

2.   DEPARTMENTS, COMMITTEES AND AGENCIES

2.1   ASSEMBLY ARRANGEMENTS COMMITTEE

Convener:	Mrs Judith J.H. Pearson LLB LLM
Vice-Convener:	Rev. Fiona E. Smith LLB BD
Secretary:	Principal Clerk
	Tel. 0131-240 2240
	E-mail: pc@churchofscotland.org.uk

Further information:
www.churchofscotland.org.uk > About us > General Assembly
www.churchofscotland.org.uk > About us > Councils, committees > Committees > Assembly Arrangements

2.2 CENTRAL PROPERTIES DEPARTMENT

Remit: to provide property, facilities and health and safety services to the Councils and Departments of the central administration of the Church.

Property, Health and Safety Manager: Colin Wallace
Property, Health and Safety Officer: Jacqueline Collins
Property Officer: Eunice Hessell
Support Assistant: Joyce Anderson

Contact: Tel: 0131-240 2254
E-mail: cpd@churchofscotland.org.uk

2.3 CHURCH OF SCOTLAND TRUST

Chairman: Mr JoŸ M. Hodge WS
Vice-Chairman: Mr Thomas C Watson
Treasurer: Mrs Anne F. Macintosh BA CA
Secretary and Clerk: Mrs Jennifer M. Hamilton BA NP
Tel: 0131-240 2222
E-mail: jhamilton@churchofscotland.org.uk

Further information:
www.churchofscotland.org.uk > About us > Councils, committees > Departments > Church of Scotland Trust

2.4 COMMUNICATIONS DEPARTMENT

Acting Communications Officer: Jane Bristow
Acting Communications Manager: Helen Silvis 0131 240 2268
Senior Media Relations Officer: Cameron Brooks 0131 240 2278
Senior Media Relations Officer: Andrew Harris 0131 240 2204
Web Editor: Jason Derr
Web Developer: Alan Murray
Design Team Leader: Chris Flexen
Senior Designer: Steve Walker

Contact Media Relations after hours: (Mbl) 07854 783539
Contact department: 0131-240 2268
Further information:
www.churchofscotland.org.uk > About us > Councils, committees > Departments > Communications

2.5   ECUMENICAL RELATIONS COMMITTEE

The Committee includes six members appointed by the General Assembly, each attached to one of the five Councils of the Church and the Theological Forum, plus representatives of other denominations in Scotland and Church of Scotland members elected to British and international ecumenical bodies. The Church of Scotland trustee of ACTS and the co-chair of the Joint Commission on Doctrine attend as co-opted members. The General Secretary of ACTS attends as a corresponding member.

Convener: Rev. Alison P. McDonald MA BD
Vice-Convener: Rev. Calum I. MacLeod BA BD
Secretary and Ecumenical Officer: Rev. Dr JoŸ L. McPake
Senior Administrator: Miss Rosalind Milne

Contact: ecumenical@churchofscotland.org.uk
               Tel. 0131-240 2208

Further information:
www.churchofscotland.org.uk > About us > Councils, committees > Committees > Ecumenical Relations Committee
www.churchofscotland.org.uk > Connect > Ecumenism
www.churchofscotland.org.uk > Resources > Subjects > Ecumenical Resources
World Council of Churches: www.oikumene.org
Churches Together in Britain and Ireland: www.ctbi.org.uk
Action of Churches Together in Scotland: www.acts-scotland.org
For other international ecumenical bodies see Committee's web pages as above
See also 'Other Churches in the United Kingdom' page 20

2.6   FORCES CHAPLAINS COMMITTEE

Convener: Rev. Gordon T. Craig BD DipMin
Vice-Convener: Rev. JoŸ A.H. Murdoch BA BD DPSS
Secretary: Mr JoŸ K. Thomson, Ministries Council
                 Tel: 0131-225 5722
                 E-mail: jthomson@churchofscotland.org.uk

Further information:
www.churchofscotland.org.uk > About us > Councils, committees > Forces Chaplains Committee
A list of Chaplains is found on page 262

2.7 GENERAL TRUSTEES

Chairman:	Mr Raymond K. Young CBE BArch FRIAS
Vice-Chairman:	Mr Roger G.G. Dodd DipBldgCons(RICS) FRICS
Secretary and Clerk:	Mr David D. Robertson LLB NP
Depute Secretary and Clerk:	Mr Keith S. Mason LLB NP
Assistant Secretaries:	Ms Claire L. Cowell LLB (Glebes)
	Mrs Morag J. Menneer BSc MRICS (Glebes)
	Mr Brian D. Waller LLB (Ecclesiastical Buildings)
	Mr. Neil Page BSc MCIOB
Safe Buildings Consultant:	Mr Brian Auld ChEHO MREHIS FRSPH GradIOSH
Energy Conservation:	Mr Robert Lindores FInstPa
Treasurer:	Mrs Anne F. Macintosh BA CA
Finance Manager:	Mr Alex Semple FCCA

Buildings insurance, all enquiries to	Church of Scotland Insurance Services Ltd. 121 George Street, Edinburgh EH2 4YN Tel: 0131-220 4119 E-mail: enquiries@cosic.co.uk

Contact: gentrustees@churchofscotland.org.uk   0131-225 5722 ext. 2261
Further information:
www.churchofscotland.org.uk > About us > Councils, committees > Departments > General Trustees

---

2.8 THE GUILD

The Church of Scotland Guild is a movement within the Church of Scotland whose aim is 'to invite and encourage both women and men to commit their lives to Jesus Christ and to enable them to express their faith in worship, prayer and action'.

Convener:	Marge Paterson
Vice-Convener:	Patricia Robertson
General Secretary:	Iain W. Whyte BA DCE DMS

Contact: Tel: 0131-240 2217
E-mail: guild@churchofscotland.org.uk

Further information:
www.cos-guild.org.uk
www.churchofscotland.org.uk > Serve > The Guild

2.9   HOUSING AND LOAN FUND

Chairman: Rev. Ian Taylor BD ThM
Deputy Chairman: Rev. MaryAnn R. Rennie BD MTh
Secretary: Lin J. Macmillan MA
                        Tel: 0131-225 5722 ext. 2310
                        E-mail: lmacmillan@churchofscotland.org.uk
Property Manager: Hilary J. Hardy
Property Assistant: JoŸ Lunn

Further information:
www.churchofscotland.org.uk > About us > Councils, committees > Departments > Housing and Loan Fund

2.10   HUMAN RESOURCES DEPARTMENT

Head of Human Resources: Elaine McCloghry
Human Resources Managers: Daran Golby (Ministries)
                                    Karen Smith

Contact: Tel: 0131-240 2270
                E-mail: hr@churchofscotland.org.uk

2.11   INFORMATION TECHNOLOGY DEPARTMENT

Information TecŸology Manager: David Malcolm
                                        Tel: 0131-240 2247

Contact: Tel: 0131-240 2245
                E-mail: itdept@churchofscotland.org.uk
Further information:
www.churchofscotland.org.uk > About us > Councils, committees > Committees > IT

2.12   INVESTORS TRUST

Chairman:	Ms Catherine Y. Alexander
Vice-Chairman:	Mr Brian J. Duffin
Treasurer:	Mrs Anne F. Macintosh BA CA
Secretary:	Mrs Nicola Robertson
	E-mail: investorstrust@churchofscotland.org.uk

Further information:
www.churchofscotland.org.uk > About us > Councils, committees > Departments > Investors Trust

2.13   LAW DEPARTMENT

Solicitor of the Church and of the General Trustees:	Miss Mary Macleod LLB NP
Depute Solicitor:	Mrs Jennifer Hamilton BA NP
Senior Solicitor:	Mrs Elspeth Annan LLB NP
Solicitors:	Miss Susan Killean LLB NP
	Mrs Anne Steele LLB NP
	Mrs Jennifer Campbell LLB LLM NP
	Gregor Buick LLB WS NP
	Mrs Madelaine Sproule LLB NP
	Gordon Barclay LLB BSc MSc MPhil PhD
	David Stihler LLB MA

Contact: Tel: 0131-225 5722 ext. 2230; Fax: 0131-240 2246.
E-mail: lawdept@churchofscotland.org.uk

Further information:
www.churchofscotland.org.uk > About us > Councils, committees > Committees > Law

2.14   LEGAL QUESTIONS COMMITTEE

The Committee's remit is to advise the General Assembly on questions of Church and Constitutional Law, assist Agencies of the Assembly in preparing and interpreting legislation, compile statistics and arrange for the care of Church Records.

Convener:	Rev. George S. Cowie BSc BD
Vice-Convener:	Rev. Alistair S. May LLB BD PhD
Secretary:	Principal Clerk
Acting Depute Clerk:	Ms Christine Paterson LLB DipLP

2.20 SAFEGUARDING SERVICE

The service ensures that the Church has robust structures and policies in place for the prevention of harm and abuse of children and adults at risk; and to ensure a timely and appropriate response when harm or abuse is witnessed, suspected or reported.

Convener: Rev. Dr Karen K. Campbell
Vice-Convener: Mrs Caroline Deerin
Service Manager: Ms Julie Main BA DipSW

Contact: Tel: 0131-240 2256
              E-mail: safeguarding@churchofscotland.org.uk

Further Information:
www.churchofscotland.org.uk > About us > Councils, committees > Departments > Safeguarding Service

2.21 SAINT ANDREW PRESS

Saint Andrew Press is managed on behalf of the Church of Scotland by Hymns Ancient and Modern Ltd and publishes a broad range of books and resources, ranging from the much-loved William Barclay series of New Testament *Daily Study Bible* commentaries to the *Pilgrim Guide to Scotland*. The full catalogue can be viewed on the Saint Andrew Press website (see below).

Contact: Christine Smith, Publishing Director (Tel: 0207 776 7546; E-mail: christine@ hymnsam.co.uk)

Further information: www.standrewpress.com

2.22 SCOTTISH CHURCHES PARLIAMENTARY OFFICE
121 George Street, Edinburgh EH2 4YN

The Office exists to build fruitful relationships between the Churches and the Scottish and UK Parliaments and Governments, seeking to engage reflectively in the political process, translate their commitment to the welfare of Scotland into parliamentary debate, and contribute their experience and faith-based reflection on it to the decision-making process.

Scottish Churches Parliamentary Officer: Chloe Clemmons MA MA (Human Rights)
                                              E-mail: chloeclemmons@scpo.scot
Research and Resource Development Officer: Irene Mackinnon
                                              E-mail: irenemackinnon@scpo.scot

Contact: Tel: 0131-240 2276

Further information:
www.churchofscotland.org.uk > Speak out > Politics and Government
www.actsparl.org

2.23   SCOTTISH STORYTELLING CENTRE (THE NETHERBOW)
43–45 High Street, Edinburgh EH1 1SR

The integrated facilities of the **Netherbow Theatre** and the **JoŸ Knox House Museum**, together with the outstanding conference and reception areas, form an important cultural and visitor centre on the Royal Mile in Edinburgh and provide advice and assistance nationally in the use of the arts in a diversity of settings. Mission and Discipleship Council are pleased to host TRACS (Traditional Arts and Culture Scotland), a grant-funded body who provide an extensive cultural and literary programme.

Contact: Tels: 0131-556 9579, Fax: 0131-652 3273
E-mail: reception@scottishstorytellingcentre.com

Further information:
www.tracscotland.org/scottish-storytelling-centre

2.24   STEWARDSHIP AND FINANCE DEPARTMENT

General Treasurer: Mrs Anne F. Macintosh BA CA
Head of Stewardship: Vacant
Deputy Treasurer (Congregational
    Finance):   Mr Archie McDowall BA CA
Deputy Treasurer (Unincorporated
    Councils and Committees):   Mr Bob Cowan BCom CA
Finance Managers: Mrs Elaine Macadie BA CA
                                            Mrs Catriona M. Scrimgeour BSc ACA
                                            Mr Alex Semple FCCA
                                            Mrs Leanne Thompson BSc CA
Pensions Accountant: Mrs Kay C. Hastie BSc CA

Contact: E-mail: sfadmin@churchofscotland.org.uk
Further information and details of local consultants:
www.churchofscotland.org.uk > About us > Councils, committees > Departments > Stewardship and Budget
www.churchofscotland.org.uk > Resources > Subjects > National Stewardship Programme

2.25   THEOLOGICAL FORUM

The purpose of the Forum is to continue to develop and bring to expression doctrinal understanding of the Church with reference to Scripture and to the confessional standards of the Church of Scotland, and the implications of this for worship and witness in and beyond contemporary Scotland. It responds to requests to undertake enquiries as they arise, draws the Church's attention to particular matters requiring theological work, and promotes theological reflection throughout the Church.

Convener: Rev. Donald G. MacEwan MA BD PhD
Vice-Convener: Sarah Lane Ritchie BA MDiv MSc PhD
Secretary: Nathalie A. Mareš MA MTh

Contact: NMareš@churchofscotland.org.uk
Further Information:
www.churchofscotland.org.uk > About us > Councils, committees > Committees > Theological Forum

SECTION 2

General Information

(1) THE CHURCH OF SCOTLAND AND THE GAELIC LANGUAGE
THE VERY REVD DR ANGUS MORRISON

Seirbhis Ghàidhlig an Àrd-sheanaidh
Mar as àbhaist, chumadh seirbhis Ghàidhlig ann an Eaglais nam Manach Liath ann an Dùn Èideann air Didòmhnaich an Àrd-sheanaidh. Air ceann an adhraidh am-bliadhna agus a' searmonachadh bha an t-Urramach Ùisdean Murchadh Stiùbhart, ministear paraistean Ùige agus Beàrnaraigh an Leòdhas. A' togail an fhuinn bha Alasdair MacLeòid. Chaidh na Sgiobtaran a leughadh le Dòmhnall Iain Dòmhnallach. Mar a tha air tachairt bho chionn grunn bhliadhnachan a-nis, sheinn Còisir Ghàidhlig Lodainn aig toiseach agus deireadh na seirbhis. Sheinn Joanne Mhoireach laoidh. Rinn Modaràtair an Àrd-sheanaidh, an t-Oll. Urr. Derek Browning, am Beannachadh.
An dèidh an adhraidh fhuair an luchd-adhraidh cuireadh gu greim-bìdh agus bha cothrom aca a bhith a' còmhradh agus a' conaltradh.
Tha Eaglais nam Manach Liath air tè de na h-eaglaisean aig Eaglais na h-Alba anns na bailtean mòra far a bheil seirbhis Ghàidhlig air a cumail a h-uile seachdain. Tha seirbhis Ghàidhlig gach Sàbaid cuideachd ann an Eaglais Chaluim Chille ann an Glaschu.

Anns na Meadhanan
Bidh ministearan agus buill eile bho Eaglais na h-Alba a' gabhail pàirt ann am prògraman spioradail air an rèidio agus air an telebhisean.
Bidh mòran ag èisdeachd ri Dèanamaid Adhradh air an rèidio madainn agus feasgar na Sàbaid. Air an oidhche bidh seirbhisean à tasglann a' BhBC air an craobh-sgaoileadh, cuid mhath dhiubh bho Eaglais na h-Alba.
Gach latha tron t-seachdain tha Smuain na Maidne ga chraoladh air Rèidio nan Gàidheal. Tha daoine nach eil air chomas seirbhisean eaglais a fhrithealadh a' dèanamh fiughair ris na prògraman spioradail seo.
Bidh am BBC a' toirt fiosrachaidh seachad mu sheirbhisean Gàidhlig a tha air an cumail air feadh na dùthcha.

Na Duilleagan Gàidhlig
A h-uile mìos tha Eaglais na h-Alba air a bhith a' foillseachadh dhuilleagan Gàidhlig an lùib na h-iris mhìosail Life and Work. Bidh cuid mhath de luchd-ionnsachaidh agus feadhainn bho eaglaisean eile a' leughadh nan Duilleag.
Faodar Na Duilleagan a' leughadh cuideachd ann an roinn leasachaidh Gàidhlig de'n larach-lion Life and Work.

A' Dèanamh Adhartas leis a' Ghàidhlig anns an Eaglais
Ann an 2015 chumadh Co-labhairt chudromach anns an robh rannsachadh ga dhèanamh air suidheachadh na Gàidhlig ann an Eaglais na h-Alba. Thugadh An Ciad Ceum air a' cho-labhairt seo.
Mar ath cheum chaidh Buidheann Ghàidhlig Eaglais na h-Alba, a bha air a bhith tàmhach airson beagan bhliadhnaichean, a shuidheachadh a-rithisd. Is e amas na Buidhne cleachdadh na Gàidhlig ann am beatha agus obair na h-Eaglaise a bhrosnachadh agus goireasan iomchaidh, a chumas taic ris an amas seo, a leasachadh.
Bho chaidh Àrd Sheanadh 2016 air adhart, chaidh coinneamhan de'n Bhuidheann a chumail ann an diofar cheàrnaidhean de'n dùthaich, nam measg Dùn Èideann, Inbhir Nis, Caolas Loch Aillse, Sabhal Mòr Ostaig anns an Eilean Sgitheanach, agus Steòrnabhagh.
Anns a' chiad dhol-a-mach, tha a' Bhuidheann ag amas air Plana Gàidhlig airson Eaglais na h-Alba a dheasachadh. Thathas an dùil gum bi am Plana deiseil airson gun teid fhoillseachadh aig Àrd Sheanadh 2018.

General Assembly Gaelic Service

As always, there was a Gaelic service on the Sunday of the General Assembly in Greyfriars Kirk in Edinburgh. Conducting the service and preaching the sermon was the Rev. Hugh Maurice Stewart, minister of the parishes of Uig and Bernera in Lewis. The precentor was Alasdair Macleod. The Scriptures were read by Donald John Macdonald. As has happened for a number of years, the Lothian Gaelic Choir sang at the beginning and conclusion of the service. Joanne Murray sang a hymn. The Moderator, the Right Rev. Dr Derek Browning, pronounced the benediction.

Following the service, worshippers were invited to a light lunch when they had opportunity for conversation and fellowship.

Greyfriars Kirk is one of the Church of Scotland congregations in the cities which hold weekly Gaelic services. A Gaelic service is also held each Sunday in St Columba's church in Glasgow.

The Media

Ministers and members of the Church of Scotland regularly take part in Gaelic religious programmes on radio and television. The weekly Gaelic service on radio, Dèanamaid Adhradh, broadcast each Sunday morning and repeated in the afternoon, attracts a large audience. Each Sunday evening, services are broadcast from the BBC archives, a good number of them from the Church of Scotland.

The BBC gives information about Gaelic services taking place in different parts of the country.

The Gaelic Supplement

The Church of Scotland publishes a Gaelic supplement each month which is distributed free of charge with *Life and Work*. Learners of Gaelic and members of other churches are regular readers of the Gaelic supplement. The Duilleagan can also be read in the Gaelic supplement section of the *Life and Work* website.

Advancing Gaelic in the Church

In 2015, an important Conference was held to consider the place of Gaelic in the Church of Scotland. The Conference was called An Ciad Ceum (The First Step).

As a subsequent step, the Gaelic Group of the Church of Scotland, which had been dormant for a few years, was reconstituted. The aim of the Group is to encourage the use of Gaelic in the life and work of the Church and to develop suitable resources in support of this aim.

Since the General Assembly of 2016, meetings of the Gaelic Group have been held in different parts of the country, including Edinburgh, Inverness, Kyle of Lochalsh, at Sabhal Mòr Ostaig on Skye, and Stornoway.

As a first priority the Group aim to produce a Gaelic Plan for the Church of Scotland. It is hoped that the Plan will be ready for publication by the General Assembly of 2018.

(2) OTHER CHURCHES IN THE UNITED KINGDOM

ACTION OF CHURCHES TOGETHER IN SCOTLAND (ACTS)
Eaglaisean Còmhla n Gnìomh an Alba
General Secretary: Rev Matthew Z. Ross LLB BD MTh FSAScot, Jubilee House, Forthside Way,
    Stirling FK8 1QZ (Tel: 01259 216980; E-mail: matthewross@acts-scotland.org; Website:
    www.acts-scotland.org).

THE UNITED FREE CHURCH OF SCOTLAND
General Secretary: Rev. John Fulton BSc BD, United Free Church Offices, 11 Newton Place,
    Glasgow G3 7PR (Tel: 0141-332 3435; E-mail: office@ufcos.org.uk).

THE FREE CHURCH OF SCOTLAND
Principal Clerk: Rev. Callum Macleod, 15 North Bank Street, The Mound, Edinburgh EH1 2LS
    (Tel: 0131-226 5286; E-mail: offices@freechurch.org).

FREE CHURCH OF SCOTLAND (CONTINUING)
Principal Clerk: Rev. John MacLeod, Free Church Manse, Portmahomack, Tain IV20 1YL (Tel:
    01862 871467; E-mail: principalclerk@fccontinuing.org).

THE FREE PRESBYTERIAN CHURCH OF SCOTLAND
Clerk of Synod: Rev. Keith Watkins, 252 Briercliffe Road, Burnley BB10 2DQ; E-mail:
    kmwatkins@fpchurch.org.uk.

ASSOCIATED PRESBYTERIAN CHURCHES
Clerk of Presbytery: Rev. J.R. Ross Macaskill, Bruach Taibh, 2 Borve, Arnisort, Isle of Skye IV51
    9PS (Tel: 01470 582264; E-mail: emailjrrm@gmail.com).

THE REFORMED PRESBYTERIAN CHURCH OF SCOTLAND
Clerk of Presbytery: Rev. Peter Loughridge, 3b West Pilton Terrace, Edinburgh EH4 4GY (Tel:
    07791 369626; E-mail: peterloughridge@hotmail.com)

THE PRESBYTERIAN CHURCH IN IRELAND
Clerk of the General Assembly and General Secretary: Rev. Trevor Gribben, Assembly
    Buildings, 2–10 Fisherwick Place, Belfast BT1 6DW (Tel: 028 9041 7208; E-mail: clerk@
    presbyterianireland.org).

THE PRESBYTERIAN CHURCH OF WALES
General Secretary: Rev. Meiron Morris, Tabernacle Chapel, 81 Merthyr Road, Whitchurch, Cardiff
    CF14 1DD (Tel: 02920 627465; E-mail: swyddfa.office@ebcpcw.org.uk).

THE UNITED REFORMED CHURCH
General Secretary: Rev. John Proctor, 86 Tavistock Place, London WC1H 9RT (Tel: 020 7916
    2020; Fax: 020 7916 2021; E-mail: john.proctor@urc.org.uk).

UNITED REFORMED CHURCH SYNOD OF SCOTLAND
Synod Clerk: Mr Bill Robson, United Reformed Church, 113 West Regent Street, Glasgow G1
    2RU (Tel: 0141-248 5382; E-mail: brobson@urcscotland.org.uk).

BAPTIST UNION OF SCOTLAND
General Director: Rev. Alan Donaldson, 48 Speirs Wharf, Glasgow G4 9TH (Tel: 0141-423 6169; E-mail: admin@scottishbaptist.org.uk).

CONGREGATIONAL FEDERATION IN SCOTLAND
Chair: Rev. May-Kane Logan, 93 Cartside Road, Busby, Glasgow G76 8QD (Tel: 0141-237 1349; E-mail: maycital@virginmedia.com).

RELIGIOUS SOCIETY OF FRIENDS (QUAKERS)
Clerk to the General Meeting for Scotland: Adwoa Bittle (Ms), 4 Burnside Park, Pitcairngreen, Perth PH1 3BF (Tel: 01738 583108; E-mail: adwoabittle@hotmail.co.uk).

ROMAN CATHOLIC CHURCH
Mgr Hugh Bradley, General Secretary, Bishops' Conference of Scotland, 64 Aitken Street, Airdrie ML6 6LT (Tel: 01236 764061; E-mail: gensec@bcos.org.uk).

THE SALVATION ARMY
Lt-Col. Carol Bailey, Secretary for Scotland and Divisional Commander East Scotland Division, Scotland Office, 12A Dryden Road, Loanhead EH20 9LZ (Tel: 0131-440 9101; E-mail: carol.bailey@salvationarmy.org.uk).

SCOTTISH EPISCOPAL CHURCH
Secretary General: Mr John F. Stuart, 21 Grosvenor Crescent, Edinburgh EH12 5EE (Tel: 0131-225 6357; E-mail: secgen@scotland.anglican.org).

THE SYNOD OF THE METHODIST CHURCH IN SCOTLAND
District Administrator: Mrs Fiona Inglis, Methodist Church Office, Old Churches House, Kirk Street, Dunblane FK15 0AJ (Tel/Fax: 01786 820295; E-mail: fiona@methodistchurch.plus.com).

GENERAL SYNOD OF THE CHURCH OF ENGLAND
Secretary General: Mr William Nye, Church House, Great Smith Street, London SW1P 3NZ (Tel: 020 7898 1000; E-mail: enquiry@churchofengland.org).

---

(3) OVERSEAS CHURCHES

See www.churchofscotland.org.uk > Serve > World Mission > Our partner churches

---

(4) HER MAJESTY'S HOUSEHOLD IN SCOTLAND
ECCLESIASTICAL

Dean of the Order of the Thistle and Dean of the Chapel Royal:	Very Rev. Prof. Iain R. Torrance TD DPhil DD DTheol LHD FRSE

Domestic Chaplains:	Rev. Kenneth I. Mackenzie DL BD CPS
	Rev. Neil N. Gardner MA BD RNR

Chaplains in Ordinary:	Rev. Norman W. Drummond CBE MA BD DUniv FRSE
	Rev. James M. Gibson TD LTh LRAM
	Very Rev. Angus Morrison MA BD PhD
	Very Rev. E. Lorna Hood OBE MA BD DD
	Rev. Alistair G. Bennett BSc BD
	Rev. Susan M. Brown BD DipMin
	Very Rev. John P. Chalmers BD CPS DD
	Rev. Prof. David A.S. Fergusson
	OBE MA BD DPhil DD FBA FRSE

Extra Chaplains:	Rev. Alwyn J.C. Macfarlane MA
	Rev. John MacLeod MA
	Very Rev. James A. Simpson BSc BD STM DD
	Very Rev. James Harkness KCVO CB OBE MA DD
	Rev. John L. Paterson MA BD STM
	Rev. Charles Robertson LVO MA
	Very Rev. John B. Cairns KCVO LTh LLB LLD DD
	Very Rev. Gilleasbuig I. Macmillan
	KCVO MA BD Drhc DD FRSE HRSA FRCSEd
	Very Rev. Finlay A.J. Macdonald MA BD PhD DD
	Rev. Alastair H. Symington MA BD

(5) RECENT LORD HIGH COMMISSIONERS
TO THE GENERAL ASSEMBLY

1990/91	The Rt Hon. Donald MacArthur Ross FRSE
1992/93	The Rt Hon. Lord Macfarlane of Bearsden KT FRSE
1994/95	Lady Marion Fraser KT
1996	Her Royal Highness the Princess Royal LT LG GCVO
1997	The Rt Hon. Lord Macfarlane of Bearsden KT FRSE
1998/99	The Rt Hon. Lord Hogg of Cumbernauld
2000	His Royal Highness the Prince Charles, Duke of Rothesay KG KT GCB OM
2001/02	The Rt Hon. Viscount Younger of Leckie
	Her Majesty the Queen attended the opening of the General Assembly of 2002
2003/04	The Rt Hon. Lord Steel of Aikwood KT KBE
2005/06	The Rt Hon. Lord Mackay of Clashfern KT
2007	His Royal Highness the Prince Andrew, Duke of York KG KCVO
2008/09	The Rt Hon. George Reid PC MA
2010/11	Lord Wilson of Tillyorn KT GCMG PRSE
2012/13	The Rt Hon. Lord Selkirk of Douglas QC MA LLB
2014	His Royal Highness the Prince Edward, Earl of Wessex KG GCVO

2015	The Rt Hon. Lord Hope of Craighead KT PC FRSE
2016	The Rt Hon. Lord Hope of Craighead KT PC FRSE
2017	Her Royal Highness the Princess Royal KG KT GCVO QSO

For Lord High Commissioners prior to 1990 see www.churchofscotland.org.uk/resources/
yearbook > Section 2.4

---

(6) RECENT MODERATORS
OF THE GENERAL ASSEMBLY

1987	Duncan Shaw of Chapelverna Bundesverdienstkreutz PhD ThDr Drhc, Edinburgh: Craigentinny St Christopher's
1988	James A. Whyte MA LLD DD DUniv, University of St Andrews
1989	William J.G. McDonald MA BD DD, Edinburgh: Mayfield
1990	Robert Davidson MA BD DD FRSE, University of Glasgow
1991	William B.R. Macmillan MA BD LLD DD, Dundee: St Mary's
1992	Hugh R. Wyllie MA DD FCIBS, Hamilton: Old Parish Church
1993	James L. Weatherhead CBE MA LLB DD, Principal Clerk of Assembly
1994	James A. Simpson BSc BD STM DD, Dornoch Cathedral
1995	James Harkness KCVO CB OBE MA DD, Chaplain General (Emeritus)
1996	John H. McIndoe MA BD STM DD, London: St Columba's linked with Newcastle: St Andrew's
1997	Alexander McDonald BA DUniv CMIWSc, General Secretary, Department of Ministry
1998	Alan Main TD MA BD STM PhD DD, University of Aberdeen
1999	John B. Cairns KCVO LTh LLB LLD DD, Dumbarton: Riverside
2000	Andrew R.C. McLellan CBE MA BD STM DD, Edinburgh: St Andrew's and St George's
2001	John D. Miller BA BD DD, Glasgow: Castlemilk East
2002	Finlay A.J. Macdonald MA BD PhD DD, Principal Clerk of Assembly
2003	Iain R. Torrance TD DPhil DD DTheol LHD FRSE, University of Aberdeen
2004	Alison Elliot OBE MA MSc PhD LLD DD FRSE, Associate Director CTPI
2005	David W. Lacy BA BD DLitt DL, Kilmarnock: Henderson
2006	Alan D. McDonald LLB BD MTh DLitt DD, Cameron linked with St Andrews: St Leonard's
2007	Sheilagh M. Kesting BA BD DD DSG, Secretary of Ecumenical Relations Committee
2008	David W. Lunan MA BD DUniv DLitt DD, Clerk to the Presbytery of Glasgow
2009	William C. Hewitt BD DipPS, Greenock: Westburn
2010	John C. Christie BSc BD MSB CBiol, Interim Minister
2011	A. David K. Arnott MA BD, St Andrews: Hope Park with Strathkinness
2012	Albert O. Bogle BD MTh, Bo'ness: St Andrew's
2013	E. Lorna Hood OBE MA BD DD, Renfrew: North
2014	John P. Chalmers BD CPS DD, Principal Clerk of Assembly
2015	Angus Morrison MA BD PhD, Orwell and Portmoak

2016   G. Russell Barr BA BD Mth Dmin, Edinburgh: Cramond
2017   Derek Browning MA BD Dmin

For Moderators prior to 1987 see www.churchofscotland.org.uk/yearbook > Section 2.5

MATTER OF PRECEDENCE

The Lord High Commissioner to the General Assembly of the Church of Scotland (while the Assembly is sitting) ranks next to the Sovereign and the Duke of Edinburgh and before the rest of the Royal Family.

The Moderator of the General Assembly of the Church of Scotland ranks next to the Lord Chancellor of Great Britain and before the Keeper of the Great Seal of Scotland (the First Minister) and the Dukes.

(7) SCOTTISH DIVINITY FACULTIES
[* denotes a Minister of the Church of Scotland]

ABERDEEN
(School of Divinity, History and Philosophy)
50–52 College Bounds, Old Aberdeen AB24 3DS
(Tel: 01224 272366; Fax: 01224 273750; E-mail: divinity@abdn.ac.uk)

Master of Christ's College: Rev. Prof. John Swinton* BD PhD RNM RNMD
                                  (E-mail: christs-college@abdn.ac.uk)
Head of School: Prof. John Morrison MA PhD
Deputy Head of School: Prof. Paul Nimmo MA DipIA, BD ThM PhD

For teaching staff and further information see www.abdn.ac.uk/sdhp/

ST ANDREWS
(University College of St Mary)
St Mary's College, St Andrews, Fife KY16 9JU
(Tel: 01334 462850/1; Fax: 01334 462852; E-mail: divinity@st-andrews.ac.uk)

Principal and Head of School: Rev. Stephen Holmes BA MA MTh PhD

For teaching staff and further information see www.st-andrews.ac.uk/divinity/

EDINBURGH
(School of Divinity and New College)
New College, Mound Place, Edinburgh EH1 2LX
(Tel: 0131-650 8959; Fax: 0131-650 7952; E-mail: divinity@ed.ac.uk)

Head of School:	Prof. Graham Paul Foster BD MSt PhD
Principal of New College:	Rev. Professor David A.S. Fergusson* OBE MA BD DPhil DD FBA FRSE
Assistant Principal of New College:	Rev. Alison M. Jack* MA BD PhD

For teaching staff and further information see www.ed.ac.uk/schools-departments/divinity/

GLASGOW
School of Critical Studies
Theology and Religious Studies Subject Area
4 The Square, University of Glasgow, Glasgow G12 8QQ
(Tel: 0141-330 6526; Fax: 0141-330 4943)

Head of Subject:	Rev. Canon Dr Charlotte Methuen
Principal of Trinity College:	Rev. Doug Gay* MA BD PhD

For teaching staff and further information see www.gla.ac.uk Subjects A-Z. Theology and Religious Studies

HIGHLAND THEOLOGICAL COLLEGE UHI
High Street, Dingwall IV15 9HA
(Tel: 01349 780000; Fax: 01349 780001;
E-mail: htc@uhi.ac.uk)

Principal of HTC:	Rev. Hector Morrison* BSc BD MTh
Vice-Principal of HTC:	Jamie Grant PhD MA LLB

For teaching staff and further information see www.htc.uhi.ac.uk

(8) SOCIETIES AND ASSOCIATIONS

The undernoted list shows the name of the Association, along with the name and address of the Secretary.

1. INTER-CHURCH ASSOCIATIONS

ACTION OF CHURCHES TOGETHER IN SCOTLAND (ACTS) – Eaglaisean Còmhla an Gnìomh an Alba – was formed in 1990 as Scotland's national ecumenical instrument. It brings together nine denominations in Scotland who share a desire for greater oneness between churches, a growth of understanding and common life between churches, and unified action in proclaiming and responding to the gospel in the whole of life. General Secretary: Rev Matthew Z. Ross LLB BD MTh FSAScot, Jubilee House, Forthside Way, Stirling, FK8 1QZ (Tel: 01259 216980; E-mail: matthewross@acts-scotland.org; Website: www.acts-scotland.org).

The FELLOWSHIP OF ST ANDREW: The fellowship promotes dialogue between Churches of the east and the west in Scotland. Further information available from the Secretary, Rev. John G. Pickles, 1 Annerley Road, Annan DG12 6HE (Tel: 01461 202626; E-mail: jgpickles@hotmail.com).

The FELLOWSHIP OF ST THOMAS: An ecumenical association formed to promote informed interest in and to learn from the experience of Churches in South Asia (India, Pakistan, Bangladesh, Nepal, Sri Lanka and Burma (Myanmar)). Secretary: Rev. Val Nellist, 28 Glamis Gardens, Dalgety Bay, Dunfermline KY11 9TD (Tel: 01383 824066; E-mail: valnellist@btinternet.com; Website: www.fost.org.uk).

FRONTIER YOUTH TRUST: Encourages, resources and supports churches, organisations and individuals working with young people (in particular, disadvantaged young people). Through the StreetSpace initiative, the Trust is able to help churches to explore new ways of engaging young people in the community around mission and fresh expressions of church. All correspondence to: Frontier Youth Trust, 202 Bradford Court, 123/131 Bradford Street, Birmingham B12 0NS (Tel: 0121-771 2328; E-mail: frontier@fyt.org.uk; Website: www. fyt.org.uk). For information on StreetSpace, contact Clare McCormack (E-mail: scotland@ streetspace.org.uk).

INTERSERVE SCOTLAND: We are part of Interserve, an international, evangelical and interdenominational organisation with 160 years of Christian service. The purpose of Interserve is 'to make Jesus Christ known through *wholistic* ministry in partnership with the global church, among the neediest peoples of Asia and the Arab world', and our vision is 'Lives and communities transformed through encounter with Jesus Christ'. Interserve supports over 800 people in cross-cultural ministry in a wide range of work including children and youth, the environment, evangelism, Bible training, engineering, agriculture, business development and health. We rely on supporters in Scotland and Ireland to join us. Director: Grace Penney, 4 Blairtummock Place, Panorama Business Village, Queenslie, Glasgow G33 4EN (Tel: 0141-781 1982; Fax: 0141-781 1572; E-mail: info@issi.org.uk; Website: www.interservescotlandandireland.org).

IONA COMMUNITY: We are an ecumenical Christian community with a dispersed worldwide membership of Full Members, Associate Members and Friends. Inspired by our faith and loving concern for the world and its people, we pursue justice and peace in and through community. Our new Glasgow centre hosts a growing programme of events, our work with young people, Wild Goose Publications and the Wild Goose Resource Group. The Iona Community also welcomes guests to share in the common life in the Abbey and MacLeod Centre, Iona and Camas outdoor adventure centre, Mull. Leader: Dr Michael Marten, 21 Carlton Court, Glasgow, G5 9JP (Tel: 0141 429 7281, Website: www.iona.org.uk; E-mail: admin@iona.org.uk; Facebook: Iona Community; Twitter: @ionacommunity). Island Centres Director: Rev Rosie Magee, Iona Abbey, Isle of Iona, Argyll, PA76 6SN (Tel: 01681 700404, E-mail: enquiries@iona.org.uk).

PLACE FOR HOPE: A body with its roots in the Church of Scotland and now an independent charity, its vision is for a world where people embrace the transformational potential of conflict and nurture the art of peacebuilding. Place for Hope accompanies and equips people and faith communities where relationships have become impaired and helps them move towards living well with difference. Through a skilled and highly trained team we aim to accompany groups navigating conflict and difficult conversations and to resource the church and wider faith communities with peacemakers. If you are aware of conflict or difficulty within your faith community and would appreciate support, or wish to encourage your church or faith group to host a community dialogue, invite us to deliver a training or workshop session to your Kirk Session or Presbytery – it is never too early for a conversation about how we may help; you may also develop your own skills through our open access training courses. (Tel: 07884 580359; E-mail: info@placeforhope.org.uk; Website: www.placeforhope.org.uk).

The ST COLM'S FELLOWSHIP: An association for all from any denomination who have trained, studied or been resident at St Colm's, either when it was a college or later as International House. There is an annual retreat and a meeting for Commemoration; and some local groups meet on a regular basis. Hon. Secretary: Margaret Nutter, 'Kilmorich', 14 Balloch Road, Balloch G83 8SR (Tel: 01389 754505; E-mail: maenutter@gmail.com).

SCOTTISH CHURCHES HOUSING ACTION: Unites the Scottish Churches in tackling homelessness; supports local volunteering to assist homeless people; advises on using property for affordable housing. Chief Executive: Alastair Cameron, 44 Hanover Street, Edinburgh EH2 2DR (Tel: 0131-477 4500; E-mail: info@churches-housing.org; Website: www.churches-housing.org).

SCOTTISH CHURCHES ORGANIST TRAINING SCHEME (SCOTS): Established in 1997 as an initiative of the then Panel on Worship, along with the Royal School of Church Music's Scottish Committee and the Scottish Federation of Organists, this is a self-propelled scheme by which a pianist who seeks competence on the organ – and organists who wish to develop their skills – can follow a three-stage syllabus, receiving a certificate at each stage. Participants each have an Adviser whom they meet occasionally for assessment, and also take part in one of the three or four Local Organ Workshops which are held in different parts of Scotland each year. There is a regular e-newsletter, *Scots Wha Play*. Costs are kept low. SCOTS is an ecumenical scheme. Information from Douglas Galbraith (Tel: 01592 752403; E-mail: dgalbraith@hotmail.com; Website: www.scotsorgan.org.uk > SCOTS).

SCOTTISH JOINT COMMITTEE ON RELIGIOUS AND MORAL EDUCATION: This is an interfaith body that began as a joint partnership between the Educational Institute of Scotland and the Church of Scotland to provide resources, training and support for the work of religious and moral education in schools. Mr Andrew Tomlinson, 121 George Street, Edinburgh EH2 4YN (Tel: 0131-225 5722; E-mail: atomlinson@churchofscotland.org.uk), and Mr Lachlan Bradley, 6 Clairmont Gardens, Glasgow G3 7LW (Tel: 0141-353 3595).

SCRIPTURE UNION SCOTLAND: 70 Milton Street, Glasgow G4 0HR (Tel: 0141-332 1162; Fax: 0141-352 7600; E-mail: info@suscotland.org.uk; Website: www.suscotland.org. uk). Scripture Union Scotland's vision is to see the children and young people of Scotland exploring the Bible and responding to the significance of Jesus. SU Scotland works in schools running SU groups and supporting Curriculum for Excellence. Its two activity centres, Lendrick Muir and Alltnacriche, accommodate school groups and weekends away during term-time. During the school holidays it runs an extensive programme of events for school-age children – including residential holidays (some focused on disadvantaged children and young people), missions and church-based holiday clubs. In addition, it runs discipleship and training programmes for young people and is committed to promoting prayer for, and by, the young people of Scotland through a range of national prayer events and the *Pray for Schools Scotland* initiative.

STUDENT CHRISTIAN MOVEMENT: National Co-ordinator: Hilary Topp, SCM, Grays Court, 3 Nursery Road, Edgbaston, Birmingham B15 3JX (Tel: 0121-426 4918; E-mail: scm@movement.org.uk; Website: www.movement.org.uk). SCM is a student-led movement inspired by Jesus to act for justice and show God's love in the world. As a community we come together to pray, worship and explore faith in an open and non-judgemental environment. The movement is made up of a network of groups and individual members across Britain, as well as link churches and affiliated chaplaincies. As a national movement we come together at regional and national events to learn more about our faith and spend time as a community, and we take action on issues of social justice chosen by our members. SCM provides resources and training to student groups, churches and chaplaincies on student outreach and engagement, leadership and social action.

UCCF: THE CHRISTIAN UNIONS: Blue Boar House, 5 Blue Boar Street, Oxford OX1 4EE (Tel: 01865 253678; E-mail: email@uccf.org.uk). UCCF is a fellowship of students, staff and supporters. Christian Unions are mission teams operating in universities and colleges, supported by the local church, and resourced by UCCF staff. This fellowship exists to proclaim the gospel of Jesus Christ in the student world.

WORLD DAY OF PRAYER: SCOTTISH COMMITTEE: Convener: Mrs Margaret Broster, Bryn a Glyn, 27b Braehead, Beith KA15 1EF, (Tel: 01505 503300; E-mail margaretbroster@ hotmail.co.uk). Secretary: Marjorie Paton, Muldoanich, Stirling Street, Blackford, Auchterarder PH4 1QG (Tel: 01764 682234; E-mail: marjoriepaton.wdp@btinternet. com; Website: www.wdpscotland.org.uk).

YMCA SCOTLAND: Offers support, training and guidance to churches seeking to reach out to love and serve young people's needs. Chief Executive – National General Secretary: Mrs Kerry Reilly, James Love House, 11 Rutland Street, Edinburgh EH1 2DQ (Tel: 0131-228 1464; E-mail: kerry@ymcascotland.org; Website: www.ymcascotland.org).

YOUTH FOR CHRIST: Youth for Christ is a national Christian charity committed to taking the Good News of Jesus Christ relevantly to every young person in Great Britain. In

Scotland there are 6 locally governed, staffed and financed centres, communicating and demonstrating the Christian faith. Local Ministries Director: Lauren Fox (Tel: 0121 502 9620; E-mail: lauren.fox@yfc.co.uk; Website: www.yfc.co.uk/local-centres/scotland).

2. CHURCH OF SCOTLAND SOCIETIES

CHURCH OF SCOTLAND ABSTAINERS' ASSOCIATION: Recognising that alcohol is a major – indeed a growing – problem within Scotland, the aim of the Church of Scotland Abstainers' Association, with its motto 'Abstinence makes sense', is to encourage more people to choose a healthy alcohol-free lifestyle. Further details are available from 'Blochairn', 17A Culduthel Road, Inverness IV24 4AG (Website: www.kirkabstainers.org.uk).

The CHURCH OF SCOTLAND CHAPLAINS' ASSOCIATION: The Association consists of serving and retired chaplains to HM Forces. It holds an annual meeting and lunch on Shrove Tuesday, and organises the annual Service of Remembrance in St Giles' Cathedral on Chaplains' Day of the General Assembly. Hon. Secretary: Rev. Neil N. Gardner MA BD RNR, The Manse of Canongate, Edinburgh EH8 8BR (Tel: 0131-556 3515; E-mail: nng22@btinternet.com).

The CHURCH OF SCOTLAND RETIRED MINISTERS' ASSOCIATION: The Association meets in St. Andrew's and St. George's West Church, George St., Edinburgh, normally on the first Monday of the month, from October to April. The group is becoming increasingly ecumenical. Meetings include a talk, which can be on a wide variety of topics, which is followed by afternoon tea. Details of the programme from Hon. Secretary: Rev. David Dutton, 13 Acredales, Haddington EH41 4NT (Tel: 01620 825999; E-mail: duttondw@gmail.com).

The CHURCH SERVICE SOCIETY: Founded in 1865 to study the development of Christian worship through the ages and in the Reformed tradition, and to work towards renewal in contemporary worship. It has published since 1928, and continues to publish, a liturgical journal, archived on its website. Secretary: Rev. Dr Douglas Galbraith (Tel: 01592 752403; E-mail: dgalbraith@hotmail.com; Website: www.churchservicesociety.org).

FORUM OF GENERAL ASSEMBLY AND PRESBYTERY CLERKS: Secretary: Rev. David W. Clark, 3 Ritchie Avenue, Cardross, Dumbarton G82 5LL (Tel: 01389 849319; E-mail: dumbarton@churchofscotland.org.uk).

COVENANT FELLOWSHIP SCOTLAND (formerly FORWARD TOGETHER): An organisation for evangelicals within the Church of Scotland. Contact the Director, Mr Eric C. Smith (Tel: 07715 665728; E-mail: director@covenantfellowshipscotland.com), or the Chairman, Rev. Prof. Andrew T.B. McGowan (Tel: 01463 238770; E-mail: amcgowan@churchofscotland.org.uk; Website: http://covenantfellowshipscotland.com).

The FRIENDS OF TABEETHA SCHOOL, JAFFA: President: Mr Donald Burgess. Hon. Secretary: Rev. Iain F. Paton, Muldoanich, Stirling Street, Blackford, Auchterarder PH4 1QG (Tel: 01764 682234; E-mail: iain.f.paton@btinternet.com).

The IRISH GATHERING: Secretary: Rev. William McLaren, 23 Shamrock Street, Dundee DD4 7AH (Tel: 01382 459119; E-mail: WMcLaren@churchofscotland.org.uk).

SCOTTISH CHURCH SOCIETY: Founded in 1892 to 'defend and advance Catholic doctrine as set forth in the Ancient Creeds and embodied in the Standards of the Church of Scotland', the Society meets for worship and discussion at All Saints' Tide, holds a Lenten Quiet Day, an AGM, and other meetings by arrangement; all are open to non members. Secretary: Rev. W. Gerald Jones MA BD MTh, The Manse, Patna Road, Kirkmichael, Maybole KA19 7PJ (Tel: 01655 750286; E-mail: WJones@churchofscotland.org.uk).

SCOTTISH CHURCH THEOLOGY SOCIETY: Rev. Alexander Shuttleworth, 62 Toll Road, Kincardine, Alloa FK10 4QZ (Tel: 01259 731002; E-mail: AShuttleworth@churchofscotland.org.uk). The Society encourages theological exploration and discussion of the main issues confronting the Church in the twenty-first century.

SOCIETY OF FRIENDS OF ST ANDREW'S JERUSALEM: Hon. Secretary and Membership Secretary: Walter T. Dunlop, c/o World Mission Council, 121 George Street, Edinburgh, EH2 4YN. In co-operation with the World Mission Council, the Society seeks to provide support for the work of the Congregation of St Andrew's Scots Memorial Church, Jerusalem, and St Andrew's Guesthouse.

3. BIBLE SOCIETIES

The SCOTTISH BIBLE SOCIETY: Chief Executive: Elaine Duncan, 7 Hampton Terrace, Edinburgh EH12 5XU (Tel: 0131-337 9701; E-mail: info@scottishbiblesociety.org).

WEST OF SCOTLAND BIBLE SOCIETY: Secretary: Rev. Finlay Mackenzie, 6 Shaw Road, Milngavie, Glasgow G62 6LU (Tel: 07817 680011; E-mail: f.c.mack51@gmail.com; Website: www.westofscotlandbiblesociety.com).

4. GENERAL

The BOYS' BRIGADE: Scottish Headquarters, Carronvale House, Carronvale Road, Larbert FK5 3LH (Tel: 01324 562008; Fax: 01324 552323; E-mail: scottishhq@boys-brigade.org.uk).

BROKEN RITES: Support group for divorced and separated clergy spouses (Tel: 01896 759254; E-mail: eshirleydouglas@hotmail.co.uk; Website: www.brokenrites.org).

CHRISTIAN AID SCOTLAND: Sally Foster-Fulton, Head of Christian Aid Scotland, Sycamore House, 290 Bath Street, Glasgow G2 4JR (Tel: 0141-221 7475; E-mail: glasgow@christian-aid.org). Edinburgh Office: Tel: 0131-220 1254.

CHRISTIAN ENDEAVOUR IN SCOTLAND: Challenging and encouraging children and young people in the service of Christ and the Church, especially through the CE Award Scheme: 16 Queen Street, Alloa FK10 2AR (Tel: 01259 215101; E-mail: admin@cescotland.org; Website: www.cescotland.org).

DAYONE CHRISTIAN MINISTRIES: Ryelands Road, Leominster, Herefordshire HR6 8NZ. Contact Mark Roberts for further information (Tel: 01568 613740; E-mail: mark@dayone.co.uk).

ECO-CONGREGATION SCOTLAND: 121 George Street, Edinburgh EH2 4YN (Tel: 0131-240 2274; E-mail: manager@ecocongregationscotland.org; Website: www.ecocongregation

scotland.org). Eco-Congregation Scotland is the largest movement of community-based environment groups in Scotland. We offer a programme to help congregations reduce their impact on climate change and live sustainably in a world of limited resources.

GIRLGUIDING SCOTLAND: 16 Coates Crescent, Edinburgh EH3 7AH (Tel: 0131-226 4511; Fax: 0131-220 4828; E-mail: administrator@girlguiding-scot.org.uk; Website: www. girlguidingscotland.org.uk).

GIRLS' BRIGADE SCOTLAND: 11A Woodside Crescent, Glasgow G3 7UL (Tel: 0141-332 1765; E-mail: enquiries@girls-brigade-scotland.org.uk; Website: www.girls-brigade-scotland.org.uk).

The LEPROSY MISSION SCOTLAND: Suite 2, Earlsgate Lodge, Livilands Lane, Stirling FK8 2BG (Tel: 01786 449266; E-mail: contactus@tlmscotland.org.uk; Website: www.tlmscotland.org.uk). Working in over 30 countries, the Leprosy Mission is a global fellowship united by our Christian faith and commitment to seeing leprosy defeated and lives transformed.

RELATIONSHIPS SCOTLAND: Chief Executive: Mr Stuart Valentine, 18 York Place, Edinburgh EH1 3EP (Tel: 0345 119 2020; Fax: 0345 119 6089; E-mail: enquiries@ relationships-scotland.org.uk; Website: www.relationships-scotland.org.uk).

SCOTTISH CHURCH HISTORY SOCIETY: Secretary: Dr Eleanor M. Harris, E-mail: eleanormharris@gmail.com.

SCOTTISH EVANGELICAL THEOLOGY SOCIETY: Secretary: Rev. M.G. Smith, 0/2, 2008 Maryhill Road, Glasgow G20 0AB (Tel: 0141 570 8680; E-mail: sets.secretary@gmail. com; Website: www.s-e-t-s.org.uk).

The SCOTTISH REFORMATION SOCIETY: Chairman: Rev. Dr S. James Millar. Vice-Chairman: Rev. John J. Murray. Secretary: Rev. Dr Douglas Somerset. Treasurer: Rev. Andrew W.F. Coghill, The Magdalen Chapel, 41 Cowgate, Edinburgh EH1 1JR (Tel: 0131-220 1450; E-mail: info@scottishreformationsociety.org; Website: www.scottishreformationsociety.org).

SCOUTS SCOTLAND: Scottish Headquarters, Fordell Firs, Hillend, Dunfermline KY11 7HQ (Tel: 01383 419073; E-mail: shq@scouts.scot; Website: www.scouts.scot).

The SOCIETY IN SCOTLAND FOR PROPAGATING CHRISTIAN KNOWLEDGE: Chairman: Rev. Michael W. Frew; Secretary: Tom Hamilton, SSPCK, c/o Shepherd and Wedderburn LLP, 1 Exchange Crescent, Edinburgh EH3 8UL (Tel: 0131-473 5487; Website: www.sspck.co.uk; E-mail: SSPCK@shepwedd.co.uk).

TEARFUND: 100 Church Road, Teddington TW11 8QE (Tel: 0208 977 9144). Director: Lynne Paterson, Tearfund Scotland, Challenge House, 29 Canal Street, Glasgow G4 0AD (Tel: 0141-332 3621; E-mail: scotland@tearfund.org; Website: www.tearfund.org/scotland).

The WALDENSIAN MISSIONS AID SOCIETY FOR WORK IN ITALY: David A. Lamb SSC, 36 Liberton Drive, Edinburgh EH16 6NN (Tel: 0131-664 3059; E-mail: david@dlamb. co.uk; Website: www.scottishwaldensian.org.uk).

YOUTH SCOTLAND: Balfour House, 19 Bonnington Grove, Edinburgh EH6 4BL (Tel: 0131-554 2561; Fax: 0131-454 3438; E-mail: office@youthscotland.org.uk; Website: www.youthscotland.org.uk).

THE YOUNG WOMEN'S MOVEMENT: Director: Jackie Scutt, Third Floor, Princes House, 5 Shandwick Place, Edinburgh EH2 4RG (Tel: 0131-652 0248; E-mail: admin@ywcascotland.org; Website: www.ywcascotland.org).

(9) TRUSTS AND FUNDS

ABERNETHY ADVENTURE CENTRES: Full board residential accommodation and adventure activities available for all Church groups, plus a range of Christian summer camps at our four centres across Scotland. Tel: 01479 818005; E-mail: marketing@abernethy.org.uk; Website: www.abernethy.org.uk).

The ARROL TRUST: The Arrol Trust gives small grants to young people between the ages of 16 and 25 for the purposes of travel which will provide education or work experience. Potential recipients would be young people with disabilities or who would for financial reasons be otherwise unable to undertake projects. It is expected that projects would be beneficial not only to applicants but also to the wider community. Application forms are available from Callum S. Kennedy WS, Lindsays WS, Caledonian Exchange, 19A Canning Street, Edinburgh EH3 8HE (Tel: 0131-229 1212).

The BAIRD TRUST: Assists in the building and repair of churches and halls, and generally assists the work of the Church of Scotland. Apply to Iain A.T. Mowat CA, 182 Bath Street, Glasgow G2 4HG (Tel: 0141-332 0476; E-mail: info@bairdtrust.org.uk; Website: www.bairdtrust.org.uk).

The Rev. Alexander BARCLAY BEQUEST: Assists a family member of a deceased minister of the Church of Scotland who at the time of his/her death was acting as his/her housekeeper and who is in needy circumstances, and in certain circumstances assists Ministers, Deacons, Ministries Development Staff and their spouses facing financial hardship. Applications should be made to the Secretary and Clerk, The Church of Scotland Trust, 121 George Street, Edinburgh EH2 4YN (Tel: 0131-240 2222; E-mail: jhamilton@churchofscotland.org.uk) or the Pastoral Support Team, 121 George Street, Edinburgh EH2 4YN (Tel: 0131-225 5722).

BELLAHOUSTON BEQUEST FUND: Gives grants to Protestant evangelical denominations in the City of Glasgow and certain areas within five miles of the city boundary for building and repairing churches and halls and the promotion of religion. Apply to Mr Donald B. Reid, Mitchells Roberton, 36 North Hanover Street, Glasgow G1 2AD (Tel: 0141-552 3422; E-mail: info@mitchells-roberton.co.uk).

BEQUEST FUND FOR MINISTERS: Provides financial assistance to ministers in outlying districts towards the cost of manse furnishings, pastoral efficiency aids, and personal and family medical or educational (including university) costs. Apply to A. Linda Parkhill CA, 60 Wellington Street, Glasgow G2 6HJ (Tel: 0141-226 4994; E-mail: mail@parkhillmackie.co.uk).

CARNEGIE TRUST FOR THE UNIVERSITIES OF SCOTLAND: In cases of hardship, the Carnegie Trust is prepared to consider applications by students of Scottish birth or extraction (at least one parent born in Scotland), or who have had at least two years' education at a secondary school in Scotland, for financial assistance with the payment of their fees for a first degree at a Scottish university. For further details, students should apply to the Secretary, Carnegie Trust for the Universities of Scotland, Andrew Carnegie House, Pittencrieff Street, Dunfermline KY12 8AW (Tel: 01383 724990; E-mail: admin@carnegie-trust.org; Website: www.carnegie-trust.org).

CHURCH OF SCOTLAND INSURANCE SERVICES LTD: Arranges Church property and liabilities insurance in its capacity of Insurance Intermediary; also arranges other classes of business including household insurance for members and adherents of the Church of Scotland and insurances for charities. It pays its distributable profits to the Church of Scotland through Gift Aid. It is authorised and regulated by the Financial Conduct Authority. Contact 121 George Street, Edinburgh EH2 4YN (Tel: 0131-220 4119; Fax: 0131-220 3113; E-mail: k.roberts@cosic.co.uk; Website: www.cosic.co.uk).

CHURCH OF SCOTLAND MINISTRY BENEVOLENT FUND: Makes grants to retired men and women who have been ordained or commissioned for the ministry of the Church of Scotland and to widows, widowers, orphans, spouses or children of such, who are in need. Apply to Elaine Macadie BA CA, Assistant Treasurer (Ministries), 121 George Street, Edinburgh EH2 4YN (Tel: 0131-225 5722).

The CINTRA BEQUEST: See 'Tod Endowment Trust …' entry below.

CLARK BURSARY: Awarded to accepted candidate(s) for the ministry of the Church of Scotland whose studies for the ministry are pursued at the University of Aberdeen. Applications or recommendations for the Bursary to the Clerk to the Presbytery of Aberdeen, Mastrick Church, Greenfern Road, Aberdeen AB16 6TR.

CRAIGCROOK MORTIFICATION: Pensions are paid to poor men and women over 60 years old, born in Scotland or who have resided in Scotland for not less than ten years. At present, pensions amount to £1,000–£1,500 p.a. Ministers are invited to notify the Clerk and Factor, Mrs Fiona M.M. Watson CA, Exchange Place 3, Semple Street, Edinburgh EH3 8BL (Tel: 0131-473 3500; E-mail: charity@scott-moncrieff.com) of deserving persons and should be prepared to act as a referee on the application form.

CROMBIE SCHOLARSHIP: Provides grants annually on the nomination of the Deans of Faculty of Divinity of the Universities of St Andrews, Glasgow, Aberdeen and Edinburgh, who each nominate one matriculated student who has taken a University course in Greek (Classical or Hellenistic) and Hebrew. Award by recommendation only.

The DRUMMOND TRUST: Makes grants towards the cost of publication of books of 'sound Christian doctrine and outreach'. The Trustees are also willing to receive grant requests towards the cost of audio-visual programme material, but not equipment, software but not hardware. Requests for application forms should be made to the Secretaries, Hill and Robb Limited, 3 Pitt Terrace, Stirling FK8 2EY (Tel: 01786 450985; E-mail: douglaswhyte@hillandrobb.co.uk). Manuscripts should *not* be sent.

The DUNCAN McCLEMENTS TRUST FOR ECUMENICAL TRAINING: Makes grants towards the cost of attendance at ecumenical assemblies and conferences; gatherings of young people; short courses or conferences promoting ecumenical understanding. Also to enable schools to organise one-off events to promote better understanding among differing communities and cultures with different religious backgrounds. The Trust also helps towards the cost of resources and study materials. Enquiries to: Committee on Ecumenical Relations, Church of Scotland, 121 George Street, Edinburgh EH2 4YN (E-mail: ecumenical@churchofscotland.org.uk; Tel: 0131-240 2208).

The David DUNCAN TRUST: Makes grants annually to students for the ministry and students in training to become deacons in the Church of Scotland in the Faculties of Arts and Divinity. Preference is given to those born or educated within the bounds of the former Presbytery of Arbroath. Applications not later than 31 October to Thorntons Law LLP, Brothockbank House, Arbroath DD11 1NE (reference: G.J.M. Dunlop; Tel: 01241 872683; E-mail: gdunlop@ thorntons-law.co.uk).

ERSKINE CUNNINGHAM HILL TRUST: Donates 50% of its annual income to the central funds of the Church of Scotland and 50% to other charities. Individual donations are in the region of £1,000. Priority is given to charities administered by voluntary or honorary officials, in particular charities registered and operating in Scotland and relating to the elderly, young people, ex-service personnel or seafarers. Application forms from the Secretary, Nicola Robertson, 121 George Street, Edinburgh EH2 4YN (Tel: 0131-225 5722; E-mail: nrobertson@cofscotland.org.uk).

ESDAILE TRUST: Assists the education and advancement of daughters of ministers, missionaries and widowed deaconesses of the Church of Scotland between 12 and 25 years of age. Applications are to be lodged by 31 May in each year with the Clerk and Treasurer, Mrs Fiona M.M. Watson CA, Exchange Place 3, Semple Street, Edinburgh EH3 8BL (Tel: 0131-473 3500; E-mail: charity@scott-moncrieff.com).

FERGUSON BEQUEST FUND: Assists with the building and repair of churches and halls and, more generally, with the work of the Church of Scotland. Priority is given to the Counties of Ayr, Kirkcudbright, Wigtown, Lanark, Dunbarton and Renfrew, and to Greenock, Glasgow, Falkirk and Ardrossan; applications are, however, accepted from across Scotland. Apply to Iain A.T. Mowat CA, 182 Bath Street, Glasgow G2 4HG (Tel: 0141-332 0476; E-mail: info@ fergusonbequestfund.org.uk; Website: www.fergusonbequestfund.org.uk).

GEIKIE BEQUEST: Makes small grants to students for the ministry, including students studying for entry to the University, preference being given to those not eligible for SAAS awards. Apply to Elaine Macadie BA CA, Assistant Treasurer (Ministries), 121 George Street, Edinburgh EH2 4YN by September for distribution in November each year.

James GILLAN'S BURSARY FUND: Bursaries are available for male or female students for the ministry who were born or whose parents or parent have resided and had their home for not less than three years continually in the old counties of Moray or Nairn. Apply to Mr Donald Prentice, St Leonard's, Nelson Road, Forres IV36 IDR (Tel: 01309 672380).

The GLASGOW SOCIETY OF THE SONS AND DAUGHTERS OF MINISTERS OF THE CHURCH OF SCOTLAND: The Society's primary purpose is to grant financial assistance to children (no matter what age) of deceased ministers of the Church of Scotland. Applications are to be submitted by 1 February in each year. To the extent that funds are available, grants are also given for the children of ministers or retired ministers, although such grants are normally restricted to university and college students. These latter grants are considered in conjunction with the Edinburgh-based Society. Limited funds are also available for individual application for special needs or projects. Applications are to be submitted by 31 May in each year. Emergency applications can be dealt with at any time when need arises. Application forms may be obtained from the Secretary and Treasurer, Mrs Fiona M.M. Watson CA, Exchange Place 3, Semple Street, Edinburgh EH3 8BL (Tel: 0131-473 3500; E-mail: charity@scott-moncrieff.com).

HAMILTON BURSARY TRUST: Awarded, subject to the intention to serve overseas under the Church of Scotland World Mission Council or to serve with some other Overseas Mission Agency approved by the Council, to a student at the University of Aberdeen (failing which to Accepted Candidate(s) for the Ministry of the Church of Scotland whose studies for the Ministry are pursued at Aberdeen University). Applications or recommendations for the Bursary to the Clerk to the Presbytery of Aberdeen, Mastrick Church, Greenfern Road, Aberdeen AB16 6TR.

Martin HARCUS BEQUEST: Makes annual grants to candidates for the ministry resident within the Presbytery of Edinburgh and currently under the jurisdiction of the Presbytery. Applications to the Principal's Secretary, New College, Mound Place, Edinburgh EH1 2LX (E-mail: k.mclean@ed.ac.uk) by 15 October.

The HOPE TRUST: Gives some support to organisations involved in combating drink and drugs, and has as its main purpose the promotion of the Reformed tradition throughout the world. There is also a Scholarship programme for Postgraduate Theology Study in Scotland. Apply to Robert P. Miller SSC LLB, Glenorchy House, 20 Union Street, Edinburgh EH1 3LR; tel. 0131-226 5151, fax 0131-225 2608.

KEAY THOM TRUST: The principal purposes of the Keay Thom Trust are:
1.   To benefit the widows, daughters or other dependent female relatives of deceased ministers, or wives of ministers who are now divorced or separated, all of whom have supported the minister in the fulfilment of his duties and who, by reason of death, divorce or separation, have been required to leave the manse. The Trust can assist them in the purchase of a house or by providing financial or material assistance whether it be for the provision of accommodation or not.
2.   To assist in the education or training of the above female relatives or any other children of deceased ministers.
Further information and application forms are available from Miller Hendry, Solicitors, 10 Blackfriars Street, Perth PH1 5NS (Tel: 01738 637311; E-mail: johnthom@millerhendry.co.uk).

LADIES' GAELIC SCHOOLS AND HIGHLAND BURSARY ASSOCIATION: Distributes money to students, preferably with a Highland/Gaelic background, who are training to be ministers in the Church of Scotland. Apply by 15 October in each year to the Secretary, Mrs Marion McGill, 61 Ladysmith Road, Edinburgh EH9 3EY (Tel: 0131 667 4243; E-mail: marionmcgill61@gmail.com).

The LYALL BEQUEST (Scottish Charity Number SC005542): Offers grants to ministers:
1.   Grants to individual ministers, couples and families, for a holiday for a minimum of seven nights. No reapplication within a three-year period; and thereafter a 50 per cent grant to those reapplying.
2.   Grants towards sickness and convalescence costs so far as not covered by the National Health Service. Applications should be made to the Secretary and Clerk, The Church of

Scotland Trust, 121 George Street, Edinburgh EH2 4YN (Tel: 0131-240 2222; E-mail: jhamilton@churchofscotland.org.uk).

REV DR MACINNES AND MRS MACINNES TRUST: Provides grants to (1) retired ministers who have spent part of their ministry in the Counties of Nairn, Ross & Cromarty or Argyll and are solely dependent upon their pensions and preaching fees and (2) widows or widowers of such ministers solely dependent on their pensions. Applications should be made to the Secretary and Clerk, The Church of Scotland Trust, 121 George Street, Edinburgh EH2 4YN (Tel: 0131-240 2222; E-mail: jhamilton@churchofscotland.org.uk).

Gillian MACLAINE BURSARY FUND: Open to candidates for the ministry of the Church of Scotland of Scottish or Canadian nationality. Preference is given to Gaelic-speakers. Application forms available from Dr Christopher T. Brett MA PhD, Clerk to the Presbytery of Argyll, Minahey Cottage, Kames, Tighnabruaich PA21 2AD (Tel: 01700 811142; E-mail: argyll@ churchofscotland.org.uk). Closing date for receipt of applications is 31 October.

The E. McLAREN FUND: The persons intended to be benefited are widows and unmarried ladies, preference being given to ladies above 40 years of age in the following order:
(a) Widows and daughters of Officers in the Highland Regiment, and
(b) Widows and daughters of Scotsmen.
Further details from the Secretary, The E. McLaren Fund, Messrs Wright, Johnston & Mackenzie LLP, Solicitors, 302 St Vincent Street, Glasgow G2 5RZ (Tel: 0141-248 3434; Fax: 0141-221 1226; E-mail: rmd@wjm.co.uk).

THE MEIKLE AND PATON FUND: Currently a limited number of 2017 grants are available from the trust fund to Ministers and staff employed by the Central Services Committee. The grant will take the form of a reduction in the cost of staying at hotels owned by the Crieff Hydro group - Crieff Hydro; Murraypark Hotel, Crieff; Peebles Hydro; Park Hotel, Peebles; Ballachulish Hotel and Isle of Glencoe Hotel. Grants are applied for at the time of booking at the hotel. During the course of the year further information will be placed in the Trusts and Funds section of the Year Book pages on the Church of Scotland's website about grants in 2018: www.churchofscotland. org.uk > Resources > Yearbook.

MORGAN BURSARY FUND: Makes grants to candidates for the Church of Scotland ministry studying at the University of Glasgow. Apply to the Clerk to the Presbytery of Glasgow, 260 Bath Street, Glasgow G2 4JP (Tel: 0141-332 6606). Closing date October 31.

NEW MINISTERS' FURNISHING LOAN FUND: Makes loans (of £1,000) to ministers in their first charge to assist with furnishing the manse. Apply to Elaine Macadie, Assistant Treasurer (Ministries), 121 George Street, Edinburgh EH2 4YN.

NOVUM TRUST: Provides small short-term grants – typically between £200 and £2,500 – to initiate projects in Christian action and research which cannot readily be financed from other sources. Trustees welcome applications from projects that are essentially Scottish, are distinctively new, and are focused on the welfare of young people, on the training of lay people or on new ways of communicating the Christian faith. The Trust cannot support large building projects, staff salaries or individuals applying for maintenance during courses or training. Application forms and guidance notes from novumt@cofscotland.org.uk or Mrs Susan Masterton, Blair Cadell WS, The Bond House, 5 Breadalbane Street, Edinburgh EH6 5JH (Tel: 0131-555 5800; Website: www.novum.org.uk).

PARK MEMORIAL BURSARY FUND: Provides grants for the benefit of candidates for the ministry of the Church of Scotland from the Presbytery of Glasgow under full-time training. Apply to the Clerk to the Presbytery of Glasgow, 260 Bath Street, Glasgow   G2 4JP (Tel: 0141-332 6606). Closing date November 15.

PATON TRUST: Assists ministers in ill health to have a recuperative holiday outwith, and free from the cares of, their parishes. Apply to Alan S. Cunningham CA, Alexander Sloan, Chartered Accountants, 38 Cadogan Street, Glasgow   G2 7HF (Tel: 0141-204 8989; Fax: 0141-248 9931; E-mail: alan.cunningham@alexandersloan.co.uk).

PRESBYTERY OF ARGYLL BURSARY FUND: Open to students who have been accepted as candidates for the ministry and the readership of the Church of Scotland. Preference is given to applicants who are natives of the bounds of the Presbytery, or are resident within the bounds of the Presbytery, or who have a strong connection with the bounds of the Presbytery. Application forms available from Dr Christopher T. Brett MA PhD, Clerk to the Presbytery of Argyll, Minahey Cottage, Kames, Tighnabruaich PA21 2AD (Tel: 01700 811142; E-mail: argyll@ churchofscotland.org.uk). Closing date for receipt of applications is 31 October.

Margaret and John ROSS TRAVELLING FUND: Offers grants to ministers and their spouses for travelling and other expenses for trips to the Holy Land where the purpose is recuperation or relaxation. Applications should be made to the Secretary and Clerk, The Church of Scotland Trust, 121 George Street, Edinburgh EH2 4YN (Tel: 0131-240 2222; E-mail: jhamilton@churchofscotland.org.uk).

SCOTLAND'S CHURCHES TRUST: Assists, through grants, with the preservation of the fabric of buildings in use for public worship by any denomination. Also supports the playing of church organs by grants for public concerts, and through tuition bursaries for suitably proficient piano or organ players wishing to improve skills or techniques. SCT promotes visitor interest in churches through the trust's Pilgrim Journeys covering Scotland. Criteria and how to apply at www.scotlandschurchestrust.org.uk. Scotland's Churches Trust, 15 North Bank Street, Edinburgh EH1 2LP (E-mail: info@scotlandschurchestrust.org.uk).

SCOTTISH CHURCHES HOUSE LEGACY RESERVE: Aim – to enable Scotland's churches and Christian organisations to resource new ways of ecumenical working. Between 1960 and 2011, the former Scottish Churches House in Dunblane was a centre for ecumenical encounter, sharing, challenge and development – the Legacy Reserve aims to continue this ethos. Applications are invited for the funding of projects; completed application forms must be submitted no later than 5th January in any year. Property schemes (such as repairs or purchase) are not eligible. Further details and application forms are available from the General Secretary, Action of Churches Together in Scotland, Jubilee House, Forthside Way, STIRLING FK8 1QZ. Telephone 01259 216980. E-mail: matthewross@acts-scotland.org.

SMIETON FUND: Makes small holiday grants to ministers. Administered at the discretion of the pastoral staff, who will give priority in cases of need. Applications to the Vocations and Support Secretary, Ministries Council, 121 George Street, Edinburgh EH2 4YN (E-mail: pastoralsupport@ churchofscotland.org.uk).

Mary Davidson SMITH CLERICAL AND EDUCATIONAL FUND FOR ABERDEENSHIRE: Assists ministers who have been ordained for five years or over and are in full charge of a congregation in Aberdeen, Aberdeenshire and the north, to purchase books, or to travel for educational purposes, and assists their children with scholarships for further education or vocational training. Apply to Alan J. Innes MA LLB, 100 Union Street, Aberdeen AB10 1QR (Tel: 01224 428000).

The SOCIETY FOR THE BENEFIT OF THE SONS AND DAUGHTERS OF THE CLERGY OF THE CHURCH OF SCOTLAND: Annual grants are made to assist in the education of the children (normally between the ages of 12 and 25 years) of ministers of the Church of Scotland. The Society also gives grants to aged and infirm daughters of ministers and ministers' unmarried daughters and sisters who are in need. Applications are to be lodged by 31 May in each year with the Secretary and Treasurer, Mrs Fiona M.M. Watson CA, Exchange Place 3, Semple Street, Edinburgh EH3 8BL (Tel: 0131-473 3500; E-mail: charity@scott-moncrieff.com).

The Nan STEVENSON CHARITABLE TRUST FOR RETIRED MINISTERS: Provides houses, or loans to purchase houses, on similar terms to the Housing and Loan Fund, for any retired paid church worker with a North Ayrshire connection. Secretary and Treasurer: Mrs Christine Thomas, 73 Castlebay Court, Largs KA30 8DP (Tel: 01475 329336, 07891 838778 (Mbl); E-mail cathomas@gmail.com).

Miss M.E. SWINTON PATERSON'S CHARITABLE TRUST: The Trust can give modest grants to support smaller congregations in urban or rural areas who require to fund essential maintenance or improvement works at their buildings. Apply to Mr Callum S. Kennedy WS, Messrs Lindsays WS, Caledonian Exchange, 19A Canning Street, Edinburgh EH3 8HE (Tel: 0131-229 1212).

SYNOD OF GRAMPIAN CHILDREN OF THE CLERGY FUND: Makes annual grants to children of deceased ministers. Apply to Rev. Iain U. Thomson, Clerk and Treasurer, 4 Keirhill Gardens, Westhill AB32 6AZ (Tel: 01224 746743).

SYNOD OF GRAMPIAN WIDOWS' FUND: Makes annual grants (currently £275 p.a.) to widows or widowers of deceased ministers who have served in a charge in the former Synod. Apply to Rev. Iain U. Thomson, Clerk and Treasurer, 4 Keirhill Gardens, Westhill AB32 6AZ (Tel: 01224 746743).

TOD ENDOWMENT TRUST; CINTRA BEQUEST; TOD ENDOWMENT SCOTLAND HOLIDAY FUND: The Trustees of the Cintra Bequest and of the Tod Endowment Scotland Holiday Fund can consider an application for a grant from the Tod Endowment funds from any ordained or commissioned minister or deacon in Scotland of at least two years' standing before the date of application, to assist with the cost of the beneficiary and his or her spouse or partner and dependants obtaining rest and recuperation in Scotland. The Trustees of the Tod Endowment Scotland Holiday Fund can also consider an application from an ordained or commissioned minister or deacon who has retired. Application forms are available from Mrs Jennifer Hamilton, Deputy Solicitor (for the Cintra Bequest), and from Elaine Macadie BA CA, Assistant Treasurer (Ministries) (for the Tod Endowment Scotland Holiday Fund). The address in both cases is 121 George Street, Edinburgh EH2 4YN (Tel: 0131-225 5722). (Attention is drawn to the separate entry above for the Church of Scotland Ministry Benevolent Fund.)

STEPHEN WILLIAMSON & ALEX BALFOUR FUND: Offers grants to Ministers in Scotland, with first priority being given to Ministers in the Presbytery of Angus, followed by the Presbyteries in Fife, to assist with the cost of educational school/ college/university trips for sons and daughters of the Manse who are under 25 years and in full time education. Application for trips in any year will be considered by the Trustees in the January of that year, when the income of the previous financial year will be awarded in grants. The applications for trips in that calendar year must be submitted by 31 December of the preceding year. If funds still remain for distribution after the allocation of grants in January further applications for that year will be considered. Applications from the Presbyteries of Angus, Dunfermline, Kirkcaldy and St Andrews will be considered at any time of year as the Trustees have retained income for these grants. Applications should be made to the Secretary and Clerk, The Church of Scotland Trust, 121 George Street, Edinburgh EH2 4YN (Tel: 0131-240 2222; E-mail: jhamilton@ churchofscotland.org.uk).

(10) LONG SERVICE CERTIFICATES

Long Service Certificates, signed by the Moderator, have to date been available for presentation to elders and others in respect of not less than thirty years of service. At the General Assembly of 2015, it was agreed that further certificates could be issued at intervals of ten years thereafter. It should be noted that the period is years of *service*, not (for example) years of ordination in the case of an elder. In the case of Sunday School teachers and Bible Class leaders, the qualifying period is twenty-one years of service. Certificates are not issued posthumously, nor is it possible to make exceptions to the rules, for example by recognising quality of service in order to reduce the qualifying period, or by reducing the qualifying period on compassionate grounds, such as serious illness. Applications for Long Service Certificates should be made in writing to the Principal Clerk at 121 George Street, Edinburgh EH2 4YN by the parish minister, or by the session clerk on behalf of the Kirk Session. Certificates are not issued from this office to the individual recipients, nor should individuals make application themselves.

(11) RECORDS OF THE CHURCH OF SCOTLAND

Church records more than fifty years old, unless still in use, should be sent or delivered to the Principal Clerk for onward transmission to the National Records of Scotland. Where ministers or session clerks are approached by a local repository seeking a transfer of their records, they should inform the Principal Clerk, who will take the matter up with the National Records of Scotland.

Where a temporary retransmission of records is sought, it is extremely helpful if notice can be given three months in advance so that appropriate procedures can be carried out satisfactorily.

SECTION 3

Church Procedure

A. THE MINISTER AND BAPTISM

See www.churchofscotland.org.uk > Resources > Yearbook > Section 3A

B. THE MINISTER AND MARRIAGE

See www.churchofscotland.org.uk > Resources > Yearbook > Section 3B

C. CONDUCT OF MARRIAGE SERVICES (CODE OF GOOD PRACTICE)

See www.churchofscotland.org.uk > Resources > Yearbook > Section 3C

D. MARRIAGE AND CIVIL PARTNERSHIP (SCOTLAND) ACT 2014

See www.churchofscotland.org.uk > Resources > Yearbook > Section 3D

E. CONDUCT OF FUNERAL SERVICES: FEES

See www.churchofscotland.org.uk > Resources > Yearbook > Section 3E

F. PULPIT SUPPLY FEES AND EXPENSES

See www.churchofscotland.org.uk > Resources > Yearbook > Section 3F

G. PROCEDURE IN A VACANCY

A full coverage can be found in two handbooks listed under *Interim Moderators and Nominating Committees* on the Ministries Resources pages on the Church of Scotland website:
www.churchofscotland.org.uk > Resources > Subjects > Ministries resources > Interim Moderators and Nominating Committees
See also www.churchofscotland.org.uk > Serve > Ministries Council > Partnership Development > Locum Appointment Guidance

SECTION 4

General Assembly 2017

Report from the General Assembly 2017
Theme: Word of Life

There is one aspect of the Church of Scotland meeting in General Assembly which never fails to strike first-time Commissioners, and that is the way the world keeps breaking in. They come to realise that, far from the Church withdrawing to put its house in order, humanity in all its brokenness, need – and promise – forces its way through to engage its feelings, deepen its prayers and craft its deliverances. This invariably happens in three ways: 1) as riding on the agenda itself as Councils and Committees report, 2) as disrupting the business through the morning's news, and 3) as made visible and tangible in the presence of delegates and guests from situations of conflict, persecution and loss.

1

In St Giles', the Moderator called the Church to become more 'porous', ready to be challenged and changed by the clamour of voices outside its own fellowship. The Assembly is living proof and symbol of this, not making decisions from a distance but forced to engage with life 'as it happens'. The Convener of the Church and Society Council opened his speech by quoting the late Carl Sandburg:

> *The single clenched fist, lifted and ready,*
> *Or the open, asking hand, held out and waiting.*
> *Choose.*
> *For we meet by one or the other,*

These words, he suggested, express the contrast between the world as it is becoming and the world as Christ would like it to be, and his report, and that of other Councils and bodies, addressed the fallow ground between.

Continuing their *Speak Out: 10,000 Voices for Change* programme, the Church and Society Council played a spotlight on many aspects of our local and global common life, examples being the uglier aspects of Brexit, gender injustice, human trafficking, asylum seekers and refugees, welfare reform, and the search for an economy driven by equality, and many of these issues were to make further appearance during the week. That these concerns are lodged firmly within the Gospel and the spiritual life of the Church was underlined by the section calling for a recovery of Pilgrimage as a contemporary discipline, where travellers on the human journey could encounter and become open to each other and to the living Christ.

Then there was the Guild, famous for its cycles of ground-breaking projects at home and abroad, of which two examples were the battle against female genital mutilation in Kenya and the provision of solar ovens in Bolivia. Later, in a joint report with the National Youth Assembly, we were challenged to develop genuine *inter*generational activity (as opposed to *multi*generational) between people of all ages. The NYA took up the tale in its own 'superbly presented' report, embracing issues such as mental health, young suicide, and gender non-conformity. At the close of the Guild report, the Moderator and his Chaplains were presented with Guild mugs [Moderator – 'This will go very nicely with my Chateau Margaux'].

The World Mission Council took the theme of Women in the World Church, proving with examples that empowering women is one of the most effective ways of addressing and eradicating poverty. (And how many of us know the theological writings of Calvin's contemporary, Marie Dentière?) Into this debate came also South Sudan, 'a forgotten place, a forgotten war and a forgotten nation' (Principal Clerk), Coptic Christians in Egypt (to be again in the news later in the week) and the increase of HIV among young people in Zambia. The Council's joint report with Church and Society on the centenary this year of the Balfour Declaration gave rise to much debate, and a proposed strategic review of possible ways forward was welcomed.

The work of the Social Care Council (CrossReach) spilled over into other areas of the agenda, mentioned by the retiring Moderator and by the Lord High Commissioner, HRH the Princess Royal, who spoke very warmly of that work in one of her engaging and spontaneous addresses. The Council report particularly highlighted three projects: the Daisy Chain Early Years Project, helping families from many backgrounds and cultures to build positive relationships; the Prison Visitors' Support Centre at Perth Prison (later commended by former Moderator Andrew McLellan, latterly HM Inspector of Prisons), and the Heart for Art projects, now 11 in number, where people with dementia can take part in therapeutic art sessions. At the Heart and Soul event, launching CrossReach's imaginative Grey Cake Campaign, a cake was cut by the Lord High Commissioner and Moderator (who in a Bake Off had earlier been a gallant second – of two – to the Moderator of the Youth Assembly). The colourful centre blanketed with grey icing is to symbolise what it is like to live under a fog of depression and anxiety (affecting 1 in 4 Scots at some time) and the campaign invites communities across Scotland to hold grey cake bake sales to raise funds for local support services.

2

The most dramatic examples this year of the world 'gate-crashing' the Assembly was the terrorist attack on a crowded music concert in Manchester with a predominantly young audience, prompting a moving statement from the Moderator, prayer and, later, a resolution and a silence. When it was found that one young victim was from one of the Church's island parishes, the Moderator spoke with the minister by telephone, promising the Assembly's support to church and community there. Then on the last day was the news of the killing and wounding of Coptic Christians in Egypt. A third example was the direct impingement on the Assembly's work of world tensions evidenced in the two seats left empty at the front of the Hall throughout the week in silent reminder of the invitees who had been refused visas by their governments, Syria and South Sudan.

3

One of the things that distinguish the Assembly from pretty much all other such gatherings is the high number of overseas and ecumenical guests, and their welcome and often moving contributions provide the third way in which the life of the world penetrates the Assembly Hall, bringing as they do first hand accounts of the difficulties they encounter and navigate. Among other specially-invited guests was the Director of Christian Aid ('we are your international development agency'), who, from her visits overseas gave vivid examples of one of the Moderator's eloquent 'words for life' at each morning worship: that we do not act 'for' others (able to remain detached) but 'with' them. She commented: 'You cannot return from a place like South Sudan and not be changed.'

Frequently, the Assembly 'spies' celebrities in the gallery who are guests at the Palace, which in recent years have included Archbishop Tutu, Gordon Brown, the Chief Rabbi, the Coptic bishop for the UK, and more than one Archbishop of Canterbury, who are called down to speak and who are listened to with courtesy. This year it was Prince Ghazi bin Muhammad of Jordan, a leading scholar of Islamic philosophy, who called on us all to break our dependency on social media and the internet and to study to understand each other's cultures and philosophies. "For in reading; in beneficial knowledge; in wisdom, there may also lie ... solutions to many other of our looming problems. ... The only prayer for 'more' in the Qur'an is: *My Lord, increase me in knowledge*." It is noticeable that the applause which invariably greets all of the Assembly's guests is particularly warm, eloquent of welcome, attention, support, and hope.

Other Councils and Committees

But for a church to be porous it has also to be structured, and with a spiritual depth that the Lord High Commissioner identified as so much needed in the contemporary world. Other Councils were working to this end: the provision of and support for ministry to resource such a body (the Ministries Council with its emphasis on the ministry of all God's people and its adventurous approach in alternative models of ministry, the Panel on Review and Reform's significant Path of Renewal programme to support congregations through change, the Council of Assembly with its call to prayer). To continue to nourish this, the Mission and Discipleship Council has provided channels and processes to lead to a deeper conversation within the church, a sharing of stories, so that its members can draw life and insight from each other.

Much awaited was the report of the Theological Forum, returning as requested to the controversial matter of the conduct of same-sex marriages, now recognised in Scots Law. Described as an 'approach', and written from the perspective of 'constrained difference' – i.e. seeking areas of allowable disagreement with the tradition of the Church as a whole, it was a substantial statement, albeit concise. Following a passionate and searching debate, the Assembly instructed its Legal Questions Committee to study the matters which would have to be addressed in permitting ministers and deacons to officiate at such marriage ceremonies. The Ecumenical Relations Committee was also asked to invite comment and feedback from our ecumenical partners.

In the encouraging report of this last committee, it was clear how the Church's relations with other churches were becoming more central to its work. Much of the credit is due to the recently retired Secretary and Ecumenical Officer, Sheilagh Kesting, and she was congratulated on being raised by the Pope to become a Dame of the Order of St Gregory, a rare distinction for a Presbyterian minister [Moderator: 'There is nothing like a dame!'].

Reports from many other committees were heard with equal appreciation of their importance in the housekeeping of the Church, but special mention may be made of the pageantry of the Chaplains to the Services and the signing by the Assembly, in common with other bodies, of a new Armed Forces Covenant, which promises fair treatment to veterans and their families, astonishingly now ten percent of the population.

Other sub themes were woven through the Assembly, one of them being Principal Clerks. As the Assembly gathered on the first day, they heard of the death that morning of James Weatherhead, wise guide of Church and Assembly for eleven years. On the final day, they bade a fond farewell to JoŸ Chalmers at the end of his memorable tenure of this office, while in between, on the 'fringe', there was launched Finlay Macdonald's forensic examination of the life and times of the Kirk through five centuries. Another sub theme was the expression of gratitude to other long-term servants of the Assembly: Alison Murray, guardian and guide to successive Moderators; David McColl, Assembly Officer for the past 17 years; Roddy MacLeod, editor of the Gaelic supplement to *Life and Work* over 37 years. A notable and welcome strand running through the whole was the Moderator's gift of finding the humour that lurked within the ordinary.

This was also the first Assembly whose entire proceedings were being made available online for the first time. It was probably also the first time that a Moderator was serenaded with 'Happy birthday to you' [Moderator: 'You are very naughty commissioners – but thank you!'].

The Editor

SECTION 5

Presbytery Lists

See overleaf for an explanation of the two parts of each list; a Key to Abbreviations; and a list of the Presbyteries in their numerical order.

SECTION 5 – PRESBYTERY LISTS

In each Presbytery list, the congregations ('charges') are listed in alphabetical order. In a linked charge, the names appear under the first named congregation. Under the name of the congregation will be found the name of the minister and, where applicable, that of an associate minister, ordained local minister, auxiliary minister and member of the Diaconate. The years indicated after a minister's name in the congregational section of each Presbytery list are the year of ordination (column 1) and the year of current appointment (column 2). Where only one date is given, it is both the year of ordination and the year of appointment. For an ordained local minister, the date is of ordination.

In the second part of each Presbytery list, those named, who are either engaged in ministry other than parish or are retired, are listed alphabetically. The first date is the year of ordination, and the following date is the year of appointment or retirement. If the person concerned is retired, then the appointment last held will be shown in brackets.

KEY TO ABBREVIATIONS

(E)   Indicates a Church Extension charge.
(NCD) Indicates a New Charge Development.
(GD)   Indicates a charge where it is desirable that the minister should have a knowledge of Gaelic.
(GE)   Indicates a charge where public worship must be regularly conducted in Gaelic.
(H)   Indicates that a Hearing Aid Loop system has been installed. In Linked charges, the (H) is placed beside the appropriate building as far as possible.
(L)   Indicates that a Chair Lift has been installed.

PRESBYTERY NUMBERS

1	Edinburgh	18	Dumbarton
2	West Lothian	19	Argyll
3	Lothian	20	
4	Melrose and Peebles	21	
5	Duns	22	Falkirk
6	Jedburgh	23	Stirling
7	Annandale and Eskdale	24	Dunfermline
8	Dumfries and Kirkcudbright	25	Kirkcaldy
9	Wigtown and Stranraer	26	St Andrews
10	Ayr	27	Dunkeld and Meigle
11	Irvine and Kilmarnock	28	Perth
12	Ardrossan	29	Dundee
13	Lanark	30	Angus
14	Greenock and Paisley	31	Aberdeen
15		32	Kincardine and Deeside
16	Glasgow	33	Gordon
17	Hamilton	34	Buchan
		35	Moray
		36	Abernethy
		37	Inverness
		38	Lochaber
		39	Ross
		40	Sutherland
		41	Caithness
		42	Lochcarron – Skye
		43	Uist
		44	Lewis
		45	Orkney
		46	Shetland
		47	England
		48	International Charges
		49	Jerusalem

(1) EDINBURGH

The Presbytery meets at St Catherine's Argyle Church, Edinburgh, on (2017) 7 November, 5 December (in the Moderator's church), and (2018) on 6 February, 20 March, 1 May and 19 June.

Clerk:	REV. MARJORY McPHERSON LLB BD MTh	10/1 Palmerston Place, Edinburgh EH12 5AA [E-mail: edinburgh@churchofscotland.org.uk]	0131-225 9137
Depute Clerk:	HAZEL HASTIE MA CQSW PhD AIWS	17 West Court, Edinburgh EH16 4EB [E-mail: HHastie@churchofscotland.org.uk]	07827 314374 (Mbl)

1 Edinburgh: Albany Deaf Church of Edinburgh (H) (0131-444 2054)

Rosemary A. Addis (Mrs) BD	2014	c/o Ministries Council, 121 George Street, Edinburgh EH2 4YN [E-mail: RAddis@churchofscotland.org.uk]	07738 983393 (Mbl)

(Albany Deaf Church is a Mission Initiative of Edinburgh: St Andrew's and St George's West)

2 Edinburgh: Balerno (H)

Andre J. Groenewald BA BD MDiv DD	1994	2016	3 Johnsonburn Road, Balerno EH14 7DN [E-mail: AGroenewald@churchofscotland.org.uk]	0131-449 3830

3 Edinburgh: Barclay Viewforth (0131-229 6810) (E-mail: admin@barclaychurch.org.uk)

Samuel A.R. Torrens BD	1995	2005	113 Meadowspot, Edinburgh EH10 5UY [E-mail: STorrens@churchofscotland.org.uk]	0131-478 2376

4 Edinburgh: Blackhall St Columba's (0131-332 4431) (E-mail: secretary@blackhallstcolumba.org.uk)

Benjamin J.A. Abeledo BTh DipTh	1991	2016	5 Blinkbonny Crescent, Edinburgh EH4 3NB [E-mail: BAbeledo@churchofscotland.org.uk]	0131-343 3708

5 Edinburgh: Bristo Memorial Craigmillar

Drausio P. Goncalves	2008	2013	72 Blackchapel Close, Edinburgh EH15 3SL [E-mail: DGoncalves@churchofscotland.org.uk]	0131-657 3266

6 Edinburgh: Broughton St Mary's (H) (0131-556 4786)

Graham G. McGeoch MA BTh MTh	2009	2013	103 East Claremont Street, Edinburgh EH7 4JA [E-mail: GMcGeoch@churchofscotland.org.uk]	0131-556 7313

7 Edinburgh: Canongate (H)

Neil N. Gardner MA BD RNR	1991	2006	The Manse of Canongate, Edinburgh EH8 8BR [E-mail: NGardner@churchofscotland.org.uk]	0131-556 3515

8   Edinburgh: Carrick Knowe (H) (0131-334 1505) (E-mail: ckchurch@talktalk.net)
Fiona M. Mathieson (Mrs)   1988   2001   21 Traquair Park West, Edinburgh EH12 7AN   0131-334 9774
BEd BD PGCommEd MTh   [E-mail: FMathieson@churchofscotland.org.uk]

9   Edinburgh: Colinton (H) (0131-441 2232) (E-mail: church.office@colinton-parish.com)
Rolf H. Billes BD   1996   2009   The Manse, Colinton, Edinburgh EH13 0JR   0131-466 8384
                                                  [E-mail: RBilles@churchofscotland.org.uk]
Gayle J.A. Taylor (Mrs) MA BD   1999   2009   Colinton Parish Church, Dell Road, Edinburgh EH13 0JR   0131-441 2232
(Associate Minister)   [E-mail: GTaylor@churchofscotland.org.uk]

10   Edinburgh: Corstorphine Craigsbank (H) (0131-334 6365)
Stewart M. McPherson BD CertMin 1991   2003   17 Craigs Bank, Edinburgh EH12 8HD   0131-467 6826
                                                  [E-mail: SMcPherson@churchofscotland.org.uk]   07814 901429 (Mbl)

11   Edinburgh: Corstorphine Old (H) (0131-334 7864) (E-mail: corold@aol.com)
Moira McDonald MA BD   1997   2005   23 Manse Road, Edinburgh EH12 7SW   0131-476 5893
                                                  [E-mail: MMcDonald@churchofscotland.org.uk]

12   Edinburgh: Corstorphine St Anne's (0131-316 4740) (E-mail: office@stannes.corstorphine.org.uk)
James J. Griggs BD MTh   2011   2013   1/5 Morham Gait, Edinburgh EH10 5GH   0131-466 3269
                                                  [E-mail: JGriggs@churchofscotland.org.uk]

13   Edinburgh: Corstorphine St Ninian's (H) (0131-539 6204) (E-mail: office@st-ninians.co.uk)
James D. Aitken BD   2002   2017   17 Templeland Road, Edinburgh EH12 8RZ   0131-334 2978
                                                  [E-mail: JAitken@churchofscotland.org.uk]

14   Edinburgh: Craiglockhart (H) (E-mail: office@craiglockhartchurch.org)
Gordon Kennedy BSc BD MTh   1993   2012   20 Craiglockhart Quadrant, Edinburgh EH14 1HD   0131-444 1615
                                                  [E-mail: GKennedy@churchofscotland.org.uk]

15   Edinburgh: Craigmillar Park (H) (0131-667 5862) (E-mail: cpkirk@btinternet.com)
Vacant   14 Hallhead Road, Edinburgh EH16 5QJ   0131-667 1623

16   Edinburgh: Cramond (H) (E-mail: cramond.kirk@blueyonder.co.uk)
G. Russell Barr BA BD MTh DMin 1979   1993   Manse of Cramond, Edinburgh EH4 6NS   0131-336 2036
                                                  [E-mail: GBarr@churchofscotland.org.uk]

17 Edinburgh: Currie (H) (0131-451 5141) (E-mail: currie_kirk@btconnect.com)
V. Easter Smart BA MDiv DMin   1996   2015   43 Lanark Road West, Currie EH14 5JX   0131-449 4719
                                                       [E-mail: ESmart@churchofscotland.org.uk]

18 Edinburgh: Dalmeny linked with Edinburgh: Queensferry
David C. Cameron BD CertMin   1993   2009   1 Station Road, South Queensferry EH30 9HY   0131-331 1100
                                                       [E-mail: DavidCCameron@churchofscotland.org.uk]

19 Edinburgh: Davidson's Mains (H) (0131-312 6282) (E-mail: life@dmainschurch.plus.com)
Daniel Robertson BA BD   2009   2016   1 Hillpark Terrace, Edinburgh EH4 7SX   0131-336 3078
                                                       [E-mail: Daniel.Robertson@churchofscotland.org.uk] 07909 840654 (Mbl)

20 Edinburgh: Drylaw (0131-343 6643)
Jenny M. Williams BSc CQSW BD   1996   2017   15 House o' Hill Gardens, Edinburgh EH4 2AR   0131-531 5786
(Transition Minister)   [E-mail: JWilliams@churchofscotland.org.uk]

21 Edinburgh: Duddingston (H) (E-mail: dodinskirk@aol.com)
James A.P. Jack   1989   2001   Manse of Duddington, Old Church Lane, Edinburgh EH15 3PX   0131-661 4240
BSc BArch BD DMin RIBA ARIAS   [E-mail: JJack@churchofscotland.org.uk]

22 Edinburgh: Fairmilehead (H) (0131-445 2374) (E-mail: office@fhpc.org.uk)
Vacant

23 Edinburgh: Gorgie Dalry Stenhouse (H) (0131-337 7936)
Peter I. Barber MA BD   1984   1995   90 Myreside Road, Edinburgh EH10 5BZ   0131-337 2284
                                                       [E-mail: PBarber@churchofscotland.org.uk]

24 Edinburgh: Gracemount linked with Edinburgh: Liberton
John N. Young MA BD PhD   1996   7 Kirk Park, Edinburgh EH16 6HZ   0131-664 3067
                                                       [E-mail: JYoung@churchofscotland.org.uk]

(Gracemount is the new designation for Kaimes Lockhart Memorial)

25 Edinburgh: Granton (H) (0131-552 3033)
Norman A. Smith MA BD   1997   2005   8 Wardie Crescent, Edinburgh EH5 1AG   0131-551 2159
                                                       [E-mail: NSmith@churchofscotland.org.uk]
Emma McDonald BD   2013   2017   c/o Granton Parish Church, Boswall Parkway, Edinburgh EH5 2DA   0131-552 3033
(Associate Minister)   [E-mail: EMcDonald@churchofscotland.org.uk]

26 Edinburgh: Greenbank (H) (0131-447 9969) (E-mail: greenbankchurch@btconnect.com; Website: www.greenbankchurch.org)
Vacant
William H. Stone BA MDiv ThM   2012   112 Greenbank Crescent, Edinburgh EH10 5SZ   0131-447 4032
(Youth Minister)   19 Caiystane Terrace, Edinburgh EH10 6SR   0131-629 1610
[E-mail: billstoneiii@gmail.com]   07883 815598 (Mbl)

27 Edinburgh: Greenside (H) (0131-556 5588)
Guardianship of the Presbytery   80 Pilrig Street, Edinburgh EH6 5AS   0131-554 3277 (Tel/Fax)

28 Edinburgh: Greyfriars Kirk (GE) (H) (0131-225 1900) (E-mail: enquiries@greyfriarskirk.com)
Richard E. Frazer BA BD DMin   1986   2003   12 Tantallon Place, Edinburgh EH9 1NZ   0131-667 6610
[E-mail: RFrazer@churchofscotland.org.uk]

29 Edinburgh: High (St Giles') (0131-225 4363) (E-mail: info@stgilescathedral.org.uk)
Calum I. MacLeod BA BD   1996   2014   St Giles' Cathedral, Edinburgh EH1 1RE   0131-225 4363
[E-mail: CMacLeod@churchofscotland.org.uk]
Helen J.R. Alexander BD DipSW   1981   2012   7 Polwarth Place, Edinburgh EH11 1LG   0131-346 0685
(Assistant Minister)   [E-mail: st_giles_cathedral@btconnect.com]

30 Edinburgh: Holy Trinity (H) (0131-442 3304)
Ian MacDonald BD MTh   2005   2017   5 Baberton Mains Terrace, Edinburgh EH14 3DG   0131-281 6153
[E-mail: Ian.Angus.MacDonald@churchofscotland.org.uk]

31 Edinburgh: Inverleith St Serf's (H)
Joanne G. Foster (Mrs)   1996   2012   78 Pilrig Street, Edinburgh EH6 5AS   0131-561 1392
DipTMus BD AdvDipCouns   [E-mail: JFoster@churchofscotland.org.uk]

32 Edinburgh: Juniper Green (H)
James S. Dewar MA BD   1983   2000   476 Lanark Road, Juniper Green, Edinburgh EH14 5BQ   0131-453 3494
[E-mail: JDewar@churchofscotland.org.uk]

33 Edinburgh: Kirkliston
Margaret R. Lane (Mrs) BA BD MTh   2009   43 Main Street, Kirkliston EH29 9AF   0131-333 3298
[E-mail: MLane@churchofscotland.org.uk]   07795 481441 (Mbl)

34 Edinburgh: Leith North (H) (0131-553 7378) (E-mail: nlpc-office@btinternet.com)
Alexander T. McAspurren BD MTh   2002   2011   6 Craighall Gardens, Edinburgh EH6 4RJ   0131-551 5252
[E-mail: AMcAspurren@churchofscotland.org.uk]

35 **Edinburgh: Leith St Andrew's (H)**
A. Robert A. Mackenzie LLB BD   1993   2013
30 Lochend Road, Edinburgh EH6 8BS
[E-mail: AMacKenzie@churchofscotland.org.uk]
0131-553 2122

36 **Edinburgh: Leith South (H) (0131-554 2578) (E-mail: slpc@dial.pipex.com)**
John S. (Iain) May BSc MBA BD   2012
37 Claremont Road, Edinburgh EH6 7NN
[E-mail: JMay@churchofscotland.org.uk]
0131-554 3062

37 **Edinburgh: Leith Wardie (H) (0131-551 3847) (E-mail: churchoffice@wardie.org.uk)**
Ute Jaeger-Fleming MTh CPS   2008   2015
35 Lomond Road, Edinburgh EH5 3JN
[E-mail: UJaeger-Fleming@churchofscotland.org.uk]
0131-552 0190

38 **Edinburgh: Liberton (H)** See Edinburgh: Gracemount

39 **Edinburgh: Liberton Northfield (H) (0131-551 3847)**
Michael A. Taylor DipTh MPhil   2006   2015
9 Claverhouse Drive, Edinburgh EH16 6BR
[E-mail: MTaylor@churchofscotland.org.uk]
0131-664 5490
07479 985075 (Mbl)

40 **Edinburgh: Marchmont St Giles' (H) (0131-447 4359)**
Karen K. Campbell BD MTh DMin   1997   2002
2 Trotter Haugh, Edinburgh EH9 2GZ
[E-mail: KKCampbell@churchofscotland.org.uk]
0131-447 2834

41 **Edinburgh: Mayfield Salisbury (0131-667 1522)**
Scott S. McKenna BA BD MTh MPhil   1994
26 Seton Place, Edinburgh EH9 2JT
[E-mail: SMcKenna@churchofscotland.org.uk]
0131-667 1286

42 **Edinburgh: Meadowbank**
R. Russell McLarty MA BD   1985   2017
(Transition Minister)
9 Sanderson's Wynd, Tranent EH33 1DA
[E-mail: RussellMcLarty@churchofscotland.org.uk]
01875   614496
07751   755986 (Mbl)
(New charge formed by a union between Edinburgh: Holyrood Abbey and Edinburgh: London Road)

43 **Edinburgh: Morningside (H) (0131-447 6745) (E-mail: office@morningsideparishchurch.org.uk)**
Derek Browning MA BD DMin   1987   2001
20 Braidburn Crescent, Edinburgh EH10 6EN
[E-mail: Derek.Browning@churchofscotland.org.uk]
0131-447 1617

44 **Edinburgh: Morningside United (H) (0131-447 3152)**
Steven Manders LLB BD STB MTh   2008   2015
1 Midmar Avenue, Edinburgh EH10 6BS
[E-mail: stevenmanders@hotmail.com]
0131-447 7943
07808 476733 (Mbl)
Morningside United is a Local Ecumenical Project shared with the United Reformed Church

45 **Edinburgh: Murrayfield (H) (0131-337 1091) (E-mail: mpchurch@btconnect.com)**
Keith Edwin Graham MA PGDip BD   2008   2014   45 Murrayfield Gardens, Edinburgh EH12 6DH
[E-mail: KEGraham@churchofscotland.org.uk]
   0131-337 1364

46 **Edinburgh: Newhaven (H)**
Peter Bluett   2007   158 Granton Road, Edinburgh EH5 3RF
[E-mail: PBluett@churchofscotland.org.uk]
   0131-476 5212

47 **Edinburgh: Old Kirk and Muirhouse (H)**
Stephen Ashley-Emery BD DPS   2006   2016   2 Thornyhall, Dalkeith EH22 2ND
[E-mail: SEmery@churchofscotland.org.uk]
   07713 613069 (Mbl)

48 **Edinburgh: Palmerston Place (H) (0131-220 1690) (E-mail: admin@palmerstonplacechurch.com)**
Colin A.M. Sinclair BA BD   1981   1996   30B Cluny Gardens, Edinburgh EH10 6BJ
[E-mail: CSinclair@churchofscotland.org.uk]
   0131-447 9598
   0131-225 3312 (Fax)

49 **Edinburgh: Pilrig St Paul's (0131-553 1876)**
Mark M. Foster BSc BD   1998   2013   78 Pilrig Street, Edinburgh EH6 5AS
[E-mail: MFoster@churchofscotland.org.uk]
   0131-332 5736

50 **Edinburgh: Polwarth (H) (0131-346 2711) (E-mail: polwarthchurch@tiscali.co.uk)**
Jack Holt BSc BD MTh   1985   2011   88 Craiglockhart Road, Edinburgh EH14 1EP
[E-mail: JHolt@churchofscotland.org.uk]
   0131-441 6105

51 **Edinburgh: Portobello and Joppa (H) (0131-669 3641)**
Stewart G. Weaver BA BD PhD   2003   2014   6 St Mary's Place, Edinburgh EH15 2QF
[E-mail: SWeaver@churchofscotland.org.uk]
   0131-669 2410

Laurens De Jager PgDip MDiv BTh   2013   2015   1 Brunstane Road North, Edinburgh EH15 2DL
[E-mail: LDeJager@churchofscotland.org.uk]
   07521 426644 (Mbl)

52 **Edinburgh: Priestfield (H) (0131-667 5644)**
Vacant   13 Lady Road, Edinburgh EH16 5PA
   0131-468 1254

53 **Edinburgh: Queensferry (H)** See Edinburgh: Dalmeny

54 Edinburgh: Ratho
Ian J. Wells BD   1999
2 Freelands Road, Ratho, Newbridge EH28 8NP
[E-mail: IWells@churchofscotland.org.uk]
0131-333 1346

55 Edinburgh: Reid Memorial (H) (0131-662 1203) (E-mail: reid.memorial@btinternet.com)
Vacant
20 Wilton Road, Edinburgh EH16 5NX
0131-667 3981

56 Edinburgh: Richmond Craigmillar (H) (0131-661 6561)
Elizabeth M. Henderson   1985   1997
MA BD MTh
Manse of Duddingston, Old Church Lane, Edinburgh EH15 3PX
[E-mail: EHenderson@churchofscotland.org.uk]
0131-661 4240

57 Edinburgh: St Andrew's and St George's West (H) (0131-225 3847) (E-mail: info@standrewsandstgeorges.org.uk)
Ian Y. Gilmour BD   1985   2011
25 Comely Bank, Edinburgh EH4 1AJ
[E-mail: IGilmour@churchofscotland.org.uk]
0131-332 5848

58 Edinburgh: St Andrew's Clermiston
Alistair H. Keil BD DipMin   1989
87 Drum Brae South, Edinburgh EH12 8TD
[E-mail: AKeil@churchofscotland.org.uk]
0131-339 4149

59 Edinburgh: St Catherine's Argyle (H) (0131-667 7220)
Stuart D. Irvin BD   2013   2016
5 Palmerston Road, Edinburgh EH9 1TL
[E-mail: SIrvin@churchofscotland.org.uk]
0131-667 9344

60 Edinburgh: St Cuthbert's (H) (0131-229 1142) (E-mail: office@st-cuthberts.net)
Peter Sutton
St Cuthbert's Church, 5 Lothian Road, Edinburgh EH1 2EP
[E-mail: PSutton@churchofscotland.org.uk]
07718 311319 (Mbl)

61 Edinburgh: St David's Broomhouse (H) (0131-443 9851)
Michael J. Mair BD   2014
33 Traquair Park West, Edinburgh EH12 7AN
[E-mail: MMair@churchofscotland.org.uk]
0131-334 1730

62 Edinburgh: St John's Colinton Mains
Peter Nelson BSc BD   2015
2 Caiystane Terrace, Edinburgh EH10 6SR
[E-mail: PNelson@churchofscotland.org.uk]
07500 057889 (Mbl)

63 Edinburgh: St Margaret's (H) (0131-554 7400) (E-mail: stm.parish@virgin.net)
Carolyn (Carol) H.M. Ford DSD RSAMD   2003   43 Moira Terrace, Edinburgh EH7 6TD
BD   [E-mail: CFord@churchofscotland.org.uk]
0131-669 7329

64 Edinburgh: St Martin's
William M. Wishart BD   2017   1 Toll House Gardens, Tranent EH33 2QQ
                                              [E-mail: BWishart@churchofscotland.org.uk]
01875 704071

65 Edinburgh: St Michael's (H) (E-mail: office@stmichaels-kirk.co.uk)
Vacant   9 Merchiston Gardens, Edinburgh EH10 5DD
0131-346 1970

66 Edinburgh: St Nicholas' Sighthill
Thomas M. Kisitu MTh PhD   2015   122 Sighthill Loan, Edinburgh EH11 4NT
                                                    [E-mail: TMKisitu@churchofscotland.org.uk]
0131-442 3978

67 Edinburgh: St Stephen's Comely Bank (0131-315 4616)
George Vidits BD MTh   2000   2015   8 Blinkbonny Crescent, Edinburgh EH4 3NB
                                                        [E-mail: GVidits@churchofscotland.org.uk]
0131-332 3364

68 Edinburgh: Slateford Longstone
Vacant   50 Kingsknowe Road South, Edinburgh EH14 2JW
0131-466 5308

69 Edinburgh: Stockbridge (H) (0131-552 8738) (E-mail: stockbridgechurch@btconnect.com)
John A. Cowie BSc BD   1983   2013   19 Eildon Street, Edinburgh EH3 5JU
                                                        [E-mail: JCowie@churchofscotland.org.uk]
0131-557 6052
07506 104416 (Mbl)

70 Edinburgh: The Tron Kirk (Gilmerton and Moredun)
Cameron Mackenzie BD   1997   2010   467 Gilmerton Road, Edinburgh EH17 7JG
                                                        [E-mail: Cammy.Mackenzie@churchofscotland.org.uk]
0131-664 7538

Janet R. McKenzie (Mrs)   2016   80C Colinton Road, Edinburgh EH14 1DD
   (Ordained Local Minister)   [E-mail: JMcKenzie@churchofscotland.org.uk]
0131-444 2054
07980 884653 (Mbl)
Liz Crocker DipComEd DCS   77c Craigcrook Road, Edinburgh EH4 3PH
                                              [E-mail: ECrocker@churchofscotland.org.uk]
0131-332 0227

71 Edinburgh: Willowbrae (H) (0131-661 8259) 1986 2017 19 Abercorn Road, Edinburgh EH8 7DP 0131-652 2938
A. Malcolm Ramsay BA LLB DipMin
(Transitional Minister)
(Edinburgh: Willowbrae is a new charge formed by the union of Edinburgh: Craigentinny St Christopher's and Edinburgh: New Restalrig)

Name	Ord	Ind	Charge/Position	Address	Tel
Abernethy, William LTh	1979	1993	(Glenrothes: St Margaret's)	120/1 Willowbrae Road, Edinburgh EH8 7HW	0131-661 0390
Alexander, Ian W. BA BD STM	1990	2010	World Mission Council	121 George Street, Edinburgh EH2 4YN [E-mail: IAlexander@churchofscotland.org.uk]	0131-225 5722
Anderson, Robert S. BD	1988	1997	(Scottish Churches World Exchange)		
Armitage, William L. BSc BD	1976	2006	(Edinburgh: London Road)	Flat 7, 4 Papermill Wynd, Edinburgh EH7 4GJ [E-mail: bill@billarm.plus.com]	0131-558 8534
Baird, Kenneth S. MSc PhD BD MIMarEST	1998	2009	(Edinburgh: Leith North)	3 Maule Terrace, Gullane EH31 2DB	01620 843447
Barrington, Charles W.H. MA BD	1997	2007	(Associate: Edinburgh: Balerno)	502 Lanark Road, Edinburgh EH14 5DH	0131-453 4826
Beckett, David M. BA BD	1964	2002	(Edinburgh: Greyfriars, Tolbooth and Highland Kirk)	1F1, 31 Sciennes Road, Edinburgh EH9 1NT [E-mail: davidbecket3@aol.com]	0131-667 2672
Bicket, Matthew S. BD	1989	2017	(Carnoustie: Panbride)	9/2 Connaught Place, Edinburgh EH6 4RQ	0131-552 8781
Blakey, Ronald S. MA BD MTh	1962	2000	(Assembly Council)	24 Kimmerghame Place, Edinburgh EH4 2GE [E-mail: kathleen.blakey@gmail.com]	0131-343 6352 (Mbl) 07851 598101
Booth, Jennifer (Mrs) BD	1996	2004	(Associate: Leith South)	39 Lilyhill Terrace, Edinburgh EH8 7DR	0131-661 3813 (Mbl) 07735 749594
Borthwick, Kenneth S. MA BD	1983	2016	(Edinburgh: Holy Trinity)	34 Rodger Crescent, Armadale EH48 3GR [E-mail: kennysamuel@aol.com]	
Boyd, Kenneth M. (Prof.) MA BD PhD FRCPE	1970	1996	University of Edinburgh: Medical Ethics	1 Doune Terrace, Edinburgh EH3 6DY [E-mail: k.boyd@ed.ac.uk]	0131-225 6485
Brady, Ian D. BSc ARCST BD	1967	2001	(Edinburgh: Corstorphine Old)	28 Frankfield Crescent, Dalgety Bay, Dunfermline KY11 9LW [E-mail: bradye500@gmail.com]	01383 825104
Brook, Stanley A. BD MTh	1977	2016	(Newport-on-Tay)	4 Scotstoun Green, South Queensferry EH30 9YA [E-mail: stan_brook@btinternet.com]	0131-331 4237
Brown, William D. MA	1963	1989	(Wishaw: Thornlie)	9/3 Craigend Park, Edinburgh EH16 5XY [E-mail: wdbrown@surefish.co.uk]	0131-672 2936
Brown, William D. BD CQSW	1987	2013	(Edinburgh: Murrayfield)	79 Carnbee Park, Edinburgh EH16 6GG [E-mail: wdb@talktalk.net]	0131-261 7297
Cameron, G. Gordon MA BD STM	1957	1997	(Juniper Green)	10 Beechwood Gardens, Stirling FK8 2AX	01786 472934
Cameron, John W.M. MA BD	1957	1996	(Liberton)	10 Plewlands Gardens, Edinburgh EH10 5JP	0131-447 1277
Chalmers, Murray MA	1965	2006	(Hospital Chaplain)	8 Easter Warriston, Edinburgh EH7 4QX	0131-552 4211
Clark, Christine M. (Mrs) BA BD MTh	2006	2013	Hospital Chaplain	40 Pentland Avenue, Edinburgh EH13 0HY [E-mail: christine.clark7@aol.co.uk]	
Clinkenbeard, William W. BSc BD STM	1966	2000	(Edinburgh: Carrick Knowe)	3/17 Western Harbour Breakwater, Edinburgh EH6 6PA [E-mail: bjclinks@compuserve.com]	
Cook, John MA BD	1967	2005	(Edinburgh: Leith St Andrew's)	26 Silverknowes Court, Edinburgh EH4 5NR	0131-312 8447
Curran, Elizabeth M. (Miss) BD	1995	2008	(Aberlour)	Blackford Grange, 39/2 Blackford Avenue, Edinburgh EH9 3HN [E-mail: ecurran8@aol.com]	0131-664 1358

Name & Qualifications			Position	Address	Tel
Cuthell, Tom C. MA BD MTh	1965	2007	(Edinburgh: St Cuthbert's)	Flat 10, 2 Kingsburgh Crescent, Waterfront, Edinburgh EH5 1JS	0131-476 3864
Davidson, D. Hugh MA	1965	2009	(Edinburgh: Inverleith)	Flat 1/2, 22 Summerside Place, Edinburgh EH6 4NZ [E-mail: hdavidson35@btinternet.com]	0131-554 8420
Davidson, Ian M.P. MBE MA BD	1954	1994	(Stirling: Allan Park South with Church of the Holy Rude)	13/8 Craigend Park, Edinburgh EH16 5XX	0131-664 0074
Dawson, Michael S. BTech BD	1979	2005	(Associate: Edinburgh: Holy Trinity)	9 The Broich, Alva FK12 5NR [E-mail: mixpen.dawson@btinternet.com]	01259 769309
Dilbey, Mary D. (Miss) BD	1997	2002	(West Kirk of Calder)	41 Bonaly Rise, Edinburgh EH13 0QU	0131-441 9092
Donald, Alistair P. MA PhD BD	1999	2009	Chaplain: Heriot-Watt University	The Chaplaincy, Heriot-Watt University, Edinburgh EH14 4AS [E-mail: a.p.donald@hw.ac.uk]	0131-451 4508
Douglas, Alexander B. BD	1979	2014	(Edinburgh: Blackhall St Columba's)	15 Inchview Gardens, Dalgety Bay, Dunfermline KY11 9SA [E-mail: alexandjill@douglas.net]	01383 242872
Douglas, Colin R. MA BD STM	1969	2007	(Livingston Ecumenical Parish)	34 West Pilton Gardens, Edinburgh EH4 4EQ [E-mail: colin.r.douglas@gmail.com]	0131-551 3808
Doyle, Ian B. MA BD PhD	1946	1991	(Department of National Mission)	21 Lygon Road, Edinburgh EH16 5QD	0131-667 2697
Drummond, Rhoda (Miss) DCS			(Deacon)	Flat K, 23 Grange Loan, Edinburgh EH9 2ER	0131-668 3631
Dunn, W. Iain C. DA LTh	1983	1998	(Pilrig and Dalmeny Street)	10 Fox Covert Avenue, Edinburgh EH12 6UQ	0131-334 1665
Embleton, Brian M. BD	1976	2015	(Edinburgh: Reid Memorial)	54 Edinburgh Road, Peebles EH45 8EB [E-mail: bmembleton@gmail.com]	01721 602157
Embleton, Sara R. (Mrs) BA BD MTh	1988	2010	(Edinburgh: Leith St Serf's)	54 Edinburgh Road, Peebles EH45 8EB [E-mail: srembleton@gmail.com]	01721 602157
Evans, Mark BSc MSc DCS	2006		Head of Spiritual Care NHS Fife	13 Easter Drylaw Drive, Edinburgh EH4 2QA [E-mail: mark.evans59@nhs.net]	(Home) 0131-343 3089 (Office) 01383 674136
Farquharson, Gordon MA BD DipEd	1998	2007	(Stonehaven: Dunnottar)	26 Learmonth Court, Edinburgh EH4 1PB [E-mail: gfarqu@talktalk.net]	0131-343 1047
Faulds, Norman L. MA BD FSAScot	1968	2000	(Aberlady with Gullane)	10 West Fenton Court, West Fenton, North Berwick EH39 5AE	01620 842331
Fergusson, David A.S. (Prof.) OBE MA BD DPhil DD FBA FRSE	1984	2000	University of Edinburgh	23 Riselaw Crescent, Edinburgh EH10 6HN	0131-447 4022
Forrester, Margaret R. (Mrs) MA BD DD	1974	2003	(Edinburgh: St Michael's)	25 Kingsburgh Road, Edinburgh EH12 6DZ [E-mail: margaret@rosskeen.org.uk]	0131-337 5646
Fraser, Liam J. LLB BD MTh PhD	2017		Pioneer Minister, Campus Ministry	[E-mail: lfraser@churchofscotland.org.uk]	
Fraser, Shirley A. (Miss) MA BD	1992	2008	(Scottish Field Director: Friends International)	6/50 Roseburn Drive, Edinburgh EH12 5NS	0131-347 1400
Frew, Michael W. BSc BD	1978	2017	(Edinburgh: Slateford Longstone)	37 Swanston Terrace, Edinburgh EH10 7DN	(Mbl) 07712 162375
Gardner, John V.	1997	2003	(Glamis, Inverarity and Kinnettles)	75/1 Lockharton Avenue, Edinburgh EH14 1BD [E-mail: jvgardner66@googlemail.com]	0131-443 7126
Gordon, Margaret (Mrs) DCS	1974	2009	(Edinburgh: Currie)	92 Lanark Road West, Currie EH14 5LA	0131-449 2554
Gordon, Tom MA BD	1967	2008	(Chaplain: Marie Curie Hospice, Edinburgh)	22 Gosford Road, Port Seton, Prestonpans EH32 0HF	01875 812262
Graham, W. Peter MA BD			(Presbytery Clerk)	23/6 East Comiston, Edinburgh EH10 6RZ	0131-445 5763
Hardman Moore, Susan (Prof.) BA PGCE MA PhD	2013		Ordained Local Minister	c/o New College, Mound Place, Edinburgh EH1 2LX [E-mail: SHardman-Moore@churchofscotland.org.uk]	0131-650 8908 (Mbl) 07811 345699
Harkness, James CB OBE QHC MA DD	1961	1995	(Chaplain General: Army)	13 Saxe Coburg Place, Edinburgh EH3 5BR	0131-343 1297

Name			Position	Address	Phone
Herbold Ross, Kristina M.	2008	2016	Workplace Chaplain	Old Parish Church Office, 2a Costorphine High Street, Edinburgh EH12 7ST [E-mail: kristina.ross@wpcscotland.co.uk]	(Mbl) 07702 863342
Hill, J. William BA BD	1967	2001	(Edinburgh: Corstorphine St Anne's)	33/9 Murrayfield Road, Edinburgh EH12 6EP	0131-629 0233
Inglis, Ann (Mrs) LLB BD	1986	2015	(Langton and Lammermuir Kirk)	34 Echline View, South Queensferry EH30 9XL [E-mail: revainglis@gmail.com]	
Irving, William D. LTh	1985	2005	(Golspie)	122 Swanston Muir, Edinburgh EH10 7HY	0131-441 3384
Jeffrey, Eric W.S. JP MA	1954	1994	(Edinburgh: Bristo Memorial)	18 Gillespie Crescent, Edinburgh EH10 4HT	0131-229 7815
Kingston, David V.F. BD DipPTh	1993	2015	(Chaplain: Army)	2 Cleuch Avenue, North Middleton, Gorebridge EH23 4RP	01875 822026
Lamont, Stewart J. BSc BD	1972	2015	(Arbirlot with Carmyllie)	13/1 Grosvenor Crescent, Edinburgh EH12 5EL [E-mail: lamontsj@gmail.com]	(Mbl) 07557 532012
Lawson, Kenneth C. MA BD	1963	1999	(Adviser in Adult Education)	56 Easter Drylaw View, Edinburgh EH4 2QP	0131-539 3311
Logan, Anne T. (Mrs) MA BD MTh DMin	1981	2012	(Edinburgh: Stockbridge)	Sunnyside Cottage, 18 Upper Broomieknowe, Lasswade EH18 1LP [E-mail: annetlogan@blueyonder.co.uk]	0131-663 9550
McCabe, George	1963	1996	(Airdrie High)	The Elms Care Home, White House Loan, Edinburgh EH9 2EX	
Macdonald, Finlay A.J. MA BD PhD DD	1971	2010	(Principal Clerk)	8 St Ronan's Way, Innerleithen EH44 6RG [E-mail: finlay_macdonald@btinternet.com]	01896 831631
Macdonald, Peter J. BD	1986	2017	(Leader of the Iona Community)	63 Jim Bush Drive, Prestonpans EH32 9GB [E-mail: petermacdonald166@me.com]	01875 819655 (Mbl) 07946 715166
Macdonald, William J. BD	1976	2002	(Board of National Mission: New Charge Development)	1/13 North Werber Park, Edinburgh EH4 1SY	0131-332 0254
MacGregor, Margaret S. (Miss) MA BD DipEd	1985	1994	(Calcutta)	16 Learmonth Court, Edinburgh EH4 1PB	0131-332 1089
McGregor, Alistair G.C. QC BD	1987	2002	(Edinburgh: Leith North)	22 Primrose Bank Road, Edinburgh EH5 3JG	0131-551 2802
McGregor, T. Stewart MBE MA BD	1957	1998	(Chaplain: Edinburgh Royal Infirmary)	19 Lonsdale Terrace, Edinburgh EH3 9HL [E-mail: cetsm@uwclub.net]	0131-229 5332
MacKay, Stewart A.	2009		Chaplain: Army	3 Bn Black Watch, Royal Regiment of Scotland, Fort George, Ardersier, Inverness IV1 2TD	
Mackenzie, James G. BA BD	1980	2005	(Jersey: St Columba's)	26 Drylaw Crescent, Edinburgh EH4 2AU [E-mail: jgrmackenzie@jerseymail.co.uk]	0131-332 3720
Maclean, Ailsa G. (Mrs) BD DipCE	1979	1988	Chaplain: George Heriot's School	28 Swan Spring Avenue, Edinburgh EH10 6NJ	0131-445 1320
Macmillan, Gilleasbuig I. KCVO MA BD DHtc DD FRSE HRSA FRCSEd	1969	2013	(Edinburgh: High (St Giles'))	207 Dalkeith Road, Edinburgh EH16 5DS	0131-667 5732
MacMurchie, F. Lynne LLB BD	1998	2003	Healthcare Chaplain	Edinburgh Community Mental Health Chaplaincy, 41 George IV Bridge, Edinburgh EH1 1EL [E-mail: gmacmillan1@btinternet.com]	0131-220 5150
McNab, John L. MA BD	1997	2014	Ministries Council	121 George Street, Edinburgh EH2 4YN	0131-225 5722
McPake, John M. LTh	2000	2014	(Edinburgh: Liberton Northfield)	9 Claverhouse Drive, Edinburgh EH16 6BR [E-mail: john_mcpake9@yahoo.co.uk]	0131-658 1754
McPheat, Elspeth DCS			Deaconess: CrossReach	11/5 New Orchardfield, Edinburgh EH6 5ET [E-mail: elspeth176@sky.com]	0131-554 4143
McPhee, Duncan C. MA BD	1953	1993	(Department of National Mission)	8 Belvedere Park, Edinburgh EH6 4LR	0131-552 6784
Macpherson, Colin C.R. MA BD	1958	1996	(Dunfermline St Margaret's)	7 Eva Place, Edinburgh EH9 3ET	0131-667 1456
McPherson, Marjory (Mrs) LLB BD MTh	1990	2017	Presbytery Clerk	17 Craigs Bank, Edinburgh EH12 8HD [E-mail: MMcPherson@churchofscotland.org.uk]	0131-467 6826

Name			Position	Address / Contact	Tel
Mathieson, Angus R. MA BD	1988	1998	Ministries Council	21 Traquair Park West, Edinburgh EH12 7AN	0131-334 9774
Moir, Ian A. MA BD	1962	2000	(Adviser for Urban Priority Areas)	28/6 Comely Bank Avenue, Edinburgh EH4 1EL	0131-332 2748
Monteith, W. Graham BD PhD	1974	1994	(Flotta and Fara with Hoy and Walls)	20/3 Grandfield, Edinburgh EH6 4TL	0131-552 2564
Morrison, Mary B. (Mrs) MA BD DipEd	1978	2000	(Edinburgh: Stenhouse St Aidan's)	174 Craigcrook Road, Edinburgh EH4 3PP	0131-336 4706
Moyes, Sheila A. (Miss) DCS (Deacon)					
Mulligan, Anne MA DCS			(Deacon: Hospital Chaplain)	27A Craigour Avenue, Edinburgh EH17 1NH [E-mail: mulliganne@aol.com]	0131-664 3426
Munro, George A.M.	1968	2000	(Edinburgh: Cluny)	108 Caiyside, Edinburgh EH10 7HR	0131-445 5829
Munro, John P.L. MA BD PhD	1977	2007	(Kinross)	5 Marchmont Crescent, Edinburgh EH9 1HN [E-mail: jplmunro@yahoo.co.uk]	0131-623 0198
Munro, John R. BD	1976	2017	(Edinburgh: Fairmilehead)	23 Braid Farm Road, Edinburgh EH10 6LE [E-mail: revjohnmunro@hotmail.com]	0131-446 9363
Murrie, John BD	1953	1996	(Kirkliston)	31 Nicol Road, The Whins, Broxburn EH52 6JJ	01506 852464
Orr, Sheena BA MSc MBA BD	2011	2015	Prison Chaplain	HM Prison, Edinburgh EH11 3LN [E-mail: sheens59@gmail.com]	0131-444 3115 (Mbl) 07922 649160
Paterson, Douglas S. MA BD	1976	2010	(Edinburgh: St Colm's)	4 Ards Place, High Street, Aberlady EH32 0DB	01875 870192
Plate, Maria A.G. (Miss) LTh BA	1983	2000	(South Ronaldsay and Burray)	Flat 29, 77 Barnton Park View, Edinburgh EH4 6EL	0131-339 8539
Rennie, Agnes M. (Miss) DCS	1982	2000	(Deacon)	3/1 Craigmillar Court, Edinburgh EH16 4AD	0131-661 8475
Ridland, Alistair K. MA BD	1965	2005	Chaplain: Western General Hospital	13 Stewart Place, Kirkliston EH29 0BQ	0131-333 2711
Robertson, Charles LVO MA			(Edinburgh: Canongate)	3 Ross Gardens, Edinburgh EH9 3BS [E-mail: canongate1@aol.com]	0131-662 9025
Robertson, Norma P. (Miss) BD DMin MTh	1993	2002	(Kincardine O'Neil with Lumphanan)	Flat 5, 2 Burnbrae Drive, Grovewood Hill, Edinburgh EH12 8AS	0131-339 6701
Robertson, Pauline (Mrs) DCS BA CertTheol			Port Chaplain, Sailors' Society	6 Ashville Terrace, Edinburgh EH6 8DD [E-mail: probertson@sailors-society.org]	0131-554 6564
Ross, Keith W. MA BD	1984	2015	(Congregational Development Officer)	Easter Bavelaw Ho, Pentland Hills Regional Park, Balerno EH14 7JS [E-mail:keithwross@outlook.com]	(Mbl) 07759 436303 (Mbl) 07855 163449
Ross, Matthew Z. LLB BD MTh FSAScot	1998	2014	General Secretary, Action of Churches Together in Scotland (ACTS)	Jubilee House, Forthside Way, Stirling FK8 1QZ [E-mail: matthewross@acts-scotland.org]	01259 222360 (Mbl) 07711 706950
Schofield, Melville F. MA	1960	2000	(Chaplain: Western General Hospital)	25 Rowantree Grove, Currie EH14 5AT	0131-449 4745
Scott, Ian G. BSc BD STM	1965	2006	(Edinburgh: Greenbank)	50 Forthview Walk, Tranent EH33 1FE [E-mail: igscott50@btinternet.com]	01875 612907
Scott, Jayne E. BA MEd MBA	1988	2016	Secretary, Ministries Council	121 George Street, Edinburgh EH2 4YN [E-mail: JScott@churchofscotland.org.uk]	0131-225 5722
Scott, Martin C. DipMusEd RSAM BD PhD	1986	2016	Secretary, Council of Assembly	121 George Street, Edinburgh EH2 4YN [E-mail: MScott@churchofscotland.org.uk]	0131-225 5722
Smith, Angus MA LTh	1965	2006	(Chaplain to the Oil Industry)	3/7 West Powburn, West Savile Gait, Edinburgh EH9 3EW	0131-667 1761
Stark, Suzi BD	2013	2016	Hospice Chaplain	St Columba's Hospice, 15 Boswall Road, Edinburgh EH5 3RW [E-mail: SStark@churchofscotland.org.uk]	0131-551 1381
Steele, Marilynn J. (Mrs) BD DCS			(Deacon)	2 Northfield Gardens, Prestonpans EH32 9LQ [E-mail: marilynnsteele@aol.com]	01875 811497

Name			Position	Address	Telephone
Stephen, Donald M. TD MA BD ThM	1962	2001	(Edinburgh: Marchmont St Giles')	10 Hawkhead Crescent, Edinburgh EH16 6LR [E-mail: donaldmstephen@gmail.com]	0131-658 1216
Stevenson, John MA BD PhD	1963	2001	(Department of Education)	12 Swanston Gardens, Edinburgh EH10 7DL	0131-445 3960
Stewart, Alexander T. MA BD FSAScot	1995	2016	(Edinburgh: Costorphine St. Ninian's)	36 Viewlands Terrace, Perth PH1 1BZ [E-mail: alex.t.stewart@blueyonder.co.uk]	01738 566675
Stewart, Lezley J. BD ThM MTh	2000	2017	Ministries Council	121 George Street, Edinburgh EH2 4YN [E-mail: LStewart@churchofscotland.org.uk]	0131-225 5722
Stirling, A. Douglas BSc	1956	1994	(Rhu and Shandon)	162 Avontoun Park, Linlithgow EH49 6QH	01506 845021
Stitt, Ronald J. Maxwell LTh BA ThM BREd DMin FSAScot	1977	2012	(Hamilton: Gilmour and Whitehill)	413 Gilmerton Road, Edinburgh EH17 7JJ	
Tait, John M. BSc BD	1985	2012	(Edinburgh: Pilrig St Paul's)	82 Greenend Gardens, Edinburgh EH17 7QH [E-mail: johnmtait@me.com]	0131-258 9105
Taylor, William R. MA BD MTh	1983	2004	Chaplaincy Adviser (Church of Scotland): Scottish Prison Service	Calton House, 5 Redheughs Rigg, South Gyle, Edinburgh EH12 9DQ [E-mail: bill.taylor@sps.pnn.gov.uk]	0131-244 8640
Teague, Yvonne (Mrs) DCS			(Board of Ministry)	46 Craigcrook Avenue, Edinburgh EH4 3PX [E-mail: y.teague.1@blueyonder.co.uk]	0131-336 3113
Telfer, Iain J.M. BD DPS	1978	2001	Chaplain: Royal Infirmary	Royal Infirmary of Edinburgh, 51 Little France Crescent, Edinburgh EH16 4SA	0131-242 1997
Thom, Helen (Miss) BA DipEd MA DCS			(Deacon)	84 Great King Street, Edinburgh EH3 6QU	0131-556 5687
Thomson, Donald M. BD	1975	2013	(Tullibody: St Serf's)	50 Sighthill Road, Edinburgh EH11 4NY [E-mail: donniethomson@tiscali.co.uk]	
Tweedie, Fiona BSc PhD	2011		Ordained Local Minister: Mission Statistics Co-ordinator	121 George Street, Edinburgh EH2 4YN [E-mail: FTweedie@churchofscotland.org.uk]	0131-225 5722
Watson, Nigel G. MA	1998	2012	(Associate: East Kilbride: Old/Stewartfield/West)	7 St Catherine's Place, Edinburgh EH9 1NU [E-mail: nigel.g.watson@gmail.com]	0131-662 4191
Webster, Peter BD	1977	2014	(Edinburgh: Portbello St James')	51 Kempock Street, Gourock PA19 1NF [E-mail: peterwebster101@hotmail.com]	01475 321916
Whyte, George J. BSc BD DMin	1981	2017	Principal Clerk	Church Offices, 121 George Street, Edinburgh EH2 4YN [E-mail: GWhyte@churchofscotland.org.uk]	0131-240 2240
Whyte, Iain A. BA BD STM PhD	1968	2005	(Community Mental Health Chaplain)	14 Carlingnose Point, North Queensferry, Inverkeithing KY11 1ER [E-mail: iainisabel@whytes28.fsnet.co.uk]	01383 410732
Wigglesworth, J. Christopher MBE BSc PhD BD	1968	1999	(St Andrew's College, Selly Oak)	12 Leven Terrace, Edinburgh EH3 9LW [E-mail: wiggles@talk21.com]	0131-228 6335
Wilson, John M. MA	1964	1995	(Adviser in Religious Education)	27 Bellfield Street, Edinburgh EH15 2BR	0131-669 5257
Wynne, Alistair T.E. BA BD	1982	2009	(Nicosia Community Church, Cyprus)	Flat 6, 14 Burnbrae Drive, Edinburgh EH12 8AS [E-mail: awynne2@googlemail.com]	0131-339 6462
Young, Alexander W. BD DipMin	1988	2016	(Head of Spiritual Care: NHS Lothian)	32 Lindsay Circus, The Hawthorns, Rosewell EH24 9EP	

EDINBURGH ADDRESSES

Church	Address
Albany	
Balerno	Johnsburn Road, Balerno
Barclay Viewforth	82 Montrose Terrace
Blackhall St Columba's	Barclay Place
Bristo Memorial	Queensferry Road
Broughton St Mary's	Peffermill Road, Craigmillar
Canongate	Bellevue Crescent
Carrick Knowe	Canongate
Colinton	North Saughton Road
Corstorphine	Dell Road
Craigsbank	Craig's Crescent
Old	Kirk Loan
St Anne's	Kaimes Road
St Ninian's	St John's Road
Craiglockhart	Craiglockhart Avenue
Craigmillar Park	Craigmillar Park
Cramond	Cramond Glebe Road
Currie	Kirkgate, Currie
Davidson's Mains	Quality Street
Dean	Dean Path
Drylaw	Groathill Road North
Duddingston	Old Church Lane, Duddingston
Fairmilehead	Frogston Road West, Fairmilehead
Gorgie Dalry Stenhouse	Gorgie Road
Edgar Hall	Chesser Avenue

Church	Address
Gracemount	Gracemount Drive
Granton	Boswall Parkway
Greenbank	Braidburn Terrace
Greenside	Royal Terrace
Greyfriars Kirk	Greyfriars Place
High (St Giles')	High Street
Holy Trinity	Hailesland Place, Wester Hailes
Inverleith St Serf's	Ferry Road
Juniper Green	Lanark Road, Juniper Green
Kirkliston	The Square, Kirkliston
Leith	
North	Madeira Street off Ferry Road
St Andrew's	Easter Road
South	Kirkgate, Leith
Wardie	Primrosebank Road
Liberton	Kirkgate, Liberton
Northfield	Gilmerton Road, Liberton
London Road	London Road
Marchmont St Giles'	Kilgraston Road
Mayfield Salisbury	Mayfield Road x West Mayfield
Meadowbank	Dalziel Place x London Road
Morningside	Cluny Gardens
Morningside United	Bruntsfield Place x Chamberlain Rd
Murrayfield	Abinger Gardens
Newhaven	Craighall Road
Old Kirk and Muirhouse	Pennywell Gardens
Palmerston Place	Palmerston Place
Pilrig St Paul's	Pilrig Street

Church	Address
Polwarth	Polwarth Terrace x Harrison Road
Portobello and Joppa	Abercorn Terrace
Priestfield	Dalkeith Road x Marchhall Place
Queensferry	The Loan, South Queensferry
Ratho	Baird Road, Ratho
Reid Memorial	West Savile Terrace
Richmond Craigmillar	Niddrie Mains Road
St Andrew's and St George's West	George Street
St Andrew's Clermiston	Clermiston View
St Catherine's Argyle	Grange Road x Chalmers Crescent
St Cuthbert's	Lothian Road
St David's Broomhouse	Broomhouse Crescent
St John's Colinton Mains	Oxgangs Road North
St Margaret's	Restalrig Road South
St Martin's	Magdalene Drive
St Michael's	Slateford Road
St Nicholas' Sighthill	Calder Road
St Stephen's Comely Bank	Comely Bank
Slateford Longstone	Kingsknowe Road North
Stockbridge	Saxe Coburg Street
The Tron Kirk (Gilmerton and Moredun)	Craigour Gardens and Ravenscroft Street
Willowbrae	Willowbrae Road

(2) WEST LOTHIAN

Meets in the church of the incoming Moderator on the first Tuesday of September and in St John's Church Hall, Bathgate, on the first Tuesday of every other month, except December, when the meeting is on the second Tuesday, and January, July and August, when there is no meeting.

Clerk: REV. DUNCAN SHAW BD MTh   St John's Manse, Mid Street, Bathgate EH48 1QD   01506 653146
[E-mail: westlothian@churchofscotland.org.uk]

Abercorn (H) linked with Pardovan, Kingscavil (H) and Winchburgh (H)
A. Scott Marshall DipComm BD   1984   1998   The Manse, Winchburgh, Broxburn EH52 6TT   01506 890919
[E-mail: SMarshall@churchofscotland.org.uk]

Armadale (H) Julia C. Wiley (Ms) MA(CE) MDiv	1998	2010	70 Mount Pleasant, Armadale, Bathgate EH48 3HB [E-mail: JWiley@churchofscotland.org.uk]	01501 730358
Margaret Corrie (Miss) DCS			44 Sunnyside Street, Camelon, Falkirk FK1 4BH [E-mail: MCorrie@churchofscotland.org.uk]	07955 633969 (Mbl)
Avonbridge (H) linked with Torphichen (H) Ann Lyall DCS (Interim Deacon)			Manse Road, Torphichen, Bathgate EH48 4LT [E-mail: ALyall@churchofscotland.org.uk]	
Bathgate: Boghall (H) Christopher Galbraith BA LLB BD	2012		1 Manse Place, Ash Grove, Bathgate EH48 1NJ [E-mail: CGalbraith@churchofscotland.org.uk]	01506 652715
Bathgate: High (H) Sandra Black BSc BD (Interim Minister)	1988	2017	36 Glencairn Drive, Glasgow G41 4PW [E-mail: SBlack@churchofscotland.org.uk]	07703 822057 (Mbl)
Bathgate: St John's (H) Duncan Shaw BD MTh	1975	1978	St John's Manse, Mid Street, Bathgate EH48 1QD [E-mail: westlothian@churchofscotland.org.uk]	01506 653146
Blackburn and Seafield (H) Vacant			The Manse, 5 MacDonald Gardens, Blackburn, Bathgate EH47 7RE	01506 652825
Blackridge (H) linked with Harthill: St Andrew's (H) Vacant			East Main Street, Harthill, Shotts ML7 5QW	01501 751239
Breich Valley (H) Robert J. Malloch BD	1987	2013	Breich Valley Manse, Stoneyburn, Bathgate EH47 8AU [E-mail: RMalloch@churchofscotland.org.uk]	01501 763142
Broxburn (H) Jacobus Boonzaaier BA BCom(OR) BD MDiv PhD	1995	2015	2 Church Street, Broxburn EH52 5EL [E-mail: JBoonzaaier@churchofscotland.org.uk]	01506 337560
Fauldhouse: St Andrew's (H) Vacant			7 Glebe Court, Fauldhouse, Bathgate EH47 9DX	01501 771190

Harthill: St Andrew's See Blackridge

Kirknewton (H) and East Calder (H)
Vacant
Brenda Robson PhD   2005   2014   8 Manse Court, East Calder, Livingston EH53 0HF   01506 884585
(Auxiliary Minister)   2 Baird Road, Ratho, Newbridge EH28 8RA   0131-333 2746
[E-mail: BRobson@churchofscotland.org.uk]

Kirk of Calder (H)
John M. Povey MA BD   1981   19 Maryfield Park, Mid Calder, Livingston EH53 0SB   01506 882495
[E-mail: JPovey@churchofscotland.org.uk]

Kay McIntosh (Mrs) DCS   4 Jacklin Green, Livingston EH54 8PZ   01506 440543
[E-mail: kay@backedge.co.uk]

Linlithgow: St Michael's (H) (E-mail: info@stmichaels-parish.org.uk)
D. Stewart Gillan BSc MDiv PhD   1985   2004   St Michael's Manse, Kirkgate, Linlithgow EH49 7AL   01506 842195
[E-mail: SGillan@churchofscotland.org.uk]

Cheryl McKellar-Young (Mrs) BA BD   2013   c/o Cross House, The Cross, Linlithgow EH49 7AL   01506 842188
(Associate Minister)   [E-mail: CMcKellarYoung@churchofscotland.org.uk]

Thomas S. Riddell BSc CEng FIChemE   1993   1994   4 The Malings, Linlithgow EH49 6DS   01506 843251
(Auxiliary Minister)   [E-mail: TRiddell@churchofscotland.org.uk]

Linlithgow: St Ninian's Craigmailen (H)
W. Richard Houston BSc BD   1998   2004   29 Philip Avenue, Linlithgow EH49 7BH   01506 202246
[E-mail: WHouston@churchofscotland.org.uk]

Livingston: Old (H)
Nelu I. Balaj BD MA ThD   2010   2017   Manse of Livingston, Charlesfield Lane, Livingston EH54 7AJ   01506 411888
[E-mail: NBalaj@churchofscotland.org.uk]

Gordon J. Pennykid BD DCS   2015   8 Glenfield, Livingston EH54 7BG   07747 652652 (Mbl)
[E-mail: GPennykid@churchofscotland.org.uk]

Livingston United
Ronald G. Greig MA BD   1987   2008   2 Eastcroft Court, Livingston EH54 7ET   01506 467426
[E-mail: RGreig@churchofscotland.org.uk]

Stephanie Njeru BA   13 Eastcroft Court, Livingston EH54 7ET   01506 461020
[E-mail: stephanie.njeru@methodist.org.uk]

Livingston United is a Local Ecumenical Project shared with the Scottish Episcopal, Methodist and United Reformed Churches

Pardovan, Kingscavil and Winchburgh See Abercorn

Polbeth Harwood linked with West Kirk of Calder (H)

Jonanda Groenewald BA BD MTh DD	1999	2014	8 Manse Court, East Calder, Livingston EH53 0HF [E-mail: JGroenewald@churchofscotland.org.uk]	01506 884802

Strathbrock (H)

Marc B. Kenton BTh MTh	1997	2009	1 Manse Park, Uphall, Broxburn EH52 6NX [E-mail: MKenton@churchofscotland.org.uk]	01506 852550

Torphichen See Avonbridge

Uphall: South (H)

Ian D. Maxwell MA BD PhD	1977	2013	8 Fernlea, Uphall, Broxburn EH52 6DF [E-mail: IMaxwell@churchofscotland.org.uk]	01506 239840

West Kirk of Calder (H) See Polbeth Harwood

Whitburn: Brucefield (H)

Alexander M. Roger BD PhD	1982	2014	48 Gleneagles Court, Whitburn, Bathgate EH47 8PG [E-mail: ARoger@churchofscotland.org.uk]	01501 229354

Whitburn: South (H)

Angus Kerr BD CertMin ThM DMin	1983	2013	5 Mansewood Crescent, Whitburn, Bathgate EH47 8HA [E-mail: AKerr@churchofscotland.org.uk]	01501 740333

Black, David W. BSc BD	1968	2008	(Strathbrock)	66 Bridge Street, Newbridge EH28 8SH [E-mail: dw.black666@yahoo.co.uk]	0131-333 2609
Darroch, Richard J.G. BD MTh MA(CMS)	1993	2010	(Whitburn: Brucefield)	23 Barnes Green, Livingston EH54 8PP [E-mail: richdarr@aol.com]	01506 436648
Dunleavy, Suzanne BD DipEd	1990	2016	(Bridge of Weir: St Machar's Ranfurly)	44 Tantallon Gardens, Bellsquarry, Livingston EH54 9AT [E-mail: suzanne.dunleavy@btinternet.com]	
Dunphy, Rhona (Mrs) BD DPTheol DrPhil	2005	2016	Ministries Council	92 The Vennel, Linlithgow EH49 7ET [E-mail: RDunphy@churchofscotland.org.uk]	(Mbl) 07791 007158 01506 412020
Jamieson, Gordon D. MA BD	1974	2012	(Head of Stewardship)	41 Goldpark Place, Livingston EH54 6LW [E-mail: gdj1949@talktalk.net]	
Mackay, Kenneth J. MA BD	1971	2007	(Edinburgh: St Nicholas' Sighthill)	46 Chuckethall Road, Livingston EH54 8FB [E-mail: kmth_mackay@yahoo.co.uk]	01506 410884
MacLaine, Marilyn (Mrs) LTh	1995	2009	(Inchinnan)	37 Bankton Brae, Livingston EH54 9LA [E-mail: marilynmaclaine@btinternet.com]	01506 400619
MacRae, Norman I. LTh	1966	2003	(Inverness: Trinity)	144 Hope Park Gardens, Bathgate EH48 2QX [E-mail: normanmacrae@talktalk.com]	01506 635254
Merrilees, Ann (Miss) DCS			(Deacon)	23 Cuthill Brae, West Calder EH55 8QE [E-mail: ann@merrilees_freeserve.co.uk]	01501 762909
Morrison, Iain C. BA BD	1990	2003	(Linlithgow: St Ninian's Craigmailen)	Whaligoe, 53 Eastcroft Drive, Polmont, Falkirk FK2 0SU [E-mail: iain@kirkweb.org]	01324 713249

Nelson, Georgina MA BD PhD DipEd	1990	1995	Hospital Chaplain	63 Hawthorn Bank, Seafield, Bathgate EH47 7EB	01506 670391
Nicol, Robert M.	1984	1996	(Jersey: St Columba's)	59 Kinloch View, Blackness Road, Linlithgow EH49 7HT [E-mail: revrob.nicol@tiscali.co.uk]	
Orr, J. McMichael MA BD PhD	1949	1986	(Aberfoyle with Port of Menteith)	17a St Ninians Way, Linlithgow EH49 7HL [E-mail: mikeandmargorr@googlemail.com]	01506 840515
Smith, Graham W. BA BD FSAScot	1995	2016	(Livingston: Old)	76 Bankton Park East, Livingston EH54 9BN [E-mail: gsmith2014@hotmail.com]	01506 442917
Thomson, Phyllis (Miss) DCS	2003	2010	(Deacon)	63 Caroline Park, Mid Calder, Livingston EH53 0SJ	01506 883207
Trimble, Robert DCS			(Deacon)	5 Templar Rise, Dedridge, Livingston EH54 6PJ	01506 412504
Walker, Ian BD MEd DipMS	1973	2007	(Rutherglen: Wardlawhill)	92 Carseknowe, Linlithgow EH49 7LG [E-mail: walk102822@aol.com]	01506 844412

(3) LOTHIAN

Meets at Musselburgh: St Andrew's High Parish Church at 7pm on the last Thursday in February, April, June and November, and in a different church on the last Thursday in September.

Clerk: MR JOHN D. McCULLOCH DL 20 Tipperwell Way, Howgate, Penicuik EH26 8QP 01968 676300
[E-mail: lothian@churchofscotland.org.uk]

Depute Clerk: REV MICHAEL D. WATSON 47 Crichton Terrace, Pathhead EH37 5QZ 01875 320043
[E-mail: MWatson@churchofscotland.org.uk]

Aberlady (H) linked with Gullane (H)

| Brian C. Hilsley LLB BD | 1990 | 2015 | The Manse, Hummel Road, Gullane EH31 2BG [E-mail: BHilsley@churchofscotland.org.uk] | 01620 843192 |

Athelstaneford linked with Whitekirk and Tyninghame

| Joanne H.G. Evans-Boiten BD | 2004 | 2009 | The Manse, Athelstaneford, North Berwick EH39 5BE [E-mail: JEvans-Boiten@churchofscotland.org.uk] | 01620 880378 |

Belhaven (H) linked with Spott

| Vacant | | | The Manse, Belhaven Road, Dunbar EH42 1NH | 01368 863098 |

Bilston linked with Glencorse (H) linked with Roslin (H)

| John R. Wells BD DipMin | 1991 | 2005 | 31A Manse Road, Roslin EH25 9LG [E-mail: JWells@churchofscotland.org.uk] | 0131-440 2012 |

Bonnyrigg (H)
John Mitchell LTh CertMin — 1991 — 9 Viewbank View, Bonnyrigg EH19 2HU [E-mail: JMitchell@churchofscotland.org.uk] — 0131-663 8287 (Tel/Fax)

Cockenzie and Port Seton: Chalmers Memorial (H)
Vacant — 2 Links Road, Port Seton, Prestonpans EH32 0HA — 01875 819254

Cockenzie and Port Seton: Old (H)
Guardianship of the Presbytery

Cockpen and Carrington (H) linked with Lasswade (H) and Rosewell (H)
Lorna M. Souter MA BD MSc — 2016 — 11 Pendreich Terrace, Bonnyrigg EH19 2DT [E-mail: LSouter@churchofscotland.org.uk]
Elisabeth G.B. Spence BD DipEd — 1995 2016 — 18 Castell Maynes Avenue, Bonnyrigg EH19 3RW [E-mail: ESpence@churchofscotland.org.uk] — 07889 566418 (Mbl), 07432 528205
(Pioneer Minister, Hopefield Connections)

Dalkeith: St John's and King's Park (H)
Keith L. Mack BD MTh DPS — 2002 — 13 Weir Crescent, Dalkeith EH22 3JN [E-mail: KMack@churchofscotland.org.uk] — 0131-454 0206

Dalkeith: St Nicholas' Buccleuch (H)
Alexander G. Horsburgh MA BD — 1995 2004 — 16 New Street, Musselburgh EH21 6JP [E-mail: AHorsburgh@churchofscotland.org.uk] — 0131-653 3318

Dirleton (H) linked with North Berwick: Abbey (H) (Office: 01620 892800) (E-mail: abbeychurch@btconnect.com)
David J. Graham BSc BD PhD — 1982 1998 — Sydserff, Old Abbey Road, North Berwick EH39 4BP [E-mail: DGraham@churchofscotland.org.uk] — 01620 840878

Dunbar (H)
Gordon Stevenson BSc BD — 2010 — The Manse, 10 Bayswell Road, Dunbar EH42 1AB [E-mail: GStevenson@churchofscotland.org.uk] — 01368 865482

Dunglass
Suzanne G. Fletcher (Mrs) BA MDiv MA — 2001 2011 — The Manse, Cockburnspath TD13 5XZ [E-mail: SFletcher@churchofscotland.org.uk] — 01368 830713

Garvald and Morham linked with Haddington: West (H)
John Vischer — 1993 2011 — 15 West Road, Haddington EH41 3RD [E-mail: JVischer@churchofscotland.org.uk] — 01620 822213

Gladsmuir linked with Longniddry (H)
Robin E. Hill LLB BD PhD   2004   The Manse, Elcho Road, Longniddry EH32 0LB   01875 853195
                                                     [E-mail: RHill@churchofscotland.org.uk]

Glencorse (H) See Bilston

Gorebridge (H)
Mark S. Nicholas MA BD   1999   100 Hunterfield Road, Gorebridge EH23 4TT   01875 820387
                                                     [E-mail: MNicholas@churchofscotland.org.uk]

Gullane See Aberlady

Haddington: St Mary's (H)
Jennifer Macrae (Mrs) MA BD   1998   2007   1 Nungate Gardens, Haddington EH41 4EE   01620 823109
                                                     [E-mail: JMacrae@churchofscotland.org.uk]

Haddington: West See Garvald and Morham

Howgate (H) linked with Penicuik: South (H)
Ian A. Cathcart BSc BD   1994   2007   15 Stevenson Road, Penicuik EH26 0LU   01968 674692
                                                     [E-mail: ICathcart@churchofscotland.org.uk]

Humbie linked with Yester, Bolton and Saltoun
Anikó Schuetz Bradwell MA BD   2015   The Manse, Tweeddale Avenue, Gifford, Haddington EH41 4QN
                                                     [E-mail: ASchuetzBradwell@churchofscotland.org.uk]

Lasswade and Rosewell See Cockpen and Carrington

Loanhead
Graham L. Duffin BSc BD DipEd   1989   2001   120 The Loan, Loanhead EH20 9AJ   0131-448 2459
                                                      [E-mail: GDuffin@churchofscotland.org.uk]

Longniddry See Gladsmuir

Musselburgh: Northesk (H)
Alison P. McDonald MA BD   1991   1998   16 New Street, Musselburgh EH21 6JP   0131-665 2128
                                                      [E-mail: Alison.McDonald@churchofscotland.org.uk]

Musselburgh: St Andrew's High (H) (0131-665 7239)
Yvonne E.S. Atkins (Mrs) BD   1997   2004   8 Ferguson Drive, Musselburgh EH21 6XA
[E-mail: YAtkins@churchofscotland.org.uk]   0131-665 1124

Musselburgh: St Clement's and St Ninian's
Guardianship of the Presbytery

Musselburgh: St Michael's Inveresk
Malcolm Lyon BD   2007   2017   5 Crookston Ct., Crookston Rd., Inveresk, Musselburgh EH21 7TR   0131-653 2411
[E-mail: MLyon@churchofscotland.org.uk]

Newbattle (H) (Website: http://freespace.virgin.net/newbattle.focus)
Vacant
Frederick Harrison   2013   33 Castle Avenue, Gorebridge EH23 4TH   01875 820908
(Ordained Local Minister)   [E-mail: FHarrison@churchofscotland.org.uk]
Malcolm T. Muir   2001   2015   Mayfield and Easthouses Church, Bogwood Court, Mayfield,   0131-663 3245
(Associate Minister)   EH22 5DG   07920 855467 (Mbl)
    [E-mail: MMuir@churchofscotland.org.uk]

Newton
Guardianship of the Presbytery
Andrew Don MBA   2006   5 Eskvale Court, Penicuik EH26 8HT   0131-663 3845
(Ordained Local Minister)   [E-mail: ADon@churchofscotland.org.uk]   01968 675766

North Berwick: Abbey See Dirleton

North Berwick: St Andrew Blackadder (H) (E-mail: admin@standrewblackadder.org.uk) (Website: www.standrewblackadder.org.uk)
Neil J. Dougall BD   1991   2003   7 Marine Parade, North Berwick EH39 4LD   01620 892132
    [E-mail: NDougall@churchofscotland.org.uk]

Ormiston linked with Pencaitland
David J. Torrance BD DipMin   1993   2009   The Manse, Pencaitland, Tranent EH34 5DL   01875 340963
    [E-mail: DTorrance@churchofscotland.org.uk]

Pencaitland See Ormiston

Penicuik: North (H) (Website: www.pnk.org.uk)
Ruth D. Halley BEd BD PGCM   2012   93 John Street, Penicuik EH26 8AG   01968 675761
    [E-mail: RHalley@churchofscotland.org.uk]   07530 307413 (Mbl)

Penicuik: St Mungo's (H)
John C.C. Urquhart MA MA BD   2010   2017   10 Fletcher Grove, Penicuik EH26 0JT   01968 382116
[E-mail: JCUrquhart@churchofscotland.org.uk]

Penicuik: South See Howgate

Prestonpans: Prestongrange
Kenneth W Donald BA BD   1982   2014   The Manse, East Loan, Prestonpans EH32 9ED   01875 813643
[E-mail: KDonald@churchofscotland.org.uk]

Roslin See Bilston
Spott See Belhaven

Tranent
Erica M Wishart (Mrs) MA BD   2014   1 Toll House Gardens, Tranent EH33 2QQ   01875 704071
[E-mail: EWishart@churchofscotland.org.uk]

Traprain
David D. Scott BSc BD   1981   2010   The Manse, Preston Road, East Linton EH40 3DS   01620 860227 (Tel/Fax)
[E-mail: DDScott@churchofscotland.org.uk]

Tyne Valley Parish (H)
Vacant   Cranstoun Cottage, Ford, Pathhead EH37 5RE   01875 320314
June E. Johnston BSc MEd BD   2013   49 Braeside Road South, Gorebridge EH23 4DL   01875 823086
(Ordained Local Minister)   [E-mail: June.Johnston@churchofscotland.org.uk]   07754 448889 (Mbl)

Whitekirk and Tyninghame See Athelstaneford
Yester Bolton and Saltoun See Humbie

Name				Address	Tel
Allison, Ann BSc PhD BD	2000	2017	(Crail with Kingsbarns)	99 Coalgate Avenue, Tranent EH33 1JW [E-mail: revann@sky.com]	01875 571778
Andrews, J. Edward MA BD DipCG FSAScot	1985	2005	(Armadale)	Dunnichen, 1B Cameron Road, Nairn IV12 5NS [E-mail: edward.andrews@btinternet.com]	01667 459466 07808 720708 (Mbl)
Bayne, Angus L. LTh BEd MTh	1969	2005	(Edinburgh: Bristo Memorial Craigmillar)	14 Myredale, Bonnyrigg EH19 3NW [E-mail: angus@mccookies.com]	0131-663 6871
Berry, Geoff T. BD BSc	2009	2011	Chaplain: Army	38 Muirfield Drive, Gullane EH31 2HJ [E-mail: geofftalk@yahoo.co.uk]	
Black, A. Graham MA	1964	2003	(Gladsmuir with Longniddry)	26 Hamilton Crescent, Gullane EH31 2HR [E-mail: grablack@btinternet.com]	01620 843899
Brown, Ronald H.	1974	1998	(Musselburgh: Northesk)	6 Monktonhall Farm Cottages, Musselburgh EH21 6RZ	0131-653 2531
Brown, William BD	1972	1997	(Edinburgh: Polwarth)	13 Thornyhall, Dalkeith EH22 2ND	0131-654 0929

Name			Charge	Address	Tel
Burt, Thomas W. BD	1982	2013	(Carlops with Kirkurd and Newlands with West Linton: St Andrew's)	7 Arkwright Court, North Berwick EH39 4RT [E-mail: tomburt@westlinton.com]	01620 895494
Cairns, John B. KCVO LTh LLB LLD DD	1974	2009	(Aberlady with Gullane)	Bell House, Roxburghe Park, Dunbar EH42 1LR [E-mail: johncairns@mail.com]	01368 862501
Coltart, Ian O. CA BD	1988	2010	(Arbirlot with Carmyllie)	25 Bothwell Gardens, Dunbar EH42 1PZ	01368 860064
Dick, Andrew B. BD DipMin	1986	2015	(Musselburgh: St Michael's Inveresk)	4 Kirkhill Court, Gorebridge EH23 4TW [E-mail: dixbit@aol.com]	01875 571223
Frail, Nicola R. BLE MBA MDiv	2000		Army Chaplain	32 Engineer Regiment, Marne Barracks, Catterick Garrison DL10 7NP [E-mail: nrfscot@hotmail.com]	
Fraser, John W. MA BD	1974	2011	(Penicuik: North)	66 Camus Avenue, Edinburgh EH10 6QX [E-mail: jjjj2005@hotmail.co.uk]	0131-623 0647
Glover, Robert L. BMus BD MTh ARCO	1971	2010	(Cockenzie and Port Seton: Chalmers Memorial)	12 Seton Wynd, Port Seton, Prestonpans EH32 0TY [E-mail: rlglover@btinternet.com]	01875 818759
Hutchison, Alan E.W.			(Deacon)	132 Lochbridge Road, North Berwick EH39 4DR	01620 894077
Jones, Anne M. (Mrs) BD	1998	2002	(Hospital Chaplain)	7 North Elphinstone Farm, Tranent EH33 2ND [E-mail: revamjones@aol.com]	01875 614442
Kellock, Chris N. MA BD	1998	2012	Army Chaplain	1 Plantation Road, Tidworth SP9 7SJ	01980 601070
Manson, James A. LTh	1981	2004	(Glencorse with Roslin)	31 Nursery Gardens, Kilmarnock KA1 3JA [E-mail: james.manson@virgin.net]	01563 535430
Pirie, Donald LTh	1975	2006	(Bolton and Saltoun with Humbie with Yester)	46 Caiystane Avenue, Edinburgh EH10 6SH	0131-445 2654
Simpson, Robert R. BA BD	1994	2014	(Callander)	10 Bellsmains, Gorebridge EH23 4QD [E-mail: robert@pansmanse.co.uk]	01875 820843
Stein, Jock MA BD	1973	2008	(Tulliallan and Kincardine)	35 Dunbar Road, Haddington EH41 3PJ [E-mail: jstein@handselpress.org.uk]	01620 824896
Stein, Margaret E. (Mrs) DA BD DipRE	1984	2008	(Tulliallan and Kincardine)	35 Dunbar Road, Haddington EH41 3PJ [E-mail: margaretestein@hotmail.com]	01620 824896
Steven, Gordon R. BD DCS			(Deacon)	51 Nantwich Drive, Edinburgh EH7 6RB [E-mail: grsteven@btinternet.com]	0131-669 2054 (Mbl) 07904 385256
Swan, Andrew F. BD	1983	2000	(Loanhead)	Park View, 2 Park Place, Lanark ML11 9HH	
Torrance, David W. MA BD	1955	1991	(Earlston)	38 Forth Street, North Berwick EH39 4JQ [E-mail: torrance103@btinternet.com]	(Tel/Fax) 01620 895109
Underwood, Florence A. (Mrs) BD	1992	2006	(Assistant, Gladsmuir with Longniddry)	18 Covenanters Rise, Pitreavie Castle, Dunfermline KY11 8SQ	01383 740745
Watson, Michael D.		2013	Ordained Local Minister: Depute Clerk	47 Crichton Terrace, Edinburgh EH37 5QZ [E-mail: MWatson@churchofscotland.org.uk]	01875 320043

(4) MELROSE AND PEEBLES

Meets at Innerleithen on the first Tuesday of February, March, May, October, November and December, and on the fourth Tuesday of June, and in places to be appointed on the first Tuesday of September.

Clerk: REV. VICTORIA LINFORD LLB BD   The Manse, 209 Galashiels Road, Stow, Galashiels TD1 2RE   01578 730237
[E-mail: melrosepeebles@churchofscotland.org.uk]

Depute Clerk: REV. JULIE M. RENNICK BTh   The Manse, High Street, Earlston TD4 6DE   01896 849236
[E-mail: JRennick@churchofscotland.org.uk]

Ashkirk linked with Selkirk (H)
Margaret D.J. Steele (Miss) BSc BD   2000   2011   1 Loanside, Selkirk TD7 4DJ   01750 23308
[E-mail: MSteele@churchofscotland.org.uk]

Bowden (H) and Melrose (H)
Rosemary Frew (Mrs) MA BD   1988   2017   The Manse, Tweedmount Road, Melrose TD6 9ST   01896 822217
[E-mail: RFrew@churchofscotland.org.uk]

Broughton, Glenholm and Kilbucho (H) linked with Skirling linked with Stobo and Drumelzier linked with Tweedsmuir (H)
Vacant   The Manse, Broughton, Biggar ML12 6HQ   01899 830331

Caddonfoot (H) linked with Galashiels: Trinity (H) (01896 752967)
Elspeth Harley BA MTh   1991   2014   8 Mossilee Road, Galashiels TD1 1NF   01896 758485
[E-mail: EHarley@churchofscotland.org.uk]

Carlops linked with Kirkurd and Newlands (H) linked with West Linton: St Andrew's (H)
Vacant   The Manse, Main Street, West Linton EH46 7EE   01968 660221

Channelkirk and Lauder
Marion (Rae) Clark MA BD   2014   The Manse, Brownsmuir Park, Lauder TD2 6QD   01578 718996
[E-mail: RClark@churchofscotland.org.uk]

Earlston
Julie M. Rennick (Mrs) BTh   2005   2011   The Manse, High Street, Earlston TD4 6DE   01896 849236
[E-mail: JRennick@churchofscotland.org.uk]

Eddleston (H) linked with Peebles: Old (H)
Malcolm M. Macdougall BD MTh DipCE   1981   2001   7 Clement Gunn Square, Peebles EH45 8LW   01721 720568
[E-mail: MMacdougall@churchofscotland.org.uk]

Pamela D. Strachan (Lady) MA (Cantab)   2015   Glenhighton, Broughton, Biggar ML12 6JF   01899 830423
(Ordained Local Minister)   [E-mail: PStrachan@churchofscotland.org.uk]   07837 873688 (Mbl)

Ettrick and Yarrow
Samuel Siroky BA MTh   2003   Yarrow Manse, Yarrow, Selkirk TD7 5LA   01750 82336
          [E-mail: SSiroky@churchofscotland.org.uk]

Galashiels: Old Parish and St Paul's (H) linked with Galashiels: St John's (H)
Leon Keller BA BD DipTheol PhD   1988   2015   Woodlea, Abbotsview Drive, Galashiels TD1 3SL   01896 753029
          [E-mail: LKeller@churchofscotland.org.uk]

Galashiels: St John's See Galashiels: Old Parish and St Paul's
Galashiels: Trinity See Caddonfoot

Innerleithen (H), Traquair and Walkerburn
Janice M. Faris (Mrs) BSc BD   1991   2001   The Manse, 1 Millwell Park, Innerleithen, Peebles   EH44 6JF   01896 830309
          [E-mail: JFaris@churchofscotland.org.uk]

Kirkurd and Newlands See Carlops

Lyne and Manor linked with Peebles: St Andrew's Leckie (H) (01721 723121)
Malcolm S. Jefferson   2012   Mansefield, Innerleithen Road, Peebles   EH45 8BE   01721 725148
          [E-mail: MJefferson@churchofscotland.org.uk]

Maxton and Mertoun linked with Newtown linked with St Boswells
Sheila W. Moir (Ms) MTheol   2008   7 Strae Brigs, St Boswells, Melrose TD6 0DH   01835 822255
          [E-mail: SMoir@churchofscotland.org.uk]

Newtown See Maxton and Mertoun
Peebles: Old See Eddleston
Peebles: St Andrew's Leckie See Lyne and Manor
St Boswells See Maxton and Mertoun
Selkirk See Ashkirk
Skirling See Broughton, Glenholm and Kilbucho
Stobo and Drumelzier See Broughton, Glenholm and Kilbucho

Stow: St Mary of Wedale and Heriot
Victoria J. Linford (Mrs) LLB BD   2010   The Manse, 209 Galashiels Road, Stow, Galashiels TD1 2RE   01578 730237
          [E-mail: VLinford@churchofscotland.org.uk]

Tweedsmuir See Broughton, Glenholm and Kilbucho
West Linton: St Andrew's See Carlops

Name			Charge / Role	Address	Telephone
Arnott, A. David K. MA BD	1971	2010	(St Andrews: Hope Park with Strathkinness)	53 Whitehaugh Park, Peebles EH45 9DB [E-mail: adka53@btinternet.com]	01721 725979 (Mbl) 07759 709205
Bowie, Adam McC.	1976	1996	(Cavers and Kirkton with Hobkirk and Southdean)		
Cashman, P. Hamilton BSc	1985	1998	(Dirleton with North Berwick: Abbey)	Glenbield, Redpath, Earlston TD4 6AD 38 Abbotsford Road, Galashiels TD1 3HR [E-mail: mcashman@tiscali.co.uk]	01896 848173 01896 752711
Cutler, James S.H. BD CEng MIStructE	1986	2011	(Black Mount with Culter with Libberton and Quothquan)	12 Kittlegairy Place, Peebles EH45 9LW [E-mail: revjc@btinternet.com]	01721 723950
Devenny, Robert P.	2002	2017	(Head of Spiritual Care, NHS Borders)	Blakeburn Cottage, Wester Housebyres, Melrose TD6 9BW	01896 822350
Dick, J. Ronald BD	1973	1996	(Hospital Chaplain)	5 Georgefield Farm Cottages, Earlston TD4 6BH	01896 848956
Dobie, Rachel J.W. (Mrs) LTh	1991	2008	(Broughton, Glenholm and Kilbucho with Skirling with Stobo and Drumelzier with Tweedsmuir)	20 Moss Side Crescent, Biggar ML12 6GE [E-mail: revracheldobie@talktalk.net]	01899 229244
Dodd, Marion E. (Miss) MA BD LRAM	1988	2010	(Kelso: Old and Sprouston)	Esdaile, Tweedmount Road, Melrose TD6 9ST [E-mail: mariondodd@btinternet.com]	01896 822446
Duncan, Charles A. MA	1956	1992	(Heriot with Stow: St Mary of Wedale)	10 Elm Grove, Galashiels TD1 3JA	01896 753261
Hardie, H. Warner BD	1979	2005	(Blackridge with Harthill: St Andrew's)	Keswick Cottage, Kingsmuir Drive, Peebles EH45 9AA [E-mail: hardies@bigfoot.com]	01721 724003
Hogg, Thomas M. BD	1986	2007	(Tranent)	22 Douglas Place, Galashiels TD1 3BT	01896 759381
Hughes, Barry MA	2011		Ordained Local Minister	Dunslair, Cardrona Way, Cardrona, Peebles EH45 9LD [E-mail: BHughes@churchofscotland.org.uk]	01896 831197
Kellet, John M. MA	1962	1995	(Leith: South)	4 High Cottages, Walkerburn EH43 6AZ	01896 870351
Kennon, Stanley BA BD RN	1992	2000	Chaplain: Royal Navy	Britannia Royal Naval College, Dartmouth TQ6 0HJ [E-mail: brnc-csf@fleetfost.mod.gov.uk]	
Lawrie, Bruce B. BD	1974	2012	(Duffus, Spynie and Hopeman)	5 Thorncroft, Scotts Place, Selkirk TD7 4LN [E-mail: thorncroft54@gmail.com]	01750 725427
MacFarlane, David C. MA	1957	1997	(Eddleston with Peebles: Old)	Lorimer House Nursing Home, 491 Lanark Road, Edinburgh EH14 5DQ	
Milloy, A. Miller DPE LTh DipTrMan	1979	2012	(General Secretary: United Bible Societies)	18 Kittlegairy Crescent, Peebles EH45 9NJ [E-mail: ammilloy@aol.com]	01721 723380
Moore, W. Haisley MA	1966	1996	(Secretary: The Boys' Brigade)	26 Tweedbank Avenue, Tweedbank, Galashiels TD1 3SP	01896 668577
Munson, Winnie (Ms) BD	1996	2006	(Delting with Northmavine)	6 St Cuthbert's Drive, St Boswells, Melrose TD6 0DF	01835 823375
Norman, Nancy M. (Miss) BA MDiv MTh	1988	2012	(Lyne and Manor)	25 March Street, Peebles EH45 8EP [E-mail: nancy.norman1@googlemail.com]	01721 721699
Rae, Andrew W.	1951	1987	(Annan: St Andrew's Greenknowe Erskine)	Roseneuk, Tweedside Road, Newtown St Boswells TD6 0PQ	01835 823783
Rennie, John D. MA	1962	1996	(Broughton, Glenholm and Kilbucho with Skirling with Stobo and Drumelzier with Tweedsmuir)	29/1 Rosetta Road, Peebles EH45 8HJ [E-mail: tworennies@talktalk.net]	01721 720963
Riddell, John A. MA BD	1967	2006	(Jedburgh: Trinity)	Orchid Cottage, Gingham Row, Earlston TD4 6ET	01896 848784
Steele, Leslie M. MA BD	1973	2013	(Galashiels: Old and St Paul's)	25 Bardfield Road, Colchester CO2 8LW [E-mail: lms@hotmail.co.uk]	01206 621939 (Mbl) 07786 797974
Taverner, Glyn R. MA BD	1957	1995	(Maxton and Mertoun with St Boswells)	Woodcot Cottage, Waverley Road, Innerleithen EH44 6QW	01896 830156
Wallace, James H. MA BD	1973	2011	(Peebles: St Andrew's Leckie)	52 Waverley Mills, Innerleithen EH44 6RH [E-mail: jimwallace121@btinternet.com]	01896 831637

(5) DUNS

Meets at Duns, in the Parish Church hall, normally on the first Saturday of February, the first Tuesdays of September and December, and in places to be appointed on the first Tuesday of May. It meets for conference, worship and training events throughout the year.

Clerk: DR H. DANE SHERRARD Mount Pleasant Granary, Mount Pleasant Farm, Duns TD11 3HU   **01361 882254**
[E-mail: duns@churchofscotland.org.uk]   **07582 468468**

Ayton (H) and District Church
Norman R. Whyte BD MTh DipMin   1982   2006   The Manse, Beanburn, Ayton, Eyemouth TD14 5QY   01890 781333
[E-mail: NWhyte@churchofscotland.org.uk]
(New charge formed by the union of Ayton and Burnmouth, Foulden and Mordington, and Grantshouse, Houndwood and Reston)

Berwick-upon-Tweed: St Andrew's Wallace Green (H) and Lowick
Adam J.J. Hood MA BD DPhil   1989   2012   3 Meadow Grange, Berwick-upon-Tweed TD15 1NW   01289 332787
[E-mail: AHood@churchofscotland.org.uk]

Chirnside linked with Hutton and Fishwick and Paxton
Vacant   Parish Church Manse, The Glebe, Chirnside, Duns TD11 3XL   01890 819109

Coldingham and St Abbs linked with Eyemouth
Andrew Haddow BEng BD   2012   The Manse, Victoria Road, Eyemouth TD14 5JD   01890 750327
[E-mail: AHaddow@churchofscotland.org.uk]

Coldstream and District Parishes (H) linked with Eccles and Leitholm
David J. Taverner MCIBS ACIS BD   1996   2011   36 Bennecourt Drive, Coldstream TD12 4BY   01890 883887
[E-mail: DTaverner@churchofscotland.org.uk]
(The charge of Coldstream and District Parishes is formed by a union between Coldstream, Swinton and Ladykirk with Whitsome)

Duns and District Parishes
Stephen A. Blakey BSc BD   1977   2012   The Manse, Castle Street, Duns TD11 3DG   01361 883755
[E-mail: SBlakey@churchofscotland.org.uk]   0771 254 2518 (Mbl)
(New charge formed by the union between Duns and District Parishes and Langton and Lammermuir Kirk)

Eccles and Leitholm See Coldstream

Eyemouth See Coldingham and St Abbs   (New charge formed by the union of Eccles and Leitholm)

Fogo
Guardianship of the Presbytery

Gordon: St Michael's linked with Greenlaw (H) linked with Legerwood linked with Westruther
Thomas S. Nicholson BD DPS   1982   1995   The Manse, Todholes, Greenlaw, Duns TD10 6XD   01361 810316
[E-mail: TNicholson@churchofscotland.org.uk]

Greenlaw See Gordon: St Michael's
Hutton and Fishwick and Paxton See Chirnside
Legerwood See Gordon: St Michael's
Westruther See Gordon: St Michael's

Name			Charge	Address	Phone
Cartwright, Alan C.D. BSc BD	1976	2016	(Fogo and Swinton with Ladykirk and Whitsome with Leitholm)	Drungray, Edrom, Duns TD11 3PX [E-mail: merse.minister@btinternet.com]	01890 819191
Gaddes, Donald R.	1961	1994	(Kelso: North and Ednam)	2 Teindhill Green, Duns TD11 3DX [E-mail: drgaddes@btinternet.com]	01361 883172
Gale, Ronald A.A. LTh	1982	1995	(Dunoon: Old and St Cuthbert's)	55 Lennel Mount, Coldstream TD12 4NS [E-mail: rgale89@aol.com]	01890 883699
Higham, Robert D. BD	1985	2002	(Tiree)	36 Low Greens, Berwick-upon-Tweed TD15 1LZ	01289 302392
Hope, Geraldine H. (Mrs) MA BD	1986	2007	(Foulden and Mordington with Hutton and Fishwick and Paxton)	4 Well Court, Chirnside, Duns TD11 3UD [E-mail: geraldine.hope@virgin.net]	01890 818134
Kerr, Andrew MA BLitt	1948	1991	(Kilbarchan: West)	4 Lairds Gate, Port Glasgow Road, Kilmacolm PA13 4EX	01507 874852
Landale, William S.	2005		Auxiliary Minister	Green Hope Guest House, Ellemford, Duns TD11 3SG [E-mail: WLandale@churchofscotland.org.uk]	01361 890242
Lindsay, Daniel G. BD	1978	2011	(Coldingham and St Abbs with Eyemouth)	18 Hallidown Crescent, Eyemouth TD14 5TB	01890 751389
McKichan, Alistair J. MA BD	1984	2015	(Kirkconnel)	The Wyld, Horndean, Berwick-upon-Tweed TD15 1XU [E-mail: alistairjmck@btinternet.com]	01289 382745
Murray, Duncan E. BA BD	1970	2012	(Bonkyl and Preston with Chirnside with Edrom Allanton)	Beech Cottage, York Road, Knaresborough HG5 0TT [E-mail: duncanemurray@tiscali.co.uk]	01423 313287
Neill, Bruce F. MA BD	1966	2007	(Maxton and Mertoun with Newtown with St Boswells)	18 Brierydean, St Abbs, Eyemouth TD14 5PQ [E-mail: bneill@phonecoop.coop]	01890 771569
Paterson, William BD	1977	2001	(Bonkyl and Preston with Chirnside with Edrom Allanton)	Benachie, Gavinton, Duns TD11 3QT [E-mail: billdm.paterson@btinternet.com]	01361 882727
Sherrard, H. Dane BD DMin	1971	2013	Presbytery Clerk	Mount Pleasant Granary, Mount Pleasant Farm, Duns TD11 4HU [E-mail: dane@mountpleasantgranary.net]	01361 882254 / 07801 939138 (Mbl)
Shields, John M. MBE LTh	1972	2007	(Channelkirk and Lauder)	12 Eden Park, Ednam, Kelso TD5 7RG [E-mail: john.shields118@btinternet.com]	01573 229015
Walker, Kenneth D.F. MA BD PhD	1976	2008	(Athelstaneford with Whitekirk and Tyninghame)	Allanbank Kothi, Allanton, Duns TD11 3PY [E-mail: walkerkenneth49@gmail.com]	01890 817102
Walker, Veronica (Mrs) BSc BD			Licentiate	Allanbank Kothi, Allanton, Duns TD11 3PY [E-mail: walkerkenneth49@gmail.com]	01890 817102

(6) JEDBURGH

Meets at various venues on the first Wednesday of February, March, May, September, October, November and December and on the last Wednesday of June.

Clerk   REV. LISA-JANE RANKINE BD CPS
4 Wilton Terrace, Hawick TD9 8BE
[E-mail: jedburgh@churchofscotland.org.uk]
01450 370744

Ale and Teviot United (H) (Website: www.aleandteviot.org.uk)
Frank Campbell   1989   1991   22 The Glebe, Ancrum, Jedburgh TD8 6UX   01835 830318
[E-mail: FCampbell@churchofscotland.org.uk]

Cavers and Kirkton linked with Hawick: Trinity (H)
Michael D. Scouler MBE BSc BD   1988   2009   Trinity Manse, Howdenburn, Hawick TD9 8PH   01450 378248
[E-mail: MScouler@churchofscotland.org.uk]

Cheviot Churches (H) (Website: www.cheviotchurches.org)
Vacant

Hawick: Burnfoot (Website: www.burnfootparishchurch.org.uk)
Charles J. Finnie LTh DPS   1991   1997   29 Wilton Hill, Hawick TD9 8BA   01450 373181
[E-mail: CFinnie@churchofscotland.org.uk]

Hawick: St Mary's and Old (H) linked with Hawick: Teviot (H) and Roberton
Alistair W. Cook BSc CA BD   2008   2017   4 Heronhill Close, Hawick TD9 9RA   01450 378175 / 07802 616352 (Mbl)
[E-mail: ACook@churchofscotland.org.uk]

Hawick: Teviot and Roberton See Hawick: St Mary's and Old
Hawick: Trinity See Cavers and Kirkton

Hawick: Wilton linked with Teviothead
Lisa-Jane Rankin BD CPS   2003   4 Wilton Hill Terrace, Hawick TD9 8BE   01450 370744
[E-mail: LRankin@churchofscotland.org.uk]

Hobkirk and Southdean (Website: www.hobkirkruberslaw.org) linked with Ruberslaw (Website: www.hobkirkruberslaw.org)
Douglas A.O. Nicol MA BD   1974   2009   The Manse, Denholm, Hawick TD9 8NB   01450 870268
[E-mail: Douglas.Nicol@churchofscotland.org.uk]

Jedburgh: Old and Trinity (Website: www.jedburgh-parish.org.uk)
Vacant   The Manse, Honeyfield Drive, Jedburgh TD8 6LQ   01835 863417

Kelso Country Churches linked with Oxnam
Vacant

Kelso: North (H) and Ednam (H) (01573 224154) (E-mail: office@kelsonorthandednam.org.uk) (Website: www.kelsonorthandednam.org.uk)
Anna S. Rodwell BD DipMin   1998   2016   The Manse, 24 Forestfield, Kelso TD5 7BX   01573 224248
    [E-mail: ARodwell@churchofscotland.org.uk]   07765 169826 (Mbl)

Kelso: Old and Sprouston
Vacant

Ruberslaw See Hobkirk and Southdean
Teviothead See Hawick: Wilton

Combe, Neil R. BSc MSc BD	1984	2015	(Hawick: St Mary's and Old with Hawick: Teviot and Roberton)	2 Abbotsview Gardens, Galashiels TD1 3ER [E-mail: neil.combe@btinternet.com]	01896 755869
McHaffie, Robin D. BD	1979	2016	(Cheviot Churches)	Shepherd's Cottage, Castle Heaton, Cornhill-on-Tweed TD12 4XQ	
McNicol, Bruce	1967	2006	(Jedburgh: Old and Edgerston)	42 Dounehill, Jedburgh TD8 6LJ [E-mail: mcnicol942@gmail.com]	01835 862991
Stewart, Una B. (Ms) BD DipEd	1995	2014	(Law)	10 Inch Park, Kelso TD5 7BQ [E-mail: rev.ubs@virgin.net]	01573 219231

HAWICK ADDRESSES

Burnfoot	Fraser Avenue	St Mary's and Old	Kirk Wynd
		Teviot	off Buccleuch Road
		Trinity	Central Square
		Wilton	Princes Street

(7) ANNANDALE AND ESKDALE

Meets on the first Tuesday of February, May, September and December, and the third Tuesday of March, June and October. The September meeting is held in the Moderator's charge. The other meetings are held in Dryfesdale Church Hall, Lockerbie, except for the June meeting, which is separately announced.

Clerk: REV. ADAM J. DILLON BD ThM

3 Ladyknowe, Moffat DG10 9DY
[E-mail: annandaleeskdale@churchofscotland.org.uk]

01683 221370

Annan: Old (H) linked with Dornock
Vacant

12 Plumdon Park Avenue, Annan DG12 6EY

01461 201405

Annan: St Andrew's (H) linked with Brydekirk
John G. Pickles BD MTh MSc   2011

1 Annerley Road, Annan DG12 6HE
[E-mail: JPickles@churchofscotland.org.uk]

01461 202626

Applegarth, Sibbaldbie (H) and Johnstone linked with Lochmaben (H)
Paul R. Read BSc MA(Th)   2000   2013

The Manse, Barrashead, Lochmaben, Lockerbie DG11 1QF
[E-mail: PRead@churchofscotland.org.uk]

01387 810640

Brydekirk See Annan: St Andrew's

Canonbie United (H) linked with Liddesdale (H)
Brian Ian Murray BD   2002   2016

23 Langholm Street, Newcastleton TD9 0QX
[E-mail: BMurray@churchofscotland.org.uk]
Canonbie United is a Local Ecumenical Project shared with the United Free Church

01387 375242

Dalton and Hightae linked with St Mungo
Vacant

The Manse, Hightae, Lockerbie DG11 1JL

01387 811499

Dornock See Annan: Old

Gretna: Old (H), Gretna: St Andrew's (H), Half Morton and Kirkpatrick Fleming
C. Bryan Haston LTh   1975

The Manse, Gretna Green, Gretna DG16 5DU
[E-mail: CBHaston@churchofscotland.org.uk]

01461 338313

Eric T. Dempster   2016
(Ordained Local Minister)

Annanside, Wamphray, Moffat DG10 9LZ
[E-mail: EDempster@churchofscotland.org.uk]

01576 470496

Hoddom, Kirtle-Eaglesfield and Middlebie
Frances M. Henderson BA BD PhD   2006   2013   The Manse, Main Road, Ecclefechan, Lockerbie DG11 3BU   01576 300108
[E-mail: FHenderson@churchofscotland.org.uk]

Kirkpatrick Juxta linked with Moffat: St Andrew's (H) linked with Wamphray
Adam J. Dillon BD ThM   2003   2008   The Manse, 1 Meadowbank, Moffat DG10 9LR   01683 220128
[E-mail: ADillon@churchofscotland.org.uk]

Langholm Eskdalemuir Ewes and Westerkirk
I. Scott McCarthy BD   2010   The Manse, Langholm DG13 0BL   01387 380252
[E-mail: ISMcCarthy@churchofscotland.org.uk]

Liddesdale See Canonbie United
Lochmaben See Applegarth, Sibbaldbie and Johnstone

Lockerbie: Dryfesdale, Hutton and Corrie
Vacant

Moffat: St Andrew's See Kirkpatrick Juxta
St Mungo See Dalton

The Border Kirk (Church office: Chapel Street, Carlisle CA1 1JA; Tel: 01228 591757)
David G. Pitkeathly LLB BD   1996   2007   95 Pinecroft, Carlisle CA3 0DB   01228 593243
[E-mail: DPitkeathly@churchofscotland.org.uk]

Tundergarth
Guardianship of the Presbytery

Wamphray See Kirkpatrick Juxta

Annand, James M. MA BD   1955 1995   (Lockerbie: Dryfesdale)   Dere Cottage, 48 Main Street, Newstead, Melrose TD6 9DX   0131-225 3393
Beveridge, S. Edwin P. BA   1959 2004   (Brydekirk with Hoddom)   19 Rothesay Terrace, Edinburgh EH3 7RY   (Mbl) 07543 796820
Brydson, Angela (Mrs) DCS   Deacon   52 Victoria Park, Lockerbie DG11 2AY
[E-mail: ABrydson@churchofscotland.org.uk]
Byers, Mairi C. (Mrs) BTh CPS   1992 1998   (Jura)   Meadowbank, Plumdon Road, Annan DG12 6SJ   01461 206512
[E-mail: aljbyers@hotmail.com]

Name	Years	Description	Address	Phone
Dawson, Morag A. BD MTh	1999 2016	(Dalton l/w Hightae l/w St Mungo)	34 Kennedy Crescent, Tranent EH33 1DP [E-mail: moragdawscn@yahoo.co.uk]	
Gibb, J. Daniel M. BA LTh	1994 2006	(Aberfoyle with Port of Menteith)	1 Beechfield. Newtor Aycliffe DL5 7AX [E-mail: dannygibb@hotmail.co.uk]	
Harvey, P. Ruth (Ms) MA BD	2009 2012	Place for Hope	Croslands, Beacon Street, Penrith CA11 7TZ [E-mail: ruth.harvey@placeforhope.org.uk]	01768 840749 (Mbl) 07403 638339
MacPherson, Duncan J. BSc BD	1993 2002	Chaplain: Army	MP413, Kentigern House, 65 Brown Street, Glasgow G2 8EX	01750 52324
Ross, Alan C. CA BD	1988 2007	(Eskdalemuir with Hutton and Corrie with Tundergarth)	Yarra, Ettrickbridge, Selkirk TD7 5JN [E-mail: alkaross@ao .com]	
Seaman, Ronald S. MA	1967 2007	(Dornock)	1 Springfield Farm Court, Springfield, Gretna DG16 5EH	01461 337228
Steenbergen, Pauline (Ms) MA BD	1996 2012	Hospice Chaplain	Eden Valley Hospice, Durdar Road, Carlisle CA2 4SD [E-mail: pauline.steenbergen@edenvalleyhospice.co.uk]	01228 817609
Vivers, Katherine A.	2004	Auxiliary Minister	Blacket House, Eaglesfield, Lockerbie DG11 3AA [E-mail: KVivers@churchofscotland.org.uk]	01461 500412 (Mbl) 07748 233011

(8) DUMFRIES AND KIRKCUDBRIGHT

Meets at Dumfries on the last Wednesday of February, April, June, September and November.

Clerk: REV. WILLIAM T. HOGG MA BD   St Bride's Manse, Glasgow Road, Sanquhar DG4 6BZ   **01659 50247**
[E-mail: dumfrieskirkcudbright@churchofscotland.org.uk]

Depute Clerk: REV. DONALD CAMPBELL BD   St George's Church, 50 George Street, Dumfries DG1 1EJ   **01387 252965**
[E-mail: DCampbell@churchofscotland.org.uk]

Balmaclellan and Kells (H) linked with Carsphairn (H) linked with Dalry (H)
David S. Bartholomew BSc MSc PhD BD   1994   The Manse, Dalry, Castle Douglas DG7 3PJ   01644 430380
[E-mail: DBartholomew@churchofscotland.org.uk]

Caerlaverock linked with Dumfries: St Mary's-Greyfriars' (H)
David D.J. Logan MStJ BD MA   2009   2016   4 Georgetown Crescent, Dumfries DG1 4EQ   01387 270128
[E-mail: DLogan@churchofscotland.org.uk]   07793 542411   (Mbl)

Carsphairn See Balmaclellan and Kells

Castle Douglas (H) linked with The Bengairn Parishes
Vacant
Oonagh Dee — 2016 — 1 Castle View, Castle Douglas DG7 1BG
(Ordained Local Minister)
Kendoon, Merse Way, Kippford, Dalbeattie DG5 4LL
[E-mail: ODee@churchofscotland.org.uk]
01556 505983
01556 620001

Closeburn linked with Kirkmahoe
Vacant — The Manse, Kirkmahoe, Dumfries DG1 1ST — 01387 710572

Colvend, Southwick and Kirkbean
James F. Gatherer BD — 1984 2003 — The Manse, Colvend, Dalbeattie DG5 4QN
[E-mail: JGatherer@churchofscotland.org.uk] — 01556 630255

Corsock and Kirkpatrick Durham linked with Crossmichael, Parton and Balmaghie
Sally Russell BTh MTh — 2006 — Knockdrocket, Clarebrand, Castle Douglas DG7 3AH
[E-mail: SRussell@churchofscotland.org.uk] — 01556 503645

Crossmichael, Parton and Balmaghie See Corsock and Kirkpatrick Durham

Cummertrees, Mouswald and Ruthwell (H)
Vacant — The Manse, Ruthwell, Dumfries DG1 4NP — 01387 870217

Dalbeattie (H) and Kirkgunzeon linked with Urr (H)
Fiona A. Wilson (Mrs) BD — 2008 2014 — 36 Mill Street, Dalbeattie DG5 4HE
[E-mail: FWilson@churchofscotland.org.uk] — 01556 610708

Dalry See Balmaclellan and Kells

Dumfries: Maxwelltown West (H)
Vacant — Maxwelltown West Manse, 11 Laurieknowe, Dumfries DG2 7AH — 01387 247538

Dumfries: Northwest
Neil G. Campbell BA BD — 1988 2006 — c/o Church Office, Dumfries Northwest Church, Lochside Road,
Dumfries DG2 0DZ
[E-mail: NCampbell@churchofscotland.org.uk] — 01387 249964

Dumfries: St George's (H)
Donald Campbell BD — 1997 — 9 Nunholm Park, Dumfries DG1 1JP
[E-mail: DCampbell@churchofscotland.org.uk] — 01387 252965

Dumfries: St Mary's-Greyfriars' See Caerlaverock

Dumfries: St Michael's and South

Maurice S. Bond MTh BA DipEd PhD	1981	1999	39 Cardoness Street, Dumfries DG1 3AL [E-mail: MBond@churchofscotland.org.uk]	01387 253849

Dumfries: Troqueer (H)

John R. Notman BSc BD	1990	2015	Troqueer Manse, Troqueer Road, Dumfries DG2 7DF [E-mail: JNotman@churchofscotland.org.uk]	01387 253043

Dunscore linked with Glencairn and Moniaive

Joachim J.H. du Plessis BA BD MTh	1975	2013	Wallaceton, Auldgirth, Dumfries DG2 0TJ [E-mail: JduPlessis@churchofscotland.org.uk]	01387 820245

Durisdeer linked with Penpont, Keir and Tynron linked with Thornhill (H)

J. Stuart Mill MA MBA BD	1976	2013	The Manse, Manse Park, Thornhill DG3 5ER [E-mail: JMill@churchofscotland.org.uk]	01848 331191

Gatehouse and Borgue linked with Tarff and Twynholm

Valerie J. Ott (Mrs) BA BD	2002	The Manse, Planetree Park, Gatehouse of Fleet, Castle Douglas DG7 2EQ [E-mail: VOtt@churchofscotland.org.uk]	01557 814233

Glencairn and Moniaive See Dunscore

Irongray, Lochrutton and Terregles

Gary J. Peacock MA BD MTh	2015	The Manse, Shawhead, Dumfries DG2 9SJ [E-mail: GPeacock@churchofscotland.org.uk]	01387 730759

Kirkconnel (H) linked with Sanquhar: St Bride's (H)

William T. Hogg MA BD	1979	2000	St Bride's Manse, Glasgow Road, Sanquhar DG6 6BZ [E-mail: WHogg@churchofscotland.org.uk]	01659 50247

Kirkcudbright (H)

John K. Collard MA BD (Interim Minister)	1986	2017	6 Bourtree Avenue, Kirkcudbright DG6 4AU [E-mail: JCollard@churchofscotland.org.uk]	01557 330489

Kirkmahoe See Closeburn

Kirkmichael, Tinwald and Torthorwald
Vacant — Manse of Tinwald, Tinwald, Dumfries DG1 3PL — 01387 710246

Lochend and New Abbey
Maureen M. Duncan (Mrs) BD — 1996 2014 — New Abbey Manse, 32 Main Street, New Abbey, Dumfries DG2 8BY [E-mail: revmo@talktalk.net] — 01387 850490

Penpont, Keir and Tynron See Durisdeer

Sanquhar: St Bride's (H) See Kirkconnel

Tarff and Twynholm See Gatehouse and Borgue
The Bengairn Parishes See Castle Douglas
Thornhill See Durisdeer
Urr See Dalbeattie and Kirkgunzeon

Name			Charge	Address	Telephone
Bennett, David K.P. BA	1974	2000	(Kirkpatrick Irongray with Lochrutton with Terregles)	53 Anne Arundel Court, Heathhall, Dumfries DG1 3SL	01387 257755
Finch, Graham S. MA BD	1977	2016	(Cadder)	32a St Mary Street, Kirkcudbright DG6 4DN [E-mail: gsf231@gmail.com]	01557 620123
Hammond, Richard J. BA BD	1993	2007	(Kirkmahoe)	3 Marchfield Mount, Marchfield, Dumfries DG1 1SE [E-mail: libby.hammond@virgin.net]	(Mbl) 07764 465783
Holland, William MA	1967	2009	(Lochend and New Abbey)	Ardshean, 55 Georgetown Road, Dumfries DG1 4DD [E-mail: billholland55@btinternet.com]	01387 256131
Irving, Douglas R. LLB BD WS	1984	2016	(Kirkcudbright)	17 Galla Crescent, Dalbeattie DG5 4JY [E-mail: douglas.irving@outlook.com]	(Mbl) 07766 531732 / 01556 610156
Kelly, William W. BSc BD	1994	2014	(Dumfries: Troqueer)	6 Vitality Way, Craigie, Perth, WA 6025, Australia [E-mail: ww.kelly@btinternet.com]	
Mack, Elizabeth A. (Miss) DipEd	1994	2011	(Auxiliary Minister)	24 Roberts Crescent, Dumfries DG2 7RS [E-mail: mackliz@btinternet.com]	01387 264847
McKay, David M. MA BD	1979	2007	(Kirkpatrick Juxta with Moffat: St Andrew's with Wamphray)	20 Auld Brig View, Auldgirth, Dumfries DG2 0XE [E-mail: davidmckay20@tiscali.co.uk]	01387 740013
McKenzie, William M. DA	1958	1993	(Dumfries: Troqueer)	41 Kingholm Road, Dumfries DG1 4SR [E-mail: mckenzie.dumfries@btinternet.com]	01387 253688
McLauchlan, Mary C. (Mrs) LTh	1997	2013	(Mochrum)	3 Ayr Street, Moniaive, Thornhill DG3 4HP [E-mail: mary@revmother.co.uk]	01848 200786
Owen, John J.C. LTh	1967	2001	(Applegarth and Sibbaldbie with Lochmaben)	5 Galla Avenue, Dalbeattie DG5 4JZ [E-mail: jj.owen@onetel.net]	01556 612125

Sutherland, Colin A. LTh	1995 2007	(Blantyre: Livingstone Memorial)	71 Caulstran Road, Dumfries DG2 9FJ [E-mail: colin.csutherland@btinternet.com]	01387 279954
Wallace, Mhairi (Mrs)	2013	Ordained Local Minister	5 Dee Road, Kirkcudbright DG6 4HQ [E-mail: MWallace@churchofscotland.org.uk]	(Mbl) 07701 375064
Williamson, James BA BD	1986 2009	(Cummertrees with Mouswald with Ruthwell)	12 Mulberry Drive, Dunfermline KY11 8BZ [E-mail: jimwill@remkirk.fsnet.co.uk]	01383 734872
Wotherspoon, Robert C. LTh	1976 1998	(Corsock and Kirkpatrick Durham with Crossmichael and Parton)	7 Hillowton Drive, Castle Douglas DG7 1LL [E-mail: robert.wotherspoon@tiscali.co.uk]	01556 502267

DUMFRIES ADDRESSES

Maxwelltown West	Laurieknowe	
Northwest	Lochside Road	
St George's	George Street	
St Mary's-Greyfriars	St Mary's Street	
St Michael's and South	St Michael's Street	
Troqueer	Troqueer Road	

(9) WIGTOWN AND STRANRAER

Meets at Glenluce, in the church hall, on the first Tuesday of March, October and December for ordinary business; on the first Tuesday of September for formal business followed by meetings of committees; on the first Tuesday of November, February and May for worship followed by meetings of committees; and at a church designated by the Moderator on the first Tuesday of June for Holy Communion followed by ordinary business.

Clerk:	MR SAM SCOBIE	40 Clenoch Parks Road, Stranraer DG9 7QT [E-mail: wigtownstranraer@churchofscotland.org.uk]	01776 703975

Ervie Kirkcolm linked with Leswalt

Vacant	Ervie Manse, Stranraer DG9 0QZ	01776 854225

Glasserton and Isle of Whithorn linked with Whithorn: St Ninian's Priory

Alexander I. Currie BD CPS	1990	The Manse, Whithorn, Newton Stewart DG8 8PT [E-mail: ACurrie@churchofscotland.org.uk]	01988 500267

Inch linked with Portpatrick linked with Stranraer: Trinity (H)

John H. Burns BSc BD	1985 1988	Bayview Road, Stranraer DG9 8BE [E-mail: JBurns@churchofscotland.org.uk]	01776 702383

Kirkcowan (H) linked with Wigtown (H)

Name			Address	Telephone
Eric Boyle BA MTh	2006		Seaview Manse, Church Lane, Wigtown, Newton Stewart DG8 9HT [E-mail: EBoyle@churchofscotland.org.uk]	01988 402314

Kirkinner linked with Mochrum linked with Sorbie (H)

Name			Address	Telephone
Jeffrey M. Mead BD	1978	1986	The Manse, Kirkinner, Newton Stewart DG8 9AL [E-mail: JMead@churchofscotland.org.uk]	01988 840643
Joyce Harvey (Mrs) (Ordained Local Minister)	2013		4a Allanfield Place, Newton Stewart DG8 6BS [E-mail: JHarvey@churchofscotland.org.uk]	01671 403693

Kirkmabreck linked with Monigaff (H)

Name			Address	Telephone
Stuart Farmes	2011	2014	Creebridge, Newton Stewart DG8 6NR [E-mail: SFarmes@churchofscotland.org.uk]	01671 403361

Kirkmaiden (H) linked with Stoneykirk

Name			Address	Telephone
Christopher Wallace BD DipMin	1988	2016	Church Road, Sandhead, Stranraer DG9 9JJ [E-mail: Christopher.Wallace@churchofscotland.org.uk]	01776 830757

Leswalt See Ervie Kirkcolm

Luce Valley

Name			Address	Telephone
Stephen Ogston MPhys MSc BD	2009	2017	Glenluce, Newton Stewart DG8 0PU [E-mail: SOgston@churchofscotland.org.uk]	01581 300319

(New charge formed by the union between Old Luce and New Luce)

Mochrum See Kirkinner
Monigaff See Kirkmabreck

Penninghame (H)

Name			Address	Telephone
Edward D. Lyons BD MTh	2007		The Manse, 1A Corvisel Road, Newton Stewart DG8 6LW [E-mail: ELyons@churchofscotland.org.uk]	01671 404425

Portpatrick See Inch
Sorbie See Kirkinner
Stoneykirk See Kirkmaiden

Stranraer: High Kirk (H)
Vacant   Stoneleigh, Whitehouse Road, Stranraer   DG9 0JB   01776 700616

Stranraer: Trinity See Inch
Whithorn: St Ninian's Priory See Glasserton and Isle of Whithorn
Wigtown See Kirkcowan

Aiken, Peter W.I.	1996	2013	(Kirkmabreck with Monigaff)	Garroch, Viewhills Road, Newton Stewart DG8 6JA [E-mail: revpetevon@gmail.com]	
Baker, Carolyn M. (Mrs) BD	1997	2008	(Ochiltree with Stair)	Clanary. 1 Maxwell Drive, Newton Stewart DG8 6EL [E-mail: cncbaker@btinternet.com]	
Bellis, Pamela A. BA	2014		Ordained Local Minister	Maughold, Low Killantrae, Port William, Newton Stewart DG8 9QR [E-mail: PBellis@churchofscotland.org.uk]	01988 700590
Cairns, Alexander B. MA	1957	2009	(Turin)	Beechwood, Main Street, Sandhead, Stranraer DG9 9JG [E-mail: dorothycairns@aol.com]	01776 830389
Sheppard, Michael J. BD	1987	2016	(Ervie, Kirkcolm with Leswalt)	4 Mill Street, Mrummore, Stranraer DG9 9PS [E-mail: michael.sheppard00@gmail.com]	01776 840369

(10) AYR

Meets in the Carrick Centre, Maybole (except as shown), on the first Tuesday of September, the first Tuesday of October (in Girvan: North), the fourth Tuesday of December, (2018) the first Tuesday of March, the first Tuesday of May, and the third Tuesday of June (in the Moderator's church). A conference is held in January.

Clerk: REV. KENNETH C. ELLIOTT   BD BA CertMin   68 St Quivox Road, Prestwick   KA9 1JF   [E-mail: ayr@churchofscotland.org.uk]   01292 478788
Presbytery Office: Prestwick South Parish Church, 50 Main Street, Prestwick   KA9 1NX   01292 678556

Alloway (H)
Neil A. McNaught BD MA   1987   1999   1A Parkview, Alloway, Ayr   KA7 4QG   [E-mail: NMcNaught@churchofscotland.org.uk]   01292 441252

Annbank (H) linked with Tarbolton
Vacant   The Manse, Tarbolton, Mauchline   KA5 5QL   01292 540969

Auchinleck (H) linked with Catrine
Stephen F. Clipston MA BD — 1982 — 2006 — 28 Mauchline Road, Auchinleck KA18 2BN
[E-mail: SClipston@churchofscotland.org.uk] — 01290 424776

Ayr: Auld Kirk of Ayr (St John the Baptist) (H)
David R. Gemmell MA BD — 1991 — 1999 — 58 Monument Road, Ayr KA7 2UB
[E-mail: DGemmell@churchofscotland.org.uk] — 01292 262580 (Tel/Fax)

Ayr: Castlehill (H)
Vacant — 3 Old Hillfoot Road, Ayr KA7 3LW — 01292 263001

Ayr: Newton Wallacetown (H)
Abi T. Ngunga GTh LTh MDiv MTh PhD — 2001 — 2014 — 9 Nursery Grove, Ayr KA7 3PH
[E-mail: ANgunga@churchofscotland.org.uk] — 01292 264251

Ayr: St Andrew's (H)
Morag Garrett (Mrs) BD — 2011 — 2013 — 31 Bellevue Crescent, Ayr KA7 2DP
[E-mail: MGarrett@churchofscotland.org.uk] — 01292 261472

Ayr: St Columba (H)
Fraser R. Aitken MA BD — 1978 — 1991 — 3 Upper Crofts, Alloway, Ayr KA7 4QX
[E-mail: FAitken@churchofscotland.org.uk] — 01292 443747

Ayr: St James' (H)
Barbara V. Suchanek-Seitz Cert Min DTh — 2016 — 1 Prestwick Road, Ayr KA8 8LD
[E-mail: BSuchanek-Seitz@churchofscotland.org.uk] — 01292 262420

Ayr: St Leonard's (H) linked with Dalrymple
Brian Hendrie BD — 1992 — 2015 — 35 Roman Road, Ayr KA7 3SZ
[E-mail: BHendrie@churchofscotland.org.uk] — 01292 283825

Ayr: St Quivox (H)
Vacant — 11 Springfield Avenue, Prestwick KA9 2HA — 01292 478306

Ballantrae (H) linked with St Colmon (Arnsheen Barrhill and Colmonell)
Vacant — The Manse, 1 The Vennel, Ballantrae, Girvan KA26 0NH — 01465 831252

Barr linked with Dailly linked with Girvan: South
Ian K. McLachlan MA BD   1999   30 Henrietta Street, Girvan KA26 9AL   01465 713370
[E-mail: IMcLachlan@churchofscotland.org.uk]

Catrine See Auchinleck

Coylton linked with Drongan: The Schaw Kirk
Vacant   4 Hamilton Place, Coylton, Ayr KA6 6JQ   01292 571442
Douglas T. Moore   2003   2015   9 Midton Avenue, Prestwick KA9 1PU   01292 671352
(Auxiliary Minister)   [E-mail: douglastmoore@hotmail.com]

Craigie Symington linked with Prestwick South (H) (E-mail: office@pwksouth.plus.com)
Kenneth C. Elliott BD BA Cert Min   1989   68 St Quivox Road, Prestwick KA9 1JF   01292 478788
[E-mail: KElliott@churchofscotland.org.uk]
Tom McLeod   2014   2015   3 Martnaham Drive, Coylton KA6 6JE   01292 570100
(Ordained Local Minister)   [E-mail: tamlin410@btinternet.com]

Crosshill (H) linked with Maybole
Vacant   The Manse, 16 McAdam Way, Maybole KA19 8FD   01655 883710

Dailly See Barr

Dalmellington linked with Patna Waterside
Vacant   4 Carsphairn Road, Dalmellington, Ayr KA6 7RE   01292 551503

Dalrymple See Ayr: St Leonard's
Drongan: The Schaw Kirk See Coylton

Dundonald (H)
Robert Mayes BD   1982   1988   64 Main Street, Dundonald, Kilmarnock KA2 9HG   01563 850243
[E-mail: RMayes@churchofscotland.org.uk]

Fisherton (H) linked with Kirkoswald (H)
Ian R. Stirling BSc BD MTh MSc   1990   2016   The Manse, Kirkoswald, Maybole KA19 8HZ   01655 760532
[E-mail: IStirling@churchofscotland.org.uk]

Girvan: North (Old and St Andrew's) (H)
Richard G. Moffat BD   1994   2013   38 The Avenue, Girvan KA26 9DS   01465 713203
[E-mail: RMoffat@churchofscotland.org.uk]

Girvan: South See Barr

Kirkmichael linked with Straiton: St Cuthbert's	1984			
W. Gerald Jones MA BD MTh		The Manse, Patna Road, Kirkmichael, Maybole KA19 7PJ [E-mail: WJones@churchofscotland.org.uk]	01655 750286

Kirkoswald See Fisherton

Lugar linked with Old Cumnock: Old (H)	1994		
John W. Paterson BSc BD DipEd		33 Barrhill Road, Cumnock KA18 1PJ [E-mail: JPaterson@churchofscotland.org.uk]	01290 420769

Mauchline (H) linked with Sorn	1991 2011		
David A. Albon BA MCS		4 Westside Gardens, Mauchline KA5 5DJ [E-mail: DAlbon@churchofscotland.org.uk]	01290 518528

Maybole See Crosshill

Monkton and Prestwick: North (H)	2010		
David Clarkson BSc BA MTh		40 Monkton Road, Prestwick KA9 1AR [E-mail: DClarkson@churchofscotland.org.uk]	01292 471379

Muirkirk (H) linked with Old Cumnock: Trinity			
Vacant		46 Ayr Road, Cumnock KA18 1DW	01290 422145

New Cumnock (H)	2009		
Helen E. Cuthbert MA MSc BD		37 Castle, New Cumnock, Cumnock KA18 4AG [E-mail: HCuthbert@churchofscotland.org.uk]	01290 338296

Ochiltree linked with Stair			
Vacant		10 Mauchline Road, Ochiltree, Cumnock KA18 2PZ	01290 700365

Old Cumnock: Old See Lugar
Old Cumnock: Trinity See Muirkirk
Patna Waterside See Dalmellington

Prestwick: Kingcase (H) (E-mail: office@kingcase.freeserve.co.uk)
Ian Wiseman BTh DipHSW   1993 2015   15 Bellrock Avenue, Prestwick KA9 1SQ   01292 479571
[E-mail: IWiseman@churchofscotland.org.uk]

Prestwick: St Nicholas' (H)
George R. Fiddes BD   1979 1985   3 Bellevue Road, Prestwick KA9 1NW   01292 477613
[E-mail: GFiddes@churchofscotland.org.uk]

Prestwick: South See Craigie Symington
St Colmon (Arnsheen Barrhill and Colmonell) See Ballantrae
Sorn See Mauchline
Stair See Ochiltree
Straiton: St Cuthbert's See Kirkmichael
Tarbolton See Annbank

Troon: Old (H)
David B. Prentice-Hyers BA MDiv   2003 2013   85 Bentinck Drive, Troon KA10 6HZ   01292 313644
[E-mail: DPrentice-Hyers@churchofscotland.org.uk]

Troon: Portland (H)
Jamie Milliken BD   2005 2011   89 South Beach, Troon KA10 6EQ   01292 318929 / 07929 349045 (Mbl)
[E-mail: JMilliken@churchofscotland.org.uk]

Troon: St Meddan's (H) (E-mail: st.meddan@virgin.net)
Derek Peat BA BD MTh   2013   27 Bentinck Drive, Troon KA10 6HX   01292 319163
[E-mail: DPeat@churchofscotland.org.uk]

Name				Address	Telephone
Anderson, Robert A. MA BD DPhil	1980	2017	(Blackburn and Seafield)	Aiona, 8 Old Auchans View, Dundonald KA2 9EX [E-mail: robertanderson307@btinternet.com]	01563 850554 07484 206190 (Mbl)
Birse, G. Stewart CA BD BSc	1980	2013	(Ayr: Newton Wallacetown)	9 Calvinston Road, Prestwick KA9 2EL [E-mail: stewart.birse@gmail.com]	01292 864975
Blackshaw, Christopher J. BA(Theol) *Chris Blackshaw is a Methodist Minister*	2015	2017	Pioneer Minister, Farming Community	Livestock Auction Mart, Whitefordhill, Ayr KA6 5JW [E-mail: christopher.blackshaw@methodist.org.uk]	01292 262241 07989 100818 (Mbl)
Blyth, James G.S. BSc BD	1963	1986	(Glenmuick)	40 Robsland Avenue, Ayr KA7 2RW	01292 261276
Bogle, Thomas C. BD	1983	2003	(Fisherton with Maybole: West)	38 McEwan Crescent, Mossblown, Ayr KA6 5DR	01292 521215
Brown, Jack M. BSc BD	1977	2012	(Applegarth, Sibbaldbie and Johnstone with Lochmaben)	69 Berelands Road, Prestwick KA9 1ER [E-mail: jackm.brown@tiscali.co.uk]	01292 477151
Crichton, James MA BD MTh	1969	2010	(Crosshill with Dalrymple)	4B Garden Court, Ayr KA8 0AT [E-mail: crichton.james@btinternet.com]	01292 288978

Name			Charge	Address	Contact
Crumlish, Elizabeth A. BD	1995	2015	Path of Renewal Co-ordinator	53 Ayr Road, Prestwick KA9 1SY [E-mail: ECrumlish@churchofscotland.org.uk]	(Mbl) 07464 675434
Dickie, Michael M. BSc	1955	1994	(Ayr: Castlehill)	8 Noltmire Road, Ayr KA8 9ES	01292 618512
Geddes, Alexander J. MA BD	1960	1998	(Stewarton: St Columba's)	2 Gregory Street, Mauchline KA5 6BY [E-mail: sandy270736@gmail.com]	01290 518597
Gillon, D. Ritchie M. BD DipMin	1994	2017	(Paisley: St Luke's)	12 Fellhill street, Ayr KA7 3JF [E-mail: revgillon@hotmail.com]	01292 270018
Glencross, William M. LTh	1968	1999	(Bellshill: Macdonald Memorial)	1 Lochay Place, Troon KA10 7HH	01292 317097
Grant, J. Gordon MA BD PhD	1957	1997	(Edinburgh: Dean)	33 Fullarton Drive, Troon KA10 6LE	01292 311852
Guthrie, James A.	1969	2005	(Corsock and Kirkpatrick Durham with Crossmichael and Parton)	2 Barrhill Road, Pinwherry, Girvan KA26 0QE [E-mail: p.h.m.guthrie@btinternet.com]	01465 841236
Hannah, William BD MCAM MIPR	1987	2001	(Muirkirk)	8 Dovecote View, Kirkintilloch, Glasgow G66 3HY [E-mail: revbillnews@btinternet.com]	0141-776 1337
Harper, David L. BSc BD	1972	2012	(Troon: St Meddan's)	19 Calder Avenue, Troon KA10 7JT [E-mail: d.l.harper@btinternet.com]	01292 312626
Harris, Samuel McC. OStJ BA BD	1974	2010	(Rothesay: Trinity)	36 Adam Wood Court, Troon KA10 6BP	01292 319603
Jackson, Nancy	2009	2013	Auxiliary Minister	35 Auchentrae Crescent, Ayr KA7 4BD [E-mail: NJackson@churchofscotland.org.uk]	01292 263034
Johnston, William R. BD	1998	2016	(Ochiltree linked with Stair)	30 Annfield Glen Road, Ayr KA7 3RP	01292 282663
Keating, Glenda K. (Mrs) MTh	1996	2015	(Craigie Symington)	8 Wardlaw Gardens, Irvine KA11 2EW [E-mail: kirkglen@btinternet.com]	
Laing, Iain A. MA BD	1971	2009	(Bishopbriggs: Kenmuir)	9 Annfield Road, Prestwick KA9 1PP [E-mail: iandrlaing@yahoo.co.uk]	01292 471732
Lennox, Lawrie I. MA BD DipEd	1991	2006	(Cromar)	7 Carwinshoch View, Ayr KA7 4AY [E-mail: lennox127@btinternet.com]	
Lochrie, John S. BSc BD MTh PhD	1967	2008	(St Colmon)	Cosyglen, Kilkerran, Maybole KA19 8LS	01465 811262
Lynn, Robert MA BD	1984	2011	(Ayr: St Leonard's with Dalrymple)	8 Kirkbrae, Maybole KA19 7ER	(Mbl) 07771 481698
McGurk, Andrew F. BD	1983	2011	(Largs: St John's)	15 Fraser Avenue, Troon KA10 6XF [E-mail: afmcg.largs@talk21.com]	01292 676008
McIntyre, Allan G. BD	1985	2017	(Greenock: St Ninian's)	9a Templehill, Troon KA10 6BQ [E-mail: agmcintyre@lineone.net]	(Mbl) 07876 445626
McNidder, Roderick H. BD	1987	1997	Chaplain: NHS Ayrshire and Arran Trust	6 Hollow Park, Alloway, Ayr KA7 4SR [E-mail: roddymcnidder@sky.com]	01292 442554
McPhail, Andrew M. BA	1968	2002	(Ayr: Wallacetown)	25 Maybole Road, Ayr KA7 2QA	01292 282108
Matthews, John C. MA BD OBE	1992	2010	(Glasgow: Ruchill Kelvinside)	12 Arrol Drive, Ayr KA7 4AF [E-mail: mejohnmatthews@gmail.com]	01292 264382
Mealyea, Harry B. BArch BD	1984	2011	(Ayr: St Andrew's)	38 Rosamunde Pilcher Drive, Longforgan, Dundee DD2 5EF [E-mail: mealyeal@sky.com]	
Morrison, Alistair H. BTh DipYCS	1985	2004	(Paisley: St Mark's Oldhall)	92 St Leonard's Road, Ayr KA7 2PU [E-mail: alistairmorrison@supanet.com]	01292 266021
Ness, David T. LTh	1972	2008	(Ayr: St Quivox)	17 Winston Avenue, Prestwick KA9 2EZ [E-mail: dtness@tiscali.co.uk]	

Paterson, John L. MA BD STM	1964	2003	(Linlithgow: St Michael's)	9 The Pines, Murdoch's Loan, Alloway, Ayr KA7 4WD [E-mail: revianpaterson@hotmail.co.uk]	01292 443615
Rae, Scott M. MBE BD CPS	1976	2016	(Muirkirk with Old Cumnock: Trinity)	2 Primrose Place, Kilmarnock KA1 2RR [E-mail: scottrae1@btopenworld.com]	01563 532711
Russell, Paul R. MA BD	1984	2006	Hospital Chaplain	23 Nursery Wynd, Ayr KA7 3NZ	01292 618020
Sanderson, Alastair M. BA LTh	1971	2007	(Craigie with Symington)	26 Main Street, Monkton, Prestwick KA9 2QL [E-mail: alel@sanderson29.fsnet.co.uk]	01292 475819
Simpson, Edward V. BSc BD	1972	2009	(Glasgow: Giffnock South)	8 Paddock View, Thorntoun, Crosshouse, Kilmarnock KA2 0BH [E-mail: eddie.simpson3@talktalk.net]	01563 522841
Smith, Elizabeth (Mrs) BD	1996	2009	(Fauldhouse: St Andrew's)	16 McIntyre Road, Prestwick KA9 1BE [E-mail: smithrevb@btinternet.com]	01292 471588
Symington, Alastair H. MA BD	1972	2012	(Troon: Old)	1 Cavendish Place, Troon KA10 6JG [E-mail: revdahs@virginmedia.com]	01292 312556
Wilkinson, Arrick D. BSc BD	2000	2013	(Fisherton with Kirkoswald)	Dunwhinny, Main Street, Ballantrae, Girvan KA26 0NB [E-mail: arrick@dunwhinny-plus.com]	01465 831704
Young, Rona M. (Mrs) BD DipEd	1991	2015	(Ayr: St Quivox)	16 Macintyre Road, Prestwick KA9 1BE [E-mail: revronyoung@hotmail.com]	
Yorke, Kenneth B.	1982	2009	(Dalmellington with Patna Waterside)	13 Annfield Terrace, Prestwick KA9 1PS [E-mail: kenneth.yorke@googlemail.com]	(Mbl) 07766 320525

AYR ADDRESSES

Ayr

Auld Kirk	Kirkport (116 High Street)
Castlehill	Castlehill Road x Hillfoot Road
Newton Wallacetown	Main Street
St Andrew's	Park Circus
St Columba	Midton Road x Carrick Park
St James'	Prestwick Road x Falkland Park Road
St Leonard's	St Leonard's Road x Monument Road

Girvan

North	Montgomerie Street
South	Stair Park

Prestwick

Kingcase	Waterloo Road
Monkton and Prestwick North	Monkton Road
St Nicholas	Main Street
South	Main Street

Troon

Old	Ayr Street
Portland	St Meddan's Street
St Meddan's	St Meddan's Street

(11) IRVINE AND KILMARNOCK

The Presbytery meets at 7:00pm in the Howard Centre, Portland Road, Kilmarnock, on the first Tuesday in September, December and March and on the fourth Tuesday in June for ordinary business, and at different locations on the first Tuesday in October, November, February and May for mission. The September meeting commences with the celebration of Holy Communion.

Clerk:	MR I. STEUART DEY LLB	72 Dundonald Road, Kilmarnock KA1 1RZ [E-mail: steuart.dey@btinternet.com]	01563 521686 (Home)
	REV. H. TAYLOR BROWN BD CertMin	14 McLelland Drive, Kilmarnock KA1 1SE [E-mail: HBrown@churchofscotland.org.uk]	01563 529920 (Home)
Presbytery Office:		Howard Centre, 5 Portland Road, Kilmarnock KA1 2BT [E-mail: irvinekilmarnock@churchofscotland.org.uk]	01563 526295 (Office)

The Presbytery office is staffed each Tuesday, Wednesday and Thursday from 9am until 12:30pm.

Ayrshire Mission to the Deaf
| Richard C. Durno DSW CQSW | 1989 | 2013 | 31 Springfield Road, Bishopbriggs,
Glasgow G64 1PJ
[E-mail: richard.durno@btinternet.com] | (Voice/Text/Fax) 0141-772 1052
(Voice/Text/Voicemail) (Mbl) 07748 607721 |

Caldwell linked with Dunlop
| Alison McBrier MA BD | 2011 | 2017 | 4 Dampark, Dunlop, Kilmarnock KA3 4BZ
[E-mail: AMcBrier@churchofscotland.org.uk] | 01560 673686 |

Crosshouse (H)
| T. Edward Marshall BD | 1987 | 2007 | 27 Kilmarnock Road, Crosshouse, Kilmarnock KA2 0EZ
[E-mail: TMarshall@churchofscotland.org.uk] | 01563 524089 |

Darvel (01560 322924)
| Charles Lines BA | | 2010 | 46 West Main Street, Darvel KA17 0AQ
[E-mail: CLines@churchofscotland.org.uk] | 01560 322924 |

Dreghorn and Springside
Vacant

Dunlop See Caldwell

Fenwick (H) linked with Kilmarnock: Riccarton
| Colin A. Strong BSc BD | 1989 | 2007 | 2 Jasmine Road, Kilmarnock KA1 2HD
[E-mail: CStrong@churchofscotland.org.uk] | 01563 549490 |

Galston (H) (01563 820136) Kristina I. Hine BS MDiv	2011	2016	60 Brewland Street, Galston KA4 8DX [E-mail: KHine@churchofscotland.org.uk]	01563 821549
Hurlford (H) Vacant	1996		12 Main Road, Crookedholm, Kilmarnock KA3 6JT	01563 535673
Irvine: Fullarton (H) (Website: www.fullartonchurch.co.uk) Neil Urquhart BD DipMin	1989		48 Waterside, Irvine KA12 8QJ [E-mail: NUrquhart@churchofscotland.org.uk]	01294 279909
Irvine: Girdle Toll (H) (Website: www.girdletoll.fsbusiness.co.uk) Vacant			2 Littlestane Rise, Irvine KA11 2BJ	01294 213565
Irvine: Mure (H) Vacant			9 West Road, Irvine KA12 8RE	01294 279916
Irvine: Old (H) (01294 273503) Vacant			22 Kirk Vennel, Irvine KA12 0DQ	01294 279265
Irvine: Relief Bourtreehill (H) Andrew R. Black BD	1987	2003	4 Kames Court, Irvine KA11 1RT [E-mail: ABlack@churchofscotland.org.uk]	01294 216939
Irvine: St Andrew's (H) (01294 276051) Ian W. Benzie BD	1999	2008	St Andrew's Manse, 206 Bank Street, Irvine KA12 0YD [E-mail: Ian.Benzie@churchofscotland.org.uk]	01294 216139
Kilmarnock: Kay Park (H) (01563 574106) (Website: www.kayparkparishchurch.co.uk) Vacant			52 London Road, Kilmarnock KA3 7AJ	01563 523113 (Tel/Fax)
Kilmarnock: New Laigh Kirk (H) David S. Cameron BD	2001	2009	1 Holmes Farm Road, Kilmarnock KA1 1TP [E-mail: David.Cameron@churchofscotland.org.uk]	01563 525416
Kilmarnock: Riccarton (H) See Fenwick				

Kilmarnock: St Andrew's and St Marnock's
James McNaughtan BD DipMin   1983   2008   35 South Gargieston Drive, Kilmarnock KA1 1TB   01563 521665
[E-mail: JMcNaughtan@churchofscotland.org.uk]

Kilmarnock: St John's Onthank (H)
Allison E. Becker BA MDiv   2015   2017   84 Wardneuk Drive, Kilmarnock KA3 2EX   07716 162380 (Mbl)
[E-mail: ABecker@churchofscotland.org.uk]

Kilmarnock: St Kentigern's (Website: www.stkentigern.org.uk)
Vacant   1 Thirdpart Place, Kilmarnock KA1 1UL   01563 571280

Kilmarnock: South (01563 524705)
H. Taylor Brown BD CertMin   1997   2012   14 McLelland Drive, Kilmarnock KA1 1SE   01563 529920
[E-mail: HBrown@churchofscotland.org.uk]

Kilmaurs: St Maur's Glencairn (H)
John A. Urquhart BD   1993   9 Standalane, Kilmaurs, Kilmarnock KA3 2NB   01563 538289
[E-mail: John.Urquhart@churchofscotland.org.uk]

Newmilns: Loudoun (H)
Vacant   Loudoun Manse, 116A Loudoun Road, Newmilns KA16 9HH   01560 320174

Stewarton: John Knox
Gavin A. Niven BSc MSc BD   2010   27 Avenue Street, Stewarton, Kilmarnock KA3 5AP   01560 482418
[E-mail: GNiven@churchofscotland.org.uk]

Stewarton: St Columba's (H)
Vacant   1 Kirk Glebe, Stewarton, Kilmarnock KA3 5BJ   01560 485113

Black, Sandra (Mrs)   2013   Ordained Local Minister   5 Doon Place, Troon KA10 7EQ   01292 220075
[E-mail: Sandra.Black@churchofscotland.org.uk]

Brockie, Colin G.F.   1967 2007   (Presbytery Clerk)   36 Braehead Court, Kilmarnock KA3 7AB   01563 559960
BSc(Eng) BD SOSc   [E-mail: revcol@revcol.demon.co.uk]

Campbell, John A. JP FIEM   1984 1998   (Irvine: St Andrew's)   Flowerdale, Balmoral Road, Rattray, Blairgowrie PH10 7AF   01250 872795
[E-mail: exrevjack@aol.com]

Cant, Thomas M. MA BD	1965 2004	(Paisley: Laigh Kirk)	3 Meikle Cutstraw, Stewarton, Kilmarnock KA3 5HU [E-mail: revtmcant@aol.com]	01560 480566
Christie, Robert S. MA BD ThM	1964 2001	(Kilmarnock: West High)	24 Homeroyal House, 2 Chalmers Crescent, Edinburgh EH9 1TP	(Mbl) 07956 557087
Clancy, P. Jill (Mrs) BD DipMin	2000 2017	Prison Chaplain	27 Cross Street, Galston KA4 8AA [E-mail: jgibson@totalise.co.uk]	
Davidson, James BD DipAFH	1989 2002	(Wishaw: Old)	13 Redburn Place, Irvine KA12 9BQ	01294 312515
Garrity, T. Alan W. BSc BD MTh	1969 2008	(Bermuda)	17 Solomon's View, Dunlop, Kilmarnock KA3 4ES [E-mail: alangarrity@btinternet.com]	01560 486879
Gillon, C. Blair BD	1975 2007	(Glasgow: Ibrox)	East Muirshiel Farmhouse, Dunlop, Kilmarnock KA3 4EJ [E-mail: blairg2011@hotmail.co.uk]	01560 483778
Godfrey, Linda BSc BD	2012 2014	(Ayr: St Leonard's with Dalrymple)	9 Taybank Drive, Ayr KA7 4RL [E-mail: godfreykayak@aol.com]	(Mbl) 07825 663866
Hall, William M. BD	1972 2010	(Kilmarnock: Old High Kirk)	33 Cairns Terrace, Kilmarnock KA1 2JG [E-mail: revwillie@talk.talk.net]	01563 525080
Hare, Malcolm M.W. BA BD	1956 1994	(Kilmarnock: St Kentigern's)	Flat 5, The Courtyard, Auchlochan, Lesmahagow, Lanark ML11 0GS	
Hewitt, William C. BD DipPS	1977 2012	(Presbytery Clerk)	60 Woodlands Grove, Kilmarnock KA3 1TZ [E-mail: billhewitt1@bt.internet.com]	01563 533312
Horsburgh, Gary E. BA	1977 2015	(Dreghorn and Springside)	1 Woodlands Grove, Kilmarnock KA3 1TY [E-mail: garyhorsburgh@hotmail.co.uk]	01563 624508
Hosain Lamarti, Samuel BD MTh PhD	1979 2006	(Stewarton: John Knox)	7 Dalwhinnie Crescent, Kilmarnock KA3 1QS [E-mail: samlamar@pobroadband.co.uk]	01563 529632
Huggett, Judith A. (Miss) BA BD	1990 1998	Lead Chaplain, NHS Ayrshire and Arran	4 Westmoor Crescent, Kilmarnock KA1 1TX [E-mail: judith.huggett@aaaht.scotnhs.uk]	
Lacy, David BA BD Dlitt DL	1976 2017	(Kilmarnock: Kay Park)	4 Cairns Terrace, Kilmarnock KA1 2JG [E-mail: DLacy@churchofscotland.org.uk]	01563 624034 / 0797 476 0272
Lind, George K. BD MCIBS	1998 2017	(Stewarton: St. Columba's)	Endrig, 98 Loudoun Road, Newmilns KA16 9HQ [E-mail: gklind@gmail.com]	(Mbl) 07872 051432
McAllister, Anne C. BSc DipEd CCS	2013	Ordained Local Minister	39 Bowes Rigg, Stewarton, Kilmarnock KA3 5EN [E-mail: AMcAllister@churchofscotland.org.uk]	01560 483191
McCulloch, James D. BD MIOP MIP3 FSAScot	1996 2016	(Hurlford)	18 Edradour Place, Dunsmuir Park, Kilmarnock KA3 1US [E-mail: mccullochmanse1@btinternet.com]	01563 535833
MacDonald, James M. BD ThM	1964 1987	(Kilmarnock: St John's Onthank)	29 Carmel Place, Kilmaurs, Kilmarnock KA3 2QU	01563 525254
Scott, Thomas T.	1968 1989	(Kilmarnock: St Marnock's)	6 North Hamilton Place, Kilmarnock KA1 2QN [E-mail: tomtscott@btinternet.com]	01563 531415
Shaw, Catherine A.M. MA	1998 2006	(Auxiliary Minister)	40 Merrygreen Place, Stewarton, Kilmarnock KA3 5EP [E-mail: catherine.shaw@tesco.net]	01560 483352
Urquhart, Barbara (Mrs) DCS		(Deacon)	9 Standalane, Kilmaurs, Kilmarnock KA3 2NB [E-mail: barbararurquhart1@gmail.com]	01563 538289
Watt, Kim	2015	Ordained Local Minister	Reddans Park Gate, The Crescent, Stewarton, Kilmarnock KA3 5AY [E-mail: KWatt@churchofscotland.org.uk]	01560 482267
Welsh, Alex M. MA BD	1979 2007	Hospital Chaplain	8 Greenside Avenue, Prestwick KA9 2HB [E-mail: alexandevelyn@hotmail.com]	01292 475341

IRVINE and KILMARNOCK ADDRESSES

Irvine
Dreghorn and Springside — Townfoot x Station Brae
Fullarton — Marress Road x Church Street
Girdle Toll — Bryce Knox Court
Mure — West Road
Old — Kirkgate

Relief Bourtreehill — Crofthead, Bourtreehill
St Andrew's — Caldon Road x Oaklands Ave

Kilmarnock
Ayrshire Mission to the Deaf — 10 Clark Street
Kay Park — London Road
Kilmarnock South — Whatrigs Road

New Laigh Kirk — John Dickie Street
Riccarton — Old Street
St Andrew's and St Marnock's — St Marnock Street
St John's Onthank — 84 Wardneuk Street

(12) ARDROSSAN

Meets at Saltcoats, New Trinity, on the first Tuesday of February, March, April, May, September, October, November and December, and on the second Tuesday of June.

Clerk: MRS JEAN C. Q. HUNTER BD The Manse, Shiskine, Isle of Arran KA27 8EP 01770 860380
[E-mail: ardrossan@churchofscotland.org.uk] 07961 299907 (Mbl)

Ardrossan: Park (01294 463711)
Tanya Webster BCom DipAcc BD 2011 35 Ardneil Court, Ardrossan KA22 7NQ 01294 538903
[E-mail: TWebster@churchofscotland.org.uk]

Ardrossan and Saltcoats: Kirkgate (H) (01294 472001) (Website: www.kirkgate.org.uk)
Dorothy A. Granger BA BD 2009 10 Seafield Drive, Ardrossan KA22 8NU 01294 463571
[E-mail: DGranger@churchofscotland.org.uk] 07918 077877 (Mbl)

Beith (H) (01505 502686)
Roderick I.T. MacDonald BD CertMin 1992 2 Glebe Court, Beith KA15 1ET 01505 503858
[E-mail: RMacDonald@churchofscotland.org.uk]

Fiona Blair DCS 2005 9 West Road, Irvine KA12 8RE 07495 673428 (Mbl)
[E-mail: FBlair@churchofscotland.org.uk]

Brodick linked with Corrie linked with Lochranza and Pirnmill linked with Shiskine (H)
R. Angus Adamson BD 2006 4 Manse Crescent, Brodick, Isle of Arran KA27 8AS 01770 302334
[E-mail: RAdamson@churchofscotland.org.uk]

Corrie See Brodick

Cumbrae linked with Largs: St John's (H) (01475 674468)
Jonathan C. Fleming MA BD   2012   2017
1 Newhaven Grove, Largs KA30 8NS
[E-mail: JFleming@churchofscotland.org.uk]
01475 329933

Dalry: St Margaret's
Vacant
33 Templand Crescent, Dalry KA24 5EZ
01294 832747

Dalry: Trinity (H)
Martin Thomson BSc DipEd BD   1988   2004
Trinity Manse, West Kilbride Road, Dalry KA24 5DX
[E-mail: MThomson@churchofscotland.org.uk]
01294 832363

Fairlie (H) linked with Largs: St Columba's
Vacant
14 Fairlieburne Gardens, Fairlie, Largs KA29 0ER
01475 568515

Kilbirnie: Auld Kirk (H)
David Whiteman BD   1998   2015
49 Holmhead, Kilbirnie KA25 6BS
[E-mail: DWhiteman@churchofscotland.org.uk]
01505 682342

Kilbirnie: St Columba's (H) (01505 685239)
Fiona C. Ross (Miss) BD DipMin   1996   2004
Manse of St Columba's, Dipple Road, Kilbirnie KA25 7IU
[E-mail: FRoss@churchofscotland.org.uk]
01505 683342

Kilmory linked with Lamlash
Lily F. McKinnon (Mrs) MA BD PGCE   1993   2015
The Manse, Lamlash, Isle of Arran KA27 8LE
[E-mail: LMcKinnon@churchofscotland.org.uk]
01770 600074

Kilwinning: Mansefield Trinity (01294 550746)
Vacant
47 Meadowfoot Road, West Kilbride KA23 9BU
01294 822224

Kilwinning: Old
Jeanette Whitecross BD   2002   2011
54 Dalry Road, Kilwinning KA13 7HE
[E-mail: JWhitecross@churchofscotland.org.uk]
01294 552606
Isobel Beck BD DCS
6 Patrick Avenue, Stevenston KA20 4AW
[E-mail: IBeck@churchofscotland.org.uk]
07919 193425

Lamlash See Kilmory

Largs: Clark Memorial (H) (01475 675186)
T. David Watson BSc BD   1988   2014   31 Douglas Street, Largs KA30 8PT   01475 672370
[E-mail: DWatson@churchofscotland.org.uk]

Largs: St Columba's (01475 686212) See Fairlie
Largs: St John's See Cumbrae
Lochranza and Pirnmill See Brodick

Saltcoats: North (01294 464679)
Alexander B. Noble MA BD ThM   1982   2003   25 Longfield Avenue, Saltcoats KA21 6DR   01294 604923
[E-mail: ANoble@churchofscotland.org.uk]

Saltcoats: St Cuthbert's (H)
Vacant   10 Kennedy Road, Saltcoats KA21 5SF   01294 696030

Shiskine See Brodick

Stevenston: Ardeer linked with Stevenston: Livingstone (H)
David A. Sutherland BD   1997   2017   8 Priest Hill View, Stevenston KA20 4AT   01294 608993
[E-mail: DSutherland@churchofscotland.org.uk]

Stevenston: High (H) (Website: www.highkirk.com)
M. Scott Cameron MA BD   2002   Glencairn Street, Stevenston KA20 3DL   01294 463356
[E-mail: Scott.Cameron@churchofscotland.org.uk]

Stevenston: Livingstone See Stevenston: Ardeer

West Kilbride (H) (Website: www.westkilbrideparishchurch.org.uk)
James J. McNay MA BD   2008   The Manse, Goldenberry Avenue, West Kilbride KA23 9LJ   01294 823186
[E-mail: JMcNay@churchofscotland.org.uk]
Mandy R. Hickman RGN   2013   Lagnaleon, 4 Wilson Street, Largs KA30 9AQ   01475 675347
(Ordained Local Minister)   [E-mail: MHickman@churchofscotland.org.uk]   07743 760792 (Mbl)

Whiting Bay and Kildonan
Elizabeth R.L. Watson (Miss) BA BD   1981   1982   The Manse, Whiting Bay, Brodick, Isle of Arran KA27 8RE   01770 700289
[E-mail: EWatson@churchofscotland.org.uk]

Buchanan, John DCS			(Deacon)	57 Strathclyde House, Shore Road, Skelmorlie PA17 5EH	01475 522525
Cruickshank, Norman BA BD	1983	2006	(West Kilbride: Overton)	24D Faulds Wynd, Seamill, West Kilbride KA23 9FA	01294 822239
Currie, Ian S. MBE BD	1975	2010	(The United Church of Bute)	15 Northfield Park, Largs KA30 8NZ [E-mail: ianscurrie@tiscali.co.uk]	(Mbl) 07764 254300
Dailly, John R. BD DipPS	1979	2007	(Chaplain: Army)	2 Curtis Close, Pound Street, Warminster, Wiltshire BA12 9NN	
Davidson, Amelia (Mrs) BD	2004	2011	(Coatbridge: Calder)	11 St Mary's Place, Saltcoats KA21 5NY	01475 674870
Drysdale, James H. LTh	1987	2006	(Blackbraes and Shieldhill)	10 John Clark Street, Largs KA30 9AH	01294 472991
Falconer, Alan D. MA BD DLitt DD	1972	2011	(Aberdeen: St Machar's Cathedral)	18 North Crescent Road, Ardrossan KA22 8NA [E-mail: alanfalconer@gmx.com]	
Finlay, William P. MA BD	1968	2000	(Glasgow: Townhead Blochairn)	High Corrie, Brodick, Isle of Arran KA27 8JB	01770 810689
Ford, Alan A. BD	1977	2013	(Glasgow: Springburn)	14 Corsankell Wynd, Saltcoats KA21 6HY [E-mail: alan.andy@btinternet.com]	01294 465740
Gordon, David C.	1953	1988	(Gigha and Cara)	South Beach House, South Crescent Road, Ardrossan KA22 8DU	
Harbison, David J.H.	1958	1998	(Beith: High with Beith: Trinity)	42 Mill Park, Dalry KA24 5BB [E-mail: djh@harbi.fsnet.co.uk]	01294 834092
Hebenton, David J. MA BD	1958	2002	(Ayton and Burnmouth with Grantshouse and Houndwood and Reston)	22B Faulds Wynd, Seamill, West Kilbride KA23 9FA	01294 829228
Howie, Marion L.K. (Mrs) MA ARCS	1992		Auxiliary Minister	51 High Road, Stevenston KA20 3DY [E-mail: MHowie@churchofscotland.org.uk]	01294 466571
McCallum, Alexander D. BD	1987	2005	(Saltcoats: New Trinity)	59 Woodcroft Avenue, Largs KA30 9EW [E-mail: sandyandjose@madasafish.com]	01475 670133
McCance, Andrew M. BSc	1986	1995	(Coatbridge: Middle)	6A Douglas Place, Largs KA30 8PU	01475 673303
Mackay, Marjory H. (Mrs) BD DipEd CCE	1998	2008	(Cumbrae)	4 Golf Road, Millport, Isle of Cumbrae KA28 0HB [E-mail: marjory.mackay@gmail.com]	01475 530388
MacKinnon, Ronald M. DCS				32 Strathclyde House, Shore Road, Skelmorlie PA17 5AN [E-mail: ronnie@ronniemac.plus.com]	01475 521333 (Mbl) 07594 427960
MacLeod, Ian LTh BA MTh PhD	1969	2006	(Brodick with Corrie)	Cromla Cottage, Corrie, Isle of Arran KA27 8JB [E-mail: i.macleod829@btinternet.com]	01770 810237
Mitchell, D. Ross BA BD	1972	2007	(West Kilbride: St Andrew's)	11 Dunbar Gardens, Saltcoats KA21 6GJ [E-mail: ross.mitchell@virgin.net]	
Mitchell, Sheila M. BD MTh	1995	2015	Head of Programme, NHS Health and Social Care Chaplaincy and Spiritual Care	2 Central Quay, 89 Hydepark St., Glasgow G3 8BW	(Mbl) 07769 367615
Paterson, John H. BD	1977	2000	(Kirkintilloch: St David's Memorial Park)	Creag Bhan, Golf Course Road, Whiting Bay, Isle of Arran KA27 8QT	01770 700569
Roy, Iain M. MA BD	1960	1997	(Stevenston: Livingstone)	2 The Fieldings, Dunlop, Kilmarnock KA3 4AU	01560 483072
Taylor, Andrew S. BTh FPhS	1959	1992	(Greenock Union)	9 Raillies Avenue, Largs KA30 8QY [E-mail: andrew.taylor_123@btinternet.com]	01475 674709
Travers, Robert BA BD	1993	2015	(Irvine Old)	74 Caledonian Road, Stevenston KA20 3LF [E-mail: robertravers@live.co.uk]	01294 279265
Ward, Alan H. MA BD	1978	2013	(Interim Minister)	47 Meadowfoot Road, West Kilbride KA23 9BU	01475 822244 (Mbl) 07709 906130

(13) LANARK

Meets on the first Tuesday of February, March, May, September, October, November and December, and on the third Tuesday of June.

Clerk pro tem: REV. BRYAN KERR BA BD

Greyfriars Manse, 3 Bellefield Way, Lanark ML11 7NW
[E-mail: lanark@churchofscotland.org.uk]

01555 663363

Biggar (H) linked with Black Mount
Mike Fucella BD MTh   1997   2013   'Candlemas', 6C Leafield Road, Biggar ML12 6AY
[E-mail: MFucella@churchofscotland.org.uk]   01899 229291

Black Mount See Biggar

Cairngryffe linked with Libberton and Quothquan (H) linked with Symington (The Tinto Parishes)
George C. Shand MA BD   1981   2014   16 Abington Road, Symington, Biggar ML12 6JX
[E-mail: George.Shand@churchofscotland.org.uk]   01899 309400

Carluke: Kirkton (H) (Church office: 01555 750778) (Website: www.kirktonchurch.co.uk)
Iain D. Cunningham MA BD   1979   1987   9 Station Road, Carluke ML8 5AA
[E-mail: ICunningham@churchofscotland.org.uk]   01555 771262

Carluke: St Andrew's (H)
Helen E. Jamieson (Mrs) BD DipEd   1989   120 Clyde Street, Carluke ML8 5BG
[E-mail: HJamieson@churchofscotland.org.uk]   01555 771218

Carluke: St John's (H) (Website: www.carluke-stjohns.org.uk)
Elijah O. Obinna BA MTh PhD   2016   2016   18 Old Bridgend, Carluke ML8 4HN
[E-mail: EObinna@churchofscotland.org.uk]   01555 752389

Carnwath (H) linked with Carstairs
Maudeen I. MacDougall BA BD MTh   1978   2016   11 Range View, Cleghorn, Carstairs, Lanark ML11 8TF
[E-mail: Maudeen.MacDougall@churchofscotland.org.uk]   01555 871258

Carstairs See Carnwath

Coalburn (H) linked with Lesmahagow: Old (H) (Church office: 01555 892425)
Vacant   9 Elm Bank, Lesmahagow, Lanark ML11 0EA

Crossford (H) linked with Kirkfieldbank Steven Reid BAcc CA BD	1989 1997	74 Lanark Road, Crossford, Carluke ML8 5RE [E-mail: SReid@churchofscotland.org.uk]	01555 860415
Forth: St Paul's (H) (Website: www.forthstpauls.com) Elspeth J. MacLean (Mrs) BVMS BD	2011 2015	22 Lea Rig, Forth, Lanark ML11 8EA [E-mail: EMacLean@churchofscotland.org.uk]	01555 812832
Kirkfieldbank See Crossford			
Kirkmuirhill (H) Vacant		The Manse, 2 Lanark Road, Kirkmuirhill, Lanark ML11 9RB	01555 892409
Lanark: Greyfriars (Church office: 01555 661510) (Website: www.lanarkgreyfriars.com) Bryan Kerr BA BD	2002 2007	Greyfriars Manse, 3 Bellefield Way, Lanark ML11 7NW [E-mail: BKerr@churchofscotland.org.uk]	01555 663363
Lanark: St Nicholas' (H) Louise E. Mackay BSc BD	2017	2 Kaimhill Court, Lanark ML11 9HU	01555 661936
Law Vacant		3 Shawgill Court, Law, Carluke ML8 5SJ	01698 373180
Lesmahagow: Abbeygreen David S. Carmichael	1982	Abbeygreen Manse, Lesmahagow, Lanark ML11 0DB [E-mail: David.Carmichael@churchofscotland.org.uk]	01555 893384
Lesmahagow: Old See Coalburn **Libberton and Quothquan** See Cairngryffe **Symington** See Cairngryffe			
The Douglas Valley Church (Church office: 01555 850000) (Website: www.douglasvalleychurch.org) Vacant		The Manse, Douglas, Lanark ML11 0RB	01555 851213
Upper Clyde Nikki Macdonald BD MTh PhD	2014	31 Carlisle Road, Crawford, Biggar ML12 6TP [E-mail: NMacdonald@churchofscotland.org.uk]	01864 502139

Name	Years	Position	Address	Telephone
Clelland, Elizabeth (Mrs) BD	2002 2012	Resident Chaplain, Divine Healing Fellowship (Scotland)	Braehead House Christian Healing and Retreat Centre, Braidwood Road, Crossford, Carluke ML8 5NQ [E-mail: liz_clelland@yahoo.co.uk]	01555 860716
Cowell, Susan G. (Miss) BA BD	1986 1998	(Budapest)	3 Gavel Lane, Regency Gardens, Lanark ML11 9FB	01555 665509
Easton, David J.C. MA BD	1965 2005	(Burnside–Blairbeth)	Rowanbank, Cormiston Road, Quothquan, Biggar ML12 6ND [E-mail: deaston@btinternet.com]	01899 308459
Findlay, Henry J.W. MA BD	1965 2005	(Wishaw: St Mark's)	2 Alba Gardens, Carluke ML8 5US	01555 759995
Houston, Graham R. BSc BD MTh PhD	1978 2011	(Cairngryffe with Symington)	3 Alder Lane, Beechtrees, Lanark ML11 9FT [E-mail: gandih6156@btinternet.com]	01555 678004
McPake, John L. BA BD PhD	1987 2017	Ecumenical Officer, Church of Scotland	121 George Street, Edinburgh EH2 4YN [E-mail: JMcPake@churchofscotland.org.uk]	0131-240 2208
McPherson, D. Cameron BSc BD DMin	1982 2015	(Dalserf)	6 Moa Court, Blackwood, Lanark ML11 9GF [E-mail: revcam@btinternet.com]	(Mbl) 07852 123956
Pacitti, Stephen A. MA	1963 2003	(Black Mount with Culter with Libberton and Quothquan)	157 Nithsdale Road, Glasgow G41 5RD	0141-423 5972
Seath, Thomas J.G.	1980 1992	(Motherwell: Manse Road)	Flat 11, Wallace Court, South Vennel, Lanark ML11 7LL	01555 665399
Young, David A.	1972 2003	(Kirkmuirhill)	110 Carlisle Road, Blackwood, Lanark ML11 9RT [E-mail: david@aol.com]	01555 893357

(14) GREENOCK AND PAISLEY

Meets on the second Tuesday of September, October, November, December, February, March, April and May, and on the third Tuesday of June.

Clerk:	REV. PETER McENHILL BD PhD		The Presbytery Office (see below) [E-mail: greenockpaisley@churchofscotland.org.uk]	
Presbytery Office:			'Homelea', Faith Avenue, Quarrier's Village, Bridge of Weir PA11 3SX	01505 615033 (Tel) 01505 615088 (Fax)

Barrhead: Bourock (H) (0141-881 9813)
Pamela Gordon BD — 2006 2014 — 14 Maxton Avenue, Barrhead, Glasgow G78 1DY [E-mail: PGordon@churchofscotland.org.uk] — 0141-881 8736

Barrhead: St Andrew's (H) (0141-881 8442)
James S.A. Cowan BD DipMin — 1986 1998 — 10 Arthurlie Avenue, Barrhead, Glasgow G78 2BU [E-mail: JCowan@churchofscotland.org.uk] — 0141-881 3457

Bishopton (H) (Office: 01505 862583)
Yvonne Smith BSc BD | 2017 | The Manse, Newton Road, Bishopton PA7 5JP | 01505 862161
[E-mail: YSmith@churchofscotland.org.uk]

Bridge of Weir: Freeland (H) (01505 612610)
Kenneth N. Gray BA BD | 1988 | 15 Lawmarnock Crescent, Bridge of Weir PA11 3AS | 01505 690918
[E-mail: aandkgray@btinternet.com]

Bridge of Weir: St Machar's Ranfurly (01505 614364)
Hanneke Marshall (Mrs) MTh MA PGCE | 2017 | 9 Glen Brae, Bridge of Weir PA11 3BH | 01505 612975
CertMin
[E-mail: Hanneke.Marshall@churchofscotland.org.uk]

Elderslie Kirk (H) (01505 323348)
Robin N. Allison BD DipMin | 1994 | 2005 | 282 Main Road, Elderslie, Johnstone PA5 9EF | 01505 321767
[E-mail: RAllison@churchofscotland.org.uk]

Erskine (0141-812 4620)
Vacant | | | The Manse, 7 Leven Place, Linburn, Erskine PA8 6AS | 0141-570 8103

Gourock: Old Gourock and Ashton (H)
David W. G. Burt BD DipMin | 1989 | 2014 | 331 Eldon Street, Gourock PA16 7QN | 01475 633914
[E-mail: DBurt@churchofscotland.org.uk]

Gourock: St John's (H)
Vacant | | | 6 Barrhill Road, Gourock PA19 1JX | 01475 632143

Greenock: East End linked with Greenock: Mount Kirk
Francis E. Murphy BEng DipDSE BD | 2006 | 76 Finnart Street, Greenock PA16 8HJ | 01475 722338
[E-mail: FMurphy@churchofscotland.org.uk]

Greenock: Lyle Kirk
Owen Derrick MDiv MASFL | 2007 | 39 Fox Street, Greenock PA16 8PD | 01475 717229
[E-mail: ODerrick@churchofscotland.org.uk] | 07840 983657 (Mbl)
Eileen Manson (Mrs) DipCE | 1994 | 2014 | 1 Cambridge Avenue, Gourock PA19 1XT | 01475 632401
(Auxiliary Minister)
[E-mail: EManson@churchofscotland.org.uk]

Greenock: Mount Kirk See Greenock: East End

Greenock: St Margaret's (01475 781953) Morris C. Coull BD	1974	2014	105 Finnart Street, Greenock PA16 8HN [E-mail: MCoull@churchofscotland.org.uk]	01475 892874
Greenock: St Ninian's Vacant			5 Auchmead Road, Greenock PA16 0PY	01475 631878
Greenock: Wellpark Mid Kirk Alan K. Sorensen BD MTh DipMin FSAScot	1983	2000	101 Brisbane Street, Greenock PA16 8PA [E-mail: ASorensen@churchofscotland.org.uk]	01475 721741
Greenock: Westburn Karen E. Harbison (Mrs) MA BD	1991	2014	50 Ardgowan Street, Greenock PA16 8EP [E-mail: KHarbison@churchofscotland.org.uk]	01475 721048
Houston and Killellan (H) Vacant	1998	2007	The Manse of Houston, Main Street, Houston, Johnstone PA6 7EL	01505 612569
Howwood Guardianship of the Presbytery				
Inchinnan (H) (0141-812 1263) Ann Knox BD Cert.Healthc.Chap	2017		51 Old Greenock Road, Inchinnan, Renfrew PA4 9PH [E-mail: AKnox@churchofscotland.org.uk]	0141-389 1724 07534 900065 (Mbl)
Inverkip (H) linked with Skelmorlie and Wemyss Bay Archibald Speirs BD	1995	2013	3a Montgomery Terrace, Skelmorlie PA17 5DT [E-mail: ASpeirs@churchofscotland.org.uk]	01475 529320
Johnstone: High (H) (01505 336303) Ann C. McCool (Mrs) BD DSD IPA ALCM	1989	2001	76 North Road, Johnstone PA5 8NF [E-mail: AMcCool@churchofscotland.org.uk]	01505 320006
Johnstone: St Andrew's Trinity Charles M. Cameron BA BD PhD	1980	2013	45 Woodlands Crescent, Johnstone PA5 0AZ [E-mail: Charles.Cameron@churchofscotland.org.uk]	01505 672908

Johnstone: St Paul's (H) (01505 321632) Alistair N. Shaw MA BD MTh PhD	1982	2003	9 Stanley Drive, Brookfield, Johnstone PA5 8UF [E-mail: Alistair.Shaw@churchofscotland.org.uk]	01505 320060
Kilbarchan Stephen J. Smith BSc BD	1993	2015	The Manse, Church Street, Kilbarchan, Johnstone PA10 2JQ [E-mail: SSmith@churchofscotland.org.uk] (New charge formed by the union of Kilbarchan: East and Kilbarchan: West)	01505 702621
Kilmacolm: Old (H) (01505 8739911) Peter McEnhill BD PhD	1992	2007	The Old Kirk Manse, Glencairn Road, Kilmacolm PA13 4NJ [E-mail: PMcEnhill@churchofscotland.org.uk]	01505 873174
Kilmacolm: St Columba (H) R. Douglas Cranston MA BD	1986	1992	6 Churchill Road, Kilmacolm PA13 4LH [E-mail: RCranston@churchofscotland.org.uk]	01505 873271
Langbank linked with Port Glasgow: St Andrew's (H) Vacant			St Andrew's Manse, Barr's Brae, Port Glasgow PA14 5QA	01475 741486
Linwood (H) (01505 328802) Eileen M. Ross (Mrs) BD MTh	2005	2008	1 John Neilson Avenue, Paisley PA1 2SX [E-mail: ERoss@churchofscotland.org.uk]	0141-887 2801
Lochwinnoch Guardianship of the Presbytery				
Neilston (0141-881 9445) Fiona E. Maxwell BA BD	2004	2013	The Manse, Neilston Road, Neilston, Glasgow G78 3NP [E-mail: FMaxwell@churchofscotland.org.uk]	0141-258 0805
Paisley: Abbey (H) (Tel: 0141-889 7654; Fax: 0141-887 3929) Alan D. Birss MA BD	1979	1988	15 Main Road, Castlehead, Paisley PA2 6AJ [E-mail: ABirss@churchofscotland.org.uk]	0141-889 3587
Paisley: Glenburn (0141-884 2602) Vacant			10 Hawick Avenue, Paisley PA2 9LD	0141-884 4903

Paisley: Lylesland (H) (0141-561 7139)
Vacant — 36 Potterhill Avenue, Paisley PA2 8BA — 0141-561 9277

Paisley: Martyrs' Sandyford (0141-889 6603)
Kenneth A.L. Mayne BA MSc CertEd — 1976 — 2007 — 27 Acer Crescent, Paisley PA2 9LR
[E-mail: KMayne@churchofscotland.org.uk] — 0141-884 7400

Paisley: Oakshaw Trinity (H) (Tel: 0141-889 4010; Fax: 0141-848 5139)
Gordon B. Armstrong BD FIAB BRC — 1998 — 2012 — The Manse, 16 Golf Drive, Paisley PA1 3LA
[E-mail: GArmstrong@churchofscotland.org.uk] — 0141-887 0884
Oakshaw Trinity is a Local Ecumenical Project shared with the United Reformed Church

Paisley: St Columba Foxbar (H) (01505 812377)
Vacant — 13 Corsebar Drive, Paisley PA2 9QD — 0141-884 5826

Paisley: St Luke's (H)
Vacant — 31 Southfield Avenue, Paisley PA2 8BX — 0141-884 6215

Paisley: St Mark's Oldhall (H) (0141-882 2755)
Robert G. McFarlane BD — 2001 — 2005 — 36 Newtyle Road, Paisley PA1 3JX
[E-mail: RMcFarlane@churchofscotland.org.uk] — 0141-889 4279

Paisley: St Ninian's Ferguslie (0141-887 9436)
Guardianship of the Presbytery

Paisley: Sherwood Greenlaw (H) (0141-889 7060)
John Murning BD — 1988 — 2014 — 5 Greenlaw Drive, Paisley PA1 3RX
[E-mail: JMurning@churchofscotland.org.uk] — 0141-889 3057

Paisley: Stow Brae Kirk
Robert Craig BA BD DipRS — 2008 — 2012 — 25 John Neilson Avenue, Paisley PA1 2SX
[E-mail: RCraig@churchofscotland.org.uk] — 0141-328 6014

Paisley: Wallneuk North (0141-889 9265)
Peter G. Gill MA BA — 2008 — 5 Glenville Crescent, Paisley PA2 8TW
[E-mail: PGill@churchofscotland.org.uk] — 0141-884 4429

Port Glasgow: Hamilton Bardrainney linked with Port Glasgow: St. Martin's
Vacant   80 Bardrainney Avenue, Port Glasgow PA14 6HD   01475 701213

Port Glasgow: St Andrew's See Langbank

Port Glasgow: St Martin's See Port Glasgow: Hamilton Bardrainney

Renfrew: North (0141-885 2154)
Vacant   1 Alexandra Drive, Renfrew PA4 8UB   0141-886 2074

Renfrew: Trinity (H) (0141-885 2129)
Stuart C. Steell BD CertMin   1992   2015   25 Paisley Road, Renfrew PA4 8JH   0141-387 2464
                                                   [E-mail: SSteell@churchofscotland.org.uk]

Skelmorlie and Wemyss Bay See Inverkip

Name			Role / (Church)	Address	Telephone
Alexander, Douglas N. MA BD	1961	1999	(Bishopton)	West Morningside, Main Road, Langbank, Port Glasgow PA4 6XP	01475 540249
Armstrong, William R. BD	1979	2008	(Skelmorlie and Wemyss Bay)	25A The Lane, Skelmorlie PA17 5AR [E-mail: warmstrong17@tiscali.co.uk]	01475 520891
Bell, Ian W. LTh	1990	2011	(Erskine)	40 Brueacre Drive, Wemyss Bay PA18 6HA [E-mail: rviwbepc@ntlworld.com]	01475 529312
Bell, May (Mrs) LTh	1998	2012	(Johnstone: St Andrew's Trinity)	40 Brueacre Drive, Wemyss Bay PA18 6HA [E-mail: may.bell@ntlbusiness.com]	01475 529312
Black, Janette M.K. (Mrs) BD	1993	2006	(Assistant: Paisley: Oakshaw Trinity)	5 Craigiehall Avenue, Erskine PA8 7DB	0141-812 0794
Breingan, Mhairi	2011		Ordained Local Minister	6 Park Road, Inchinnan, Renfrew PA4 4QJ [E-mail: MBreingan@churchofscotland.org.uk]	0141-812 1425
Campbell, Donald BD	1998	2016	(Houston and Killellan)	1 Herriot Avenue, Kilbirnie KA25 7HZ [E-mail: tofua1951@btinternet.com]	01505 684147 (Mbl) 07530 394458
Cameron, Margaret (Miss) DCS			(Deacon)	2 Rowans Gate, Paisley PA2 6RD	0141-840 2479
Cherry, Alastair J. BA BD FPLD	1982	2009	(Glasgow: Penilee St Andrew's)	8 Coruisk Drive, Clarkston, Glasgow G76 7NG [E-mail: alastair.j.cherry@btinternet.com]	0141 620 3852 (Mbl) 07483 221141
Chestnut, Alexander MBE BA	1948	1987	(Greenock: St Mark's Greenbank)	5 Douglas Street, Largs KA30 8PS	01475 674168
Copland, Agnes M. (Mrs) MBE DCS	1961	1999	(Deacon)	3 Craigmuschat Road, Gourock PA19 1SE	01475 631870
Cubie, John P. MA BD			(Caldwell)	36 Winram Place, St Andrews KY16 8XH	01334 474708
Davidson, Stuart BD	2008	2017	(Pioneer Minister: Paisley North End)	25H Cross Road, Paisley PA2 9QJ [E-mail: SDavidson@churchofscotland.org.uk]	07717 503059
Easton, Lilly C. (Mrs)	1999	2012	(Renfrew: Old)	Flat 0/2, 90 Beith Street, Glasgow G11 6DG [E-mail: revlillyeaston@hotmail.co.uk]	0141-586 7628
Erskine, Morag (Miss) DCS			(Deacon)	111 Mains Drive, Park Mains, Erskine PA8 7JJ [E-mail: morag.erskine@ntlworld.com]	0141-812 6096

(16) GLASGOW

Meets at Govan and Linthouse Parish Church, Govan Cross, Glasgow (unless otherwise intimated), on the following Tuesdays: 2017: 10 October, 14 November, 12 December; 2018: 13 February, 13 March, 10 April, 8 May, 19 June.

| Clerk: | REV. GEORGE S. COWIE BSc BD | 260 Bath Street, Glasgow G2 4JP
[E-mail: glasgow@churchofscotland.org.uk]
[Website: www.presbyteryofglasgow.org.uk] | 0141-332 6606
0141-352 6646 (Fax) |
| Treasurer: | MRS ALISON WHITELAW | [E-mail: treasurer@presbyteryofglasgow.org.uk] | |

1	**Banton linked with Twechar** Vacant		
2	**Bishopbriggs: Kenmure** James Gemmell BD MTh	1999 2010	5 Marchfield, Bishopbriggs, Glasgow G64 3PP [E-mail: JGemmell@churchofscotland.org.uk]	0141-772 1468
3	**Bishopbriggs: Springfield Cambridge (0141-772 1596)** Ian Taylor BD ThM	1995 2006	64 Miller Drive, Bishopbriggs, Glasgow G64 1FB [E-mail: ITaylor@churchofscotland.org.uk]	0141-772 1540
4	**Broom (0141-639 3528)** James A.S. Boag BD CertMin	1992 2007	3 Laigh Road, Newton Mearns, Glasgow G77 5EX [E-mail: JBoag@churchofscotland.org.uk]	0141-639 2916 (Tel) 0141-639 3528 (Fax)
5	**Burnside Blairbeth (0141-634 4130)** William T.S. Wilson BSc BD	1999 2006	59 Blairbeth Road, Burnside, Glasgow G73 4JD [E-mail: WWilson@churchofscotland.org.uk]	0141-583 6470
6	**Busby (0141-644 2073)** Jeremy C. Eve BSc BD	1998	17A Carmunnock Road, Busby, Glasgow G76 8SZ [E-mail: JEve@churchofscotland.org.uk]	0141-644 3670
7	**Cadder (0141-772 7436)** John B. MacGregor BD	1999 2017	231 Kirkintilloch Road, Bishopbriggs, Glasgow G64 2JB	0141-576 7127

8   Cambuslang: Flemington Hallside
Neil M. Glover — 2005
59 Hay Crescent, Cambuslang, Glasgow G72 6QA
[E-mail: NGlover@churchofscotland.org.uk]
0141-641 1049
07779 280074 (Mbl)

9   Cambuslang Parish Church
A. Leslie Milton MA BD PhD — 1996 2008
74 Stewarton Drive, Cambuslang, Glasgow G72 8DG
[E-mail: LMilton@churchofscotland.org.uk]
0141-641 2028

David Maxwell — 2014
(Ordained Local Minister)
248 Old Castle Road, Glasgow G44 5EZ
[E-mail: DMaxwell@churchofscotland.org.uk]
0141-569 6397
07779 280074 (Mbl)

Karen M. Hamilton (Mrs) DCS
6 Beckfield Gate, Glasgow G33 1SW
[E-mail: KHamilton@churchofscotland.org.uk]
0141-558 3195
07514 402612 (Mbl)

10   Campsie (01360 310939)
Jane M. Denniston MA BD MTh — 2002 2016
19 Redhill View, Lennoxtown, Glasgow G66 7BL
[E-mail: Jane.Denniston@churchofscotland.org.uk]
01360 310846
07738 123101 (Mbl)

11   Chryston (H) (0141-779 4188)
Mark Malcolm MA BD — 1999 2008
The Manse, 109 Main Street, Chryston, Glasgow G69 9LA
[E-mail: MMalcolm@churchofscotland.org.uk]
0141-779 1436
07731 737377 (Mbl)

Mark W.J. McKeown — 2013 2014
MEng MDiv (Associate Minister)
6 Glenapp Place, Moodiesburn, Glasgow G69 0HS
[E-mail: MMcKeown@churchofscotland.org.uk]
01236 263406

12   Eaglesham (01355 302047)
Andrew J. Robertson BD — 2008 2016
The Manse, Cheapside Street, Eaglesham, Glasgow G76 0NS
[E-mail: ARobertson@churchofscotland.org.uk]
01355 303495

13   Fernhill and Cathkin
Aquila R. Singh BA PGCE BD — 2017
20 Glenlyon Place, Rutherglen, Glasgow G73 5PL
[E-mail: ASingh@churchofscotland.org.uk]
0141-389 3599

14   Gartcosh (H) (01236 873770) linked with Glenboig
David G. Slater BSc BA DipThRS — 2011
26 Inchnock Avenue, Gartcosh, Glasgow G69 8EA
[E-mail: DSlater@churchofscotland.org.uk]
01236 870331
01236 872274 (Office)

15   Giffnock: Orchardhill (0141-638 3604)
S. Grant Barclay LLB DipLP BD MSc PhD — 1995 2016
23 Huntly Avenue, Giffnock, Glasgow G46 6LW
[E-mail: GBarclay@churchofscotland.org.uk]
0141-620 3734

No.	Church / Minister	Year(s)	Address	Telephone
16	**Giffnock: South (0141-638 2599)** Catherine J. Beattie (Mrs) BD	2008 2011	164 Ayr Road, Newton Mearns, Glasgow G77 6EE [E-mail: CBeattie@churchofscotland.org.uk]	0141-258 7804
17	**Giffnock: The Park (0141-620 2204)** Calum D. Macdonald BD	1993 2001	41 Rouken Glen Road, Thornliebank, Glasgow G46 7JD [E-mail: CMacdonald@churchofscotland.org.uk]	0141-638 3023
18	**Glenboig** See Gartcosh			
19	**Greenbank (H) (0141-644 1841)** Jeanne N. Roddick BD	2003	Greenbank Manse, 38 Eaglesham Road, Clarkston, Glasgow G76 7DJ [E-mail: JRoddick@churchofscotland.org.uk]	0141-644 1395
20	**Kilsyth: Anderson** Allan S. Vint BSc BD MTh	1989 2013	Anderson Manse, Kingston Road, Kilsyth, Glasgow G65 0HR [E-mail: AVint@churchofscotland.org.uk]	01236 822345 07795 483070 (Mbl)
21	**Kilsyth: Burns and Old** Robert Johnston BD MSc FSAScot	2017	The Grange, 17 Glasgow Road, Kilsyth G65 9AE [E-mail: RJohnston@churchofscotland.org.uk]	01236 899901 07810 377582 (Mbl)
22	**Kirkintilloch: Hillhead** Guardianship of the Presbytery Bill H Finnie BA PgDipSW CertCRS (Ordained Local Minister)	2015	27 Hallside Crescent, Cambuslang, Glasgow G72 7DY [E-mail: BFinnie@churchofscotland.org.uk]	07518 357138 (Mbl)
23	**Kirkintilloch: St Columba's (H) (0141-578 0016)** Philip Wright BSc MSc PhD BTh	2017	6 Glenwood Road, Lenzie, Glasgow G66 4DS [E-mail: PWright@churchofscotland.org.uk]	07427 623393 (Mbl)
24	**Kirkintilloch: St David's Memorial Park (H) (0141-776 4989)** Vacant		2 Roman Road, Kirkintilloch, Glasgow G66 1EA	0141-776 1434
25	**Kirkintilloch: St Mary's (0141-775 1166)** Mark E. Johnstone MA BD	1993 2001	St Mary's Manse, 60 Union Street, Kirkintilloch, Glasgow G66 1DH [E-mail: Mark.Johnstone@churchofscotland.org.uk]	0141-776 1252

No.	Name	Ord.	Ind.	Address	Tel
26	**Lenzie: Old (H)** Louise J.E. McClements BD	2008	2016	41 Kirkintilloch Road, Lenzie, Glasgow G66 4LB [E-mail: LMcClements@churchofscotland.org.uk]	0141-573 5006
27	**Lenzie: Union (H) (0141-776 1046)** Daniel J.M. Carmichael MA BD	1994	2003	1 Larch Avenue, Lenzie, Glasgow G66 4HX [E-mail: DCarmichael@churchofscotland.org.uk]	0141-776 3831
28	**Maxwell Mearns Castle (Tel/Fax: 0141-639 5169)** Scott R.McL. Kirkland BD MAR	1996	2011	122 Broomfield Avenue, Newton Mearns, Glasgow G77 5JR [E-mail: SKirkland@churchofscotland.org.uk]	0141-560 5603
29	**Mearns (H) (0141-639 6555)** Joseph A. Kavanagh BD DipPTh MTh MTh	1992	1998	11 Belford Grove, Newton Mearns, Glasgow G77 5FB [E-mail: JKavanagh@churchofscotland.org.uk]	0141-384 2218
30	**Milton of Campsie (H)** Julie H.C. Moody BA BD PGCE	2006		Dunkeld, 33 Birdston Road, Milton of Campsie, Glasgow G66 8BX [E-mail: JMoody@churchofscotland.org.uk]	01360 310548 07787 184800 (Mbl)
31	**Netherlee (H) (0141-637 2503)** Thomas Nelson BSc BD	1992	2002	25 Ormonde Avenue, Netherlee, Glasgow G44 3QY [E-mail: TNelson@churchofscotland.org.uk]	0141-585 7502 (Tel/Fax)
32	**Newton Mearns (H) (0141-639 7373)** Vacant				
33	**Rutherglen: Old (H)** Malcolm (Calum) MacLeod BA BD	1979	2017	31 Highburgh Drive, Rutherglen, Glasgow G73 3RR [E-mail: Malcolm.MacLeod@churchofscotland.org.uk]	0141-534 7477
34	**Rutherglen: Stonelaw (0141-647 5113)** Alistair S. May LLB BD PhD	2002		80 Blairbeth Road, Rutherglen, Glasgow G73 4JA [E-mail: AMay@churchofscotland.org.uk]	0141-583 0157
35	**Rutherglen: West and Wardlawhill (0844 736 1470)** Malcolm Cuthbertson BA BD	1984	2017	12 Albert Drive, Rutherglen, Glasgow G73 3RT [E-mail: MCuthbertson@churchofscotland.org.uk]	07864 820612 (Mbl)

36 Stamperland (0141-637 4999) (H)
Vacant

37 Stepps (H)
Gordon MacRae BD MTh — 1985 — 2014 — 112 Jackson Drive, Crowwood Grange, Stepps, Glasgow G33 6GF [E-mail: GMacRae@churchofscotland.org.uk] — 0141-779 5742

38 Thornliebank (H)
Mike R. Gargrave BD — 2008 — 2014 — 19 Arthurlie Drive, Giffnock, Glasgow G46 6UR [E-mail: MGargrave@churchofscotland.org.uk] — 0141-880 5532

39 Torrance (01360 620970)
Nigel L. Barge BSc BD — 1991 — 1 Atholl Avenue, Torrance, Glasgow G64 4JA [E-mail: NBarge@churchofscotland.org.uk] — 01360 622379

40 Twechar See Banton

41 Williamwood (0141-638 2091)
Janet S. Mathieson MA BD — 2003 — 2015 — 125 Greenwood Road, Clarkston, Glasgow G76 7LL [E-mail: JMathieson@churchofscotland.org.uk] — 0141-579 9997

42 Glasgow: Anderston Kelvingrove (0141-221 9408)
Vacant

43 Glasgow: Baillieston Mure Memorial (0141-773 1216) linked with Glasgow: Baillieston St Andrew's
Vacant — 28 Beech Avenue, Baillieston, Glasgow G69 6LF
Alex P. Stuart — 2014 — 107 Baldorran Crescent, Balloch, Cumbernauld, Glasgow G68 9EX — 07901 802967 (Mbl)
(Ordained Local Minister) [E-mail: AStuart@churchofscotland.org.uk]

44 Glasgow: Baillieston St Andrew's See Glasgow: Baillieston Mure Memorial

45 Glasgow: Balshagray Victoria Park
Campbell Mackinnon BSc BD — 1982 — 2001 — 20 St Kilda Drive, Glasgow G14 9JN [E-mail: CMackinnon@churchofscotland.org.uk] — 0141-954 9780

46 Glasgow: Barlanark Greyfriars (0141-771 6477)
Willem J. Bezuidenhout BA BD MHEd MEd — 1977 — 2016 — 4 Rhindmuir Grove, Baillieston, Glasgow G69 6NE [E-mail: WBezuidenhout@churchofscotland.org.uk] — 0141-771 7103

47   Glasgow: Blawarthill

G. Melvyn Wood MA BD	1982	2009	46 Earlbank Avenue, Glasgow G14 9HL [E-mail: GMelvynWood@churchofscotland.org.uk]	0141-579 6521

48   Glasgow: Bridgeton St Francis in the East (H) (L) (0141-556 2830) (Church House: Tel: 0141-554 8045)

Howard R. Hudson MA BD	1982	1984	10 Albany Drive, Rutherglen, Glasgow G73 3QN [E-mail: HHudson@churchofscotland.org.uk]	0141-587 8667

49   Glasgow: Broomhill Hyndland

George C. Mackay BD CertMin CertEd DipPC	1994	2014	27 St Kilda Drive, Glasgow G14 9LN [E-mail: GMackay@churchofscotland.org.uk]	0141-959 8697 07711 569127 (Mbl)
Ruth Forsythe (Mrs) MCS (Ordained Local Minister)	2017		Flat 1/2 41 Bellwood Street, Glasgow G41 3EX [E-mail: RForsythe@churchofscotland.org.uk]	0141-649 7755

(New charge formed by the union of Glasgow: Broomhill and Glasgow: Hyndland)

50   Glasgow: Calton Parkhead (0141-554 3866)

Alison E.S. Davidge MA BD	1990	2008	98 Drumover Drive, Glasgow G31 5RP [E-mail: ADavidge@churchofscotland.org.uk]	07843 625059 (Mbl)

51   Glasgow: Cardonald (0141-882 6264)

Vacant			133 Newtyle Road, Paisley PA1 3LB	0141-887 2726

52   Glasgow: Carmunnock (0141-644 0655)

G. Gray Fletcher BSc BD	1989	2001	The Manse, 161 Waterside Road, Carmunnock, Glasgow G76 9AJ [E-mail: GFletcher@churchofscotland.org.uk]	0141-644 1578 (Tel/Fax)

53   Glasgow: Carmyle linked with Glasgow: Kenmuir Mount Vernon

Murdo MacLean BD CertMin	1997	1999	3 Meryon Road, Glasgow G32 9NW [E-mail: Murdo.MacLean@churchofscotland.org.uk]	0141-778 2625
Roland Hunt (Ordained Local Minister)	2016		4 Flora Gardens, Bishopbriggs, Glasgow G64 1DS [E-mail: RHunt@churchofscotland.org.uk]	0141-563 3257

54   Glasgow: Carntyne (0141-778 4186)

Joan Ross BSc BD PhD	1999	2016	163 Lethamhill Road, Glasgow G33 2SQ [E-mail: JRoss@churchofscotland.org.uk]	0141-770 9247
Patricia A. Carruth (Mrs) BD (Associate Minister)	1998	2014	38 Springhill Farm Road, Baillieston, Glasgow G69 6GW [E-mail: PCarruth@churchofscotland.org.uk]	0141-771 3758

(Glasgow: Carntyne is a new charge formed by the union of Glasgow: High Carntyne and Glasgow: South Carntyne)

55 Glasgow: Carnwadric
Graeme K. Bell BA BD   1983   62 Loganswell Road, Thornliebank, Glasgow G46 8AX   0141-638 5884
[E-mail: GBell@churchofscotland.org.uk]
Mary S. Gargrave (Mrs) DCS   12 Parkholm Quad, Glasgow G63 7ZH   0141-880 5532
[E-mail: Mary.Gargrave@churchofscotland.org.uk]   07896 866618 (Mbl)

56 Glasgow: Castlemilk (H) (0141-634 1480)
Sarah A. Brown (Ms)   2012   156 Old Castle Road, Glasgow G44 5TW   0141-637 5451
MA BD ThM DipYW/Theol PDCCE   07532 457245 (Mbl)
[E-mail: Sarah.Brown@churchofscotland.org.uk]

57 Glasgow: Cathcart Old (0141-637 4168)
Neil W. Galbraith BD CertMin   1987 1996   21 Courthill Avenue, Cathcart, Glasgow G44 5AA   0141-633 5248 (Tel/Fax)
[E-mail: NGalbraith@churchofscotland.org.uk]

58 Glasgow: Cathcart Trinity (H) (0141-637 6658)
Alasdair MacMillan   2015   82 Merrylee Road, Glasgow G43 2QZ   0141-633 3744
[E-mail: Alasdair.MacMillan@churchofscotland.org.uk]
Wilma Pearson (Mrs) BD   2004   90 Newlands Road, Glasgow G43 2JR   0141-632 2491
(Associate Minister)
[E-mail: WPearson@churchofscotland.org.uk]

59 Glasgow: Cathedral (High or St Mungo's) (0141-552 6891)
Vacant   41 Springfield Road, Bishopbriggs, Glasgow G64 1PL   0141-762 2719

60 Glasgow: Causeway (Tollcross)
Monica Michelin-Salomon BD   1999 2016   228 Hamilton Road, Glasgow G32 9QU   0141-778 2413
[E-mail: MMichelin-Salomon@churchofscotland.org.uk]
(New charge formed by the union of Glasgow: Shettleston Old and Glasgow: Shettleston Victoria Tollcross)

61 Glasgow: Clincarthill (H) (0141-632 4206)
Stuart Love BA MTh   2016   90 Mount Annan Drive, Glasgow G44 4RZ   0141-632 2985
[E-mail: SLove@churchofscotland.org.uk]

62 Glasgow: Colston Milton (0141-772 1922)
Christopher J. Rowe BA BD   2008   118 Birsay Road, Milton, Glasgow G22 7QP   0141-564 1138
[E-mail: CRowe@churchofscotland.org.uk]

63 Glasgow: Colston Wellpark (H)
Guardianship of the Presbytery
Leslie Grieve   2014   23 Hertford Avenue, Kelvindale, Glasgow G12 0LG   07813 255052 (Mbl)
(Ordained Local Minister)
[E-mail: LGrieve@churchofscotland.org.uk]

64 Glasgow: Cranhill (H) (0141-774 3344)
Muriel B. Pearson (Ms) MA BD PGCE — 2004 — 31 Lethamhill Crescent, Glasgow G33 2SH
[E-mail: MPearson@churchofscotland.org.uk] — 0141-770 6873 / 07951 888860 (Mbl)

65 Glasgow: Croftfoot (H) (0141-637 3913)
Robert M. Silver BA BD — 1995 2011 — 4 Inchmurrin Gardens, High Burnside, Rutherglen, Glasgow G73 5RU
[E-mail: RSilver@churchofscotland.org.uk] — 0141-258 7268

66 Glasgow: Dennistoun New (H) (0141-550 2825)
Ian M.S. McInnes BD DipMin — 1995 2008 — 31 Pencaitland Drive, Glasgow G32 8RL
[E-mail: IMcInnes@churchofscotland.org.uk] — 0141-564 6498

67 Glasgow: Drumchapel St Andrew's (0141-944 3758)
John S. Purves LLB BD — 1983 1984 — 6 Firdon Crescent, Old Drumchapel, Glasgow G15 6QQ
[E-mail: john.s.purves@talk21.com] — 0141-944 4566

68 Glasgow: Drumchapel St Mark's
Audrey J. Jamieson BD MTh — 2004 2007 — 146 Garscadden Road, Glasgow G15 6PR
[E-mail: AJamieson@churchofscotland.org.uk] — 0141-944 5440

69 Glasgow: Easterhouse (0141-771 8810)
Vacant
(New charge formed by the union of Glasgow: Lochwood and Glasgow: Easterhouse St George's and St. Peter's)

70 Glasgow: Eastwood
James R. Teasdale BA BD — 2009 2016 — 54 Mansewood Road, Eastwood, Glasgow G43 1TL
[E-mail: JTeasdale@churchofscotland.org.uk] — 0141-571 7648

71 Glasgow: Gairbraid (H)
Donald Michael MacInnes BD — 2002 2011 — 4 Blackhill Gardens, Summerston, Glasgow G23 5NE
[E-mail: DMacInnes@churchofscotland.org.uk] — 0141-946 0604

72 Glasgow: Gallowgate
Peter L.V. Davidge BD MTh — 2003 2009 — 98 Drumover Drive, Glasgow G31 5RP
[E-mail: PDavidge@churchofscotland.org.uk] — 07765 096599 (Mbl)

73 Glasgow: Garthamlock and Craigend East
Vacant

Marion Buchanan (Mrs) MA DCS			16 Almond Drive, East Kilbride, Glasgow G74 2HX [E-mail: MBuchanan@churchofscotland.org.uk]	01355 228776 / 07999 889817 (Mbl)
74 Glasgow: Gorbals				
Ian F. Galloway BA BD	1976	1996	6 Stirlingfauld Place, Gorbals, Glasgow G5 9QF [E-mail: IGalloway@churchofscotland.org.uk]	0141-649 5250
75 Glasgow: Govan and Linthouse				
Eleanor J. McMahon BEd BD (Interim Minister)	1994	2017	81 Moorpark Square, Renfrew PA4 8DB [E-mail: EMcMahon@churchofscotland.org.uk]	07974 116539 (Mbl)
Andrew Thomson BA (Assistant Minister)	1976	2010	3 Laurel Wynd, Drumsagard Village, Cambuslang, Glasgow G72 7BH [E-mail: AThomson@churchofscotland.org.uk]	0141-641 2936 / 07772 502774 (Mbl)
John Paul Cathcart DCS			9 Glen More, East Kilbride, Glasgow G74 2AP [E-mail: John.Cathcart@churchofscotland.org.uk]	01355 243970 / 07708 396074 (Mbl)
76 Glasgow: Hillington Park (H)				
Vacant			61 Ralston Avenue, Glasgow G52 3NB	0141-882 7000
77 Glasgow: Ibrox (H) (0141-427 0896)				
Vacant			59 Langhaul Road, Glasgow G53 7SE	0141-883 7744
78 Glasgow: John Ross Memorial Church for Deaf People (Voice Text: 0141-420 1391; Fax: 0141-420 3778)				
Richard C. Durno DSW CQSW	1989	1998	31 Springfield Road, Bishopbriggs, Glasgow G64 1PJ (Voice/Text/Fax) (Voice/Text/Voicemail) [E-mail: richard.durno@btinternet.com]	0141-772 1052 / 07748 607721 (Mbl)
79 Glasgow: Jordanhill (Tel: 0141-959 2496)				
Bruce H Sinclair BA BD	2009	2015	12 Priorwood Gardens, Academy Park, Glasgow G13 1GD [E-mail: BSinclair@churchofscotland.org.uk]	0141-959 1310
80 Glasgow: Kelvinbridge (0141-339 1750)				
Gordon Kirkwood BSc BD PGCE MTh	1987	2013	Flat 2/2, 94 Hyndland Road, Glasgow G12 9PZ [E-mail: GKirkwood@churchofscotland.org.uk]	0141-334 5352
Cathie H. McLaughlin (Mrs) (Ordained Local Minister)	2014		8 Lamlash Place, Glasgow G33 3XH [E-mail: CMcLaughlin@churchofscotland.org.uk]	0141-774 2483

81 Glasgow: Kelvinside Hillhead (0141-334 2788)
Vacant
Roger D. Sturrock (Prof.) BD MD FCRP 2014 36 Thomson Drive, Bearsden, Glasgow G61 3PA 0141-942 7412
(Ordained Local Minister) [E-mail: RSturrock@churchofscotland.org.uk]

82 Glasgow: Kenmuir Mount Vernon See Glasgow: Carmyle

83 Glasgow: King's Park (H) (0141-636 8688)
Sandra Boyd (Mrs) BEd BD 2007 1101 Aikenhead Road, Glasgow G44 5SL 0141-637 2803
[E-mail: SBoyd@churchofscotland.org.uk]

84 Glasgow: Kinning Park (0141-427 3063)
Margaret H. Johnston BD 1988 2000 168 Arbroath Avenue, Cardonald, Glasgow G52 3HH 0141-810 3782
[E-mail: MHJohnston@churchofscotland.org.uk]

85 Glasgow: Knightswood St Margaret's (H)
Alexander M. Fraser BD DipMin 1985 2009 26 Airthrey Avenue, Glasgow G14 9LJ 0141-959 7075
[E-mail: AFraser@churchofscotland.org.uk]

86 Glasgow: Langside (0141-632 7520)
David N. McLachlan BD 1985 2004 36 Madison Avenue, Glasgow G44 5AQ 0141-637 0797
[E-mail: DMcLachlan@churchofscotland.org.uk]

87 Glasgow: Maryhill (H) (0141-946 3512)
Stuart C. Matthews BD MA 2006 251 Milngavie Road, Bearsden, Glasgow G61 3DQ 0141-942 0804
[E-mail: SMatthews@churchofscotland.org.uk]
James Hamilton DCS 6 Beckfield Gate, Glasgow G33 1SW 0141-558 3195
[E-mail: James.Hamilton@churchofscotland.org.uk] 07584 137314 (Mbl)

88 Glasgow: Merrylea (0141-637 2009)
David P. Hood BD CertMin DipIOB(Scot) 1997 2001 4 Pilmuir Avenue, Glasgow G44 3HX 0141-637 6700
[E-mail: DHood@churchofscotland.org.uk]

89 Glasgow: Mosspark (H) (0141-882 2240)
Vacant

90 Glasgow: Newlands South (H) (0141-632 3055)
R. Stuart M. Fulton BA BD 1991 2017 24 Monreith Road, Glasgow G43 2NY 0141-632 2588

No.	Congregation / Minister		Address	Telephone
91	**Glasgow: Partick South (H)** James Andrew McIntyre BD	2010	3 Branklyn Crescent, Glasgow G13 1GJ [E-mail: Andy.McIntyre@churchofscotland.org.uk]	0141-959 3732
92	**Glasgow: Partick Trinity (H)** Vacant		99 Balshagray Avenue, Glasgow G11 7EQ	0141-576 7149
93	**Glasgow: Pollokshaws (0141-649 1879)** Roy J.M. Henderson MA BD DipMin	1987 2013	33 Mannering Road, Glasgow G41 3SW [E-mail: RHenderson@churchofscotland.org.uk]	0141-632 8768
94	**Glasgow: Pollokshields (H)** David R. Black MA BD	1986 1997	36 Glencairn Drive, Glasgow G41 4PW [E-mail: DBlack@churchofscotland.org.uk]	0141-423 4000
95	**Glasgow: Possilpark (0141-336 8028)** Rosalind (Linda) E. Pollock (Miss) BD ThM ThM	2001 2014	108 Erradale Street, Lambhill, Glasgow G22 6PT [E-mail: RPollock@churchofscotland.org.uk]	0141-336 6909
96	**Glasgow: Queen's Park Govanhill (0141-423 3654)** Elijah W. Smith BA MLitt	2015	32 Queen Mary Avenue, Crosshill, Glasgow G42 8DT [E-mail: E.Smith@churchofscotland.org.uk]	07975 998382 (Mbl)
97	**Glasgow: Renfield St Stephen's (Tel: 0141-332 4293; Fax: 0141-332 8482)** Vacant		101 Hill Street, Glasgow G3 6TY	0141-353 0349
98	**Glasgow: Robroyston (0141-558 8414)** Jonathan A. Keefe BSc BD	2009	7 Beckfield Drive, Glasgow G33 1SR [E-mail: JKeefe@churchofscotland.org.uk]	0141-558 2952
99	**Glasgow: Ruchazie (0141-774 2759)** Vacant			
100	**Glasgow: Ruchill Kelvinside (0141-946 0466)** Mark Lowey BD DipTh	2012 2013	41 Mitre Road, Glasgow G14 9LE [E-mail: MLowey@churchofscotland.org.uk]	0141-959 6718

101 Glasgow: St Andrew and St Nicholas
Lyn Peden (Mrs) BD   2010   2015
80 Tweedsmuir Road, Glasgow G52 2RX
[E-mail: LPeden@churchofscotland.org.uk]
0141-883 9873

102 Glasgow: St Andrew's East (0141-554 1485)
Barbara D. Quigley (Mrs)   1979   2011
MTheol ThM DPS
43 Broompark Drive, Glasgow G31 2JB
[E-mail: BQuigley@churchofscotland.org.uk]
0141-237 7982

103 Glasgow: St Christopher's Priesthill and Nitshill (0141-881 6541)
Douglas M. Nicol BD CA   1987   1996
36 Springkell Drive, Glasgow G41 4EZ
[E-mail: DNicol@churchofscotland.org.uk]
0141-427 7877

104 Glasgow: St Columba (GE) (0141-221 3305)
Vacant

105 Glasgow: St David's Knightswood (0141-954 1081)
Graham M. Thain LLB BD   1988   1999
60 Southbrae Drive, Glasgow G13 1QD
[E-mail: GThain@churchofscotland.org.uk]
0141-959 2904

106 Glasgow: St Enoch's Hogganfield (H) (Tel: 0141-770 5694; Fax: 0870 284 0084) (E-mail: church@st-enoch.org.uk)
(Website: www.stenochshogganfield.org.uk)
Elaine H. MacRae (Mrs) BD   1985   2017
112 Jackson Drive, Crowwood Grange, Stepps, Glasgow G33 6GF
[E-mail: EMacRae@churchofscotland.org.uk]
0141-779 5742
07834 269487 (Mbl)

107 Glasgow: St George's Tron (0141-221 2141)
Alastair S. Duncan MA BD   1989   2013
(Transition Minister)
29 Hertford Avenue, Glasgow G12 0LG
[E-mail: ADuncan@churchofscotland.org.uk]
07968 852083 (Mbl)

108 Glasgow: St James' (Pollok) (0141-882 4984)
John W. Mann BSc MDiv DMin   2004
30 Ralston Avenue, Glasgow G52 3NA
[E-mail: John.Mann@churchofscotland.org.uk]
0141-883 7405

109 Glasgow: St John's Renfield (0141-339 7021) (Website: www.stjohns-renfield.org.uk)
Vacant
26 Leicester Avenue, Glasgow G12 0LU
0141-339 4637

110 Glasgow: St Paul's (0141-770 8559)
Daniel Manastireanu BA MTh   2010   2014
38 Lochview Drive, Glasgow G33 1QF
[E-mail: DManastireanu@churchofscotland.org.uk]
0141-770 1561

111 Glasgow: St Rollox (0141-558 1809)
Jane M. Howitt   1996   2016   42 Melville Gardens, Bishopbriggs, Glasgow G64 3DE   0141-581 0050
(Transition Minister)   [E-mail: JHowitt@churchofscotland.org.uk]

112 Glasgow: Sandyford Henderson Memorial (H) (L)
Vacant   66 Woodend Drive, Glasgow G13 1TG   0141-954 9013

113 Glasgow: Sandyhills (0141-778 3415)
Vacant   60 Wester Road, Glasgow G32 9JJ   0141-778 2174

114 Glasgow: Scotstoun
Richard Cameron BD DipMin   2000   15 Northland Drive, Glasgow G14 9BE   0141-959 4637
                                            [E-mail: RCameron@churchofscotland.org.uk]

115 Glasgow: Shawlands Trinity
Valerie J. Duff (Miss) DMin   1993   2014   29 St Ronan's Drive, Glasgow G41 3SQ   0141-258 6782
                                            [E-mail: VDuff@churchofscotland.org.uk]
(New charge formed by the union of Glasgow: **Shawlands** and Glasgow: **South Shawlands**)

116 Glasgow: Sherbrooke St Gilbert's (H) (0141-427 1968)
Thomas L. Pollock   1982   2003   114 Springkell Avenue, Glasgow G41 4EW   0141-427 2094
BA BD MTh FSAScot JP   [E-mail: TPollock@churchofscotland.org.uk]

117 Glasgow: Shettleston New (0141-778 0857)
W. Louis T. Reddick MA BD   2017   211 Sandyhills Road, Glasgow G32 9NB   0141-778 1286
                                            [E-mail: LReddick@churchofscotland.org.uk]   0784 308 3548 (Mbl)

118 Glasgow: Springburn (H) (0141-557 2345)
Brian M. Casey MA BD   2014   c/o Springburn Parish Church, 180 Springburn Way,   07703 166772 (Mbl)
                                            Glasgow G21 1TU
                                            [E-mail: BCasey@churchofscotland.org.uk]

119 Glasgow: Temple Anniesland (0141-959 1814)
Fiona M.E. Gardner (Mrs) BD MA MLitt 1997 2011   76 Victoria Park Drive North, Glasgow G14 9PJ   0141-959 5647
                                            [E-mail: FGardner@churchofscotland.org.uk]

120 Glasgow: Toryglen (H)
Ada V. MacLeod MA BD PgCE — 2013 2015 — 31 Highburgh Drive, Rutherglen, Glasgow G73 3RR
[E-mail: AVMacLeod@churchofscotland.org.uk] — 07900 254959 (Mbl)

121 Glasgow: Trinity Possil and Henry Drummond
Richard G. Buckley BD MTh — 1990 1995 — 50 Highfield Drive, Glasgow G12 0HL
[E-mail: RBuckley@churchofscotland.org.uk] — 0141-339 2870

122 Glasgow: Tron St Mary's (0141-558 1011)
Rhona E. Graham BA BD — 2015 — 30 Louden Hill Road, Robroyston, Glasgow G33 1GA
[E-mail: RGraham@churchofscotland.org.uk] — 0141-389 8816

123 Glasgow: Wallacewell (New Charge Development)
Daniel L. Frank BA MDiv DMin — 1984 2011 — 8 Streamfield Gate, Glasgow G33 1SJ
[E-mail: DFrank@churchofscotland.org.uk] — 0141-585 0283

124 Glasgow: Wellington (H) (0141-339 0454)
Vacant — 31 Hughenden Gardens, Glasgow G12 9YH — 0141-334 2343
Roger Sturrock (Prof.) BD MD FCRP — 2014 — 36 Thomson Drive, Bearsden, Glasgow G61 3PA — 0141-942 7412
(Ordained Local Minister) [E-mail: RSturrock@churchofscotland.org.uk]

125 Glasgow: Whiteinch (Website: www.whiteinchcofs.co.uk)
Alan McWilliam BD MTh — 1993 2000 — 65 Victoria Park Drive South, Glasgow G14 9NX
[E-mail: AMcWilliam@churchofscotland.org.uk] — 0141-576 9020

126 Glasgow: Yoker
Karen E. Hendry BSc BD — 2005 — 15 Coldingham Avenue, Glasgow G14 0PX
[E-mail: KHendry@churchofscotland.org.uk] — 0141-952 3620

Alexander, Eric J. MA BD — 1958 1997 — (Glasgow: St George's Tron) — 77 Norwood Park, Bearsden, Glasgow G61 2RZ — 0141-942 4404
Allen, Martin A.W. MA BD ThM — 1977 2007 — (Chryston) — Lealenge, 85 High Barrwood Road, Kilsyth, Glasgow G65 0EE — 01236 826616
Alston, William G. — 1961 2009 — (Glasgow: North Kelvinside) — Flat 0/2, 5 Knightswood Court, Glasgow G13 2XN — 0141-959 3113
[E-mail: williamalston@hotmail.com]
Bayes, Muriel C. (Mrs) DCS — (Deacon) — Flat 6, Carlton Court, 10 Fenwick Road, Glasgow G46 6AN — 0141-633 0865
Beaton, Margaret S. (Miss) DCS — (Deacon) — 64 Gardenside Grove, Carmyle, Glasgow G32 8EZ — 0141-646 2297
[E-mail: margaretbeaton54@hotmail.com] — 07796 642382 (Mbl)
Bell, John L. MA BD FRSCM DUniv — 1978 1988 — Iona Community — Flat 2/1, 31 Lansdowne Crescent, Glasgow G20 6NH — 0141-334 0688
Birch, James PgDip FRSA FIOC — 2001 2007 — (Auxiliary Minister) — 1 Kirkhill Grove, Cambuslang, Glasgow G72 8EH — 0141-583 1722

Black, William B. MA BD	1972	2011	(Stornoway: High)	33 Tankerland Road, Glasgow G44 4EN [E-mail: revwillieblack@gmail.com]	0141-637 4717
Blount, A. Sheila (Mrs) BD BA	1978	2010	(Cupar: St John's and Dairsie United)	28 Alcaig Road, Mosspark, Glasgow G52 1NH [E-mail: asblount@orange.net]	0141-419 9746
Blount, Graham K. LLB BD PhD	1976	2016	(Presbytery Clerk)	28 Alcaig Road, Mosspark, Glasgow G52 1NH [E-mail: Graham.Blount@churchofscotland.org.uk]	0141-419 0746
Brain, Isobel J. (Mrs) MA	1987	1997	(Ballantrae)	10/11 Maxwell Street, Edinburgh EH10 5GZ	0131-466 6115
Brice, Dennis G. BSc BD	1981		(Taiwan)	8 Parkwood Close, Broxbourne, Herts EN10 7PF [E-mail: dbrice1@comcast.net]	
Bryden, William A. BD	1977	1984	(Yoker: Old with St Matthew's)	145 Bearsden Road, Glasgow G13 1BS	0141-959 5213
Bull, Alister W. BD DipMin MTh PhD	1994	2013	Mission and Discipleship Council	121 George Street, Edinburgh EH2 4YN [E-mail: ABull@churchofscotland.org.uk]	0131-225 5722
Campbell, A. Iain MA DipEd	1961	1997	(Busby)	430 Clarkston Road, Glasgow G44 3QF [E-mail: bellmac@againternet.co.uk]	0141-637 7460
Campbell, John MA BA BSc	1973	2009	(Caldwell)	96 Boghead Road, Lenzie, Glasgow G66 4BN [E-mail: johncampbell.lenzie@gmail.com]	0141-776 0874
Cartlidge, Graham R.G. MA BD STM	1977	2015	(Glasgow: Eastwood)	5 Briar Grove, Newlands, Glasgow G43 2TG	0141-637 3228
Clark, Douglas W. LTh	1993	2015	(Lenzie: Old)	1/3, 39 Saltmarsh Drive, Lenzie, Glasgow G66 3NR [E-mail: douglaswclark@hotmail.com]	0141-776 1298
Cowie, George S. BSc BD	1991	2006	Presbytery Clerk	120e Southbrae Drive, Glasgow G13 1TZ [E-mail: GCowie@churchofscotland.org.uk]	0141-332 6066
Cowie, Marian (Mrs) MA BD MTh	1990	2012	(Aberdeen: Mid Stockett)	120e Southbrae Drive, Glasgow G12 1TZ [E-mail: mcowieou@aol.com]	(Mbl) 07740 174969
Cunningham, Alexander MA BD	1961	2002	(Presbytery Clerk)	18 Lady Jane Gate, Bothwell, Glasgow G71 8BW	01698 811051
Cunningham, James S.A. MA BD BLitt PhD	1992	2000	(Glasgow: Barlanark Greyfriars)	'Kirkland', 5 Inveresk Place, Coatbridge ML5 2DA	01236 421541
Drummond, John W. MA BD	1971	2011	(Rutherglen: West and Wardlawhill)	25 Kingsburn Drive, Rutherglen, Glasgow G73 2AN	0141-571 6002
Duff, T. Malcolm F. MA BD	1985	2009	(Glasgow: Queen's Park)	54 Hawkhead Road, Paisley PA1 3NB	0141-570 0614
Dutch, Morris M. BD BA Dip BTI	1998	2013	(Costa del Sol)	41 Baronald Drive, Glasgow G12 0HN [E-mail: mmdutch@yahoo.co.uk]	(Mbl) 07846 926584 / 0141-357 2286
Farrington, Alexandra LTh	2003	2015	(Campsie)	'Glenburn', High Banton, Kilsyth G65 0RA [E-mail: revsfarrington@aol.co.uk]	01236 824516
Ferguson, James B. LTh	1972	2002	(Lenzie: Union)	3 Bridgeway Place, Kirkintilloch, Glasgow G66 3HW [E-mail: revferg@btinternet.com]	0141-588 5868
Ferguson, William B. BA BD	1971	2012	(Glasgow: Broomhill)	20 Swift Crescent, Knightswood Gate, Glasgow G13 4QL	0141-954 6655
Fleming, Alexander F. MA BD	1966	1995	(Strathblane)	11 Bankwood Drive, Kilsyth, Glasgow G65 0GZ	01236 821461
Forrest, Martin R. BA MA BD	1988	2012	Prison Chaplain	4/1, 7 Blochairn Place, Glasgow G21 2EB [E-mail: martinrforrest@gmail.com]	0141-552 1132
Forsyth, Sandy LLB BD DipLP PhD	2009	2013	(Associate: Kirkintilloch: St David's Memorial Park)	48 Kerr Street, Kirkintilloch, Glasgow G66 1JZ [E-mail: sandyforsyth67@hotmail.co.uk]	0141-777 8194 / (Mbl) 07739 639037
Foster-Fulton, Sally BA BD	1999	2016	Head of Christian Aid Scotland	24 Monreith Road, Glasgow G43 2NY [E-mail: sallyfulton01@gmail.com]	(Mbl) 07850 937226

Galloway, Kathy (Mrs) BD DD	1977	2002	(Head of Christian Aid Scotland)	20 Hamilton Park Avenue, Glasgow G12 8UU [E-mail: kathygalloway200@btinternet.com]	0141-357 4079
Gay, Douglas C. MA BD PhD	1998	2005	University of Glasgow	1F, 16 Royal Terrace, Glasgow G3 7NY [E-mail: douggay@mac.com]	0141-332 4040 (Mbl) 07971 321452
Gibson, H. Marshall MA BD	1957	1996	(Glasgow: St Thomas' Gallowgate)	39 Burnbroom Drive, Glasgow G69 7XG	0141-771 0749
Grant, David I.M. MA BD	1969	2003	(Dalry: Trinity)	8 Mossbank Drive, Glasgow G33 1LS	0141-770 7186
Gray, Christine M. (Mrs)			(Deacon)	11 Woodside Avenue, Thornliebank, Glasgow G46 7HR	0141-571 1008
Green, Alex H. MA BD	1986	2010	(Strathblane)	44 Laburnum Drive, Milton of Campsie, Glasgow G66 8HY [E-mail: lesvert@btinternet.com]	01360 313001
Gregson, Elizabeth M. (Mrs) BD	1996	2001	(Glasgow: Drumchapel St Andrew's)	17 Westfields, Bishopbriggs, Glasgow G64 3PL	0141-563 1918
Haley, Derek BD DPS	1960	1999	(Chaplain: Gartnavel Royal)	9 Kinnaird Crescent, Bearsden, Glasgow G61 2BN	0141-942 9281
Harvey, W. John BA BD DD	1965	2002	(Edinburgh: Corstorphine Craigsbank)	501 Shields Road, Glasgow G41 2RF	0141-429 3774
Hazlett, W. Ian P. (Prof.-Emer.) BA BD Dr theol DLitt DD		2009	University of Glasgow	587 Shields Road, Glasgow G41 2RW [E-mail: ian.hazlett@glasgow.ac.uk]	0141-423 7461 (Work) 0141-330 5155
Hope, Evelyn P. (Miss) BA BD	1990	1998	(Wishaw: Thornlie)	Flat 0/1, 48 Moss Side Road, Glasgow G41 3UA	0141-649 1522
Houston, Thomas C. BA	1975	2004	(Glasgow: Priesthill and Nitshill)	63 Broomhouse Crescent, Uddingston, Glasgow G71 7RE	0141-771 0577
Hughes, Helen (Miss) DCS			(Deacon)	2/2, 43 Burnbank Terrace, Glasgow G20 6UQ [E-mail: helhug35@gmail.com]	0141-333 9459 (Mbl) 07752 604817
Hunter, Alastair G. MSc BD	1976	1980	(University of Glasgow)	487 Shields Road, Glasgow G41 2RG	0141-429 1687
Johnston, Robert W.M. MA BD STM	1964	1999	(Glasgow: Temple Anniesland)	13 Kilmardinny Crescent, Bearsden, Glasgow G61 3NP	0141-931 5862
Johnstone, H. Martin J. MA BD MTh PhD	1989	2000	Church and Society Council	3/1, 952 Pollokshaws Road, Glasgow G41 2ET [E-mail: MJohnstone@churchofscotland.org.uk]	0141-636 5819
Lang, I. Pat (Miss) BSc	1996	2003	(Dunoon: The High Kirk)	37 Crawford Drive, Glasgow G15 6TW	0141-944 2240
Levison, Chris L. MA BD	1972	1998	(Health Care Chaplaincy Training and Development Officer)	Gardenfield, Nine Mile Burn, Penicuik EH26 9LT	01968 674566 (Mbl) 07879 812816
Lloyd, John M. BD CertMin	1984	2009	(Glasgow: Croftfoot)	17 Acacia Way, Cambuslang, Glasgow G72 7ZY	0141-772 0149
Love, Joanna (Ms) BSc DCS			Iona Community: Wild Goose Resource Group	92 Everard Drive, Glasgow G21 1XQ [E-mail: jo@wildgoose.scot]	0141-429 7281 (Office)
Lunan, David W. MA BD DUniv DLitt DD	1970	2002	(Presbytery Clerk)	30 Mill Road, Banton, Glasgow G65 0RD	01236 824110
MacBain, Ian W. BD	1971	1993	(Coatbridge: Coatdyke)	24 Thornyburn Drive, Baillieston, Glasgow G69 7ER	0141-771 7030
McChlery, Lynn M. BA BD	2005	2015	(Eaglesham)	62 Grenville Drive, Cambuslang, Glasgow G72 8DP [E-mail: lmcchlery@btinternet.com]	0141-643 9730 (Mbl) 07748 118008
MacDonald, Anne (Miss) BA DCS			Healthcare Chaplain	c/o Leverndale Hospital, Glasgow G53 7TU [E-mail: anne.macdonald2@ggc.scot.nhs.uk]	0141-211 6695 (Mbl) 07976 786174
MacDonald, Kenneth MA BA	2001	2006	(Auxiliary Minister)	5 Henderland Road, Bearsden, Glasgow G61 1AH	0141-943 1103
McDougall, Hilary N. (Mrs) MA PGCE BD	2002	2013	Congregational Facilitator: Presbytery of Glasgow	16 Central Court, Central Avenue, Cambuslang G72 8DJ [E-mail: hilary@presbyteryofglasgow.org.uk]	0141-641 8574 (Mbl) 07539 321832
MacFadyen, Anne M. (Mrs) BSc BD FSAScot		1995	(Auxiliary Minister)	295 Mearns Road, Glasgow G77 5LT	0141-639 3605
Mackenzie, Gordon R. BScAgr BD	1977	2014	(Chapelhall)	16 Crowhill Road, Bishopbriggs, Glasgow G64 1QY [E-mail: rev.g.mackenzie@btopenworld.com]	0141-772 6052

Name	Years	Charge / Status	Address & E-mail	Tel.
MacKinnon, Charles M. BD	1989 2009	(Kilsyth: Anderson)	36 Hilton Terrace, Bishopbriggs, Glasgow G64 3HB [E-mail: cm.ccmackinnon@gmail.com]	0141-772 3811
McLachlan, Eric BD MTh	1978 2005	(Glasgow: Cardonald)	16 Kinpurnie Road, Paisley PA1 3HH [E-mail: eric.janis@btinternet.com]	0141-810 5789
McLachlan, T. Alastair BSc	1972 2009	(Craignish with Kilbrandon and Kilchattan with Kilninver and Kilmelford)	9 Alder Road, Milton of Campsie, Glasgow G66 8HH [E-mail: talastair@btinternet.com]	01360 319861
McLaren, D. Muir MA BD MTh PhD	1971 2001	(Glasgow: Mosspark)	House 44, 145 Shawhill Road, Glasgow G43 1SX [E-mail: muir44@yahoo.co.uk]	(Mbl) 07931 155779
McLellan, Margaret DCS		Deacon	18 Broom Road East, Newton Mearns, Glasgow G77 5SD [E-mail: margaretmclellan@rocketmail.com]	0141-639 6853
Macleod, Donald BD LRAM DRSAM	1987 2008	(Blairgowrie)	9 Millersneuk Avenue, Lenzie G66 5HJ [E-mail: donmac2@sky.com]	0141-776 6235
MacLeod, Iain A.	2012	Ordained Local Minister	6 Hallydown Drive, Glasgow G13 1UF [E-mail: IMacLeod@churchofscotland.org.uk]	(Mbl) 07795 014889
MacLeod-Mair, Alisdair T. MEd DipTheol	2001 2012	(Glasgow: Baillieston St Andrew's)	2/2, 44 Leven Street, Pollokshields, Glasgow G41 2JE [E-mail: revalisdair@hotmail.com]	0141-423 9600
MacMahon, Janet P.H. (Mrs) MSc BD	1992 2010	(Kilmaronock Gartocharn)	14 Hillfoot Drive, Bearsden, Glasgow G61 3QQ [E-mail: janetmacmahon@yahoo.co.uk]	0141-942 8611
Macnaughton, J.A. MA BD	1949 1989	(Glasgow: Hyndland)	Lilyburn Care Home, 100 Birdston Road, Milton of Campsie, Glasgow G66 8BY	(Mbl) 07811 621671
MacPherson, James B. DCS	1984 2001	(Deacon)	0/1, 104 Cartside Street, Glasgow G42 9TQ [E-mail: tom@gallus.org.uk]	0141-616 6468
MacQuarrie, Stuart JP BD BSc MBA	1988	Chaplain: Glasgow University	The Chaplaincy Centre, University of Glasgow, Glasgow G12 8QQ	0141-330 5419
MacQuien, Duncan DCS	1994 2005	(Deacon)	35 Criffel Road, Mount Vernon, Glasgow G32 9JE	0141-575 1137
Martindale, John P.F. BD	1971 2007	(Glasgow: Sandyhills)	Flat 3/2, 25 Albert Avenue, Glasgow G42 8RB	0141-433 4367
Miller, John D. BA BD DD	1976 2008	(Glasgow: Castlemilk East)	98 Kirkcaldy Road, Glasgow G41 4LD [E-mail: rev.john.miller@zol.co.zw]	0141-423 0221
Moffat, Thomas BSc BD	1993 2015	(Culross and Torryburn)	Flat 8/1, 8 Cranston Street, Glasgow G3 8GG	0141-248 1886
Moore, William B.		(Prison Chaplain: Low Moss)	10 South Dumbreck Road, Kilsyth, Glasgow G65 9LX	01236 821918
Ninian, Esther J. (Miss) MA BD	1953 1996	(Newton Mearns)	21 St Ronan's Drive, Burnside, Rutherglen G73 3SR [E-mail: estheninian5914@btinternet.com]	0141-647 9720
Philip, George M. MA	1971 2010	(Glasgow: Sandyford Henderson Memorial)	44 Beech Avenue, Bearsden, Glasgow G61 3EX	0141-942 1327
Raeburn, Alan C. MA BD	1967 1999	(Glasgow: Battlefield East)	3 Orchard Gardens, Strathaven ML10 6UN [E-mail: acraeburn@hotmail.com]	(Mbl) 07709 552161
Ramsay, W.G.		(Glasgow: Springburn)	53 Kelvinvale, Kirkintilloch, Glasgow G66 1RD [E-mail: billram@btopenworld.com]	0141-776 2915
Ramsden, Iain R. MStJ BTh	1999 2013	(Killearnan with Knockbain)	Flat 1/1, 15 Cardon Square, Renfrew PA4 8BY [E-mail: s4rev@sky.com]	(Mbl) 07795 972560
Ross, Donald M. MA	1953 1994	(Industrial Mission Organiser)	14 Cartsbridge Road, Busby, Glasgow G76 8DH	0141-644 2220
Ross, James MA BD	1968 1998	(Kilsyth: Anderson)	53 Turnberry Gardens, Westerwood, Cumbernauld, Glasgow G68 0AY	01236 730501
Shackleton, Scott J.S. QCVS BA BD	1993 2010	Chaplain, Royal Navy	MOD Academy, Amport House, Amport, Andover SP11 8BG [E-mail: shackletonscott@hotmail.com]	

Name			Charge	Address	Phone
Shackleton, William	1960	1996	(Greenock: Wellpark West)	3 Tynwald Avenue, Burnside, Glasgow G73 4RN	0141-569 9407
Smeed, Alex W. MA BD	2008	2013	(Glasgow: Whiteinch: Associate)	3/1, 24 Thornwood Road, Glasgow G11 7RB [E-mail: alexsmeed@yahoo.co.uk]	0141-337 3878 (Mbl) 07709 756495
Smith, G. Stewart MA BD STM	1966	2006	(Glasgow: King's Park)	33 Brent Road, Stewartfield, East Kilbride, Glasgow G74 4RA [E-mail: stewartandmary@googlemail.com]	(Tel/Fax) 01355 226718
Spencer, John MA BD	1962	2001	(Dumfries: Lincluden with Holywood)	10 Kinkell Gardens, Kirkintilloch, Glasgow G66 2HJ	0141-777 8935
Spiers, John M. LTh MTh	1972	2004	(Giffnock: Orchardhill)	58 Woodlands Road, Thornliebank, Glasgow G46 7JQ	(Tel/Fax) 0141-638 0632
Stewart, Diane E. BD	1988	2006	(Milton of Campsie)	4 Miller Gardens, Bishopbriggs, Glasgow G64 1FG [E-mail: destewart@givemail.co.uk]	0141-762 1358
Stewart, Norma D. (Miss) MA MEd BD MTh	1977	2000	(Glasgow: Strathbungo Queen's Park)	127 Nether Auldhouse Road, Glasgow G43 2YS	0141-637 6956
Sutherland, David A.	2001		Auxiliary Minister	3/1, 145 Broomhill Drive, Glasgow G11 7ND [E-mail: dave.a.sutherland@gmail.com]	0141-357 2058
Sutherland, Denis I.	1963	1995	(Glasgow: Hutchesontown)	56 Lime Crescent, Cumbernauld, Glasgow G67 3PQ	01236 731723
Turner, Angus BD	1976	1998	(Industrial Chaplain)	46 Keir Street, Pollokshields, Glasgow G41 2LA	0141-424 0493
Tuton, Robert M. MA	1957	1995	(Glasgow: Shettleston Old)	6 Holmwood Gardens, Uddingston, Glasgow G71 7BH	01698 321108
Walker, Linda	2008	2013	Auxiliary Minister	18 Valeview Terrace, Glasgow G42 9LA [E-mail: LWalker@churchofscotland.org.uk]	0141-649 1340
Walton, Ainslie MA MEd	1954	1995	(University of Aberdeen)	501 Shields Road, Glasgow G41 2RF [E-mail: revainslie@aol.com]	0141-420 3327
White, C. Peter BVMS BD MRCVS	1974	2011	(Glasgow: Sandyford Henderson Memorial)	2 Hawthorn Place, Torrance, Glasgow G64 4EA [E-mail: revcpw@gmail.com]	01360 622680
Whiteford, John D. MA BD	1989	2016	(Glasgow: Newlands South)	42 Maxwell Drive, East Kilbride, Glasgow G74 4HJ [E-mail: jwhiteford@hotmail.com]	(Mbl) 07809 290806
Whitley, Laurence A.B. MA BD PhD DLitt HonFRCPSG	1975	2017	(Glasgow: Cathedral)	35 Springfield Road, Bishopbriggs, Glasgow G64 1PL [E-mail: labwhitley@btinternet.com]	(Mbl) 07870 733721
Whyte, James BD	1981	2011	(Fairlie)	32 Torburn Avenue, Giffnock, Glasgow G46 7RB [E-mail: jameswhyte89@btinternet.com]	0141 620 3043
Wilson, John BD	1985	2010	(Glasgow: Temple Anniesland)	4 Carron Crescent, Bearsden, Glasgow G61 1HJ [E-mail: revjwilson@btinternet.com]	0141-931 5609
Younger, Adah (Mrs) BD	1978	2004	(Glasgow: Dennistoun Central)	7 Gartocher Terrace, Glasgow G32 0HE	0141-774 6475

GLASGOW ADDRESSES

Banton	Kelvinhead Road, Banton	
Bishopbriggs Kenmure	Viewfield Road, Bishopbriggs	
Springfield Cambridge	The Leys, off Springfield Road	
Broom	Mearns Road, Newton Mearns	
Burnside Blairbeth	Church Avenue, Burnside	Kirkriggs Avenue, Blairbeth
Busby	Church Road, Busby	
Cadder	Cadder Road, Bishopbriggs	
Cambuslang Flemington Hallside	Hutchinson Place	
Parish	Arnott Way	
Campsie	Main Street, Lennoxtown	
Chryston	Main Street, Chryston	
Eaglesham	Montgomery Street, Eaglesham	
Fernhill and Cathkin	Neilvaig Drive	
Gartcosh	113 Lochend Road, Gartcosh	
Giffnock Orchardhill	Church Road	
South	Eastwood Toll	

The Park	Ravenscliffe Drive
Glenboig	Main Street, Glenboig
Greenbank	Eaglesham Road, Clarkston
Kilsyth	
Anderson	Kingston Road, Kilsyth
Burns and Old	Church Street, Kilsyth
Kirkintilloch	
Hillhead	Newdyke Road, Kirkintilloch
St Columba's	Waterside Road nr Auld Aisle Road
St David's Mem Pk	Alexandra Street
St Mary's	Cowgate
Lenzie	
Old	Kirkintilloch Road x Garngaber Ave
Union	65 Kirkintilloch Road
Maxwell	
Mearns Castle	Waterfoot Road
Mearns	Mearns Road, Newton Mearns
Milton of Campsie	Antermony Road, Milton of Campsie
Netherlee	Ormonde Drive x Ormonde Avenue
Newton Mearns	Ayr Road, Newton Mearns
Rutherglen	
Old	Main Street at Queen Street
Stonelaw	Stonelaw Road x Dryburgh Avenue
West and Wardlawhill	3 Western Avenue
Stamperland	Stamperland Gardens, Clarkston
Stepps	Whitehill Avenue
Thornliebank	61 Spiersbridge Road
Torrance	School Road, Torrance
Twechar	Main Street, Twechar
Williamwood	4 Vardar Avenue, Clarkston
Glasgow	
Anderston Kelvingrove	759 Argyle St x Elderslie St
Baillieston	
Mure Memorial	Maxwell Drive, Garrowhill
St Andrew's	Bredisholm Road
Balshagray Victoria Pk	218–230 Broomhill Drive
Barlanark Greyfriars	Edinburgh Rd x Hallhill Rd (365)

Blawarthill	Millbrix Avenue
Bridgeton St Francis in the East	26 Queen Mary Street
Broomhill	64–66 Randolph Rd (x Marlborough Ave)
Calton Parkhead	122 Helenvale Street
Cardonald	2155 Paisley Road West
Carmunnock	Kirk Road, Carmunnock
Carmyle	155 Carmyle Avenue
Carntyne	358 Carntynehall Road
Carnwadric	556 Boydstone Road, Thornliebank
Castlemilk	Carmunnock Road
Cathcart Old	119 Carmunnock Road
Trinity	90 Clarkston Road
Cathedral	Cathedral Square, 2 Castle Street
Causeway Church, Tollcross	1134 Tollcross Road
Clincarthill	1216 Cathcart Road
Colston Milton	Egilsay Crescent
Colston Wellpark	1378 Springburn Road
Cranhill	109 Bellrock St (at Bellrock Cr)
Croftfoot	Croftpark Ave x Crofthill Road
Dennistoun New	9 Armadale Street
Drumchapel St Andrew's	153 Garscadden Road
St Mark's	281 Kinfauns Drive
Easterhouse	Boyndie Street
Eastwood	Mansewood Road
Gairbraid	1517 Maryhill Road
Gallowgate	David Street
Garthamlock and Craigend East	46 Porchester Street
Gorbals	1 Errol Gardens
Govan and Linthouse	Govan Cross
Hillington Park	24 Berryknowes Road
Hyndland	79 Hyndland Rd, opp Novar Dr
Ibrox	Carillon Road x Clifford Street
John Ross Memorial	100 Norfolk Street
Jordanhill	28 Woodend Drive (x Munro Road)

Kelvinbridge	Belmont Street at Belmont Bridge
Kelvinside Hillhead	Observatory Road
Kenmuir Mount Vernon	2405 London Road, Mount Vernon
King's Park	242 Castlemilk Road
Kinning Park	Eaglesham Place
Knightswood St Margaret's	2000 Great Western Road
Langside	167–169 Ledard Road (x Lochleven Road)
Maryhill	1990 Maryhill Road
Merrylea	78 Merrylee Road
Mosspark	167 Ashkirk Drive
Newlands South	Riverside Road x Langside Drive
Partick South	259 Dumbarton Road
Trinity	20 Lawrence Street x Elie Street
Pollokshaws	223 Shawbridge Street
Pollokshields	Albert Drive x Shields Road
Possilpark	124 Saracen Street
Queen's Park Govanhill	170 Queen's Drive
Renfield St Stephen's	260 Bath Street
Robroyston	34 Saughs Road
Ruchazie	4 Elibank Street (x Milncroft Road)
Ruchill Kelvinside	Shakespeare Street nr Maryhill Rd and 10 Kelbourne Street (two buildings)
St Andrew and St Nicholas	Bowfield Road x Bowfield Avenue
St Andrew's East	224 Hartlaw Crescent
St Christopher's Priesthill and Nitshill	681 Alexandra Parade
Priesthill building	100 Priesthill Rd (x Muirshiel Cr)
Nitshill building	36 Dove Street
St Christopher's	Meikle Road
St Columba	300 St Vincent Street
St David's Knightswood	66 Boreland Drive (nr Lincoln Avenue)
St Enoch's Hogganfield	860 Cumbernauld Road
St George's Tron	163 Buchanan Street
St James' (Pollok)	Lyoncross Road x Byrebush Road
St John's Renfield	22 Beaconsfield Road

St Paul's	30 Langdale St (x Greenrig St)	Shettleston New	679 Old Shettleston Road	Wellington	University Ave x Southpark Avenue
St Rollox	9 Fountainwell Road	Springburn	180 Springburn Way	Whiteinch	1a Northinch Court
Sandyford Henderson Memorial	Kelvinhaugh Street at Argyle Street	Temple Anniesland	869 Crow Road	Yoker	10 Hawick Street
Sandyhills	28 Baillieston Rd nr Sandyhills Rd	Toryglen	Glenmore Ave nr Prospecthill Road		
Scotstoun	Earlbank Avenue x Ormiston Avenue	Trinity Possil and Henry Drummond	2 Crowhill Street (x Broadholm Street)		
Shawlands	Shawlands Cross (1114 Pollokshaws Road)	Tron St Mary's	128 Red Road		
Sherbrooke St Gilbert's	Nithsdale Rd x Sherbrooke Avenue	Wallacewell	57 Northgate Rd., Balornock		

(17) HAMILTON

Meets at Motherwell: Dalziel St Andrew's Parish Church Halls, on the first Tuesday of February, March, May, September, October, November and December, and on the third Tuesday of June.

Presbytery Office: 353 Orbiston Street, Motherwell ML1 1QW — 01698 259135
[E-mail: hamilton@churchofscotland.org.uk]
[E-mail: clerk@presbyteryofhamilton.co.uk]

Clerk: REV. GORDON A. McCRACKEN BD CertMin DMin — c/o The Presbytery Office

Presbytery Treasurer: MR ROBERT A. ALLAN — 7 Graham Place, Ashgill, Larkhall ML9 3BA — 01698 883246
[E-mail: Fallan3246@aol.com]

1 Airdrie: Cairnlea (H) (01236 762101) linked with Calderbank
Vacant — 38 Commonhead Street, Airdrie ML6 6NS — 01236 609584
(Airdrie: Cairnlea is formed by the union between Airdrie: Broomknoll and Airdrie: Flowerhill)

2 Airdrie: Clarkston
F. Derek Gunn BD   1986   2009 — Clarkston Manse, Forrest Street, Airdrie ML6 7BE — 01236 603146
[E-mail: DGunn@churchofscotland.org.uk]

3 Airdrie: High linked with Caldercruix and Longriggend
Ian R.W. McDonald BSc BD PhD   2007 — 17 Etive Drive, Airdrie ML6 9QL — 01236 760023
[E-mail: IMcDonald@churchofscotland.org.uk]

#				Address / E-mail	Tel
4	**Airdrie: Jackson** Kay Gilchrist (Miss) BD	1996	2008	48 Dunrobin Road, Airdrie ML6 8LR [E-mail: KGilchrist@churchofscotland.org.uk]	01236 760154
5	**Airdrie: New Monkland (H) linked with Greengairs** William Jackson BD CertMin	1994	2015	3 Dykehead Crescent, Airdrie ML6 6PU [E-mail: WJackson@churchofscotland.org.uk]	01236 761723
6	**Airdrie: St Columba's** Margaret F. Currie BEd BD	1980	1987	52 Kennedy Drive, Airdrie ML6 9AW [E-mail: MCurrie@churchofscotland.org.uk]	01236 763173
7	**Airdrie: The New Wellwynd** Robert A. Hamilton BA BD	1995	2001	20 Arthur Avenue, Airdrie ML6 9EZ [E-mail: RHamilton@churchofscotland.org.uk]	01236 763022
8	**Bargeddie (H)** Vacant			The Manse, Manse Road, Bargeddie, Baillieston, Glasgow G69 6UB	0141-771 1322
9	**Bellshill: Central** Kevin M. de Beer BTh	1995	2016	32 Adamson Street, Bellshill ML4 1DT [E-mail: KdeBeer@churchofscotland.org.uk]	01698 841176 07555 265609 (Mbl)
10	**Bellshill: West (H) (01698 747581)** Calum Stark LLB BD	2011	2015	16 Croftpark Street, Bellshill ML4 1EY [E-mail: CStark@churchofscotland.org.uk]	01698 842877
11	**Blantyre: Livingstone Memorial linked with Blantyre St Andrew's** Murdo C. Macdonald MA BD	2017		332 Glasgow Road, Blantyre, Glasgow G72 9LQ [E-mail: MurdoCMacdonald@churchofscotland.org.uk]	01698 769699
12	**Blantyre: Old (H)** Sarah L. Ross (Mrs) BD MTh PGDip	2004	2013	The Manse, Craigmuir Road, High Blantyre, Glasgow G72 9UA [E-mail: SRoss@churchofscotland.org.uk]	01698 769046
13	**Blantyre: St Andrew's** See Blantyre: Livingstone Mermorial Vacant				

14 Bothwell (H)
James M. Gibson TD LTh LRAM   1978   1989   Manse Avenue, Bothwell, Glasgow G71 8PQ   01698 853189 (Tel)
[E-mail: JGibson@churchofscotland.org.uk]   01698 854903 (Fax)

15 Calderbank See Airdrie: Cairnlea

16 Caldercruix and Longriggend (H) See Airdrie: High

17 Chapelhall (H) linked with Kirk o' Shotts (H)
Vacant   The Manse, Russell Street, Chapelhall, Airdrie ML6 8SG   01236 763439

18 Chapelton linked with Strathaven: Rankin (H)
Shaw J. Paterson BSc BD MSc   1991   15 Lethame Road, Strathaven ML10 6AD   01357 520019 (Tel)
[E-mail: SPaterson@churchofscotland.org.uk]   01357 529316 (Fax)

19 Cleland (H) linked with Wishaw: St Mark's
Graham Austin BD   1997   2008   3 Laburnum Crescent, Wishaw ML2 7EH   01698 384596
[E-mail: GAustin@churchofscotland.org.uk]

20 Coatbridge: Blairhill Dundyvan (H) linked with Coatbridge: Middle
Vacant   1 Nelson Terrace, East Kilbride, Glasgow G74 2EY   01355 520093

21 Coatbridge: Calder (H) linked with Coatbridge: Old Monkland
Vacant   26 Bute Street, Coatbridge ML5 4HF   01236 421516

22 Coatbridge: Middle See Coatbridge: Blairhill Dundyvan

23 Coatbridge: New St Andrew's
Fiona Nicolson BA BD   1996   2005   77 Eglinton Street, Coatbridge ML5 3JF   01236 437271
[E-mail: FNicolson@churchofscotland.org.uk]

24 Coatbridge: Old Monkland See Coatbridge: Calder

25 Coatbridge: Townhead (H)
Ecilo Selemani LTh MTh   1993   2004   Crinan Crescent, Coatbridge ML5 2LH   01236 702914
[E-mail: ESelemani@churchofscotland.org.uk]

26 Dalserf
Vacant
Manse Brae, Dalserf, Larkhall ML9 3BN
01698 882195

27 East Kilbride: Claremont (H) (01355 238088)
Gordon R. Palmer MA BD STM   1986   2003
17 Deveron Road, East Kilbride, Glasgow G74 2HR
[E-mail: GPalmer@churchofscotland.org.uk]
01355 248526

28 East Kilbride: Greenhills (E) (01355 221746)
John Brewster MA BD DipEd   1988
21 Turnberry Place, East Kilbride, Glasgow G75 8TB
[E-mail: JBrewster@churchofscotland.org.uk]
01355 242564

29 East Kilbride: Moncreiff (H) (01355 223328)
Neil Buchanan BD   1991   2011
16 Almond Drive, East Kilbride, Glasgow G74 2HX
[E-mail: NBuchanan@churchofscotland.org.uk]
01355 238639

30 East Kilbride: Mossneuk (01355 260954)
Vacant
30 Eden Grove, Mossneuk, East Kilbride, Glasgow G75 8XU
01355 234196

31 East Kilbride: Old (H) (01355 279004)
Anne S. Paton BA BD   2001
40 Maxwell Drive, East Kilbride, Glasgow G74 4HJ
[E-mail: APaton@churchofscotland.org.uk]
01355 220732

32 East Kilbride: South (H)
Terry Ann Taylor BA MTh   2005   2017
7 Clamps Wood, St Leonard's, East Kilbride, Glasgow G74 2HB
[E-mail: TTaylor@churchofscotland.org.uk]
01355 902758

33 East Kilbride: Stewartfield (New Charge Development)
Douglas W. Wallace MA BD   1981   2001
8 Thistle Place, Stewartfield, East Kilbride, Glasgow G74 4RH
[E-mail: DWallace@churchofscotland.org.uk]
01355 260879

34 East Kilbride: West (H)
Mahboob Masih BA MDiv MTh   1999   2008
4 East Milton Grove, East Kilbride, Glasgow G75 8FN
[E-mail: MMasih@churchofscotland.org.uk]
01355 224469

35 East Kilbride: Westwood (H) (01355 245657)
Kevin Mackenzie BD DPS   1989   1996
16 Inglewood Crescent, East Kilbride, Glasgow G75 8QD
[E-mail: Kevin.MacKenzie@churchofscotland.org.uk]
01355 223992

No.	Charge / Minister	Ord.	App.	Address / E-mail	Tel.
36	**Glassford linked with Strathaven: East** William T. Stewart BD	1980		68 Townhead Street, Strathaven ML10 6DJ [E-mail: WStewart@churchofscotland.org.uk]	01357 521138
37	**Greengairs** See Airdrie: New Monkland				
38	**Hamilton: Cadzow (H) (01698 428695)** John W. Carswell BS MDiv	1996	2009	3 Carlisle Road, Hamilton ML3 7BZ [E-mail: JCarswell@churchofscotland.org.uk]	01698 426682
39	**Hamilton: Gilmour and Whitehill (H) linked with Hamilton: West** Vacant				
40	**Hamilton: Hillhouse** Christopher A. Rankine MA MTh PgDE	2016		66 Wellhall Road, Hamilton ML3 9BY [E-mail: CRankine@churchofscotland.org.uk]	01698 327579
41	**Hamilton: Old (H) (01698 281905)** I. Ross Blackman BSc MBA BD	2015		1 Chateau Grove, Hamilton ML3 7DS [E-mail: RBlackman@churchofscotland.org.uk] (This congregation has united with the congregation of Hamilton: North)	01698 640185
42	**Hamilton: St John's (H) (01698 283492)** Joanne C. Hood (Miss) MA BD	2003	2012	9 Shearer Avenue, Ferniegair, Hamilton ML3 7FX [E-mail: JHood@churchofscotland.org.uk]	01698 425002
43	**Hamilton: South (H) (01698 281014) linked with Quarter** Donald R. Lawrie		2012	The Manse, Limekilnburn Road, Quarter, Hamilton ML3 7XA [E-mail: DLawrie@churchofscotland.org.uk]	01698 424511
44	**Hamilton: Trinity (01698 284254)** S. Lindsay A. Turnbull BSc BD	2014		69 Buchan Street, Hamilton ML3 8JY [E-mail: Lindsay.Turnbull@churchofscotland.org.uk]	01698 284919
45	**Hamilton: West (H) (01698 284670)** See Hamilton: Gilmour and Whitehill				

46 Holytown linked with New Stevenston: Wrangholm Kirk
Caryl A.E. Kyle (Mrs) BD DipEd   2008   The Manse, 260 Edinburgh Road, Holytown, Motherwell ML1 5RU   01698 832622
[E-mail: CKyle@churchofscotland.org.uk]

47 Kirk o' Shotts (H)   See Chapelhall

48 Larkhall: Chalmers (H)
Vacant   Quarry Road, Larkhall ML9 1HH   01698 882238

49 Larkhall: St Machan's (H)
Alastair McKillop BD DipMin   1995   2004   2 Orchard Gate, Larkhall ML9 1HG   01698 321976
[E-mail: AMcKillop@churchofscotland.org.uk]

50 Larkhall: Trinity
Vacant   13 Machan Avenue, Larkhall ML9 2HE   01698 881401

51 Motherwell: Crosshill (H) linked with Motherwell: St Margaret's
Gavin W.G. Black BD   2006   15 Orchard Street, Motherwell ML1 3JE   01698 263410
[E-mail: GBlack@churchofscotland.org.uk]

52 Motherwell: Dalziel St Andrew's (H) (01698 264097)
Derek W. Hughes BSc BD DipEd   1990   1996   4 Pollock Street, Motherwell ML1 1LP   01698 263414
[E-mail: DHughes@churchofscotland.org.uk]

53 Motherwell: North
Derek H.N. Pope BD   1987   1995   35 Birrens Road, Motherwell ML1 3NS   01698 266716
[E-mail: DPope@churchofscotland.org.uk]

54 Motherwell: St Margaret's   See Motherwell: Crosshill

55 Motherwell: St Mary's (H)
Bryce Calder MA BD   1995   2017   19 Orchard Street, Motherwell ML1 3JE   07986 144834
[E-mail: BCalder@churchofscotland.org.uk]

No.	Name / Minister	Ordained	Inducted	Address / E-mail	Telephone
56	**Motherwell: South (H)** Alan W Gibson BA BD	2001	2016	62 Manse Road, Motherwell ML1 2PT [E-mail: Alan.Gibson@churchofscotland.org.uk]	01698 239279
57	**Newarthill and Carfin** Elaine W. McKinnon MA BD	1988	2014	Church Street, Newarthill, Motherwell ML1 5HS [E-mail: EMcKinnon@churchofscotland.org.uk]	01698 296850
58	**Newmains: Bonkle (H) linked with Newmains: Coltness Memorial (H)** Graham Raeburn MTh	2004		5 Kirkgate, Newmains, Wishaw ML2 9BT [E-mail: GRaeburn@churchofscotland.org.uk]	01698 383858
59	**Newmains: Coltness Memorial** See Newmains: Bonkle				
60	**New Stevenston: Wrangholm Kirk** See Holytown				
61	**Overtown** Lorna I. MacDougall MA DipGC BD	2003	2017	The Manse, 146 Main Street, Overtown, Wishaw ML2 0QP [E-mail: LMacDougall@churchofscotland.org.uk]	01698 352090
62	**Quarter** See Hamilton: South				
63	**Shotts: Calderhead Erskine** Allan B. Brown BD MTh	1995	2010	The Manse, 9 Kirk Road, Shotts ML7 5ET [E-mail: ABrown@churchofscotland.org.uk]	01501 823204 07578 448655 (Mbl)
64	**Stonehouse: St Ninian's (H)** Stewart J. Cutler BA Msc DipHE	2017		4 Hamilton Way, Stonehouse, Larkhall ML9 3PU [E-mail: revstewartcutler@gmail.com]	01698 791508
	Stonehouse: St Ninian's is a Local Ecumenical Partnership shared with the United Reformed Church				
65	**Strathaven: Avendale Old and Drumclog (H) (01357 529748)** Alan B. Telfer BA BD	1983	2010	4 Fortrose Gardens, Strathaven ML10 6SH [E-mail: ATelfer@churchofscotland.org.uk]	01357 523031
66	**Strathaven: East** See Glassford				

No.	Charge / Minister	Ordained	Inducted	Address	Tel
67	**Strathaven: Rankin** See Chapelton				
68	**Uddingston: Burnhead (H)** Les N. Brunger BD	2010		90 Laburnum Road, Uddingston, Glasgow G71 5DB [E-mail: LBrunger@churchofscotland.org.uk]	01698 813716
69	**Uddingston: Old (H) (01698 814015)** Fiona L.J. McKibbin (Mrs) MA BD	2011		1 Belmont Avenue, Uddingston, Glasgow G71 7AX [E-mail: FMcKibbin@churchofscotland.org.uk]	01698 814757
70	**Uddingston: Viewpark (H)** Michael G. Lyall BD	1993	2001	14 Holmbrae Road, Uddingston, Glasgow G71 6AP [E-mail: MLyall@churchofscotland.org.uk]	01698 813113
71	**Wishaw: Cambusnethan North (H)** Mhorag Macdonald (Ms) MA BD	1989		350 Kirk Road, Wishaw ML2 8LH [E-mail: Mhorag.Macdonald@churchofscotland.org.uk]	01698 381305
72	**Wishaw: Cambusnethan Old and Morningside** Vacant			22 Coronation Street, Wishaw ML2 8LF	01698 384235
73	**Wishaw: Craigneuk and Belhaven (H) linked with Wishaw: Old** Vacant			130 Glen Road, Wishaw ML2 7NP	01698 375134
74	**Wishaw: Old (H) (01698 376080)** See Wishaw: Craigneuk and Belhaven				
75	**Wishaw: St Mark's** See Cleland				
76	**Wishaw: South Wishaw (H) (01698 375306)** Terence C. Moran BD CertMin	1995	2015	3 Walter Street, Wishaw ML2 8LQ [E-mail: TMoran@churchofscotland.org.uk]	01698 767459

Barrie, Arthur P. LTh	1973 2007	(Hamilton: Cadzow)	30 Airbles Crescent, Motherwell ML1 3AR [E-mail: elizabethbarrie@ymail.com]	01698 261147

Baxendale, Georgina M. (Mrs) BD	1981	2014	(Motherwell: South)	32 Meadowhead Road, Plains, Airdrie ML6 7HG [E-mail: georgiebaxendale6@tiscali.co.uk]	01555 759063
Buck, Maxine	2007		Auxiliary Minister	Brownlee House, Mauldslie Road, Carluke ML8 5HW [E-mail: MBuck@churchofscotland.org.uk]	
Colvin, Sharon E.F. (Mrs) BD LRAM LTCL	1985	2007	(Airdrie: Jackson)	25 Balblair Road, Airdrie ML6 6GQ [E-mail: dibleycol@hotmail.com]	01236 590796
Cook, J. Stanley BD Dip PSS	1974	2001	(Hamilton: West)	Mansend, 137A Old Manse Road, Netherton, Wishaw ML2 0EW [E-mail: stancook@blueyonder.co.uk]	01698 299600
Donaldson, George M. MA BD	1984	2015	(Caldercruix and Longriggend)	4 Toul Gardens, Motherwell ML1 2FE [E-mail: g.donaldson505@btinternet.com]	01698 239477
Doyle, David W. MA BD	1977	2014	(Motherwell: St Mary's)	76 Kethers Street, Motherwell ML1 3HN	01698 263472
Gordon, Alasdair B. BD LLB EdD	1970	1980	(Aberdeen: Summerhill)	Flat 1, 13 Auchingramont Road, Hamilton ML3 6JP [E-mail: alasdairbgordon@hotmail.com]	01698 200561 (Mbl) 07768 897843
Grant, Paul G.R. BD MTh	2003	2015	Hospital Chaplain	67 Newfield Road, Stonehouse ML9 3HH [E-mail: paul.grant@ggc-scot.nhs.co.uk]	0141-211 4661 (work)
Grier, James BD	1991	2005	(Coatbridge: Middle)	14 Love Drive, Bellshill ML4 1BY	01698 742545
Hunter, James E. LTh	1974	1997	(Blantyre: Livingstone Memorial)	57 Dalwhinnie Avenue, Blantyre, Glasgow G72 9NQ	01698 826177
Kent, Robert M. MA BD	1973	2011	(Hamilton: St John's)	48 Fyne Crescent, Larkhall ML9 2UX [E-mail: robertmkent@talktalk.net]	01698 769244
Lusk, Alastair S. BD	1974	2010	(East Kilbride: Moncreiff)	9 MacFie Place, Stewartfield, East Kilbride, Glasgow G74 4TY	01698 384610
McAlpine, John BSc	1988	2004	(Auxiliary Minister)	Braeside, 201 Bonkle Road, Newmains, Wishaw ML2 9AA	(Mbl) 07918 600720
McCracken, Gordon A. BD CertMin DMin	1988	2015	Presbytery Clerk	1 Kenilworth Road, Lanark ML11 7BL	
McDonald, John A. MA BD	1978	1997	(Cumbernauld: Condorrat)	17 Thomson Drive, Bellshill ML4 3ND	01698 827358
McKee, Norman B. BD	1987	2010	(Uddingston: Old)	148 Station Road, Blantyre, Glasgow G72 9BW [E-mail: normanmckee946@btinternet.com]	
MacKenzie, Ian C. MA BD	1970	2011	(Interim Minister)	21 Wilson Street, Motherwell ML1 1NP [E-mail: iancmac@blueyonder.co.uk]	01698 301230
McKenzie, Raymond D. BD	1978	2012	(Hamilton: Burnbank with Hamilton: North)	25 Austine Drive, Hamilton ML3 7YE [E-mail: rdmackenzie@hotmail.co.uk]	
MacLeod, Norman BTh	1999	2013	(Hamilton: St Andrew's)	15 Bent Road, Hamilton ML3 6QB [E-mail: normanmacleod@blueyonder.co.uk]	01698 283264
McPake, John L. BA BD PhD	1987	2017	Ecumenical Officer, Church of Scotland	121 George Street, Edinburgh EH2 4YN [E-mail: JMcPake@churchofscotland.org.uk]	0131-240 2208
Melrose, J.H. Loudon MA BD MEd	1955	1996	(Gourock: Old Gourock and Ashton [Assoc])	1 Laverock Avenue, Hamilton ML3 7DD	01698 427958
Moore, Agnes A. (Miss) BD	1987	2014	(Bellshill: West)	10 Carr Quadrant, Mossend, Bellshill ML4 1HZ [E-mail: revamoore2@tiscali.co.uk]	01698 841558
Munton, James G. BA	1969	2002	(Coatbridge: Old Monkland)	2 Moorcroft Drive, Airdrie ML6 8ES [E-mail: revjgm1@gmail.com]	01236 754848
Murdoch, Iain C. MA LLB DipEd BD	1995	2017	(Wishaw: Cambusnethan Old and Morningside)	22 Coronation Street, Wishaw ML2 8LF [E-mail: iaincmurdoch@btopenworld.com]	01698 384235
Murphy, Jim	2014		Ordained Local Minister	10 Hillview Crescent, Bellshill ML4 1NX [E-mail: JMurphy@churchofscotland.org.uk]	01698 740189

Name	Years		Charge	Address	Phone
Price, Peter O. CBE QHC BA FPhS	1960	1996	(Blantyre: Old)	22 Old Bothwell Road, Bothwell, Glasgow G71 8AW [E-mail: peteroprice@aol.com]	01698 854032
Rogerson, Stuart D. BSc BD	1980	2001	(Strathaven: West)	17 Westfield Park, Strathaven ML10 6XH [E-mail: srogerson@cnetwork.co.uk]	01357 523321
Salmond, James S. BA BD MTh ThD	1979	2003	(Holytown)	165 Torbothie Road, Shotts ML7 5NE	01698 870598
Spence, Sheila M. (Mrs) MA BD	1979	2010	(Kirk o' Shotts)	6 Drumbowie Crescent, Salsburgh, Shotts ML7 4NP	01698 817582
Stevenson, John LTh	1998	2006	(Cambuslang: St Andrew's)	20 Knowehead Gardens, Uddingston, Glasgow G71 7PY [E-mail therev20@sky.com]	
Thomson, John M.A. TD JP BD ThM	1978	2014	(Hamilton: Old)	8 Skylands Place, Hamilton ML3 8SB [E-mail: jt@john1949.plus.com]	01698 422511
Waddell, Elizabeth A. (Mrs) BD	1999	2014	(Hamilton: West)	114 Branchalfield, Wishaw ML2 8QD [E-mail: elizabethwaddell@tiscali.co.uk]	01698 382909
Wilson, James H. LTh	1970	1996	(Cleland)	21 Austine Drive, Hamilton ML3 7YE [E-mail: wilsonjh@blueyonder.co.uk]	01698 457042
Wyllie, Hugh R. MA DD FCIBS	1962	2000	(Hamilton: Old)	18 Chantinghall Road, Hamilton ML3 8NP	01698 420002
Zambonini, James LIADip	1997	2015	(Auxiliary Minister)	100 Old Manse Road, Wishaw ML2 0EP	01698 350889

HAMILTON ADDRESSES

Airdrie
Cairnlea — 89 Graham Street
Clarkston — Forrest Street
High — North Bridge Street
Jackson — Glen Road
New Monkland — Glenmavis
St Columba's — Thrashbush Road
The New Wellwynd — Wellwynd

Coatbridge
Blairhill Dundyvan — Blairhill Street
Calder — Calder Street
Middle — Bank Street
New St Andrew's — Church Street
Old Monkland — Woodside Street
Townhead — Crinan Crescent

East Kilbride
Claremont — High Common Road, St Leonard's
Greenhills — Greenhills Centre
Moncreiff — Calderwood Road
Mossneuk — Eden Drive
Old — Montgomery Street
South — Baird Hill, Murray
West — Kittoch Street
Westwood — Belmont Drive, Westwood

Hamilton
Cadzow — Woodside Walk
Gilmour and Whitehill — Glasgow Road, Burnbank / Abbotsford Road, Whitehill
Hillhouse — Clerkwell Road
Old — Leechlee Road
St John's — Duke Street
South — Strathaven Road
Trinity — Neilsland Square off Neilsland Road
West — Burnbank Road

Motherwell
Crosshill — Windmillhill Street x
Dalziel St Andrew's — Airbles Street
North — Merry Street and Muir Street
St Margaret's — Chesters Crescent
St Mary's — Shields Road
South — Avon Street
Gavin Street

Uddingston
Burnhead — Laburnum Road
Old — Old Glasgow Road
Viewpark — Old Edinburgh Road

Wishaw
Cambusnethan North — Kirk Road
Cambusnethan Old — Kirk Road
Craigneuk and Belhaven — Craigneuk Street
St Mark's — Main Street
Old — Coltness Road
South Wishaw — East Academy Street

(18) DUMBARTON

Meets at Dumbarton, in Riverside Church Halls, on the first Tuesday of February, March, April (if required), May, September, October (if required), November and December, and on the third Tuesday of June at the incoming Moderator's church for the installation of the Moderator.

Clerk:	REV. DAVID W. CLARK MA BD			3 Ritchie Avenue, Cardross, Dumbarton G82 5LL [E-mail: dumbarton@churchofscotland.org.uk]	01389 849319
Alexandria Elizabeth W. Houston MA BD DipEd	1985	1995	32 Ledrish Avenue, Balloch, Alexandria G83 8JB [E-mail: WHouston@churchofscotland.org.uk]	01389 751933
Arrochar linked with Luss Vacant			The Manse, Luss, Alexandria G83 8NZ	01436 860240
Baldernock (H) linked with Milngavie: St Paul's (H) (0141-956 4405) Fergus C. Buchanan MA BD MTh	1982	1988	8 Buchanan Street, Milngavie, Glasgow G62 8DD [E-mail: Fergus.Buchanan@churchofscotland.org.uk]	0141-956 1043
Bearsden: Baljaffray (H) Ian McEwan BSc PhD BD FRSE	2008		5 Fintry Gardens, Bearsden, Glasgow G61 4RJ [E-mail: IMcEwan@churchofscotland.org.uk]	0141-942 0366
Bearsden: Cross (H) Graeme R. Wilson MCIBS BD ThM	2006	2013	61 Drymen Road, Bearsden, Glasgow G61 2SU [E-mail: GWilson@churchofscotland.org.uk]	0141-942 0507
Bearsden: Killermont (H) Alan J. Hamilton LLB BD PhD	2003		8 Clathic Avenue, Bearsden, Glasgow G61 2HF [E-mail: AHamilton@churchofscotland.org.uk]	0141-942 0021
Bearsden: New Kilpatrick (H) (0141-942 8827) (E-mail: mail@nkchurch.org.uk) Roderick G. Hamilton MA BD	1992	2011	51 Manse Road, Bearsden, Glasgow G61 3PN [E-mail: Roddy.Hamilton@churchofscotland.org.uk]	0141-942 0035

Bearsden: Westerton Fairlie Memorial (H) (0141-942 6960)
Christine M. Goldie LLB BD MTh DMin   1984   2008   3 Cannieshurn Road, Bearsden, Glasgow G61 1PW   0141-942 2672
[E-mail: CGoldie@churchofscotland.org.uk]

Bonhill (H) (01389 756516) linked with Renton: Trinity (H)
Barbara A. O'Donnell BD PGSE   2007   2016   Ashbank, 258 Main Street, Alexandria G83 0NU   01389 752356 / 07889 251912 (Mbl)
[E-mail: BODonnell@churchofscotland.org.uk]

Cardross (H) (01389 841322)
Margaret McArthur BD DipMin   1995   2015   16 Bainfield Road, Cardross G82 5JQ   01389 849329 / 07799 556367 (Mbl)
[E-mail: MMcArthur@churchofscotland.org.uk]

Clydebank: Waterfront linked with Dalmuir: Barclay (0141-941 3988)
Ruth H.B. Morrison MA BD PhD   2009   2014   16 Parkhall Road, Dalmuir, Clydebank G81 3RJ   0141-941 3317
[E-mail: RMorrison@churchofscotland.org.uk]

Margaret A.E. Nutter   2014   2017   Kilmorich, 14 Balloch Road, Balloch, Alexandria G83 8SR   01389 754505
[E-mail: MNutter@churchofscotland.org.uk]
(Ordained Local Minister)

(Clydebank: Waterfront is formed by the union of Clydebank: Abbotsford and Clydebank: St Cuthbert's)

Clydebank: Faifley
Gregor McIntyre BSc BD   1991   Kirklea, Cochno Road, Hardgate, Clydebank G81 6PT   01389 876836
[E-mail: Gregor.McIntyre@churchofscotland.org.uk]

Clydebank: Kilbowie St Andrew's linked with Clydebank: Radnor Park (H)
Margaret J.B. Yule BD   1992   11 Tiree Gardens, Old Kilpatrick, Glasgow G60 5AT   01389 875599
[E-mail: MYule@churchofscotland.org.uk]

Clydebank: Radnor Park   See Clydebank: Kilbowie St Andrew's

Craigrownie linked with Garelochhead (01436 810589) linked with Rosneath: St Modan's (H)
Christine M. Murdoch   1999   2015   The Manse, Argyll Road, Kilcreggan, Helensburgh G84 0JW   01436 842274 / 07973 331890 (Mbl)
[E-mail: CMurdoch@churchofscotland.org.uk]

Ann J. Cameron (Mrs) CertCS DCE TEFL   2005   2017   Water's Edge, Ferry Road, Rosneath, Helensburgh G84 0RS   01436 831800
[E-mail: ACameron@churchofscotland.org.uk]
(Auxiliary Minister)

Dalmuir: Barclay   See Clydebank: Waterfront

Dumbarton: Riverside (H) (01389 742551) linked with Dumbarton: West Kirk (H)
C. Ian W. Johnson MA BD   1997   2014   18 Castle Road, Dumbarton G82 1JF   01389 726685
[E-mail: CJohnson@churchofscotland.org.uk]

Dumbarton: St Andrew's (H)
Vacant
Ishbel A.R. Robertson MA BD   2013   2015   17 Mansewood Drive, Dumbarton G82 3EU   01389 726715
(Ordained Local Minister)   Oakdene, 81 Bonhill Road, Dumbarton G82 2DU   01389 763436
[E-mail: IRobertson@churchofscotland.org.uk]

Dumbarton: West Kirk See Dumbarton: Riverside

Duntocher
Vacant

Garelochhead See Craigrownie

Helensburgh linked with Rhu and Shandon
David T. Young BA BD MTh   2007   2015   35 East Argyle Street, Helensburgh G84 8UP   01436 673365
[E-mail: DYoung@churchofscotland.org.uk]   07508 628133 (Mbl)
Tina Kemp MA   2005   2017   12 Oaktree Gardens, Dumbarton G82 1EU   01389 730477
(Auxiliary Minister)   [E-mail: TKemp@churchofscotland.org.uk]

Jamestown (H)
Vacant   26 Kessog's Gardens, Balloch, Alexandria G83 8QJ   01389 756447

Kilmaronock Gartocharn
Guardianship of the Presbytery

Luss See Arrochar

Milngavie: Cairns (H) (0141-956 4868)
Andrew Frater BA BD MTh   1987   1994   4 Cairns Drive, Milngavie, Glasgow G62 8AJ   0141-956 1717
[E-mail: AFrater@churchofscotland.org.uk]

Milngavie: St Luke's (0141-956 4226)
Ramsay B. Shields BA BD   1990   1997   70 Hunter Road, Milngavie, Glasgow G62 7BY   0141-577 9171 (Tel)
[E-mail: RShields@churchofscotland.org.uk]   0141-577 9181 (Fax)

Milngavie: St Paul's (H) See Baldernock

Old Kilpatrick Bowling
Vacant   The Manse, Old Kilpatrick, Glasgow G60 5JQ

Renton: Trinity See Bonhill
Rhu and Shandon See Helensburgh
Rosneath: St Modan's See Craigrownie

Booth, Frederick M. LTh	1970	2005	(Helensburgh: St Columba)	Achnashie Coach House, Clynder, Helensburgh G84 0QD [E-mail: boothef@btinternet.com]	01436 831858
Christie, John C. BSc BD MSB CBiol	1990	2014	(Interim Minister)	10 Cumberland Avenue, Helensburgh G84 8QG [E-mail: rev.jcc@btinternet.com]	01436 674078 (Mbl) 07711 336392
Clark, David W. MA BD	1975	2014	(Helensburgh: St Andrew's Kirk with Rhu and Shandon)	3 Ritchie Avenue, Cardross, Dumbarton G82 5LL [E-mail: clarkdw@talktalk.net]	01389 849319
Crombie, William D. MA BD	1947	1987	(Glasgow: Calton New with St Andrew's)	9 Fairview Court, 46 Main Street, Milngavie, Glasgow G62 6BU	0141-956 1898
Dalton, Mark BD DipMin RN		2002	Chaplain: Royal Navy	HM Naval Base Clyde, Faslane, Helensburgh G84 8HL [E-mail: mark.dalton242@mod.gov.uk]	01436 674321 ext. 6216
Hamilton, David G. MA BD	1971	2004	(Braes of Rannoch with Foss and Rannoch)	79 Finlay Rise, Milngavie, Glasgow G62 6QL [E-mail: davidhamilton40@googlemail.com]	0141-956 4202
Harris, John W.F. MA	1967	2012	(Bearsden: Cross)	68 Mitre Road, Glasgow G14 9LL [E-mail: jwfh@sky.com]	0141-321 1061
Lees, Andrew P. BD	1984	2017	(Baldernock)	58 Lindores Drive, Stepps G33 6PD [E-mail: andrew.lees@yahoo.co.uk]	0141-389 5840
McCutcheon, John		2014	Ordained Local Minister	Flat 2/6 Parkview, Milton Brae, Milton, Dumbarton G82 2TT [E-mail: JMcCutcheon@churchofscotland.org.uk]	01389 739034
McIntyre, J. Ainslie MA BD	1963	1984	(University of Glasgow)	60 Bonnaughton Road, Bearsden, Glasgow G61 4DB [E-mail: jamcintyre@hotmail.com]	0141-942 5143
Martin, James MA BD DD	1946	1987	(Glasgow: High Carntyne)	Westerton Care Home, 116 Maxwell Avenue, Bearsden, Glasgow G61 1HU	(Mbl) 07826 013266
Miller, Ian H. BA BD	1975	2012	(Bonhill)	Derand, Queen Street, Alexandria G83 0AS [E-mail: revianmiller@btinternet.com]	01389 753039
Moore, Norma MA BD	1995	2017	(Jamestown)	25 Miller Street, Dumbarton G82 2JA [E-mail: norma-moore@sky.com]	
Munro, David P. MA BD STM	1953	1996	(Bearsden: North)	14 Birch Road, Killearn, Glasgow G63 9SQ [E-mail: david.munro1929@btinternet.com]	01360 550098
Ramage, Alastair E. MA BA ADB CertEd		1996	Auxiliary Minister	16 Claremont Gardens, Milngavie, Glasgow G62 6PG [E-mail: sueandalastairramage@btinternet.com]	0141-956 2897
Steven, Harold A.M. MStl LTh FSA Scot	1970	2001	(Baldernock)	9 Cairnhill Road, Bearsden, Glasgow G61 1AT [E-mail: harold.allison.steven@gmail.com]	0141-942 1598

Wilson, John BD	1985 2010	(Glasgow: Temple Anniesland)	4 Carron Crescent, Bearsden, Glasgow G61 1HJ	0141-931 5609
			[E-mail: revjwilson@btinternet.com]	
Wright, Malcolm LTh	1970 2003	(Craigrownie with Rosneath: St Modan's)	30 Clairinsh, Drumkinnon Gate, Balloch, Alexandria G83 8SE	01389 720338
			[E-mail: malcolmcatherine@msn.com]	

DUMBARTON ADDRESSES

Bearsden
Baljaffray	Grampian Way
Cross	Drymen Road
Killermont	Rannoch Drive
New Kilpatrick	Manse Road
Westerton	Crarae Avenue

Clydebank
Faifley	Faifley Road
Kilbowie St Andrew's	Kilbowie Road
Radnor Park	Radnor Street
Waterfront	Town Centre

Dumbarton
Riverside	High Street
St Andrew's	Aitkenbar Circle

Helensburgh
West Kirk	West Bridgend
	Colquhoun Square

Milngavie
Cairns	Buchanan Street
St Luke's	Kirk Street
St Paul's	Strathblane Road

(19) ARGYLL

Meets in the Village Hall, Tarbert, Loch Fyne, Argyll on the first Tuesday or Wednesday of March, June, September and December. For details, contact the Presbytery Clerk.

Clerk:	DR CHRISTOPHER T. BRETT MA PhD	Minahey Cottage, Kames, Tighnabruaich PA21 2AD	01700 811142
		[E-mail: argyll@churchofscotland.org.uk]	
Treasurer:	MRS PAMELA A. GIBSON	Allt Ban, Portsonachan, Dalmally PA33 1BJ	01866 833344
		[E-mail: justpam1@tesco.net]	

Appin linked with Lismore

Iain C. Barclay MBE TD MA BD MTh MPhil PhD FRSA	1976	2015	The Manse, Appin PA38 4DD	(Appin) 01631 730143
				(Lismore) 01631 760077
			[E-mail: ICBarclay@churchofscotland.org.uk]	

Ardchattan (H)

Jeffrey A. McCormick BD	1984	Ardchattan Manse, North Connel, Oban PA37 1RG	01631 710364
		[E-mail: JMcCormick@churchofscotland.org.uk]	

Ardrishaig (H) linked with South Knapdale

David Carruthers BD	1998	The Manse, Park Road, Ardrishaig, Lochgilphead PA30 8HE	01546 603269
		[E-mail: DCarruthers@churchofscotland.org.uk]	

Barra (GD) linked with South Uist (GD)
Lindsay Schluter ThE CertMin PhD   1995   2016
The Manse, Cuithir, Isle of Barra HS9 5XU   01871 810230
[E-mail: LSchluter@churchofscotland.org.uk]   07835 913963 (Mbl)

Campbeltown: Highland (H)
Vacant
Highland Church Manse, Kirk Street, Campbeltown PA28 6BN   01586 551146

Campbeltown: Lorne and Lowland (H)
Philip D. Wallace BSc BTh DTS   1998   2004
Lorne and Lowland Manse, Castlehill, Campbeltown PA28 6AN   01586 552468
[E-mail: PWallace@churchofscotland.org.uk]

Coll linked with Connel
Vacant
St Oran's Manse, Connel, Oban PA37 1PJ   (Connel) 01631 710242
                                                                 (Coll) 01879 230366

Colonsay and Oronsay (Website: www.islandchurches.org.uk)
Guardianship of the Presbytery

Connel See Coll

Craignish linked with Kilbrandon and Kilchattan linked with Kilninver and Kilmelford (Netherlorn)
Kenneth R. Ross BA BD PhD   1982   2010
The Manse, Kilmelford, Oban PA34 4XA   01852 200565
[E-mail: KRoss@churchofscotland.org.uk]

Cumlodden, Lochfyneside and Lochgair linked with Glenaray and Inveraray (West Lochfyneside)
Roderick D.M. Campbell OStJ TD BD   1975   2015
DMin FSAScot
The Manse, Inveraray PA32 8XT   01499 302295
[E-mail: Roderick.Campbell@churchofscotland.org.uk]   07469 186495 (Mbl)

Dunoon: St John's linked with Kirn (H) and Sandbank (H) (Central Cowal)
Vacant
The Manse, 13 Dhailling Park, Hunter Street, Kirn, Dunoon
PA23 8FB   01369 702256

Glenda M. McLaren (Ms) DCS
5 Allan Terrace, Sandbank, Dunoon PA23 8PR   01369 704168
[E-mail: Glenda.McLaren@churchofscotland.org.uk]

Dunoon: The High Kirk (H) linked with Innellan (H) linked with Toward (H) (South-East Cowal)
Aileen M. Robson (Miss) BD   2003   2011
7A Mathieson Lane, Innellan, Dunoon PA23 7SH   01369 830276
[E-mail: ARobson@churchofscotland.org.uk]

Ruth I. Griffiths (Mrs) 2004 Kirkwood, Mathieson Lane, Innellan, Dunoon PA23 7TA 01369 830145
(Auxiliary Minister) [E-mail: RGriffiths@churchofscotland.org.uk]

Gigha and Cara (H) (GD) linked with Kilcalmonell linked with Killean and Kilchenzie (H)
Vacant The Manse, Muasdale, Tarbert, Argyll PA29 6XD 01583 421432

Glassary, Kilmartin and Ford linked with North Knapdale
Clifford R. Acklam BD MTh 1997 2010 The Manse, Kilmichael Glassary, Lochgilphead PA31 8QA 01546 606926
[E-mail: CAcklam@churchofscotland.org.uk]

Glenaray and Inveraray See Cumlodden, Lochfyneside and Lochgair

Glenorchy and Innishael linked with Strathfillan
Vacant The Manse, Dalmally PA33 1AA 01838 200207

Innellan See Dunoon: The High Kirk

Iona linked with Kilfinichen and Kilvickeon and the Ross of Mull
Vacant The Manse, Bunessan, Isle of Mull PA67 6DW 01681 700227

Jura (GD) linked with Kilarrow (H) linked with Kildalton and Oa (GD) (H)
Vacant The Manse, Bowmore, Isle of Islay PA43 7LH 01496 810271

Kilarrow See Jura
Kilbrandon and Kilchattan See Craignish
Kilcalmonell See Gigha and Cara

Kilchoman (GD) linked with Kilmeny linked with Portnahaven (GD)
Valerie G.C. Watson MA BD STM 1987 2013 The Manse, Port Charlotte, Isle of Islay PA48 7TW 01496 850241
[E-mail: VWatson@churchofscotland.org.uk]

Kilchrenan and Dalavich linked with Muckairn
Vacant Muckairn Manse, Taynuilt PA35 1HW 01866 822204

Kildalton and Oa See Jura

Kilfinan linked with Kilmodan and Colintraive linked with Kyles (H) (West Cowal)
David Mitchell BD DipPTheol MSc 1988 2006 West Cowal Manse, Kames, Tighnabruaich PA21 2AD 01700 811045
[E-mail: DMitchell@churchofscotland.org.uk]

Kilfinichen and Kilvickeon and the Ross of Mull See Iona
Killean and Kilchenzie See Gigha and Cara
Kilmeny See Kilchoman
Kilmodan and Colintraive See Kilfinan

Kilmore (GD) and Oban (Website: www.obanchurch.com)
Dugald J.R. Cameron BD DipMin MTh 1990 2007 Kilmore and Oban Manse, Ganavan Road, Oban PA34 5TU 01631 566253
[E-mail: Dugald.Cameron@churchofscotland.org.uk]

Christine P. Fulcher BEd 2012 2014 St Blaan's Manse, Southend, Campbeltown PA28 6RQ 01586 830504
(Ordained Local Minister)
[E-mail: CFulcher@churchofscotland.org.uk]

Kilmun, Strone and Ardentinny: The Shore Kirk (H)
David Mill KJSJ MA BD 1978 2010 The Manse, Blairmore, Dunoon PA23 8TE 01369 840313
[E-mail: DMill@churchofscotland.org.uk]

Kilninian and Kilmore linked with Salen (H) and Ulva linked with Tobermory (GD) (H) linked with Torosay (H) and Kinlochspelvie (North Mull)
John H. Paton BSc BD 1983 2013 The Manse, Gruline Road, Salen, Aros, Isle of Mull PA72 6XF 01680 300001
[E-mail: JPaton@churchofscotland.org.uk]

Kilninver and Kilmelford See Craignish
Kirn See Dunoon: St John's
Kyles See Kilfinan
Lismore See Appin

Lochgilphead
Hilda C. Smith (Miss) MA BD MSc 1992 2005 Parish Church Manse, Manse Brae, Lochgilphead PA31 8QZ 01546 602238
[E-mail: HSmith@churchofscotland.org.uk]

Lochgoilhead (H) and Kilmorich linked with Strachur and Strathlachlan (Upper Cowal)
Robert K. Mackenzie MA BD PhD 1976 1998 The Manse, Strachur, Cairndow PA27 8DG 01369 860246
[E-mail: RKMackenzie@churchofscotland.org.uk]

Muckairn See Kilchrenan and Dalavich
North Knapdale See Glassary, Kilmartin and Ford
Portnahaven See Kilchoman

Rothesay: Trinity (H) (Website: www.rothesaytrinity.org)
Vacant
12 Crichton Road, Rothesay, Isle of Bute PA20 9JR
01700 503010

Saddell and Carradale (H) linked with Southend (H)
Stephen Fulcher BA MA   1993   2012
St Blaan's Manse, Southend, Campbeltown PA28 6RQ
[E-mail: SFulcher@churchofscotland.org.uk]
01586 830504

Salen and Ulva See Kilninian and Kilmore
Sandbank See Dunoon: St John's

Skipness linked with Tarbert, Loch Fyne and Kilberry (H)
Vacant
The Manse, Cambeltown Road, Tarbert, Argyll PA29 6SX
01880 821012

Southend See Saddell and Carradale
South Knapdale See Ardrishaig
South Uist See Barra
Strachur and Strathlachlan See Lochgoilhead and Kilmorich
Strathfillan See Glenorchy and Innishael
Strone and Ardentinny See Kilmun
Tarbert, Loch Fyne and Kilberry See Skipness

The United Church of Bute
John Owain Jones MA BD FSAScot   1981   2011
10 Bishop Terrace, Rothesay, Isle of Bute PA20 9HF
[E-mail: JJones@churchofscotland.org.uk]
01700 504502

Tiree (GD)
Vacant
The Manse, Scarinish, Isle of Tiree PA77 6TN
01879 220377

Tobermory See Kilninian and Kilmore
Torosay and Kinlochspelvie See Kilninian and Kilmore
Toward See Dunoon: The High Kirk

Beautyman, Paul H. MA BD	1993	2009	Youth Adviser	130b John Street, Dunoon PA23 7BN [E-mail: PBeautyman@churchofscotland.org.uk]	(Mbl) 07596 164112
Bell, Douglas W. MA LLB BD	1975	1993	(Alexandria: North)	3 Cairnbaan Lea, Cairnbaan, Lochgilphead PA31 8BA	01546 606815
Bristow, W.H.G. BEd HDipRE DipSpecEd	1951	2002	(Chaplain: Army)	Cnoc Ban, Southend, Campbeltown PA28 6RQ	01586 830667
Cringles, George G. BD	1981	2017	(Coll with Connel)	The Moorings, Ganavan Road, Oban PA34 5TU [E-mail: george.cringles@gmail.com]	01631 564215
Crossan, William	2014		Ordained Local Minister	Gowanbank, Kilkerran Road, Campbeltown PA28 6JL	01586 553453
Dunlop, Alistair J. MA	1965	2004	(Saddell and Carradale)	8 Pipers Road, Cairnbaan, Lochgilphead PA31 8UF [E-mail: dunrevn@btinternet.com]	01546 600316
Earl, Jenny MA BD	2007	2015	(Kelso Country Churches with Kelso: Old and Sprouston)	1 The Steadings, Achavaich, Isle of Iona PA76 6SW [E-mail: jennyearl@btinternet.com]	(Mbl) 07769 994680
Forrest, Alan B. MA	1956	1993	(Uphall: South)	126 Shore Road, Innellan, Dunoon PA23 7SX	01369 830424
Gibson, Elizabeth A. (Mrs) MA MLitt BD	2003	2013	Locum Minister	Mo Dhachaidh, Lochdon, Isle of Mull PA64 6AP [E-mail: egibson@churchofscotland.org.uk]	01680 812541
Gibson, Frank S. BL BD STM DSW A DD	1963	1995	(Kilarrow with Kilmeny)	1/7 Joppa Station Place, Edinburgh EH15 2QU	01369 704495
Goss, Alister J. BD DMin	1975	2009	(Industrial Chaplain)	24 Albert Place, Ardnadam, Sandbank, Dunoon PA23 8QF [E-mail: scimwest@hotmail.com]	
Gray, William LTh	1971	2006	(Kilberry with Tarbert)	Lochnagar, Longsdale Road, Oban PA34 5DZ [E-mail: gray98@hotmail.com]	01631 567471
Henderson, Grahame McL. BD	1974	2008	(Kirn)	6 Gerhallow, Bullwood Road, Dunoon PA23 7QB [E-mail: ghende5884@aol.com]	01369 702433
Hood, Catriona A.	2006		Auxiliary Minister	Rose Cottage, Whitehouse, Tarbert PA29 6EP [E-mail: CHood@churchofscotland.org.uk]	01880 730366
Hood, H. Stanley C. MA BD	1966	2000	(London: Crown Court)	10 Dalriada Place, Kilmichael Glassary, Lochgilphead PA31 8QA	01546 606168
Lamont, Archibald MA	1952	1994	(Kilcalmonell with Skipness)	22 Bonnyton Drive, Eaglesham, Glasgow G76 0LU	
Lind, Michael J. LLB BD	1984	2012	(Campbeltown: Highland)	Maybank, Station Road, Conon Bridge, Dingwall IV7 8BJ [E-mail: mijylind@gmail.com]	
Macfarlane, James PhD	1991	2011	(Lochgoilhead and Kilmorich)	'Lindores', 11 Bullwood Road, Dunoon PA23 7QJ [E-mail: mac.farlane@btinternet.com]	01369 710626
McIvor, Anne (Miss) SRD BD	1996	2013	(Gigha and Cara)	20 Albyn Avenue, Campbeltown PA28 6LY [E-mail: annemcivor@btinternet.com]	(Mbl) 07901 964825
MacLeod, Roderick MBE MA BD PhD(Edin) PhD(Open)	1966	2011	(Cumlodden, Lochfyneside and Lochgair)	Creag-nam-Barnach, Furnace, Inveraray PA32 8XU [E-mail: mail@revroddy.co.uk]	01499 500629
Marshall, Freda (Mrs) BD FCII	1993	2005	(Colonsay and Oronsay with Kilbrandon and Kilchattan)	Allt Mhaluidh, Glenview, Dalmally PA33 1BE [E-mail: mail@freda.org.uk]	01838 200693
Millar, Margaret R.M. (Miss) BTh	1977	2008	(Kilchrenan and Dalavich with Muckairn)	Fearnoch Cottage, Fearnoch, Taynuilt PA35 1JB [E-mail: macoje@aol.com]	01866 822416
Morrison, Angus W. MA BD	1959	1999	(Kildalton and Oa)	1 Livingstone Way, Port Ellen, Isle of Islay PA42 7EP	01496 300043
Park, Peter B. BD MCIBS	1997	2014	(Fraserburgh: Old)	Hillview, 24 McKelvie Road, Oban PA34 4GB [E-mail: peterpark9@btinternet.com]	01631 565849
Ritchie, Walter M.	1973	1999	(Uphall: South)	Hazel Cottage, Barr Mor View, Kilmartin, Lochgilphead PA31 8UN	01546 510343

Scott, Randolph MA BD	1991 2013	(Jersey: St Columba's)	18 Lochan Avenue, Kirn, Dunoon PA23 8HT [E-mail: rev.rs@hotmail.com]	01369 703175
Stewart, Joseph LTh	1979 2011	(Dunoon: St John's with Sandbank)	7 Glenmorag Avenue, Dunoon PA23 7LG	01369 703438
Taylor, Alan T. BD	1980 2005	(Isle of Mull Parishes)	Erray Road, Tobermory, Isle of Mull PA75 6PS	01688 302496
Wilkinson, W. Brian MA BD	1968 2007	(Glenaray and Inveraray)	3 Achlonan, Taynuilt PA35 1JJ [E-mail: williambrian35@btinternet.com]	01866 822036

ARGYLL Communion Sundays

Parish	Communion Sundays	Parish	Communion Sundays	Parish	Communion Sundays
Ardrishaig	4th Apr, 1st Nov	Jura	Passion Sun., 2nd Jul, 3rd Nov	North Knapdale	3rd Oct, 2nd May
Barra	2nd Mar, June, Sep, Easter, Advent	Kilarrow	1st Mar, Jun, Sep, Dec	Portnahaven	3rd Jul
Campbeltown		Kilcalmonell	1st Jul, 3rd Nov	Rothesay: Trinity	1st Feb, Jun, Nov
Highland	1st May, Nov	Kilchoman	1st Jul, 2nd Dec, Easter	Saddell and Carradale	2nd May, 1st Nov
Lorne and Lowland	1st May, Nov	Kildalton and Oa	Last Jan, Jun, Oct, Easter	Sandbank	1st Jan, May, Nov
Craignish	1st Jun, Nov	Kilfinan	Last Apr, Oct	Skipness	2nd May, Nov
Cumlodden, Lochfyneside and Lochgair	1st May, 3rd Nov	Killean and Kilchenzie	1st Mar, Jul, Oct	Southend	1st Jun, Dec
Dunoon		Kilmeny	2nd May, 3rd Nov	South Knapdale	4th Apr, 1st Nov
St John's	1st Mar, Jun, Nov	Kilmodan and Colintraive	1st Apr, Sep	South Uist	
The High Kirk	1st Feb, Jun, Oct	Kilmun	Last Jun, Nov	Howmore	1st Jun
Gigha and Cara	1st May, Nov	Kilninver and Kilmelford	Last Feb, Jun, Oct	Daliburgh	1st Sep
Glassary, Kilmartin and Ford	1st Apr, Sep	Kirn	2nd Jun, Oct	Strachur and Strathlachlan	1st Mar, Jun, Nov
Glenaray and Inveraray	1st Apr, Jul, Oct, Dec	Kyles	1st May, Nov	Strone and Ardentinny	Last Feb, Jun, Oct
Innellan	1st Mar, Jun, Sep, Dec	Lochgair	Last Apr, Oct	Tarbert and Kilberry	1st May, Oct
Inverlussa and Bellanoch	2nd May, Nov	Lochgilphead	2nd Oct (Gaelic), 1st Apr, Nov	Tayvallich	2nd May, Nov
		Lochgoilhead and Kilmorich	1st Aug, Easter	The United Church of Bute	1st Feb, Jun, Nov
				Toward	Last Feb, May, Aug, Nov

(22) FALKIRK

Meets at Falkirk Trinity Parish Church on the first Tuesday of September, December, March and May, on the fourth Tuesday of October and January and on the third Tuesday of June.

Clerk:	REV. ANDREW SARLE BSc BD	114 High Station Road, Falkirk FK1 5LN [E-mail: falkirk@churchofscotland.org.uk]	07565 362074 (Mbl)
Depute Clerk:	MR CHRISTOPHER DUNN	3b Afton Road, Cumbernauld G67 2DS [E-mail: depclerk@falkirkpresbytery.org]	01236 720874
Treasurer:	MR ARTHUR PRIESTLY	32 Broomhill Avenue, Larbert FK5 3EH [E-mail: treasurer@falkirkpresbytery.org]	01324 557142

Airth (H)

James F. Todd BD CPS	1984	2012	The Manse, Airth, Falkirk FK2 8LS [E-mail: JTodd@churchofscotland.org.uk]	01324 831120

Blackbraes and Shieldhill linked with Muiravonside

Vacant			81 Stevenson Avenue, Polmont, Falkirk FK2 0GU	01324 717757

Bo'ness: Old (H)

Amanda J. MacQuarrie MA PGCE MTh	2014	2016	10 Dundas Street, Bo'ness EH51 0DG [E-mail: AMacQuarrie@churchofscotland.org.uk]	01506 204585

Bo'ness: St Andrew's (Website: www.standonline.org.uk) (01506 825803)

Graham D. Astles BD MSc	2007	2016	St Andrew's Manse, 11 Erngath Road, Bo'ness EH51 9DP [E-mail: GAstles@churchofscotland.org.uk]	01506 822195

Bonnybridge: St Helen's (H) (Website: www.bbshnc.com)

George MacDonald BTh	2004	2009	The Manse, 32 Reilly Gardens, High Bonnybridge FK4 2BB [E-mail: GMacDonald@churchofscotland.org.uk]	01324 874807

Bothkennar and Carronshore

Andrew J. Moore BSc BD	2007		11 Hunter Place, Greenmount Park, Carronshore, Falkirk FK2 8QS [E-mail: AMoore@churchofscotland.org.uk]	01324 570525

Brightons (H)

Vacant			The Manse, Maddiston Road, Brightons, Falkirk FK2 0JP	01324 712062

Carriden (H)

Vacant			The Spires, Foredale Terrace, Carriden, Bo'ness EH51 9LW	01506 822141

Cumbernauld: Abronhill (H)

Joyce A. Keyes (Mrs) BD	1996	2003	26 Ash Road, Cumbernauld, Glasgow G67 3ED [E-mail: JKeyes@churchofscotland.org.uk]	01236 723833

Cumbernauld: Condorrat (H)

Grace I.M. Saunders BSc BTh	2007	2011	11 Rosehill Drive, Cumbernauld, Glasgow G67 4EQ [E-mail: GSaunders@churchofscotland.org.uk]	01236 452090

Marion Perry (Mrs) (Auxiliary Minister) 2009 2013 17a Tarbolton Road, Cumbernauld, Glasgow G67 2AJ
[E-mail: MPerry@churchofscotland.org.uk] 01236 898519
07563 180662 (Mbl)

Cumbernauld: Kildrum (H)
Vacant 64 Southfield Road, Balloch, Cumbernauld, Glasgow G68 9DZ 01236 723204
David Nicholson DCS 2D Doonside, Kildrum, Cumbernauld, Glasgow G67 2HX 01236 732260
[E-mail: DNicholson@churchofscotland.org.uk]

Cumbernauld: Old (H) (Website: www.cumbernauldold.org.uk)
Elspeth M McKay LLB LLM PGCert BD 2014 2017 The Manse, 23 Baronhill, Cumbernauld, Glasgow G67 2SD 01236 728853
[E-mail: EMckay@churchofscotland.org.uk]
Valerie S. Cuthbertson (Miss) DCS 105 Bellshill Road, Motherwell ML1 3SJ 01698 259001
[E-mail: VCuthbertson@churchofscotland.org.uk]

Cumbernauld: St Mungo's
Vacant 18 Fergusson Road, Cumbernauld, Glasgow G67 1LS 01236 721513

Denny: Old linked with Haggs
Vacant 31 Duke Street, Denny FK6 6NR 01324 824508
Alexena (Sandra) Mathers 10 Ercall Road, Brightons, Falkirk FK2 0RS 01324 872253
(Ordained Local Minister) 2015 [E-mail: SMathers@churchofscotland.org.uk]

Denny: Westpark (H) (Website: www.westparkchurch.org.uk)
D. I. Kipchumba Too BTh MTh MSc 13 Baxter Crescent, Denny FK6 5EZ 01324 882220
[E-mail: KToo@churchofscotland.org.uk] 07340 868067

Dunipace (H)
Jean W. Gallacher (Miss) 1989 The Manse, 239 Stirling Street, Dunipace, Denny FK6 6QJ 01324 824540
BD CMin CTheol DMin [E-mail: JGallacher@churchofscotland.org.uk]

Falkirk: Bainsford
Vacant 1 Valleyview Place, Newcarron Village, Falkirk FK2 7JB 01324 621648
Andrew Sarle BSc BD 114 High Station Road, Falkirk FK1 5LN
(Ordained Local Minister) 2013 [E-mail: ASarle@churchofscotland.org.uk]

Falkirk: Camelon (Church office: 01324 870011)
Stuart W. Sharp MTheol DipPA — 2001 — 30 Cotland Drive, Falkirk FK2 7GE
[E-mail: SSharp@churchofscotland.org.uk] — 01324 623631

Falkirk: Grahamston United (H)
Ian Wilkie BD PGCE — 2001 2007 — 16 Cromwell Road, Falkirk FK1 1SF
[E-mail: IWilkie@churchofscotland.org.uk] — 01324 624461 / 07877 803280 (Mbl)
Grahamston United is a Local Ecumenical Project shared with the Methodist and United Reformed Churches

Falkirk: Laurieston linked with Redding and Westquarter
J. Mary Henderson MA BD DipEd PhD — 1990 2009 — 11 Polmont Road, Laurieston, Falkirk FK2 9QQ
[E-mail: JMary.Henderson@churchofscotland.org.uk] — 01324 621196

Falkirk: St Andrew's West (H)
Alastair M. Horne BSc BD — 1989 1997 — 1 Maggiewood's Loan, Falkirk FK1 5SJ
[E-mail: AHorne@churchofscotland.org.uk] — 01324 623308

Falkirk: St James'
Vacant

Falkirk: Trinity (H)
Robert S.T. Allan LLB DipLP BD — 1991 2003 — 9 Major's Loan, Falkirk FK1 5QF
[E-mail: RAllan@churchofscotland.org.uk] — 01324 625124
Kathryn Brown (Mrs) (Ordained Local Minister) — 2014 — 1 Callendar Park Walk, Callendar Grange, Falkirk FK1 1TA
[E-mail: KBrown@churchofscotland.org.uk] — 01324 617352

Grangemouth: Abbotsgrange
Aftab Gohar MA MDiv PgDip — 1995 2010 — 8 Naismith Court, Grangemouth FK3 9BQ
[E-mail: AGohar@churchofscotland.org.uk] — 01324 482109 / 07528 143784 (Mbl)

Grangemouth: Kirk of the Holy Rood
Vacant — The Manse, Bowhouse Road, Grangemouth FK3 0EX — 01324 471595

Grangemouth: Zetland (H)
Alison A. Meikle (Mrs) BD — 1999 2015 — Ronaldshay Crescent, Grangemouth FK3 9JH
[E-mail: AMeikle@churchofscotland.org.uk] — 01324 336729

Haggs (H) See Denny: Old

Larbert: East
Melville D. Crosthwaite BD DipEd DipMin 1984 1995 1 Cortachy Avenue, Carron, Falkirk FK2 8DH
[E-mail: MCrosthwaite@churchofscotland.org.uk] 01324 562402

Larbert: Old (H)
Vacant The Manse, 38 South Broomage Avenue, Larbert FK5 3ED 01324 872760

Larbert: West (H)
Vacant 11 Carronvale Road, Larbert FK5 3LZ 01324 562878

Muiravonside See Blackbraes and Shieldhill

Polmont: Old
Deborah L. van Welie (Ms) MTheol 2015 3 Orchard Grove, Polmont, Falkirk FK2 0XE
[E-mail: DLVanWelie@churchofscotland.org.uk] 01324 713427

Redding and Westquarter See Falkirk: Laurieston

Sanctuary First
Albert O. Bogle BD MTh 1981 2016 49a Kenilworth Road, Bridge of Allan FK9 4RS
[E-mail: albertbogle@mac.com] 07715 374557 (Mbl)

Slamannan
Vacant
Monica MacDonald (Mrs) 2014 32 Reilly Gardens, High Bonnybridge, Bonnybridge FK4 2BB
  (Ordained Local Minister) [E-mail: Monica.MacDonald@churchofscotland.org.uk] 01324 874807

Stenhouse and Carron (H)
William Thomson BD 2001 2007 The Manse, 21 Tipperary Place, Stenhousemuir, Larbert FK5 4SX
[E-mail: WThomson@churchofscotland.org.uk] 01324 416628

Black, Ian W. MA BD 1976 2013 (Grangemouth: Zetland) Flat 1R, 2 Carrickvale Court, Carrickstone, Cumbernauld,
Glasgow G68 0LA
[E-mail: iwblack@hotmail.com] 01236 453370

Brown, T. John MA BD	1995	2006	(Tullibody: St Serf's)	1 Callendar Park Walk, Callendar Grange, Falkirk FK1 1TA [E-mail: johnbrown1cpw@talktalk.net]	01324 617352
Campbell-Jack, W.C. BD MTh PhD	1979	2011	(Glasgow: Possilpark)	35 Castle Avenue, Airth, Falkirk FK2 8GA [E-mail: c.c-j@homecall.co.uk]	01324 832011
Chalmers, George A. MA BD MLitt	1962	2002	(Catrine with Sorn)	3 Cricket Place, Brightons, Falkirk FK2 0HZ [E-mail: andychristie747@yahoo.com]	01324 712030
Christie, Helen F. (Mrs) BD	1998	2015	(Haggs)		
Hardie, Robert K. MA BD	1968	2005	(Stenhouse and Carron)	33 Palace Street, Berwick-upon-Tweed TD15 1HN	
Job, Anne J. BSc BD	1993	2010	(Kirkcaldy: Viewforth with Thornton)	5 Carse View, Airth, Falkirk FK2 8NY [E-mail: aj@ajjob.co.uk]	01875 615851
Macaulay, Glendon BD	1999	2012	(Falkirk: Erskine)	43 Gavin's Lee, Tranent EH33 2AP [E-mail: gd.macaulay@btinternet.com]	
McCallum, John	1962	1998	(Falkirk: Irving Camelon)	11 Bumbrae Gardens, Falkirk FK1 5SB	01324 619766
McDonald, William G. MA BD	1959	1975	(Falkirk: Grahamston United)	3 Kinkell Terrace, St Andrews KY16 8DL	01334 479770
McDowall, Ronald J. BD	1980	2001	(Falkirk: Laurieston with Redding and Westquarter)	'Kailas', Windsor Road, Falkirk FK1 5EJ	01324 871947
Mathers, Daniel L. BD	1982	2001	(Grangemouth: Charing Cross and West)	10 Ercall Road, Brightons, Falkirk FK2 0RS	01324 872253
Maxton, Ronald M. MA	1955	1995	(Dollar: Associate)	16 Tygetshaugh Court, Thistle Avenue, Dunipace FK6 6LQ	01324 822752
Miller, Elsie M. (Miss) DCS			(Deacon)	30 Swinton Avenue, Rowansbank, Baillieston, Glasgow G69 6JR	0141-771 0857
Ross, Evan J. LTh	1986	1998	(Cowdenbeath: West with Mossgreen and Crossgates)	5 Arneil Place, Brightons, Falkirk FK2 0NJ	01324 719936
Scott, Donald H. BA BD	1983	2002	Chaplain: HMYOI Polmont	14 Gibsongray Street, Falkirk FK2 0AB [E-mail: donaldhscott@hotmail.com]	01324 722241
Smith, Richard BD	1976	2002	(Denny: Old)	Easter Wayside, 46 Kennedy Way, Airth, Falkirk FK2 8GB [E-mail: richards@uklinux.net]	01324 831386
Wandrum, David C.	1993		Auxiliary Minister	5 Cawder View, Carrickstone Meadows, Cumbernauld, Glasgow G68 0BN [E-mail: DWandrum@churchofscotland.org.uk]	01236 723288
Wilson, Phyllis M. (Mrs) DipCom DipRE	1985	2006	(Motherwell: South Dalziel)	'Landemer', 17 Sneddon Place, Airth, Falkirk FK2 8GH [E-mail: thomas.wilson38@btinternet.com]	01324 832257

FALKIRK ADDRESSES

Blackbraes and Shieldhill	Main St x Anderson Cr	Kirk of the Holy Rood	Bowhouse Road
Bo'ness: Old	Panbrae Road	Zetland	Ronaldshay Crescent
St Andrew's	Grahamsdyke Avenue	Haggs	Glasgow Road
Carriden	Carriden Brae	Larbert: East	Kirk Avenue
Cumbernauld: Abronhill	Larch Road	Old	Denny Road x Stirling Road
Condorrat	Main Road	West	Main Street
Kildrum	Clouden Road	Muiravonside	off Vellore Road
Old	Baronhill	Polmont: Old	Kirk Entry/Bo'ness Road
St Mungo's	St Mungo's Road	Redding and Westquarter	Main Street
Denny: Old	Denny Cross	Slamannan	Manse Place
Westpark	Duke Street	Stenhouse and Carron	Church Street
Dunipace	Stirling Street		
Falkirk: Bainsford	Hendry Street, Bainsford		
Camelon	Dorror Road		
Grahamston United	Bute Street		
Laurieston	Main Falkirk Road		
St Andrew's West	Newmarket Street		
St James'	Thornhill Road x Firs Street		
Trinity	Kirk Wynd		
Grangemouth: Abbotsgrange	Abbot's Road		

(23) STIRLING

Meets at the Moderator's church on the second Thursday of September, and at Bridge of Allan Parish Church on the second Thursday of February, March, April, May, June, October, November and December.

Clerk:	REV. ALAN F. MILLER BA MA BD	7 Windsor Place, Stirling FK8 2HY [E-mail:AMiller@churchofscotland.org.uk]	01786 465166
Depute Clerk:	MR EDWARD MORTON	22 Torry Drive, Alva FK12 5LN [E-mail: edmort@aol.com]	01259 760861 07525 005028 (Mbl) 01259 762262
Treasurer:	MR MARTIN DUNSMORE	60 Brookfield Place, Alva FK12 5AT [E-mail: m.dunsmore53@btinternet.com]	
Presbytery Office:		St Columba's Church, Park Terrace, Stirling FK8 2NA [E-mail: stirling@churchofscotland.org.uk]	01786 447575

Aberfoyle (H) linked with Port of Menteith (H) (Website: www.aberfoyleportchurches.org.uk)
Vacant   The Manse, Lochard Road, Aberfoyle, Stirling FK8 3SZ   01877 382391

Alloa: Ludgate (Website: www.alloaludgatechurch.org.uk)
Vacant   28 Alloa Park Drive, Alloa FK10 1QY   01259 212709

Alloa: St Mungo's (H) (Website: www.stmungosparish.org.uk)
Sang Y. Cha BD MTh   2011   37A Claremont, Alloa FK10 2DG   01259 213872
                                                        [E-mail: SCha@churchofscotland.org.uk]

Alva (Website: www.alvaparishchurch.org.uk)
James N.R. McNeil BSc BD   1990   1997   34 Ochil Road, Alva FK12 5JT   01259 760262
                                                        [E-mail: JMcNeil@churchofscotland.org.uk]

Balfron (Website: www.balfronchurch.org.uk) linked with Fintry (H) (Website: www.fintrykirk.btck.org.uk)
Sigrid Marten   1997   2013   7 Station Road, Balfron, Glasgow G63 0SX   01360 440285
                                                        [E-mail: SMarten@churchofscotland.org.uk]

Balquhidder linked with Killin and Ardeonaig (H)
Russel Moffat BD MTh PhD   1986   2016   The Manse, Killin FK21 8TN   01567 820247
                                                        [E-mail: Russel.Moffat@churchofscotland.org.uk]

Bannockburn: Allan (H) (Website: www.allanchurch.org.uk)
Vacant
The Manse, Bogend Road, Bannockburn, Stirling FK7 8NP   01786 814692

Bannockburn: Ladywell (H) (Website: www.ladywellchurch.co.uk)
Elizabeth M.D. Robertson (Miss) BD CertMin   1997
57 The Firs, Bannockburn FK7 0EG   01786 812467
[E-mail: ERobertson@churchofscotland.org.uk]

Bridge of Allan (H) (01786 834155) (Website: www.bridgeofallanparishchurch.org.uk)
Rev. Daniel (Dan) J. Harper BSc BD   2016
29 Keir Street, Bridge of Allan, Stirling FK9 4QJ   01786 832753
[E-mail: DHarper@churchofscotland.org.uk]

Buchanan linked with Drymen (Website: www.drymenchurch.org)
Alexander J. MacPherson BD   1986   1997
Buchanan Manse, Drymen, Glasgow G63 0AQ   01360 870212
[E-mail: AMacPherson@churchofscotland.org.uk]

Buchlyvie (H) linked with Gartmore (H)
Vacant
112 Jackson Drive, Crowwood Grange, Stepps, Glasgow G33 6GF   0141-779 5742

Callander (H) (Tel/Fax: 01877 331409) (Website: www.callanderkirk.org.uk)
Vacant
3 Aveland Park Road, Callander FK17 8FD   01877 330097

Cambusbarron: The Bruce Memorial (H) (Website: www.cambusbarronchurch.org)
Graham P. Nash MA BD   2006   2012
14 Woodside Court, Cambusbarron, Stirling FK7 9PH   01786 442068
[E-mail: GPNash@churchofscotland.org.uk]

Clackmannan (H) (Website: www.clackmannankirk.org.uk)
Scott Raby LTh   1991   2007
The Manse, Port Street, Clackmannan FK10 4JH   01259 211255
[E-mail: SRaby@churchofscotland.org.uk]

Cowie (H) and Plean See Bannockburn: Allan

Dollar (H) linked with Glendevon linked with Muckhart (Website: www.dollarparishchurch.org.uk)
Vacant
2 Princes Crescent East, Dollar FK14 7BU   01259 743593

Drymen See Buchanan

Dunblane: Cathedral (H) (Website: www.dunblanecathedral.org.uk)

Colin C. Renwick BMus BD   1989   2014   Cathedral Manse, The Cross, Dunblane FK15 0AQ   01786 822205
                                                  [E-mail: CRenwick@churchofscotland.org.uk]

Dorothy U. Anderson (Mrs) LLB DipPL BD   2006   2017   Invereith, Stirling Road, Doune FK16 6AA   01786 841706
(Associate Minister)   [E-mail: DAnderson@churchofscotland.org.uk]

Dunblane: St Blane's (H) linked with Lecropt (H) (Website: www.lecroptkirk.org.uk)

Gary J. Caldwell BSc BD   2007   2015   46 Kellie Wynd, Dunblane FK15 0NR   01786 825324
                                                [E-mail: GCaldwell@churchofscotland.org.uk]

Fallin

Vacant   5 Fincastle Place, Cowie, Stirling FK7 7DS   01786 818413

Fintry See Balfron

Gargunnock linked with Kilmadock linked with Kincardine-in-Menteith (Website: blairdrummondchurches.org.uk)

Andrew B. Campbell BD DPS MTh   1979   2011   The Manse, Manse Brae, Gargunnock. Stirling FK8 3BQ   01786 860678
                                                      [E-mail: ACampbell@churchofscotland.org.uk]   07523 420079 (Mbl)

Lynne Mack (Mrs)   2013   36 Middleton, Menstrie FK11 7HD   01259 761465
(Ordained Local Minister)   [E-mail: LMack@churchofscotland.org.uk]

Gartmore See Buchlyvie
Glendevon See Dollar

Killearn (H) (Website: www.killearnkirk.org.uk)

Vacant   2 The Oaks, Killearn, Glasgow G63 9SF   01360 550045

Killin and Ardeonaig See Balquhidder
Kilmadock See Gargunnock
Kincardine-in-Menteith See Gargunnock

Kippen (H) linked with Norrieston

Ellen Larson Davidson BA MDiv   2007   2015   The Manse, Main Street, Kippen, Stirling FK8 3DN   01786 871249
                                                      [E-mail: ELarsonDavidson@churchofscotland.org.uk]

Lecropt See Dunblane: St Blane's

Logie (H) (Website: sms-test.webplus.net)
Vacant
Anne F. Shearer BA DipEd   2010   21 Craiglea, Causewayhead, Stirling FK9 5EE   01786 463060
(Auxilliary Minister)   10 Colsnaur, Menstrie FK11 7HG   01259 769176
                                         [E-mail: AShearer@churchofscotland.org.uk]

Menstrie (H) (Website: www.menstrieparishchurch.co.uk)
Maggie R. Roderick BA BD FRSA FTSI   2010   2015   The Manse, 7 Long Row, Menstrie FK11 7BA   01259 761372
                                                       [E-mail: MRoderick@churchofscotland.org.uk]

Muckhart See Dollar
Norrieston See Kippen
Port of Menteith See Aberfoyle

Sauchie and Coalsnaughton
Margaret Shuttleworth MA BD   2013   62 Toll Road, Kincardine, Alloa FK10 4QZ   01259 731002
                                       [E-mail: MShuttleworth@churchofscotland.org.uk]

Stirling: Allan Park South (H) (Website: www.apschurch.com)
Alistair Cowper BSc BD   2011   22 Laurelhill Place, Stirling FK8 2JH   01786 358872
                                  [E-mail: ACowper@churchofscotland.org.uk]   07791 524504 (Mbl)

Stirling: Church of the Holy Rude (H) (Website: http://holyrude.org) linked with Stirling: Viewfield Erskine (H)
Alan F. Miller BA MA BD   2000   2010   7 Windsor Place, Stirling FK8 2HY   01786 465166
                                           [E-mail: AMiller@churchofscotland.org.uk]

Stirling: North (H) (01786 463376) (Website: www.northparishchurch.com)
Scott McInnes MEng BD   2016   18 Shirras Brae Road, Stirling FK7 0BA   01786 357428
                                 [E-mail: SMcInnes@churchofscotland.org.uk]

Stirling: St Columba's (H) (01786 449516) (Website: www.stcolumbasstirling.org.uk)
Alexander M. Millar MA BD MBA   1980   2010   St Columba's Manse, 5 Clifford Road, Stirling FK8 2AQ   01786 469979
                                                 [E-mail: Alexander.Millar@churchofscotland.org.uk]

Stirling: St Mark's (Website: www.stmarksstirling.org.uk)
Vacant
Jean T. Porter (Mrs) BD DCS   10 Laidlaw Street, Stirling FK8 1ZS
                               3 Cochrie Place, Tullibody FK10 2RR   07729 316321 (Mbl)
                               [E-mail: JPorter@churchofscotland.org.uk]

Stirling: St Ninians Old (H) (Website: www.stniniansold.org.uk)
Gary J. McIntyre BD DipMin   1993   1998   7 Randolph Road, Stirling FK8 2AJ
[E-mail: GMcIntyre@churchofscotland.org.uk]   01786 474421

Stirling: Viewfield Erskine See Stirling: Church of the Holy Rude

Strathblane (H) (Website: www.strathblanekirk.org.uk)
Murdo M. Campbell BD DipMin   1997   2017   2 Campsie Road, Strathblane, Glasgow G63 9AB
[E-mail: MCampbell@churchofscotland.org.uk]   01360 770226

Tillicoultry (H) (Website: www.tillicoultryparishchurch.co.uk)
Alison E.P. Britchfield (Mrs) MA BD   1987   2013   The Manse, 17 Dollar Road, Tillicoultry FK13 6PD
[E-mail: ABritchfield@churchofscotland.org.uk]   01259 750340

Tullibody: St Serf's (H)
Drew Barrie BSc BD   1984   2016   16 Menstrie Road, Tullibody, Alloa FK10 2RG
[E-mail: DBarrie@churchofscotland.org.uk]   01259 729804

Aitken, E. Douglas MA	1961	1998	(Clackmannan)	1 Dolan Grove, Saline, Dunfermline KY12 9UP [E-mail: douglasaitken14@btinternet.com]	01383 852730
Allen, Valerie L. (Ms) BMus MDiv DMin	1990	2016	Presbytery Chaplain	16 Pine Court, Doune FK16 6JE [E-mail: vl2allen@btinternet.com]	01786 842577 (Mbl) 07801 291538
Barr, John BSc PhD BD	1958	1979	(Kilmacolm: Old)	6 Ferry Court, Stirling FK9 5GJ [E-mail: kilbrandon@btinternet.com]	01786 472286
Begg, Richard MA BD	2008	2016	Army Chaplain	12 Whiteyetts Drive, Sauchie FK10 3GE [E-mail: rbegg711@aol.com]	
Boyd, Ronald M.H. BD DipTheol	1995	2010	Chaplain, Queen Victoria School	6 Victoria Green, Queen Victoria School, Dunblane FK15 0JY [E-mail: ron.boyd@qvs.crg.uk]	(Mbl) 07766 004292
Brown, James H. BD	1977	2005	(Helensburgh: Park)	14 Gullipen View, Callander FK17 8HN [E-mail: revjimhbrown@yahoo.co.uk]	01877 339425
Cloggie, June (Mrs)	1997	2006	(Auxiliary Minister)	11A Tulipan Crescent, Callander FK17 8AR [E-mail: david.cloggie@hotmail.co.uk]	01877 331021
Cochrane, James P.N. LTh	1994	2012	(Tillicoultry)	12 Sandpiper Meadow, Alloa Park, Alloa FK10 1QU [E-mail: jamescochrane@pobroadband.co.uk]	01259 218883
Cook, Helen (Mrs) BD	1974	2012	Hospital Chaplain	60 Pelstream Avenue, Stirling FK7 0BG [E-mail: revhcook@btinternet.com]	01786 464128
Dunnett, Alan L. LLB BD	1994	2016	(Cowie and Plean with Fallin)	9 Tulipan Crescent, Callander FK17 8AR [E-mail: alan.dunnett@sky.com]	01877 339640
Dunnett, Linda BA DCS	1994	2016		9 Tulipan Crescent, Callander FK17 8AR [E-mail: lindadunnett@sky.com]	01877 339640 (Mbl) 07838 041683

Foggie, Janet P. MA BD PhD	2003	2017	Pioneer Minister, Stirling University	Pioneer Office, Logie Kirk Halls, 15–17 Alloa Road, Stirling FK9 5LH [E-mail: JFoggie@churchofscotland.org.uk]	(Mbl) 07899 349246
Gaston, A. Ray C. MA BD	1969	2002	(Leuchars: St Athernase)	'Hamewith', 13 Manse Road, Dollar FK14 7AL [E-mail: gaston.arthur@yahoo.co.uk]	01259 743202
Gillespie, Irene C. (Mrs) BD	1991	2007	(Tiree)	39 King O'Muirs Drive, Tullibody, Alloa FK10 3AY [E-mail: revicg@btinternet.com]	01259 723937
Gilmour, William M. MA BD	1969	2008	(Lecropt)	14 Pine Court, Doune FK16 6JE	01786 842928
Goodison, Michael J. BSc BD	2013		Chaplain: Army	27 Hunter Crescent, Leuchars KY16 0JP [E-mail: mike.goodison@btinternet.com]	
Goring, Iain M. BSc BD	1976	2015	(Interim Minister)	4 Argyle Grove, Dunblane FK15 9DU [E-mail: imgoring@gmail.com]	01259 821688
Izett, William A.F.	1968	2000	(Law)	1 Duke Street, Clackmannan FK10 4EF [E-mail: william.izett@talktalk.net]	01259 724203
Jack, Alison M. MA BD PhD	1998	2001	Assistant Principal and Lecturer, New College, Edinburgh	5 Murdoch Terrace, Dunblane FK15 9JE [E-mail: alisonmjack809@btinternet.com]	01786 826953
Landels, James BD CertMin	1990	2015	(Bannockburn: Allan)	11 Ardgay Place, Bonnybridge, Falkirk FK4 2FH [E-mail: revjimlandels@icloud.com]	01324 810685 (Mbl) 07860 944266
MacCormick, Moira G. BA LTh	1986	2003	(Buchlyvie with Gartmore)	12 Rankine Wynd, Tullibody, Alloa FK10 2UW [E-mail: mgmaccormick@o2.co.uk]	01259 724619
McIntosh, Hamish N.M. MA	1949	1987	(Fintry)	9 Abbeyfield House, 17 Allan Park, Stirling FK8 2QG	01786 479294
McKenzie, Alan BSc BD	1988	2013	(Bellshill: Macdonald Memorial with Bellshill: Orbiston)	89 Drip Road, Stirling FK8 1RN [E-mail: rev.a.mckenzie@btopenworld.com]	01786 430450
Malloch, Philip R.M. LLB BD	1970	2009	(Killearn)	8 Michael McParland Drive, Torrance, Glasgow G64 4EE [E-mail: pmalloch@mac.com]	01360 620089
Mathew, J. Gordon MA BD	1973	2011	(Buckie: North)	45 Westhaugh Road, Stirling FK9 5GF [E-mail: jg.matthew@btinternet.com]	01786 445951
Millar, Jennifer M. (Mrs) BD DipMin	1986	1995	Teacher: Religious and Moral Education	5 Clifford Road, Stirling FK8 2AQ [E-mail: ajrmillar@blueyonder.co.uk]	01786 469979
Mitchell, Alexander B. BD	1981	2014	(Dunblane: St Blane's)	24 Hebridean Gardens, Crieff PH7 3BP [E-mail: alex.mitchell6@btopenworld.com]	01764 652241
Ogilvie, C. (Mrs)	1999	2015	(Cumbernauld: Old)	Seberham Flat, 1A Bridge Street, Dollar FK14 7DF [E-mail: catriona.ogilvie1@btinternet.com]	01259 742155
Ovens, Samuel B. BD	1982	1993	(Slamannan)	21 Bevan Drive, Alva FK12 5PD	01259 763456
Parker, Carol Ann (Mrs) BEd BD	2009	2017	(Alloa Ludgate)	The Cottages, Dornoch Firth Caravan Park, Meikle Ferry South, Tain IV19 1JX	01862 892292
Pryde, W. Kenneth DA BD	1994	2012	(Foveran)	Corrie, 7 Alloa Road, Woodside, Cambus FK10 2NT [E-mail: CParker@churchofscotland.org.uk]	01259 721562
Rose, Dennis S. LTh	1996	2016	(Arbuthnott, Bervie and Kinneff)	69 Blackthorn Grove, Menstrie FK11 7DX [E-mail: wkpryde@hotmail.com]	01259 692451
Russell, Kenneth G. BD CCE	1986	2013	Prison Chaplain	Chaplaincy Centre, HM Prison Perth, 3 Edinburgh Road, Perth PH2 7JH [E-mail: kenneth.russell@sps.pnn.gov.uk]	01738 458216
Sangster, Ernest G. MA BD ThM	1958	1997	(Alva)	6 Lawhill Road, Dollar FK14 7BG [E-mail: dennis2327@aol.com]	01259 742344

Scott, James F.	1957 1997	(Dyce)	5 Gullipen View, Callander FK17 8HN	01877 330565
Sewell, Paul M.N. MA BD	1970 2010	(Berwick-upon-Tweed: St Andrew's Wallace Green and Lowick)	7 Bohun Court, Stirling FK7 7UT [E-mail: paulmsewell@btinternet.com]	01786 489969
Sherry, George T. LTh	1977 2004	(Menstrie)	4 Woodburn Way, Alva FK12 5LB [E-mail: gandmns@btinternet.com]	01259 763779
Sinclair, James H. MA BD DipMin	1966 2004	(Auchencairn and Rerrick with Buittle and Kelton)	16 Delaney Court, Alloa FK10 1RB	01259 729001
Thomson, Raymond BD DipMin	1992 2013	(Slamannan)	8 Rhodders Grove, Alva FK12 5ER	01259 769083
Wilson, Hazel MA BD DMS	1991 2015	(Dundee: Lochee)	2 Boe Court, Springfield Terrace, Dunblane FK15 9LU [E-mail: hmwilson704@gmail.com]	01786 825850

STIRLING ADDRESSES

Allan Park South	Dumbarton Road	North	Springfield Road	St Ninians Old	Kirk Wynd, St Ninians
Holy Rude	St John Street	St Columba's	Park Terrace	Viewfield Erskine	Barnton Street
		St Mark's	Drip Road		

(24) DUNFERMLINE

Meets at Dunfermline in St Andrew's Erskine Church, Robertson Road, on the first Thursday of each month, except January, July and August when there is no meeting, and June when it meets on the last Thursday.

Clerk:	REV. IAIN M. GREENSHIELDS BD DipRS ACMA MSc MTh DD	38 Garvock Hill, Dunfermline KY12 7UU [E-mail: dunfermline@churchofscotland.org.uk]	01383 741495 (Office) 01383 723955 (Home)

Aberdour: St Fillan's (H) (Website: www.stfillans.presbytery.org)

Peter S. Gerbrandy-Baird MA BD MSc FRSA FRGS	2004	St Fillan's Manse, 36 Bellhouse Road, Aberdour, Fife KY3 0TL [E-mail: PGerbrandy-Baird@churchofscotland.org.uk]	01383 861522

Beath and Cowdenbeath: North (H)

David W. Redmayne BSc BD	2001	10 Stuart Place, Cowdenbeath KY4 9BN [E-mail: DRedmayne@churchofscotland.org.uk]	01383 511033

Cairneyhill (H) (01383 882352) linked with Limekilns (H) (01383 873337)
Norman M. Grant BD — 1990 — The Manse, 10 Church Street, Limekilns, Dunfermline KY11 3HT — 01383 872341
[E-mail: NGrant@churchofscotland.org.uk]

Carnock and Oakley (H)
Vacant — The Manse, Main Street, Carnock, Dunfermline KY12 9JG — 01383 850327

Cowdenbeath: Trinity (H)
Gavin R. Boswell BTheol — 1993 2013 — 2 Glenfield Road, Cowdenbeath KY4 9EL — 01383 510696
[E-mail: GBoswell@churchofscotland.org.uk]
John Wyllie (Pastoral Assistant) — 51 Seafar Street, Kelty KY4 0JX — 01383 839200

Culross and Torryburn (H)
Vacant — The Manse, Culross, Dunfermline KY12 8JD — 01383 880231

Dalgety (H) (01383 824092) (E-mail: office@dalgety-church.co.uk) (Website: www.dalgety-church.co.uk)
Christine Sime (Miss) BSc BD — 1994 2012 — 9 St Colme Drive, Dalgety Bay, Dunfermline KY11 9LQ — 01383 822316
[E-mail: CSime@churchofscotland.org.uk]

Dunfermline: Abbey (H) (Website: www.dunfabbey.freeserve.co.uk)
MaryAnn R. Rennie (Mrs) BD MTh — 1998 2012 — 3 Perdieus Mount, Dunfermline KY12 7XE — 01383 727311
[E-mail: MARennie@churchofscotland.org.uk]

Dunfermline: East
Andrew A. Morrice MA BD — 1999 2010 — 9 Dover Drive, Dunfermline KY11 8HQ — 01383 223144 / 07815 719301 (Mbl)
[E-mail: AMorrice@churchofscotland.org.uk]

Dunfermline: Gillespie Memorial (H) (01383 621253) (E-mail: gillespie.church@btopenworld.com)
Vacant — 4 Killin Court, Dunfermline KY12 7XF — 01383 723329

Dunfermline: North
Ian G. Thom BSc PhD BD — 1990 2007 — 13 Barbour Grove, Dunfermline KY12 9YB — 01383 733471
[E-mail: IThom@churchofscotland.org.uk]

Dunfermline: St Andrew's Erskine (01383 841660)
Muriel F. Willoughby (Mrs) MA BD — 2006 2013 — 71A Townhill Road, Dunfermline KY12 0BN — 01383 738487
[E-mail: MWilloughby@churchofscotland.org.uk]

Dunfermline: St Leonard's (01383 620106) (E-mail: office@stleonardsparishchurch.org.uk) (Website: www.stleonardsparishchurch.org.uk)
Monika R. Redman BA BD   2003   2014   12 Torvean Place, Dunfermline KY11 4YY   01383 300092
[E-mail: MRedman@churchofscotland.org.uk]

Dunfermline: St Margaret's
Iain M. Greenshields   1984   2007   38 Garvock Hill, Dunfermline KY12 7UU   01383 723955
BD DipRS ACMA MSc MTh DD   07427 477575 (Mbl)
[E-mail: IGreenshields@churchofscotland.org.uk]

Dunfermline: St Ninian's
Vacant   51 St John's Drive, Dunfermline KY12 7TL   01383 722256

Dunfermline: Townhill and Kingseat (H)
Jean A. Kirkwood BSc PhD BD   2015   7 Lochwood Park, Kingseat, Dunfermline KY12 0UX   01383 723691
[E-mail: JKirkwood@churchofscotland.org.uk]

Inverkeithing linked with North Queensferry
Colin M. Alston BMus BD BN RN   1975   2012   1 Dover Way, Dunfermline KY11 8HR   01383 621050
[E-mail: CAlston@churchofscotland.org.uk]

Kelty (Website: www.keltykirk.org.uk)
Hugh D. Steele LTh DipMin   1994   2013   15 Arlick Road, Kelty KY4 0BH   01383 831362
[E-mail: HSteele@churchofscotland.org.uk]

Limekilns See Cairneyhill

Lochgelly and Benarty: St Serf's
Vacant   82 Main Street, Lochgelly KY5 9AA   01592 780435
Pamela Scott (Mrs) DCS   177 Primrose Avenue, Rosyth KY11 2TZ   01383 410530
[E-mail: PScott@churchofscotland.org.uk]   07548 819334 (Mbl)

North Queensferry See Inverkeithing

Rosyth
Violet C.C. McKay (Mrs) BD   1988   2002   42 Woodside Avenue, Rosyth KY11 2LA   01383 412776
[E-mail: VMcKay@churchofscotland.org.uk]
Morag Crawford (Miss) MSc DCS   118 Wester Drylaw Place, Edinburgh EH4 2TG   0131-332 2253
[E-mail: MCrawford@churchofscotland.org.uk]   07970 982563 (Mbl)

Saline and Blairingone linked with Tulliallan and Kincardine

Alexander Shuttleworth MA BD	2004	2013		62 Toll Road, Kincardine, Alloa FK10 4QZ [E-mail: AShuttleworth@churchofscotland.org.uk]	01259 731002

Tulliallan and Kincardine See Saline and Blairingone

Name			Charge	Address	Phone
Almond, David M. BD	1996	2016	(Kirkmahoe)	2 Carlingnose Part, North Queensferry KY11 1EX [E-mail: almonddavid242@gmail.com]	01383 616073
Bjarnason, Sven S. CandTheol	1974	2011	(Tomintoul, Glenlivet and Inveraven)	14 Edward Street, Dunfermline KY12 0JW [E-mail: sven@bjarnason.org.uk]	01383 724625
Boyle, Robert P. LTh	1990	2010	(Saline and Blairingone)	43 Dunipace Crescent, Dunfermline KY12 7JE [E-mail: boab.boyle@btinternet.com]	01383 740980
Brown, Peter MA BD FRAScot	1953	1987	(Holm)	24 Inchmickery Avenue, Dalgety Bay, Dunfermline KY11 5NF	01383 822456
Chalmers, John P. BD CPS DD	1979	1995	(Principal Clerk)	10 Liggars Place, Dunfermline KY12 7XZ	01383 739130
Farquhar, William E. BA BD	1987	2006	(Dunfermline: Townhill and Kingseat)	29 Queens Drive, Middlewich, Cheshire CW10 0DG	01606 835097
Jenkins, Gordon F.C. MA BD PhD	1968	2006	(Dunfermline: North)	20 Lumsden Park, Cupar KY15 5YL [E-mail: jenkinsgordon1@sky.com]	01334 652548
Jessamine, Alistair L. MA BD	1979	2011	(Dunfermline: Abbey)	11 Gallowhill Farm Cottages, Strathaven ML10 6BZ [E-mail: chatty.1@talktalk.net]	01357 520934
Johnston, Thomas N. LTh	1972	2008	(Edinburgh: Priestfield)	71 Main Street, Newmills, Dunfermline KY12 8ST [E-mail: tomjohnston@blueyonder.co.uk]	01383 889240
Kenny, Elizabeth S.S. BD RGN SCM	1989	2010	(Carnock and Oakley)	5 Cobden Court, Crossgates, Cowdenbeath KY4 8AU [E-mail: esskenny@btinternet.com]	(Mbl) 07831 763494
Laidlaw, Victor W.N. BD	1975	2008	(Edinburgh: St Catherine's Argyle)	9 Tern Road, Dunfermline KY11 8GA	01383 620134
Leitch, D. Graham MA BD	1974	2012	(Tyne Valley Parish)	9 St Margaret Wynd, Dunfermline KY12 0UT [E-mail: dgrahamleitch@gmail.com]	01383 249245
McCulloch, William B BD	1997	2016	(Rome: St Andrew's)	81 Meldrum Court, Dunfermline KY11 4XR [E-mail: revwbmculloch@hotmail.com]	01383 730305
McDonald, Tom BD	1994	2015	(Kelso: North and Ednam)	12 Woodmill Grove, Dunfermline KY11 4JR [E-mail: revtomparadise12@gmail.com]	01383 695365
McLellan, Andrew R.C. CBE MA BD STM DD	1970	2002	(HM Inspector of Prisons)	4 Liggars Place, Dunfermline KY12 7XZ	01383 725959
Paterson, Andrew E. JP	1994		Auxiliary Minister	6 The Willows, Kelty KY4 0FQ [E-mail: APaterson@churchofscotland.org.uk]	01383 830998
Reid, A. Gordon BSc BD	1982	2008	(Dunfermline: Gillespie Memorial)	7 Arkleston Crescent, Paisley PA3 4TG [E-mail: reid501@fsmail.net]	0141-842 1542 (Mbl) 07773 300989
Reid, David MSc LTh FSAScot	1961	1992	(St Monans with Largoward)	North Lethans, Saline, Dunfermline KY12 9TE	01383 733144
Sutherland, Iain A. BSc BD	1996	2014	(Dunfermline: Gillespie Memorial)	64 Beech Court, Rosyth KY11 2ZP [E-mail: RevISutherland@aol.com]	(Mbl) 07843 089598
Watt, Robert J. BD	1994	2009	(Dumbarton: Riverside)	101 Birrell Drive, Dunfermline KY11 8FA [E-mail: robertwatt101@gmail.com]	01383 735417 (Mbl) 07753 683717

Whyte, Isabel H. (Mrs) BD | 1993 | (Chaplain: Queen Margaret Hospital, Dunfermline) | 14 Carlingnose Point, North Queensferry, Inverkeithing KY11 1ER | 01383 410732
[E-mail: iainisabel@whytes28.fsnet.co.uk]

(25) KIRKCALDY

Meets at Kirkcaldy, in the St Bryce Kirk Centre, on the first Tuesday of March, September and December, and on the last Tuesday of June. It meets also on the first Tuesday of November for Holy Communion and a conference at the church of the Moderator.

Clerk: **REV. ALAN W.D. KIMMITT BSc BD** — **40 Liberton Drive, Glenrothes KY6 3PB** — **01592 742233**
[E-mail: kirkcaldy@churchofscotland.org.uk]

Depute Clerk: **REV. ROBIN J. McALPINE BDS BD MTh** — **25 Bennochy Avenue, Kirkcaldy KY2 5QE** — **01592 643558**
[E-mail: RMcAlpine@churchofscotland.org.uk]

Auchterderran Kinglassie
Vacant — 7 Woodend Road, Cardenden, Lochgelly KY5 0NE — 01592 720202

Auchtertool linked with Kirkcaldy: Linktown (H) (01592 641080)
Catriona M. Morrison (Mrs) MA BD | 1995 | 2000 | 16 Raith Crescent, Kirkcaldy KY2 5NN — 01592 265536
[E-mail: CMorrison@churchofscotland.org.uk]
Marc Prowe — 16 Raith Crescent, Kirkcaldy KY2 5NN — 01592 265536
[E-mail: MProwe@churchofscotland.org.uk]

Buckhaven (01592 715577) and Wemyss
Wilma R.C. Cairns (Miss) BD | 1999 | 2004 | 33 Main Road, East Wemyss, Kirkcaldy KY1 4RE — 01592 712870
[E-mail: WCairns@churchofscotland.org.uk]
Jacqueline Thomson (Mrs) MTh DCS — 16 Aitken Place, Coaltown of Wemyss, Kirkcaldy KY1 4PA — 01592 653995 / 07806 776560 (Mbl)
[E-mail: Jacqueline.Thomson@churchofscotland.org.uk]

Burntisland (H)
Alan Sharp BSc BD | 1980 | 2001 | 21 Ramsay Crescent, Burntisland KY3 9JL — 01592 874303
[E-mail: ASharp@churchofscotland.org.uk]

Dysart: St Clair (H)
Lynn Brady BD DipMin (Interim Minister) | 1996 | 2017 | 42 Craigfoot Walk, Kirkcaldy KY1 1GA — 01592 561967
[E-mail: LBrady@churchofscotland.org.uk]

Glenrothes: Christ's Kirk (H)
Vacant
12 The Limekilns, Glenrothes KY6 3QJ
0800 566 8242

Glenrothes: St Columba's (01592 752539) (Rothes Trinity Parish Grouping)
Alan W.D. Kimmitt BSc BD 2013
40 Liberton Drive, Glenrothes KY6 3PB
[E-mail: Alan.Kimmitt@churchofscotland.org.uk]
01592 742233

Glenrothes: St Margaret's (H) (01592 328162)
Eileen Miller BD MBACP (Snr. Accred.) 2014
DipCouns DipComEd
8 Alburne Park, Glenrothes KY7 5RB
[E-mail: EMiller@churchofscotland.org.uk]
01592 752241

Glenrothes: St Ninian's (H) (01592 610560) (E-mail: office@stninians.co.uk) (Rothes Trinity Parish Grouping)
David J. Smith BD DipMin 1992 2017
1 Cawdor Drive, Glenrothes KY6 2HN
[E-mail: David.Smith@churchofscotland.org.uk]
01592 611963

Kennoway, Windygates and Balgonie: St Kenneth's (01333 351372) (E-mail: stkennethsparish@gmail.com)
Vacant
2 Fernhill Gardens, Windygates, Leven KY8 5DZ
01333 352329

Kinghorn
James Reid BD 1985 1997
17 Myre Crescent, Kinghorn, Burntisland KY3 9UB
[E-mail: JReid@churchofscotland.org.uk]
01592 890269

Kirkcaldy: Abbotshall (H) (Website: www.abbotshallchurch.org.uk)
Vacant
83 Milton Road, Kirkcaldy KY1 1TP
01592 260315

Kirkcaldy: Bennochy
Robin J. McAlpine BDS BD MTh 1988 2011
25 Bennochy Avenue, Kirkcaldy KY2 5QE
[E-mail: RMcAlpine@churchofscotland.org.uk]
01592 643518

Kirkcaldy: Linktown See Auchtertool

Kirkcaldy: Pathhead (H) (Tel/Fax: 01592 204635) (E-mail: pathheadchurch@btinternet.com) (Website: www.pathheadparishchurch.co.uk)
Andrew C. Donald BD DPS 1992 2005
73 Loughborough Road, Kirkcaldy KY1 3DB
[E-mail: ADonald@churchofscotland.org.uk]
01592 652215

Kirkcaldy: St Bryce Kirk (H) (01592 640016) (E-mail: office@stbrycekirk.org.uk)
J. Kenneth (Ken) Froude MA BD   1979   6 East Fergus Place, Kirkcaldy KY1 1XT
[E-mail: JFroude@churchofscotland.org.uk]   01592 264480

Kirkcaldy: Templehall (H)
Anthony J.R. Fowler BSc BD   1982   2004   35 Appin Crescent, Kirkcaldy KY2 6EJ
[E-mail: AFowler@churchofscotland.org.uk]   01592 260156

Kirkcaldy: Torbain
Ian J. Elston BD MTh   1999   91 Sauchenbush Road, Kirkcaldy KY2 5RN
[E-mail: IElston@churchofscotland.org.uk]   01592 263015

Michael Allardyce MA MPhil PGCertTHE FHEA   2014   26 Parbroath Road, Glenrothes KY7 4TH
(Ordained Local Minister)   [E-mail: MAllardice@churchofscotland.org.uk]   01592 772280 / 07936 203465 (Mbl)

Leslie: Trinity (Rothes Trinity Parish Grouping)
Guardianship of the Presbytery

Leven
Gilbert C. Nisbet CA BD   1993   2007   5 Forman Road, Leven KY8 4HH
[E-mail: GNisbet@churchofscotland.org.uk]   01333 303339

Markinch and Thornton
Carolann Erskine BD DipPSRP   2009   2016   7 Guthrie Crescent, Markinch, Glenrothes KY7 6AY
[E-mail: CErskine@churchofscotland.org.uk]   01592 758264

Methil: Wellesley (H)
Gillian Paterson (Mrs) BD   2010   10 Vettriano Vale, Leven KY8 4GD
[E-mail: GPaterson@churchofscotland.org.uk]   01333 423147

Methilhill and Denbeath
Elisabeth F. Cranfield (Ms) MA BD   1988   9 Chemiss Road, Methilhill, Leven KY8 2BS
[E-mail: ECranfield@churchofscotland.org.uk]   01592 713142

Adams, David G. BD   1991 2011   (Cowdenbeath: Trinity)   13 Fernhill Gardens, Windygates, Leven KY8 5DZ
[E-mail: adams.69@btinternet.com]   01333 351214

Collins, Mitchell BD CPS   1996 2005   (Creich, Flisk and Kilmany with Monimail)   6 Netherby Park, Glenrothes KY6 3PL
[E-mail: collinsmit@aol.com]   01592 742915

Name	Ord.	Current	Congregation	Address	Tel
Elston, Peter K.	1963	2000	(Dalgety)	6 Cairngorm Crescent, Kirkcaldy KY2 5RF [E-mail: peterkelston@btinternet.com]	01592 205622
Ferguson, David J.	1966	2001	(Bellie with Speymouth)	4 Russell Gardens, Ladybank, Cupar KY15 7LT	01337 831406
Forrester, Ian L. MA	1964	1996	(Friockheim Kinnell with Inverkeilor and Lunan)		
Forsyth, Alexander R. TD BA MTh	1973	2013	(Markinch)	8 Bennochy Avenue, Kirkcaldy KY2 5QE; 49 Scaraben Crescent, Formonthills, Glenrothes KY6 3HL [E-mail: alex@arforsyth.com]	01592 260251; 01592 749049; (Mbl) 07756 239021
Galbraith, D. Douglas MA BD BMus MPhil ARSCM PhD	1965	2008	Editor: *The Year Book*	34 Balbirnie Street, Markinch, Glenrothes KY7 6DA [E-mail: dgalbraith@hotmail.com]	01592 752403
Gisbey, John E. MA BD MSc DipEd	1964	2002	(Thornhill)	Whitemyre House, 28 St Andrews Road, Largoward, Leven KY9 1HZ	01334 840540
Gordon, Ian D. LTh	1972	2001	(Markinch)	2 Somerville Way, Glenrothes KY7 5GE	01592 742487
Houghton, Christine (Mrs) BD	1997	2010	(Whitburn: South)	39 Cedar Crescent, Thornton, Kirkcaldy KY1 4BE [E-mail: c.houghton1@btinternet.com]	01592 772823
McLeod, Alistair G.	1988	2005	(Glenrothes: St Columba's)	13 Greenmantle Way, Glenrothes KY6 3QG [E-mail: alistairmcleod1936@gmail.com]	01592 744558
McNaught, Samuel M. MA BD MTh	1968	2002	(Kirkcaldy: St John's)	6 Munro Court, Glenrothes KY7 5GD [E-mail: sjmcnaught@btinternet.com]	01592 742352
Munro, Andrew MA BD PhD	1972	2000	(Glencaple with Lowther)	7 Dunvegan Avenue, Kirkcaldy KY2 5SG [E-mail: am.smm@blueyonder.co.uk]	01592 566129
Nicol, George G. BD DPhil	1982	2013	(Falkland with Freuchie)	48 Fidra Avenue, Burntisland KY3 0AZ [E-mail: ggnicol@totalise.co.uk]	01592 873258
Paterson, Maureen (Mrs) BSc	1992	2010	(Auxiliary Minister)	91 Dalmahoy Crescent, Kirkcaldy KY2 6TA [E-mail: m.e.paterson@blueyonder.co.uk]	01592 262300
Roy, Allistair BD DipSW PgDip	2007	2016	(Glenrothes: St Ninian's)	39 Ravenswood Drive, Glenrothes KY6 2PA [E-mail: minister@revroy.co.uk]	
Templeton, James L. BSc BD	1975	2012	(Innerleven: East)	29 Coldstream Avenue, Leven KY8 5TN [E-mail: jamietempleton@btinternet.com]	01333 427102
Thomson, John D. BD	1985	2005	(Kirkcaldy: Pathhead)	3 Tottenham Court, Hill Street, Dysart, Kirkcaldy KY1 2XY [E-mail: j.thomson10@sky.com]	01592 655313; (Mbl) 07885 414979
Tomlinson, Bryan L. TD	1969	2003	(Kirkcaldy: Abbotshall)	2 Duddingston Drive, Kirkcaldy KY2 6JP [E-mail: abbkirk@blueyonder.co.uk]	01592 564843
Wilson, Tilly (Miss) MTh	1990	2012	(Dysart)	6 Citron Glebe, Kirkcaldy KY1 2NF [E-mail: tillywilson1@sky.com]	01592 263134
Wright Lynda BEd DCS			Community Chaplaincy Listening (Scotland): National Coordinator	71a Broomhill Avenue, Burntisland KY3 0BP	07835 303395

KIRKCALDY ADDRESSES

Abbotshall — Abbotshall Road

Bennochy	Elgin Street	Templehall	Beauly Place
Linktown	Nicol Street x High Street	Torbain	Lindores Drive
Pathhead	Harriet Street x Church Street	Viewforth	Viewforth Street x Viewforth Terrace
St Bryce Kirk	St Brycedale Avenue x Kirk Wynd		

(26) ST ANDREWS

Meets at Cupar, in St John's Church Hall, on the first Wednesday of February, May, September, October, November and December, and on the last Wednesday of June.

| Clerk: | REV. NIGEL J. ROBB FCP MA BD ThM MTh | Presbytery Office, The Basement, 1 Howard Place, St Andrews KY16 9HL [E-mail: standrews@churchofscotland.org.uk] | 01334 461300 |
| Depute Clerk: | MRS CATHERINE WILSON MBE BSc FInstP | 5 Taeping Close, Cellardyke, Anstruther KY10 3YL [E-mail: catherine.wilson15@btinternet.com] | 01333 310936 |

Abdie and Dunbog (H) linked with Newburgh (H)
Vacant

2 Guthrie Court, Cupar Road, Newburgh, Cupar KY14 6HA   01337 842228

Anstruther and Cellardyke (H) St Ayle linked with Kilrenny
Arthur A. Christie BD   1997   2009

16 Taeping Close, Cellardyke, Anstruther KY10 3YL [E-mail: AChristie@churchofscotland.org.uk]   01333 313917

(Anstruther and Cellardyke: St Ayle is formed by the union of Anstruther and Cellardyke)

Auchtermuchty (H) linked with Edenshead and Strathmiglo
Vacant

The Manse, Kirk Wynd, Strathmiglo, Cupar KY14 7QS   01337 860256

Balmerino (H) linked with Wormit (H)
James Connolly   1982   2004
DipTh CertMin MA(Theol) DMin

5 Westwater Place, Newport-on-Tay DD6 8NS [E-mail: JConnolly@churchofscotland.org.uk]   01382 542626

Boarhills and Dunino linked with St Andrews: Holy Trinity
Vacant

Cameron linked with St Andrews: St Leonard's (H) (01334 478702) (E-mail: stlencam@btconnect.com)
Graeme W. Beebee BD   1993   2017

1 Cairnhill Gardens, St Andrews KY16 8QY [E-mail: GBeebee@churchofscotland.org.uk]   01334 472793

Carnbee linked with Pittenweem
Margaret E.S. Rose BD   2007

29 Milton Road, Pittenweem, Anstruther KY10 2LN [E-mail: MRose@churchofscotland.org.uk]   01333 312838

Ceres, Kemback and Springfield
James W. Campbell BD   1995   2010   The Manse, St Andrews Road, Ceres, Cupar KY15 5NQ   01334 829350
[E-mail: James.Campbell@churchofscotland.org.uk]

Crail linked with Kingsbarns (H)
Vacant   The Manse, St Andrews Road, Crail, Anstruther KY10 3UH   01333 451986

Creich, Flisk and Kilmany
Guardianship of the Presbytery

Cupar: Old (H) and St Michael of Tarvit linked with Monimail
Jeffrey A. Martin BA MDiv   1991   2016   76 Hogarth Drive, Cupar KY15 5YU   01334 656181
[E-mail: JMartin@churchofscotland.org.uk]

Cupar: St John's and Dairsie United   The Manse, 23 Hogarth Drive, Cupar KY15 5YH   01334 650751

Edenshead and Strathmiglo See Auchtermuchty

East Neuk Trinity (H) linked with St Monans (H)
Vacant
(East Neuk Trinity was formerly known as Elie Kilconquhar and Colinsburgh)

Falkland linked with Freuchie (H)
Vacant   1 Newton Road, Falkland, Cupar KY15 7AQ   01337 858557
Susan Thorburn MTh   2014   3 Daleally Farm Cottages, St Madoes Road, Errol, Perth PH2 7TJ   01821 642681
(Ordained Local Minister)   [E-mail: SThorburn@churchofscotland.org.uk]

Freuchie See Falkland

Howe of Fife
William F. Hunter MA BD   1986   2011   The Manse, 83 Church Street, Ladybank, Cupar KY15 7ND   01337 832717
[E-mail: WHunter@churchofscotland.org.uk]

Kilrenny See Anstruther and Cellardyke: St Ayle
Kingsbarns See Crail

Largo
Vacant

(Largo is formed by the union of Largo and Newburn and Largo: St David's)

Largoward (H)
Guardianship of the Presbytery
Peter W. Mills CB BD DD CPS   1984   2013   The Manse, St Monans, Anstruther KY10 2DD   01333 730135
(Locum Minister)   [E-mail: PMills@churchofscotland.org.uk]

Leuchars: St Athernase
John C. Duncan BD MPhil   1979   2016   7 David Wilson Park, Balmullo, St Andrews KY16 0NP   01334 870038
[E-mail: JDuncan@churchofscotland.org.uk]

Monimail See Cupar: Old
Newburgh See Abdie and Dunbog

Newport-on-Tay (H)
Amos Chewachong   2017   17 East Station Place, Newport-on-Tay DD6 8EG   01382 542893
[E-mail: AChewachong@churchofscotland.org.uk]

Pittenweem See Carnbee

St Andrews: Holy Trinity See Boarhills and Dunino

St Andrews: Hope Park and Martyrs (H) linked with Strathkinness
Allan McCafferty BSc BD   1993   2011   20 Priory Gardens, St Andrews KY16 8XX   01334 478287 (Tel/Fax)
[E-mail: AMcCafferty@churchofscotland.org.uk]

St Andrews: St Leonard's See Cameron
St Monans See East Neuk Trinity
Strathkinness See St Andrews: Hope Park and Martyrs

Tayport
Brian H. Oxburgh BSc BD   1980   2011   27 Bell Street, Tayport DD6 9AP   01382 553879
[E-mail: BOxburgh@churchofscotland.org.uk]

Wormit See Balmerino

Name	Ord/Ind	Position	Address / E-mail	Telephone
Alexander, James S. MA BD BA PhD	1966 1973	(University of St Andrews)	5 Strathkinness High Road, St Andrews KY16 9RP	01334 472680
Barron, Jane L. (Mrs) BA DipEd BD	1999 2013	(Aberdeen: St Machar's Cathedral)	Denhead Old Farm, St Andrews KY16 8PA [E-mail: livialouise888@gmail.com]	01334 850135 (Mbl) 07545 904541
Bradley, Ian C. MA BD DPhil	1990	(Principal, St Mary's College)	4 Donaldson Gardens, St Andrews KY16 9DN [E-mail: icb@st-andrews.ac.uk]	01334 475389
Cameron, John U. BA BSc PhD BD ThD	1974 2008	(Dundee: Broughty Ferry St Stephen's and West)	10 Howard Place, St Andrews KY16 9HL [E-mail: jucameron@yahoo.co.uk]	01334 474474
Clark, David M. MA BD	1989 2013	(Dundee: The Steeple)	2b Rose Street, St Monans, Anstruther KY10 2BQ [E-mail: dmclark72@gmail.com]	01333 738034
Connolly, Daniel BD DipTheol Dip Min	1983	Army Chaplain	2 Cairngreen, Cupar KY15 2SY [E-mail: dannyconnolly@hotmail.co.uk]	(Mbl) 07951 078478
Douglas, Peter C. JP	1966 1993	(Boarhills with Dunino)	12 Greyfriars Gardens, St Andrews KY16 8DR	01334 475868
Earnshaw, Philip BA BSc BD	1986 1996	(Glasgow: Pollokshields)	22 Castle Street, St Monans, Anstruther KY10 2AP	01333 730640
Fairlie, George BD BVMS MRCVS	1971 2002	(Crail with Kingsbarns)	41 Warrack Street, St Andrews KY16 8DR	01334 475868
Fraser, Ann G. BD CertMin	1990 2007	(Auchtermuchty)	24 Irvine Crescent, St Andrews KY16 8LG [E-mail: anngilfraser@btinternet.com]	01334 461329
Galloway, Robert W.C. LTh	1970 1998	(Cromarty)	22 Haughgate, Leven KY8 4SG	01333 426223
Gordon, Peter M. MA BD	1958 1995	(Airdrie: West)	3 Cupar Road, Cuparmuir, Cupar KY15 5RH [E-mail: machrie@madasafish.com]	01334 652341
Hamilton, Ian W.F. BD LTh ALCM AVCM	1978 2012	(Nairn: Old)	Mossneuk, 5 Windsor Gardens, St Andrews KY16 8XL [E-mail: reviwfh@btinternet.com]	01334 477745
Harrison, Cameron	2006	(Auxiliary Minister)	Woodfield House, Priormuir, St Andrews KY16 8LP	01334 478067
Jeffrey, Kenneth S. BA BD PhD	2002 2014	University of Aberdeen	The North Steading, Dalgairn, Cupar KY15 4PH [E-mail: ksjeffrey@btopenworld.com]	01334 653196
MacEwan, Donald G. MA BD PhD	2001 2012	Chaplain: University of St Andrews	Chaplaincy Centre, 3A St Mary's Place, St Andrews KY16 9UY [E-mail: dgm21@st-andrews.ac.uk]	01334 462865 (Mbl) 07713 322036
McGregor, Duncan J. MIFM	1982 1996	(Channelkirk with Lauder: Old)	14 Mount Melville, St Andrews KY16 8NG	01334 478314
McKinmon, Eric BA BD MTh PhD	1983 2014	(Cargill Burrelton with Collace)	14 Marionfield Place, Cupar KY15 5JN [E-mail: ericmckinmon@gmail.com]	01334 659650
McLean, John P. BSc BPhil BD	1994 2013	(Glenrothes: St Margaret's)	72 Lawmill Gardens, St Andrews KY16 8QS [E-mail: john@mcleanmail.me.uk]	01334 470803
Meager, Peter MA BD CertMgmt(Open)	1971 1998	(Elie with Kilconquhar and Colinsburgh)	7 Lorraine Drive, Cupar KY15 5DY [E-mail: meager52@btinternet.com]	01334 656991
Mills, Peter W. CB BD DD CPS	1984 2017	(Largoward with St Monans)	The Manse, St Monans, Anstruther KY10 2DD [E-mail: PMills@churchofscotland.org.uk]	01333 730135
Neilson, Peter MA BD MTh	1975 2006	(Mission Consultant)	Linne Bheag, 2 School Green, Anstruther KY10 3HF [E-mail: neilson.peter@btinternet.com]	01333 310477 (Mbl) 07818 418608
Reid, Alan A.S. MA BD STM	1962 1995	(Bridge of Allan: Chalmers)	Wayside Cottage, Bridgend, Ceres, Cupar KY15 5LS	01334 828509
Robb, Nigel J. FCP MA BD ThM MTh	1981 2014	Presbytery Clerk	Presbytery Office, Hope Park and Martyrs' Church, 1 Howard Place, St Andrews KY16 9UY	(Mbl) 07966 286958
Strong, Clifford LTh	1983 1995	(Creich, Flisk and Kilmany with Monimail)	60 Maryknowe, Gauldry, Newport-on-Tay DD6 8SL [E-mail: cliffstrongman@btinternet.com]	01382 330445

Torrance, Alan J. (Prof.) MA BD DrTheol 1984 1999   University of St Andrews   Kincaple House, Kincaple, St Andrews KY16 9SH   (Home) 01334 850755 / (Office) 01334 462843

Unsworth, Ruth BA BD CertMHS PgDipCBP BABCP 1984   (Mbl) 07894 802119
5 Lindsay Gardens, St Andrews KY16 8XB [E-mail: RUnsworth@churchofscotland.org.uk]

Walker, James B. MA BD DPhil 1975 2011 (Chaplain: University of St Andrews)   5 Priestden Park, St Andrews KY16 8DL 01334 472839

Wotherspoon, Ian G. BA LTh 1967 2004 (Coatbridge: St Andrew's)   12 Cherry Lane, Cupar KY15 5DA 01334 650710
[E-mail: wotherspoonrig@aol.com]

(27) DUNKELD AND MEIGLE

Meets at Pitlochry on the first Tuesday of February, September and December, on the third Tuesday of April and the fourth Tuesday of October, and at the Moderator's church on the third Tuesday of June.

Clerk:	REV. JOHN RUSSELL MA	Kilblaan, Gladstone Terrace, Birnam, Dunkeld PH8 0DP [E-mail: dunkeldmeigle@churchofscotland.org.uk]	01350 728896
Depute Clerk:	REV. R. FRASER PENNY BA BD	Cathedral Manse, Dunkeld PH8 0AW [E-mail: RPenny@churchofscotland.org.uk]	01350 727249

Aberfeldy (H) linked with Dull and Weem (H) linked with Grantully, Logierait and Strathtay
Vacant   The Manse, Taybridge Terrace, Aberfeldy PH15 2BS

Alyth (H)
Michael J. Erskine MA BD 1985 2012 The Manse, Cambridge Street, Alyth, Blairgowrie PH11 8AW 01828 632238
[E-mail: MErskine@churchofscotland.org.uk]

Ardler, Kettins and Meigle
Alison Notman BD 2014 The Manse, Dundee Road, Meigle, Blairgowrie PH12 8SB 01828 640074
[E-mail: ANotman@churchofscotland.org.uk]

Bendochy linked with Coupar Angus: Abbey
Andrew F. Graham BTh DPS 2001 2016 Caddam Road, Coupar Angus, Blairgowrie PH13 9EF 01828 627864
[E-mail: Andrew.Graham@churchofscotland.org.uk]

Blair Atholl and Struan linked with Braes of Rannoch linked with Foss and Rannoch (H)
Vacant   The Manse, Blair Atholl, Pitlochry PH18 5SX 01796 481213

Blairgowrie
Harry Mowbray BD CA — 2003 — 2008 — The Manse, Upper David Street, Blairgowrie PH10 6HB [E-mail: HMowbray@churchofscotland.org.uk] — 01250 872146

Braes of Rannoch linked with Foss and Rannoch (H) See Blair Atholl and Struan

Caputh and Clunie (H) linked with Kinclaven (H)
Peggy Ewart-Roberts BA BD — 2003 — 2011 — Cara Beag, Essendy Road, Blairgowrie PH10 6QU [E-mail: PEwart-Roberts@churchofscotland.org.uk] — 01250 876897

Coupar Angus: Abbey See Bendochy
Dull and Weem See Aberfeldy

Dunkeld (H)
R. Fraser Penny BA BD — 1984 — 2001 — Cathedral Manse, Dunkeld PH8 0AW [E-mail: RPenny@churchofscotland.org.uk] — 01350 727249

Fortingall and Glenlyon linked with Kenmore and Lawers (H)
Anne J. Brennan BSc BD MTh — 1999 — The Manse, Balnaskeag, Kenmore, Aberfeldy PH15 2HB [E-mail: ABrennan@churchofscotland.org.uk] — 01887 830218

Foss and Rannoch See Blair Atholl and Struan
Grantully, Logierait and Strathtay See Aberfeldy
Kenmore and Lawers See Fortingall and Glenlyon
Kinclaven See Caputh and Clunie

Kirkmichael, Straloch and Glenshee linked with Rattray (H)
Linda Stewart (Mrs) BD — 1996 — 2012 — The Manse, Alyth Road, Rattray, Blairgowrie PH10 7HF [E-mail: Linda.Stewart@churchofscotland.org.uk] — 01250 872462

Pitlochry (H) (01796 472160)
Mary M. Haddow (Mrs) BD — 2001 — 2012 — Manse Road, Moulin, Pitlochry PH16 5EP [E-mail: MHaddow@churchofscotland.org.uk] — 01796 472774

Rattray See Kirkmichael, Straloch and Glenshee

Tenandry
Guardianship of the Presbytery

Name	Dates	Charge	Address	Tel
Campbell, Richard S. LTh	1993 2010	(Gargunnock with Kilmadock with Kincardine-in-Menteith)	3 David Farquharson Road, Blairgowrie PH10 6FD [E-mail: revrichards@yahoo.co.uk]	01250 876386
Cassells, Alexander K. MA BD	1961 1997	(Leuchars: St Athernase and Guardbridge)	Alt-Na-Feidh, Bridge of Cally, Blairgowrie PH10 7JL	(Mbl) 07816 043968
Ewart, William BSc BD	1972 2010	(Caputh and Clunie with Kinclaven)	Cara Beag, Essendy Road, Blairgowrie PH10 6QU [E-mail: ewe1@btinternet.com]	01250 876897
Knox, John W. MTheol	1992 1997	(Lochgelly: Macainsh)	Heatherlea, Main Street, Ardler, Blairgowrie PH12 8SR	01828 640731
McAlister, D.J.B. MA BD PhD	1951 1989	(North Berwick: Blackadder)	2 Duff Avenue, Moulin, Pitlochry PH16 5EN	01796 473591
MacRae, Malcolm H. MA PhD	1971 2010	(Kirkmichael, Straloch and Glenshee with Rattray)	10B Victoria Place, Stirling FK8 2QU [E-mail: malcolm.macrae1@btopenworld.com]	01786 465547
Nelson, Robert C. BA BD	1980 2010	(Isle of Mull, Kilninian and Kilmore with Salen and Ulva with Tobermory with Torosay and Kinlochspelvie)	St Colme's, Perth Road, Birnam, Dunkeld PH8 0BH [E-mail: rcnelson49@btinternet.com]	01350 727455
Nicol, Robert D.	2013	Ordained Local Minister	Rappla Lodge, Camserney, Aberfeldy PH15 2JF [E-mail: RNicol@churchofscotland.org.uk]	01887 820242
Ormiston, Hugh C. BSc BD MPhil PhD	1969 2004	(Kirkmichael, Straloch and Glenshee with Rattray)	Cedar Lea, Main Road, Woodside, Blairgowrie PH13 9NP	01828 670539
Robertson, Matthew LTh	1968 2002	(Cawdor with Croy and Dalcross)	Inver, Strathtay, Pitlochry PH9 0PG	01887 840780
Rooney, Malcolm I.G. DPE BEd BD	1993 2017	(The Glens and Kirriemuir: Old)	23 Mart Lane, Northmuir, Kirriemuir DD8 4TL [E-mail: malc.rooney@gmail.com]	01575 575334 / 07909 993233
Russell, John MA	1959 2000	Presbytery Clerk	Kilblaan, Gladstone Terrace, Birnam, Dunkeld PH8 0DP	(Mbl) 01350 728896
Shannon, W.G. MA BD	1955 1998	(Pitlochry)	19 Knockard Road, Pitlochry PH16 5HJ	01796 473533
Sloan, Robert BD	1997 2014	(Fauldhouse St Andrew's)	3 Gean Grove, Blairgowrie PH10 6TL.	01250 875286
Steele, Grace M.F. MA BTh	2014	Ordained Local Minister	12a Farragon Drive, Aberfeldy PH15 2BQ [E-mail: GSteele@churchofscotland.org.uk]	01887 820025
Tait, Thomas W. BD MBE	1972 1997	(Rattray)	3 Rosemount Park, Blairgowrie PH10 6TZ	01250 874833
Whyte, William B. BD	1973 2003	(Nairn: St Ninian's)	The Old Inn, Park Hill Road, Rattray, Blairgowrie PH10 7DS	01250 874401
Wilson, John M. MA BD	1967 2004	(Altnaharra and Farr)	Berbice, The Terrace, Blair Atholl, Pitlochry PH18 5SZ	01796 481619
Wilson, Mary D. (Mrs) RGN SCM DTM	1990 2004	(Auxiliary Minister)	Berbice, The Terrace, Blair Atholl, Pitlochry PH18 5SZ	01796 481619

(28) PERTH

Meets at 10am on the second Saturday of September, December, March, and June at Kinross and other venues within the bounds.

Clerk:	REV. J. COLIN CASKIE BA BD	209 High Street, Perth PH1 5PB [E-mail: perth@churchofscotland.org.uk]	
Presbytery Office:			01738 451177

1. Aberdalgie (H) and Forteviot (H) linked with Aberuthven and Dunning (H)
James W. Aitchison BD   1993   2015   The Manse, Aberdalgie, Perth PH2 0QD   01738 446771
[E-mail: JAitchison@churchofscotland.org.uk]

2. Abernethy and Dron and Arngask
Vacant   3 Manse Road, Abernethy, Perth PH2 9JP   01738 850938

3. Aberuthven and Dunning See Aberdalgie and Forteviot

4. Almondbank Tibbermore linked with Methven and Logiealmond
Vacant   The Manse, Pitcairngreen, Perth PH1 3EA   01738 583217

5. Ardoch (H) linked with Blackford (H)
Mairi Perkins BA BTh   2012   2016   Manse of Ardoch, Feddoch Road, Braco, Dunblane FK15 5RE   01786 880948
[E-mail: MPerkins@churchofscotland.org.uk]

6. Auchterarder (H)
Robert D. Barlow   2010   2013   22 Kirkfield Place, Auchterarder PH3 1FP   01764 662399
BA BSc MSc PhD CChem MRSC   [E-mail: RBarlow@churchofscotland.org.uk]

7. Auchtergaven and Moneydie linked with Redgorton and Stanley
Adrian J. Lough BD   2012   22 King Street, Stanley, Perth PH1 4ND   01738 827952
[E-mail: ALough@churchofscotland.org.uk]

8. Blackford See Ardoch

9. Cargill Burrelton linked with Collace
Steven Thomson BSc BD   2001   2016   The Manse, Manse Road, Woodside, Blairgowrie PH13 9NQ   01828 670384
[E-mail: SThomson@churchofscotland.org.uk]

10. Cleish (H) linked with Fossoway: St Serf's and Devonside
Elisabeth M. Stenhouse BD   2006   2014   Station House, Station Road, Crook of Devon, Kinross KY13 0PG   01577 842128
[E-mail: EStenhouse@churchofscotland.org.uk]

11. Collace See Cargill Burrelton

12 **Comrie (H) linked with Dundurn (H)**
Graham McWilliams BSc BD   2005   The Manse, Strowan Road, Comrie, Crieff PH6 2ES   01764 670076
[E-mail: GMcWilliams@churchofscotland.org.uk]

13 **Crieff (H)**
Andrew J. Philip BSc BD   1996   2013   8 Strathearn Terrace, Crieff PH7 3AQ   01764 218976
[E-mail: APhilip@churchofscotland.org.uk]

14 **Dunbarney (H) and Forgandenny**
Allan J. Wilson BSc MEd BD   2007   Dunbarney Manse, Manse Road, Bridge of Earn, Perth PH2 9DY   01738 812211
[E-mail: AWilson@churchofscotland.org.uk]

15 **Dundurn** See Comrie

16 **Errol (H) linked with Kilspindie and Rait**
John Macgregor BD   2001   2016   South Bank, Errol, Perth PH2 7PZ   01821 642279
[E-mail: John.Macgregor@churchofscotland.org.uk]

17 **Fossoway: St Serf's and Devonside** See Cleish

18 **Fowlis Wester, Madderty, and Monzie linked with Gask (H)**
David W. Denniston BD DipMin   1981   2016   Beechview, Abercairney, Crieff PH7 3NF   01764 652116
(Interim Minister)   07903 926727 (Mbl)
[E-mail: DDenniston@churchofscotland.org.uk]

19 **Gask** See Fowlis Wester, Madderty and Monzie
Kilspindie and Rait See Errol

20 **Kinross (H) (Office: 01577 862570)**
Alan D. Reid MA BD   1989   2009   15 Green Wood, Kinross KY13 8FG   01577 862952
[E-mail: AReid@churchofscotland.org.uk]

21 **Methven and Logiealmond** See Almondbank Tibbermore

22 **Muthill (H) linked with Trinity Gask and Kinkell**
Klaus O.F. Buwert LLB BD DMin   1984   2013   The Manse, Station Road, Muthill, Crieff PH5 2AR   01764 681205
[E-mail: KBuwert@churchofscotland.org.uk]

Orwell (H) and Portmoak (H) (Office: 01577 862100)
Angus Morrison MA BD PhD 1979 2011
41 Auld Mart Road, Milnathort, Kinross KY13 9FR
[E-mail: AMorrison@churchofscotland.org.uk]
01577 863461

Perth: Craigie and Moncreiffe
Vacant
Robert F. Wilkie 2011
(Auxiliary Minister)
The Manse, 46 Abbot Street, Perth PH2 0EE　01738 623748
24 Huntingtower Road, Perth PH1 2JS　01738 628301
[E-mail: RWilkie@churchofscotland.org.uk]

Perth: Kinnoull (H)
Graham W. Crawford BSc BD STM 1991 2016
1 Mount Tabor Avenue, Perth PH2 7BT　01738 626046
[E-mail: GCrawford@churchofscotland.org.uk]　07817 504042 (Mbl)
Timothy E.G. Fletcher BA FCMA 1998
(Auxiliary Minister)
3 Ardchoille Park, Perth PH2 7TL　01738 638189
[E-mail: TFletcher@churchofscotland.org.uk]　07747 013985 (Mbl)

Perth: Letham St Mark's (H) (Office: 01738 446377)
James C. Stewart BD DipMin 1997
35 Rose Crescent, Perth PH1 1NT　01738 624167
[E-mail: JStewart@churchofscotland.org.uk]
Kenneth D. McKay DCS
11F Balgowan Road, Perth PH1 2JG　01738 621169
[E-mail: Kenneth.McKay@churchofscotland.org.uk]　07843 883042 (Mbl)

Perth: North (Office: 01738 622298)
Vacant

Perth: Riverside (Office: 01738 622341)
David R. Rankin MA BD 2009 2014
44 Hay Street, Perth PH1 5HS　07810 008754 (Mbl)
[E-mail: DRankin@churchofscotland.org.uk]

Perth: St John's Kirk of Perth (H) (01738 626159) linked with Perth: St Leonard's-in-the-Fields (H) (01738 632238)
John A.H. Murdoch BA BD DPSS 1979 2016
Ferntower, Kinfauns Holdings, Perth PH2 7JY　01738 628378
[E-mail: JMurdoch@churchofscotland.org.uk]　07578 558978 (Mbl)

Perth: St Leonard's-in-the-Fields See Perth: St John's Kirk of Perth

Perth: St Matthew's (Office: 01738 636757; Vestry: 01738 630725)
Scott Burton BD DipMin 1999 2007
23 Kincarrathie Crescent, Perth PH2 7HH　01738 626828
[E-mail: SBurton@churchofscotland.org.uk]

32 Redgorton and Stanley See Auchtergaven and Moneydie

33 St Madoes and Kinfauns
Marc F. Bircham BD MTh	2000	Glencarse, Perth PH2 7NF [E-mail: MBircham@churchofscotland.org.uk]	01738 860837

34 Scone and St Martins
Vacant
Alan Livingstone (Ordained Local Minister)	2013	Meadowside, Lawnmuir, Methven, Perth PH1 3SZ [E-mail: ALivingstone@churchofscotland.org.uk]	01738 840682

Trinity Gask and Kinkell See Muthill

34 congregations – 27 charges.

Name			Charge	Address	Phone
Ballentine, Ann M. MA BD	1981	2007	(Kirknewton and East Calder)	17 Nellfield Road, Crieff PH7 3DU [E-mail: annmballentine@gmail.com]	01764 652567
Barr, T. Leslie LTh	1969	1997	(Kinross)	8 Fairfield Road, Kelty KY4 0BY [E-mail: leslie_barr@yahoo.com]	01383 839330
Bertram, Thomas A.	1972	1995	(Patna Waterside)	3 Scrimgeour's Corner, 29 West High Street, Crieff PH7 4AP	01764 652066
Brown, Elizabeth JP RGN	1996	2007	(Auxiliary Minister)	8 Viewlands Place, Perth PH1 1BS [E-mail: liz.brown@blueyonder.co.uk]	01738 552391
Brown, Marina D. MA BD MTh	2000	2012	(Hawick: St Mary's and Old)	Moneydie School Cottage, Luncarty, Perth PH1 3HZ [E-mail: revmdb1711@btinternet.com]	01738 582163
Buchan, William DipTheol BD	1987	2001	(Kilwinning: Abbey)	34 Bridgewater Avenue, Auchterarder PH3 1DQ [E-mail: billbuchan3@btinternet.com]	01764 660306
Cairns, Evelyn BD	2004	2012	(Chaplain: Rachel House)	15 Talla Park, Kinross KY13 8AB [E-mail: revelyn@btinternet.com]	01577 863990
Caskie, J. Colin BA BD	1977	2012	Presbytery Clerk	13 Anderson Drive, Perth PH1 1JZ [E-mail: jcolincaskie@gmail.com]	01738 445543
Coleman, Sidney H. BA BD MTh	1961	2001	(Glasgow: Merrylea)	'Blaven', 11 Clyde Place, Perth PH2 0EZ [E-mail: sidney.coleman@blueyonder.co.uk]	01738 565072
Craig, Joan H. MTheol	1986	2005	(Orkney: East Mainland)	7 Jedburgh Place, Perth PH1 1SJ [E-mail: joanhcraig@btinternet.com]	01738 580180
Donaldson, Robert B. BSocSc	1953	1997	(Kilchoman with Portnahaven)	11 Strathearn Court, Crieff PH7 3DS	01764 654976
Dunn, W. Stuart LTh	1970	2006	(Motherwell: Crosshill)	10 Macrostie Gardens, Crieff PH7 4LP	01764 655178
Fleming, Hamish K. MA	1966	2001	(Banchory Ternan: East)	36 Earnmuir Road, Comrie, Crieff PH6 2EY [E-mail: hamishnan@gmail.com]	01764 679178
Gilchrist, Ewen J. BD DipMin DipComm	1982	2017	(Cults)	9 David Douglas Avenue, Scone PH2 6QQ [E-mail: ewengilchrist@btconnect.com]	(Mbl) 07747 746418
Graham, Sydney S. DipYL MPhil BD	1987	2009	(Iona with Kilfinichen and Kilvickeon and the Ross of Mull)	'Aspen', Milton Road, Luncarty, Perth PH1 3ES [E-mail: syd@sydgraham.plus.com]	01738 829350

Name	Ordained	Retired/Role	Address	Telephone
Gregory, J.C. LTh	1968 1992	(Blantyre: St Andrew's)	2 Southlands Road, Auchterarder PH3 1BA	01764 664594
Gunn, Alexander M. MA BD	1967 2006	(Aberfeldy with Amulree and Strathbraan with Dull and Weem)	'Navarone', 12 Cornhill Road, Perth PH1 1LR [E-mail: sandygunn@btinternet.com]	01738 443216
Halliday, Archibald R. BD MTh	1964 1999	(Duffus, Spynie and Hopeman)	8 Turretbank Drive, Crieff PH7 4LW [E-mail: roberthalliday343@btinternet.com]	01764 656464
Kelly, T. Clifford	1973 1995	(Ferintosh)	20 Whinfield Drive, Kinross KY13 8UB	01577 864946
Lawson, James B. MA BD	1961 2002	(South Uist)	4 Cowden Way, Comrie, Crieff PH6 2NW [E-mail: james.lawson7@btopenworld.com]	01764 679180
Lawson, Ronald G. MA BD	1964 1999	(Greenock: Wellpark Mid Kirk)	6 East Brougham Street, Stanley, Perth PH1 4NJ	01738 828871
McCarthy, David J. BSc BD	1985 2014	Mission and Discipleship Council	121 George Street, Edinburgh EH2 4YN [E-mail: DMcCarthy@churchofscotland.org.uk]	0131-225 5722
McCormick, Alastair F.	1962 1998	(Creich with Rosehall)	14 Balmanno Park, Bridge of Earn, Perth PH2 9RJ	01738 813588
McCrum, Robert BSc BD	1982 2014	(Ayr: St James')	28 Rose Crescent, Perth PH1 1NT [E-mail: robert.mccrum@virgin.net]	01738 447906
McCrum, Scott BD	2015 2017	(Glenrothes: Christ's Kirk)	26 Arthur Park, Perth PH2 0TB [E-mail: SMcCrum@churchofscotland.org.uk]	
MacDonald, James W. BD	1976 2012	(Crieff)	'Mingulay', 29 Hebridean Gardens, Crieff PH7 3BP [E-mail: rev_up@btinternet.com]	01764 654500
McFadzean, Iain MA BD	1989 2010	National Director: Workplace Chaplaincy (Scotland)	2 Lowfield Crescent, Luncarty, Perth PH13FG [E-mail: iain.mcfadzean@wpcscotland.co.uk]	01738 827338 (Mbl) 07969 227696
McGregor, William LTh	1987 2003	(Auchtergaven and Moneydie)	'Ard Choille', 7 Taypark Road, Luncarty, Perth PH1 3FE [E-mail: bill.mcgregor7@btinternet.com]	01738 827866
McIntosh, Colin G. MA BD	1976 2013	(Dunblane: Cathedral)	Drumhead Cottage, Drum, Kinross KY13 0PR [E-mail: colinmcintosh4@btinternet.com]	01577 840012
MacLaughlan, Grant BA BD	1998 2017	Community Worker, Perth Tulloch Net	Unit 2, Tulloch Square, Perth PH1 2PW [E-mail: grantmac.tullochnet@gmail.com]	01738 562731 (Mbl) 07790 518041
MacMillan, Riada M. BD	1991 1998	(Perth: Craigend Moncreiffe with Rhynd)	73 Muirend Gardens, Perth PH1 1JR	01738 628867
McNaughton, David J.H. BA CA	1976 1995	(Killin and Ardeonaig)	14 Rankine Court, Wormit, Newport-on-Tay DD6 8TA	
Main, Douglas M. BD	1986 2014	(Errol with Kilspindie and Rait)	14 Madoch Road, St Madoes, Perth PH2 7TT [E-mail: revdmain@sky.com]	01738 860867
Malcolm, Alistair BD DPS	1976 2012	(Inverness: Inshes)	11 Kinclaven Gardens, Murthly, Perth PH1 4EX [E-mail: amalcolm067@btinternet.com]	01738 710979
Michie, Margaret	2013	Ordained Local Minister: Loch Leven Parish Grouping	3 Loch Leven Court, Wester Balgedie, Kinross KY13 9NE [E-mail: margaretmichie@btinternet.com]	01592 840602
Millar, Archibald E. DipTh	1965 1991	(Perth: St Stephen's)	7 Maple Place, Perth PH1 1RT	01738 621813
Milne, Robert B. BTh	1999 2017	(Broughton, Glenholm and Kilbucho with Skirling with Stobo and Drumelzier with Tweedsmuir)	3 Mid Square, Comrie PH6 2EG [E-mail: rbmilne@aol.com]	
Mitchell, Alexander B. BD	1981 2014	(Dunblane: St Blane's)	24 Hebridean Gardens, Crieff PH7 3BP [E-mail: alex.mitchell6@btopenworld.com]	01764 652241
Munro, Gillian BSc BD	1989 2003	Head of Spiritual Care, NHS Tayside	Royal Victoria Hospital, Dundee DD2 1SP	01382 423116
Munro, Patricia BSc DCS		(Deacon)	4 Hewat Place, Perth PH1 2UD [E-mail: patmunrodcs@gmail.com]	01738 443088 (Mbl) 07814 836314

Paton, Iain F. BD FCIS	1980	2006	(Elie with Kilconquhar and Colinsburgh)	Muldoanich, Stirling Street, Blackford, Auchterarder PH4 1QG [E-mail: iain.f.paton@btinternet.com]	01764 682234
Pattison, Kenneth J. MA BD STM	1967	2004	(Kilmuir and Logie Easter)	2 Castle Way, St Madoes, Glencarse, Perth PH2 7NY [E-mail: k_pattison@btinternet.com]	01738 860340
Philip, Elizabeth DCS MA BA PGCSE			Deacon	8 Strathearn Terrace, Crieff PH7 3AQ [E-mail: ephilipstitch@gmail.com]	01764 218976 (Mbl) 07970 767851
Philip, Michael R. BD	1978	2014	(Falkirk: Bainsford)	9 Muir Bank, Scone, Perth PH2 6SZ [E-mail: mrphilip@blueyonder.co.uk]	01738 564533 (Mbl) 07776 011601
Redpath, James G. BD DipPTh	1988	2016	(Auchtermuchty with Edenshead and Strathmiglo)	9 Beveridge Place, Kinross KY13 8QY [E-mail: JRedpath@churchofscotland.org.uk]	(Mbl) 07713 919442
Searle, David C. MA DipTh	1965	2003	(Warden: Rutherford House)	Stonefall Lodge, 30 Abbey Lane, Grange, Errol PH2 7GB [E-mail: dcs@davidsearle.plus.com]	01821 641004
Simpson, James A. BSc BD STM DD	1960	2000	(Dornoch Cathedral)	'Dornoch', Perth Road, Bankfoot, Perth PH1 4ED [E-mail: ja@simpsondornoch.co.uk]	01738 787710
Sloan, Robert P. MA BD	1968	2007	(Braemar and Crathie)	1 Broomhill Avenue, Perth PH1 1EN [E-mail: sloan12@virginmedia.com]	01738 443904
Souter, David I. BD	1996	2015	(Perth: Kinnoull)	Duncairn, 2 Gowrie Farm, Perth PH1 4PP [E-mail: d.souter@blueyonder.co.uk]	
Stenhouse, W. Duncan MA BD	1989	2006	(Dunbarney and Forgandenny)	32 Sandport Gait, Kinross KY13 8FB	01577 866992
Stewart, Anne E. BD CertMin	1998		Prison Chaplain	35 Rose Crescent, Perth PH1 1NT [E-mail: anne.stewart2@sps.pnn.gov.uk]	01738 624167
Stewart, Gordon G. MA	1961	2000	(Perth: St Leonard's-in-the-Fields and Trinity)	'Balnoe', South Street, Rattray, Blairgowrie PH10 7BZ	01250 870626
Stewart, Robin J. MA BD STM	1959	1995	(Orwell with Portmoak)	'Oakbrae', Perth Road, Murthly, Perth PH1 4HF	01738 710220
Thomson, J. Bruce MA BD	1972	2009	(Scone: Old)	47 Elm Street, Errol, Perth PH2 7SQ [E-mail: RevBruceThomson@aol.com]	01821 641039 (Mbl) 07850 846404
Thomson, Peter D. MA BD	1968	2004	(Comrie with Dundurn)	34 Queen Street, Perth PH2 0EJ [E-mail: peterthomson208@btinternet.com]	01738 622418
Wallace, Catherine PGDipC DCS			Deacon	21 Durley Dene Crescent, Bridge of Earn PH2 9RD [E-mail: samesky2407@aol.com]	01738 621709
Wallace, James K. MA BD STM	1988	2015	Scotus Tours	21 Durley Dene Crescent, Bridge of Earn PH2 9RD [E-mail: jkwministry@hotmail.com]	01738 621709
Wylie, Jonathan BSc BD MTh	2000	2015	Chaplain	Strathallan School, Forgandenny, Perth PH2 9EG [E-mail: chaplain@strathallan.co.uk]	01738 815098

PERTH ADDRESSES

Craigie	Abbot Street	Letham St Mark's	Rannoch Road	St John's	St John's Street
Kinnoull	Dundee Rd near Queen's Bridge	Moncreiffe	Glenbruar Crescent	St Leonard's-in-the-Fields	Marshall Place
		North	Mill Street near Kinnoull Street	St Matthew's	Tay Street
		Riverside	Bute Drive		

(29) DUNDEE

Meets at Dundee: The Steeple, Nethergate, on the second Wednesday of February, March, May, September, November and December, and on the fourth Wednesday of June.

Clerk:	REV. JAMES L. WILSON BD CPS	[E-mail: dundee@churchofscotland.org.uk]	
Depute Clerk:	MR COLIN D. WILSON	[E-mail: cd.wilson663@tiscali.co.uk]	07885 618659 (Mobile) 01382 774059
Presbytery Office:		Whitfield Parish Church, Haddington Crescent, Dundee DD4 0NA	01382 503012

Abernyte linked with Inchture and Kinnaird linked with Longforgan (H)
Marjory A. MacLean LLB BD PhD   1991   2011   The Manse, Longforgan, Dundee DD2 5HB   01382 360238
[E-mail: MMaclean@churchofscotland.org.uk]

Auchterhouse (H) linked with Monikie and Newbigging and Murroes and Tealing (H)
Vacant

Dundee: Balgay (H)
Vacant   150 City Road, Dundee DD2 2PW   01382 669600

Dundee: Barnhill St Margaret's (H) (01382 737294) (E-mail: church.office@btconnect.com)
Vacant   2 St Margaret's Lane, Barnhill, Dundee DD5 2PQ   01382 779278

Dundee: Broughty Ferry New Kirk (H)
Catherine E.E. Collins (Mrs) MA BD   1993   2006   New Kirk Manse, 25 Ballinard Gardens, Broughty Ferry, Dundee DD5 1BZ   01382 778874
[E-mail: CCollins@churchofscotland.org.uk]

Dundee: Broughty Ferry St James' (H)
Vacant   2 Ferry Road, Monifieth, Dundee DD5 4NT   01382 534468

Dundee: Broughty Ferry St Luke's and Queen Street (01382 732094)
C. Graham D. Taylor BSc BD FIAB   2001   22 Albert Road, Broughty Ferry, Dundee DD5 1AZ   01382 779212
[E-mail: CTaylor@churchofscotland.org.uk]

Dundee: Broughty Ferry St Stephen's and West (H) linked with Dundee: Dundee (St Mary's) (H) (01382 226271)
Keith F. Hall MA BD   1980   1994   33 Strathern Road, West Ferry, Dundee DD5 1PP   01382 778808
[E-mail: KHall@churchofscotland.org.uk]

Dundee: Camperdown (H) (01382 623958)
Vacant
Camperdown Manse, Myrekirk Road, Dundee DD2 4SF

Dundee: Chalmers-Ardler (H)
Kenneth D. Stott MA BD
1989   1997
The Manse, Turnberry Avenue, Dundee DD2 3TP
[E-mail: KStott@churchofscotland.org.uk]
01382 827439

Dundee: Coldside
Anthony P. Thornthwaite MTh
1995   2011
9 Abercorn Street, Dundee DD4 7HY
[E-mail: AThornthwaite@churchofscotland.org.uk]
01382 458314

Dundee: Craigiebank (H) (01382 731173) linked with Dundee: Douglas and Mid Craigie
Edith F. McMillan (Mrs) MA BD
1981   1999
19 Americanmuir Road, Dundee DD3 9AA
[E-mail: EMcMillan@churchofscotland.org.uk]
01382 812423

Dundee: Douglas and Mid Craigie See Dundee: Craigiebank

Dundee: Downfield Mains (H) (01382 810624/812166)
Nathan S. McConnell BS MA ThM
2005   2016
9 Elgin Street, Dundee DD3 8NL
[E-mail: NMcConnell@churchofscotland.org.uk]
01382 690196

Dundee: Dundee (St Mary's) See Dundee: Broughty Ferry St Stephen's and West

Dundee: Fintry Parish Church
Colin M. Brough BSc BD
1998   2002
4 Clive Street, Dundee DD4 7AW
[E-mail: CBrough@churchofscotland.org.uk]
01382 458629

Dundee: Lochee (H)
Vacant
Willie Strachan MBA DipY&C
(Ordained Local Minister)
2013
32 Clayhills Drive, Dundee DD2 1SX
Ladywell House, Lucky Slap, Monikie, Dundee DD5 3QG
[E-mail: WStrachan@churchofscotland.org.uk]
01382 561989
01382 370286

Dundee: Logie and St John's Cross (H) (01382 668700)
David T. Gray BArch BD
2010   2014
7 Hyndford Street, Dundee DD2 1HQ
[E-mail: DGray@churchofscotland.org.uk]
01382 668853

Charge and Minister	Ordained/Inducted	Address	Telephone
Dundee: Meadowside St Paul's (H) (01382 225420) Vacant		36 Blackness Avenue, Dundee DD2 1HH	01382 668828
Dundee: Menzieshill Robert Mallinson BD	2010	The Manse, Charleston Drive, Dundee DD2 4ED [E-mail: RMallinson@churchofscotland.org.uk]	01382 667446 07595 249089 (Mbl)
Dundee: St Andrew's (H) (01382 224860) Vacant		39 Tullideph Road, Dundee DD2 2JD	01382 660152
Dundee: St David's High Kirk (H) Vacant		6 Adelaide Place, Dundee DD3 6LF	01382 322955
Dundee: The Steeple (H) (01382 200031) Robert A. Calvert BSc BD DMin	1983 2014	128 Arbroath Road, Dundee DD4 7HR [E-mail: RCalvert@churchofscotland.org.uk]	01382 522837 07532 029343 (Mbl)
Dundee: Stobswell (H) (01382 461397) William McLaren MA BD	1990 2007	23 Shamrock Street, Dundee DD4 7AH [E-mail: WMcLaren@churchofscotland.org.uk]	01382 459119
Dundee: Strathmartine (H) (01382 825817) Stewart McMillan BD	1983 1990	19 Americanmuir Road, Dundee DD3 9AA [E-mail: SMcMillan@churchofscotland.org.uk]	01382 812423
Dundee: Trinity (H) Vacant		65 Clepington Road, Dundee DD4 7BQ	01382 458764
Dundee: West Vacant			
Dundee: Whitfield (H) (01382 503012) James L. Wilson BD CPS	1986 2001	53 Old Craigie Road, Dundee DD4 7JD [E-mail: James.Wilson@churchofscotland.org.uk]	01382 459249

Fowlis and Liff linked with Lundie and Muirhead (H)

Donna M. Hays (Mrs) MTheol DipEd DipTMHA	2004		149 Coupar Angus Road, Muirhead of Liff, Dundee DD2 5QN [E-mail: DHays@churchofscotland.org.uk]	01382 580210

Inchture and Kinnaird See Abernyte

Invergowrie (H)

Robert J. Ramsay LLB NP BD	1986	1997	2 Boniface Place, Invergowrie, Dundee DD2 5DW [E-mail: RRamsay@churchofscotland.org.uk]	01382 561118

Longforgan See Abernyte
Lundie and Muirhead See Fowlis and Liff

Monifieth (H)

Vacant			8 Church Street, Monifieth, Dundee DD5 4JP	01382 532607

Monikie and Newbigging and Murroes and Tealing See Auchterhouse

Allan, Jean (Mrs) DCS			(Deacon) — 12C Hindmarsh Avenue, Dundee DD3 7LW [E-mail: jeannieallan45@googlemail.com]	01382 827299 (Mbl) 07709 959474
Barrett, Leslie M. BD FRICS	1991	2014	(Chaplain: University of Abertay, Dundee) — Dunelm Cottage, Logie, Cupar KY15 4SJ [E-mail: lesliembarrett@btinternet.com]	01334 870396
Campbell, Gordon MA BD CDipAF DipHSM CMgr MCMI MIHM AssocCIPD AFRIN ARSGS FRGS FSAScot	2001		Auxiliary Minister: Chaplain: University of Dundee — 2 Falkland Place, Kingoodie, Invergowrie, Dundee DD2 5DY [E-mail: g.a.campbell@dundee.ac.uk]	01382 561383
Collins, David A. BSc BD	1993	2016	(Auchterhouse with Monikie and Newbigging and Murroes and Tealing) — New Kirk Manse, 25 Ballinard Gardens, Broughty Ferry, Dundee DD5 1BZ [E-mail: revdacollins@btinternet.com]	01382 778874
Craik, Sheila (Mrs) BD	1989	2001	(Dundee: Camperdown) — 35 Haldane Terrace, Dundee DD3 0HT	01382 802078
Cramb, Erik M. LTh	1973	1989	(Industrial Mission Organiser) — Flat 35, Braehead, Methven Walk, Dundee DD2 3FJ [E-mail: erikcramb@aol.com]	01382 526196
Donald, Robert M. LTh BA	1969	2005	(Kilmodan and Colintraive) — 2 Blacklaw Drive, Birkhill, Dundee DD2 5RJ [E-mail: robandmoiradorald@yahoo.co.uk]	01382 581337
Douglas, Fiona C. MBE MA BD PhD	1989	1997	Chaplain: University of Dundee — 10 Springfield, Dundee DD1 4JE [E-mail: f.c.douglas@dundee.ac.uk]	01382 384157

Name		Ord.	Charge/Role	Address	Tel
Fraser, Donald W.	MA	1958 2010	(Monifieth)	1 Blake Avenue, Broughty Ferry, Dundee DD5 3LH [E-mail: fraserdonald37@yahoo.co.uk]	01382 477491 (Mbl) 07531 863316
Galbraith, W. James L.	BSc BD MICE	1973 1996	(Kilchrenan and Dalavich with Muckairn)	586 Brook Street, Broughty Ferry, Dundee DD5 2EA	01382 732110
Greaves, Andrew T.	BD	1985 2016	(Dundee: West)	Wards of Keithock, Brechin DD9 7PZ	01356 624479
Ingram, J.R.		1954 1978	(Chaplain: RAF)	48 Marlee Road, Broughty Ferry, Dundee DD5 3EX	01382 736400
Jamieson, David B.	MA BD STM	1974 2011	(Monifieth)	8A Albert Street, Monifieth, Dundee DD5 4JS	01382 532772
Kay, Elizabeth (Miss)	DipYCS	1993 2007	(Auxiliary Minister)	1 Kintail Walk, Inchture, Perth PH14 9RY [E-mail: ekay007@btinternet.com]	01828 686029
Laidlaw, John J.	MA	1964 1973	(Adviser in Religious Education)	14 Dalhousie Road, Barnhill, Dundee DD5 2SQ	01382 477458
Laing, David J.H.	BD DPS	1976 2014	(Dundee: Trinity)	18 Kerrington Crescent, Barnhill, Dundee DD5 2TN [E-mail: david.laing@live.co.uk]	01382 739586
Lillie, Fiona L. (Mrs)	BA BD MLitt	1995 2017	(Glasgow: St John's Renfield)	4 McVicars Lane, Dundee DD1 4LH [E-mail:fionalillie@btinternet.com]	01382 229082
McLeod, David C.	BSc MEng BD	1969 2001	(Dundee: Fairmuir)	6 Carseview Gardens, Dundee DD2 1NE	01382 641371
McMillan, Charles D.	LTh	1979 2004	(Elgin: High)	11 Troon Terrace, The Orchard, Ardler, Dundee DD2 3FX	01382 831358
Mair, Michael V.A.	MA BD	1967 2007	(Craigiebank with Dundee: Douglas and Mid Craigie)	48 Panmure Street, Monifieth DD5 4EH [E-mail: mvamair@gmail.com]	01382 530538
Martin, Janie (Miss)	DCS		(Deacon)	16 Wentworth Road, Ardler, Dundee DD2 8SD [E-mail: janimar@aol.com]	01382 813786
Mitchell, Jack	MA BD CTh	1987 1996	(Dundee: Menzieshill)	29 Carrick Gardens, Ayr KA7 2RT	
Paton, Marion J. (Miss)	MA BMus BD	1991 2017	(Dundee: St David's High Kirk)	18 Winram Place, St Andrews KY16 8XH [E-mail: sdhkrev@googlemail.com]	01334 208743
Powrie, James E.	LTh	1969 1995	(Dundee: Chalmers-Ardler)	3 Kirktonhill Road, Kirriemuir DD8 4HU	01575 572503
Rae, Robert	LTh	1968 1983	(Chaplain: Dundee Acute Hospitals)	14 Nedderton View, Liff, Dundee DD3 5RU	01382 581790
Reid, R. Gordon	BSc BD MIET	1993 2010	(Carriden)	6 Bayview Place, Monifieth, Dundee DD5 4TN [E-mail: GordonReid@aol.com]	01382 520519 (Mbl) 07952 349884
Robertson, James H.	BSc BD	1975 2014	(Culloden: The Barn)	'Far End', 35 Mains Terrace, Dundee DD4 7BZ [E-mail: jimrob838@gmail.com]	01382 522773 (Mbl) 07595 465838
Robson, George K.	LTh DPS BA	1983 2011	(Dundee: Balgay)	11 Ceres Crescent, Broughty Ferry, Dundee DD5 3JN [E-mail: gkrobson@virginmedia.com]	01382 901212
Rose, Lewis (Mr)	DCS		(Deacon)	6 Gauldie Crescent, Dundee DD3 0RR [E-mail: lewis_rose48@yahoo.co.uk]	01382 816580 (Mbl) 07899 790466
Scott, James	MA BD	1973 2010	(Drumoak-Durris)	3 Blake Place, Broughty Ferry, Dundee DD5 3LQ [E-mail: jimscott73@yahoo.co.uk]	01382 739595
Scoular, Stanley		1963 2000	(Rosyth)	31 Duns Crescent, Dundee DD4 0RY	01382 501653
Strickland, Alexander	LTh	1971 2005	(Dairsie with Kemback with Strathkinness)	12 Ballumbie Braes, Dundee DD4 0UN	01382 685539
Taylor Caroline (Mrs)		1995 2014	(Leuchars: St Athernase)	The Old Dairy, 15 Forthill Road, Broughty Ferry, Dundee DD5 3DH [E-mail: caro234@btinternet.com]	01382 770198

DUNDEE ADDRESSES

Balgay	200 Lochee Road	Coldside	Isla Street x Main Street	Meadowside St Paul's	114 Nethergate
Barnhill St Margaret's	10 Invermark Terrace	Craigiebank	Craigie Avenue at Greendykes Road	Menzieshill	Charleston Drive, Menzieshill
Broughty Ferry		Douglas and Mid Craigie	Balbeggie Place/ Longtown Terrace	St Andrew's	2 King Street
New Kirk	370 Queen Street	Downfield Mains	Haldane Street off Strathmartine Road	St David's High Kirk	119A Kinghorne Road
St James'	5 Fort Street	Dundee (St Mary's)	Nethergate	Steeple	Nethergate
St Luke's and Queen Street	5 West Queen Street	Fintry	Fintry Road x Fintry Drive	Stobswell	170 Albert Street
St Stephen's and West	96 Dundee Road	Lochee	191 High Street, Lochee	Strathmartine	507 Strathmartine Road
Camperdown	22 Brownhill Road	Logie and St John's Cross	Shaftesbury Rd x Blackness Ave	Trinity	73 Crescent Street
Chalmers-Ardler	Turnberry Avenue			West	130 Perth Road
				Whitfield	Haddington Crescent

(30) ANGUS

Meets at Forfar in St Margaret's Church Hall on the first Tuesday of February, March, May, September, November and December, and on the last Tuesday of June.

Clerk: **REV IAN A. McLEAN BSc BD DMin** [E-mail: angus@churchofscotland.org.uk]
Depute Clerk: **RODERICK J. GRAHAME BD CPS DMin** [E-mail:RGrahame@churchofscotland.org.uk]
Presbytery Office: **St Margaret's Church, West High Street, Forfar DD8 1BJ** **01307 464224**

Aberlemno (H) linked with Guthrie and Rescobie
Brian Ramsay BD DPS MLitt   1980   1984   The Manse, Guthrie, Forfar DD8 2TP   01241 828243
[E-mail: BRamsay@churchofscotland.org.uk]

Arbirlot linked with Carmyllie
Brian Dingwall BTh CQSW   1999   2016   The Manse, Arbirlot, Arbroath DD11 2NX   01241 879800
[E-mail: brian.d12@btinternet.com]   07906 656847 (Mbl)

Arbroath: Knox's (H) linked with Arbroath: St Vigeans (H)
Vacant   The Manse, St Vigeans, Arbroath DD11 4RF   01241 873206

Arbroath: Old and Abbey (H) (Church office: 01241 877068)
Dolly Purnell BD   2003   2014   51 Cliffburn Road, Arbroath DD11 5BA   01241 872196 (Tel/Fax)
[E-mail: DPurnell@churchofscotland.org.uk]

Arbroath: St Andrew's (H) (E-mail: office@arbroathstandrews.org.uk)
W. Martin Fair BA BD DMin — 1992 — 92 Grampian Gardens, Arbroath DD11 4AQ [E-mail: MFair@churchofscotland.org.uk] — 01241 873238 (Tel/Fax)

Arbroath: St Vigeans See Arbroath: Knox's

Arbroath: West Kirk (H)
Alasdair G. Graham BD DipMin — 1981 1986 — 1 Charles Avenue, Arbroath DD11 2EY [E-mail: AGraham@churchofscotland.org.uk] — 01241 872244

Barry linked with Carnoustie
Michael S. Goss BD DPS — 1991 2003 — 44 Terrace Road, Carnoustie DD7 7AR [E-mail: MGoss@churchofscotland.org.uk] — 01241 410194 / 07787 141567 (Mbl)
Dougal Edwards BTh (Ordained Local Minister) — 2013 — 25 Mackenzie Street, Carnoustie DD7 6HD [E-mail: DEdwards@churchofscotland.org.uk] — 01241 852666

Brechin: Cathedral (H) (Cathedral office: 01356 629360) (Website: www.brechincathedral.org.uk)
Roderick J. Grahame BD CPS DMin — 1991 2010 — Chanonry Wynd, Brechin DD9 6JS [E-mail: RGrahame@churchofscotland.org.uk] — 01356 624980

Brechin: Gardner Memorial (H) linked with Farnell
Jane M. Blackley MA BD — 2009 — 15 Caldhame Gardens, Brechin DD9 7JJ [E-mail: JBlackley@churchofscotland.org.uk] — 01356 622034

Carmyllie See Arbirlot
Carnoustie See Barry

Carnoustie: Panbride (H)
Vacant — 8 Arbroath Road, Carnoustie DD7 6BL — 01241 854478 (Tel) / 01241 855088 (Fax)

Colliston linked with Friockheim Kinnell linked with Inverkeilor and Lunan (H)
Peter A. Phillips BA — 1995 2004 — The Manse, Inverkeilor, Arbroath DD11 5SA [E-mail: PPhillips@churchofscotland.org.uk] — 01241 830464

Dun and Hillside
Fiona C. Bullock (Mrs) MA LLB BD — 2014 — 4 Manse Road, Hillside, Montrose DD10 9FB [E-mail: FBullock@churchofscotland.org.uk] — 01674 830288

Dunnichen, Letham and Kirkden
Dale London BTh FSAScot   2011   2013   7 Braehead Road, Letham, Forfar DD8 2PG   01307 818025
[E-mail: DLondon@churchofscotland.org.uk]

Eassie, Nevay and Newtyle
Carleen J. Robertson (Miss) BD   1992   2 Kirkton Road, Newtyle, Blairgowrie PH12 8TS   01828 650461
[E-mail: CRobertson@churchofscotland.org.uk]

Edzell Lethnot Glenesk (H) linked with Fern Careston Menmuir
A.S. Wayne Pearce MA PhD   2002   2017   19 Lethnot Road, Edzell, Brechin DD9 7TG   01356 648117
[E-mail: ASWaynePearce@churchofscotland.org.uk]

Farnell See Brechin: Gardner Memorial
Fern Careston Menmuir See Edzell Lethnot Glenesk

Forfar: East and Old (H)
Barbara Ann Sweetin BD   2011   The Manse, Lour Road, Forfar DD8 2BB   01307 248228
[E-mail: BSweetin@churchofscotland.org.uk]

Forfar: Lowson Memorial (H)
Karen Fenwick PhD MPhil BSc BD   2006   1 Jamieson Street, Forfar DD8 2HY   01307 468585
[E-mail: KFenwick@churchofscotland.org.uk]

Forfar: St Margaret's (H) (Church office: 01307 464224)
Margaret J. Hunt (Mrs) MA BD   2014   St Margaret's Manse, 15 Potters Park Crescent, Forfar DD8 1HH   01307 462044
[E-mail: MHunt@churchofscotland.org.uk]

Friockheim Kinnell See Colliston

Glamis (H), Inverarity and Kinnettles
Guardianship of the Presbytery   (See Eassie, Nevay and Newtyle)

Guthrie and Rescobie See Aberlemno
Inverkeilor and Lunan See Colliston

Kirriemuir: St Andrew's (H) linked with Oathlaw Tannadice
2012

John K. Orr BD MTh	26 Quarry Park, Kirriemuir DD8 4DR [E-mail: JOrr@churchofscotland.org.uk]	01575 572610

Montrose: Old and St Andrew's

Ian A. McLean BSc BD DMin	1981	2008	2 Rosehill Road, Montrose DD10 8ST [E-mail: IMcLean@churchofscotland.org.uk]	01674 672447

Montrose: South and Ferryden

Geoffrey Redmayne BSc BD MPhil	2000	2016	Inchbrayock Manse, Usan, Montrose DD10 9SD [E-mail: GRedmayne@churchofscotland.org.uk]	01674 675634

Oathlaw Tannadice See Kirriemuir: St Andrew's

The Glens and Kirriemuir: Old (H) (Church office: 01575 572819) (Website: www.gkopc.co.uk)
Guardianship of the Presbytery

Linda Stevens (Mrs) BSc BD PgDip (Team Minister)	2006	17 North Latch Road, Brechin DD9 6LE [E-mail: LStevens@churchofscotland.org.uk]	01356 623415 07801 192730 (Mbl)

The Isla Parishes

Vacant	Balduff House, Kilry, Blairgowrie PH11 8HS	01575 560268

Butters, David	1964	1998	(Turriff: St Ninian's and Forglen)	68A Millgate, Friockheim, Arbroath DD11 4TN	01241 828030
Drysdale, James P.R.	1967	1999	(Brechin: Gardner Memorial)	51 Airlie Street, Brechin DD9 6JX	01356 625201
Duncan, Robert F. MTheol	1986	2001	(Lochgelly: St Andrew's)	25 Rowan Avenue, Kirriemuir DD8 4TB	01575 573973
Gray, Ian	2013		(OLM) Children and Family Worker, Arbroath: Knox's with St Vigeans	The Mallards, 15 Rossie Island Road, Montrose DD10 9NH [E-mail: IGray@churchofscotland.org.uk]	01674 677126
Gough, Ian G. MA BD MTh DMin	1974	2009	(Arbroath: Knox's with Arbroath: St Vigeans)	23 Keptie Road, Arbroath DD11 3ED [E-mail: iangough@btinternet.com]	(Mbl) 07891 838379
Hastie, George I. MA BD	1971	2009	(Mearns Coastal)	23 Borrowfield Crescent, Montrose DD10 9BR	01674 672290
Hodge, William N.T.	1966	1995	(Longside)	19 Craigengar Park, Craigshill, Livingston EH54 5NY	01506 435813
Milton, Eric G. RD	1963	1994	(Blairdaff)	16 Bruce Court, Links Parade, Carnoustie DD7 7JE	01241 854928
Morrice, Alastair M. MA BD	1968	2002	(Rutherglen: Stonelaw)	5 Brechin Road, Kirriemuir DD8 4BX [E-mail: ambishkek@swissmail.org]	01575 574102
Norrie, Graham MA BD	1967	2007	(Forfar: East and Old)	'Novar', 14A Wyllie Street, Forfar DD8 3DN [E-mail: grahamnorrie@hotmail.com]	01307 468152

Reid, Albert B. BD BSc	1966 2001	(Ardler, Kettins and Meigle)	1 Mary Countess Way, Glamis, Forfar DD8 1RF [E-mail: abreid@btinternet.com]	01307 840213
Robertson, George R. LTh	1985 2004	(Udny and Pitmedden)	3 Slateford Gardens, Edzell, Brechin DD9 7SX [E-mail: geomag.robertson@btinternet.com]	01356 647322
Smith, Hamish G.	1965 1993	(Auchterless with Rothienorman)	11A Guthrie Street, Letham, Forfar DD8 2PS	01307 818973
Thomas, Martyn R.H. CEng MIStructE	1987 2002	(Fowlis and Liff with Lundie and Muirhead of Liff)	14 Kirkgait, Letham, Forfar DD8 2XQ [E-mail: martyn.thomas@mypostoffice.co.uk]	01307 818084
Thomas, Shirley A. (Mrs) DipSocSci AMIA (Aux)	2000 2006	(Auxiliary Minister)	14 Kirkgait, Letham, Forfar DD8 2XQ [E-mail: martyn.thomas@mypostoffice.co.uk]	01307 818084
Watt, Alan G.N. MTh CQSW DipCommEd	1996 2009	(Edzell Lethnot Glenesk with Fern Careston Menmuir)	16 Thornton Place, Forfar DD8 1HG [E-mail: watt455@btinternet.com]	01307 461686
Webster, Allan F. MA BD	1978 2013	(Workplace Chaplain)	42 McCulloch Drive, Forfar DD8 2EB [E-mail: allanfwebster@aol.com]	01307 464252 (Mbl) 07546 276725
Youngson, Peter	1961 1996	(Kirriemuir: St Andrew's)	'Coreen', Woodside, Northmuir, Kirriemuir DD8 4PG	01575 572832

ANGUS ADDRESSES

Arbroath:	Knox's	Howard Street
	Old and Abbey	West Abbey Street
	St Andrew's	Hamilton Green
	West Kirk	Keptie Street
Brechin:	Cathedral	Bishops Close
	Gardner Memorial	South Esk Street
Carnoustie:		Dundee Street
	Panbride	Arbroath Road
Forfar:	East and Old	East High Street
	Lowson Memorial	Jamieson Street
	St Margaret's	West High Street
Kirriemuir:	Old	High Street
	St Andrew's	Glamis Road
Montrose:	Melville South	Castle Street
	Old and St Andrew's	High Street

(31) ABERDEEN

Meets on the first Tuesday of February, March, May, September, October, November and December, and on the fourth Tuesday of June. The venue varies.

Clerk:	REV. JOHN A. FERGUSON BD DipMin DMin	
Administrator:	MRS CHERYL MARWICK-WATT BA	
Treasurer:	MR ALAN MORRISON	
Presbytery Office:	Mastrick Church, Greenfern Road, Aberdeen AB16 6TR [E-mail: aberdeen@churchofscotland.org.uk]	01224 698119

Aberdeen: Bridge of Don Oldmachar (01224 709299) (Website: www.oldmacharchurch.org)

David J. Stewart BD MTh DipMin	2000 2012	60 Newburgh Circle, Aberdeen AB22 8QZ [E-mail: DStewart@churchofscotland.org.uk]	01224 823283

Aberdeen: Craigiebuckler (H) (01224 315649) (Website: www.craigiebuckler.org)
Kenneth L. Petrie MA BD   1984   1999   185 Springfield Road, Aberdeen AB15 8AA   01224 315125
[E-mail: KPetrie@churchofscotland.org.uk]

Aberdeen: Ferryhill (H) (01224 213093) (Website: www.ferryhillparishchurch.org)
J. Peter N. Johnston BSc BD   2001   2013   54 Polmuir Road, Aberdeen AB11 7RT   01224 949192
[E-mail: PJohnston@churchofscotland.org.uk]

Aberdeen: Garthdee (H)
Vacant   53 Springfield Avenue, Aberdeen AB15 8JJ   01224 312706

Aberdeen: High Hilton (H) (01224 494717) (Website: www.highhilton.zyberweb.com)
G. Hutton B. Steel MA BD   1982   2013   24 Rosehill Drive, Aberdeen AB24 4JJ   01224 493552
[E-mail: Hutton.Steel@churchofscotland.org.uk]

Aberdeen: Holburn West (H) (01224 571120) (Website: www.holburnwestchurch.org.uk)
Duncan C. Eddie MA BD   1992   1999   31 Cranford Road, Aberdeen AB10 7NJ   01224 325873
[E-mail: DEddie@churchofscotland.org.uk]

Aberdeen: Mannofield (H) (01224 310087) (E-mail: office@mannofieldchurch.org.uk) (Website: www.mannofieldchurch.org.uk)
Keith T. Blackwood BD DipMin   1997   2007   21 Forest Avenue, Aberdeen AB15 4TU   01224 315748
[E-mail: KBlackwood@churchofscotland.org.uk]
Getliffe, Dot (Mrs) DCS BA BD DipEd   Mannofield Parish Church, Gt Western Road, Aberdeen AB10 6UZ   01224 310087
[E-mail: DGetliffe@churchofscotland.org.uk]

Aberdeen: Mastrick (H) (01224 694121)
Susan J. Sutherland (Mrs) BD   2009   8 Corse Wynd, Kingswells, Aberdeen AB15 8TP   01224 279562
[E-mail: SSutherland@churchofscotland.org.uk]

Aberdeen: Middlefield (H)
Vacant

Aberdeen: Midstocket (01224 319519) (Website: www.midstocketchurch.org.uk)
Sarah E.C. Nicol (Mrs) BSc BD MTh   1985   2013   182 Midstocket Road, Aberdeen AB15 5HS   01224 561358
[E-mail: SNicol@churchofscotland.org.uk]

Aberdeen: Northfield (01224 692332)
Scott C. Guy BD   1989   1998   28 Byron Crescent, Aberdeen AB16 7EX   01224 692332
                                                                   [E-mail: SGuy@churchofscotland.org.uk]

Aberdeen: Queen Street (01224 643567) (Website: www.queenstreetchurch.org.uk)
Vacant   51 Osborne Place, Aberdeen AB25 2BX   01224 646429

Aberdeen: Queen's Cross (H) (01224 644742) (Website: www.queenscrosschurch.org.uk)
Scott M. Rennie MA BD STM   1999   2009   1 St Swithin Street, Aberdeen AB10 6XH   01224 322549
                                                                   [E-mail: SRennie@churchofscotland.org.uk]

Aberdeen: Rubislaw (H) (01224 645477) (Website: rubislawparishchurchofscotland.org.uk)
Robert L. Smith BS MTh PhD   2000   2013   45 Rubislaw Den South, Aberdeen AB15 4BD   01224 314773
                                                                   [E-mail: RSmith@churchofscotland.org.uk]

Aberdeen: Ruthrieston West (Website: www.ruthriestonwestchurch.org.uk)
Benjamin D.W. Byun BS MDiv MTh PhD   1992   2008   53 Springfield Avenue, Aberdeen AB15 8JJ   01224 312706
                                                                   [E-mail: BByun@churchofscotland.org.uk]

Aberdeen: St Columba's Bridge of Don (H) (01224 825653) (Website: http://stcolumbaschurch.org.uk)
Louis Kinsey BD DipMin TD   1991   151 Jesmond Avenue, Aberdeen AB22 8UG   01224 705337
                                                                   [E-mail: LKinsey@churchofscotland.org.uk]

Aberdeen: St George's Tillydrone (H) (01224 482204) (Website: http://tillydrone.church)
James J.C.M. Weir BD   1991   2003   127 Clifton Road, Aberdeen AB24 4RH   01224 483976
                                                                   [E-mail: JWeir@churchofscotland.org.uk]

Aberdeen: St John's Church for Deaf People
Mary Whittaker   2011   11 Templand Road, Lhanbryde, Elgin IV30 8BR   (text only) (Mbl) 07810 420106
   (Auxiliary Minister)
or contact St Mark's, below.

Aberdeen: St Machar's Cathedral (H) (01224 485988) (Website: www.stmachar.com)
Barry W. Dunsmore MA BD   1982   2015   39 Woodstock Road, Aberdeen AB15 5EX   01224 314596
                                                                   [E-mail: BDunsmore@churchofscotland.org.uk]

Aberdeen: St Mark's (H) (01224 640672) (Website: www.stmarksaberdeen.org.uk)
Vacant
65 Mile-end Avenue, Aberdeen AB15 5PT

01224 641578

Aberdeen: St Mary's (H) (01224 487227)
Elsie J. Fortune (Mrs) BSc BD   2003
456 King Street, Aberdeen AB24 3DE
[E-mail: EFortune@churchofscotland.org.uk]

01224 633778

Aberdeen: St Nicholas Kincorth, South of (Website: www.southstnicholas.org.uk)
Edward C. McKenna BD DPS   1989   2002
The Manse, Kincorth Circle, Aberdeen AB12 5NX
[E-mail: EMcKenna@churchofscotland.org.uk]

01224 872820

Aberdeen: St Nicholas Uniting, Kirk of (H) (01224 643494) (Website: www.kirk-of-st-nicholas.org.uk)
B. Stephen C. Taylor BA BBS MA MDiv   1984   2005
12 Louisville Avenue, Aberdeen AB15 4TX
[E-mail: BSCTaylor@churchofscotland.org.uk]
St Nicholas Uniting is a Local Ecumenical Project shared with the United Reformed Church

01224 314318
01224 649242 (Fax)

Aberdeen: St Stephen's (H) (01224 624443) (Website: www.st-stephens.co.uk)
Maggie Whyte BD   2010
6 Belvidere Street, Aberdeen AB25 2QS
[E-mail: Maggie.Whyte@churchofscotland.org.uk]

01224 635694

Aberdeen: South Holburn (H) (01224 211730) (Website: www.southholburn.org)
Vacant
54 Woodstock Road, Aberdeen AB15 5JF

01224 315042

Aberdeen: Stockethill (Website: www.stockethillchurch.org.uk)
Ian M. Aitken MA BD   1999
52 Ashgrove Road West, Aberdeen AB16 5EE
[E-mail: IAitken@churchofscotland.org.uk]

01224 686929

Aberdeen: Summerhill (H) (Website: www.summerhillchurch.org.uk)
Michael R.R. Shewan MA BD CPS   1985   2010
36 Stronsay Drive, Aberdeen AB15 6JL
[E-mail: MShewan@churchofscotland.org.uk]

01224 324669

Aberdeen: Torry St Fittick's (H) (01224 899183) (Website: www.torrychurch.org.uk)
Edmond Gatima BEng BD MSc MPhil PhD   2013
11 Devanha Gardens East, Aberdeen AB11 7UN
[E-mail: EGatima@churchofscotland.org.uk]

01224 588245

Aberdeen: Woodside (H) (01224 277249) (Website: www.woodsidechurch.co.uk)
Markus Auffermann DipTheol   1999   2006   322 Clifton Road, Aberdeen AB24 4HQ   01224 484562
[E-mail: MAuffermann@churchofscotland.org.uk]

Bucksburn Stoneywood (H) (01224 712411) (Website: www.bucksburnstoneywoodchurch.com)
Nigel Parker BD MTh DMin   1994   23 Polo Park, Stoneywood, Aberdeen AB21 9JW   01224 712635
[E-mail: NParker@churchofscotland.org.uk]

Cults (H) (01224 869028) (Website: www.cultsparishchurch.co.uk)
Vacant   1 Cairnlee Terrace, Bieldside, Aberdeen AB15 9AE   01224 861692

Dyce (H) (01224 771295) (Website: www.dyceparishchurch.org.uk)
Manson C. Merchant BD CPS   1992   2008   100 Burnside Road, Dyce, Aberdeen AB21 7HA   01224 722380
[E-mail: MMerchant@churchofscotland.org.uk]

Kingswells (Website: www.kingswellschurch.com)
Alisa L. McDonald BA MDiv   2008   2013   Kingswells Manse, Lang Stracht, Aberdeen AB15 8PN   01224 740229
[E-mail: Alisa.McDonald@churchofscotland.org.uk]

Newhills (H) (Tel/Fax: 01224 716161)
Hugh M. Wallace MA BD   1980   2007   Newhills Manse, Bucksburn, Aberdeen AB21 9SS   01224 710318
[E-mail: HWallace@churchofscotland.org.uk]

Peterculter (H) (01224 735845) (Website: http://culterkirk.co.uk)
John A. Ferguson BD DipMin DMin   1988   1999   7 Howie Lane, Peterculter AB14 0LJ   01224 735041
[E-mail: JFerguson@churchofscotland.org.uk]

Craig, Gordon T. BD DipMin   1988   2012   Chaplain to UK Oil and Gas Industry   c/o Total E and P (UK) plc, Altens Industrial Estate, Crawpeel Road, Aberdeen AB12 3FG   01224 297532
[E-mail: gordon.craig@ukoilandgaschaplaincy.com]

Deans, Graham D.S. MA BD MTh MLitt DMin   1978   2017   (Aberdeen: Queen Street)   38 Sir Thomas Elder Way, Kirkcaldy KY2 6ZS   01592 641429
[E-mail: graham.deans@btopenworld.com]

Falconer, James B. BD   1982   1991   Hospital Chaplain   3 Brimmond Walk, Westhill AB32 6XH   01224 744621
Garden, Margaret J. (Miss) BD   1993   2009   (Cushnie and Tough)   26 Earns Heugh Circle, Cove Bay, Aberdeen AB12 3PY
[E-mail: revmjgarden@gmail.com]

Goldie, George D. ALCM   1953   1995   (Aberdeen: Greyfriars)   27 Broomhill Avenue, Aberdeen AB10 6JL   01224 322503
Gordon, Laurie Y.   1960   1995   (Aberdeen: John Knox)   1 Alder Drive, Portlethen, Aberdeen AB12 4WA   01224 782703

Grainger, Harvey L. LTh	1975	2004	(Kingswells)	13 St Ronan's Crescent, Peterculter, Aberdeen AB14 0RL [E-mail: harveygrainger@btinternet.com] — 01224 739824
Haddow, Angus H. BSc	1963	1999	(Methlick)	25 Lerwick Road, Aberdeen AB16 6RF — (Mbl) 07768 333216; 01224 696362
Hobson, Diane L. (Mrs) BA BD	2002	2017	(Aberdeen: St Mark's)	Buttercup Meadow, 5 Lower Westerland Barn, Marldon Village, Paignton TQ3 1RU [E-mail: DHobson@churchofscotland.org.uk] — (Mbl) 07850 962007
Hutchison, David S. BSc BD ThM	1991	1999	(Aberdeen: Torry St Fittick's)	The Den of Keithfield, Tarves, Ellon AB41 7NU — 01651 851501
Lundie, Ann V. (Miss) DCS			(Deacon)	20 Langdykes Drive, Cove, Aberdeen AB12 3HW [E-mail: ann.lundie@btopenworld.com] — 01224 898416
Maciver, Norman MA BD DMin	1976	2006	(Newhills)	4 Mundi Crescent, Newmachar, Aberdeen AB21 0LY [E-mail: norirene@aol.com] — 01651 869434
Main, Alan (Prof.) TD MA BD STM PhD DD	1963	2001	(University of Aberdeen)	Kirkfield, Barthol Chapel, Inverurie AB51 8TD [E-mail: amain@talktalk.net] — 01651 806773
Montgomerie, Jean B. (Miss) MA BD	1973	2005	(Forfar: St Margaret's)	12 St Ronan's Place, Peterculter, Aberdeen AB14 0QX [E-mail: revjeanb@tiscali.co.uk] — 01224 732350
Munro, Flora BD DMin	1993	2015	(Portlethen)	87 Gairn Terrace, Aberdeen AB10 6AY [E-mail: floramunro@aol.com] — (Mbl) 07762 966393
Phillippo, Michael MTh BSc BVetMed MRCVS	2003		(Auxiliary Minister)	25 Deeside Crescent, Aberdeen AB15 7PT [E-mail: phillippo@btinternet.com] — 01224 318317
Richardson, Thomas C. LTh ThB	1971	2004	(Cults: West)	19 Kinkell Road, Aberdeen AB15 8HR [E-mail: tomandpatrich@gmail.com] — 01224 315328
Rodgers, D. Mark BA BD MTh	1987	2003	Head of Spiritual Care, NHS Grampian	63 Cordiner Place, Hilton, Aberdeen AB24 4SB [E-mail: mrodgers@nhs.net] — 01224 379135
Sefton, Henry R. MA BD STM PhD	1957	1992	(University of Aberdeen)	25 Albury Place, Aberdeen AB11 6TQ — 01224 572305
Sheret, Brian S. MA BD DPhil	1982	2009	(Glasgow: Drumchapel Drumry St Mary's)	59 Airyhall Crescent, Aberdeen AB15 7QS — 01224 323032
Somevi, Joseph K. BSc MSc (Oxon) PhD MRICS MRTPI MIEMA CertCRS	2015		Ordained Local Minister	97 Ashwood Road, Bridge of Don, Aberdeen AB22 8QX [E-mail: JSomevi@churchofscotland.org.uk] — 01224 826362; (Mbl) 07886 533259
Stewart, James C. MA BD STM FSAScot	1960	2000	(Aberdeen: Kirk of St Nicholas)	54 Murray Terrace, Aberdeen AB11 7SB [E-mail: study@jascstewart.co.uk] — 01224 587071
Swan, David BVMS BD	2005		(Aberdeen: Cove)	250/3 Lanark Road, Edinburgh EH14 2LR [E-mail: davidswan97@gmail.com] — (Mbl) 07944 598988
Swinton, John (Prof.) BD PhD	1999		University of Aberdeen	51 Newburgh Circle, Bridge of Don, Aberdeen AB22 8XA [E-mail: j.swinton@abdn.ac.uk] — 01224 825637
Torrance, Iain R. (Prof.) TD DPhil DD DTheol LHD FRSE	1982	2012	(President: Princeton Theological Seminary)	25 The Causeway, Duddingston Village, Edinburgh EH15 3QA [E-mail: irt@ptsem.edu] — 0131-661 3092
Wilson, Thomas F. BD	1984	1996	Education	55 Allison Close, Cove, Aberdeen AB12 3WG — 01224 873501
Youngson, Elizabeth J.B. BD	1996	2015	(Aberdeen: Mastrick)	47 Corse Drive, The Links, Dubford, Aberdeen AB23 8LN [E-mail: elizabeth.youngson@btinternet.com] — (Mbl) 07788 294745

ABERDEEN ADDRESSES

Bridge of Don	Mastrick	Greenfern Road	St Machar's	The Chanonry
Oldmachar	Ashwood Park	Middlefield	Manor Avenue	St Mark's	Rosemount Viaduct
Craigiebuckler	Springfield Road	Midstocket	Mid Stocket Road	St Mary's	King Street
Cults	Quarry Road, Cults	New Stockethill		St Nicholas Kincorth,
Dyce	Victoria Street, Dyce	Northfield	Byron Crescent	South of	Kincorth Circle
Ferryhill	Fonthill Road x Polmuir Road	Peterculter	Craigton Crescent	St Nicholas Uniting,
Garthdee	Ramsay Gardens	Queen Street	Queen Street	Kirk of	Union Street
High Hilton	Hilton Drive	Queen's Cross	Albyn Place	St Stephen's	Powis Place
Holburn West	Great Western Road	Rubislaw	Queen's Gardens	South Holburn	Holburn Street
Kingswells	Old Skene Road, Kingswells	Ruthrieston West	Broomhill Road	Summerhill	Stronsay Drive
Mannofield	Great Western Road x Craigton Road	St Columba's	Braehead Way, Bridge of Don	Torry St Fittick's	Walker Road
		St George's	Hayton Road, Tillydrone	Woodside	Church Street, Woodside
		St John's for the Deaf	at St Mark's		

(32) KINCARDINE AND DEESIDE

Meets in various locations as arranged on the first Tuesday of September, October, November, December, March and May, and on the last Tuesday of June at 7pm.

Clerk: **REV. HUGH CONKEY BSc BD**   **39 St Ternans Road, Newtonhill, Stonehaven AB39 3PF**   **01569 739297**
[E-mail: kincardinedeeside@churchofscotland.org.uk]

Aberluthnott linked with Laurencekirk (H)
Ronald Gall BSc BD   1985   2001   Aberdeen Road, Laurencekirk AB30 1AJ   01561 378838
[E-mail: RGall@churchofscotland.org.uk]

Aboyne-Dinnet (H) (01339 886989) linked with Cromar (E-mail: aboynedinnet.cos@virgin.net)
Frank Ribbons MA BD DipEd   1985   2011   49 Charlton Crescent, Aboyne AB34 5GN   01339 887267
[E-mail: FRibbons@churchofscotland.org.uk]

Arbuthnott, Bervie and Kinneff
Vacant   10 Kirkburn, Inverbervie, Montrose DD10 0RT   01561 362560

Banchory-Ternan: East (H) (01330 820380) (E-mail: banchoryeastchurchoffice@btconnect.com)
Alan J.S. Murray BSc BD PhD   2003   2013   East Manse, Station Road, Banchory AB31 5YP   01330 822481
[E-mail: AJSMurray@churchofscotland.org.uk]

Banchory-Ternan: West (H)
Antony A. Stephen MA BD — 2001 2011 — The Manse, 2 Wilson Road, Banchory AB31 5UY [E-mail: TStephen@churchofscotland.org.uk] — 01330 822811

Birse and Feughside
Vacant — The Manse, Finzean, Banchory AB31 6PB — 01330 850776

Braemar and Crathie
Kenneth I. Mackenzie DL BD CPS — 1990 2005 — The Manse, Crathie, Ballater AB35 5UL [E-mail: KMacKenzie@churchofscotland.org.uk] — 01339 742208

Cromar See Aboyne-Dinnet

Drumoak (H)-Durris (H)
Jean A. Boyd MSc BSc BA — 2016 — 26 Sunnyside Drive, Drumoak, Banchory AB31 3EW [E-mail: JBoyd@churchofscotland.org.uk] — 01330 811031

Glenmuick (Ballater) (H)
David L.C. Barr — 2014 — The Manse, Craigendarroch Walk, Ballater AB35 5ZB [E-mail: DBarr@churchofscotland.org.uk] — 01339 756111

Laurencekirk See Aberluthnott

Maryculter Trinity (01224 735983) (E-mail: thechurchoffice@tiscali.co.uk)
Melvyn J. Griffiths BTh DipTheol DMin — 1978 2014 — The Manse, Kirkton of Maryculter, Aberdeen AB12 5FS [E-mail: MGriffiths@churchofscotland.org.uk] — 01224 730150

Mearns Coastal
Guardianship of the Presbytery — The Manse, Kirkton, St Cyrus, Montrose DD10 0BW — 01674 850880

Mid Deeside
Alexander C. Wark MA BD STM — 1982 2012 — The Manse, Torphins, Banchory AB31 4GQ [E-mail: AWark@churchofscotland.org.uk] — 01339 882276

Newtonhill
Hugh Conkey BSc BD — 1987 2001 — 39 St Ternans Road, Newtonhill, Stonehaven AB39 3PF [E-mail: HConkey@churchofscotland.org.uk] — 01569 730143

Portlethen (H) (01224 782883)
Vacant
Rodolphe Blanchard-Kowal   18 Rowanbank Road, Portlethen, Aberdeen AB12 4NX   01224 780211
(Exchange Minister)   [E-mail: RKowal@churchofscotland.org.uk]

Stonehaven: Dunnottar (H) linked with Stonehaven: South (H)
Rosslyn P. Duncan BD MTh   2007   Dunnottar Manse, Stonehaven AB39 3XL   01569 762166
                                     [E-mail: RDuncan@churchofscotland.org.uk]

Stonehaven: Fetteresso (H) (01569 767689) (E-mail: fetteresso.office@btinternet.com)
Fyfe Blair BA BD DMin   1989 2009   11 South Lodge Drive, Stonehaven AB39 2PN   01569 762876
                                        [E-mail: Fyfe.Blair@churchofscotland.org.uk]

Stonehaven: South See Stonehaven: Dunnottar

West Mearns
Brian D. Smith BD (Hons)   1990 2016   The Manse, Fettercairn,   01561 340203
                                           Laurencekirk AB30 1UE
                                           [E-mail: BSmith@churchofscotland.org.uk]

Name			Charge	Address	Tel
Broadley, Linda J. (Mrs) LTh DipEd	1996	2013	(Dun and Hillside)	Snaefell, Lochside Road, St Cyrus, Montrose DD10 0DB [E-mail: lindabroadley@btinternet.com]	01674 850141
Brown, J.W.S. BTh	1960	1995	(Cromar)	10 Forestside Road, Banchory AB31 5ZH [E-mail: iainisobel@aol.com]	01330 824353
Christie, Andrew C. LTh	1975	2000	(Banchory-Devenick and Maryculter/Cookney)	17 Broadstraik Close, Elrick, Aberdeen AB32 6JP	01224 746888
Dempster, Colin J. BD CertMin	1990	2016	(Mearns Coastal)	16 Kippford Street, Monifieth DD5 4TT [E-mail: coldcoast@btinternet.com]	01382 532368
Hamilton, Helen (Miss) BD	1991	2003	(Glasgow: St James' Pollok)	The Cottage, West Tilbouries, Maryculter, Aberdeen AB12 5GD	01224 739632
Lamb, A. Douglas MA	1964	2002	(Dalry: St Margaret's)	9 Luther Drive, Laurencekirk AB30 1FE [E-mail: lamb.edzell@talk21.com]	01561 376816
Smith, Albert E. BD	1983	2006	(Methlick)	42 Haulkerton Crescent, Laurencekirk AB30 1FB [E-mail: aesmith42@googlemail.com]	01561 376111
Wallace, William F. BDS BD	1968	2008	(Wick: Pulteneytown and Thrumster)	Lachan Cottage, 29 Station Road, Banchory AB31 5XX [E-mail: williamwallace39@talktalk.net]	01330 822259

(33) GORDON

Meets at various locations on the first Tuesday of February, March, April, May, September, October, November and December, and on the last Tuesday of June.

Clerk:	REV. G. EUAN D. GLEN BSc BD			The Manse, 26 St Ninians, Monymusk, Inverurie AB51 7HF [E-mail: gordon@churchofscotland.org.uk]	01467 651470
Barthol Chapel linked with Tarves					
Alison I. Swindells (Mrs) LLB BD		1998	2016	8 Murray Avenue, Tarves, Ellon AB41 7LZ	01651 851250
Belhelvie (H)					
Paul McKeown BSc PhD BD		2000	2005	Belhelvie Manse, Balmedie, Aberdeen AB23 8YR [E-mail: PMcKeown@churchofscotland.org.uk]	01358 742227
Blairdaff and Chapel of Garioch					
Martyn S. Sanders BA CertEd		2015		The Manse, Chapel of Garioch, Inverurie AB51 5HE [E-mail: MSanders@churchofscotland.org.uk]	01467 681619 07814 164373 (Mbl)
Cluny (H) linked with Monymusk (H)					
G. Euan D. Glen BSc BD		1992		The Manse, 26 St Ninians, Monymusk, Inverurie AB51 7HF [E-mail: GGlen@churchofscotland.org.uk]	01467 651470
Culsalmond and Rayne linked with Daviot (H)					
Mary M. Cranfield MA BD DMin		1989		The Manse, Daviot, Inverurie AB51 0HY [E-mail: MCranfield@churchofscotland.org.uk]	01467 671241
Cushnie and Tough (R) (H)					
Rosemary Legge (Mrs) BSc BD MTh		1992	2010	The Manse, Muir of Fowlis, Alford AB33 8JU [E-mail: RLegge@churchofscotland.org.uk]	01975 581239
Daviot See Culsalmond and Rayne					
Echt and Midmar (H)					
Vacant				The Manse, Echt, Westhill AB32 7AB (New charge formed by a union between Echt and Midmar)	01330 860004

Charge / Minister	Ordained	Inducted	Address	Telephone
Ellon Alastair J. Bruce BD MTh PGCE	2015		The Manse, 12 Union Street, Ellon AB41 9BA [E-mail: ABruce@churchofscotland.org.uk]	01358 723787
Fintray Kinellar Keithhall Sean Swindells BD DipMin MTh	1996	2016	8 Murray Avenue, Tarves, Ellon AB41 7LZ	01651 851295
Foveran Richard M.C. Reid BSc BD MTh	1991	2013	The Manse, Foveran, Ellon AB41 6AP [E-mail: RReid@churchofscotland.org.uk]	01358 789288
Howe Trinity John A. Cook MA BD	1986	2000	The Manse, 110 Main Street, Alford AB33 8AD [E-mail: John.Cook@churchofscotland.org.uk]	01975 562282
Huntly Cairnie Glass Thomas R. Calder LLB BD WS	1994		The Manse, Queen Street, Huntly AB54 8EB [E-mail: TCalder@churchofscotland.org.uk]	01466 792630
Insch-Leslie-Premnay-Oyne (H) Kay Gauld BD STM PhD	1999	2015	66 Denwell Road, Insch AB52 6LH [E-mail: KGauld@churchofscotland.org.uk]	01464 820404
Inverurie: St Andrew's (Website: standrewschurchinverurie.org.uk) Vacant			27 Buchan Drive, Newmachar, Aberdeen AB21 0NR	01651 862281
Inverurie: West Vacant			West Manse, 1 Westburn Place, Inverurie AB51 5QS	01467 620285
Kennay Joshua M. Mikelson	2008	2015	15 Kirkland, Kemnay, Inverurie AB51 5QD [E-mail: JMikelson@churchofscotland.org.uk]	01467 642219 (Tel/Fax)
Kintore (H) Neil W. Meyer BD MTh	2000	2014	28 Oakhill Road, Kintore, Inverurie AB51 0FH [E-mail: NMeyer@churchofscotland.org.uk]	01467 632219

Meldrum and Bourtie				
Alison Jaffrey (Mrs) MA BD FSAScot	1990	2010	The Manse, Urquhart Road, Oldmeldrum, Inverurie AB51 0EX [E-mail: AJaffrey@churchofscotland.org.uk]	01651 872250
Methlick				
William A. Stalder BA MDiv MLitt PhD	2014		The Manse, Manse Road, Methlick, Ellon AB41 7DG [E-mail: WStalder@churchofscotland.org.uk]	01651 806264
Monymusk See Cluny				
New Machar				
Douglas G. McNab BA BD	1999	2010	The New Manse, Newmachar, Aberdeen AB21 0RD [E-mail: DMcNab@churchofscotland.org.uk]	01651 862278
Noth				
Regine U. Cheyne (Mrs) MA BSc BD	1988	2010	Manse of Noth, Kennethmont, Huntly AB54 4NP [E-mail: RCheyne@churchofscotland.org.uk]	01464 831690
Skene (H)				
Stella Campbell MA (Oxon) BD	2012		The Manse, Manse Road, Kirkton of Skene, Westhill AB32 6LX [E-mail: SCampbell@churchofscotland.org.uk]	01224 745955
Marion G. Stewart (Miss) DCS			Kirk Cottage, Kirkton of Skene, Westhill AB32 6XE [E-mail: MStewart@churchofscotland.org.uk]	01224 743407
Strathbogie Drumblade				
Neil I.M. MacGregor BD	1995		49 Deveron Park, Huntly AB54 8UZ [E-mail: NMacGregor@churchofscotland.org.uk]	01466 792702
Tarves See Barthol Chapel				
Udny and Pitmedden				
Gillean P. MacLean (Ms) BA BD	1994	2013	The Manse, Manse Road, Udny Green, Ellon AB41 7RS [E-mail: GMacLean@churchofscotland.org.uk]	01651 843794
Upper Donside (H) (E-mail: upperdonsideparishchurch@btinternet.com)				
Vacant			The Manse, Lumsden, Huntly AB54 4GQ	01464 861757

Name			Charge	Address	Phone
Craggs, Sheila (Mrs)	2001	2008	(Auxiliary Minister)	7 Morar Court, Ellon AB41 9GG	01358 723055
Craig, Anthony J.D. BD	1987	2009	(Glasgow: Maryhill)	4 Hightown, Colliston, Ellon AB41 8RS [E-mail: craig.glasgow@gmx.net]	01358 751247
Dryden, Ian MA DipEd	1988	2001	(New Machar)	16 Glenhome Gardens, Dyce, Aberdeen AB21 7FG [E-mail: ian@idryden.freeserve.co.uk]	01224 722820
Greig, Alan BSc BD	1977	2017	(Interim Minister)	1 Dunnydeer Place, Insch AB52 6HP [E-mail: greig@kincarr.free-online.co.uk]	01464 821332
Groves, Ian B BD CPS	1989	2016	(Inverurie West)	28 Parkhill Circle, Dyce, Aberdeen AB21 7FN [E-mail: IGroves@churchofscotland.org.uk]	01224 774380
Hawthorn, Daniel MA BD DMin	1965	2004	(Belhelvie)	7 Crimond Drive, Ellon AB41 8BT [E-mail: donhawthorn@compuserve.com]	01358 723981
Irvine, Carl	2017		Ordained Local Minister	Northside of Glack, Meikle Wartle, Inverurie AB51 5AR [E-mail: CIrvine@churchofscotland.org.uk]	01467 671135
Jones, Robert A. LTh CA	1966	1997	(Marnoch)	13 Gordon Terrace, Inverurie AB51 4GT	01467 622691
Kiehlmann, Peter	2016		Ordained Local Minister	8 Main Street, Newburgh, Ellon AB41 6BP	01358 789235
Macalister, Eleanor	1994	2006	(Ellon)	Quarryview, Ythan Bank, Ellon AB41 7TH [E-mail: macal1ster@aol.com]	01358 761402
Mack, John C. JP	1985	2008	(Auxiliary Minister)	The Willows, Auchlever, Insch AB52 6QB	01464 820387
McLeish, Robert S.	1970	2000	(Insch-Leslie-Premnay-Oyne)	19 Western Road, Insch AB52 6JR	01464 820749
Rodger, Matthew A. BD	1978	1999	(Ellon)	15 Meadowlands Drive, Westhill AB32 6EJ	01224 743184
Stoddart, A. Grainger	1975	2001	(Meldrum and Bourtie)	6 Mayfield Gardens, Insch AB52 6XL	01464 821124
Thomson, Iain U. MA BD	1970	2011	(Skene)	4 Keirhill Gardens, Westhill AB32 6AZ [E-mail: iainuthomson@googlemail.com]	01224 746743

(34) BUCHAN

Meets at St Kane's Centre, New Deer, Turriff on the first Tuesday of February, March, May, September, October, November and December, and on the third Tuesday of June.

Clerk:	REV. SHEILA M. KIRK BA LLB BD	The Manse, Old Deer, Peterhead AB42 5JB [E-mail: buchan@churchofscotland.org.uk]	01771 623582

Aberdour linked with Pitsligo
Vacant

31 Blairmore Park, Rosehearty, Fraserburgh AB43 7NZ   01346 571823

Auchaber United linked with Auchterless
Stephen J. Potts BA — 2012 — The Manse, Auchterless, Turriff AB53 8BA [E-mail: SPotts@churchofscotland.org.uk] — 01888 511058

Auchterless See Auchaber United

Banff linked with King Edward
David I.W. Locke MA MSc BD — 2000 2012 — 7 Colleonard Road, Banff AB45 1DZ [E-mail: DLocke@churchofscotland.org.uk] — 01261 812107 / 07776 448301 (Mbl)

Crimond linked with Lonmay
Vacant — The Manse, Crimond, Fraserburgh AB43 8QJ — 01346 532431

Cruden (H)
Vacant — The Manse, Hatton, Peterhead AB42 0QQ — 01779 841229

Deer (H)
Sheila M. Kirk BA LLB BD — 2007 2010 — The Manse, Old Deer, Peterhead AB42 5JB [E-mail: SKirk@churchofscotland.org.uk] — 01771 623582

Fraserburgh: Old
Vacant — 4 Robbie's Road, Fraserburgh AB43 7AF — 01346 515332

Fraserburgh: South (H) linked with Inverallochy and Rathen: East
Ronald F. Yule — 1982 — 15 Victoria Street, Fraserburgh AB43 9PJ [E-mail: RYule@churchofscotland.org.uk] — 01346 518244

Fraserburgh: West (H) linked with Rathen: West
Vacant — 4 Kirkton Gardens, Fraserburgh AB43 8TU — 01346 513303

Fyvie linked with Rothienorman
Vacant — The Manse, Fyvie, Turriff AB53 8RD — 01651 891230

Inverallochy and Rathen: East See Fraserburgh: South
King Edward See Banff

Longside
Robert A. Fowlie BD — 2007 — The Manse, Old Deer, Peterhead AB42 5JB [E-mail: RFowlie@churchofscotland.org.uk] — 01771 622228

Lonmay See Crimond

Macduff
Hugh O'Brien CSS MTheol — 2001 2016 — 10 Ross Street, Macduff AB44 1NS — 01261 832316

Marnoch
Alan Macgregor BA BD PhD — 1992 2013 — Marnoch Manse, 53 South Street, Aberchirder, Huntly AB54 7TS [E-mail: AMacgregor@churchofscotland.org.uk] — 01466 781143

Maud and Savoch linked with New Deer: St Kane's
Vacant — The Manse, New Deer, Turriff AB53 6TD — 01771 644216

Monquhitter and New Byth linked with Turriff: St Andrew's
James Cook MA MDiv — 1999 2002 — St Andrew's Manse, Balmellie Road, Turriff AB53 4SP [E-mail: JCook@churchofscotland.org.uk] — 01888 560304

New Deer: St Kane's See Maud and Savoch

New Pitsligo linked with Strichen and Tyrie
Vacant
William Stewart — 2015 — Kingsville, Strichen, Fraserburgh AB43 6SQ — 01771 637365
(Ordained Local Minister) — Denend, Strichen, Fraserburgh AB43 6RN [E-mail: billandjunes@live.co.uk] — 01771 637256

Ordiquhill and Cornhill (H) linked with Whitehills
W. Myburgh Verster BA BTh LTh MTh — 1981 2011 — 6 Craigneen Place, Whitehills, Banff AB45 2NE [E-mail: WVerster@churchofscotland.org.uk] — 01261 861317

Peterhead: New
Vacant — 1 Hawthorn Road, Peterhead AB42 2DW
(New charge formed by the union of Peterhead: Old and Peterhead: Trinity)

Peterhead: St Andrew's (H)
Vacant — 1 Landale Road, Peterhead AB42 1QN — 01779 238200

Pitsligo See Aberdour

Portsoy
Vacant — The Manse, 4 Seafield Terrace, Portsoy, Banff AB45 2QB — 01261 842272

Rathen: West See Fraserburgh: West
Rothienorman See Fyvie

St Fergus
Jeffrey Tippner BA MDiv MCS PhD   1991 2012 — 26 Newton Road, St Fergus, Peterhead AB42 3DD — 01779 838287
[E-mail: JTippner@churchofscotland.org.uk]

Sandhaven
Vacant

Strichen and Tyrie See New Pitsligo
Turriff: St Andrew's See Monquhitter and New Byth

Turriff: St Ninian's and Forglen (H) (L)
Kevin R. Gruer BSc BA   2011 — 4 Deveronside Drive, Turriff AB53 4SP — 01888 563850
[E-mail: KGruer@churchofscotland]

Whitehills See Ordiquhill and Cornhill

Coutts, Fred MA BD	1973	1989	(Hospital Chaplain)	Ladebank, 1 Manse Place, Hatton, Peterhead AB42 0UQ [E-mail: fred.coutts@btinternet.com]	01779 841320
Fawkes, G.M. Allan BA BSc JP	1979	2000	(Lonmay with Rathen: West)	3 Northfield Gardens, Hatton, Peterhead AB42 0SW [E-mail: afawkes@aol.com]	01779 841814
McMillan, William J. CA LTh BD	1969	2004	(Sandsting and Aithsting with Walls and Sandness)	7 Ardinn Drive, Turriff AB53 4PR [E-mail: revbillymcmillan@aol.com]	01888 560727
Macnee, Iain LTh BD MA PhD	1975	2011	(New Pitsligo with Strichen and Tyrie)	Wardend Cottage, Alvah, Banff AB45 3TR [E-mail: macneeiain4@googlemail.com]	01261 815647
Noble, George S. DipTh	1972	2000	(Carfin with Newarthill)	Craigowan, 3 Main Street, Inverallochy, Fraserburgh AB43 8XX	01346 582749
Ross, David S. MSc PhD BD	1978	2013	(Prison Chaplain Service)	3–5 Abbey Street, Old Deer, Peterhead AB42 5LN [E-mail: padsross@btinternet.com]	01771 623994

Ross, William B. LTh CPS	1988 2016	(Aberdour with Pitsligo)	31 Blairmore Park, Rosehearty, Fraserburgh AB43 7NZ [E-mail: williamross278@btinternet.com]	01346 571823
Thorburn, Robert J. BD	1978 2017	(Fyvie with Rothienorman)	12 Slackadale Gardens, Turriff AB53 4UA [E-mail: rjthorburn@aol.com]	
van Sittert, Paul BA BD	1997 2011	Chaplain: Army	4Bn The Royal Regiment of Scotland, Bourlon Barracks, Plumer Road, Catterick Garrison DL9 3AD [E-mail: padre.pvs@gmail.com]	

(35) MORAY

Meets at St Andrew's-Lhanbryd and Urquhart on the first Tuesday of February, March, May, September, October, November and December, and at the Moderator's church on the fourth Tuesday of June.

Clerk:	REV. ALASTAIR H. GRAY MA BD	North Manse, Church Road, Keith AB55 5FX [E-mail: moray@churchofscotland.org.uk]	**01542 886840** **07944 287777 (Mbl)**

Aberlour (H)

Shuna M. Dicks BSc BD	2010	The Manse, Mary Avenue, Aberlour AB38 9QU [E-mail: SDicks@churchofscotland.org.uk]	01340 871687

Alves and Burghead linked with Kinloss and Findhorn

Louis C. Bezuidenhout BA MA BD DD	1978 2014	The Manse, 4 Manse Road, Kinloss, Forres IV36 3GH [E-mail: LBezuidenhout@churchofscotland.org.uk]	01309 690474

Bellie and Speymouth

Vacant		11 The Square, Fochabers IV32 7DG	01343 820256

Birnie and Pluscarden linked with Elgin: High

Stuart M. Duff BA	1997 2014	The Manse, Daisy Bank, 5 Forteath Avenue, Elgin IV30 1TQ [E-mail: SDuff@churchofscotland.org.uk]	01343 545703

Buckie: North (H) linked with Rathven

Isabel C. Buchan (Mrs) BSc BD RE(PgCE)	1975 2013	The Manse, 14 St Peter's Road, Buckie AB56 1DL [E-mail: IBuchan@churchofscotland.org.uk]	01542 832118

Buckie: South and West (H) linked with Enzie

Vacant		Craigendarroch, 14 Cliff Terrace, Buckie AB56 1LX	01542 833775

Cullen and Deskford (Website: www.cullen-deskford-church.org.uk)

Douglas F. Stevenson BD DipMin	1991	2010	14 Seafield Road, Cullen, Buckie AB56 4AF 01542 841963
			[E-mail: DStevenson@churchofscotland.org.uk]

Dallas linked with Forres: St Leonard's (H) linked with Rafford

Donald K. Prentice BSc BD	1989	2010	St Leonard's Manse, Nelson Road, Forres IV36 1DR 01309 672380
			[E-mail: DPrentice@churchofscotland.org.uk]
Anne Attenburrow BSc MB ChB	2006	2013	4 Jock Inksons Brae, Elgin IV30 1QE 01343 552330
(Auxiliary Minister)			[E-mail: AAttenburrow@churchofscotland.org.uk]
John A. Morrison BSc BA PGCE		2013	35 Kirkton Place, Elgin IV30 6JR 01343 550199
(Ordained Local Minister)			[E-mail: JMorrison@churchofscotland.org.uk]

Duffus, Spynie and Hopeman (H) (Website: www.duffusparish.co.uk)

Jennifer M. Adams BEng BD	2013	The Manse, Duffus, Elgin IV30 5QP 01343 830276
		[E-mail: JAdams@churchofscotland.org.uk]

Dyke linked with Edinkillie

Vacant	Manse of Dyke, Brodie, Forres IV36 2TD 01309 641239

Edinkillie See Dyke

Elgin: High See Birnie and Pluscarden

Elgin: St Giles' (H) and St Columba's South (01343 551501) (Office: Williamson Hall, Duff Avenue, Elgin IV30 1QS)

Deon Oelofse BA MDiv LTh MTh	2002	2017	18 Reidhaven Street, Elgin IV30 1QH 01343 208786
			[E-mail: DOelofse@churchofscotland.org.uk]
Sonia Palmer		2017	94 Ashgrove Park, Elgin IV30 1UT 07748 700929 (Mbl)
(Ordained Local Minister)			[E-mail: Sonia.Palmer@churchofscotland.org.uk]

Enzie See Buckie: South and West

Findochty linked with Portknockie

Vacant	20 Netherton Terrace, Findochty, Buckie AB56 4QD 01542 833180

Forres: St Laurence (H)

Barry J. Boyd LTh DPS	1993	12 Mackenzie Drive, Forres IV36 2JP 01309 672260
		[E-mail: BBoyd@churchofscotland.org.uk] 07778 731018 (Mbl)

Forres: St Leonard's See Dallas

Keith: North, Newmill, Boharm and Rothiemay (H) (01542 886390)
Alastair H. Gray MA BD   1978   2015   North Manse, Church Road, Keith AB55 5BR   01542 886840
[E-mail: AGray@churchofscotland.org.uk]

Keith: St Rufus, Botriphnie and Grange (H)
Vacant   St Rufus' Manse, Church Road, Keith AB55 5BR   01542 882799

Kinloss and Findhorn See Alves and Burghead

Knockando, Elchies and Archiestown (H) linked with Rothes (Website: www.moraykirk.co.uk)
Robert J.M. Anderson BD FInstLM   1993   2000   The Manse, Rothes, Aberlour AB38 7AF   01340 831381
[E-mail: RJMAnderson@churchofscotland.org.uk]

Lossiemouth: St Gerardine's High (H) linked with Lossiemouth: St James
Geoffrey D. McKee BA   1997   2014   The Manse, St Gerardine's Road, Lossiemouth IV31 6RA   01343 208852
[E-mail: GMcKee@churchofscotland.org.uk]

Lossiemouth: St James' See Lossiemouth: St Gerardine's High

Mortlach and Cabrach (H)
Vacant   Mortlach Manse, Dufftown, Keith AB55 4AR   01340 820380

Portknockie See Findochty
Rafford See Dallas
Rathven See Buckie: North
Rothes See Knockando, Elchies and Archiestown

St Andrew's-Lhanbryd (H) and Urquhart
Vacant   39 St Andrews Road, Lhanbryde, Elgin IV30 8PU   01343 843765

Bain, Brian LTh   1980 2007   (Gask with Methven and Logiealmond)   Bayview, 13 Stewart Street, Portgordon, Buckie AB56 5QT   01542 831215
[E-mail: bricoreen@gmail.com]

Buchan, Alexander MA BD PGCE   1975 1992   (North Ronaldsay with Sanday)   The Manse, 14 St Peter's Road, Buckie AB56 1DL   01542 832118
[E-mail: revabuchan@bluebucket.org]

Davidson, A.A.B. MA BD   1960 1997   (Grange with Rothiemay)   11 Sutors Rise, Nairn IV12 5BU   01343 820937
King, Margaret MA DCS   (Deacon)   56 Murrayfield, Fochabers IV32 7EZ
[E-mail: margaretrking@tiscali.co.uk]

Morton, Alasdair J. MA BD DipEd FEIS   1960 2000   (Bowden with Newtown)   16 St Leonard's Road, Forres IV36 1DW   01309 671719
[E-mail: alasgilmor@hotmail.co.uk]

Morton, Gillian M. (Mrs) MA BD PGCE	1983 1996	(Hospital Chaplain)	16 St Leonard's Road, Forres IV36 1DW [E-mail: gillianmorton@hotmail.co.uk]	01309 671719
Munro, Sheila BD	1995 2016	RAF Station Chaplain	RAF Lossiemouth, Elgin IV31 6SD [E-mail: sheila.munro781@mod.gov.uk]	01343 817180
Poole, Ann McColl (Mrs) DipEd ACE LTh	1983 2003	(Dyke with Edinkillie)	Kirkside Cottage, Dyke, Forres IV36 2TF	01309 641046
Robertson, Peter BSc BD	1988 1998	(Dallas with Forres: St Leonard's with Rafford)	17 Ferryhill Road, Forres IV36 2GY [E-mail: peterrobertsonforres@talktalk.net]	01309 676769
Rollo, George B. BD	1974 2010	(Elgin: St Giles' and St Columba's South)	'Struan', 13 Meadow View, Hopeman, Elgin IV30 5PL [E-mail: rollo@gmail.com]	01343 835226
Smith, Hugh M.C. LTh	1973 2013	(Mortlach and Cabrach)	6 Concraig Walk, Kingswells, Aberdeen AB15 8DU	01224 745275
Smith, Morris BD	1988 2013	(Cromdale and Advie with Dulnain Bridge with Grantown-on-Spey)	1 Urquhart Grove, New Elgin IV30 8TB [E-mail: mosmith.themanse@btinternet.com]	01343 545019
Watts, Anthony BD DipTechEd JP	1999 2013	(Glenmuick Ballater)	7 Cumiskie Crescent, Forres IV36 2QB [E-mail: tony.watts6@btinternet.com]	
Whyte, David LTh	1993 2011	(Boat of Garten, Duthil and Kincardine)	1 Lemanfield Crescent, Garmouth, Fochabers IV32 7LS [E-mail: whytedj@btinternet.com]	01343 870667
Wright, David L. MA BD	1957 1998	(Stornoway: St Columba)	84 Wyvis Drive, Nairn IV12 4TP	01667 451613

(36) ABERNETHY

Meets at Boat of Garten on the first Tuesday of February, March, May, September, October, November and December, and on the last Tuesday of June.

Clerk: REV JAMES A.I. McEWAN MA BD   Rapness, Station Road, Nethy Bridge PA25 3DN [E-mail: abernethy@churchofscotland.org.uk]   01479 821116

Abernethy (H) linked with Boat of Garten (H), Carrbridge (H) and Kincardine
Donald K. Walker BD   1979   2013   The Manse, Deshar Road, Boat of Garten PH24 3BN [E-mail: DWalker@churchofscotland.org.uk]   01479 831252

Alvie and Insh (H) linked with Rothiemurchus and Aviemore (H)
Vacant   The Manse, 8 Dalfaber Park, Aviemore PH22 1QF   01479 810280

Boat of Garten (H), Carrbridge (H) and Kincardine See Abernethy

Cromdale (H) and Advie linked with Dulnain Bridge (H) linked with Grantown-on-Spey (H)
Gordon Strang   2014   The Manse, Golf Course Road, Grantown-on-Spey PH26 3HY [E-mail: GStrang@churchofscotland.org.uk]   01479 872084

Dulnain Bridge See Cromdale and Advie
Grantown-on-Spey See Cromdale and Advie

Kingussie (H)
Alison H. Burnside (Mrs) MA BD   1991   2013   The Manse, 18 Hillside Avenue, Kingussie PH21 1PA   01540 662327
[E-mail: ABurnside@churchofscotland.org.uk]

Laggan (H) linked with Newtonmore: St Bride's (H)
Catherine A. Buchan (Mrs) MA MDiv   2002   2009   The Manse, Fort William Road, Newtonmore PH20 1DG   01540 673238
[E-mail: CBuchan@churchofscotland.org.uk]

Newtonmore: St Bride's See Laggan
Rothiemurchus and Aviemore See Alvie and Insh

Tomintoul (H), Glenlivet and Inveraven
Vacant   The Manse, Tomintoul, Ballindalloch AB37 9HA   01807 580254

Atkinson, Graham MA BD MTh   2006 2017   (Glasgow: Sandyhills)   15 Lockhart Place, Aviemore PH22 1SW   07715 108837
[E-mail: gtatkinson75@yahoo.co.uk]

Duncanson, Mary (Ms) BTh   2013   Ordained Local Minister: Presbytery Pastoral Support   3 Balmenach Road, Cromdale, Grantown-on-Spey PH26 3LJ   01479 872165
[E-mail: MDuncanson@churchofscotland.org.uk]

MacEwan, James A.I. MA BD   1973 2012   (Abernethy with Cromdale and Advie)   Rapness, Station Road, Nethy Bridge PH25 3DN   01479 821116
[E-mail: wurrus@hotmail.co.uk]

Ritchie, Christine A.Y. (Mrs) BD DipMin   2002 2012   (Braes of Rannoch with Foss and Rannoch)   25 Beachen Court, Grantown-on-Spey PH26 3JD   01479 873419
[E-mail: cayritchie@bt.internet.com]

Thomson, Mary Ellen (Mrs)   2013   Ordained Local Minister   Riverside Flat, Gynack Street, Kingussie PH21 1EL   01540 661772
[E-mail: Mary.Thomson@churchofscotland.org.uk]

Wallace, Sheila D. (Mrs) DCS BA BD   Deacon   Beannach Cottage, Spey Avenue, Boat of Garten PH24 3BE   01479 831548
(Mbl) 07733 243046
[E-mail: sheilad.wallace53@gmail.com]

(37) INVERNESS

Meets at Inverness, in Inverness: Inshes (2017) on the second Saturday of September, the third Tuesday of November, (2018) the second Saturday in March and the last Tuesday in June; Saturday meetings preceded by a presbytery conference.

Clerk: REV. TREVOR G. HUNT BA BD   7 Woodville Court, Culduthel Avenue, Inverness IV2 6BX   01463 250355
[E-mail: inverness@churchofscotland.org.uk]   07753 423333 (Mbl)

Ardersier (H) linked with Petty
Robert Cleland — 1997 — 2014
The Manse, Ardersier, Inverness IV2 7SX
[E-mail: RCleland@churchofscotland.org.uk]
01667 462224

Auldearn and Dalmore linked with Nairn: St Ninian's (H)
Thomas M. Bryson BD — 1997 — 2015
The Manse, Auldearn, Nairn IV12 5SX
[E-mail: TBryson@churchofscotland.org.uk]
01667 451675

Cawdor (H) linked with Croy and Dalcross (H)
Robert E. Brookes BD — 2009 — 2016
The Manse, Croy, Inverness IV2 5PH
[E-mail: RBrookes@churchofscotland.org.uk]
01667 493717

Croy and Dalcross See Cawdor

Culloden: The Barn (H)
Michael Robertson BA — 2014
45 Oakdene Court, Culloden IV2 7XL
[E-mail: Mike.Robertson@churchofscotland.org.uk]
01463 795430
07740 984395 (Mbl)

Daviot and Dunlichity linked with Moy, Dalarossie and Tomatin
Vacant
The Manse, Daviot, Inverness IV2 5XL
01463 772242

Dores and Boleskine
Vacant

Inverness: Crown (H) (01463 231140)
Peter H. Donald MA PhD BD — 1991 — 1998
39 Southside Road, Inverness IV2 4XA
[E-mail: PDonald@churchofscotland.org.uk]
01463 230537

Inverness: Dalneigh and Bona (GD) (H)
Vacant
9 St Mungo Road, Inverness IV3 5AS
01463 232339

Inverness: East (H)
Andrew T.B. McGowan (Prof.) — 1979 — 2009
BD STM PhD
2 Victoria Drive, Inverness IV2 3QD
[E-mail: AMcGowan@churchofscotland.org.uk]
01463 238770

Inverness: Hilton
Duncan A.C. MacPherson LLB BD — 1994
66 Culduthel Mains Crescent, Inverness IV2 6RG
[E-mail: DMacPherson@churchofscotland.org.uk]
01463 231417

Name			Address	Telephone
Jonathan Fraser MA(Div) MTh ThM (Associate Minister)	2012		9 Broom Drive, Inverness IV2 4EG [E-mail: jonathan@hiltonchurch.org.uk]	07749 539981 (Mbl)
Inverness: Inshes (H) David S. Scott MA BD	1987	2013	48 Redwood Crescent, Milton of Leys, Inverness IV2 6HB [E-mail: David.Scott@churchofscotland.org.uk]	01463 772402
Farquhar A.M. Forbes MA BD (Associate Minister)	2016		The Heights, Inverarnie, Inverness IV2 6XA [E-mail: FForbes@churchofscotland.org.uk]	01808 521450
Inverness: Kinmylies (H) Andrew Barrie BD	2013		2 Balnafettack Place, Inverness IV3 8TQ [E-mail: Andrew.Barrie@churchofscotland.org.uk]	01463 224307
Inverness: Ness Bank (H) Fiona E. Smith (Mrs) LLB BD	2010		15 Ballifeary Road, Inverness IV3 5PJ [E-mail: FSmith@churchofscotland.org.uk]	01463 234653
Inverness: Old High St Stephen's Peter W. Nimmo BD ThM	1996	2004	24 Damfield Road, Inverness IV2 3HU [E-mail: PNimmo@churchofscotland.org.uk]	01463 250802
Inverness: St Columba (New Charge Development) (H) Scott A. McRoberts BD MTh	2012		20 Bramble Close, Inverness IV2 6BS [E-mail: SMcRoberts@churchofscotland.org.uk]	01463 230308 / 07535 290092 (Mbl)
Inverness: Trinity (H) Alistair Murray BD	1984	2004	60 Kenneth Street, Inverness IV3 5PZ [E-mail: Alistair.Murray@churchofscotland.org.uk]	01463 234756
Kilmorack and Erchless Ian A. Manson BA BD	1989	2016	'Roselynn', Croyard Road, Beauly IV4 7DJ [E-mail: IManson@churchofscotland.org.uk]	01463 783824
Kiltarlity linked with Kirkhill Jonathan W. Humphrey BSc BD PhD	2015		Wardlaw Manse, Wardlaw Road, Kirkhill, Inverness IV5 7NZ [E-mail: JHumphrey@churchofscotland.org.uk]	01463 831662

Kirkhill See Kiltarlity
Moy, Dalarossie and Tomatin See Daviot and Dunlichity

Nairn: Old (H) (01667 452382)

Alison C. Mehigan BD DPS	2003	2015		15 Chattan Gardens, Nairn IV12 4QP [E-mail: AMehigan@churchofscotland.org.uk]	01667 453777

Nairn: St Ninian's See Auldearn and Dalmore
Petty See Ardersier

Urquhart and Glenmoriston (H)

Hugh F. Watt BD DPS DMin	1986	1996		Blairbeg, Drumnadrochit, Inverness IV3 6UG [E-mail: HWatt@churchofscotland.org.uk]	01456 450231

Archer, Morven (Mrs)	2013		Ordained Local Minister	42 Firthview Drive, Inverness IV3 8QE [E-mail: MArcher@churchofscotland.org.uk]	01463 237840
Black, Archibald T. BSc	1964	1997	(Inverness: Ness Bank)	16 Elm Park, Inverness IV2 4WN	01463 230588
Brown, Derek G. BD DipMin DMin	1989	1994	Lead Chaplain: NHS Highland	Cathedral Manse, Cnoc-an-Lobht, Dornoch IV25 3HN [E-mail: derek.brown1@nhs.net]	01862 810296
Buell, F. Bart BA MDiv	1980	1995	(Urquhart and Glenmoriston)	6 Towerhill Place, Cradlehall, Inverness IV2 5FN [E-mail: bartbuell@talktalk.net]	01463 794634
Campbell, Reginald F.	1979	2015	(Urquhart and Glenmoriston)	12 Alloway Drive, Kirkcaldy KY2 6DX [E-mail: campbell578@talktalk.net]	
Chisholm, Archibald F. MA	1957	1997	(Braes of Rannoch with Foss and Rannoch)	32 Seabank Road, Nairn IV12 4EU	01667 452001
Craw, John DCS			(Deacon)	5 Larchfield Court, Nairn IV12 4SS [E-mail: johncraw607@btinternet.com]	(Mbl) 07544 761653
Hunt, Trevor G. BA BD	1986	2011	(Evie with Firth with Rendall)	7 Woodville Court, Culduthel Avenue, Inverness IV2 6BX [E-mail: trevorhunt@gmail.com]	01463 250355
Jeffrey, Stewart D. BSc BD	1962	1997	(Banff with King Edward)	10 Grigor Drive, Inverness IV2 4LP [E-mail: stewart.jeffrey@talktalk.net]	(Mbl) 07753 423333
Livesley, Anthony LTh	1979	1997	(Kiltearn)	87 Beech Avenue, Nairn IV12 4ST [E-mail: tonylivesley@googlemail.com]	01463 230085
Lyon, Andrew LTh	1971	2007	(Fraserburgh West with Rathen West)	20 Barnview, Culloden, Inverness IV2 7EX [E-mail: andrewlyon70@hotmail.co.uk]	01667 455126
Mackenzie, Seoras L. BD	1996	1998	Chaplain: Army	39 Engr Regt (Air Support), Kinloss Barracks, Kinloss, Forres IV36 3XL	01463 559609
MacQuarrie, Donald A. BSc BD	1979	2012	(Fort William: Duncansburgh MacIntosh with Kilmonivaig)	Birch Cottage, 4 Craigrorie, North Kessock, Inverness IV1 3XH [E-mail: pdmacq@ukgateway.net]	01463 731050
McRoberts, T. Douglas BD CPS FRSA	1975	2014	(Malta)	24 Redwood Avenue, Inverness IV2 6HA [E-mail: doug.mcroberts@btinternet.com]	01463 772594

Name	Dates	Role / (Charge)	Address	Telephone
Mitchell, Joyce (Mrs) DCS	1994	(Deacon)	Sunnybank, Farr, Inverness IV2 6XG [E-mail: joyce@mitchell71.freeserve.co.uk]	01808 521285
Morrison, Hector BSc BD MTh	1981 1994	Principal: Highland Theological College (Melness and Eriboll with Tongue)	24 Oak Avenue, Inverness IV2 4NX	01463 238561
Rettie, James A. BTh	1981 1999		2 Trantham Drive, Westhill, Inverness IV2 5QT	01463 798896
Ritchie, Bruce BSc BD PhD	1977 2014	(Dingwall: Castle Street)	16 Brinckman Terrace, Westhill, Inverness IV2 5BL	01463 791389
Robertson, Fergus A. MA BD	1971 2010	(Inverness: Dalneigh and Bona)	16 Druid Temple Way, Inverness IV2 6UQ [E-mail: brucezomba@hotmail.com] [E-mail: faavrobertscn@yahoo.co.uk]	01463 718462
Stirling, G. Alan S. MA	1960 1999	(Leochel Cushnie and Lynturk with Tough)	97 Lochlann Road, Culloden, Inverness IV2 7HJ	01463 798313
Turner, Fraser K. LTh	1994 2007	(Kiltarlity with Kirkhill)	20 Caulfield Avenue, Inverness IV2 5GA [E-mail: fraseratq@yahoo.co.uk]	01463 794004
Warwick, Ivan C. MA BD TD	1980	Army Chaplain	Ardcruidh Croft, Heights of Dochcarty, Dingwall, IV15 9UF [E-mail: L70rev@btinternet.com]	01349 861464 (Mbl) 07787 535083
Waugh, John L. LTh	1973 2002	(Ardclach with Auldearn and Dalmore)	58 Wyvis Drive, Nairn IV12 4TP [E-mail: jwaugh334@btinternet.com]	(Tel/Fax) 01667 456397
Younger, Alastair S. BScEcon ASCC	1969 2008	(Inverness: St Columba High)	33 Duke's View, Slackbuie, Inverness IV2 6BB [E-mail: younger873@btinternet.com]	01463 242873

INVERNESS ADDRESSES

Inverness

Crown	Kingsmills Road x Midmills Road
Dalneigh and Bona	St Mary's Avenue
East	Academy Street x Margaret Street
Hilton	Druid Road x Tomatin Road
Inshes	Inshes Retail Park
Kinmylies	Kinmylies Way
Ness Bank	Ness Bank x Castle Road
St Stephen's	Old Edinburgh Road x Southside Road
The Old High	Church Street x Church Lane
Trinity	Huntly Place x Upper Kessock Street

Nairn

Old	Academy Street x Seabank Road
St Ninian's	High Street x Queen Street

(38) LOCHABER

Meets at Caol, Fort William, in Kilmallie Church Hall at 6pm, on the first Tuesday of September and December, on the last Tuesday of October and on the fourth Tuesday of March. The June meeting is held at 6pm on the first Tuesday in the church of the incoming Moderator.

Clerk:	REV DONALD G. B. McCORKINDALE BD DipMin	The Manse, 2 The Meadows, Strontian, Acharacle PH36 4HZ [E-mail: lochaber@churchofscotland.org.uk]	01967 402234
Treasurer:	MRS CONNIE ANDERSON	Darach, Duror PA38 4BS [E-mail : faoconnie@gmail.com]	01631 740334

Acharacle (H) linked with Ardnamurchan
Fiona Ogg (Mrs) BA BD   2012   The Manse, Acharacle PH36 4JU   01967 431654
                                                        [E-mail: Fiona.Ogg@churchofscotland.org.uk]

Ardgour and Kingairloch linked with Morvern linked with Strontian
Donald G.B. McCorkindale BD DipMin   1992   2011   The Manse, 2 The Meadows, Strontian, Acharacle PH36 4HZ   01967 402234
                                                        [E-mail: DMcCorkindale@churchofscotland.org.uk]

Ardnamurchan See Acharacle

Duror (H) linked with Glencoe: St Munda's (H)
Alexander C. Stoddart BD   2001   2016   9 Cameron Brae, Kentallen, Duror PA38 4BF   01631 740285
                                                        [E-mail: AStoddart@churchofscotland.org.uk]

Fort Augustus linked with Glengarry
Vacant   The Manse, Fort Augustus PH32 4BH   01320 366210

Fort William: Duncansburgh MacIntosh (H) linked with Kilmonivaig
Richard Baxter MA BD   1997   2016   The Manse, The Parade, Fort William PH33 6BA   01397 702297
                                                        [E-mail: RBaxter@churchofscotland.org.uk]   07958 541418 (Mbl)

Glencoe: St Munda's See Duror
Glengarry See Fort Augustus

Kilmallie
Richard T. Corbett BSc MSc PhD BD   1992   2005   Kilmallie Manse, Corpach, Fort William PH33 7JS   01397 772736
                                                        [E-mail: RCorbett@churchofscotland.org.uk]

Kilmonivaig See Fort William: Duncansburgh MacIntosh

Kinlochleven (H) linked with Nether Lochaber (H)
Malcolm A. Kinnear MA BD PhD   2010   The Manse, Lochaber Road, Kinlochleven PH50 4QW   01855 831227
                                                        [E-mail: MKinnear@churchofscotland.org.uk]

Morvern See Ardgour
Nether Lochaber See Kinlochleven

North West Lochaber

Edgar J. Ogston BSc BD	1976	2013	Church of Scotland Manse, Annie's Brae, Mallaig PH41 4RG [E-mail: EOgston@churchofscotland.org.uk]	01687 460042

Strontian See Ardgour

Anderson, David M. MSc FCOptom	1984	2012	(Ordained Local Minister)	'Mirlos', 1 Dumfries Place, Fort William PH33 6UQ [E-mail: David.Anderson@churchofscotland.org.uk]	01397 702091
Lamb, Alan H.W. BA MTh	1959	2005	(Associate Minister)	Smiddy House, Arisaig PH39 4NH [E-mail: h.a.lamb@handelamb.plus.com]	01687 450227
Millar, John L. MA BD	1981	1990	(Fort William: Duncansburgh with Kilmonivaig)	Flat 0/1, 12 Chesterfield Gardens, Glasgow G12 0BF [E-mail: johnmillar123@btinternet.com]	0141-339 4098
Muirhead, Morag (Mrs)		2013	Ordained Local Minister	6 Dumbarton Road, Fort William PH33 6UU [E-mail: MMuirhead@churchofscotland.org.uk]	01397 703643
Rae, Peter C. BSc BD	1968	2000	(Beath and Cowdenbeath: North)	8 Wether Road, Great Cambourne, Cambridgeshire CB23 5DT [E-mail: rae.fairview@btinternet.com]	01954 710079
Varwell, Adrian P.J. BA BD PhD	1983	2011	(Fort Augustus with Glengarry)	19 Enrick Crescent, Kilmore, Drumnadrochit, Inverness IV63 6TP [E-mail: adrian.varwell@btinternet.com]	01456 459352
Winning, A. Ann MA DipEd BD	1984	2006	(Morvern)	'Westering', 13C Carnoch, Glencoe, Ballachulish PH49 4HQ [E-mail: awinning009@btinternet.com]	01855 811929

LOCHABER Communion Sundays Please consult the Presbytery website: www.cofslochaber.co.uk

(39) ROSS

Meets on the first Tuesday of September in the church of the incoming Moderator, and in Dingwall: Castle Street Church on the first Tuesday of October, November, December, February, March and May, and on the last Tuesday of June.

Clerk:	**MR RONALD W. GUNSTONE BSc**		**20 Bellfield Road, North Kessock, Inverness IV1 3XU** **[E-mail: ross@churchofscotland.org.uk]**	**01463 731337**

Alness
Vacant

Michael J. Macdonald (Auxiliary Minister)	2004	2014	27 Darroch Brae, Alness IV17 0SD 73 Firhill, Alness IV17 0RT [E-mail: Michael.Macdonald@churchofscotland.org.uk]	01349 882238 01349 884268

Avoch linked with Fortrose and Rosemarkie
Vacant — 5 Ness Way, Fortrose IV10 8SS — 01381 621433

Contin (H) linked with Foddery and Strathpeffer (H)
Vacant — The Manse, Contin, Strathpeffer IV14 9ES — 01997 421028

Cromarty linked with Resolis and Urquhart
Terrance Burns BA MA — 2014 2017 — The Manse, Culbokie, Dingwall IV7 8JN
[E-mail: TBurns@churchofscotland.org.uk] — 01349 877452

Dingwall: Castle Street (H)
Stephen Macdonald BD MTh — 2008 2014 — 16 Achany Road, Dingwall IV15 9JB
[E-mail: SMacdonald@churchofscotland.org.uk] — 01349 866792 / 07570 804193 (Mbl)

Dingwall: St Clement's (H)
Bruce Dempsey BD — 1997 2014 — 8 Castlehill Road, Dingwall IV15 9PB
[E-mail: BDempsey@churchofscotland.org.uk] — 01349 292055

Fearn Abbey and Nigg linked with Tarbat
Robert G.D.W. Pickles BD MPhil ThD — 2003 2015 — Church of Scotland Manse, Fearn, Tain IV20 1WN
[E-mail: RPickles@churchofscotland.org.uk] — 01862 832282

Ferintosh
Vacant — Ferintosh Manse, Leanaig Road, Conon Bridge, Dingwall IV7 8BE — 01349 861275

Fodderty and Strathpeffer See Contin
Fortrose and Rosemarkie See Avoch

Invergordon
Kenneth Donald MacLeod BD CPS — 1989 2000 — The Manse, Cromlet Drive, Invergordon IV18 0BA
[E-mail: KMacLeod@churchofscotland.org.uk] — 01349 852273

Killearnan (H) linked with Knockbain (H)
Susan Cord — 2016 — 14 First Field Avenue, North Kessock, Inverness IV1 3JB
[E-mail: SCord@churchofscotland.org.uk] — 01463 731930

Kilmuir and Logie Easter
Vacant
The Manse, Delny, Invergordon IV18 0NW — 01862 842280

Kiltearn (H)
Donald A. MacSween BD   1991   1998
The Manse, Swordale Road, Evanton, Dingwall IV16 9UZ
[E-mail: DMacSween@churchofscotland.org.uk] — 01349 830472

Knockbain See Killearnan

Lochbroom and Ullapool (GD)
Vacant
The New Manse, Garve Road, Ullapool IV26 2SX — 01854 613146

Resolis and Urquhart See Cromarty

Rosskeen
Vacant
Rosskeen Manse, Perrins Road, Alness IV17 0XG — 01349 882265

Tain
Andrew P. Fothergill BA   2012   2017
14 Kingsway Avenue, Tain IV19 1NJ
[E-mail: AFothergill@churchofscotland.org.uk] — 01862 892296

Tarbat See Fearn Abbey and Nigg

Urray and Kilchrist
Scott Polworth LLB BD   2009
The Manse, Corrie Road, Muir of Ord IV6 7TL
[E-mail: SPolworth@churchofscotland.org.uk] — 01463 870259

Archer, Nicholas D.C. BA BD   1971 1992   (Dores and Boleskine)
2 Aldie Cottages, Tain IV19 1LZ
[E-mail: na.2ac777@btinternet.com] — 01862 821494

Bissett, James   2016   Ordained Local Minister
14 First Field Avenue, North Kessock, Inverness IV1 3JB
[E-mail: JBissett@churchofscotland.org.uk] — 01463 731930

Dupar, Kenneth W. BA BD PhD   1965 1993   (Christ's College, Aberdeen)
The Old Manse, The Causeway, Cromarty IV11 8XJ — 01381 600428
Forsyth, James LTh   1970 2000   (Fearn Abbey with Nigg Chapelhill)
Rhives Lodge, Golspie, Sutherland KW10 6DD
Greer, A. David C.   1956 1996   (Barra)
17 Duthac Wynd, Tain IV19 1LP
[E-mail: greer2@talktalk.net] — 01862 892065

Horne, Douglas A. BD	1977 2009	(Tain)	151 Holm Farm Road, Culduthel, Inverness IV2 6BF [E-mail: douglas.horne@talktalk.net]	01463 712677
Jones, Robert BSc BD	1990 2017	(Rosskeen)	3 Grantown Avenue, Airdrie ML6 8HH [E-mail: rob2jones@btinternet.com]	(Mbl) 07761 782714
Lincoln, John MPhil BD	1986 2014	(Balquhidder with Killin and Ardeonaig)	59 Obsdale Park, Alness IV17 0TR [E-mail: johnlincoln@minister.com]	01349 882791
McDonald, Alan D. LLB BD MTh DLitt DD	1979 2016	(Cameron with St Andrews: St Leonard's)	7 Duke Street, Cromarty IV11 8YH [E-mail: alan.d.mcdonald@talk21.com]	01381 600954
MacKinnon, R.M. LTh	1968 1995	(Kilmuir and Logie Easter)	27 Riverford Crescent, Conon Bridge, Dingwall IV7 8HL	01349 866293
MacLennan, Alasdair J. BD DCE	1978 2001	(Resolis and Urquhart)	Airdale, Seaforth Road, Muir of Ord IV6 7TA	01463 870704
Macleod, John MA	1959 1993	(Resolis and Urquhart)	'Benview', 19 Balvaird, Muir of Ord IV6 7RG [E-mail: sheilaandjohn@yahoo.co.uk]	01463 871286
Munro, James A. BA BD DMS	1979 2013	(Port Glasgow: Hamilton Bardrainney)	1 Wyvis Crescent, Conon Bridge, Dingwall IV7 8BZ [E-mail: james781munro@btinternet.com]	01349 865752
Rattenbury, Carol	2017	Ordained Local Minister	Balloan Farm House, Alcaig, Conon Bridge, Dingwall IV7 8HU [E-mail: CRattenbury@churchofscotland.org.uk]	01349 877323
Scott, David V. BTh	1994 2014	(Fearn Abbey and Nigg with Tarbat)	29 Sunnyside, Culloden Moor, Inverness IV2 5ES	01463 795802
Smith, Russel BD	1994 2013	(Dingwall: St Clement's)	1 School Road, Conon Bridge, Dingwall IV7 8AE [E-mail: russanttwo@btinternet.com]	01349 861011

(40) SUTHERLAND

Meets at Lairg on the first Tuesday of March, May, September, November and December, and on the first Tuesday of June at the Moderator's church.

| Clerk: | REV. STEWART GOUDIE BSc BD | 1977 | 2017 | St Andrew's Manse, Tongue, Lairg IV27 4XL [E-mail: sutherland@churchofscotland.org.uk] | 01847 611230 (Tel/Fax) 07957 237757 (Mbl) |

Altnaharra and Farr
Beverly W. Cushman MA MDiv BA PhD | 1977 2017 | The Manse, Bettyhill, Thurso KW14 7SS [E-mail: BCushman@churchofscotland.org.uk] | 01641 521208

Assynt and Stoer
Vacant | Canisp Road, Lochinver, Lairg IV27 4LH | 01571 844342

Clyne (H) linked with Kildonan and Loth Helmsdale (H)
Vacant | Golf Road, Brora KW9 6QS | 01408 621239

Creich See Kincardine Croick and Edderton

Dornoch Cathedral (H)
Susan M. Brown (Mrs) BD DipMin — 1985 — 1998 — Cathedral Manse, Cnoc-an-Lobht, Dornoch IV25 3HN [E-mail: Susan.Brown@churchofscotland.org.uk] — 01862 810296

Durness and Kinlochbervie
Andrea M. Boyes (Mrs) RMN BA(Theol) — 2013 — 2017 — Manse Road, Kinlochbervie, Lairg IV27 4RG [E-mail: ABoyes@churchofscotland.org.uk] — 01971 521287

Eddrachillis
John MacPherson BSc BD — 1993 — Church of Scotland Manse, Scourie, Lairg IV27 4TQ [E-mail: JMacPherson@churchofscotland.org.uk] — 01971 502431

Golspie
John B. Sterrett BA BD PhD — 2007 — The Manse, Fountain Road, Golspie KW10 6TH [E-mail: JSterret@churchofscotland.org.uk] — 01408 633295 (Tel/Fax)

Kildonan and Loth Helmsdale See Clyne

Kincardine Croick and Edderton linked with Creich linked with Rosehall
Anthony M. Jones BD DPS DipTheol CertMin FRSA — 1994 — 2010 — The Manse, Ardgay IV24 3BG [E-mail: AJones@churchofscotland.org.uk] — 01863 766285
Hilary M. Gardner (Miss) (Auxiliary Minister) — 2010 — 2012 — Cayman Lodge, Kincardine Hill, Ardgay IV24 3DJ [E-mail: HGardner@churchofscotland.org.uk] — 01863 766107

Lairg (H) linked with Rogart (H)
Vacant — The Manse, Lairg IV27 4EH

Melness and Tongue (H)
Stewart Goudie BSc BD — 2010 — St Andrew's Manse, Tongue, Lairg IV27 4XL [E-mail: SGoudie@churchofscotland.org.uk] — 01847 611230 (Tel/Fax) / 07957 237757 (Mbl)

Rogart See Lairg
Rosehall See Kincardine Croick and Edderton

Chambers, John OBE BSc	1972 2009	(Inverness: Ness Bank)	Bannlagan Lodge, 4 Earls Cross Gardens, Dornoch IV25 3NR	01862 811520
			[E-mail: chambersdornoch@btinternet.com]	
Goskirk, J.L. LTh	1968 2010	(Lairg with Rogart)	Rathvilly, Lairgmuir, Lairg IV27 4ED	01549 402569
			[E-mail: leslie_goskirk@sky.com]	
McCree, Ian W. BD	1971 2011	(Clyne with Kildonan and Loth Helmsdale)	Tigh Ardachu, Mosshill, Brora KW9 6NG	01408 621185
			[E-mail: ian@mccree.f9.co.uk]	
Stobo, Mary J. (Mrs)	2013	Ordained Local Minister: Community Healthcare Chaplain	Druim-an-Sgairnich, Ardgay IV24 3BG	01863 766868
			[E-mail: MStobo@churchofscotland.org.uk]	

(41) CAITHNESS

Meets alternately at Wick and Thurso on the first Tuesday of February, March, May, September, November and December, and the third Tuesday of June.

| Clerk: | REV. RONALD JOHNSTONE BD | 2 Comlifoot Drive, Halkirk KW12 6ZA | 01847 839033 |
| | | [E-mail: caithness@churchofscotland.org.uk] | |

Bower linked with Halkirk Westerdale linked with Watten
Vacant — The Manse, Station Road, Watten, Wick KW1 5YN — 01955 621220

Canisbay linked with Dunnet linked with Keiss linked with Olrig
Vacant — The Manse, Canisbay, Wick KW1 4YH — 01955 611756

Dunnet See Canisbay
Halkirk Westerdale See Bower
Keiss See Canisbay
Olrig See Canisbay

The North Coast Parish
Vacant — Church of Scotland Manse, Reay, Thurso KW14 7RE — 01847 811441

The Parish of Latheron
Vacant — Central Manse, Main Street, Lybster KW3 6BN — 01593 721706
[E-mail: parish-of-latheron@btconnect.com]

Thurso: St Peter's and St Andrew's (H)
David S.M. Malcolm BD 2011 2014 The Manse, 46 Rose Street, Thurso KW14 8RF 01847 895186
[E-mail: David.Malcolm@churchofscotland.org.uk]

Thurso: West (H)
Ida Tenglerova Mgr 2012 2017 Thorkel Road, Thurso KW14 7LW 01847 892663

Watten See Bower

Wick: Pulteneytown (H) and Thrumster
Vacant The Manse, Coronation Street, Wick KW1 5LS 01955 603166

Wick: St Fergus
John Nugent BD 1999 2011 Mansefield, Miller Avenue, Wick KW1 4DF 01955 602167
[E-mail: JNugent@churchofscotland.org.uk] 07511 503946 (Mbl)

Duncan, Esme (Miss) 2013 Ordained Local Minister Avalon, Upper Warse, Canisbay, Wick KW1 4YD 01955 611455
[E-mail: EDuncan@churchofscotland.org.uk]

Johnstone, Ronald BD 1977 2011 (Thurso: West) 2 Comlifoot Drive, Halkirk KW12 6ZA 01847 839033
[E-mail: ronaldjohnstone@btinternet.com]

Rennie, Lyall 2013 Ordained Local Minister Ruachmarra, Lower Warse, Canisbay, Wick KW1 4YB 01955 611756
[E-mail: LRennie@churchofscotland.org.uk]

Stewart, Heather (Mrs) 2013 Ordained Local Minister Burnthill, Thrumster, Wick KW1 5TR 01955 651717
[E-mail: Heather.Stewart@churchofscotland.org.uk] (Work) 01955 603333

Warner, Kenneth BD 1981 2008 (Halkirk and Westerdale) Kilearnan, Clayock, Halkirk KW12 6UZ 01847 831825
[E-mail: wrnrkenn@btinternet.com]

CAITHNESS Communion Sundays

Bower 1st Jul, Dec	Keiss 1st May, 3rd Nov	West 4th Mar, Jun, Nov
Canisbay 1st Jun, Nov	Latheron Apr, Jul, Sep, Nov	Watten 1st Jul, Dec
Dunnet last May, Nov	North Coast Mar, Easter, Jun, Sep, Dec	Wick: Pulteneytown and 1st Mar, Jun, Sep, Dec
Halkirk Westerdale Apr, Jul, Oct	Olrig last May, Nov	Thrumster
	Thurso: St Peter's and Mar, Jun, Sep, Dec	St Fergus Apr, Oct
	St Andrew's	

(42) LOCHCARRON – SKYE

Meets in Kyle on the first Tuesday of September, November, December, February, June, and in conference on the first Saturday in March.

Clerk: REV. JOHN W. MURRAY LLB BA — 1 Totescore, Kilmuir, Portree, Isle of Skye IV51 9YW
[E-mail: lochcarronskye@churchofscotland.org.uk]   01470 542297

Applecross, Lochcarron and Torridon (GD)
Anita Stutter Drs (MA)   2008   2017
The Manse, Colonel's Road, Lochcarron, Strathcarron IV54 8YG
[E-mail: AStutter@churchofscotland.org.uk]   01520 722783

Bracadale and Duirinish (GD)
Janet Easton-Berry BA (SocSc) BA (Theol)   1994   2016
Duirinish Manse, Dunvegan, Isle of Skye IV55 8WQ
[E-mail: JEaston-Berry@churchofscotland.ork.uk]   01470 521668

Gairloch and Dundonnell
Stuart J. Smith BEng BD MTh   1994   2016
Church of Scotland Manse, The Glebe, Gairloch IV21 2BT
[E-mail: Stuart.Smith@churchofscotland.org.uk]   01445 712645

Glenelg Kintail and Lochalsh
Vacant
The Manse, Main Street, Kyle of Lochalsh IV40 8DA
(New charge formed by the union of Glenelg and Kintail and Lochalsh)   01599 534294

Kilmuir and Stenscholl (GD)
John W. Murray LLB BA   2003   2015
1 Totescore, Kilmuir, Isle of Skye IV51 9YN
[E-mail: JMurray@churchofscotland.org.uk]   01470 542297

Portree (GD)
Sandor Fazakas BD MTh   1976   2007
Viewfield Road, Portree, Isle of Skye IV51 9ES
[E-mail: SFazakas@churchofscotland.org.uk]   01478 611868

Snizort (H) (GD)
Vacant
The Manse, Kensaleyre, Snizort, Portree, Isle of Skye IV51 9XE   01470 532453

Strath and Sleat (GD)
Rory A.R. MacLeod BA MBA BD DMin   1994   2015
The Manse, 6 Upper Breakish, Isle of Skye IV42 8PY
[E-mail: RMacLeod@churchofscotland.org.uk]   01471 822416

Anderson, Janet (Miss) DCS		(Deacon)	Creagard, 31 Lower Breakish, Isle of Skye IV42 8QA [E-mail: jaskye@hotmail.co.uk]	01471 822403
Kellas, David J. MA BD	1966 2004	(Kilfinan with Kyles)	Buarblach, Glenelg, Kyle IV40 8LA [E-mail: davidkellas@btinternet.com]	01599 522257 (Mbl) 07909 577764
McCulloch, Alen J.R. MA BD	1990 2012	(Chaplain: Royal Navy)	Aros, 6 Gifford Terrace Road, Plymouth PL3 4JE [E-mail: aviljoen90@hotmail.com]	01752 657290
Mackenzie, Hector M.	2008	Chaplain: Army	HQ Military Corrective Training Centre, Berechurch Hall Camp, Berechurch Hall Road, Colchester CO2 9NU [E-mail: mackenziehector@hotmail.com]	
Martin, George M. MA BD	1987 2005	(Applecross, Lochcarron and Torridon)	8(1) Buckingham Terrace, Edinburgh EH4 3AA	0131-343 3937
Morrison, Derek	1995 2013	(Gairloch and Dundonnell)	2 Cliffton Place, Poolewe, Achnasheen IV22 2JU [E-mail: derekmorrison1@aol.com]	01445 781333

LOCHCARRON – SKYE Communion Sundays

Applecross	1st Sep	Gairloch	3rd Jun, Nov
Amisort	3rd Mar, Sep	Glenelg	2nd Jun, Nov
Bracadale	Last Feb	Glenshiel	1st Jul
Broadford	3rd Jan, Easter, 3rd Sep	Kilmuir	1st Mar, Sep
Duirinish	4th Jun	Kintail	3rd Apr, Jul
Dundonnell	1st Aug	Kyleakin	Last Sep
Elgol		Lochalsh and Stromeferry	4th Jan, Jun, Sep, Christmas, Easter
		Lochcarron and Shieldaig	Easter; communion held on a revolving basis when there is a fifth Sunday in the month

Plockton and Kyle	2nd May, 1st Oct
Portree	Easter, Pentecost, Christmas, 2nd Mar, Aug, 1st Nov
Sleat	Last May
Snizort	1st Jan, 4th Mar
Stenscholl	1st Jun, Dec
Strath	4th Jan
Torridon and Kinlochewe	

In the Parish of Strath and Sleat, Easter communion is held on a revolving basis.

(43) UIST

Meets on the first Tuesday of February, March, September and November in Lochmaddy, and on the third Tuesday of June in Leverburgh.

Clerk:	REV. GAVIN J. ELLIOTT MA BD		5a Aird, Isle of Benbecula HS7 5LT [E-mail: uist@churchofscotland.org.uk]	01870 602726

Benbecula (GD) (H) linked with Carinish

Andrew (Drew) P. Kuzma BA	2007	2016	Church of Scotland Manse, Griminish, Isle of Benbecula HS7 5QA	01870 602180

Berneray and Lochmaddy (GD) (H) linked with Kilmuir and Paible (GD)

Vacant	Church of Scotland Manse, Paible, Isle of North Uist HS6 5HD	01876 510310

Carinish (GD) (H) See Benbecula

Church of Scotland Manse, Clachan, Locheport, Lochmaddy,
Isle of North Uist HS6 5HD   01876 580219

Kilmuir and Paible See Berneray and Lochmaddy

Manish-Scarista (GD) (H)
David Donaldson MA BD DMin   1969   2015

Church of Scotland Manse, Scarista, Isle of Harris HS3 3HX
[E-mail: DDonaldson@churchofscotland.org.uk]   01859 550200

Tarbert (GD) (H)
Ian Murdo M. Macdonald DPA BD   2001   2015

The Manse, Manse Road, Tarbert, Isle of Harris HS3 3DF
[E-mail: Ian.MacDonald@churchofscotland.org.uk]   01859 502231

Elliott, Gavin J. MA BD	1976	2015	(Ministries Council)	5a Aird, Isle of Benbecula HS7 5LT [E-mail: gavkondwani@gmail.com]	01870 602726
Macdonald, Ishabel		2011	Ordained Local Minister	'Cleat Afe Ora', 18 Carinish, Isle of North Uist HS6 5HN [E-mail: Ishie.Macdonald@churchofscotland.org.uk]	01876 580367
MacInnes, David MA BD	1966	1999	(Kilmuir and Paible)	9 Golf View Road, Kinmylies, Inverness IV3 8SZ	01463 717377
MacIver, Norman BD	1976	2011	(Tarbert)	57 Boswell Road, Wester Inshes, Inverness IV2 3EW [E-mail: norman@n-cmaciver.freeserve.co.uk]	
Morrison, Donald John		2001	Auxiliary Minister	22 Kyles, Tarbert, Isle of Harris HS3 3BS [E-mail: DMorrison@churchofscotland.org.uk]	01859 502341
Petrie, Jackie G.	1989	2011	(South Uist)	7B Malaclete, Isle of North Uist HS6 5BX [E-mail: jackiegpetrie@yahoo.com]	01876 560804
Smith, John M.	1956	1992	(Lochmaddy)	Hamersay, Clachan, Locheport, Lochmaddy, Isle of North Uist HS6 5HD	01876 580332
Smith, Murdo MA BD	1988	2011	(Manish-Scarista)	Aisgeir, 15A Upper Shader, Isle of Lewis HS3 3MX	

UIST Communion Sundays

Benbecula	2nd Mar, Sep
Berneray and Lochmaddy	4th Jun, last Oct
Carinish	4th Mar, Aug
Kilmuir and Paible	1st Jun, 3rd Nov
Manish-Scarista	3rd Apr, 1st Oct
Tarbert	2nd Mar, 3rd Sep

(44) LEWIS

Meets at Stornoway, in St Columba's Church Hall, on the second Tuesday of February, March, September and November. It also meets if required in April, June and December on dates to be decided.

Clerk: MR JOHN CUNNINGHAM

1 Raven's Lane, Stornoway, Isle of Lewis HS2 0EG
[E-mail: lewis@churchofscotland.org.uk]

0851 709977
07789 878840 (Mbl)

Barvas (GD) (H)
Dougie Wolf BA(Theol)

2017

Church of Scotland Manse, Lower Barvas, Isle of Lewis HS2 0QY
[E-mail: DWolf@churchofscotland.org.uk]

01851 840218

Carloway (GD) (H) (Office: 01851 643211)
Vacant

Church of Scotland Manse, Knock, Carloway, Isle of Lewis HS2 9AU

01851 643255

Cross Ness (GE) (H)
Vacant

Cross Manse, Swainbost, Ness, Isle of Lewis HS2 0TB

01851 810375

Kinloch (GE) (H)
Iain M. Campbell BD

2004   2008

Laxay, Lochs, Isle of Lewis HS2 9LA
[E-mail: ICampbell@churchofscotland.org.uk]

01851 830218

Knock (GE) (H)
Guardianship of the Presbytery

Lochs-Crossbost (GD) (H)
Guardianship of the Presbytery

Lochs-in-Bernera (GD) (H) linked with Uig (GE) (H)
Hugh Maurice Stewart DPA BD

2008

7 Tobson, Great Bernera, Isle of Lewis HS2 9NA
(Temporary Manse)
[E-mail: berneralwuig@btinternet.com]

01851 612466

Stornoway: High (GD) (H)
Vacant

High Manse, 1 Goathill Road, Stornoway, Isle of Lewis HS1 2NJ

01851 703106

Stornoway: Martin's Memorial (H) (Church office: 01851 700820)

Thomas MacNeil MA BD	2002	2006	Matheson Road, Stornoway, Isle of Lewis HS1 2LR	01851 704238

[E-mail: tommymacneil@hotmail.com]

Stornoway: St Columba (GD) (H) (Church office: 01851 701546)

William J. Heenan BA MTh	2012	St Columba's Manse, Lewis Street, Stornoway, Isle of Lewis HS1 2JF	01851 705933

[E-mail: WHeenan@churchofscotland.org.uk]   07837 770589 (Mbl)

Uig See Lochs-in-Bernera

Amed, Paul LTh DPS	1992	2015	(Barvas)	6 Scotland Street, Stornoway, Isle of Lewis HS1 2JQ 01851 706450

[E-mail: paulamed56@gmail.com]

Johnstone, Ben MA BD DMin	1973	2013	(Strath and Sleat)	Loch Alainn, 5 Breaclete, Great Bernera, Isle of Lewis HS2 9LT 01851 612445

[E-mail: benonbernera@gmail.com]

Maclean, Donald A. DCS	1975	2006	(Deacon)	8 Upper Barvas, Isle of Lewis HS2 0QX 01851 840454
MacLennan, Donald Angus			(Kinloch)	4 Kestrel Place, Inverness IV2 3YH 01463 243750

[E-mail: maclennankinloch@btinternet.com]   07799 668270 (Mbl)

Macleod, Gordon M. BA	2017	Healthcare Chaplain	6 Laxdale Lane, Stornoway, Isle of Lewis HS2 0DR 01851 706966

[E-mail: macleods@laxdaleholidaypark.com]

Macleod, William	1957	2006	(Uig)	54 Lower Barvas, Isle of Lewis HS2 0QY 01851 840217
Shadakshari, T.K. BTh BD MTh	1998	2006	Healthcare Chaplain	23D Benside, Newmarket, Stornoway, Isle of Lewis HS2 0DZ (Home) 01851 701727

[E-mail: tk.shadakshari@nhs.net]   (Office) 01851 704704
(Mbl) 07403 697138

LEWIS Communion Sundays

Barvas	3rd Mar, Sep
Carloway	1st Mar, last Sep
Cross Ness	2nd Mar, Oct
Kinloch	3rd Mar, 2nd Jun, 2nd Sep

Knock	3rd Apr, 1st Nov
Lochs-Crossbost	4th Mar, Sep
Lochs-in-Bernera	1st Apr, 2nd Sep

Stornoway: High	3rd Feb, last Aug
Martin's Memorial	3rd Feb, last Aug, 1st Dec, Easter
St Columba	3rd Feb, last Aug
Uig	3rd Jun, 4th Oct

(45) ORKNEY

Normally meets at Kirkwall, in the St Magnus Centre, on the first Wednesday of September, November, February, April, and the third Wednesday of June.

Clerk: DR MICHAEL PARTRIDGE

Coldomo Cottage, Stenness, Orkney KW16 3HA
[E-mail: orkney@churchofscotland.org.uk]

01856 873747

Depute Clerk: MS MARGARET A.B. SUTHERLAND LLB BA

13 Cursiter Crescent, Kirkwall, Orkney KW15 1XN
[E-mail: mabs2@tiscali.co.uk]

Birsay, Harray and Sandwick
David G. McNeish MB ChB BSc BD   2015   The Manse, North Biggings Road, Dounby, Orkney KW17 2HZ   01856 771599
[E-mail: DMcNeish@churchofscotland.org.uk]

East Mainland
Wilma A. Johnston MTheol MTh   2006   2014   The Manse, Holm, Orkney KW17 2SB   01856 781797
[E-mail: Wilma.Johnston@churchofscotland.org.uk]

Eday
Vacant

Evie (H) linked with Firth (H) (01856 761117) linked with Rendall linked with Rousay
Roy Cordukes BSc BD   2014   The Manse, Finstown, Orkney KW17 2EG   01856 761328
[E-mail: RCordukes@churchofscotland.org.uk]

Firth See Evie

Flotta linked with Hoy and Walls linked with Orphir (H) and Stenness (H)
Vacant   Stenness Manse, Stenness, Stromness, Orkney KW16 3HH

Hoy and Walls See Flotta

Kirkwall: East (H) linked with Shapinsay
Julia Meason MTh   2013   East Church Manse, Thoms Street, Kirkwall, Orkney KW15 1PF   01856 874789
[E-mail: JMeason@churchofscotland.org.uk]

Kirkwall: St Magnus Cathedral (H)
G. Fraser H. Macnaughton MA BD — 1982 2002 — Berstane Road, Kirkwall, Orkney KW15 1NA
[E-mail: FMacnaughton@churchofscotland.org.uk] — 01856 873312

North Ronaldsay
Guardianship of the Presbytery

Orphir and Stenness See Flotta

Papa Westray linked with Westray
Iain D. MacDonald BD — 1993 — The Manse, Hilldavale, Westray, Orkney KW17 2DW
[E-mail: IMacDonald@churchofscotland.org.uk] — 01857 677357 (Tel/Fax) / 07710 443780 (Mbl)

Rendall See Evie
Rousay (Church centre: 01856 821271) See Evie

Sanday
Vacant

Shapinsay See Kirkwall: East

South Ronaldsay and Burray
Vacant — St Margaret's Manse, Church Road, St Margaret's Hope, Orkney KW17 2SR — 01856 831670

Stromness (H)
John A. Butterfield BA BD MPhil — 1990 2016 — 5 Manse Lane, Stromness, Orkney KW16 3AP
[E-mail: JButterfield@churchofscotland.org.uk] — 01856 850203

Stronsay: Moncur Memorial
Vacant — The Manse, Stronsay, Orkney KW17 2SB

Westray See Papa Westray

Clark, Thomas L. BD	1985	2008	(Orphir with Stenness)	7 Headland Rise, Burghead, Elgin IV30 5HA [E-mail: toml.clark@btinternet.com]	01343 830144
Freeth, June BA MA	2015		Ordained Local Minister	Cumlaquoy, Birsay, Orkney KW17 2ND [E-mail: JFreeth@churchofscotland.org.uk]	01856 721449
Graham, Jennifer D. (Mrs) BA MDiv PhD	2000	2011	(Eday with Stronsay: Moncur Memorial)	Lodge, Stronsay, Orkney KW17 2AN [E-mail: jdgraham67@gmail.com]	01857 616487
Prentice, Martin W.M.	2013		Ordained Local Minister	Cott of Howe, Cairston, Stromness, Orkney KW16 3JU [E-mail: MPrentice@churchofscotland.org.uk]	01856 851139 (Mbl) 07795 817213
Tait, Alexander	1967	1995	(Glasgow: St Enoch's Hogganfield)	Ingermas, Evie, Orkney KW17 2PH [E-mail: jen1957@hotmail.co.uk]	01856 751477
Whitson, William S. MA	1959	1999	(Cumbernauld: St Mungo's)	2 Chapman's Brae, Bathgate EH48 4LH [E-mail: william_whitson@tiscali.co.uk]	01506 650027
Wishart, James BD	1986	2009	(Deer)	Upper Westshore, Burray, Orkney KW17 2TE [E-mail: jwishart06@btinternet.com]	01856 731672

(46) SHETLAND

Meets at Lerwick on the first Tuesday of February, April, June, September, November and December.

Clerk: REV DEBORAH J. DOBBY BD PGCE RGN RSCN The Manse, Hogalee, East Voe, Scalloway, Shetland ZE1 0UU   01595 881184
[E-mail: shetland@churchofscotland.org.uk]

Burra Isle linked with Tingwall
Deborah J. Dobby (Mrs)   2014   The Manse, 25 Hogalee, East Voe, Scalloway, Shetland ZE1 0UU   01595 881184
BA BD PGCE RGN RSCN   [E-mail: DDobby@churchofscotland.org.uk]

Delting linked with Northmavine
Vacant   The Manse, Grindwell, Brae, Shetland ZE2 9QJ   01806 522219

Dunrossness and St Ninian's inc. Fair Isle linked with Sandwick, Cunningsburgh and Quarff
Vacant

Lerwick and Bressay
Vacant   The Manse, 82 St Olaf Street, Lerwick, Shetland ZE1 0ES   01595 692125

Nesting and Lunnasting linked with Whalsay and Skerries
Irene A. Charlton (Mrs) BTh   1994 1997   The Manse, Marrister, Symbister, Whalsay, Shetland ZE2 9AE   01806 566767
[E-mail: ICharlton@churchofscotland.org.uk]

Northmavine See Delting

Sandsting and Aithsting linked with Walls and Sandness
D. Brian Dobby MA BA   1999 2014   The Manse, 25 Hogalee, East Voe, Scalloway, Shetland ZE1 0UU   01595 881184
[E-mail: BDobby@churchofscotland.org.uk]

Sandwick, Cunningsburgh and Quarff See Dunrossness and St Ninian's
Tingwall See Burra Isle

Unst and Fetlar linked with Yell
Vacant   North Isles Manse, Gutcher, Yell, Shetland ZE2 9DF   01957 744258

Walls and Sandness See Sandsting and Aithsting
Whalsay and Skerries See Nesting and Lunnasting
Yell See Unst and Fetlar

Greig, Charles H.M. MA BD	1976	2016	(Dunrossness and St Ninian's inc. Fair Isle with Sandwick, Cunningsburgh and Quarff)	6 Hayhoull Place, Bigton, Shetland ZE2 9GA [E-mail: chm.greig@btinternet.com]	01950 422468
Kirkpatrick, Alice H. (Miss) MA BD FSAScot	1987	2000	(Northmavine)	1 Daisy Park, Baltasound, Unst, Shetland ZE2 9EA	
Knox, R. Alan MA LTh AInstAM	1965	2004	(Fetlar with Unst with Yell)	27 Killyvalley Road, Garvagh, Co. Londonderry, Northern Ireland BT51 5LX	02829 558925
Lockerbie, Caroline R. BA MDiv DMin	2007	2017	(Lerwick and Bressay: Transition Minister)	[E-mail: carolinelockerbie@hotmail.com]	
Macintyre, Thomas MA BD	1972	2011	(Sandsting and Aithsting with Walls and Sandness)	Lappideks, South Voxter, Cunningsburgh, Shetland ZE2 9HF [E-mail: the2macs.macintyre@btinternet.com]	01950 477549
Smith, Catherine (Mrs) DCS			(Deacon)	21 Lingaro, Bixter, Shetland ZE2 9NN	01595 810207
Williamson, Magnus J.C.	1982	1999	(Fetlar with Yell)	Creekhaven, Houl Road, Scalloway, Shetland ZE1 0XA	01595 880023

(47) ENGLAND

Meets at London, in Crown Court Church, on the second Tuesday of February, and at St Columba's, Pont Street, on the second Tuesday of June and the second Saturday of October.

Clerk: REV. ALISTAIR CUMMING MSc CCS FInstLM   64 Prince George's Avenue, London SW20 8BH   07534 943986 (Mbl)
[E-mail: england@churchofscotland.org.uk]

Corby: St Andrew's (H)
A. Norman Nicoll BD   2003   2016   43 Hempland Close, Corby, Northants NN18 8LR   07930 988863 (Mbl)
[E-mail: NNicoll@churchofscotland.org.uk]

Corby: St Ninian's (H) (01536 265245)
Kleber Machado BTh MA MTh   1998   2012   The Manse, 46 Glyndebourne Gardens, Corby, Northants NN18 0PZ   01536 669478
[E-mail: KMachado@churchofscotland.org.uk]

Guernsey: St Andrew's in the Grange (H)
Vacant   The Manse, Le Villocq, Castel, Guernsey GY5 7SB   01481 257345

Jersey: St Columba's (H)
Graeme M. Glover   2017   18 Claremont Avenue, St Saviour, Jersey JE2 7SF   01534 730659
[E-mail: GGlover@churchofscotland.org.uk]

London: Crown Court (H) (020 7836 5643)
Philip L. Majcher BD   1982   2007   53 Sidmouth Street, London WC1H 8JX   020 7278 5022
[E-mail: PMajcher@churchofscotland.org.uk]

London: St Columba's (H) (020 7584 2321) linked with Newcastle: St Andrew's (H)
C. Angus MacLeod MA BD   1996   2012   29 Hollywood Road, Chelsea, London SW10 9HT   020 7584 2321 (Office)
[E-mail: Angus.MacLeod@churchofscotland.org.uk]
Andrea E. Price (Mrs)   1997   2014   St Columba's, Pont Street, London SW1X 0BD   020 7610 6994 (Home)
(Associate Minister)   020 7584 2321 (Office)
[E-mail: APrice@churchofscotland.org.uk]

Anderson, Andrew F. MA BD   1981 2011   (Edinburgh: Greenside)   58 Reliance Way, Oxford OX4 2FG   01865 778397
[E-mail: andrew.relianceway@gmail.com]
Anderson, David P. BSc BD   2002 2007   Army Chaplain
[E-mail: padre.anderson180@mod.gov.uk]

Name	Ordained/Inducted	Position	Address / E-mail	Telephone
Binks, Mike	2007	Auxiliary Minister	Hollybank, 10 Kingsbrook, Corby NN18 9HY [E-mail: MBinks@churchofscotland.org.uk]	(Mbl) 07590 507917
Bowie, A. Glen CBE BA BSc	1954 1984	(Principal Chaplain: RAF)	16 Weir Road, Hemingford Grey, Huntingdon PE18 9EH	01480 381425
Brown, Scott J. CBE QHC BD	1993 2015	(Chaplain of the Fleet: Royal Navy)	[E-mail: scott3568@gmail.com]	(Mbl) 07769 847876
Cairns, W. Alexander BD	1978 2006	(Corby: St Andrew's)	Kirkton House, Kirkton of Craig, Montrose DD10 9TB [E-mail: sandy.cairns@btinternet.com]	(Mbl) 07808 588045
Cameron, R. Neil	1975 1981	(Chaplain: Community)	[E-mail: neilandminacameron@yahoo.co.uk]	
Coulter, David G. QHC BA BD MDA PhD CF	1989 1994	Chaplain General, HM Land Forces	8 Ashdown Terrace, Tidworth, Wilts SP9 7SQ [E-mail: padredgcoulter@yahoo.co.uk]	01980 842175
Cumming, Alistair MSc CCS FInstLM	2010	Presbytery Clerk	64 Prince George's Avenue, London SW20 8BH [E-mail: ACumming@churchofscotland.org.uk]	020 8540 7365 (Mbl) 07534 943986
Dowswell, James A.M.	1991 2001	(Lerwick and Bressay)	Mill House, High Street, Staplehurst, Tonbridge, Kent TN12 0AU [E-mail: jdowswell@btinternet.com]	01580 891271
Fields, James MA BD STM	1988 1997	School Chaplain	The Bungalow, The Ridgeway, Mill Hill, London NW7 1QX	020 8201 1397
Francis, James BD PhD	2002 2009	Army Chaplain	37 Milburn Road, Coleraine BT52 1QT	02870 353869
Lancaster, Craig MA BD	2004 2011	RAF Chaplain	[E-mail: bzn-chaplain4@mod.gov.uk]	
Langlands, Cameron H. BD MTh ThM PhD MInstLM	1995 2012	Chaplain South London and Maudsley NHS Foundation Trust	Maudsley Hospital, Denmark Road, London SE5 8EZ	(Mbl) 07989 642544
Lovett, Mairi F. BSc BA DipPS MTh	2005 2013	Hospital Chaplain	Royal Brompton Hospital, Sydney Street, London SW3 6NP [E-mail: m.lovett@rbht.nhs.uk]	020 7352 8121 ext. 4736
Lugton, George L. MA BD	1955 1997	(Guernsey: St Andrew's in the Grange)	6 Clos de Beauvoir, Rue Cohu, Guernsey GY5 7TE	(Tel/Fax) 01481 254285
Lunn, Dorothy I.M.	2002	(Auxiliary Minister)	14 Bellerby Drive, Ouston, Co.Durham DH2 1TW [E-mail: dorothylunn@hotmail.com]	0191-492 0647
Macfarlane, Peter T. BA LTh	1970 1994	(Chaplain: Army)	4 rue de Rives, 37160 Abilly, France	
McIndoe, John H. MA BD STM DD	1966 2000	(London: St Columba's with Newcastle: St Andrew's)	5 Dunlin, Westerlands Park, Glasgow G12 0FE [E-mail: johnandeve@mcindoe555.f5net.co.uk]	0141-579 1366
MacLeod, Rory N. BA BD	1986 1992	Chaplain: Army	21 Engr Regt, Clara Barracks, Chatham Road, Ripon HG4 2RD	
McMahon, John K.S. MA BD	1998 2012	Head of Spiritual and Pastoral Care, West London Mental Health Trust	Broadmoor Hospital, Crowthorne, Berkshire RG45 7EG [E-mail: john.mcmahonrev@wlmht.nhs.uk]	01344 754098
Mather, James BA DipArch MA MBA	2010	Auxiliary Minister: University Chaplain	24 Ellison Road, Barnes, London SW13 0AD [E-mail: JMather@churchofscotland.org.uk]	(Home) 020 8876 6540 (Work) 020 7361 1670 (Mbl) 07836 715655
Middleton, Paul BMus BD ThM PhD	2000	University Lecturer	97B Whipcord Lane, Chester CH1 4DG	
Munro, Alexander W. MA BD	1978	Chaplain and Teacher of Religious Studies	Columba House, 12 Alexandra Road, Southport PR9 0NB [E-mail: revdjt@gmail.com]	01704 543044
Thom, David J. BD DipMin	1999 2015	Army Chaplain	12 Test Green, Corby, Northants NN17 2HA	01536 264018
Trevorrow, James A. LTh	1971 2003	(Glasgow: Cranhill)	[E-mail: jimtrevorrow@compuserve.com]	
Walker, R. Forbes BSc BD ThM	1987 2013	School Chaplain	Flat 5, 18 Northside Wandsworth Common, London SW18 2SL [E-mail: revrfw@gmail.com]	020 8870 0953
Wallace, Donald S.	1950 1980	(Chaplain: RAF)	7 Dellfield Close, Watford, Herts WD1 3BL	01923 223289

Ward, Michael J.
BSc BD PhD MA PGCE   1983 2009   Training and Development Officer: Presbyterian Church of Wales   Apt 6, Bryn Hedd, Conwy Road, Penmaen-mawr, Gwynedd LL34 6BS
[E-mail: revmw@btopenworld.com]   (Mbl) 07765 598816

Wood, Peter J. MA BD   1993   (College Lecturer)   97 Broad Street, Cambourne, Cambridgeshire CB23 6DH
[E-mail: pejowood@tiscali.co.uk]   01954 715558

ENGLAND – Church Addresses

Corby: St Andrew's   Occupation Road
St Ninian's   Beanfield Avenue

Liverpool: The Western Rooms, Anglican Cathedral

London: Crown Court   Crown Court WC2
St Columba's   Pont Street SW1

Newcastle: Sandyford Road

(48) PRESBYTERY OF INTERNATIONAL CHARGES

Meets over the weekend of the second Sunday of March and October, hosted by congregations in mainland Europe.

Clerk: REV. JAMES SHARP   **102 Rue des Eaux-Vives, CH-1207 Geneva, Switzerland**
[E-mail: europe@churchofscotland.org.uk]   **0041 22 786 4847**

Depute Clerk: REV. DEREK G. LAWSON   **Schiedamse Vest 121, 3012BH, Rotterdam, The Netherlands**
[E-mail: deputeclerk@europepresbytery.net]   **0031 10 412 5709**

Amsterdam: English Reformed Church
Lance Stone   BD MTh PhD   2014   Jan Willem Brouwersstraat 9, NL-1071 LH Amsterdam, The Netherlands
[E-mail: minister@ercadam.nl]
Church address: Begijnhof 48, 1012WV Amsterdam   0031 20 672 2288

Bermuda: Christ Church, Warwick (H) (001 441 236 1882)
Alistair G. Bennett BSc BD   1978   2016   The Manse, 6 Manse Road, Paget PG 01. Bermuda
Church address: Christ Church, Middle Road, Warwick, Bermuda
Mailing address: PO Box WK 130, Warwick WK BX. Bermuda
[E-mail: christchurch@logic.bm; Website: www.christchurch.bm]   001 441 236 0400

Bochum (Associated congregation)
James M. Brown MA BD   1982   Neustrasse 15, D-44787 Bochum, Germany
[E-mail: j.brown56@gmx.de]
Church address: Pauluskircke, Grabenstrasse 9, 44787 Bochum   0049 234 133 65

Brussels St Andrew's (H) (0032 2 649 02 19) Andrew Gardner BSc BD PhD	1997	2004	23 Square des Nations, B-1000 Brussels, Belgium [E-mail: minister@churchofscotland.be] Church address: Chaussée de Vieurgat 181, 1050 Brussels [E-mail: secretary@churchofscotland.be]	0032 2 672 40 56
Budapest St Columba's (0036 1 373 0725) Aaron Stevens BA MDiv MACE	2010		Stefánia út 32, H-1143, Budapest, Hungary [E-mail: revastevens@yahoo.co.uk] Church address: Vörösmarty utca 51, 1064 Budapest	(Mbl) 0036 70 615 5394
Colombo, Sri Lanka: St Andrew's Scots Kirk (0094 112 323 765) Vacant			73 Galle Road, Colpetty, Colombo 3, Sri Lanka [E-mail: minister@standrewsscotskirk.org]	0094 112 386 774
Costa del Sol Vacant			Avenida Jesus Santos Rein, 24 Edf. Lindamar 4 – 3Q, Fuengirola, 29640 Malaga, Spain Church address: Lux Mundi Ecumenical Centre, Calle Nueva 3, 29460 Fuengirola	0034 951 260 982
Geneva (0041 22 788 08 31) Laurence H. Twaddle MA BD MTh	1977	2017	6 chemin Taverney, 1218 Geneva, Switzerland [E-mail: cofsg@pingnet.ch] Church address: Auditoire de Calvin, 1 Place de la Taconnerie, Geneva	0041 22 788 08 31
Gibraltar St Andrew's Ewen MacLean BA BD	1995	2009	St Andrew's Manse, 29 Scud Hill, Gibraltar [E-mail: scotskirk@gibraltar.gi] Church address: Governor's Parade, Gibraltar	00350 200 77040
Lausanne: The Scots Kirk (H) Ian J.M. McDonald MA BD	1984	2010	26 Avenue de Rumine, CH-1005 Lausanne, Switzerland [E-mail: minister@scotskirklausanne.ch]	0041 21 323 98 28
Lisbon St Andrew's Vacant			Rua Coelho da Rocha, N°75 - 1° Campa de Ourique, 1350-073 Lisbon, Portugal [E-mail: cofslx@netcabo.pt] Church address: Rua da Arriaga, Lisbon	00351 213 951 165

Malta St Andrew's Scots Church (H)
Kim Hurst   2014   La Romagnola, 15 Triq is-Seiqja, Misrah Kola, Attard ATD 1713, Malta [E-mail: minister@saintandrewsmalta.com] Church address: 210 Old Bakery Street, Valletta, Malta   (Tel/Fax) 00356 214 15465

Paris: The Scots Kirk
Jan J. Steyn   2011   2017   10 Rue Thimonnier, F-75009 Paris, France Church address: 17 Rue Bayard, 75009 Paris [E-mail: JSteyn@churchofscotland.org.uk]   0033 1 48 78 47 94

Rome: St Andrew's
Vacant   Via XX Settembre 7, 00187 Rome, Italy   (Tel) 0039 06 482 7627 (Fax) 0039 06 487 4370

Rotterdam: Scots International Church (0031 10 412 4779)
Derek G. Lawson LLB BD   1998   2016   Church address: Schiedamse Vest 121, 3012BH Rotterdam, The Netherlands Meeuwenstraat 4A, NL-3071 PE Rotterdam, The Netherlands [E-mail: info@scotsintchurch.com]   0031 10 412 5709

Trinidad: Greyfriars St Ann's, Port of Spain l/w Arouca and Sangre Grande
Vacant   50 Frederick Street, Port of Spain, Trinidad   001 868 623 6684

Born, Irene   2008   Ordained Local Minister-worship resourcing   Bergpolderstraat 53A, NL-3038 KB Rotterdam, The Netherlands [E-mail: ibsalem@xs4all.nl]   0031 10 265 1703

Johnston, Colin D. MA BD   1986 2016   Evangelical Theological Seminary Cairo   8 El - Sekka El - Beidah Street, Abassiyya, Cairo 11381, Egypt

McLay, Neil BA BD   2006 2012   Chaplain: Army (Brussels)   Barker Barracks, Paderborn, BFPO 22

Pitkeathly, Thomas C. MA CA BD   1984 2004   77 St Thomas Road, Lytham St Anne's FY8 1JP [E-mail: tpitkeathly@yahoo.co.uk]   01253 789634

Sharp, James   2005   OLM, Presbytery Clerk   102 Rue des Eaux-Vives, 1207 Geneva, Switzerland [E-mail: jimsharp@bluewin.ch]   0041 22 786 4847

(49) JERUSALEM

Clerk: **JOANNA OAKLEY-LEVSTEIN**   St Andrew's, Galilee, PO Box 104, Tiberias 14100, Israel [E-mail: j.oak.lev@gmail.com]   00972 50 5842517

Jerusalem: St Andrew's
Paraic Reamonn BA BD
1982   2014   St Andrew's Scots Memorial Church, 1 David Remez Street,   00972 2 673 2401
                PO Box 8619, Jerusalem 91086, Israel
                [E-mail: PReamonn@churchofscotland.org.uk]

Tiberias: St Andrew's (E-mail: tiberias@churchofscotland.org.uk; Website:https://standrewsgalilee.com)
Katharine S. McDonald BA MSc BD MLitt   2012   2015   St Andrew's, Galilee, 1 Gdud Barak Street,   00972 4 671 0759
(Scottish Episcopal Church)   PO Box 104, Tiberias 14100, Israel
                                                         [E-mail: kmcdonald@churchofscotland.org.uk]

SECTION 6

Additional Lists of Personnel

LIST A – ORDAINED LOCAL MINISTERS

Further information, including E-mail addresses, may be found under the presbytery (Section 5) to which an OLM belongs, its number recorded in the final column.

NAME	ORD	ADDRESS	TEL	PR
Allardice, Michael MA MPhil PGCertTHE FHEA	2014	26 Parbroath Road, Glenrothes KY7 4TH	01592 772280	25
Archer, Morven (Mrs)	2013	42 Firthview Drive, Inverness IV3 8QE	01463 237840	37
Bellis, Pamela A. BA	2014	Maughold, Low Killantrae, Port William, Newton Stewart DG8 9QR	01988 700590	9
Bissett, James	2016	14 First Field Avenue, North Kessock, Inverness IV1 3JB	01463 731930	39
Black, Sandra (Mrs)	2013	5 Doon Place, Troon KA10 7EQ	01292 220075	10
Bom, Irene	2008	Bergpolderstraat 53A, NL–3038 KB Rotterdam, The Netherlands	0031 10 265 1703	48
Breingan, Mhairi	2011	6 Park Road, Inchinnan, Renfrew PA4 4QJ	0141-812 1425	14
Brown, Kathryn (Mrs)	2014	1 Callendar Park Walk, Callendar Grange, Falkirk FK1 1TA	01324 617352	22
Crossan, William	2014	Gowanbank, Kilkerran Road, Campbeltown PA28 6JL	01586 553453	19
Dee, Oonagh	2014	'Kendoon', Merse Way, Kippford, Dalbeattie DG5 4LL	01556 620001	8
Dempster, Eric T. MBA	2016	Amanside, Wamphray, Moffat DG10 9LZ	01576 470496	7
Don, Andrew MBA	2006	5 Eskdale Court, Penicuik EH26 8HT	01968 675766	3
Duncan, Esme (Miss)	2013	Avalon, Upper Warse, Canisbay, Wick KW1 4YD	01955 611455	41
Duncanson, Mary (Ms)	2013	3 Balmenach Road, Cromdale, Grantown-on-Spey PH26 3LJ	01479 872165	36
Edwards, Dougal BTh	2013	25 Mackenzie Street, Carnoustie DD7 6HD	01241 852666	30
Fidler, David G.	2013	48 Priory Close, Louth LN11 9AS	01507 609806	47
Finnie, Bill H. BA PgDipSW CertCRS	2015	27 Hallside Crescent, Cambuslang, Glasgow G72 7DY (Mbl)	07518 357138	16
Forsythe, Ruth MCS	2017	1/2 41 Bellwood Street, Glasgow G41 3EX	0141-649 7755	16
Freeth, June	2015	Cumlaquoy, Birsay, Orkney KW17 2ND	01856 721449	45
Fulcher, Christine	2012	St Blaan's Manse, Southend, Campbeltown PA28 6RQ	01586 830504	19
Geddes, Elizabeth (Mrs)	2013	9 Shillingworth Place, Bridge of Weir PA11 3DY	01505 612639	14
Gray, Ian	2013	'The Mallards', 15 Rossie Island Road, Montrose DD10 9NH	01674 677126	30
Grieve, Leslie E.T.	2014	23 Hertford Avenue, Kelvindale, Glasgow G12 0LG (Mbl)	07813 255052	16
Hardman Moore, Susan (Prof.) BA PGCE MA PhD	2013	c/o New College, Mound Place, Edinburgh EH1 2LX	0131-650 8908	1
Harrison, Frederick	2013	33 Castle Avenue, Gorebridge EH23 4TH	01875 820908	3
Harvey, Joyce (Mrs)	2013	4A Allanfield Place, Newton Stewart DG8 6BS	01671 403693	9
Hickman, Mandy R. RGN	2013	Lagnaleon, 4 Wilson Street, Largs KA30 9AQ	01475 675347	12
Hughes, Barry MA	2011	Dunslair, Cardrona Way, Cardrona, Peebles EH45 9LD	01896 831197	4
Hunt, Roland BSc PhD CertEd	2016	4 Flora Gardens, Bishopbriggs, Glasgow G64 1DS	0141- 5633257	16
Irvine, Carl J.	2017	Northside of Glack, Meikle Wartle, Inverurie AB51 5AR	01467 671135	33
Johnston, June E. BSc MEd BD	2013	9 Braehead Road South, Gorebridge EH23 4DL	07754 448889	3
Kiehlmann, Peter	2016	8 Main Street, Newburgh, Ellon AB41 6BP (Mbl)	01358 789235	33
Livingstone, Alan	2013	Meadowside, Lawmuir, Methven, Perth PH1 3SZ	01738 840682	28
McCutcheon, John	2014	Flat 2/6 Parkview, Milton Brae, Milton, Dumbarton G82 2TT	01389 739034	18
Macdonald, Ishabel	2011	'Cleat Afe Ora', 18 Carinish, Isle of North Uist HS6 5HN	01876 580367	43
MacDonald, Monica (Mrs)	2014	32 Reilly Gardens, High Bonnybridge, Bonnybridge FK4 2BB	01324 874807	22

Name	Year	Address	Tel	No.
Mack, Lynne (Mrs)	2013	36 Middleton, Menstrie FK11 7HD	01259 761465	23
McKenzie, Janet R. (Mrs)	2016	80C Colinton Road, Edinburgh EH14 1DD	0131-444 2054	1
McLaughlin, Cathie H. (Mrs)	2014	8 Lamlash Place, Glasgow G33 3XH	0141-774 2483 (Mbl)	16
MacLeod, Iain A.	2012	6 Hallydown Drive, Glasgow G13 1UF	07795 014889	16
McLeod, Tom	2014	3 Martnaham Drive, Coylton KA6 6JE	01292 570100	0
Mathers, Alexena (Sandra)	2015	10 Ercall, Brightons, Falkirk FK2 0RS	01324 872253	22
Maxwell, David	2014	248 Old Castle Road, Glasgow G44 5EZ	0141-569 6379	16
Michie, Margaret (Mrs)	2013	3 Loch Leven Court, Wester Balgedie, Kinross KY13 9NE	01592 840602	28
Morrison, John A. BSc BA PGCE	2013	35 Kirkton Place, Elgin IV30 6JR	01343 550199	35
Muirhead, Morag Y. (Mrs)	2013	6 Dunbarton Road, Fort William PH33 6UU	01397 703643	38
Murphy, Jim	2014	10 Hillview Crescent, Bellshill ML4 1N	01698 740189	17
Nicol, Robert D.	2013	3 Castlegreen Road, Thurso KW14 7DN		41
Noonan, Pam (Mrs)	2013	Kilmorich, 14 Balloch Road, Balloch, Alexandria G83 8SR	01389 754505	18
Nutter, Margaret A.E.	2014	94 Ashgrove Park, Elgin IV30 1UT	07748 700929 (Mbl)	35
Palmer, Sonia	2017	Ashlea, Cuil Road, Duror, Appin PA38 3DA	01631 740313 (Work)	38
Perkins, Mairi (Mrs)	2012	Cott of Howe, Cairston, Stromness, Orkney KW16 3JU	01856 851139	45
Prentice, Martin W.M.	2013	94 Ashgrove Park, Elgin IV30 1UT	07748 700929 (Mbl)	35
Palmer, Sonia	2017	Balloan Farm House, Alcaig, Conon Bridge, Dingwall IV7 8HU	01349 877323	39
Rattenbury, Carol	2013	Ruachmarra, Lower Warse, Canisbay, Wick KW1 4YB	01955 611756	41
Rennie, Lyall	2013	Oakdene, 81 Bonhill Road, Dumbarton G82 2DU	01389 763436	18
Robertson, Ishbel A.R. MA BD	2013	114 High Station Road, Falkirk FK1 5LN	01324 621648	22
Sarle, Andrew BSc BD	2005	102 Rue des Eaux-Vives, CH-1207 Geneva, Switzerland	0041 22 786 4847	48
Sharp, James	2015	97 Ashwood Road, Bridge of Don, Aberdeen AB22 8QX	01224 826362	31
Somevi, Joseph K. BSc MSc (Oxon) PhD MRICS MRTPI MIEMA CertCRS	2014	12a Farragon Drive, Aberfeldy PH15 2BQ	01887 820025	27
Steele, Grace M.F. MA	2011	143 Springfield Park, Johnstone PA5 8JT	0141-886 2131	14
Stevenson, Stuart	2013	Burnthill, Thrumster, Wick KW1 5TR	01955 651717	41
Stewart, Heather (Mrs)	2015	Denend, Strichen, Fraserburgh AB43 6RN	01771 637256	34
Stewart, William	2013	Druim-an-Sgairnich, Ardgay IV24 3BG	01863 766868	40
Stobo, Mary J. (Mrs)	2015	Glenhighton, Broughton, Biggar ML12 6JF	01899 830423	4
Strachan, Pamela D. (Lady) MA (Cantab)	2013	Ladywell House, Lucky Slap, Monikie, Dundee DD5 3QG	01382 370286	29
Strachan, Willie MBA DipY&C	2014	107 Baldorran Crescent, Cumbernauld, Glasgow G68 9EX	01236 727710	16
Stuart, Alex P.	2013	36 Thomson Drive, Bearsden, Glasgow G61 3PA	0141-942 7412	16
Sturrock, Roger D. (Prof.) BD MD FCRP	2014	Riverside Flat, Gynack Street, Kingussie PH21 1EL	01540 661772	36
Thomson, Mary Ellen (Mrs)	2014	3 Daleally Cottages, St Madoes Road, Errol, Perth PH2 7JH	01821 642681	28
Thorburn, Susan (Mrs) MTh	2011	121 George Street, Edinburgh EH2 4YN	0131-225 5722	1
Tweedie, Fiona BSc PhD	2013	5 Dee Road, Kirkcudbright DG6 4HQ	07701 375064 (Mbl)	8
Wallace, Mhairi (Mrs)	2013	47 Crichton Terrace, Pathhead EH37 5QZ	01875 320043	3
Watson, Michael D.	2015	Reddans Park Gate, The Crescent, Stewarton, Kilmarnock KA3 5AY	01560 482267	11
Watt, Kim				

ORDAINED LOCAL MINISTERS (Retired List)

Name	Ord	Address	Tel	PR
Anderson, David M. MSc FCOptom	1984	'Mirlos', 1 Dumfries Place, Fort William PH33 6UQ	01397 702091	38
McAllister, Anne C. (Mrs) BSc DipEd CCS	2013	39 Bowes Rigg, Stewarton, Kilmarnock KA3 5EN	01560 483191	11

LIST B – AUXILIARY MINISTERS

Further information, including E-mail addresses, may be found under the presbytery (Section 5) to which an Auxiliary Minister belongs, as recorded in the final column.

NAME	ORD	ADDRESS	TEL	PR
Attenburrow, Anne BSc MB ChB	2006	4 Jock Inksons Brae, Elgin IV30 1QE	01343 552330	35
Binks, Mike	2007	Hollybank, 12 Kingsbrook, Corby NN18 9HY	(Mbl) 07590 507917	47
Buck, Maxine	2007	Brownlee House, Mauldslie Road, Carluke ML8 5HW	01555 759063	17
Campbell, Gordon A. MA BD CDipAF DipHSM CMer MCMI MIHM AssocCIPD AFRIN ARSGS FRGS FSAScot				
Cumming, Alistair MSc CCS FInstLM	2001	2 Falkland Place, Kingoodie, Invergowrie, Dundee DD2 5DY	01382 561383	29
Dick, Roddy S.	2010	64 Prince George's Avenue, London SW10 8BH	0208 540 7365	47
Fletcher, Timothy E.G. BA FCMA	2010	27 Easter Crescent, Wishaw ML2 8XB	01698 383453	17
Forrest, Kenneth P. CBE BSc PhD	1998	3 Ardchoille Park, Perth PH2 7TL	01738 638189	28
Gardner, Hilary M. (Miss)	2006	5 Carruth Road, Bridge of Weir PA11 3HQ	01505 612651	14
Griffiths, Ruth I. (Mrs)	2010	Cayman Lodge, Kincardine Hill, Ardgay IV24 3DJ	01863 766107	40
Hood, Catriona A.	2004	Kirkwood, Mathieson Lane, Innellan, Dunoon PA23 7TA	01369 830145	19
Howie, Marion L.K. (Mrs) MA ARCS	2006	Rose Cottage, Whitehouse, Tarbert PA29 6EP	01880 730366	19
Jackson, Nancy	1992	51 High Road, Stevenston KA20 3DY	01294 466571	12
Kemp, Tina MA	2009	35 Auchentrae Crescent, Ayr KA7 4BD	01292 262034	10
Landale, William S.	2005	12 Oaktree Gardens, Dumbarton G82 1EU	01389 730477	18
Macdonald, Michael	2005	Green Hope Guest House, Green Hope, Duns TD11 3SG	01361 890242	5
Manson, Eileen (Mrs) DipCE	2004	73 Firhill, Alness IV17 0RT	01349 884268	39
Mather, James BA DipArch MA MBA	1994	1 Cambridge Avenue, Gourock PA19 1XT	01475 632401	14
Moore, Douglas T.	2010	24 Ellison Road, Barnes, London SW13 0AD	020 8876 6540	47
Morrison, Donald John	2003	9 Milton Avenue, Prestwick KA9 1PU	01292 671352	10
O'Donnell, Barbara BD PGSE	2001	22 Kyles, Tarbert, Isle of Harris HS3 3BS	01859 502341	43
Paterson, Andrew E. JP	2007	Ashbank, 258 Main Street, Alexandria G83 0NU	01389 752356	18
Perry, Marion (Mrs)	1994	6 The Willows, Kelty KY4 0FQ	01383 830098	24
Riddell, Thomas S. BSc CEng FIChemE	2009	17a Tarbolton Road, Cumbernauld, Glasgow G67 2AJ	01236 898519	22
Robson, Brenda PhD	1993	4 The Maltings, Linlithgow EH49 6DS	01506 843251	2
	2005	2 Baird Road, Ratho, Newbridge EH28 8RA	0131-333 2746	2
Shearer, Anne F. BA DipEd	2010	10 Colsnaur, Menstrie FK11 7HG	01259 769176	23

NAME	ORD	ADDRESS	TEL	PR
Sutherland, David A.	2001	3/1, 145 Broomhill Drive, Glasgow G11 7ND	0141-357 2058	16
Vivers, Katherine A.	2004	Blacket House, Eaglesfield, Lockerbie DG11 3AA	01461 500412	7
Walker, Linda	2008	18 Valeview Terrace, Glasgow G42 9LA	0141-649 1340	16
Wandrum, David C.	1993	5 Cawder View, Carrickstone Meadows, Cumbernauld, Glasgow G68 0BN		
Whittaker, Mary	2011	11 Templand Road, Lhanbryde, Elgin IV30 8BR (text only) (Mbl)	01236 723288 / 07810 420106	22 / 35
Wilkie, Robert F.	2011	24 Huntingtower Road, Perth PH1 2JS	01738 628301	28

AUXILIARY MINISTERS (Retired List)

NAME	ORD	ADDRESS	TEL	PR
Birch, James PgDip FRSA FIOC	2001	1 Kirkhill Grove, Cambuslang, Glasgow G72 8EH	0141-583 1722	16
Brown, Elizabeth (Mrs) JP RGN	1996	8 Viewlands Place, Perth PH1 1BS	01738 552391	28
Cloggie, June (Mrs)	1997	11A Tulipan Crescent, Callander FK17 8AR	01877 331021	23
Craggs, Sheila (Mrs)	2001	7 Morar Court, Ellon AB41 9GG	01358 723055	33
Ferguson, Archibald M. MSc PhD CEng FRINA	1989	The Whins, 2 Barrowfield, Station Road, Cardross, Dumbarton G82 5NL	01389 841517	18
Harrison, Cameron	2006	Woodfield House, Priormuir, St Andrews KY16 8LP	01334 478067	26
Jenkinson, John J. JP LTCL ALCM DipEd DipSen	1991	8 Rosehall Terrace, Falkirk FK1 1PY	01324 625498	22
Kay, Elizabeth (Miss) DipYCS	1993	1 Kintail Walk, Inchture, Perth PH14 9RY	0828 686029	29
Lunn, Dorothy	2002	14 Bellerby Drive, Ouston, Co. Durham DH2 1TW	0191-492 0647	47
McAlpine, John BSc	1988	Braeside, 201 Bonkle Road, Newmains, Wishaw ML2 9AA	01698 384610	17
MacDonald, Kenneth MA BA	2001	5 Henderland Road, Bearsden, Glasgow G61 1AH	0141-943 1103	16
MacFadyen, Anne M. (Mrs) BSc BD FSAScot	1995	295 Mearns Road, Glasgow G77 5LT	0141-639 3605	16
Mack, Elizabeth A. (Miss) DipPEd	1994	24 Roberts Crescent, Dumfries DG2 7RS	01387 264847	8
Mack, John C. JP	1985	The Willows, Auchleven, Insch AB52 6QB	01464 820387	33
Mailer, Colin	1996	Innis Chonain, Back Row, Polmont, Falkirk FK2 0RD	01324 712401	22
Munro, Mary (Mrs) BA	1993	91 Dalmahoy Crescent, Kirkcaldy KY2 6TA		9
Paterson, Maureen (Mrs) BSc	1992	25 Deeside Crescent, Aberdeen AB15 7PT	01592 262300	25
Phillippo, Michael MTh BSc BVetMed MRCVS	2003		01224 318317	31
Pot, Joost BSc	1992	[E-mail: joostpot@gmail.com]		48
Ramage, Alastair E. MA BA ADB CertEd	1996	16 Claremont Gardens, Milngavie, Glasgow G62 6PG	0141-956 2897	18
Shaw, Catherine A.M. MA	1998	40 Merrygreen Place, Stewarton, Kilmarnock KA3 5EP	01560 483352	11
Thomas, Shirley A. (Mrs) DipSocSci AMIA	2000	14 Kirkgait, Letham, Forfar DD8 2XQ	01307 818084	30
Wilson, Mary D. (Mrs) RGN SCM DTM	1990	Berbice, The Terrace, Bridge of Tilt, Blair Atholl, Pitlochry PH18 5SZ	01796 481619	27
Zambonini, James LIADip	1997	100 Old Manse Road, Netherton, Wishaw ML2 0EP	01698 350889	17

LIST C – THE DIACONATE

Fuller information, including E-mail addresses, may be found under the presbytery (Section 5) to which a Deacon belongs, whose number is recorded in the final column.

NAME	COM	APP	ADDRESS	TEL	PRES
Beck, Isobel DCS	2014	2014	16 Patrick Avenue, Stevenston KA20 4AW	(Mbl) 07919 193425	16
Blair, Fiona (Miss) DCS	1994	2010	Mure Church Manse, 9 West Road, Irvine KA12 8RE	(Mbl) 07977 235168	12
Buchanan, Marion (Mrs) MA DCS	1983	2006	16 Almond Drive, East Kilbride, Glasgow G74 2HX	(Mbl) 07999 889817	16
Brydson, Angela (Mrs) DCS	2015		52 Victoria Park, Lockerbie DG11 2AY	(Mbl) 07543 796820	7
Cathcart, John Paul (Mr) DCS	2000		9 Glen More, East Kilbride, Glasgow G74 2AP	01355 243970	16
Corrie, Margaret (Miss) DCS	1989	2013	44 Sunnyside Street, Camelon, Falkirk FK1 4BH	(Mbl) 07955 633969	2
Crawford, Morag (Miss) MSc DCS	1977	1998	118 Wester Drylaw Place, Edinburgh EH4 2TG	(Tel/Fax) 0131-332 2253	24
Crocker, Liz (Mrs) DipComEd DCS	1985	2003	77C Craigcrook Road, Edinburgh EH4 3PH	0131-332 0227	1
Cunningham, Ian (Mr) DCS	1994	2002	110 Nelson Terrace, Keith AB55 5FD		35
Cuthbertson, Valerie (Miss) DipTMus DCS	2003		105 Bellshill Road, Motherwell ML1 3SJ	01698 259001	22
Deans, Raymond (Mr) DCS	1994	2003	60 Ardmory Road, Rothesay, Isle of Bute PA20 0PG [E-mail: r.deans93@btinternet.com]	01700 504893	19
Evans, Mark (Mr) BSc MSc DCS	1988	2006	13 Easter Drylaw Drive, Edinburgh EH4 2QA	0131-343 3089	1
Gargrave, Mary (Mrs) DCS	1989	2002	12 Parkholm Quad, Glasgow G63 7ZH	0141-880 5532	16
Getliffe, Dot (Mrs) DCS BA BD DipEd	2006	2017	3 Woodview Terrace, Hamilton ML3 9DP	01698 423504	31
Hamilton, James (Mr) DCS	1997	2000	6 Beckfield Gate, Glasgow G33 1SW	0141-558 3195	16
Hamilton, Karen (Mrs) DCS	1995	2009	6 Beckfield Gate, Glasgow G33 1SW	0141-558 3195	16
Love, Joanna (Ms) BSc DCS	1992	2009	92 Everard Drive, Glasgow G21 1XQ	0141-772 0149	16
Lyall, Ann (Miss) DCS	1980	2017	The Manse, Manse Road, Torphichen, Bathgate EH48 4LT		2
MacDonald, Anne (Miss) BA DCS	1980	2002	502 Castle Gait, Paisley PA1 2PA	0141-840 1875	16
McIntosh, Kay (Mrs) DCS	1988	2013	4 Jacklin Green, Livingston EH54 8PZ	01506 440543	2
McKay, Kenneth D. (Mr) DCS	1996	1998	11F Balgowan Road, Letham, Perth PH1 2JG	01738 621169	28
McLellan, Margaret DCS	1986	2014	18 Broom Road East, Newton Mearns, Glasgow G77 5SD	0141-639 6853	16
McPheat, Elspeth (Miss) DCS	1985	2001	11/5 New Orchardfield, Edinburgh EH6 5ET	0131-554 4143	1
Nicholson, David (Mr) DCS	1994		2D Doonside, Kildrum, Cumbernauld, Glasgow G67 2HX	01236 732260	22
Ogilvie, Colin (Mr) BA DCS	1998	1993	21 Neilsland Drive, Motherwell ML1 3DZ [E-mail: colinogilvie2@gmail.com]	01698 321836	
Pennykid, Gordon J. BD DCS DCS MA BA PGCSE	2015		8 Glenfield, Livingston EH54 7BG	(Mbl) 07837 287804	2
Philip, Elizabeth (Mrs)	2007		8 Strathearn Terrace, Crieff PH7 3AQ	(Mbl) 07747 652652 / 01764 218976	28
Porter, Jean (Mrs) BD DCS	2006	2008	St Mark's Church, Drip Road, Stirling FK8 1RE	(Mbl) 07729 316321	23
Robertson, Pauline (Mrs) DCS BA CertTheol	2003	2006	6 Ashville Terrace, Edinburgh EH6 8DD	0131-554 6564	1
Scott, Pamela	2017	2017	177 Primrose Avenue, Rosyth KY11 2TZ	01383 410530	24
Stewart, Marion G. (Miss) DCS	1991	1994	Kirk Cottage, Kirkton of Skene, Westhill, Skene AB32 6XE	01224 743407	33

NAME			ADDRESS	TEL	PRES
Thomson, Jacqueline (Mrs) MTh DCS	2004	2004	16 Aitken Place, Coaltown of Wemyss, Kirkcaldy KY1 4PA	01592 653995	25
Urquhart, Barbara (Mrs) DCS	1986	2006	9 Standalane, Kilmaurs, Kilmarnock KA3 2NB	01563 538289	11
Wallace, Catherine (Mrs) PGDipC DCS	1987		21 Durley Dene Crescent, Bridge of Earn PH2 9RD	01738 621709	28
Wallace, Sheila (Mrs) DCS BA BD	2009	2011	Beannach Cottage, Spey Avenue, Boat of Garten PH24 3BE	01479 831548	36
Wilson, Glenda (Mrs) DCS	1990	2006	5 Allan Terrace, Sandbank, Dunoon PA23 8PR	01369 704168	19
Wright, Lynda (Miss) BEd DCS	1979	1992	1a Broomhill Avenue, Burntisland KY3 0BP	(Mbl) 07835 303395	25

THE DIACONATE (Retired List)

Fuller contact details are found in the presbytery, indicated by its number in the last column, in which the retired deacon has a seat. Where a retired deacon does not have a seat on presbytery, full contact details are given here.

NAME	COM	ADDRESS	TEL	PRES
Allan, Jean (Mrs) DCS	1989	12C Hindmarsh Avenue, Dundee DD3 7LW	01382 827299	29
Anderson, Janet (Miss) DCS	1979	Creagard, 31 Lower Breakish, Isle of Skye IV42 8QA	01471 822403	42
Bayes, Muriel C. (Mrs) DCS	1963	Flat 6, Carleton Court, 10 Fenwick Road, Glasgow G46 4AN	0141-633 0865	16
Beaton, Margaret (Miss) DCS	1989	64 Gardenside Grove, Carmyle, Glasgow G32 8EZ	0141-646 2297	16
Bell, Sandra (Mrs) DCS	2001	62 Loganswell Road, Thornliebank, Glasgow G46 8AX	0141-638 5884	
Black, Linda (Miss) BSc DCS	1993	148 Rowan Road, Abronhill, Cumbernauld, Glasgow G67 3DA	01236 786265	22
Buchanan, John (Mr) DCS	1988	57 Strathclyde House, Shore Road, Skelmorlie PA17 5EH	01475 522525	12
Burns, Marjory (Mrs) DCS	1997	22 Kirklee Road, Mossend, Bellshill ML4 2QN	01698 292685	
[E-mail: mburns8070@aol.co.uk]			(Mbl) 07792 843922	
Craw, John (Mr) DCS	1998	5 Larchfield Court, Nairn IV12 4SS	(Mbl) 07544 761653	37
Drummond, Rhoda (Miss) DCS	1960	Flat K, 23 Grange Loan, Edinburgh EH9 2ER	0131-668 3631	1
Dunnett, Linda (Mrs) BA DCS	1976	9 Tulipan Crescent, Callander FK17 8AR	01877 339640	23
Erskine, Morag (Miss) DCS	1979	111 Mains Drive, Park Mains, Erskine PA8 7JJ	0141-812 6096	14
Forrest, Janice (Mrs)	1990	4/1, 7 Blochairn Place, Glasgow G21 2EB	0141-552 1132	
Gordon, Fiona S. (Mrs) MA DCS	1958	Machrie, 3 Cupar Road, Cuparmuir, Cupar KY15 5RH	01334 652341	
		[E-mail: machrie@madasafish.com]		
Gordon, Margaret (Mrs) DCS	1998	92 Lanark Road West, Currie EH14 5LA	0131-449 2554	
Gray, Catherine (Miss) DCS	1969	10C Eastern View, Gourock PA19 1RJ	01475 637479	1
		[E-mail: gray_catherine2@sky.com]		
Gray, Christine M. (Mrs) DCS	1969	11 Woodside Avenue, Thornliebank, Glasgow G46 7HR	0141-571 1008	16
Gray, Greta (Miss) DCS	1992	67 Crags Avenue, Paisley PA2 6SG	0141-884 6178	14
Hughes, Helen (Miss) DCS	1977	2/2, 43 Burnbank Terrace, Glasgow G20 6UQ	0141-333 9459	16
Hutchison, Alan E.W. (Mr) DCS	1988	132 Lochbridge Road, North Berwick EH39 4DR	01620 894077	3
Johnston, Mary (Miss) DCS	1988	19 Lounsdale Drive, Paisley PA2 9ED	0141-849 1615	14

Name	Year	Address	Telephone	No.
King, Chris (Mrs) DCS	2002	28 Kilnford Drive, Dundonald, Kilmarnock KA2 9ET [E-mail: chrisking99@tiscali.co.uk]	01563 851197	
King, Margaret MA DCS	2002	56 Murrayfield, Fochabers IV32 7EZ	01343 820937	35
Lundie, Ann V. (Miss) DCS	1972	20 Langdykes Drive, Cove, Aberdeen AB12 3HW	01224 898416	31
McCully, Ann Isobel (Miss) DCS	1974	10 Broadstone Avenue, Port Glasgow PA14 5BB	01475 742240	14
MacKinnon, Ronald M. (Mr) DCS	1996	32 Strathclyde House, Shore Road, Skelmorlie PA17 5AN	01475 521333	12
MacLean, Donald A. (Mr) DCS	1988	8 Upper Barvas, Isle of Lewis HS2 0QX	01851 840454	44
McNaughton, Janette (Miss) DCS	1982	4 Dunellan Avenue, Moodiesburn, Glasgow G69 0GB	01236 870180	
MacPherson, James B. (Mr) DCS	1988	0/1, 104 Cartside Street, Glasgow G42 9TQ	0141-616 6468	16
MacQuien, Duncan (Mr) DCS	1988	35 Criffel Road, Mount Vernon, Glasgow G32 9JE	0141-575 1137	
Martin, Janie (Miss) DCS	1979	16 Wentworth Road, Dundee DD2 3SD	01382 813786	29
Merrilees, Ann (Miss) DCS	1994	23 Cuthill Brae, Willow Wood Residential Park, West Calder EH55 8QE	01501 762909	2
Miller, Elsie M. (Miss) DCS	1974	30 Swinton Avenue, Rowanbank, Baillieston, Glasgow G69 6JR	0141-771 0857	22
Mitchell, Joyce (Mrs) DCS	1994	Sunnybank, Farr, Inverness IV2 6XG	01808 521285	37
Morrison, Jean (Dr) DCS	1964	9 The Courtyard, Inchmarlo, Banchory AB31 4AZ [E-mail: morrison.jc612@btinternet.com]	01330 824426	
Moyes, Sheila (Miss) DCS	1957	27A Craigour Avenue, Edinburgh EH17 7NH	0131-664 3426	1
Mulligan, Anne MA DCS	1974	4 Hewat Place, Perth PH1 2UD	01738 443088	1
Munro, Patricia (Ms) BSc DCS	1986	93 Brisbane Street, Greenock PA16 8NY	01475 723235	28
Nicol, Joyce (Mrs) BA DCS	1974	Flat 4, Carissima Court, 99 Elmer Road, Elmer, Bognor Regis PO22 6LH	01243 858641	14
Palmer, Christine (Ms) DCS	2003	3/1 Craigmillar Court, Edinburgh EH16 4AD	0131-661 8475	
Rennie, Agnes M. (Miss) DCS	1974	6 Gauldie Crescent, Dundee DD3 0RR	01382 816580	1
Rose, Lewis (Mr) DCS	1993	1 John Neilson Avenue, Paisley PA1 2SX	0141-887 2801	29
Ross, Duncan (Mr) DCS	1996	21 Lingaro, Bixter, Shetland ZE2 9NN	01595 810207	14
Smith, Catherine (Mrs) DCS	1964	2 Northfield Gardens, Prestonpans EH32 9LQ	01875 811497	
Steele, Marilynn J. (Mrs) BD DCS	1999	51 Nantwich Drive, Edinburgh EH7 6RB	0131-669 2054	1
Steven, Gordon R. BD DCS	1997	10 Carnoustie Crescent, Greenhills, East Kilbride, Glasgow G75 8TE	01355 243095	3
Tait, Agnes (Mrs) DCS	1995	46 Craigcrook Avenue, Edinburgh EH4 3PX	0131-336 3113	
Teague, Yvonne (Mrs) DCS	1965			
Thom, Helen (Miss) BA DipEd MA DCS	1959	84 Great King Street, Edinburgh EH3 6QU	0131-556 5687	
Thomson, Phyllis (Miss) DCS	2003	63 Caroline Park, Mid Calder, Livingston EH53 0SJ	01506 883207	
Trimble, Robert DCS	1988	5 Templar Rise, Livingston EH54 6PJ	01506 412504	1
Webster, Elspeth H. (Miss) DCS	1950	82 Broomhill Avenue, Burntisland KY3 0BP	01592 873616	2
Wilson, Muriel (Miss) MA BD DCS	1997	28 Bellevue Crescent, Ayr KA7 2DR [E-mail: muriel.wilson4@btinternet.com]	01292 264939	2

THE DIACONATE (Supplementary List)

Name	Year	Address	Telephone
Carson, Christine (Miss) MA DCS	2006	36 Upper Wellhead, Limekilns, Dunfermline KY11 3JQ	01383 873131
Gilroy, Lorraine (Mrs) DCS	1988	5 Bluebell Drive, Bedworth CV12 0GE	02476 366031
Guthrie, Jennifer M. (Miss) DCS		14 Eskview Terrace, Ferryden, Montrose DD10 9RD	01674 674413

Harris, Judith (Mrs) DCS	1993	243 Western Avenue, Sandfields, Port Talbot, West Glamorgan SA12 7NF	01639 884855
Hood, Katrina (Mrs) DCS	1988	67C Farquhar Road, Edgbaston, Birmingham B18 2QP	
Hudson, Sandra (Mrs) DCS	1982	10 Albany Drive, Rutherglen, Glasgow G73 3QN	
Muir, Alison M. (Mrs) DCS	1969	77 Arthur Street, Dunfermline KY12 0JJ	
Ramsden, Christine (Miss) DCS	1978	2 Wykeham Close, Bassett, Southampton SO16 7LZ	
Walker, Wikje (Mrs) DCS	1970	24 Brodie's Yard, Queen Street, Coupar Angus PH13 9RA	01828 628251

LIST D – MINISTERS WHO HOLD PRACTISING CERTIFICATES (in accordance with Act II (2000), but who are not members of a Presbytery)

NAME	ORD	ADDRESS	TEL	PRES
Adamson, Hugh M. BD	1976	38F Mayboke Road, Ayr KA7 4SF [E-mail: hmadamson768@btinternet.com]	01292 440958	10
Aiken, Peter W.I	1996	[E-mail: revpetevon@gmail.com]		9
Aitken, Ewan R. BA BD	1992	159 Restalrig Avenue, Edinburgh EH7 6PJ	0131-467 1660	1
Alexander, William M. BD	1971	110 Fairview Circle, Danestone, Aberdeen AB22 8YR	01224 703752	31
Anderson, David MA BD	1975	Rowan Cottage, Aberlour Gardens, Aberlour AB38 9LD [E-mail: maurvid@hotmail.com]	01340 871906	35
Anderson, Kenneth G. MA BD	1967	8 School Road, Arbroath DD11 2LT	01241 874825	30
Anderson, Susan M. (Mrs) BD	1997	32 Murrayfield, Bishopbriggs, Glasgow G64 3DS [E-mail: susanbbriggs32@gmail.com]	0141-772 6338	16
Auld, A. Graeme (Prof.) MA BD PhD DLitt FSAScot FRSE	1973	Nether Swanshiel, Hobkirk, Bonchester Bridge, Hawick TD9 8JU [E-mail: a.g.auld@ed.ac.uk]	01450 860636	
Barclay, Neil W. BSc BEd BD	1986	4 Gibsongray Street, Falkirk FK2 7LN	01324 874681	22
Bardgett, Frank D. MA BD PhD	1987	Tigh an Iasgair, Street of Kincardine, Boat of Garten PH24 3BY [E-mail: tigh@bardgett.plus.com]	01479 831751	36
Bartholomew, Julia (Mrs) BSc BD	2002	Kippenhill, Dunning, Perth PH2 0RA	01764 684929	28
Beattie, Warren R. BSc BD MSc PhD	1991	Director for Mission Research, OMF International, 2 Cluny Road, Singapore 259570 [E-mail: beattiewarren@omf.net]	0065 6319 4550	1
Biddle, Lindsay (Ms)	1991	30 Ralston Avenue, Glasgow G52 3NA [E-mail: lindsaybiddle@hotmail.com]	0141-883 7405	
Birrell, John M. MA LLB BD	1974	'Hiddlehame', 5 Hewat Place, Perth PH1 2UD [E-mail: john.birrell@nhs.net]	01738 443335	28
Black, James S. BD DPS	1976	7 Breck Terrace, Penicuik EH26 0RJ [E-mail: jsb.black@btopenworld.com]	01968 677559	3
Boyd, Ian R. MA BD PhD	1989	33 Castleton Drive, Newton Mearns, Glasgow G77 3LE	0141-931 5344	16
Bradley, Andrew W. BD	1975	Flat 1/1, 38 Cairnhill View, Bearsden, Glasgow G61 1RP		31
Brown, Robert F. MA BD ThM	1971	55 Hilton Drive, Aberdeen AB24 4NJ [E-mail: Bjacob546@aol.com]	01224 491451	

Name	Year	Address	Tel	No.
Caie, Albert LTh	1983	34 Ringwell Gardens, Stonehouse, Larkhall ML9 3QW	01698 792187	17
Coogan, J. Melvyn LTh	1992	19 Glen Grove, Largs KA30 8QQ		12
Cowie, James M. BD	1977	The Blue House, 24 Cowdrait, Burnmouth, Eyemouth TD14 5SW [E-mail: jimcowie@europe.com]	01890 781394	
Cowieson, Roy J. BD	1979	2160-15 Hawk Drive, Courtenay, BC V9N 9B2, Canada [E-mail: arjay1232@gmail.com]		13
Craig, Ronald A.S. BAcc BD	1983	29 Third Avenue, Auchinloch, Kirkintilloch, Glasgow G66 5EB [E-mail: rascraig@ntlworld.com]	0141-573 9220	16
Davidson, John F. BSc DipEdTech	1970	49 Craigmill Gardens, Carnoustie DD7 6HX [E-mail: davidson900@btinternet.com]	01241 854566	30
Davidson, Mark R. MA BD STM PhD RN	2005	The Manse, Main Street, Kippen FK8 3DN [E-mail: mark.davidson122@mod.uk]	01786 871249	33
Dick, John H.A. MA MSc BD	1982	18 Fairfield Road, Kelty KY4 0BY		31
Dickson, Graham T. MA BD	1985	43 Hope Park Gardens, Bathgate EH48 2QT [E-mail: gtd194@googlemail.com]	01506 237597	2
Donaldson, Colin V.	1982	3A Playfair Terrace, St Andrews KY16 9HX	01334 472889	3
Drake, Wendy F. (Mrs) BD	1978	21 William Black Place, South Queensferry EH30 9QR [E-mail: revwdrake@hotmail.co.uk]	0131-331 1520	1
Drummond, Norman W. (Prof.) CBE MA BD DUniv FRSE	1976	c/o Columba 1400 Ltd, Staffin, Isle of Skye IV51 9JY [Email: LDunbar@churchofscotland.org.uk]	01478 611400	42
Dunbar, Linda J. BSc BA BD PhD FRHS	2000		(Mbl) 07939 496360	4
Ellis, David W. GIMechE GIProdE PhD FRHS	1962	4 Wester Tarsappie, Rhynd Road, Perth PH2 8PT	01738 449618	16
Espie, Howard	2011	1 Sprucebank Avenue, Langbank, Port Glasgow PA14 6YX [E-mail: howardespie.me.com]	01475 540391	1
Fairful, John BD	1994	12 Forth Road, Bearsden, Glasgow G61 1JT		45
Ferguson, Ronald MA BD ThM DUniv	1972	Vinbreck, Orphir, Orkney KW17 2RE [E-mail: ronbluebrazil@aol.com]	01856 811353	
Forbes, John W.A. BD	1973	Little Ennochie Steading, Finzean, Banchory AB31 6LX [E-mail: jrbbbb@icloud.com]	01330 850785	32
Fowler, Richard C.A. BSc MSc BD	1978	4 Gardentown, Whalsay, Shetland ZE2 9AB	01806 566538	46
Fraser, Ian M. MA BD PhD	1946	Flat 19, Burnside Court, 101 Brook Street, Alva FK8 5AD	01259 763809	23
Frew, John M. MA BD	1946	17 The Furrows, Walton-on-Thames KT12 3JQ		16
Gammack, George BD	1985	13A Hill Street, Broughty Ferry, Dundee DD5 2JP	01382 778636	29
Gardner, Bruce K. MA BD PhD	1988	21 Hopetown Crescent, Bucksburn, Aberdeen AB21 9QY [E-mail: drbrucegardner@aol.com]	(Mbl) 07891 186724	31
Gauld, Beverly G.D.D. MA BD	1972	7 Rowan View, Lanark ML11 9FQ	01555 665765	13
Gillies, Janet E. BD	1998	18 McIntyre Lane, Macmerry, Tranent EH33 1QL	01875 824607	3
Gordon, Elinor J. (Miss) BD	1988	6 Balgibbon Drive, Callander FK17 8EU [E-mail: elinorgordon@btinternet.com]	01877 331049	22
Grainger, Alison J. BD	1995	2 Hareburn Avenue, Avonbridge, Falkirk FK1 2NR [E-mail: revajgrainger@btinternet.com]	01324 861632	2
Grubb, George D.W. BA BD BPhil DMin	1962	10 Wellhead Close, South Queensferry EH30 9WA	0131-331 2072	1
Harper, Anne J.M. (Miss) BD STM MTh CertSocPsych	1979	122 Greenock Road, Bishopton PA7 5AS	01505 862466	16

Name	Year	Address	Tel	No.
Haslett, Howard J. BA BD	1972	26 The Maltings, Haddington EH41 4EF [E-mail: howard.haslett@btinternet.com]	01620 820292	3
Hendrie, Yvonne (Mrs) MA BD	1995	The Manse, 16 McAdam Way, Maybole KA19 8FD	01655 883710	10
Hibbert, Frederick W. BD	1986	4 Cemydd Terrace, Senghenydd, Caerphilly, Mid Glamorgan CF83 4HL	02920 831653	47
Hutcheson, Norman M. MA BD	1973	66 Maxwell Park, Dalbeattie DG5 4LS [E-mail: norman.hutcheson@gmail.com]		8
Hutchison, Alison M. (Mrs) BD DipMin	1988	Ashfield, Drumoak, Banchory AB31 5AG [E-mail: amhutch62@aol.com]	01330 811309	31
Jamieson, Esther M.M. (Mrs) BD	1984	1 Redburn, Bayview, Stornoway, Isle of Lewis HS1 2UU [E-mail: ianandejamieson@btinternet.com]	01851 704789	44
Jenkinson, John J. JP LTCL ALCM DipEd DipSen	1991	8 Rosehall Terrace, Falkirk FK1 1PY	01324 625498	22
Kelly, Ewan R. MB ChB BD PhD	1994	2/1, 117 Novar Drive, Glasgow G12 9 SZ [E-mail: ewanrkelly@outlook.com]	0141 357 2599	8
Kenny, Celia G. BA MTh MPhil PhD	1995	37 Grosvenor Road, Rathgar, Dublin 6, Ireland [E-mail: cgkenny@tcd.ie]		5
Kerr, Hugh F. MA BD	1968	134C Great Western Road, Aberdeen AB10 6QE	01224 580091	31
Kesting, Sheilagh M. BA BD DD DSG	1980	Restalrig, Chance Inn, Cupar KY15 5QJ [E-mail: smkesting@btinternet.com]	01334 829485	22
Lawrie, Robert M. BD MSc DipMin LLCM(TD) MCMI	1994	18/1 John's Place, Edinburgh EH6 7EN [E-mail: robert.lawrie@ed.ac.uk]	0131-554 9765	1
Ledgard, J. Christopher BA	1969	Streonshalh, 8 David Hume View, Chirnside, Duns TD11 3SX [E-mail: ledgard07@btinternet.com]	01890 817124	5
Leishman, James S. LTh BD MA	1969	11 Hunter Avenue, Heathhall, Dumfries DG1 3UX	01387 249241	8
Liddiard, F.G.B. MA	1957	34 Trinity Fields Crescent, Brechin DD9 6YF	01356 622966	30
Lindsay, W. Douglas BD CPS	1978	3 Drummond Place, Calderwood, East Kilbride, Glasgow G74 3AD	01355 234169	16
Lithgow, Anne R. (Mrs) MA BD	1992	13 Cameron Park, Edinburgh EH16 5JY [E-mail: anne.lithgow@btinternet.com]		3
Logan, Thomas M. LTh	1971	3 Duncan Court, Kilmarnock KA3 7TF	01563 524398	11
Lyall, David BSc BD STM PhD	1965	16 Brian Crescent, Tunbridge Wells, Kent TN4 0AP [E-mail: lyall3@gmail.com]	01892 670323	47
McAdam, David J. BSc BD (Assoc)	1990	12 Dunellan Crescent, Moodiesburn, Glasgow G69 0GA [E-mail: dmca29@hotmail.co.uk]	01236 870472	16
McDonald, Ross J. BA BD ThM RNR	1998	HMS *Dalriada*, Navy Buildings, Eldon Street, Greenock PA16 7SL [E-mail: rossjmcdonald@tiscali.co.uk]	0141-883 7545 / 07952 558767 (Mbl)	16
McFadyen, Gavin BEng BD	2006	20 Tennyson Avenue, Bridlington YO15 2EP [E-mail: mcfadyen.gavin@gmail.com]	01262 608659 / 07503 971068 (Mbl)	18
McGillivray, A. Gordon MA BD STM	1951	36 Larchfield Neuk, Balerno EH14 7NL		1
Maciver, Iain BD	2007	5 MacLeod Road, Stornoway, Isle of Lewis HS1 2HJ [E-mail: iain.maciver@hebrides.net]		44
MacKay, Alan H. BD	1974	Flat 1/1, 18 Newburgh Street, Glasgow G43 2XR [E-mail: alanhmackay@aol.com]	0141-632 0527	
McKay, Johnston R. MA BA PhD	1969	15 Montgomerie Avenue, Fairlie, Largs KA29 0EE [E-mail: johnston.mckay@btopenworld.com]	01475 568802	16

Name	Ord.	Address / E-mail	Tel	No.
McKay, Margaret MA BD MTh	1991	19 Richmond Road, Huntly AB54 8BH [E-mail: elricksmithy@yahoo.co.uk]	01466 793937	34
McKean, Alan T. BD CertMin	1982	15 Park Road, Kirn, Dunoon PA23 8JL	01369 700016	39
McKean, Martin J. BD DipMin	1984	56 Kingsknowe Drive, Edinburgh EH14 2JX	0131-466 1157	1
Mackenzie, A. Cameron MA	1955	Hedgerow, 5 Shiels Avenue, Freuchie, Cupar KY15 7JD	01337 857763	26
MacKichan, Alistair J. MA BD	1984	The Wyld, Horndean, Berwick-upon-Tweed TD15 1XJ [E-mail: alistairjmck@btinternet.com]	01289 382745	8
McLachlan, Fergus C. BD	1982	46 Queen Square, Glasgow G41 2AZ	0141-423 3830	16
McLean, Gordon LTh	1972	Beinn Dhorain, Kinnettas Square, Strathpeffer IV14 9BD [E-mail: gmaclean@hotmail.co.uk]	01997 421380	39
MacPherson, Gordon C.	1963	203 Capelrig Road, Patterton, Newton Mearns, Glasgow G77 6ND	0141-616 2107	16
McPherson, William BD DipEd	1993	83 Laburnum Avenue, Port Seton, Prestonpans EH32 0UD	01875 812252	22
McWilliam, Thomas M. MA BD	1964	Flat 3, 13 Culduthel Road, Inverness IV2 4AG [E-mail: tommcwilliam@btconnect.com]	01463 718981	39
Mailer, Colin	1996	Innis Chonain, Back Row, Polmont, Falkirk FK2 0RD	01324 712401	22
Main, Arthur W.A. BD	1954	13/3 Eildon Terrace, Edinburgh EH3 5NL	0131-556 1344	16
Manners, Stephen	1989	124 Fernieside Crescent, Edinburgh EH17 7DH [E-mail: sk.manners@me.com]	0131-468 0480	7
Masson, John D. MA BD PhD BSc	1984	2 Beechgrove, Craw Hall, Brampton CA8 1TS [E-mail: jmasson96@btinternet.com]		7
Melville, David D. BD	1989	28 Porterfield, Comrie, Dunfermline KY12 9HJ	01383 850075	24
Messeder, Lee BD PgDipMin	2003	59 Miles End, Cavalry Park, Kilsyth G65 0BH [E-mail: lee.messeder@gmail.com]	01236 820845	
Millar, Peter W. MA BD PhD	1971	6/5 Ettrickdale Place, Edinburgh EH3 5JN [E-mail: ionacottage@hotmail.com]	0131-557 0517	1
Minto, Joan E. (Mrs) MA BD	1993	139/1 New Street, Musselburgh EH21 6DH	0131-665 6736	3
Moodie, Alastair R. MA BD	1978	4 Burnbrae Road, Auchinloch, Glasgow G66 5DQ		16
Morton, Andrew Q.	1949	Sunnyside, 4A Manse Street, Aberdour, Burntisland KY3 0TY		
Muckart, Graeme W.M. MA BSc BD FRSE	1983	Kildale, Clashmore, Dornoch IV25 3RG [E-mail: gw2m.kildale@gmail.com]	01862 881715	18
Muir, Eleanor D. (Miss) MTh MSc FSAScot	1986	6 Mayfield, Lesmahagow ML11 0FH [E-mail: eleanordmuir@tiscali.co.uk]	01555 895216	40
Muir, Margaret A. (Miss) MTheol DipPTheol	1989			28
Murray, George M. MTh MA LLB BD	1995	59/4 South Beechwood, Edinburgh EH12 5YS [E-mail: george.murray7@gmail.com]	0131-313 3240	13
Neilson, Rodger BSc BD	1972	4 Waulkmill Steading, Charlestown, Dunfermline KY12 8ZS	01383 873336	34
Newell, Alison M. (Mrs) BD	1986	1A Inverleith Terrace, Edinburgh EH3 5NS [E-mail: alinewell@aol.com]	0131-556 3505	1
Newell, J. Philip MA BD PhD	1982	1A Inverleith Terrace, Edinburgh EH3 5NS	0131-556 3505	1
Newlands, George M. (Prof.) MA BD PhD DLitt FRSA FRSE	1970	12 Jamaica Street North Lane, Edinburgh EH3 6HQ		16
Nicolson, John Murdo	1997	731 16th Street North, Lethbridge, Alberta, Canada T1H 3B3		42
Notman, John R. BSc BD	1990	5 Dovecote Road, Bromsgrove, Worcs B61 7BN		47

Name	Year	Address	Telephone	No.
Owen, Catherine W. MTh	1984	10 Waverley Park, Kirkintilloch, Glasgow G66 2BP	0141-776 0407	16
Penman, Iain D. BD	1977	33/5 Carnbee Avenue, Edinburgh EH16 6GA [E-mail: iainpenmanklm@aol.com]	0131-664 0673 (Mbl) 07931 993427	1
Petrie, Ian D. MA BD	1970	27/111 West Savile Terrace, Edinburgh EH9 3DR [E-mail: idp-77@hotmail.com]	0131-237 2857	26
Pieterse, Ben BA BTh LTh	2001	15 Bakeoven Close, Seaforth Sound, Simon's Town 7975, South Africa		25
Provan, Iain W. MA BA PhD	1991	Regent College, 5800 University Boulevard, Vancouver BC V6T 2E4, Canada	001 604 224 3245	1
Risby, Lesley P. (Mrs) BD	1994	Tigh an Achaidh, 21 Fernoch Crescent, Lochgilphead PA31 8AE [E-mail: mrsrisby@hotmail.com]	01546 600464	19
Rosener, Alexandra M (Mrs)	2007	Lüttenglehn 3, 41352 Korschenbroich, Germany	0049 2182 833 9535	25
Salters, Robert B. MA BD PhD	1966	Vine Cottage, 119 South Street, St Andrews KY16 9UH	01334 473198	16
Saunders, Keith BD	1983	Western Infirmary, Dumbarton Road, Glasgow G11 6NT	0141-211 2000	17
Sawers, Hugh BA	1968	2 Rosemount Meadows, Castlepark, Bothwell, Glasgow G71 8EL	01698 853960	35
Scotland, Ronald J. BD	1993	7A Rose Avenue, Elgin IV30 1NX [E-mail: ronnieandjill@thescotlands.co.uk]	01343 543086	
Scouller, Hugh BSc BD	1985	11 Kirk View, Haddington EH41 4AN [E-mail: h.scouller@btinternet.com]		3
Shanks, Norman J. MA BD DD	1983	1 Marchmont Terrace, Glasgow G12 9LT [E-mail: rufuski@btinternet.com]	0141-339 4421	16
Shaw, D.W.D. BA BD LLB WS DD	1960	4/13 Succoth Court, Edinburgh EH12 6BZ	0131-337 2130	26
Shedden, John CBE BD DipPSS	1971	The Wold, Selsey GL5 5LJ [E-mail: rev.johnshedden@gmx.com]	01453 453047	19
Smith, Hilary W. BD DipMin MTh PhD	1999	1F1, 2 Middlefield, Edinburgh EH7 4PF [E-mail: hilaryoxfordsmith1@gmail.com]	0131-553 1174 (Mbl) 07900 896954	35
Smith, Ronald W. BA BEd BD	1979	12a Crowlista, Uig, Isle of Lewis HS2 9JF [E-mail: fraserstewart1955@hotmail.com]	01851 672413	23
Stewart, Fraser M.C. BSc BD	1980	28 Inch Crescent, Bathgate EH48 1EU [E-mail: famstewart@ormail.co.uk]	01506 653428	39
Stewart, Margaret L. (Mrs) BSc MB ChB BD	1985	Director, Center of Theological Inquiry, 50 Stockton Street, Princeton, NJ 08540, USA [E-mail: aestrachan@aol.com]		2
Storrar, William F. (Prof.) MA BD PhD	1984	2 Leafield Road, Dumfries DG1 2DS		1
Strachan, Alexander E. MA BD	1974	1 Deeside Park, Aberdeen AB15 7PQ	01387 279460	8
Strachan, David G. BD DPS	1978	'Cardenwell', Glen Drive, Dyce, Aberdeen AB21 7EN	01224 324101	31
Strachan, Ian M. MA BD	1959	29 Firthview Drive, Inverness IV3 8NS [E-mail: johntallac1@talktalk.net]	01224 772028	31
Tallach, John MA MLitt	1970		01463 418721	48
Tamas, Bertalan	1983	Pozsonyi út 34, Budapest H-1137, Hungary [E-mail: bertalantamas@hotmail.com]	0036 1 239 6315 (Mbl) 0036 30 638 6647	48
Taylor, Ian BSc MA LTh DipEd	1983	Lundie Cottage, Arncroach, Anstruther KY10 2RN	01333 720222	26
Taylor, Jane C. BD DipMin	1990	1/2 72 St Vincent Crescent, Glasgow G3 8NQ [E-mail: jane.c.taylor@btinternet.com]	0141-204 3022	16
Thomas, W. Colville ChLJ BTh BPhil DPS DSc	1964	11 Muirfield Crescent, Gullane EH31 2HN	01620 842415	3

NAME	ORD	ADDRESS	TEL	PRES
Thomson, Alexander BSc BD MPhil PhD	1973	4 Munro Street, Dornoch IV25 3RA [E-mail: alexander.thomson6@btinternet.com]	01862 811650	40
Thrower, Charles D. BSc	1965	Grange House, Wester Grangemuir, Pittenweem, Anstruther KY10 2RB [E-mail: charlesandsteph@btinternet.com]	01333 312631	26
Tollick, Frank BSc DipEd	1958	3 Bellhouse Road, Aberdour, Burntisland KY3 0TL	01383 860559	24
Turnbull, John LTh	1994	4 Rathmor Road, Biggar ML12 6QG	01899 221502	13
Turnbull, Julian S. BSc BD MSc CEng MBCS	1980	39 Suthern Yett, Prestonpans EH32 9GL [E-mail: jules@turnbull25.plus.com]	01875 818305	3
Watson, John M. LTh	1989	20 Greystone Place, Newtonhill, Stonehaven AB39 3UL [E-mail: watson-john18@sky.com]	(Mbl) 01569 730604 / 07733 334380	31
Webster, Brian G. BSc BD CEng MIET	1998	3/1 Cloch Court, 57 Albert Road, Gourock PA19 1NJ [E-mail: revwebby@aol.com]	01475 638332	23
Whitton, John P.	1977	115 Sycamore Road, Farnborough, Hants GU14 6RE	01252 674488	47
Whyte, Ron C. BD CPS	1990	13 Hillside Avenue, Kingussie PH21 1PA [E-mail: ron4xst@btinternet.com]	01540 661101	36
Wilkie, James L. MA BD	1959	7 Comely Bank Avenue, Edinburgh EH4 1EW [E-mail: jl.wilkie@btinternet.com]	(Mbl) 07979 026973 / 0131-343 1552	1
Wilson, Andrew G.N. MA BD DMin	1977	Auchintarph, Coull, Tarland, Aboyne AB34 4TT [E-mail: agn.wilson@gmail.com]	01339 880918	32
Wood, James L.K.	1967	1 Glen Drive, Dyce, Aberdeen AB21 7EN	01224 722543	31
Young, Evelyn (Mrs) BSc BD	1984	2 Priesteden Place, St Andrews KY16 8DP	01334 479662	26

LIST E – MINISTERS WHO ARE NOT MEMBERS OF A PRESBYTERY AND WHO DO NOT CURRENTLY HOLD A PRACTISING CERTIFICATE (in terms of Act II (2000))

NAME	ORD	ADDRESS	TEL	PRES
Beck, John C. BD	1975	31 The Woodlands, Stirling FK8 2LB	01738 443335	35
Birrell, Isobel (Mrs) BD	1994	'Hiddlehame', 5 Hewat Place, Perth PH1 2UD [E-mail: isobel@ibmail.org.uk]	(Mbl) 07540 797945	17
Black, W. Graham MA BD	1983	72 Linksview, Linksfield Road, Aberdeen AB24 5RG [E-mail: graham.black@virgin.net]	01224 492491	31
Breakey, Judith (Ms) LizTheol MTh DipEd	2010	[E-mail: judith.breakey@gmail.com]		16
Brown, Alastair BD	1986	52 Henderson Drive, Kintore, Inverurie AB51 0FB	01467 632787	32
Brown, R. Graeme BA BD	1961	Bring Deeps, Orphir, Orkney KW17 2LX	01856 811707	45
Brown, Joseph MA	1954	The Orchard, Hermitage Lane, Shedden Park Road, Kelso TD5 7AN	01573 223481	6
Burgess, Paul C.J. MA	1968	Springvale, Halket Road, Lugton, Kilmarnock KA3 4EE [E-mail: paulandcathie@gmail.com]	01505 850254	
Burnside, William A.M. MA BD PgCE	1990	68 Huntly Street, Inverness IV3 5JN [E-mail: bburnside@btinternet.com]		37

Name	Ord.	Address	Tel	No.
Campbell, J. Ewen R. MA BD	1967	85/15 High Street, North Berwick EH39 4HD	01620 894839	25
Christie, James LTh	1993	20 Wester Inshes Crescent, Inverness IV2 5HL		1
Cooper, George MA BD	1943	8 Leighton Square, Alyth, Blairgowrie PH11 8AQ	01828 633746	1
Craig, Eric MA BD BA	1959	5 West Relugas Road, Edinburgh EH9 2PW	0131-667 8210	26
Craig, Gordon W. MBE MA BD	1972	1 Beley Bridge, Dunino, St Andrews KY16 8LT	01334 880285	17
Cullen, William T. BA LTh	1984	6 Laurel Wynd, Cambuslang, Glasgow G72 7BA	0141-641 4337	2
Currie, Gordon C.M. MA BD	1975	43 Deanburn Park, Linlithgow EH49 6HA	01506 842759	24
Davies, Gareth W. BA BD	1979	Pitadro House, Fordell Gardens, Dunfermline KY11 7EY	01383 417634	16
Dean, Roger A.F. LTh	1983	0/2, 20 Ballogie Road, Glasgow G44 4TA [E-mail: roger.dean4@btopenworld.com]		
Dick, James S. MA BTh	1988	8 Malthouse Drive, Belper DE56 1RU		18
Dodman, R.	1983			
Donaghy, Leslie G. BD DipMin PGCE FSAScot	1990	53 Oak Avenue, East Kilbride G75 9ED [E-mail: leslie@donaghy.org.uk]	(Mbl) 07809 484812	
Douglas, Andrew M. MA	1957	219 Countesswells Road, Aberdeen AB15 7RD	01224 311932	31
Dutton, David W. BA	1973	13 Acredales, Haddington EH41 4NT [E-mail: duttondw@gmail.com]	01620 825999	9
Finlay, Quintin BA BD	1975	Ivy Cottage, Greenlees Farm, Kelso TD5 8BT	(Mbl) 07901 981171	6
Flockhart, D. Ross OBE BA BD DUniv	1956	Longwood, Humbie EH36 5PN [E-mail: rossflock@btinternet.com]	01875 833208	3
Foggitt, Eric W. MA BSc BD	1991	Christiaan de Wet Straat 19/2, 1091 NG Amsterdam, The Netherlands [E-mail: ericleric3@btinternet.com]		1
Frizzell, R. Stewart BD	1961	98 Boswell Road, Inverness IV2 3EW		
Gardner, Frank J. MA	1966	1 Levanne Place, Gourock PA16 1AX [E-mail: fjg@clyde-mail.co.uk]	01475 630187	14
Graham, A. David M. MA BD	1971	Elmhill House, 27 Shaw Crescent, Aberdeen AB25 3BE	01224 648041	31
Hamilton, David S.M. MA BD STM	1958	63 Pendreich Avenue, Bonnyrigg EH19 2EE [E-mail: dandmhamilton@gmail.com]	0131-654 2604	47
Homewood, I.M. MSc BD	1997	Ander Fließwiese 26, D-14052 Berlin, Germany [E-mail: maxhomewood@me.com]		48
Howie, William MA BD STM	1964	26 Morgan Road, Aberdeen AB16 5JY	01224 483669	31
Hudson, Eric V. LTh	1971	2 Murrayfield Drive, Bearsden, Glasgow G61 1JE	0141-942 6110	18
Huie, David F. MA BD	1962	17 St Mary's Mead, Witney OX28 4EZ	01993 778310	48
Hurst, Frederick R. MA	1965	Flat 6, 21 Bulldale Place, Glasgow G14 0NE	0141-959 2604	40
Inglis, Donald B.C. MA MEd BD	1975	39 Thomson Drive, Bearsden, Glasgow G61 3PA	0141-942 1387	18
Johnstone, William (Prof.) MA BD	1963	9/5 Mount Alvernia, Edinburgh EH16 6AW	0131-664 3140	31
Logan, Robert J.V. MA BD	1962	Lindores, 1 Murray Place, Smithton, Inverness, IV2 7PX [E-mail: rjvlogan@btinternet.com]	01463 790226	
Lynn, Joyce (Mrs) MIPM BD	1995	Flat 8, 131 St Vincent Street, Broughty Ferry, Dundee DD5 2DA	01382 690556	29
Macaskill, Donald MA BD PhD	1994			16
McClenaghan, L. Paul BA	1973	4 Glendale Gardens, Randalstown, Co. Antrim BT41 3EJ [E-mail: paul.mcclenaghan@gmail.com]	02894 478545	34
McCreadie, David W.	1961	23 Willoughby Place, Callander PH17 8DG	01877 330785	23
Macfarlane, Alwyn J.C. MA	1951	Flat 12, Homebum House, 177 Fenwick Road, Giffnock, Glasgow G46 6JD	0141-620 3235	1
Macfarlane, Thomas G. BSc PhD BD	1956	12 Elphinstone Court, Lochwinnoch Road, Kilmacolm PA13 4DW	01505 874962	14
McGill, Thomas W.	1972	Flat 75, J M Barry House, George Street, Dumfries DG1 1EA		9

Name	Year	Address	Tel	No.
McKenzie, Mary O. (Miss)	1976	4 Dunellan Avenue, Moodiesburn, Glasgow G69 0GB	01236 870180	16
Mackie, John F. BD	1979	1A Halls Close, Weldon, Corby, Northants NN17 3HH		40
Mackinnon, Thomas J.R. LTh DipMin	1996	4 Flashadder, Arnisort, Portree, Isle of Skye IV51 9PT	01470 582377	39
McLean, John MA BD	1967	16 Eastside Drive, Westhill AB32 6QN	01224 747701	33
Middleton, Jeremy R.H. LLB BD	1981	Innean Mor, Southend, Campbeltown PA28 6RF	01586 830439	19
Miller, Irene B. (Mrs) MA BD	1984	5 Braeside Park, Aberfeldy PH15 2DT	01887 829396	27
Murray, Douglas R. MA BD	1965	32 Forth Park, Bridge of Allan, Stirling FK9 5NT [E-mail: d-smurray@supanet.com]	01786 831081	23
Niven, William W. LTh	1982	4 Obsdale Park, Alness IV17 0TP	01349 884053	39
O'Leary, Thomas BD	1983	1 Carter's Place, Irvine KA12 0BU	01294 313274	11
Oliver, Gordon BD	1979	129 Knockomie Drive, Forres IV36 2HE	01309 672667	41
Olsen, Heather (Miss) BD	1978	4 Riverside Park, Lochyside, Caol, Fort William PH33 7RA	01397 700023	38
Osbeck, John R. BD	1979	15 Deeside Crescent, Aberdeen AB15 7PT	01224 315595	31
Park, Christopher BSc BD	1977	65 Moubray Road, Dalgety Bay, Dunfermline KY11 9JP [E-mail: chrispark8649@hotmail.com]	01383 821111	24
Patterson, James BSc BD	2003	c/o 9 Oakview, Balmedie, Aberdeen AB23 8SR		1
Peacock, Heather M. BSc PhD BD	2009	9 Frankscroft, Peebles EH45 9DX [E-mail: hmpeacock@btinternet.com]		32
Pryce, Stuart F.A.	1963	36 Forth Park, Bridge of Allan, Stirling FK9 5NT	01786 831026	23
Purves, John P.S. MBE BSc BD	1978	37 Hollywood, Largs KA30 8SR	01475 676180	48
Ramsay, Alan MA	1967	12 Riverside Grove, Lochyside, Caol, Fort William PH33 7RD	01397 702054	38
Reid, Janette G. (Miss) BD	1991	c/o Glasgow Presbytery Office, 260 Bath Street, Glasgow G2 4JP		16
Ritchie, Garden W.M.	1961	23 Croft Road, Kelso TD5 7EP	01573 224419	6
Robertson, Blair MA BD ThM	1990	West End Guest House, 282 High Street, Elgin IV30 1AG [E-mail@ info@westendguesthouse.co.uk]	01343 549629	
Robertson, John M. BSc BD	1975	8 North Green Drive, The Wilderness, Airth, Falkirk FK2 8RA	01324 832244	16
Robertson, Thomas G.M. LTh	1971	23 Muirend Avenue, Perth PH1 1JL	01738 624432	28
Roy, James A. MA BD	1965	'Beechwood', 7 Northview Terrace, Wormit, Newport-on-Tay DD6 8PP [E-mail: jim.roy@dundeepresbytery.org.uk]	01382 543578	29
Duncan Shaw of Chapelverna Bundesverdienstkreuz PhD ThDr Drhc	1951	4 Sydney Terrace, Edinburgh EH7 6SL		19
Sawyer, John F.A. MA BD PhD	1964	The Hemmell, North Charlton NE67 5HP	01665 579083	1
Shaw, Duncan LTh CPS	1984	73 Woodside Drive, Forres IV36 0UF		
Smith, Ralph C.P. MA STM	1960	2A Waverley Road, Eskbank, Dalkeith EH22 3DJ [E-mail: rcpsmith@waitrose.com]	0131-663 1234	
Spowart, Mary G. (Mrs) BD	1978	Aldersyde, St Abbs Road, Coldingham, Eyemouth TD14 5NR	01890 771697	26
Stewart, Charles E.	1976	105 Sinclair Street, Helensburgh G84 9HY [E-mail: c.e.stewart@btinternet.com]	01436 678113	18
Stone, W. Vernon MA BD	1949	36 Woodrow Court, Port Glasgow Road, Kilmacolm PA13 4QA [E-mail: stone@kilmacolm.fsnet.co.uk]	01505 872644	14
Sutcliffe, Clare B. BSc BD	2000	4 Dalmailing Avenue, Dreghorn, Irvine KA11 4HX		11
Taylor, David J. MA BD	1982	32 Croft an Righ, Inverkeithing KY11 1PF	01383 413227	24
Thomson, Gilbert L. BA	1965	3 Fortharfield, Freuchie, Cupar KY15 7JJ	01337 857431	25

Watson, James B. BSc	1968	3 Royal Terrace, Hutton, Berwick-upon-Tweed TD15 1TP [E-mail: jimwatson007@hotmail.com]	01289 386282	5
Webster, John G. BSc	1964	Plane Tree, King's Cross, Brodick, Isle of Arran KA27 8RG	01770 700747	16
Wedderburn, A.J.M. (Prof.) MA BA PhD	1975	Therese-Danner-Platz 3, D-80636 Munich, Germany [E-mail: ajmw42@gmx.de]	0049 89 1200 3726	
Weir, Mary K. BD PhD	1968	1249 Millar Road RR1, SITEH-46, BC V0N 1G0, Canada	001 604 947 0636	1
Westmarland, Colin A.	1971	PO Box 5, Cospicua, CSPO1, Malta	00356 216 923552	48
Wilkie, George D. OBE BL	1948	2/37 Barnton Avenue West, Edinburgh EH4 6EB	0131-339 3973	1
Wilkie, William E. LTh	1978	32 Broomfield Park, Portlethen, Aberdeen AB12 4XT	01224 782052	31
Williams, Trevor	1990	[E-mail: revtrev@btinternet.com]		
Wilson, M.	1988	37 King's Avenue, Longniddry EH32 0QN		7

LIST F – HEALTH AND SOCIAL CARE CHAPLAINS (NHS)

LOTHIAN

Interim Head of Spiritual Care   Rev. Canon Caroline Applegath
[E-mail: carrie.applegath@nhslothian.scot.nhs.uk]

Spiritual Care Office: 0131-242 1990

The Royal Infirmary of Edinburgh
51 Little France Crescent, Edinburgh EH16 4SA (0131-536 1000)

Full details of chaplains and contacts in all hospitals: www.nhslothian.scot.nhs.uk > Services > Health Services A-Z > Spiritual Care

BORDERS

Head of Spiritual Care   Vacant   Chaplaincy Centre, Borders General Hospital, Melrose TD6 9BS 01896 826564
Further information: www.nhsborders.scot.nhs.uk > Patients and Visitors > Our services > Chaplaincy Centre

DUMFRIES AND GALLOWAY

Chaplaincy Service   Macmillan Wing, Dumfries and Galloway Royal   01387 241625
Infirmary, Bankend Road, Dumfries DG1 4AP

Further information: www.nhsdg.scot.nhs.uk > Focus on > Search > Chaplaincy

AYRSHIRE AND ARRAN

Service Lead for Chaplaincy and Staff Care   Rev. Judith A. Huggett   Crosshouse Hospital, Kilmarnock KA2 0BE   01563 577301
[E-mail: judith.huggett@aaaht.scotnhs.uk]

Further information: www.nhsaaa.net > Services A-Z > Chaplaincy service

LANARKSHIRE

Head of Spiritual Care   Vacant   Law House, Airdrie Road, Carluke ML8 5EP   01698 377637
Chaplaincy Office   Law House, Airdrie Road, Carluke ML8 5EP   01698 377637

Further information: www.nhslanarkshire.org.uk > Our services A–Z > Palliative care > Palliative care support > Spiritual care

GREATER GLASGOW AND CLYDE

Head of Chaplaincy and Spiritual Care   Vacant   The Sanctuary, Queen Elizabeth University Hospital,   0141-452 3221
Govan Road, Glasgow G51 4TF
[E-mail: chaplains@ggc.scot.nhs.uk]

Further information: www.nhsggc.org.uk > Services Directory (foot of page) > Spiritual Care

FORTH VALLEY

Head of Spiritual Care   Vacant   Forth Valley Royal Hospital, Larbert FK5 4WR   01324 566071
Further information: www.nhsforthvalley.com > Services A–Z > Spiritual Care Centre

FIFE

Head of Spiritual Care   Mr Mark Evans DCS   Department of Spiritual Care, Queen Margaret Hospital,   01383 674136
Whitefield Road, Dunfermline KY12 0SU
[E-mail: mark.evans59@nhs.net]

Victoria Hospital, Kirkcaldy   Chaplain's Office   01592 648158
Queen Margaret Hospital, Dunfermline   Chaplain's Office   01383 674136
Community Chaplaincy Listening (Scotland):   Miss Lynda Wright DCS   [E-mail: lynda.wright1 @nhs.net]   (Mbl) 07835 303395
National Coordinator

Further information: www.nhsfife.org > Your Health > Support Services > Spiritual Care

TAYSIDE

Head of Spiritual Care   Rev. Gillian Munro   The Wellbeing Centre, Royal Victoria Hospital, Dundee DD2 1SP   01382 423110
[E-mail: lynne.downie@nhs.net]

Further information: www.nhstayside.scot.nhs.uk > Your Health/Wellbeing > Our Services A-Z > Spiritual Care

GRAMPIAN

Lead Chaplain   Rev. Mark Rodgers   Chaplains' Office, Aberdeen Royal Infirmary, Foresterhill, Aberdeen AB25 2ZN   01224 553166
[E-mail: nhsg.chaplaincy@nhs.net]

Further information: www.nhsgrampian.co.uk > Home > Local Services and Clinics > Spiritual Care

HIGHLAND

Lead Chaplain   Rev. Dr Derek Brown   Raigmore Hospital, Old Perth Road, Inverness IV2 3UJ   01463 704463
[E-mail: derek.brown1@nhs.net]

Further information: www.nhshighland.scot.nhs.uk > Services > All Services A-Z > NHS Chaplaincy

WESTERN ISLES HEALTH BOARD

Lead Chaplain   Rev. T. K. Shadakshari   23D Benside, Newmarket, Stornoway, Isle of Lewis HS2 0DZ   (Home) 01851 701727
(Office) 01851 704704
(Mbl) 07403 697138
[E-mail: tk.shadakshari@nhs.net]

NHS SCOTLAND

Head of Programme, Health & Social Care Chaplaincy & Spiritual Care, NHS Education for Scotland
Rev. Sheila Mitchell   3rd Floor, 2 Central Quay, 89 Hydepark Street, Glasgow G3 8BW   (Mbl) 07769 367615
[E-mail: sheila.mitchell@res.scot.nhs.uk]

LIST G – CHAPLAINS TO HM FORCES

The three columns give dates of ordination and commissioning, and branch where the chaplain is serving: Royal Navy, Army, Royal Air Force, Royal Naval Reserve, Army Reserve, Army Cadet Force, or where the person named is an Officiating Chaplain to the Military.

NAME	ORD	COM	BCH	ADDRESS
Anderson, David P. BSc BD	2002	2007	A	JSCSC Defence Academy, Shrivenham, Swindon SN6 8TS
Begg, Richard MA BD	2008	2016	A	3 Signal Regt., Picton Barracks, Bulford Barracks, Salisbury SP4 9NY
Berry, Geoff T. BD BSc	2009	2012	A	JSSU Cyprus, Mercury Barracks, Ayios Nikolaos, BFPO 59
Blackwood, Keith T. BD DipMin	1997	1977	ACF	Shetland Independent Battery, ACF, TA Centre, Fort Charlotte, Lerwick, Shetland ZE1 0JN
Blakey, Stephen A. BSc BD	1977		AR	6 Bn The Royal Regiment of Scotland, Walcheran Barracks, 122 Hotspur Street, Glasgow G20 8LQ
Blakey, Stephen A. BSc BD	1977	1977	ACF	Lothian & Borders Bn ACF, Drumshoreland House, Broxburn EH52 5PF
Blakey, Stephen B. BSc BD	1977	1977	OCM	HQ 51 Infantry Brigade & 2 SCOTS, Glencorse Barracks, Penicuik EH26 0QH
Bryson, Thomas M. BD	1997		ACF	2 Bn The Highlanders, ACF, Cadet Training Centre, Rocksley Drive, Boddam, Peterhead AB42 3BA
Bryson, Thomas M. BD	1997		OCM	51 Infantry Brigade, Forthside, Stirling FK7 7RR
Campbell, Karen K. BD MTh DMin	1997		OCM	Personnel Recovery Centre, Edinburgh
Cobain, Alan R. BD	2000	2017	AR	1 Yorks, Battlesbury Barracks, Warminster BH12 9DT
Connolly, Daniel BD DipTheol DipMin	1983		AR	Scottish and North Irish Yeomanry, Redford Barracks, Colinton Road, Edinburgh EH13 0PP
Coulter, David G. QHC BA BD MDA PhD	1989	1994	A	Chaplain General, MoD Chaplains (Army), HQ Land Forces, 2nd Floor Zone 6, Ramillies Building, Marlborough Lines, Andover, Hants SP11 8HJ
Dalton, Mark BD DipMin RN	2002		RN	HM Naval Base Clyde, Faslane, Helensburgh G84 8HL
Davidson, Mark R. MA BD STM PhD RN	2005		RN	Naval Chaplaincy Service, NCHQ, Whale Island, Portsmouth PO2 8BY
Dicks, Shuna M. BSc BD	2010		ACF	2 Bn The Highlanders, ACF, Cadet Training Centre, Rocksley Drive, Boddam, Peterhead AB42 3BA
Frail, Nicola BLE MBA MDiv	2000	2012	A	32 Engineer Regiment, Marne Barracks, Catterick Garrison, DL10 7NP
Francis, James BD PhD	2002	2009	A	MoD Chaplains (Army), HQ Land Forces, 2nd Floor Zone 6, Ramillies Building, Marlborough Lines, Andover SP11 8HJ
Gardner, Neil N. MA BD RNR	1991		OCM	Edinburgh Universities Officers' Training Corps
Gardner, Neil N. MA BD RNR	1991	2015	RNR	Honorary Chaplain, Royal Navy
Goodison, Michael J. BSc BD	2013		A	Royal Scots Dragoon Guards, Leuchars Station, Leuchars KY16 0JX
Kellock, Chris N. MA BD	1998	2012	A	1 Bn Royal Regiment of Fusiliers, Mooltan Barracks, Tidworth SP9 7SJ
Kennon, Stanley BA BD RN	1992	2000	RN	Britannia Royal Naval College, Dartmouth TO6 0HJ
Kinsey, Louis BD DipMin TD	1991		AR	205 (Scottish) Field Hospital (V), Graham House, Whitefield Road, Glasgow G51 6JU
Lancaster, Craig MA BD	2004	2011	RAF	RAF Brize Norton, Carterton OX18 3LX
McCulloch, Alen J.R. MA BD	1990		ACF	Cornwall ACF, 7 Castle Canyke Road, Bodmin PL31 1DX
MacDonald, Roderick I.T. BD CertMin	1992		ACF	West Lowland Bn, ACF, Fusilier House, Seaforth Road, Ayr KA8 9HX

MacKay, Stewart A.	2009	2009	A	3 Bn Black Watch, Royal Regiment of Scotland, Fort George, Ardersier, Inverness IV1 2TD
Mackenzie, Cameron BD	1997	2011	ACF	Lothian and Borders Bn, ACF, Drumshoreland House, Broxburn EH52 5PF
Mackenzie, Hector M.	2008	2008	A	HQ Military Corrective Training Centre, Berechurch Hall Camp, Berechurch Hall Road, Colchester CO2 9NU
Mackenzie, Seoras L. BD	1996	1998	A	39 Engr Regt (Air Support), Kinloss Barracks, Kinloss, Forres IV36 3XL
McLaren, William MA BD	1990	1990	ACF	Angus and Dundee Bn, ACF, Barry Buddon, Carnoustie DD7 7RY
McLaren, William MA BD	1990	1990	OCM	225 GS Med Regt (V), Oliver Barracks, Dalkeith Road, Dundee DD4 7DL
McLay, Neil BA BD	2006	2012	A	1 Bn Princess of Wales's Royal Regiment, Barker Barracks, Sennelager, Paderborn BFPO 22
MacLeod, Rory N. MA BD	1986	1992	AR	154 Regt RLC, Bothwell House, Elgin Street, Dunfermline KY12 7SB
MacPherson, Duncan J. BSc BD	1993	2002	A	Army Personnel Centre, MP413, Kentigern House, 65 Brown Street, Glasgow G2 8EX
Mathieson, Angus R. MA BD	1988		OCM	Edinburgh Garrison & the Personnel Recovery Unit (PRU)
Milliken, Jamie BD	2005		RNR	HMS *Dalriada*, Govan, Glasgow G51 3JH
Munro, Sheila BD	1995	2003	RAF	Station Chaplain, RAF Lossiemouth, Elgin IV31 6SD
Patterson, Philip W. BMus BD	1999	2017	A	Armour Centre, Allenby Barracks, Boyington, Wareham BH20 6JA
Prentice, Donald K. BSc BD	1989	1989	OCM	205 (Scottish) Field Hospital (V), Graham House, Whitefield Road, Glasgow G51 6JU
Rankin, Lisa-Jane BD CPS	2003	2003	OCM	2 Bn Royal Regiment of Scotland, Glencorse Barracks, Penicuik EH26 0QH
Rowe, Christopher J. BA BD	2008	2008	AR	32 (Scottish) Signal Regiment, 21 Jardine Street, Glasgow G20 6JU
Selemani, Ecilo LTh MTh	1993	2011	ACF	Glasgow and Lanark Bn, ACF, Gilbertfield Road, Cambuslang, Glasgow G72 8YP
Selemani, Ecilo LTh MTh	1993	2011	OCM	51 Infantry Brigade, Forthside, Stirling FK7 7RR
Shackleton, Scott J.S. QCVS BA RN BD PhD	1993	2010	RN	MOD Academy, Amport House, Amport, Andover SP11 8BG
Stewart, Fraser M.C. BSc BD	1980	1980	ACF	1 Bn The Highlanders, ACF, Gordonville Road, Inverness IV2 4SU
Stewart, Fraser M.C. BSc BD	1980	1980	OCM	51 Infantry Brigade, Forthside, Stirling FK7 7RR
Taylor, Gayle J.A. MA BD	1999	1999	OCM	3 Bn The Rifles, Redford Barracks, Colinton Road, Edinburgh EH13 0PP
Thom, David J. BD DipMin	1999	2015	A	Royal Logistics Corps, Princess Royal Barracks, Deepcut, Camberley GU16 6RW
van Sittert, Paul BA BD	1997	2011	A	4 Bn The Royal Regiment of Scotland, Bourlon Barracks, Plumer Road, Catterick Garrison DL9 3AD
Warwick, Ivan C. MA BD TD	1980	1980	ACF	1 Bn The Highlanders, ACF, Gordonville Road, Inverness IV2 4SU
Warwick, Ivan C. MA BD TD	1980	1980	ACF	Orkney Independent Battery, ACF, Territorial Army Centre, Weyland Park, Kirkwall KW1 5LP
Warwick, Ivan C. MA BD TD	1980	1980	OCM	Fort George and Cameron Barracks, Inverness
Wilson, Fiona A. BD	2008	2008	ACF	West Lowland Battalion, ACF, Fusilier House, Seaforth Road, Ayr KA8 9HX

LIST H – READERS

1. EDINBURGH

Brown, Ivan	4 St Cuthberts Court, Edinburgh EH13 0LG	0131-441 1245
	[E-mail: j.ivanb@btinternet.com]	(Mbl) 07730 702860
Christie, Gillian L. (Mrs)	32 Allan Park Road, Edinburgh EH14 1LJ	0131-443 4472
	[E-mail: mrsglchristie@aol.com]	(Mbl) 07914 883354

Davies, Ruth (Ms) (attached to Liberton) — 4 Hawkhead Grove, Edinburgh EH16 6LS [E-mail: ruth@ndavies.me.uk] — 0131-664 3608

Farrell, William J. — 50 Ulster Crescent, Edinburgh EH8 7JS [E-mail: w.farrell154@btinternet.com] — 0131-661 1026

Farrow, Edmund — 14 Brunswick Terrace, Edinburgh EH7 5PG [E-mail: edmundfarrow@blueyonder.co.uk] — 0131-558 8210

Johnston, Alan — 8/19 Constitution Street, Edinburgh EH6 7BT [E-mail: alanacj@cairnassoc.wanadoo.co.uk] — 0131-554 1326 (Mbl) 07901 510819

Kerrigan, Herbert A. (Prof.) MA LLB QC — Airdene, 20 Edinburgh Road, Dalkeith EH22 1JY [E-mail: kerrigan@kerriganqc.com] — 0131-660 3007 (Mbl) 07725 953772

McPherson, Alistair — 77 Bonaly Wester, Edinburgh EH13 0RQ [E-mail: amjhmcpherson@blueyonder.co.uk] — 0131-478 5384

Pearce, Martin — 4 Corbiehill Avenue, Edinburgh EH4 5DR [E-mail: martin.j-pearce@blueyonder.co.uk] — 0131-336 4864 (Mbl) 07801 717222

Sherriffs, Irene (Mrs) — 22/2 West Mill Bank, Edinburgh EH13 0QT [E-mail: reenie.sherriffs@blueyonder.co.uk] — 0131-466 9530

Tew, Helen (Mrs) — 318 Lanark Road, Edinburgh EH14 2LJ [E-mail: helentew9@gmail.com] — 0131-478 1268 (Mbl) 07986 170802

Wyllie, Anne (Miss) — 2F3, 46 Jordan Lane, Edinburgh EH10 4QX [E-mail: anne.wyllie@tiscali.co.uk] — 0131-447 9035

2. WEST LOTHIAN

Elliott, Sarah (Miss) — 105 Seafield Rows, Seafield, Bathgate EH47 7AW [E-mail: sarah.elliottf@btopenworld.com] — 01506 654950

Galloway, Brenda (Dr) — Lochend, 58 St Ninians Road, Linlithgow EH49 7BN [E-mail: bhgallo@yahoo.co.uk] — 01506 842028

Holden, Louise (Mrs) — Am Batnach, Easter Breich, West Calder EH55 8PP [E-mail: louise.holden@btinternet.com] — 01506 873030

Middleton, Alex — 19 Cramond Place, Dalgety Bay KY11 9LS [E-mail: alex.middleton@btinternet.com] — 01383 820800

Orr, Elizabeth (Mrs) — 64a Marjoribanks Street, Bathgate EH48 1AL [E-mail: liz-orr@hotmail.co.uk] — 01506 653116

Paxton, James — 5 Main Street, Longridge, Bathgate EH47 8AE [E-mail: jim_paxton@btinternet.com] — 01501 772192

Scoular, Iain W. — 15 Bonnyside Road, Bonnybridge FK4 2AD [E-mail: iain@iwsconsultants.com] — 01324 812395 (Mbl) 07717 131596

Wilkie, David — 53 Goschen Place, Broxburn EH52 5JH [E-mail: david-fmu_09@tiscali.co.uk] — 01506 854777

3. LOTHIAN

Evans, W. John IEng MIIE(Elec) — Waterlily Cottage, 10 Fenton Steading, North Berwick EH39 5AF [E-mail: jevans7is@hotmail.com] — 01620 842990

Hogg, David MA — 82 Eskhill, Penicuik EH26 8DQ [E-mail: hogg-d2@sky.com] — 01968 676350

Millan, Mary (Mrs) — 33 Polton Vale, Loanhead EH20 9DF [E-mail: marymillan@fsmail.net] — (Mbl) 07821 693946 · 0131-440 1624

Trevor, A. Hugh MA MTh — 29A Fidra Road, North Berwick EH39 4NE [E-mail: htrevor@talktalk.net] — (Mbl) 07814 466104 · 01620 894924

Yeoman, Edward T.N. FSAScot — 75 Newhailes Crescent, Musselburgh EH21 6EF [E-mail: edwardyeoman6@aol.com] — 0131-653 2291 · (Mbl) 07896 517666

4. MELROSE AND PEEBLES

Cashman, Margaret D. (Mrs) — 38 Abbotsford Road, Galashiels TD1 3HR [E-mail: mcashman@tiscali.co.uk] — 01896 752711

Selkirk, Frances (Mrs) — 2 The Glebe, Ashkirk, Selkirk TD7 4PJ [E-mail: f.selkirk@btinternet.com] — 01750 32204

5. DUNS

Landale, Alison (Mrs) — Green Hope Guest House, Ellemford, Duns TD11 3SG [E-mail: alison@greenhope.co.uk] — 01361 890242

Taylor, Christine (Mrs) — Rowardennan, Main Street, Gavinton, Duns TD11 3QT [E-mail: christine2751@btinternet.com] — 01361 882994

6. JEDBURGH

Findlay, Elizabeth (Mrs) — 7e Rose Lane, Kelso TD5 7AP [E-mail: findlay290@gmail.com] — 01573 226641

Knox, Dagmar (Mrs) — 3 Stichill Road, Ednam, Kelso TD5 7QQ [E-mail: dagmar.knox.riding@btinternet.com] — 01573 224883

7. ANNANDALE AND ESKDALE

Boncey, David — Redbrae, Beattock, Moffat DG10 9RF [E-mail: david.boncey613@btinternet.com] — 01683 300613

Brown, Martin J. — Lochhouse Farm, Beattock, Moffat DG10 9SG [E-mail: martin@lochhousefarm.com] — 01683 300451

Brown, S. Jeffrey BA — Skara Brae, 8 Ballplay Road, Moffat DG10 9JU [E-mail: sjbrown@btinternet.com] — 01683 220475

Chisholm, Dennis A.G. MA BSc — Moss-side, Hightae, Lockerbie DG11 1JR [E-mail: dchis@talktalk.net] — 01387 811803

Dodds, Alan — Trinco, Battlehill, Annan DG12 6SN [E-mail: alanandjen46@talktalk.net] — 01461 201235

Jackson, Susan (Mrs) — 48 Springbells Road, Annan DG12 6LQ — 01461 204159

Morton, Andrew A. BSc
[E-mail: peter-jackson24@sky.com]
19 Sherwood Park, Lockerbie DG11 2DX
[E-mail: andrew.a.morton@btinternet.com]
[E-mail: andrew_morton@mac.com]   01576 203164

Saville, Hilda A. (Mrs)
32 Crosslaw Burn, Moffat DG10 9LP
[E-mail: saville.c@sky.com]   01683 222854

8. DUMFRIES AND KIRKCUDBRIGHT
Corson, Gwen (Mrs)
7 Sunnybrae, Borgue, Kirkcudbright DG6 4SJ   01557 870328
Matheson, David
44 Auchenkeld Avenue, Heathhall, Dumfries DG1 3QY
Monk, Geoffrey
Ogilvie, D. Wilson MA FSAScot
Lingerwood, 2 Nelson Street, Dumfries DG2 9AY   01387 264267
Paterson, Ronald M. (Dr)
Mirkwood, Ringford, Castle Douglas DG7 2AL   01557 820202
[E-mail: mirkwoodtyke@aol.com]
Smith, Nicola (Mrs)
Brightwater Lodge, Kelton, Castle Douglas DG7 1SZ   01556 680453
[E-mail: nickysasmith@btinternet.com]

9. WIGTOWN AND STRANRAER
McQuistan, Robert
Old Schoolhouse, Carsluith, Newton Stewart DG8 7DT   01671 820327
[E-mail: mcquistan@mcquistan.plus.com]
Williams, Roy
120 Belmont Road, Stranraer DG9 7BG   01776 705762
[E-mail: roywilliams84@hotmail.com]

10. AYR
Anderson, James (Dr)
BVMS PhD DVM FRCPath FIBiol MRCVS
67 Henrietta Street, Girvan KA26 9AN   (Mbl) 01465 710059
[E-mail: jc.anderson@tesco.net]   07952 512720
Gowans, James
2 Cochrane Avenue, Dundonald, Kilmarnock KA2 9EJ   01563 850904
[E-mail: jim@luker42.freeserve.co.uk]
Jamieson, Ian A.
2 Whinfield Avenue, Prestwick KA9 2BH   (Mbl) 07985 916814
[E-mail: ian@jamieson4189.freeserve.co.uk]   01242 476898
Morrison, James
27 Monkton Road, Prestwick KA9 1AP   01292 479313
[E-mail: jim.morrison@talktalk.net]
Murphy, Ian   07773 287852
56 Lamont Crescent, Netherthird, Cumnock KA18 3DU   (Mbl) 01290 423675
[E-mail: ianm_cumnock@yahoo.co.uk]
Riome, Elizabeth (Mrs)
Monkwood Mains, Minishant, Maybole KA19 8EY   01292 443440
[E-mail: aj.riome@btinternet.com]
Stewart, Christine (Mrs)
52 Kilnford Drive, Dundonald KA2 9ET   01563 850486
[E-mail: christiestewart@btinternet.com]

11. IRVINE AND KILMARNOCK

Bircham, James F.	8 Holmlea Place, Kilmarnock KA1 1UU [E-mail:james.bircham@sky.com]	01563 532287
Cooper, Fraser	5 Balgray Way, Irvine KA11 1RP [E-mail: frasercooper@wightcablenorth.net]	01294 211235
Crosbie, Shona (Mrs)	4 Campbell Street, Darvel KA17 0DA [E-mail: fawltytowersdarvel@yahoo.co.uk]	01560 322229
Dempster, Ann (Mrs)	20 Graham Place, Kilmarnock KA3 7JN [E-mail: ademp99320@aol.com]	01563 529361 01563 534080 (Work) 07729 152945 (Mbl) 01563 540009
Gillespie, Janice (Miss)	12 Jeffrey Street, Kilmarnock KA1 4EB [E-mail: janice.gillespie@tiscali.co.uk]	01563 534431
Hamilton, Margaret A. (Mrs)	59 South Hamilton Street, Kilmarnock KA1 2DT [E-mail: tomhnltn@sky.com]	01563 534065
Jamieson, John H. BSc DEP AFBPSS	22 Moorfield Avenue, Kilmarnock KA1 1TS [E-mail: johnhjamieson@tiscali.co.uk]	01560 484331
McGeever, Gerard	23 Kinloch Avenue, Stewarton, Kilmarnock KA3 3HQ [E-mail: gerard@gmcgeever.freeserve.co.uk]	0141-847 5717 (Work) 01563 538475
MacLean, Donald	1 Four Acres Drive, Kilmaurs, Kilmarnock KA3 2ND [E-mail: donannmac@yahoo.co.uk]	01563 535305
Mills, Catherine (Mrs)	59 Crossdene Road, Crosshouse, Kilmarnock KA2 0JU [E-mail: cfmills5lib@hotmail.com]	01563 539377
Raleigh, Gavin	21 Landsborough Drive, Kilmarnock KA3 1RY [E-mail: gavin.raleigh@lineone.net]	01294 203577
Robertson, William	1 Archers Avenue, Irvine KA11 2GB [E-mail: willie.robert@yahoo.co.uk]	01294 551695
Whitelaw, David	9 Kirkhill, Kilwinning KA13 6NB [E-mail: whitelawfam@talktalk.net]	

12. ARDROSSAN

Barclay, Elizabeth (Mrs)	2 Jacks Road, Saltcoats KA21 5NT [E-mail: mfiz98@dsl.pipex.com]	01294 471855
Bruce, Andrew	57 Dockens Road, Ardrossan KA22 8JB [E-mail: andrew_bruce2@sky.com]	01294 605113
Clarke, Elizabeth (Mrs)	Swallowbrae, Torbeg, Isle of Arran KA27 8HE [E-mail: lizahclarke@gmail.com]	01770 860219 07780 574367 (Mbl)
Currie, Archie BD	55 Central Avenue, Kilbirnie KA25 6JP [E-mail: archiecurrie@yahoo.co.uk]	01505 681474 07881 452115 (Mbl)
Hunter, Jean C.Q. (Mrs) BD	Church of Scotland Manse, Shiskine, Isle of Arran KA27 3EP [E-mail: j.hunter744@btinternet.com]	01770 860380
McCool, Robert	17 McGregor Avenue, Stevenston KA20 4BA	01294 466548

Macleod, Sharon (Mrs) Creag Dhubh, Golf Course Road, Whiting Bay, Isle of Arran KA27 8QT [E-mail: macleodsharon@hotmail.com] 01770 700353
Ross, Magnus BA MEd 39 Beachway, Largs KA30 8QH [E-mail: m.b.ross@btinternet.com] 01475 689572

13. LANARK
Grant, Alan 25 Moss-side Avenue, Carluke ML8 5UG [E-mail: amgran25@aol.com] 01555 771419
Love, William 30 Barmore Avenue, Carluke ML8 4PE [E-mail: janbill130@tiscali.co.uk] 01555 751243

14. GREENOCK AND PAISLEY
Banks, Russell 18 Aboyne Drive, Paisley PA2 7SJ [E-mail: margaret.banks2@ntlworld.com] 0141-884 6925
Bird, Mary Jane
Boag, Jennifer (Miss) 11 Madeira Street, Greenock PA16 7UJ [E-mail: jenniferboag@hotmail.com] 01475 720125
Campbell, Tom BA DipCPC 3 Grahamston Place, Paisley PA2 7BY [E-mail: tomcam38@googlemail.com] 0141-840 2273
Davey, Charles L. 16 Divert Road, Gourock PA19 1DT [E-mail: charles.davey@talktalk.net] 01475 631544
Glenny, John C. 49 Cloch Road, Gourock PA19 1AT [E-mail: jacklizg@aol.com] 01475 636415
Hood, Eleanor (Mrs) 12 Clochoderick Avenue, Kilbarchan, Johnstone PA10 2AY [E-mail: eleanor.hood.kilbarchan@ntlworld.com] 01505 704208
MacDonald, Christine (Ms) 33 Collier Street, Johnstone PA5 8AG [E-mail: christine.macdonald10@ntlworld.com] 01505 355779
McFarlan, Elizabeth (Miss) 20 Fauldswood Crescent, Paisley PA2 9PA [E-mail: elizabeth.mcfarlan@ntlworld.com] 01505 358411
McHugh, Jack 'Earlshaugh', Earl Place, Bridge of Weir PA11 3HA [E-mail: jackmchugh@tiscali.co.uk] 01505 612789
Marshall, Leon M. 'Glenisla', Gryffe Road, Kilmacolm PA13 4BA [E-mail: lm@stevenson-kyles.co.uk] 01505 872417
Maxwell, Sandra A. (Mrs) BD 2 Grants Avenue, Paisley PA2 6AZ [E-mail: sandra1.maxwell@virgin.net] 0141-884 3710
Orry, Geoff 'Rhu Ellan', 4 Seaforth Crescent, Barrhead, Glasgow G78 1PL [E-mail: geoff.orry@googlemail.com] 0141-881 9748
Rankin, Kenneth 20 Bruntsfield Gardens, Glasgow G53 7QJ 0141-880 7474

16. GLASGOW
Birchall, Edwin

Brenner, David	Greenhill Lodge, 1 Old Humbie Road, Glasgow G77 5DF [E-mail: david.bremner@tiscali.co.uk]	0141-639 1742
Campbell, Jack T. BD BEd	40 Kenmure Avenue, Bishopbriggs, Glasgow G64 2DE [E-mail: jack.campbell@ntlworld.com]	0141-563 5837
Dickson, Hector M.K.	'Gwito', 61 Whitton Drive, Giffnock, Glasgow G46 6EF [E-mail: hectordickson@hotmail.com]	0141-637 0080
Fullarton, Andrew	1/1 40 Gardner Street, Partick, Glasgow G11 5DF	0141-883 9518
Graham, Morrison	8 Erskine Street, Stirling FK7 0QN	0141-579 4772 01786 609594
Grant, George	[E-mail: georgegrant@gmail.com]	(Mbl) 07921 168057
Horner, David J.	20 Ledi Road, Glasgow G43 2AJ [E-mail: djhorner@btinternet.com]	0141-637 7369
Joansson, Tordur	1/2, 18 Eglinton Court, Glasgow G5 9NE [E-mail: to41jo@yahoo.co.uk]	0141-429 6733
Kilpatrick, Mrs Joan	39 Brent Road, Regent's Park, Glasgow G46 8JG [E-mail: je-kilpatrick@sky.com]	0141-621 1809
McChlery, Stuart	62 Grenville Drive, Cambuslang, Glasgow G72 8DP [E-mail: s.mcchlery@gcu.ac.uk]	0141-643 9730
McColl, John	2FL, 53 Aberfoyle Street, Glasgow G31 3RP [E-mail: solfolly11@gmail.com]	0141-554 9881 (Mbl) 07757 303195
McFarlane, Robert	25 Avenel Road, Glasgow G13 2PB [E-mail: robertmcfrln@yahoo.co.uk]	0141-954 5540
McInally, Gordon	10 Melville Gardens, Bishopbriggs, Glasgow G64 3DF [E-mail: gmcinally@sky.com]	0141-563 2685
Mackenzie, Norman	Flat 3/2, 41 Kilmailing Road, Glasgow G44 5UH [E-mail: mackenzie799@btinternet.com]	(Mbl) 07780 733710
MacLeod, John	2 Shuna Place, Newton Mearns, Glasgow G77 6TN [E-mail: jmacleod2@sky.com]	0141-639 6862
Millar, Kathleen (Mrs)	9 Glenbank Court, Thornliebank, Glasgow G46 7EJ [E-mail: kathleen.millar@tesco.net]	0141-638 6250 (Mbl) 07793 203045
Montgomery, Hamish	13 Avon Avenue, Bearsden, Glasgow G61 2PS	0141-942 3640
Morrison, Katie (Miss)	3b Lennox Court, 16 Stockiemuir Avenue, Bearsden G61 3JL [E-mail: katiemorrison2003@hotmail.co.uk]	07852 373840
Nairne, Elizabeth	229 Southbrae Drive, Glasgow G13 1TT	(Mbl) 0141-942 3024
Nicolson, John	2 Lindsaybeg Court, Chryston, Glasgow G69 9DD [E-mail: john.c.nicolson@btinternet.com]	0141-959 5066 0141-779 2447
Phillips, John B.	2/3, 30 Handel Place, Glasgow G5 0TP [E-mail: johnphillips@fish.co.uk]	0141-429 7716
Robertson, Adam	423 Amulree Street, Glasgow G32 7SS	0141-573 6662
Robertson, Lynne M. MA MEd	2 Greenhill, Bishopbriggs, Glasgow G64 1LE [E-mail: emrobertsonmed@btinternet.com]	0141-772 1323 07720 053981
Roy, Mrs Shona	81 Busby Road, Clarkston, Glasgow G76 8BD [E-mail: theroyfamily@yahoo.co.uk]	(Mbl) 0141-644 3713

Smith, Ann — 52 Robslee Road, Thornliebank, Glasgow G46 7BX — 0141-621 0638

Stead, Mrs Mary — 9A Carrick Drive, Mount Vernon, Glasgow G32 0RW [E-mail: maystead@hotmail.co.uk] — 0141-764 1016

Stewart, James — 45 Airthrey Avenue, Glasgow G14 9LY [E-mail: jmstewart325@btinternet.com] — 0141-959 5814

Tindall, Margaret (Mrs) — 23 Ashcroft Avenue, Lennoxtown, Glasgow G65 7EN [E-mail: margarettindall@aol.com] — 01360 310911

17. HAMILTON

Allan, Angus J. — Blackburn Mill, Chapelton, Strathaven ML10 6RR [E-mail: angus.allan@hotmail.com] — 01357 528548

Beattie, Richard — 4 Bent Road, Hamilton ML3 6QB [E-mail: richardbeattie1958@hotmail.com] — 01698 420086

Bell, Sheena — 2 Langdale, East Kilbride, Glasgow G74 4RP [E-mail: belljsheena@hotmail.co.uk] — 01355 248217

Chirnside, Peter — 141 Kyle Park Drive, Uddingston, Glasgow G71 7DB — 01698 813769

Codona, Joy (Mrs) — Dykehead Farm, 300 Dykehead Road, Airdrie ML6 7SR [E-mail: jcodona772@btinternet.com] — 01236 767063 (Mbl) 07810 770609

Hastings, William Paul — 186 Glen More, East Kilbride, Glasgow G74 2AN [E-mail: wphastings@hotmail.co.uk] — 01355 521228

Hislop, Eric — 1 Castlegait, Strathaven ML10 6FF [E-mail: eric.hislop@tiscali.co.uk] — 01357 520003

Jardine, Lynette — 32 Powburn Crescent, Uddingston, Glasgow G71 7SS [E-mail: lpjardine@blueyonder.co.uk] — 01698 812404

Keir, Dickson — 46 Brackenhill Drive, Hamilton ML3 8AY [E-mail: dickson.keir@btinternet.com] — 01698 457351

McCleary, Isaac — 719 Coatbridge Road, Baillieston, Glasgow G69 7PH — 01236 421073

Preston, J. Steven — 24 Glen Prosen, East Kilbride, Glasgow G74 3TA [E-mail: steven.preston1@btinternet.com] — 01355 237359

Robertson, Rowan — 68 Townhead Road, Coatbridge ML5 2HU — 01236 425703

Stevenson, Thomas — 34 Castle Wynd, Quarter, Hamilton ML3 7XD — 01698 282263

White, Ian T. — 21 Muirhead, Stonehouse, Larkhall ML9 3HG [E-mail: iantwhite@aol.com] — 01698 792772

18. DUMBARTON

Foster, Peter — Flat 3 Templeton, 51 John Street, Helensburgh G84 8XN [E-mail: peterfostera39@btinternet.com] — 01436 678226

Galbraith, Iain B. MA MPhil MTh ThD FTCL — Beechwood, Overton Road, Alexandria G83 0LJ [E-mail: iainbg@icloud.com] — 01389 753563

Giles, Donald (Dr) — Levern House, Stuckenduff, Shandon, Helensburgh G84 8NW [E-mail: don.giles@btopenworld.com] — 01436 820565

Hart, R.J.M. BSc — 7 Kidston Drive, Helensburgh G84 8QA [E-mail: rjm7k@yahoo.com] — 01436 672039

Morgan, Richard — Amandale, School Road, Rhu, Helensburgh G84 8RS [E-mail: themorgans@hotmail.co.uk] — 01436 821269

19. ARGYLL

Alexander, John — 11 Cullipool Village, Isle of Luing, Oban PA34 4UB [E-mail: jandjalex@gmail.com] — 01852 314242

Allan, Douglas — 1 Camplen Court, Rothesay PA20 0NL [E-mail:douglasallan94@btinternet.com]

Binner, Aileen (Mrs) — 'Ailand', North Connel, Oban PA37 1QX [E-mail: binners@ailand.plus.com] — 01631 710264

Logue, David — 3 Braeface, Tayvallich, Lochgilphead PA31 8PN [E-mail: david@loguenet.co.uk] — 01546 870647

Macdonald, Duncan N. BD MBA — Clachacharra, Taynuilt PA35 1JE [E-mail: duncan@dnmacdonald.co.uk] — 01866 822651 (Mbl) 07801 439795

McFie, David — 1/1 33 Victoria Street, Rothesay PA20 0AJ [E-mail: waverley710@gmx.co.uk] — 01700 500048

MacKellar, Janet BSc — Laurel Bank, 23 George Street, Dunoon PA23 8JT [E-mail: jkmackellar@aol.com] — 01369 705549

McLellan, James A. — West Drimvore, Lochgilphead PA31 8SU [E-mail: james.mclellan8@btinternet.com] — 01546 606403

Mills, Peter A. — Northton, Ganavan, Oban PA34 5TU [E-mail: peter@peteramills.com]

Morrison, John L. — Tigh na Barnashaig, Tayvallich, Lochgilphead PA31 8PN [E-mail: jolomo@thejolomostudio.com] — 01546 870637

Ramsay, Matthew M. — Portnastorm, Carradale, Campbeltown PA28 6SB [E-mail: kintyre@fishersmensmission.org.uk] — 01583 431381

Scouller, Alastair — 15 Allanwater Appartments, Bridge of Allan, Stirling FK9 4DZ [E-mail: scouller@globalnet.co.uk] — 01786 832496

Sinclair, Margaret (Ms) — 2 Quarry Place, Furnace, Inveraray PA32 8XW [E-mail: margaret_sinclair@btinternet.com] — 01499 500633

Stather, Angela (Ms) — 1 Dunlossit Cottages, Port Askaig, Isle of Islay PA46 7RB [E-mail: angstat@btinternet.com] — 01496 840726

Thornhill, Christopher R. — 4 Ardfern Cottages, Ardfern, Lochgilphead PA31 8QN [E-mail: c.thornhill@btinternet.com] — 01852 300011

Waddell, Martin — Fasgadh, Clachan Seil, Oban PA34 4TJ [E-mail: waddell715@btinternet.com] — 01852 300395

Zielinski, Jenneffer C. (Mrs) — 26 Cromwell Street, Dunoon PA23 7AX [E-mail: jennefferzielinski@gmail.com] — 01369 706136

22. FALKIRK

Duncan, Lorna M. (Mrs) BA — Richmond, 28 Solway Drive, Head of Muir, Denny FK6 5NS — 01324 813020
[E-mail: ell.dee@blueyonder.co.uk]

McMillan, Isabelle (Mrs) — Treetops, 17 Castle Avenue, Airth FK2 8GA — (Mbl) 07896 433314

Stewart, Arthur MA — 51 Bonnymuir Crescent, Bonnybridge FK4 1GD — 01324 812667
[E-mail: arthur.stewart1@btinternet.com]

Struthers, Ivar B. — 7 McVean Place, Bonnybridge FK4 1QZ — 01324 841145
[E-mail: ivar.struthers@btinternet.com] — (Mbl) 07921 778208

23. STIRLING

Durie, Alastair (Dr) — 25 Forth Place, Stirling FK8 1UD — 01786 451029
[E-mail: acdurie@btinternet.com]

Grier, Hunter — 17 Station Road, Bannockburn, Stirling FK7 8LG — 01786 815192
[E-mail: hunter@xaltmail.com]

Tilly, Patricia (Mrs) — 25 Meiklejohn Street, Stirling FK9 5HQ — 01786 446401
[E-mail: Trishatilly@aol.com] — (Mbl) 07428 559554

Weir, Andrew (Dr) — 16 The Oaks, Killearn, Glasgow G63 9SF — 01360 550779
[E-mail: andrewweir@btinternet.com] — (Mbl) 07534 506075

24. DUNFERMLINE

Brown, Gordon — Nowell, Fossoway, Kinross KY13 0UW — 01577 840248
[E-mail: brown.nowell@hotmail.co.uk]

Conway, Bernard — 4 Centre Street, Kelty KY4 0EQ — 01383 830442
Grant, Allan — 6 Normandy Place, Rosyth KY11 2HJ — 01383 428760
[E-mail: allan75@btinternet.com]

McCafferty, Joyce (Mrs) — 53 Foulford Street, Cowdenbeath KY4 9AS — 01383 515775
McDonald, Elizabeth (Mrs) — Parleyhill, Culross, Dunfermline KY12 8JD — 01383 880231
Meiklejohn, Barry — 40 Lilac Grove, Dunfermline KY11 8AP — 01383 731550
[E-mail: barry.meiklejohn@btinternet.com]

Mitchell, Ian G. QC — 17 Carlingnose Point, North Queensferry, Inverkeithing KY11 1ER — 01383 416240
[E-mail: igmitchell@easynet.co.uk]

25. KIRKCALDY

Biernat, Ian — 2 Formonthills Road, Glenrothes KY6 3EF — 01592 655565
[E-mail: ian.biernat@btinternet.com]

26. ST ANDREWS

Elder, Morag Anne (Ms) — 5 Provost Road, Tayport DD6 9JE — 01382 552218
[E-mail: benuardin@tiscali.co.uk]

Grant, Allan	6 Normandy Place, Rosyth KY11 2HJ [E-mail: allan75@talktalk.net]	01383 428760
King, C.M. (Mrs)	8 Bankwell Road, Anstruther KY10 3DA	01333 310017
Peacock, Graham	6 Balgove Avenue, Gauldry, Newport-on-Tay DD6 8SQ [E-mail: grahampeacock6@btinternet.com]	01382 330124
Porteous, Brian	Kirkdene, Westfield Road, Cupar KY15 5DS [E-mail: brian@porteousleisure.co.uk]	01334 653561
Smith, Elspeth (Mrs)	Glentarkie Cottage, Glentarkie, Strathmiglo, Cupar KY14 7RU [E-mail: elspeth.smith@btopenworld.com]	01337 860824

27. DUNKELD AND MEIGLE

Howat, David	Lilybank Cottage, Newton Street, Blairgowrie PH10 6HZ [E-mail: david@thehowats.net]	01250 874715
Theaker, Phillip	5 Altamount Road, Blairgowrie PH10 6QL [E-mail: ptheaker@talktalk.net]	01250 871162

28. PERTH

Name	Address	Telephone
Archibald, Michael	Wychwood, Culdeesland Road, Methven, Perth PH1 3QE [E-mail: michael.archibald@gmail.com]	01738 840995
Begg, James	8 Park Village, Turretbank Road, Crieff PH7 4JN [E-mail: Bjimmy37@aol.com]	01764 655907
Benneworth, Michael	7 Hamilton Place, Perth PH1 1BB [E-mail: mbenneworth@hotmail.com]	01738 628093
Davidson, Andrew	95 Needless Road, Perth PH2 0LD [E-mail: a.r.davidson.91@cantab.net]	01738 620839
Laing, John	10 Graybank Road, Perth PH2 0GZ [E-mail: johnandmarylaing@hotmail.co.uk]	01738 623888
Ogilvie, Brian	67 Whitecraigs, Kinnesswood, Kinross KY13 9JN [E-mail: brianj.ogilvie1@btopenworld.com]	01592 840823 / (Mbl) 07815 759864
Stewart, Anne	Ballcraine, Murthly Road, Stanley, Perth PH1 4PN [E-mail: anne.stewart13@btinternet.com]	01738 828637
Yellowlees, Deirdre (Mrs)	Ringmill House, Gannochy Farm, Perth PH2 7JH [E-mail: d.yellowlees@btinternet.com]	01738 633773 / (Mbl) 07920 805399

29. DUNDEE

Name	Address	Telephone
Sharp, Gordon	6 Kelso Street, Dundee DD2 1SJ	01382 643002
Xenophontos-Hellen, Tim	Aspro Spiti, 23 Ancrum Drive, Dundee DD2 2JG [E-mail: tim.xsf@btinternet.com]	01382 630355 / (Work) 01382 567756

30. ANGUS

Beedie, Alexander W.	62 Newton Crescent, Arbroath DD11 3JZ [E-mail: bill.beedie@hotmail.co.uk]	01241 875001
Davidson, Peter I.	24 Kinnaird Place, Brechin DD9 7HF [E-mail: mail@idavidson.co.uk]	
Gray, Linda (Mrs)	8 Inchgarth Street, Forfar DD8 3LY [E-mail: lindamgray@sky.com]	01307 464039
Nicoll, Douglas	16 New Road, Forfar DD8 2AE	01307 463264
Walker, Eric	12 Orchard Brae, Kirriemuir DD8 4JY	01575 572082
Walker, Pat	12 Orchard Brae, Kirriemuir DD8 4JY	01575 572082

31. ABERDEEN

Cooper, Gordon	4 Springfield Place, Aberdeen AB15 7SF [E-mail: ga_cooper@hotmail.co.uk]	01224 316667
Gray, Peter (Prof.)	165 Countesswells Road, Aberdeen AB15 7RA [E-mail: pmdgray@bcs.org.uk]	01224 318172

32. KINCARDINE AND DEESIDE

Bell, Robert	27 Mearns Drive, Stonehaven AB39 2DZ [E-mail: r.bell282@btinternet.com]	01569 767173
Broere, Teresa (Mrs)	3 Balnastraid Cottages, Dinnet, Aboyne AB34 5NE [E-mail: broere@btinternet.com]	(Mbl) 07733 014826 / 01339 880058
Coles, Stephen	43 Mearns Walk, Laurencekirk AB30 1FA [E-mail: steve@sbcco.com]	01561 378400
McCafferty, W. John	Lynwood, Cammachmore, Stonehaven AB39 3NR [E-mail: wjmccafferty@yahoo.co.uk]	01569 730281
McLuckie, John	7 Monaltrie Close, Ballater AB35 5PT [E-mail: johnemcluckie@btinternet.com]	01339 755489
Middleton, Robin B. (Capt.)	7 St Ternan's Road, Newtonhill, Stonehaven AB39 3PF [E-mail: robbiemiddleton7@hotmail.co.uk]	01569 730852
Platt, David	2 St Michael's Road, Newtonhill, Stonehaven AB39 3RW [E-mail: daveplatt01@btinternet.com]	01569 730465
Simpson, Elizabeth (Mrs)	Connemara, 33 Golf Road, Ballater AB35 5RS [E-mail: connemara33@yahoo.com]	01339 755597

33. GORDON

Bichard, Susanna (Mrs)	Beechlee, Haddo Lane, Tarves, Ellon AB41 7JZ [E-mail: smbichard@aol.com]	01651 851345
Crouch, Simon	Greenbank, Corgarff, Strathdon AB36 8YL [E-mail: scassents@aol.com] (Mbl) 07713 101358	01975 651779

Doak, Alan B. 17 Chievres Place, Ellon AB41 9WH
[E-mail: alanbdoak@aol.com]
01358 721819

Findlay, Patricia (Mrs) Douglas View, Tullynessle, Alford AB33 8QR
[E-mail: p.a.findlay@btopenworld.com]
01975 562379

Mitchell, Jean (Mrs) 6 Cowgate, Oldmeldrum, Inverurie AB51 0EN
[E-mail: j.g.mitchell@btinternet.com]
01651 872745

Robb, Margaret (Mrs) Chrislouan, Keithhall, Inverurie AB51 0LN
[E-mail: Robbminister1@aol.com]
01651 882310

Robertson, James Y. MA 1 Nicol Road, Kintore, Inverurie AB51 0QA
[E-mail: j.robertson833@btinternet.com]
01467 633001

34. BUCHAN

Armitage, Rosaline (Mrs) Whitecairn, Blackhills, Peterhead AB42 3LR
[E-mail: r.r.armitage@btinternet.com]
01779 477267

Barker, Tim South Silverford Croft, Longmanhill, Banff AB45 3SB
[E-mail: tbarker05@aol.com]
01261 851839

Brown, Lillian (Mrs) 45 Main Street, Aberchirder, Huntly AB54 7ST
01466 780330

Forsyth, Alicia (Mrs) Rothie Inn Farm, Forgue Road, Rothienorman, Inverurie AB51 8YH
[E-mail: a.forsyth@btinternet.com]
01651 821359

Givan, James Zimra, Longmanhill, Banff AB45 3RP
[E-mail: jim.givan@btinternet.com]
01261 833318
(Mbl) 07753 458664

Grant, Margaret (Mrs) 22 Elphin Street, New Aberdour, Fraserburgh AB43 6LH
[E-mail: margaret@wilmar.demon.co.uk]
01346 561341

Higgins, Scott St Ninian's, Manse Terrace, Turriff AB53 4BA
[E-mail: mhairiandscott@btinternet.com]
01888 569103

Lumsden, Vera (Mrs) 8 Queen's Crescent, Portsoy, Banff AB45 2PX
[E-mail: ivsd@lumsden77.freeserve.co.uk]
01261 842712

McColl, John East Cairnchina, Lonmay, Fraserburgh AB43 8RH
[E-mail: solfolly11@gmail.com]
01346 532558
(Mbl) 07757 303195

MacLeod, Ali (Ms) 11 Pitfour Crescent, Fetterangus, Peterhead AB42 4EL
[E-mail: aliowl@hotmail.com]
01771 622992
(Mbl) 07821 670705

Macnee, Anthea (Mrs) Wardend Cottage, Alvah, Banff AB45 3TR
[E-mail: macneeiain4@googlemail.com]
01261 815647

Mair, Dorothy L.T. (Miss) Flat F, 15 The Quay, Newburgh, Ellon AB41 6DA
[E-mail: dorothymair2@aol.com]
01358 788832
(Mbl) 07505 051305

Noble, John M. 44 Henderson Park, Peterhead AB42 2WR
[E-mail: john_m_noble@hotmail.co.uk]
01779 472522

Ogston, Norman Rowandale, 6 Rectory Road, Turriff AB53 4SU
[E-mail: norman.ogston@gmail.com]
01888 560342

Simpson, Andrew C. 10 Wood Street, Banff AB45 1JX
[E-mail: andy.louise1@btinternet.com]
01261 812538

Smith, Ian M.G. 2 Hill Street, Cruden Bay, Peterhead AB42 0HF
01779 812698

Sneddon, Richard	100 West Road, Peterhead AB42 2AQ [E-mail: richard.sneddon@btinternet.com]	01779 480803
Taylor, Elaine (Mrs)	101 Cairntrodlie, Peterhead AB42 2AY [E-mail: elaine.taylor60@btinternet.com]	01779 472978
35. MORAY		
Forbes, Jean (Mrs)	Greenmoss, Drybridge, Buckie AB56 2JB [E-mail: dancingfeet@tinyworld.co.uk]	01542 831646 (Mbl) 07974 760337
36. ABERNETHY		
Bardgett, Alison (Mrs)	Tigh an Iasgair, Street of Kincardine, Boat of Garten PH24 3BY [E-mail: tigh@bardgett.plus.com]	01479 831751
37. INVERNESS		
Appleby, Jonathan	91 Cradlehall Park, Inverness IV2 5DB [E-mail: jon.wyvis@gmail.com]	01463 791470
Cazaly, Leonard	9 Moray Park Gardens, Culloden, Inverness IV2 7FY [E-mail: len_cazaly@lineone.net]	01463 794469
Cook, Arnett D.	66 Millerton Avenue, Inverness IV3 8RY [E-mail: arnett.cook@btinternet.com]	01463 224795
Dennis, Barry	50 Holm Park, Inverness IV2 4XU [E-mail: barry.dennis@tiscali.co.uk]	01463 225883
Innes, Derek	Allanswell, Cawdor Road, Auldearn, Nairn IV12 5TQ [E-mail: dereklinnes@btinternet.com]	(Work) 01463 663448
MacInnes, Ailsa (Mrs)	Kilmartin, 17 Southside Road, Inverness IV2 3BG [E-mail: ailsa.macinnes@btopenworld.com]	(Mbl) 01463 230321 07704 485055
Robertson, Hendry	Park House, 51 Glenurquhart Road, Inverness IV3 5PB [E-mail: hendry.robertson@connectfree.co.uk]	01463 231858 (Mbl) 07929 766102
Robertson, Stewart J.H.	21 Towerhill Drive, Cradlehall, Inverness IV2 5FD	01463 793144
Roden, Vivian (Mrs)	15 Old Mill Road, Tomatin, Inverness IV13 7YW [E-mail: vroden@btinternet.com]	01808 511355 (Mbl) 07887 704915
Todd, Iain	9 Leanach Gardens, Inverness IV2 5DD [E-mail: itoddyo@aol.com]	01463 791161
38. LOCHABER		
Chalkley, Andrew BSc	41 Hillside Road, Campbeltown PA28 6NE [E-mail: andrewjoan@googlemail.com]	
Ogston, Jean (Mrs)	Church of Scotland Manse, Annie's Brae, Mallaig PH41 4RG [E-mail: jeanogston@googlemail.com]	01687 460042
Skene, William		

| Walker, Eric | Tigh a' Chlann, Inverroy, Roy Bridge PH31 4AQ [E-mail: line15@btinternet.com] | 01397 712028 |
| Walker, Pat (Mrs) | Tigh a' Chlann, Inverroy, Roy Bridge PH31 4AQ [E-mail: pat.line15@btinternet.com] | 01397 712028 |

39. ROSS

Finlayson, Michael R.	Amberlea, Glenskiach, Evanton, Dingwall IV16 9UU [E-mail: finlayson935@btinternet.com]	01349 830598
Greer, Kathleen (Mrs) MEd	17 Duthac Wynd, Tain IV19 1LP [E-mail: greer2@talktalk.net]	01862 892065
Gunstone, Ronald W.	20 Bellfield Road, North Kessock, Inverness IV1 3XU [E-mail: ronald.gunstone@virgin.net]	01463 731337 (Mbl) 07974 443948
Jamieson, Patricia A. (Mrs)	9 Craig Avenue, Tain IV19 1JP [E-mail: hapjjam179@yahoo.co.uk]	01862 893154
McAlpine, James	5 Cromlet Park, Invergordon IV18 0RN [E-mail: jmca1@tinyworld.co.uk]	01349 852801
McCreadie, Frederick	7 Castle Gardens, Dingwall IV15 9HY [E-mail: fredmccreadie@tesco.net]	01349 862171
Munro, Irene (Mrs)	1 Wyvis Crescent, Conon Bridge, Dingwall IV15 9HY [E-mail: irenemunro@rocketmail.com]	01349 865752

40. SUTHERLAND

Baxter, A. Rosie (Dr)	Daylesford, Invershin, Lairg IV27 4ET [E-mail: drrosiereid@yahoo.co.uk]	01549 421326 (Mbl) 07748 761694
Roberts, Irene (Mrs)	Flat 4, Harbour Buildings, Main Street, Portmahomack, Tain IV20 1YG [E-mail: ireneroberts43@hotmail.com]	01862 871166 (Mbl) 07854 436854
Weidner, Karl	6 St Vincent Road, Tain IV19 1JR [E-mail: kweidner@btinternet.com]	01862 894202

41. CAITHNESS

| MacDonald, Dr Morag | Orkney View, Portskerra, Melvich KW14 7YL [E-mail: liliasmacdonald@btinternet.com] | 01641 531281 |

42. LOCHCARRON – SKYE

Lamont, John H. BD	6 Tigh na Filine, Aultbea, Achnasheen IV22 2JE [E-mail: jhlamont@btinternet.com]	(Mbl) 07714 720753
MacRae, Donald E.	Nethania, 52 Strath, Gairloch IV21 2DB [E-mail: Dmgair@aol.com]	01445 712235
Ross, R. Ian	St Conal's, Inverinate, Kyle IV40 8HB	01599 511371

43. UIST

Name	Address	Tel
Browning, Margaret (Miss)	1 Middlequarter, Sollas, Lochmaddy, Isle of North Uist HS6 5BU [E-mail: margaretckb@tiscali.co.uk]	01876 560392
Lines, Charles M.D.	Flat 1/02, 8 Queen Margaret Road, Glasgow G20 6DP	
MacAulay, John	Fernhaven, 1 Flodabay, Isle of Harris HS3 3HA	01859 530340
MacNab, Ann (Mrs)	Druim Skilivat, Scolpaig, Lochmaddy, Isle of North Uist HS6 5DH [E-mail: annabhan@hotmail.com]	01876 510701

44. LEWIS

Name	Address	Tel
Macleod, Donald	14 Balmerino Drive, Stornoway, Isle of Lewis HS1 2TD [E-mail: donaldmacleod25@btinternet.com]	01851 704516
Macmillan, Iain	34 Scotland Street, Stornoway, Isle of Lewis HS1 2JR [E-mail: macmillan@brocair.fsnet.co.uk]	01851 704826 (Mbl) 07775 027987
Murray, Angus	4 Ceann Chilleagraidh, Stornoway, Isle of Lewis HS1 2UJ [E-mail: angydmurray@btinternet.com]	01851 703550

45. ORKNEY

Name	Address	Tel
Dicken, Marion (Mrs)	12 MacDonald Park, St Margaret's Hope, Orkney KW17 2AL [E-mail: mj44@hotmail.co.uk]	01856 831687
Jones, Jo (Mrs) BA Cert Ed LRAM	Moorside, Firth, Orkney KW17 2IZ [E-mail: yetminstermusic@googlemail.com]	01856 761899
Robertson, Johan (Mrs)	Old Manse, Eday, Orkney KW17 2AA	01857 622251

46. SHETLAND

Name	Address	Tel
Harrison, Christine (Mrs) BA	Gerdavatn, Baltasound, Unst, Shetland ZE2 9DY [E-mail: chris4242@btinternet.com]	01957 711578
Smith, M. Beryl (Mrs) DCE MSc	Vakterlee, Cumliewick, Sandwick, Shetland ZE2 9HH [E-mail: beryl@brooniestaing.co.uk]	01950 431280

47. ENGLAND

Houghton, Mark (Dr)	Kentcliffe, Charney Road, Grange-over-Sands, Cumbria LA11 6BP [E-mail: mark@chaplain.me.uk]	01539 525048 (Work) 01629 813505
Menzies, Rena (Mrs)	49 Elizabeth Avenue, St Brelade's, Jersey JE3 8GR [E-mail: menzfamily@jerseymail.co.uk]	01534 741095
Milligan, Elaine (Mrs)	16 Surrey Close, Corby, Northants NN17 2TG [E-mail: elainemilligan@ntlworld.com]	01536 205259
Munro, William	35 Stour Road, Corby, Northants NN17 2HX	01536 504864

48. INTERNATIONAL CHARGES

Ross, David — Urb. El Campanario, EDF Granada, Esc. 14, Baja B, Ctra Cadiz N-340, Km 168, 29680 Estepona, Malaga, Spain [E-mail: rosselcampanario@yahoo.co.uk] (Tel/Fax) 0034 952 88 26 34

49. JERUSALEM

Oakley-Levstein, Joanna (Mrs) BA — Mevo Hamma, 12934, Israel [E-mail: j.oak.lev@gmail.com] 00972 50584 2517

ASSOCIATE (Ireland)

Binnie, Jean (Miss) — 2 Ailesbury Lawn, Dundrum, Dublin 16, Ireland [E-mail: jeanbinnie@eircom.net] 00353 1 298 7229

LIST I – MINISTRIES DEVELOPMENT STAFF

Ministries Development Staff support local congregations, parish groupings and presbyteries in a wide variety of ways, bringing expertise or experience to pastoral work, development, and outreach in congregation and community. Some of these may be ministers and deacons undertaking specialist roles; these are not listed below but are found in Section 5 (Presbyteries), with deacons also in List C of the present section.

NAME	APPOINTMENT AND PRESBYTERY	CONTACT
Adam, Pamela BD	Ellon (Gordon)	pbaker@churchofscotland.org.uk
Amanaland, John	Aberdeen: Garthdee (Aberdeen)	jamanaland@churchofscotland.org.uk
Archer, Janice	Cumbernauld: Kildrum – Admin Support Worker (Falkirk)	
Baird, Janette Y.	Glasgow: St Andrew and St Nicholas – Community Development (Glasgow)	JBaird@churchofscotland.org.uk
Baker, Paula (Mrs)	Birnie and Pluscarden l/w Elgin: High – Parish Assistant (Moray)	PBaker@churchofscotland.org.uk
Berry, Gavin R.	Arbroath Old and Abbey – Parish Assistant (Angus)	GBerry@churchofscotland.org.uk
Binnie, Michelle	Possilpark (Glasgow)	MBinnie@churchofscotland.org.uk
Boland, Susan (Mrs) DipHE(Theol)	Cumbernauld: Abronhill (Falkirk)	SBoland@churchofscotland.org.uk
Bosch, Eckhardt	Keith churches – Parish Assistant (Moray)	EBosch@churchofscotland.org.uk
Boyle, Deborah	Glasgow: Ruchill Kelvinside – Children and Family Outreach (Glasgow)	
Broere, Paula	Aberdeen: Mastrick – Parish Assistant (Aberdeen)	PBroere@churchofscotland.org.uk
Brown, Kenneth	Livingston United – Church and Community Worker (West Lothian)	Kenneth.Brown@churchofscotland.org.uk
Bruce, Nicola P.S.	Ellon – Parish Assistant, Mission Development (Gordon)	NBruce@churchofscotland.org.uk
Bruce, Stuart	Glasgow: Queen's Park Govanhill – Parish Assistant (Glasgow)	

Name	Role	Contact
Burton, Rebecca A.	Presbytery Youth and Children's Worker (Argyll)	RBurton@churchofscotland.org.uk
Campbell, Alasdair D. BA	Annan and Gretna churches – Parish Assistant (Annandale and Eskdale)	Alasdair.Campbell@churchofscotland.org.uk
Campbell, Julie	Drumchapel: St Andrew's (Glasgow)	0141-944 3758
Campbell, Neil MA	Dundee: Craigiebank l/w Douglas and Mid Craigie – Youth and Young Adult Development Worker (Dundee)	Neil.Campbell@churchofscotland.org.uk
Clark, Ross	Dundee:Fintry – Mission and Discipleship Development Worker (Dundee)	Ross.Clark@churchofscotland.org.uk
Craig, Iona S.	Glasgow: Maryhill – Volunteer Development Worker (Glasgow)	ICraig@churchofscotland.org.uk
Crawford, Fiona	Presbytery Strategy Officer (Glasgow)	FCrawford@churchofscotland.org.uk
Crossan, Morag BA	Dalmellington l/w Patna Waterside – Youth and Childen's Worker (Ayr)	MCrossan@churchofscotland.org.uk
Crumlin, Melodie BA PGMgt DipBusMgt	PEEK (Possibilities for Each and Every Kid) – Project Development Manager (Glasgow)	MCrumlin@churchofscotland.org.uk
Currie, Archie	Ardrossan Park – Outreach and Family Worker (Ardrossan)	archie.currie@churchofscotland.org.uk
Douglas, Ian	Motherwell Crosshill l/w St Margaret's – Parish Assistant (Hamilton)	IDouglas@churchofscotland.org.uk
Duncan, Emma	Montrose churches (Angus)	WMacDonald@churchofscotland.org.uk
Dungavel, Marie Claire	Dumbarton: Riverside l/w West, Development Worker (Dumbarton)	01389 742551
Eggo, Rosemary E.	North Ayr – Development and Family Worker (Ayr)	REggo@churchofscotland.org.uk
Evans, Andrew	Glasgow: Gorbals – Community Development Worker (Glasgow)	
Glen, Ewen A.	Tranent Cluster – Family and Youth Development Worker (Lothian)	EGlen@churchofscotland.org.uk
Grimmond, Shona	Arbroath: Knox's l/w St Vigeans – Family Worker (Angus)	
Finch, John BA	Gorbals Parish Church – Community Development Worker (Glasgow)	jfinch@churchofscotland.org.uk
Gray, Ian	Arbroath: Knox's l/w St Vigeans – Children and Family Worker (Angus)	IGray@churchofscotland.org.uk
Gunn, Philip BSc	Aberdeen: Mannofield – Parish Assistant (Aberdeen)	PGunn@churchofscotland.org.uk
Haringman, Paul MSc	Culloden: The Barn – Community Worker (Inverness)	Paul.Haringman@churchofscotland.org.uk
Harper, Kirsty BA	Edinburgh: Granton (Edinburgh)	KHarper@churchofscotland.org.uk
Hislop, Donna	Youth Worker (Annandale and Eskdale)	DHislop@churchofscotland.org.uk
Hunter, Jean C.Q. BD	Brodick and linked parishes – Parish Assistant (Ardrossan)	JHunter@churchofscotland.org.uk
Hutchison, John BA	Rothes Trinity Parish Grouping (Kirkcaldy)	JHutchison@churchofscotland.org.uk
Hyndman, Graham	Church House, Bridgeton – Youth Worker (Glasgow)	GHyndman@churchofscotland.org.uk
Johnston, Ashley L.	Abercorn with Pardovan, Kinscavil and Winchburgh – Family Development Worker (West Lothian)	AJohnston@churchofscotland.org.uk
Jolly, E. Anne	Glasgow: Castlemilk – Community Development Worker	Anne.Jolly@churchofscotland.org.uk
Keenan, Deborah	Glasgow: Easterhouse St George's and St Peter's (Glasgow)	DKeenan@churchofscotland.org.uk
Kennedy, Sarah	Kilmarnock New Laigh l/w Onthank – Community Development (Irvine/Kilmarnock)	SKennedy@churchofscotland.org.uk
Kerr, Fiona A.	Dalgety Bay – Parish Assistant (Dunfermline)	FKerr@churchofscotland.org.uk
Lennox, Gigha K.	Edinburgh: St David's Broomhouse – Children and Family Worker (Edinburgh)	GLennox@churchofscotland.org.uk
Knights, Chris (Rev Dr)	Musselburgh churches (Lothian)	revchrisknights@gmail.com

Name	Role	Contact
Lightbody, Philip (Rev)	Credo Centre – Mission Development (Aberdeen)	PLightbody@churchofscotland.org.uk
Livingstone, Ruth M.	Glenrothes: St Margaret's – Congregational Support Worker (Kirkcaldy)	RLivingstone@churchofscotland.org.uk
Logie, Duncan A.	Edinburgh: St Margaret's – Children, Youth and Family Worker (Edinburgh)	
Lynch, David J.	Inverness: Trinity – Children's and Family Worker (Inverness)	DLynch@churchofscotland.org.uk
McDougall, Hilary N.	Presbytery Congregational Facilitator (Glasgow)	HMacDougall@churchofscotland.org.uk
McDowell, Bonnie J.	Alloa: Ludgate and Alloa: St Mungo's – Community Development (Stirling)	BMcDowell@churchofscotland.org.uk
McElhinney, Amy	Glasgow: Carntyne – Research and Development Facilitator (Glasgow)	
McGreechin, Anne	Glasgow: Cranhill, Ruchazie and Garthamlock and Craigend East Parish Grouping (Glasgow)	AMcGreechin@churchofscotland.org.uk
McIlreavy, Gillian M.	Glasgow: Govan and Linthouse (Glasgow)	GMcIlreavy@churchofscotland.org.uk
McKay, Angus	Glasgow: Lodging House Mission (Glasgow)	AMcKay@churchofscotland.org.uk
McQuaid, Ruth Clements	Glasgow: Castlemilk – Community Arts Worker (Glasgow)	0141-634 1480
Marshall, Kirsteen	Glasgow: St Christopher's Priesthill and Nitshill – Parish Assistant (Glasgow)	
Middlemass, Deborah	Tranent Cluster (Lothian)	DMiddlemass@churchofscotland.org.uk
Mikelson, (Rev) Heather	Presbytery Mission Development Worker (Gordon)	HMikelson@churchofscotland.org.uk
Miller, Susan	Glasgow: Shettleston New – Youth and Children's Worker (Glasgow)	0141-778 0857
Mitchell, William	Aberdeen: St George's Tillydrone – Community Development Worker (Aberdeen)	WMitchell@churchofscotland.org.uk
Moodie, David	Edinburgh: Granton – Parish Assistant (Edinburgh)	DMoodie@churchofscotland.org.uk
Morrin, Jonathan	Glasgow: Barlanark Greyfriars – Youth and Children's Worker (Glasgow)	
Morrison, Iain J.	Glasgow: Colston Milton – Community Arts Worker	IMorrison@churchofscotland.org.uk
Murphy, Natasha C.	Greenock Parish Grouping – Youth and Children's Worker (Greenock/Paisley)	NMurphy@churchofscotland.org.uk
Murray, James L.	Newton and Dalkeith: St John's and King's Park – Mission and Discipleship Co-ordinator (Lothian)	James.Murray@churchofscotland.org.uk
Orr, Gillian	Presbytery Youth Worker (Abernethy)	GOrr@churchofscotland.org.uk
Philip, Darren BSc	Livingston United – Youth and Children's Worker (West Lothian)	DPhilip@churchofscotland.org.uk
Pringle, Iona M.	Kennoway, Windygates and Balgonie: St Kenneth's – Pastoral Assistant (Kirkcaldy)	IPringle@churchofscotland.org.uk
Pryde, Erica	Newbattle Parish Church – Mission and Outreach Co-ordinator (Lothian)	EPryde@churchofscotland.org.uk
Reynolds, Jessica	Inverness Trinity – Children's and Family Worker (Inverness)	07445 491132
Robertson, Douglas S. BEng BA MTh	Kaimes Lockhart Memorial – Team Leader, Project Worker (Edinburgh)	Douglas.Robertson@churchofscotland.org.uk
Robertson, Douglas J.	Baillieston – Children, Young People and Family Worker (Glasgow)	DJRobertson@churchofscotland.org.uk
Safrany, Zoltan (Rev.)	Bathgate: St John's – Parish Development Worker (West Lothian)	ZSafrany@churchofscotland.org.uk
Smith, David J.	Dundee: Lochee – Children and Young Persons Development Worker (Dundee)	DJSmith@churchofscotland.org.uk
Smith, Rebecca	Edinburgh: Richmond Craigmillar – Community Project Worker (Edinburgh)	Rebecca.Smith@churchofscotland.org.uk
Stark, Alastair BA	Glenrothes and Leslie: Youth and Children's Worker (Kirkcaldy)	AStark@churchofscotland.org.uk
Stark, Jennifer MA MATheol	Glenrothes and Leslie – Families and Projects (Kirkcaldy)	JStark@churchofscotland.org.uk

Stigant, Victoria J.	Presbytery Youth Work Facilitator (Gordon)	VStigant@churchofscotland.org.uk
Stirling, Diane BSc DipCPC BTh	Dundee: Craigiebank l/w Douglas and Mid Craigie – Parish Assistant (Dundee)	DStirling@churchofscotland.org.uk
Sutton, Naomi	Glasgow: St Christopher's Priesthill/Nitshill – Children and Families Worker (Glasgow)	
Taylor, Valerie AssocCIPD PGDip	Aberdeen: Torry St Fittick's – Ministry Assistant (Aberdeen)	VTaylor@churchofscotland.org.uk
Taylor-Smith, Moira	Edinburgh: St David's Broomhouse Pastoral Assistant (Edinburgh)	MTaylor-Smith@churchofscotland.org.uk
Temple, Tracy	Dumfries Northwest – Parish Assistant (Dumfries and Kirkcudbright)	TTemple@churchofscotland.org.uk
Thomas, Jay MA BA	Glasgow: St James' (Pollok) (Glasgow)	JThomas@churchofscotland.org.uk
Usher, Eileen	Glasgow: Cranhill, Ruchazie, Garthamlock and Craigend East Parish Grouping (Glasgow)	EUsher@churchofscotland.org.uk
Wellstood, Keith A. PGDip MICG	Perth: Riverside – Community Worker (Perth)	KWellstood@churchofscotland.org.uk
Wilson, Jeanette L.	Parish Assistant (Annandale and Eskdale, Dumfries and Kircudbright)	jlisa@tiscali.co.uk
Wilson, John K. (Kenny)	Presbytery Youth and Children's Worker (Argyll)	KWilson@churchofscotland.org.uk
Willis, Mags	Glasgow: Easterhouse (Glasgow)	mwillis@churchofscotland.org.uk
Young, Neil J.	Glasgow: St Paul's – Youth Worker (Glasgow)	NYoung@churchofscotland.org.uk

LIST J – OVERSEAS LOCATIONS

AFRICA

MALAWI

Church of Central Africa Presbyterian

Synod of Blantyre

Dr Ruth Shakespeare (2011) — Mulanje Mission Hospital, PO Box 45, Mulanje, Malawi
[E-mail: shakespeareruth@gmail.com]
(Tel) 00265 9922 61569
(Fax) 00265 1 467 022

Synod of Nkhoma

Dr David Morton (2009) — Nkhoma Hospital, PO Box 48, Nkhoma, Malawi
[E-mail: kuluva2@gmail.com]
(Tel) 00265 9940 74022

ZAMBIA

United Church of Zambia

Mr Keith and Mrs Ida Waddell — UCZ Synod, Nationalist Road at Burma Road, P.O. Box 50122, 15101 Ridgeway, Lusaka, Zambia
[E-mail: keithida2014@gmail.com]
(Tel) 00260 964 761 039

Ms Jenny Featherstone
(Ecum) (2007)

c/o Chodort Training Centre, PO Box 630451,
   Choma, Zambia
[E-mail: jenny.featherstone@googlemail.com]

(Tel) 00260 979 703 130

ASIA
NEPAL

Mr Joel Hasvenstein and Mrs Fiona Hasvenstein (2015)

c/o United Mission to Nepal, PO Box 126, Kathmandu, Nepal
(Tel: 00 977 1 4228 118)
[E-mail: joelkavari2003@gmail.com]

EUROPE
PRAGUE

David I. Sinclair BSc BD PhD DipSW

Evangelical Church of the Czech Brethren,
Jungmannova 9, CZ111 21, Prague 1
[E-mail: DSinclair@churchofscotland.org.uk]

MIDDLE EAST
EGYPT

Colin D. JoŸston MA BD

Evangelical Theological Seminary, 8 El Sekka, El Beidah Street,
Abassiyya, Cairo 11381
[E-mail: CDJoŸston@churchofscotland.org.uk]

For other European, Middle Eastern and other locations, see the Presbyteries of International Charges and Jerusalem (Section 5; 48 and 49, above)

LIST K – OVERSEAS RESIGNED AND RETIRED MISSION PARTNERS (ten or more years' service)

For a full list see: www.churchofscotland.org.uk > Resources > Yearbook > Section 6-K

LIST L – FULL-TIME WORKPLACE CHAPLAINS

CHIEF EXECUTIVE OFFICER   Rev. Iain McFadzean   iain.mcfadzean@wpcscotland.co.uk   (Mbl) 07969 227696
For a full list of Regional Organisers, Team Leaders and Chaplaincy Locations see: www.wpcscotland.co.uk > Contact Us

LIST M – PRISON CHAPLAINS

ADVISER TO SCOTTISH PRISON SERVICE   Rev. William R. Taylor   SPS HQ, Carlton House, 5 Redheughs Rigg, South Gyle,   0131-244 8745
(NATIONAL)
Edinburgh EH12 9DQ
[E-mail: bill.taylor@sps.pnn.gov.uk]

For a list of Prisons and Chaplains see: www.churchofscotland.org.uk > Resources > Yearbook > Section 6-M

LIST N – UNIVERSITY CHAPLAINS

For a list of Universities and Chaplains see: www.churchofscotland.org.uk > Resources > Yearbook > Section 6-N

LIST O – REPRESENTATIVES ON COUNCIL EDUCATION COMMITTEES

For a full list see: www.churchofscotland.org.uk > Resources > Yearbook > Section 6-O

LIST P – RETIRED LAY AGENTS

See further: www.churchofscotland.org.uk > Resources > Yearbook > Section 6-P

LIST Q – MINISTERS ORDAINED FOR SIXTY YEARS AND UPWARDS

For a full list see: www.churchofscotland.org.uk > Resources > Yearbook > Section 6-Q

LIST R – DECEASED MINISTERS AND DEACONS

The Editor has been made aware of the following ministers and deacons who have died since the publication of the previous volume of the *Year Book*.

Ainslie, William John	(Community Minister Glasgow: Easterhouse)
Aitken, Alexander Reid	(Newhaven)
Beaton, Donald	(Glenelg and Kintail)
Bonar, Alexander Fernie	(Fowlis Wester, Madderty and Monzie)
Cameron, Ian	(Kilbrandon and Kilchattan)
Cameron, Margaret DCS	
Crawford, Michael Scott Murray	(Aberdeen: St Mary's)
Creegan, Christine McLeod	(Grandtully, Logierait and Strathtay)
Davidson Kelly, Thomas Alexander	(Glasgow: Govan Old)
Davies, James McBride	(Interim Minister)
Duncan, James	(Blair Atholl and Struan)
Dougall, Elspeth Gillian	(Marchmont St Giles')
Ferguson, Archibald M.	(Auxiliary Minister)
Forrester, Duncan Baillie	(University of Edinburgh)
Gatt, David West	(Thornton)
Gibson, Ivor	(Abercorn and Dalmeny)
Guthrie, James Leslie	(Muirkirk)
Gow, Neil	(Foveran)
Hennig, Gordon	(Bellie l/w Speymouth)
Jones, Willis Arthur	(Cromarty with Resolis and Urquhart)
Kent, Arthur Francis Stoddart	(Monkton and Prestwick: North)
Kinninburgh, Elizabeth Baxter Forbes	(Birse with Finzean with Strachan)
Kirk, William Logan	(Dalton with Hightae with St Mungo)
Low, James Eric Stewart	(Tarbat)
McAlpine, Richard Haldane Martin	(Lochgoilhead and Kilmorich)
MacArthur, Allan Ian	(Applecross, Lochcarron and Torridon)
McBain, Margaret DCS	
McCallum, Moyra DCS	
McCaskill, George Ivory Lithgow	(Religious Education)
McCrorie, William	(Hospital Chaplain)
MacGregor, Robert Motherwell	(Auxiliary Minister)
McIlroy, Ian	Stranraer: High Kirk
MacMillan, William McDowall	(Kilmory with Lamlash)
MacVicar, Kenneth	(Kenmore with Lawyers with Fortingall and Glenlyon)
Morrice, William Gorman	(St John's College, Durham)
Mowatt, Gilbert Mollison	(Dundee: Albany-Butterburn)
Muir, Frederick Comery	(Stepps)

Name	Charge
Ostler, John Harkess	(Contin-Strachconon)
Oswald, John	(Muthil with Trinity Gask and Kinkell)
Palmer, Stanley William	(Kilbarchan: East)
Picken, Stuart Donald Blair	(Ardoch with Blackford)
Ramsay, Patricia	(Dundee: Balgay)
Reid, James	(Glasgow: Carmunnock)
Renton, John Paton	(Kenmay)
Ritchie, James McLaren	(Coalsnaughton)
Robb, Rodney Prentice Taylor	(Stirling St Mark's)
Robertson, Archibald	(Glasgow: Eastwood)
Robertson, Ian William	(Colvend, Southwick and Kirkbean)
Roy, Alistair Anderson	(Wick Bridge Street)
Roy, Alan John	(Aberuthven with Dunning)
Scoular, James Marshall Buttery	(Kippen)
Shewan, Frederick David Fitzgerald	(Edinburgh: Muirhouse St Andrew's)
Smith, James Sidney Allison	(Drongan: The Schaw Kirk)
Swinburne, Norman	(Sauchie)
Thomson, Margaret	(Saltcoats: Erskine)
Thorne, Leslie William	(Coatbridge: Clifton)
Underwood, Geoffrey Horne	(Cockenzie and Port Seton: Chalmers Memorial)
Watt, William Douglas	(Aboyne-Dinnet)
Weatherhead, James Leslie	(Principal Clerk)
Young, John	(Airdrie: Broomknoll with Calderbank)

SECTION 7

Legal Names and Scottish Charity Numbers for Individual Congregations

(All congregations in Scotland, and congregations furth of Scotland which are registered with OSCR, the Office of the Scottish Charity Regulator)

For a complete list of legal names see:
www.churchofscotland.org.uk > Resources > Yearbook > Section 7

Further information

All documents, as defined in the Charities References in Documents (Scotland) Regulations 2007, must specify the Charity Number, Legal Name of the congregation, any other name by which the congregation is commonly known and the fact that it is a Charity. For more information, please refer to the Law Department circular on the Regulations on the Church of Scotland website.

www.churchofscotland.org.uk > Resources > Subjects > Law Department Circulars > 'Charity Law'

SECTION 8

Church Buildings: Ordnance Survey National Grid References

Please go to: www.churchofscotland.org.uk > Resources > Yearbook > Section 8

SECTION 9

A
Discontinued Parish
and Congregational Names

The purpose of this list, compiled by Roy Pinkerton, is to assist those who are trying to identify the present-day successor of some former parish or congregation whose name is now wholly out of use and which can therefore no longer be easily traced.

Where the former name has not disappeared completely, and the whereabouts of the former parish or congregation may therefore be easily established by reference to the name of some existing parish, the former name has not been included in this list.

Present-day names, in the right-hand column of the list, may be found in the ' Index of Parishes and Places' in the print edition of the Year Book.

The list, with explanatory notes, may be found at:

www.churchofscotland.org.uk/Resources/Yearbook > Section 9

B
Recent Readjustment and Other
Congregational Changes

This is a list, also compiled by Roy Pinkerton, of parish adjustments made by presbyteries since mid-2014.

(see following pages)

The following list incorporates all instances of readjustment (i.e. union, linkage and dissolution) and certain other congregational changes, such as a change of name, which have taken place over the last three years (i.e. since the publication of the 2014–15 Year Book).

Edinburgh	**Edinburgh: Albany Deaf Church of Edinburgh** now a Mission Initiative of **Edinburgh: St Andrew's and St George's West**
	Edinburgh: Craigentinny St Christopher's and **Edinburgh: New Restalrig** united as **Edinburgh: Willowbrae**
	Edinburgh: Dean dissolved
	Edinburgh: Gorgie Dalry and **Edinburgh: Stenhouse St Aidan's** united as **Edinburgh: Gorgie Dalry Stenhouse**
	Edinburgh: Holyrood Abbey and **Edinburgh: London Road** united as **Edinburgh: Meadowbank**
	Edinburgh: Kaimes Lockhart Memorial renamed **Edinburgh: Gracemount**
West Lothian	**Livingston Ecumenical Parish** renamed **Livingston United Parish**
Lothian	**Bolton and Saltoun** and **Yester** united as **Yester, Bolton and Saltoun**
Duns	**Ayton and Burnmouth, Foulden and Mordington** and **Grantshouse and Houndwood and Reston** united as **Ayton and District Churches**
	Bonkyl and Edrom, Duns and **Langton and Lammermuir Kirk** united as **Duns and District Parishes**
	Coldstream, Ladykirk and Whitsome and **Swinton** united as **Coldstream and District Parishes**
	Eccles and **Leitholm** united as **Eccles and Leitholm**
	Fogo and Swinton linked with **Ladykirk and Whitsome** linked with **Leitholm:** linkage severed
	Fogo and **Swinton:** union dissolved
Jedburgh	**Kelso Country Churches** linked with **Kelso: Old and Sprouston**: linkage severed
	Kelso Country Churches linked with **Oxnam**
Annandale and Eskdale	**Dalton** and **Hightae** united as **Dalton and Hightae**
Dumfries and Kirkcudbright	**Balmaghie** linked with **Tarff and Twynholm**: linkage severed
	Balmaghie and **Crossmichael and Parton** united as **Crossmichael, Parton and Balmaghie**
	Borgue and **Gatehouse of Fleet** united as **Gatehouse and Borgue**

Closeburn linked with **Kirkmahoe**

Gatehouse and Borgue linked with **Tarff and Twynholm**

Kirkconnel linked with **Sanquhar: St Bride's**

Wigtown and Stranraer   **Kirkinner** linked with **Mochrum** linked with **Sorbie**

New Luce and **Old Luce** united as **Luce Valley**

Ayr   **Craigie Symington** linked with **Prestwick: South**

Irvine and Kilmarnock   **Fenwick** linked with **Kilmarnock: Riccarton**

Ardrossan   **Fairlie** linked with **Largs: St Columba's**

Lanark   **The United Church of Carstairs and Carstairs Junction** renamed **Carstairs**

Greenock and Paisley   **Howwood** linked with **Lochwinnoch**: linkage severed

Kilbarchan: East and **Kilbarchan: West** united as **Kilbarchan**

Paisley: St James dissolved

Port Glasgow: Hamilton Bardrainney linked with **Port Glasgow: St Martin's**

Glasgow   **Glasgow: Broomhill** and **Glasgow: Hyndland** united as **Glasgow: Broomhill Hyndland**

Glasgow: Easterhouse St George's and St Peter's and **Glasgow: Lochwood** united as **Glasgow: Easterhouse**

Glasgow: High Carntyne and **Glasgow: South Carntyne** united as **Glasgow: Carntyne**

Glasgow: Penilee St Andrew and **Glasgow: St Nicholas' Cardonald** united as **Glasgow: St Andrew and St Nicholas**

Glasgow: St Margaret's Tollcross Park dissolved

Glasgow: Shawlands and **Glasgow: South Shawlands** united as **Glasgow: Shawlands Trinity**

Glasgow: Shettleston Old and **Glasgow: Victoria Tollcross** united as **Glasgow: Causeway, Tollcross**

Hamilton   **Airdrie: Broomknoll** and **Airdrie: Flowerhill** united as **Airdrie: Cairnlea**

Airdrie: Cairnlea linked with **Calderbank**

Airdrie: High linked with **Caldercruix and Longriggend**

Blantyre: Livingstone Memorial linked with **Blantyre: St Andrew's**

Chapelhall linked with **Kirk o' Shotts**

Cleland linked with **Wishaw: St Mark's**

	Coatbridge: Blairhill Dundyvan linked with Coatbridge: Middle
	Hamilton: Gilmour and Whitehill linked with Hamilton: West
Dumbarton	Baldernock linked with Milngavie: St Paul's
	Clydebank: Abbotsford and Clydebank: St Cuthbert's to be united as Clydebank: Waterside
	Clydebank: St Cuthbert's linked with Duntocher: linkage severed
	Clydebank: Waterside linked with Dalmuir: Barclay
	Dumbarton: St Andrew's linked with Old Kilpatrick Bowling: linkage severed
	Helensburgh: Park and Helensburgh: St Andrew's Kirk united as Helensburgh
Argyll	Kilmun (St Munn's) and Strone and Ardentinny united as Kilmun, Strone & Ardentinny: The Shore Kirk
	Kirn and Sandbank united as Kirn and Sandbank
	Skipness linked with Tarbert, Loch Fyne and Kilberry
Falkirk	Denny: Old linked with Haggs
Stirling	Bannockburn: Allan linked with Cowie and Plean
	Cowie and Plean linked with Fallin: linkage severed
Dunfermline	Carnock and Oakley linked with Saline and Blairingone: linkage severed
	Saline and Blairingone linked with Tulliallan and Kincardine
St Andrews	Anstruther and Cellardyke united as Anstruther and Cellardyke: St Ayle
	Boarhills and Dunino linked with St Andrews: Holy Trinity
	Creich, Flisk and Kimany linked with Monimail: linkage severed
	Cupar: Old and St Michael of Tarvit linked with Monimail
	Elie, Kilconquhar and Colinsburgh renamed East Neuk Trinity and linked with St Monans
	Largo and Newburn and Largo: St David's united as Largo
	Largoward linked with St Monans: linkage severed
Dunkeld and Meigle	Aberfeldy linked with Dull and Weem linked with Grantully, Logierait and Strathtay

	Amulree and Strathbraan: linkages with **Aberfeldy** and with **Dull and Weem** severed and united with **Dunkeld** as **Dunkeld**
	Blair Atholl and Struan linked with **Tenandry**: linkage severed
	Blair Atholl and Struan linked with **Braes of Rannoch** linked with **Foss and Rannoch**
Angus	**Inchbrayock** and **Montrose: Melville South** united as **Montrose: South and Ferryden**
Aberdeen	**Aberdeen: Cove** (New Charge Development) dissolved
	Aberdeen: Garthdee linked with **Aberdeen: Ruthrieston West**: linkage severed
Kincardine and Deeside	**Banchory-Devenick and Maryculter/Cookney** renamed **Maryculter Trinity**
Gordon	**Echt** and **Midmar** united as **Echt and Midmar**
Buchan	**Gardenstown** dissolved
	Peterhead: Old and **Peterhead: Trinity** united as **Peterhead: New**
Moray	**Bellie** and **Speymouth** united as **Bellie and Speymouth**
	Lossiemouth: St Gerardine's High linked with **Lossiemouth: St James**
Abernethy	**Boat of Garten, Duthil and Kincardine** renamed **Boat of Garten, Carrbridge and Kincardine**
Lochcarron-Skye	**Glenelg and Kintail** and **Lochalsh** united as **Glenelg, Kintail and Lochalsh**
Uist	**Benbecula** linked with **Carinish**
	Berneray and Lochmaddy linked with **Kilmuir and Paible**
Orkney	**North Ronaldsay** linked with **Sanday**: linkage severed
Shetland	**Fetlar** and **Unst** united as **Unst and Fetlar**

SECTION 10

Congregational
Statistics
2016

Compiled by Sandy Gemmill

CHURCH OF SCOTLAND
Comparative Statistics: 1976–2016

	2016	2006	1996	1986	1976
Communicants	351,934	504,363	680,062	854,311	1,020,403
Elders	28,346	40,651	45,999	47,336	47,736

NOTES ON CONGREGATIONAL STATISTICS

Com   Number of communicants at 31 December 2016.

Eld   Number of elders at 31 December 2016.

G   Membership of the Guild including Young Woman's Group and others as recorded on the 2016 annual return submitted to the Guild Office.

In 16   Ordinary General Income for 2016. Ordinary General Income consists of members' offerings, contributions from congregational organisations, regular fund-raising events, income from investments, deposits and so on. This figure does not include extraordinary or special income, or income from special collections and fund-raising for other charities.

M&M   Final amount allocated to congregations after allowing for Presbytery-approved amendments up to 31 December 2016, but before deducting stipend endowments and normal allowances given for stipend purposes in a vacancy.

–18   This figure shows 'the number of children and young people aged 17 years and under who are involved in the life of the congregation'.

(NB: Figures may not be available for new charges created or for congregations which have entered into readjustment late in 2016 or during 2017. Figures might also not be available for congregations which failed to submit the appropriate schedule.)

Congregation	Com	Eld	G	In 16	M&M	–18
1. Edinburgh						
Balerno	557	72	27	131,370	72,500	36
Barclay Viewforth	314	31	-	167,239	122,292	63
Blackhall St Columba's	693	66	-	212,782	109,218	20
Bristo Memorial Craigmillar	53	6	-	57,511	31,713	50
Broughton St Mary's	186	26	-	74,311	46,592	46
Canongate	331	47	-	130,295	72,222	18
Carrick Knowe	364	48	61	63,369	40,354	277
Colinton	851	56	-	195,098	120,898	80
Corstorphine: Craigsbank	452	33	-	102,300	58,943	61
Corstorphine: Old	400	34	48	175,850	73,189	46
Corstorphine: St Anne's	354	54	62	115,232	56,924	24
Corstorphine: St Ninian's	676	81	54	172,472	93,744	55
Craiglockhart	387	47	25	142,310	99,756	60
Craigmillar Park	203	16	24	70,200	47,742	3
Cramond	991	95	-	235,812	158,001	73
Currie	490	29	60	154,334	88,111	80
Dalmeny	95	11	-	25,692	21,154	7
Queensferry	531	40	54	125,587	65,586	160
Davidson's Mains	454	71	-	205,423	120,447	80
Dean	-	-	-	-	38,423	-
Drylaw	77	18	-	19,093	9,772	1
Duddingston	434	47	31	118,959	67,129	193
Fairmilehead	528	62	29	98,995	74,509	58
Gorgie Dalry Stenhouse	252	21	-	83,853	78,766	-
Gracemount	27	3	-	17,701	1,656	10
Liberton	712	56	38	220,265	126,587	83
Granton	198	18	-	49,747	21,960	12
Greenbank	714	72	37	257,323	140,461	61
Greenside	133	26	-	-	28,767	8
Greyfriars Kirk	299	41	-	224,220	89,693	20
High (St Giles')	479	30	-	354,306	180,094	16
Holyrood Abbey	33	1	-	15,550	79,586	-
Holy Trinity	205	31	-	142,500	109,269	59
Inverleith St Serf's	341	34	22	108,128	80,524	70
Juniper Green	307	27	-	100,782	66,480	30
Kirkliston	236	31	44	95,318	57,048	12
Leith: North	199	23	-	82,842	50,447	46
Leith: St Andrew's	196	22	-	78,759	51,837	50
Leith: South	320	58	-	120,919	78,778	170
Leith: Wardie	511	47	42	169,138	86,520	90
Liberton Northfield	174	10	-	55,331	32,018	93
London Road	63	3	19	49,507	41,706	7
Marchmont St Giles'	223	30	18	113,680	71,551	64
Mayfield Salisbury	520	48	-	326,466	137,174	35
Morningside	435	59	-	193,863	115,171	103
Morningside United	101	13	-	110,336	11,965	17
Murrayfield	513	47	-	156,903	94,437	79
Newhaven	153	16	-	109,221	50,088	116

Congregation	Com	Eld	G	In 16	M&M	–18
Old Kirk and Muihouse	99	15	-	30,412	16,252	9
Palmerston Place	388	35	-	173,998	106,415	79
Pilrig St Paul's	222	17	20	50,686	29,655	2
Polwarth	188	22	13	88,816	55,194	15
Portobello and Joppa	851	79	78	231,374	141,962	197
Priestfield	120	18	21	89,483	46,906	60
Ratho	193	17	-	43,189	27,711	14
Reid Memorial	289	15	-	100,550	58,852	21
Richmond Craigmillar	92	12	-	-	4,652	6
St Andrew's and St George's West	334	47	-	277,010	161,734	69
St Andrew's Clermiston	211	11	-	-	31,772	10
St Catherine's Argyle	110	5	-	56,492	87,611	15
St Cuthbert's	304	41	-	128,706	89,890	15
St David's Broomhouse	127	12	-	30,728	16,511	24
St JoŸ's Colinton Mains	226	18	-	58,467	40,616	51
St Margaret's	209	32	18	53,568	35,346	83
St Martin's	86	12	-	22,413	3,639	28
St Michael's	326	26	30	79,912	58,216	14
St Nicholas' Sighthill	336	22	-	-	21,552	12
St Stephen's Comely Bank	189	10	-	-	74,348	27
Slateford Longstone	204	12	34	46,360	29,249	36
Stockbridge	190	19	-	83,505	57,741	22
Tron Kirk (Gilmerton and Moredun)	91	8	-	37,570	7,612	141
Willowbrae	137	15	-	55,948	51,096	4

2. West Lothian

Congregation	Com	Eld	G	In 16	M&M	–18
Abercorn	63	8	-	14,214	10,057	-
Pardovan, Kingscavil and Winchburgh	264	26	-	63,985	43,222	197
Armadale	509	43	33	85,914	46,104	197
Avonbridge	74	7	-	12,804	7,409	11
Torphichen	228	13	-	-	33,303	9
Bathgate: Boghall	236	28	21	96,443	50,193	168
Bathgate: High	476	34	34	87,119	62,000	48
Bathgate: St JoŸ's	349	26	35	71,095	37,119	120
Blackburn and Seafield	385	30	-	86,496	44,312	65
Blackridge	75	9	-	27,857	9,000	-
Harthill: St Andrew's	187	11	21	60,183	32,780	67
Breich Valley	166	11	20	31,579	21,734	12
Broxburn	349	31	50	75,034	46,338	22
Fauldhouse: St Andrew's	181	12	-	48,933	34,647	18
Kirknewton and East Calder	306	37	26	112,142	65,361	55
Kirk of Calder	519	42	19	91,782	47,955	31
Linlithgow: St Michael's	1,307	107	48	-	174,061	127
Linlithgow: St Ninian's Craigmailen	400	40	42	70,231	43,272	82
Livingston: Old	333	30	19	87,133	57,021	46
Livingston: United	299	28	-	72,020	46,392	205
Polbeth Harwood	168	18	-	28,995	14,769	9
West Kirk of Calder	245	18	14	70,258	43,812	21
Strathbrock	286	26	18	90,918	70,007	75
Uphall South	198	25	-	59,478	37,491	25

Congregation	Com	Eld	G	In 16	M&M	–18
Whitburn: Brucefield	213	18	25	106,741	49,232	99
Whitburn: South	355	27	29	78,749	50,064	94
3. Lothian						
Aberlady	201	20	-	46,583	19,322	4
Gullane	361	27	19	66,951	36,018	24
Athelstaneford	203	13	-	24,453	17,468	20
Whitekirk and Tyninghame	135	13	-	-	22,456	15
Belhaven	568	44	57	86,294	50,217	35
Spott	103	7	-	21,752	8,625	5
Bilston	89	3	15	10,506	5,068	-
Glencorse	295	13	20	26,636	15,399	4
Roslin	225	8	-	26,831	16,829	26
Bonnyrigg	627	58	44	100,971	68,894	18
Cockenzie and Port Seton: Chalmers M'rl	181	28	25	84,258	52,219	105
Cockenzie and Port Seton: Old	227	16	26	-	31,868	20
Cockpen and Carrington	193	26	44	29,270	21,813	12
Lasswade and Rosewell	275	20	-	29,614	23,505	8
Dalkeith: St JoŸ's and King's Park	479	38	24	97,237	62,427	65
Dalkeith: St Nicholas' Buccleuch	343	16	-	71,496	33,087	-
Dirleton	219	16	-	-	34,805	8
North Berwick: Abbey	270	28	39	97,810	53,863	12
Dunbar	358	22	30	106,640	72,531	84
Dunglass	276	10	-	23,000	21,554	15
Garvald and Morham	40	10	-	-	7,380	12
Haddington: West	216	17	30	54,360	40,200	17
Gladsmuir	170	12	-	-	15,098	-
Longniddry	333	43	31	77,892	48,846	25
Gorebridge	113	12	-	99,371	62,182	100
Haddington: St Mary's	505	40	-	-	57,202	65
Howgate	32	6	-	20,638	11,471	8
Penicuik: South	96	8	-	-	42,135	26
Humbie	66	8	-	-	14,967	14
Yester, Bolton and Saltoun	282	32	-	50,126	38,762	35
Loanhead	296	24	30	-	34,766	35
Musselburgh: Northesk	309	27	32	65,895	39,413	76
Musselburgh: St Andrew's High	287	28	17	64,455	42,605	-
Musselburgh: St Clement's & St Ninian's	199	13	-	-	16,718	-
Musselburgh: St Michael's Inveresk	369	37	-	79,626	50,562	10
Newbattle	351	27	17	79,974	54,998	142
Newton	111	1	-	14,700	14,261	11
North Berwick: St Andrew Blackadder	575	33	32	166,998	88,754	80
Ormiston	150	9	17	-	24,604	15
Pencaitland	159	4	-	-	27,961	17
Penicuik: North	424	32	-	72,729	47,731	64
Penicuik: St Mungo's	309	22	16	66,597	42,059	45
Prestonpans: Prestongrange	261	19	19	61,098	35,123	20
Tranent	233	13	28	55,613	31,976	60
Traprain	420	31	30	73,498	50,798	39
Tyne Valley Parish	303	23	-	75,880	53,907	107

Congregation	Com	Eld	G	In 16	M&M	–18
4. Melrose and Peebles						
Asÿirk	36	10	-	10,158	5,587	1
Selkirk	380	18	-	66,304	44,457	32
Bowden and Melrose	717	63	22	124,240	76,952	20
Broughton, Glenholm and Kilbucho	139	9	20	20,495	11,960	-
Skirling	60	5	-	7,534	5,414	2
Stobo and Drumelzier	88	8	-	19,475	12,719	3
Tweedsmuir	34	5	-	-	5,238	6
Caddonfoot	162	12	-	17,676	10,080	7
Galashiels: Trinity	392	39	25	59,200	43,640	-
Carlops	52	13	-	27,116	10,880	15
Kirkurd and Newlands	84	11	9	15,579	16,131	15
West Linton: St Andrew's	180	17	-	38,365	23,531	60
Channelkirk and Lauder	401	21	19	65,316	42,948	22
Earlston	375	22	10	53,586	35,110	54
Eddleston	100	5	-	-	9,074	14
Peebles: Old	435	36	-	-	65,951	-
Ettrick and Yarrow	190	18	-	40,226	32,989	12
Galashiels: Old and St Paul's	252	19	33	68,009	41,069	11
Galashiels: St JoŸ's	189	12	-	38,855	26,122	53
Innerleithen, Traquair and Walkerburn	344	26	41	56,061	35,716	30
Lyne and Manor	105	7	-	33,464	19,599	10
Peebles: St Andrew's Leckie	536	34	-	-	62,238	76
Maxton and Mertoun	85	11	-	-	7,301	-
Newtown	125	10	-	19,313	9,003	-
St Boswells	176	20	19	30,289	22,374	4
Stow: St Mary of Wedale and Heriot	178	12	-	36,280	24,115	9
5. Duns						
Ayton and District Churches	296	17	12	30,721	30,218	4
Berwick-upon-Tweed: St Andrew's						
Wallace Green & Lowick	307	15	-	60,335	33,363	19
Chirnside	97	8	10	15,093	8,261	22
Hutton and Fishwick and Paxton	63	6	14	-	11,489	2
Coldingham and St Abb's	69	11	-	41,232	25,567	27
Eyemouth	115	23	22	48,039	19,851	32
Coldstream and District Parishes	425	36	-	40,248	45,275	24
Eccles and Leitholm	149	15	16	16,893	15,566	2
Duns and District Parishes	669	38	44	92,550	77,415	60
Fogo	32	3	-	-	-	3
Gordon: St Michael's	66	7	-	6,924	6,515	6
Greenlaw	86	7	16	19,947	12,646	-
Legerwood	60	6	-	8,388	5,131	5
Westruther	40	7	-	5,343	4,116	30
6. Jedburgh						
Ale and Teviot United	391	26	17	47,066	39,457	13
Cavers and Kirkton	102	6	-	11,185	9,165	-
Hawick: Trinity	502	28	43	45,916	28,403	7
Cheviot Churches	297	18	31	-	49,733	25

Congregation	Com	Eld	G	In 16	M&M	–18
Hawick: Burnfoot	73	14	8	24,482	17,070	76
Hawick: St Mary's and Old	382	21	22	39,844	27,434	10
Hawick: Teviot and Roberton	256	8	7	43,820	33,435	15
Hawick: Wilton	281	24	-	48,079	29,278	34
Teviothead	55	5	-	5,062	3,522	-
Hobkirk and Southdean	130	15	13	17,983	16,262	-
Ruberslaw	245	19	11	37,650	23,187	20
Jedburgh: Old and Trinity	624	16	31	72,109	47,926	10
Kelso Country Churches	195	16	18	27,000	31,358	10
Oxnam	125	11	-	11,836	7,486	6
Kelso: Old and Sprouston	473	28	-	64,860	33,234	12
Kelso: North and Ednam	963	64	20	125,907	82,480	8

7. Annandale and Eskdale

Congregation	Com	Eld	G	In 16	M&M	–18
Annan: Old	361	46	37	70,139	42,291	20
Dornock	109	10	-	-	6,157	2
Annan: St Andrew's	601	43	51	58,966	37,819	80
Brydekirk	50	4	-	9,855	5,306	-
Applegarth, Sibbaldbie and JoŸstone	123	8	13	12,050	8,250	-
Lochmaben	250	18	36	66,904	36,216	6
Canonbie United	92	15	-	37,090	18,470	12
Liddesdale	107	7	18	28,176	20,899	-
Dalton and Hightae	178	9	-	18,600	13,723	5
St Mungo	81	11	-	14,192	9,475	-
Gretna: Old, Gretna: St Andrew's Half Morton & Kirkpatrick Fleming	312	23	22	-	40,356	80
Hoddom, Kirtle-Eaglesfield and Middlebie	209	19	14	26,095	17,167	48
Kirkpatrick Juxta	103	7	-	12,715	6,403	-
Moffat: St Andrew's	347	32	26	73,753	42,013	70
Wamphray	55	5	-	8,361	4,460	6
Langholm Eskdalemuir Ewes and Westerkirk	445	28	12	62,441	44,559	10
Lockerbie: Dryfesdale, Hutton and Corrie	708	44	34	65,418	46,377	18
The Border Kirk	297	44	27	69,327	38,019	32
Tundergarth	30	6	-	10,074	5,480	-

8. Dumfries and Kirkcudbright

Congregation	Com	Eld	G	In 16	M&M	–18
Balmaclellan and Kells	57	5	9	15,815	14,829	7
Carsphairn	87	9	-	9,529	6,174	6
Dalry	74	12	12	28,261	11,362	3
Caerlaverock	106	7	-	12,439	7,141	-
Dumfries: St Mary's-Greyfriars	407	27	33	74,401	43,293	-
Castle Douglas	362	21	22	68,578	40,994	10
The Bengairn Parishes	-	-	-	26,146	25,053	-
Closeburn	184	12	-	29,728	16,562	20
Kirkmahoe	248	13	-	24,995	19,004	3
Colvend, Southwick and Kirkbean	213	18	18	88,254	55,127	-
Corsock and Kirkpatrick Durham	85	12	9	25,757	14,180	6
Crossmichael, Parton and Balmaghie	205	11	15	26,211	24,748	-
Cummertrees, Mouswald and Ruthwell	182	21	-	-	18,968	-
Dalbeattie and Kirkgunzeon	-	-	39	50,511	37,053	-

Congregation	Com	Eld	G	In 16	M&M	–18
Urr	182	12	-	-	13,295	20
Dumfries: Maxwelltown West	553	26	32	87,169	59,440	56
Dumfries: Northwest	349	-	-	38,233	28,378	11
Dumfries: St George's	494	46	27	122,566	70,449	97
Dumfries: St Michael's and South	727	44	24	93,389	60,752	77
Dumfries: Troqueer	247	21	26	87,992	57,844	67
Dunscore	187	18	5	31,027	23,201	-
Glencairn and Moniaive	161	13	-	44,050	24,808	8
Durisdeer	148	6	-	25,572	12,406	10
Penpont, Keir and Tynron	152	10	-	-	17,942	10
Thornhill	130	10	-	27,123	25,118	-
Gatehouse and Borgue	290	20	15	51,568	34,412	-
Tarff and Twynholm	141	13	25	25,477	18,692	13
Irongray, Lochrutton and Terregles	168	24	-	-	20,408	4
Kirkconnel	250	15	-	-	22,701	-
Kirkcudbright	503	23	-	93,957	57,394	60
Kirkmichael, Tinwald & Torthorwald	387	35	19	-	42,461	6
Lochend and New Abbey	204	15	11	43,089	16,430	-
Sanquhar: St Bride's	389	24	11	45,739	28,027	30

9. Wigtown and Stranraer

Ervie Kirkcolm	174	13	-	21,918	14,218	25
Leswalt	267	-	-	29,095	16,621	-
Glasserton and Isle of Whithorn	96	6	-	-	9,359	-
Whithorn: St Ninian's Priory	303	9	17	38,730	27,036	19
Inch	218	15	10	18,036	15,270	63
Portpatrick	214	9	17	19,828	16,328	-
Stranraer: Trinty	497	40	40	88,530	65,009	35
Kirkcowan	110	10	-	34,236	20,875	9
Wigtown	157	14	12	33,741	23,766	45
Kirkinner	128	7	8	-	9,694	-
Mochrum	235	15	21	27,576	17,398	30
Sorbie	113	10	-	21,685	13,297	-
Kirkmabreck	128	11	24	19,031	11,845	-
Monigaff	211	12	-	22,027	20,374	9
Kirkmaiden	209	21	-	24,345	23,194	24
Stoneykirk	292	21	17	-	26,613	5
Luce Valley	229	20	23	39,684	32,742	13
Penninghame	405	21	23	85,326	55,916	31
Stranraer: High Kirk	535	35	20	68,468	54,388	166

10. Ayr

Alloway	1,007	98	-	219,684	122,653	450
Annbank	253	17	15	41,054	23,450	1
Tarbolton	315	27	22	54,025	37,584	12
Auchinleck	323	14	23	-	27,984	10
Catrine	112	-	-	24,177	16,730	-
Ayr: Auld Kirk of Ayr	504	-	26	79,695	55,242	-
Ayr: Castlehill	555	35	50	96,385	65,229	144
Ayr: Newton Wallacetown	382	41	53	105,941	73,799	29

Congregation	Com	Eld	G	In 16	M&M	–18
Ayr: St Andrew's	294	-	12	75,444	48,714	10
Ayr: St Columba	1,296	116	88	319,636	149,960	45
Ayr: St James'	355	39	31	82,355	46,959	150
Ayr: St Leonard's	513	-	26	78,973	47,613	-
Dalrymple	126	-	-	25,038	16,749	-
Ayr: St Quivox	233	-	-	41,327	36,641	-
Ballantrae	241	-	16	43,664	24,631	-
St Colmon (Arnsheen Barrhill and Colmonell)	226	-	-	-	16,790	-
Barr	66	-	-	2,689	3,334	-
Dailly	117	8	-	10,024	12,330	-
Girvan: South	308	-	28	35,009	21,340	-
Coylton	323	-	-	39,533	26,435	-
Drongan: The Schaw Kirk	175	16	15	37,186	23,996	76
Craigie and Symington	383	22	20	49,389	40,195	13
Prestwick: South	284	36	28	85,205	56,681	90
Crosshill	173	-	30	11,691	9,978	-
Maybole	324	-	17	69,635	44,361	-
Dalmellington	214	-	-	-	24,417	-
Patna: Waterside	135	-	-	-	15,681	-
Dundonald	456	-	45	-	53,176	-
Fisherton	106	11	-	11,881	8,310	-
Kirkoswald	209	9	21	34,681	19,277	6
Girvan: North (Old and St Andrew's)	662	-	-	81,575	43,263	-
Kirkmichael	202	14	21	26,198	14,924	6
Straiton: St Cuthbert's	165	11	17	15,957	11,484	10
Lugar	156	10	15	21,359	10,666	8
Old Cumnock: Old	341	15	32	57,160	43,891	20
Mauchline	435	-	34	74,991	51,382	-
Sorn	118	12	15	19,316	12,552	7
Monkton and Prestwick: North	313	-	25	90,040	59,058	-
Muirkirk	163	13	-	21,978	12,612	8
Old Cumnock: Trinity	314	17	33	50,560	39,009	17
New Cumnock	459	32	31	75,849	50,487	55
Ochiltree	216	21	14	28,774	23,768	25
Stair	205	14	17	34,826	24,940	24
Prestwick: Kingcase	651	-	69	118,405	83,146	-
Prestwick: St Nicholas'	600	-	41	126,245	75,197	-
Troon: Old	922	-	-	136,461	85,462	-
Troon: Portland	511	46	24	135,199	79,820	25
Troon: St Meddan's	672	83	37	152,031	102,551	115

11. Irvine and Kilmarnock

Congregation	Com	Eld	G	In 16	M&M	–18
Caldwell	221	16	-	60,777	39,848	4
Dunlop	373	34	24	84,123	44,158	25
Crosshouse	269	33	14	59,268	38,125	73
Darvel	318	26	32	53,533	31,243	48
Dreghorn and Springside	460	42	28	89,203	53,497	45
Fenwick	283	25	24	-	34,810	24
Galston	598	53	48	97,948	65,981	20
Hurlford	312	26	28	66,084	42,259	4

Congregation	Com	Eld	G	In 16	M&M	–18
Irvine: Fullarton	356	31	48	102,743	61,689	160
Irvine: Girdle Toll	154	16	20	-	21,353	80
Irvine: Mure	291	28	18	68,871	42,445	-
Irvine: Old	369	24	13	-	48,774	6
Irvine: Relief Bourtreehill	216	21	20	43,609	27,686	14
Irvine: St Andrew's	246	18	29	59,471	32,860	25
Kilmarnock: Kay Park	493	77	31	147,948	79,751	22
Kilmarnock: New Laigh Kirk	825	74	51	213,213	129,109	167
Kilmarnock: Riccarton	233	25	18	66,347	41,989	58
Kilmarnock: St Andrew's & St Marnock's	788	95	40	175,447	105,815	429
Kilmarnock: St JoŸ's Onthank	244	22	21	-	31,539	70
Kilmarnock: St Kentigern's	268	22	-	54,575	35,176	68
Kilmarnock: South	251	9	20	35,000	26,147	26
Kilmaurs: St Maur's Glencairn	287	14	26	51,753	32,264	50
Newmilns: Loudoun	178	9	-	49,160	34,769	2
Stewarton: JoŸ Knox	255	21	23	99,745	55,558	130
Stewarton: St Columba's	409	38	42	79,147	54,142	145

12. Ardrossan

Congregation	Com	Eld	G	In 16	M&M	–18
Ardrossan: Park	384	24	36	70,579	48,335	24
Ardrossan and Saltcoats Kirkgate	241	36	29	78,789	56,741	3
Beith	694	58	21	103,939	67,828	56
Brodick	123	16	-	56,839	33,860	12
Corrie	37	5	-	19,972	11,112	-
Lochranza and Pirnmill	64	13	8	21,191	13,829	4
Shiskine	65	11	14	39,596	22,093	10
Cumbrae	231	21	34	43,846	40,512	55
Largs: St JoŸ's	676	47	43	-	77,509	20
Dalry: St Margaret's	508	32	30	-	93,978	24
Dalry: Trinity	185	19	-	82,835	49,926	55
Fairlie	215	21	32	81,347	52,345	8
Largs: St Columba's	347	33	56	90,613	64,493	17
Kilbirnie: Auld Kirk	292	34	-	61,829	42,431	13
Kilbirnie: St Columba's	509	31	-	65,899	38,541	53
Kilmory	34	7	-	13,862	7,737	-
Lamlash	93	12	25	36,926	20,247	10
Kilwinning: Mansefield Trinity	198	15	23	58,067	34,295	17
Kilwinning: Old	539	51	37	108,141	68,834	18
Largs: Clark Memorial	712	90	53	162,184	85,479	36
Saltcoats: North	275	24	23	43,976	30,187	50
Saltcoats: St Cuthbert's	244	32	14	79,813	51,346	131
Stevenston: Ardeer	239	26	27	47,513	30,927	117
Stevenston: Livingstone	253	30	19	38,891	37,096	9
Stevenston: High	224	20	20	87,151	55,678	49
West Kilbride	434	45	24	106,770	77,294	40
Whiting Bay and Kildonan	87	9	-	53,798	28,892	4

13. Lanark

Congregation	Com	Eld	G	In 16	M&M	–18
Biggar	291	23	31	78,879	60,240	30
Black Mount	67	6	14	14,724	10,579	4

Congregation	Com	Eld	G	In 16	M&M	–18
Cairngryffe	147	15	12	24,974	20,955	4
Libberton and Quothquan	81	13	-	18,781	8,968	12
Symington	158	17	19	39,472	20,922	3
Carluke: Kirkton	739	51	29	135,387	74,061	380
Carluke: St Andrew's	195	13	15	47,633	32,703	15
Carluke: St JoŸ's	601	44	28	-	57,864	88
Carnwath	122	11	19	-	18,342	3
Carstairs	183	16	19	45,285	31,482	99
Coalburn	113	8	14	17,095	11,807	15
Lesmahagow: Old	361	19	17	-	54,239	24
Crossford	142	6	-	37,582	19,521	62
Kirkfieldbank	74	6	-	19,264	9,166	-
Forth: St Paul's	325	24	37	62,620	33,405	120
Kirkmuirhill	139	13	41	72,370	65,805	115
Lanark: Greyfriars	529	49	29	112,411	52,844	183
Lanark: St Nicholas'	485	42	19	107,080	65,037	47
Law	179	7	20	57,259	28,040	94
Lesmahagow: Abbeygreen	175	14	-	58,728	50,511	155
The Douglas Valley Church	290	24	32	52,453	36,835	5
Upper Clyde	181	12	18	27,008	21,558	14

14. Greenock and Paisley

Congregation	Com	Eld	G	In 16	M&M	–18
Barrhead: Bourock	432	38	36	-	56,966	225
Barrhead: St Andrew's	440	43	36	148,416	92,389	261
Bishopton	599	53	-	106,012	58,280	64
Bridge of Weir: Freeland	390	-	-	118,632	80,491	-
Bridge of Weir: St Machar's Ranfurly	331	32	25	94,025	60,429	169
Elderslie Kirk	438	42	37	100,270	68,789	155
Erskine	338	33	52	97,402	64,525	250
Gourock: Old Gourock and Ashton	638	51	22	125,967	73,564	210
Gourock: St JoŸ's	440	62	14	139,619	73,026	250
Greenock: East End	56	-	-	-	5,645	-
Greenock: Lyle Kirk	757	50	31	-	99,531	93
Greenock: Mount Kirk	310	-	-	57,413	44,200	-
Greenock: St Margaret's	170	29	-	42,253	18,655	25
Greenock: St Ninian's	226	17	-	58,936	17,852	38
Greenock: Wellpark Mid Kirk	475	50	13	-	64,080	70
Greenock: Westburn	617	80	23	122,998	83,365	120
Houston and Killellan	667	64	71	145,433	86,221	150
Howwood	139	10	19	44,826	26,720	10
Lochwinnoch	92	11	-	37,144	27,898	152
Inchinnan	254	25	24	-	42,980	148
Inverkip	297	32	23	72,226	40,463	21
Skelmorlie and Wemyss Bay	246	38	-	89,879	52,758	6
JoŸstone: High	216	32	26	98,481	62,042	73
JoŸstone: St Andrew's Trinity	203	27	-	39,705	28,324	63
JoŸstone: St Paul's	379	66	-	77,546	48,241	154
Kilbarchan	657	61	46	109,027	96,354	110
Kilmacolm: Old	395	42	-	127,759	77,721	30
Kilmacolm: St Columba	173	16	-	-	61,326	4

Congregation	Com	Eld	G	In 16	M&M	–18
Langbank	128	15	-	33,715	23,262	17
Port Glasgow: St Andrew's	439	62	28	83,802	50,503	319
Linwood	200	21	28	43,935	35,146	12
Neilston	450	34	22	109,757	70,655	225
Paisley: Abbey	688	41	-	138,750	101,916	86
Paisley: Glenburn	172	14	-	45,697	29,755	11
Paisley: Lylesland	289	42	28	95,977	60,774	34
Paisley: Martyrs' Sandyford	398	60	27	111,074	76,862	126
Paisley: Oakshaw Trinity	453	61	-	155,144	59,807	33
Paisley: St Columba Foxbar	152	17	-	30,353	22,268	-
Paisley: St James'	192	-	-	-	46,468	-
Paisley: St Luke's	189	24	-	-	36,108	13
Paisley: St Mark's Oldhall	448	55	50	110,905	69,900	29
Paisley: St Ninian's Ferguslie	44	-	-	-	4,500	6
Paisley: Sherwood Greenlaw	553	68	31	126,506	69,691	150
Paisley: Stow Brae Kirk	329	67	48	101,295	61,713	21
Paisley: Wallneuk North	356	21	-	56,441	42,684	14
Port Glasgow: Hamilton Bardrainney	234	19	15	47,616	25,593	11
Port Glasgow: St Martin's	144	9	-	26,584	14,954	16
Renfrew: North	634	71	32	114,515	75,420	138
Renfrew: Trinity	348	28	37	92,630	65,094	19

16. Glasgow

Congregation	Com	Eld	G	In 16	M&M	–18
Banton	61	8	-	9,652	6,330	-
Twechar	69	11	-	17,376	10,620	-
Bishopbriggs: Kenmure	259	17	39	84,596	64,293	80
Bishopbriggs: Springfield Cambridge	623	-	89	120,421	80,795	-
Broom	516	56	24	120,119	82,241	418
Burnside Blairbeth	554	40	86	255,763	146,111	244
Busby	222	35	23	74,020	48,727	15
Cadder	629	79	50	-	95,464	155
Cambuslang: Flemington Hallside	298	-	27	57,533	35,475	-
Cambuslang Parish Church	653	-	35	122,185	87,448	-
Campsie	143	14	19	57,934	37,315	70
Chryston	574	23	18	196,609	116,792	80
Eaglesham	502	45	40	142,882	91,008	180
Fernhill and CatҮin	239	20	20	52,023	37,368	78
Gartcosh	135	13	-	25,571	15,430	82
Glenboig	103	10	-	19,813	8,624	7
Giffnock: Orchardhill	418	-	12	160,914	82,234	-
Giffnock: South	594	79	40	179,692	106,691	35
Giffnock: The Park	243	23	-	81,759	46,531	76
Greenbank	842	78	65	231,065	130,193	350
Kilsyth: Anderson	289	22	60	-	46,996	135
Kilsyth: Burns and Old	364	28	30	81,162	52,708	58
Kirkintilloch: Hillhead	65	8	12	23,040	8,304	-
Kirkintilloch: St Columba's	220	36	30	88,130	56,638	30
Kirkintilloch: St David's Memorial Park	535	46	31	102,662	50,400	102
Kirkintilloch: St Mary's	670	42	29	106,039	78,688	24
Lenzie: Old	420	40	-	111,086	72,536	96

Congregation	Com	Eld	G	In 16	M&M	–18
Lenzie: Union	586	59	72	189,038	106,795	240
Maxwell Mearns Castle	252	31	-	168,034	96,723	206
Mearns	722	40	-	-	120,541	48
Milton of Campsie	306	30	43	66,638	45,569	88
Netherlee	605	66	33	202,113	118,708	291
Newton Mearns	377	32	31	116,902	69,360	93
Rutherglen: Old	287	28	-	66,396	40,115	34
Rutherglen: Stonelaw	296	37	-	-	84,239	61
Rutherglen: West and Wardlawhill	444	47	40	74,217	52,637	171
Stamperland	326	30	19	75,816	44,040	60
Stepps	209	23	-	60,585	34,489	102
Thornliebank	122	12	29	43,361	26,038	35
Torrance	200	17	-	101,596	58,916	105
Williamwood	409	67	33	110,837	66,517	192
Glasgow: Anderston Kelvingrove	48	-	8	-	19,344	8
Glasgow: Baillieston Mure Memorial	355	37	75	84,840	58,435	202
Glasgow: Baillieston St Andrew's	260	23	29	-	42,541	136
Glasgow: Balshagray Victoria Park	138	27	15	91,930	63,169	34
Glasgow: Barlanark Greyfriars	91	13	9	-	20,447	190
Glasgow: Blawarthill	167	-	20	-	18,045	-
Glasgow: Bridgeton St Francis in the East	79	15	16	33,261	21,912	8
Glasgow: Broomhill	383	57	35	128,265	84,531	176
Glasgow: Hyndland	225	-	-	85,999	52,772	-
Glasgow: Calton Parkhead	84	-	-	-	5,425	-
Glasgow: Cardonald	330	46	-	104,589	71,358	90
Glasgow: Carmunnock	284	23	19	46,899	33,340	55
Glasgow: Carmyle	84	5	-	23,486	11,397	25
Glasgow: Kenmuir Mount Vernon	117	9	20	58,879	34,428	40
Glasgow: Carntyne	300	-	37	63,866	52,231	25
Glasgow: Carnwadric	146	-	-	33,370	22,481	-
Glasgow: Castlemilk	137	17	14	-	18,615	15
Glasgow: Cathcart Old	252	-	26	84,871	61,985	-
Glasgow: Cathcart Trinity	420	55	38	210,486	119,352	97
Glasgow: Cathedral (High or St Mungo's)	394	38	-	103,160	70,004	24
Glasgow: Causeway (Tollcross)	285	15	25	103,542	49,807	-
Glasgow: Clincarthill	230	33	37	90,199	65,159	103
Glasgow: Colston Milton	58	-	-	19,684	8,136	-
Glasgow: Colston Wellpark	93	12	-	23,018	15,118	54
Glasgow: Cranhill	44	8	-	-	3,142	80
Glasgow: Croftfoot	253	33	31	-	48,617	112
Glasgow: Dennistoun New	170	33	-	80,379	60,861	8
Glasgow: Drumchapel St Andrew's	176	-	-	-	41,387	-
Glasgow: Drumchapel St Mark's	71	-	-	15,059	1,111	-
Glasgow: Easterhouse	51	6	-	-	8,386	127
Glasgow: Eastwood	212	-	19	82,761	61,802	-
Glasgow: Gairbraid	119	-	-	33,306	24,029	-
Glasgow: Gallowgate	50	-	-	27,991	13,432	-
Glasgow: Garthamlock and Craigend East	56	-	-	-	2,244	-
Glasgow: Gorbals	93	-	-	66,058	19,418	-
Glasgow: Govan and Linthouse	186	47	44	-	58,770	276

Congregation	Com	Eld	G	In 16	M&M	–18
Glasgow: Hillington Park	265	32	43	68,951	44,386	110
Glasgow: Ibrox	127	-	15	61,383	32,576	-
Glasgow: JoŸ Ross Memorial (For Deaf People)	53	4	-	-	-	-
Glasgow: Jordanhill	365	57	24	176,980	102,727	40
Glasgow: Kelvinbridge	69	26	-	36,585	37,059	45
Glasgow: Kelvinside Hillhead	151	23	-	68,598	43,877	60
Glasgow: King's Park	561	67	41	139,930	88,195	111
Glasgow: Kinning Park	130	13	-	36,075	22,585	-
Glasgow: Knightswood St Margaret's	178	20	-	47,302	27,470	7
Glasgow: Langside	204	-	-	83,603	55,866	-
Glasgow: Maryhill	133	15	12	-	23,770	94
Glasgow: Merrylea	268	55	24	76,229	48,129	30
Glasgow: Mosspark	100	22	25	62,198	32,472	44
Glasgow: Newlands South	417	55	-	132,322	90,622	29
Glasgow: Partick South	120	19	-	60,632	44,928	25
Glasgow: Partick Trinity	167	-	-	-	58,347	-
Glasgow: Pollokshaws	113	22	-	47,644	25,224	16
Glasgow: Pollokshields	164	30	21	-	57,090	60
Glasgow: Possilpark	100	19	12	-	18,421	35
Glasgow: Queen's Park Govanhill	231	27	32	95,458	78,481	12
Glasgow: Renfield St Stephen's	136	20	18	-	44,763	10
Glasgow: Robroyston	43	-	-	30,977	3,200	17
Glasgow: Ruchazie	26	8	-	-	3,112	120
Glasgow: Ruchill Kelvinside	73	15	-	-	37,841	25
Glasgow: St Andrew and St Nicholas	-	-	9	-	59,484	-
Glasgow: St Andrew's East	61	12	21	34,691	22,760	50
Glasgow: St Christopher's Priesthill and Nitshill	202	20	-	32,769	29,594	14
Glasgow: St Columba	135	15	-	-	17,294	18
Glasgow: St David's Knightswood	217	17	28	77,094	60,696	22
Glasgow: St Enoch's Hogganfield	115	16	25	32,732	26,877	6
Glasgow: St George's Tron	380	-	-	-	100	-
Glasgow: St James' (Pollok)	155	22	37	45,913	30,820	79
Glasgow: St JoŸ's Renfield	291	45	-	142,682	84,073	132
Glasgow: St Margaret's Tollcross Park	131	-	-	-	8,155	-
Glasgow: St Paul's	55	6	-	10,517	3,851	204
Glasgow: St Rollox	72	6	-	38,845	21,698	30
Glasgow: Sandyford Henderson Memorial	201	-	-	-	106,911	-
Glasgow: Sandyhills	238	27	43	83,000	49,044	26
Glasgow: Scotstoun	98	5	-	-	37,868	90
Glasgow: Shawlands	202	21	-	79,594	55,110	37
Glasgow: South Shawlands	148	19	-	53,434	42,185	70
Glasgow: Sherbrooke St Gilbert's	252	38	-	133,597	92,497	20
Glasgow: Shettleston New	208	30	25	-	49,988	78
Glasgow: Springburn	204	-	21	-	38,586	-
Glasgow: Temple Anniesland	270	22	39	102,315	59,074	115
Glasgow: Toryglen	93	10	-	16,160	8,546	12
Glasgow: Trinity Possil and Henry Drummond	62	6	-	49,682	37,508	3
Glasgow: Tron St Mary's	100	18	-	38,698	26,980	34
Glasgow: Wallacewell	126	-	-	-	1,263	25
Glasgow: Wellington	172	31	-	-	71,095	22

Congregation	Com	Eld	G	In 16	M&M	–18
Glasgow: Whiteinch	75	6	-	-	34,464	28
Glasgow: Yoker	94	-	-	25,814	14,845	-

17. Hamilton

Congregation	Com	Eld	G	In 16	M&M	–18
Airdrie: Cairnlea	583	49	25	128,439	94,699	110
Calderbank	120	9	16	26,739	12,450	-
Airdrie: Clarkston	343	36	19	72,503	42,154	149
Airdrie: High	286	32	-	-	40,830	-
Caldercruix and Longriggend	169	9	-	54,824	36,561	57
Airdrie: Jackson	331	48	23	89,037	52,129	212
Airdrie: New Monkland	281	29	25	68,105	36,423	131
Greengairs	119	9	-	26,226	13,444	8
Airdrie: St Columba's	212	11	-	19,942	12,559	2
Airdrie: The New Wellwynd	723	93	-	169,380	86,458	109
Bargeddie	86	7	-	-	41,132	9
Bellshill: Central	164	30	22	56,990	34,221	14
Bellshill: West	468	38	18	73,825	43,756	24
Blantyre: Livingstone Memorial	202	21	19	56,148	30,868	200
Blantyre: Old	254	18	33	67,649	43,108	45
Blantyre: St Andrew's	182	21	-	48,788	33,135	14
Bothwell	483	55	39	117,118	63,572	137
Chapelhall	207	21	22	41,407	27,751	62
Chapelton	155	16	19	26,320	17,476	29
Strathaven: Rankin	496	55	30	118,237	51,218	190
Cleland	155	10	-	25,653	15,596	14
Wishaw: St Mark's	302	30	40	72,306	45,910	120
Coatbridge: Blairhill Dundyvan	257	22	19	57,833	34,704	98
Coatbridge: Middle	316	36	34	44,224	37,069	134
Coatbridge: Calder	318	16	20	51,895	33,344	-
Coatbridge: Old Monkland	104	20	-	50,583	35,297	40
Coatbridge: New St Andrew's	675	76	27	113,443	72,985	232
Coatbridge: Townhead	124	18	-	34,838	26,493	36
Dalserf	201	17	21	66,923	54,898	10
East Kilbride: Claremont	405	44	-	136,764	75,947	150
East Kilbride: Greenhills	176	12	20	36,808	20,726	12
East Kilbride: Moncrieff	609	59	44	117,518	72,563	185
East Kilbride: Mossneuk	249	11	-	27,132	18,611	80
East Kilbride: Old	667	64	38	-	70,908	30
East Kilbride: South	224	31	-	-	51,741	8
East Kilbride: Stewartfield	26	4	-	16,910	6,600	7
East Kilbride: West	290	29	31	-	43,987	60
East Kilbride: Westwood	340	34	-	80,520	52,074	40
Glasford	115	6	15	22,806	11,858	-
Strathaven: East	280	31	29	60,886	38,241	29
Hamilton: Cadzow	410	54	49	116,515	79,964	125
Hamilton: Gilmour and Whitehill	143	24	-	33,450	30,600	80
Hamilton: West	207	27	-	70,871	40,019	48
Hamilton: Hillhouse	369	41	-	86,521	57,416	180
Hamilton: Old	491	81	18	-	90,811	47
Hamilton: St JoŸ's	510	55	63	-	72,503	266

Congregation	Com	Eld	G	In 16	M&M	–18
Hamilton: South	189	22	27	56,009	39,837	20
Quarter	93	13	-	26,219	15,274	-
Hamilton: Trinity	286	21	-	56,381	34,327	76
Holytown	169	16	21	47,978	31,299	85
New Stevenston: Wrangholm Kirk	94	12	20	35,947	23,988	14
Kirk o' Shotts	164	11	-	24,275	18,295	14
Larkhall: Chalmers	99	11	21	31,935	19,620	86
Larkhall: St Machan's	404	60	37	103,335	64,491	125
Larkhall: Trinity	166	16	30	82,433	30,334	132
Motherwell: Crosshill	303	55	53	100,221	57,985	90
Motherwell: St Margaret's	355	15	-	42,509	26,255	10
Motherwell: Dalziel St Andrew's	494	61	37	136,290	77,709	245
Motherwell: North	122	24	27	45,986	32,595	90
Motherwell: St Mary's	697	94	64	175,451	85,135	285
Motherwell: South	380	53	60	-	70,522	120
Newarthill and Carfin	354	30	19	77,089	38,198	28
Newmains: Bonkle	121	18	-	35,253	21,060	36
Newmains: Coltness Memorial	189	20	12	-	37,731	63
Overtown	247	30	49	48,916	26,439	110
Shotts: Calderhead Erskine	416	34	31	88,785	53,977	16
Stonehouse: St Ninian's	403	46	35	-	48,573	25
Strathaven: Avendale Old and Drumclog	560	52	38	159,045	78,664	16
Uddingston: Burnhead	255	19	9	50,738	30,509	81
Uddingston: Old	447	51	39	135,217	77,623	45
Uddingston: Viewpark	420	70	16	114,945	60,547	170
Wishaw: Cambusnethan North	425	50	-	74,420	45,931	80
Wishaw: Cambusnethan Old & Morningside	386	35	17	81,028	58,880	180
Wishaw: Craigneuk and Belhaven	140	28	-	41,032	31,443	12
Wishaw: Old	200	29	-	36,004	23,605	50
Wishaw: South Wishaw	396	19	25	87,807	56,301	15

18. Dumbarton

Alexandria	261	25	25	75,659	45,866	26
Arrochar	61	13	9	-	12,721	-
Luss	98	15	13	42,484	27,312	-
Baldernock	181	17	-	36,055	24,442	17
Bearsden: Baljaffray	355	25	37	82,439	50,364	60
Bearsden: Cross	763	79	29	164,242	103,900	34
Bearsden: Killermont	587	53	48	185,738	91,777	70
Bearsden: New Kilpatrick	1,332	128	108	311,553	172,258	60
Bearsden: Westerton Fairlie Memorial	355	41	54	112,994	57,887	40
Bonhill	495	55	-	-	46,351	85
Renton: Trinity	244	12	-	-	21,994	2
Cardross	380	36	31	88,799	53,093	40
Clydebank: Abbotsford	137	15	-	44,012	29,597	33
Dalmuir: Barclay	182	15	-	46,329	28,857	27
Clydebank: Faifley	177	-	33	42,157	27,677	-
Clydebank: Kilbowie St Andrew's	256	21	24	46,172	30,046	145
Clydebank: Radnor Park	132	22	17	45,260	29,480	-
Clydebank: St Cuthbert's	42	11	-	11,753	10,872	1

Congregation	Com	Eld	G	In 16	M&M	–18
Duntocher	204	26	43	36,567	24,371	1
Craigrownie	147	17	-	36,159	30,396	6
Garelochhead	146	13	-	-	39,942	40
Rosneath: St Modan's	112	12	14	22,982	16,658	3
Dumbarton: Riverside	486	61	51	112,919	72,723	261
Dumbarton: West Kirk	272	23	-	-	31,284	100
Dumbarton: St Andrew's	107	22	-	32,932	17,686	-
Old Kilpatrick Bowling	230	21	21	-	40,764	87
Helensburgh	1,013	73	39	-	153,978	22
Rhu and Shandon	265	20	30	64,870	40,394	8
Jamestown	178	20	15	-	29,786	3
Kilmaronock Gartocharn	211	12	-	28,497	19,199	8
Milngavie: Cairns	359	36	-	156,881	85,565	9
Milngavie: St Luke's	358	18	-	76,555	53,079	28
Milngavie: St Paul's	866	81	89	207,424	118,733	180

19 Argyll

Congregation	Com	Eld	G	In 16	M&M	–18
Appin	96	12	23	26,609	14,363	10
Lismore	39	6	8	15,423	8,603	-
Ardchattan	96	9	-	-	17,247	33
Ardrishaig	127	19	31	37,856	21,755	-
South Knapdale	34	4	-	-	5,272	-
Barra	44	3	-	12,036	10,455	30
South Uist	51	10	-	19,309	11,136	6
Campbeltown: Highland	382	30	-	43,880	31,522	14
Campbeltown: Lorne and Lowland	754	52	31	81,633	55,076	125
Coll	17	3	-	4,808	1,805	-
Connel	114	19	11	44,944	27,453	15
Colonsay and Oronsay	13	2	-	-	5,654	-
Craignish	46	9	-	11,121	7,076	2
Kilbrandon and Kilchattan	93	18	-	30,848	22,822	17
Kilninver and Kilmelford	55	5	-	-	8,029	10
Cumlodden, Lochfyneside and Lochgair	85	-	16	24,563	15,945	-
Glenaray and Inveraray	101	-	-	31,371	18,925	-
Dunoon: St JoŸ's	167	22	28	40,775	29,382	-
Kirn	269	26	-	53,451	37,041	15
Sandbank	92	-	-	10,714	7,434	-
Dunoon: The High Kirk	297	29	28	-	43,771	1
Innellan	54	7	-	17,110	11,507	6
Toward	57	8	-	-	12,286	9
Gigha and Cara	33	6	-	7,887	6,495	7
Kilcalmonell	43	12	9	8,871	5,369	3
Killean and Kilchenzie	121	13	15	24,224	15,314	30
Glassary, Kilmartin and Ford	94	10	-	-	16,001	10
North Knapdale	51	8	-	25,756	20,495	17
Glenorchy and Innishael	58	6	-	-	7,063	-
Strathfillan	43	6	-	-	6,482	-
Iona	11	5	-	-	7,512	-
Kilfinichen & Kilvickeon & the Ross of Mull	33	5	-	7,469	3,521	-
Jura	24	5	-	7,538	6,146	-

Congregation	Com	Eld	G	In 16	M&M	–18
Kilarrow	43	14	-	29,345	20,507	5
Kildalton and Oa	83	16	-	-	26,123	10
Kilchoman	72	12	-	16,408	19,390	15
Kilmeny	28	5	-	13,006	7,071	-
Portnahaven	26	5	13	17,714	3,388	4
Kilchrenan and Dalavich	23	7	-	13,783	9,779	-
Muckairn	119	17	7	28,722	18,483	-
Kilfinan	29	4	-	6,898	3,614	-
Kilmodan and Colintraive	78	10	-	20,390	13,362	15
Kyles	100	17	-	26,889	19,492	50
Kilmore and Oban	462	48	26	81,875	61,451	35
Kilmun (St Munn's)	68	7	10	12,113	12,390	-
Strone and Ardentinny	104	10	-	26,279	24,316	4
Kilninian and Kilmore	24	5	-	12,869	5,111	-
Salen and Ulva	30	5	-	-	9,014	7
Tobermory	65	12	-	25,609	19,026	13
Torosay and Kinlochspelvie	23	-	-	-	4,413	-
Lochgilphead	216	-	22	-	22,256	-
Lochgoilhead and Kilmorich	58	9	-	20,469	19,221	7
Strachur and Strachlachlan	116	12	16	19,736	20,960	-
Rothesay: Trinity	330	37	14	63,062	41,107	53
Saddell and Carradale	187	15	20	33,795	22,130	20
Southend	224	13	13	34,915	20,781	1
Skipness	19	4	-	10,806	4,249	5
Tarbert, Loch Fyne and Kilberry	113	12	22	40,745	29,127	4
The United Church of Bute	493	33	38	70,847	52,688	82
Tiree	73	10	10	-	15,291	2
22. Falkirk						
Airth	147	9	18	-	26,782	47
Blackbraes and Shieldhill	155	23	21	32,072	19,151	2
Muiravonside	184	20	-	-	27,087	2
Bo'ness: Old	326	25	8	49,899	39,361	22
Bo'ness: St Andrew's	384	22	-	66,242	53,341	75
Bonnybridge: St Helen's	303	14	-	45,399	35,312	6
BotÝennar and Carronshore	205	18	-	39,456	21,594	14
Brightons	608	37	57	132,229	81,372	205
Carriden	387	41	23	63,926	43,387	9
Cumbernauld: Abronhill	199	16	27	60,560	42,964	60
Cumbernauld: Condorrat	304	24	36	72,663	45,114	119
Cumbernauld: Kildrum	259	28	-	58,864	38,685	135
Cumbernauld: Old	296	42	-	-	47,151	82
Cumbernauld: St Mungo's	176	34	-	39,306	31,243	16
Denny: Old	323	42	23	62,815	49,785	30
Haggs	227	25	-	-	25,202	43
Denny: Westpark	445	31	31	90,709	64,262	120
Dunipace	328	24	-	63,032	36,660	72
Falkirk: Bainsford	121	12	-	47,256	23,194	90
Falkirk: St James'	229	-	-	29,348	23,912	-
Falkirk: Camelon	271	17	-	-	48,566	16

Congregation	Com	Eld	G	In 16	M&M	–18
Falkirk: Grahamston United	302	43	23	-	42,492	46
Falkirk: Laurieston	208	20	24	-	24,884	4
Redding and Westquarter	149	13	-	28,797	16,646	3
Falkirk: St Andrew's West	421	30	-	79,378	55,782	28
Falkirk: Trinity	-	-	15	165,192	106,427	-
Grangemouth: Abbotsgrange	349	46	-	68,021	47,759	92
Grangemouth: Kirk of the Holy Rood	335	29	-	57,521	35,738	24
Grangemouth: Zetland	695	68	55	116,962	70,355	163
Larbert: East	618	54	40	128,268	76,225	97
Larbert: Old	310	21	-	70,535	46,234	82
Larbert: West	357	34	34	77,835	46,631	135
Polmont: Old	356	25	43	105,702	53,113	87
Slamannan	209	8	-	23,561	17,411	12
Stenhouse and Carron	342	32	-	-	48,582	9

23. Stirling

Congregation	Com	Eld	G	In 16	M&M	–18
Aberfoyle	83	7	20	20,796	10,884	6
Port of Menteith	55	6	-	14,711	5,497	-
Alloa: Ludgate	292	20	19	67,879	46,915	12
Alloa: St Mungo's	327	44	41	-	44,351	16
Alva	463	51	29	75,747	47,508	96
Balfron	134	16	13	46,003	26,067	16
Fintry	106	12	17	19,448	18,059	3
Balquhidder	54	2	-	10,412	11,460	-
Killin and Ardeonaig	82	6	7	23,781	13,197	5
Bannockburn: Allan	279	34	-	55,520	35,171	-
Bannockburn: Ladywell	381	18	-	-	17,512	20
Bridge of Allan	681	47	76	112,679	83,767	79
Buchanan	96	8	-	20,571	10,450	4
Drymen	252	23	-	72,689	40,557	36
Buchlyvie	202	15	15	26,453	21,390	19
Gartmore	58	13	-	18,276	15,987	5
Callander	526	21	31	93,890	71,148	55
Cambusbarron: The Bruce Memorial	296	21	-	96,659	34,899	32
Clackmannan	367	24	23	-	51,365	51
Cowie and Plean	174	9	-	18,258	8,788	-
Fallin	244	7	-	-	20,438	65
Dollar	235	26	61	89,911	60,909	4
Glendevon	38	3	-	5,438	3,431	-
Muckhart	82	6	-	20,762	16,724	10
Dunblane: Cathedral	799	74	43	224,582	125,979	257
Dunblane: St Blane's	304	33	34	118,978	58,999	30
Lecropt	153	15	-	43,939	27,955	10
Gargunnock	131	9	-	24,474	21,375	19
Kilmadock	92	12	-	17,883	14,261	-
Kincardine-in-Menteith	75	6	-	17,021	12,682	8
Killearn	354	23	43	88,105	65,312	48
Kippen	199	16	17	28,865	20,275	-
Norrieston	94	10	10	19,856	14,506	2
Logie	516	58	30	95,721	61,898	31

Congregation	Com	Eld	G	In 16	M&M	–18
Menstrie	347	22	25	67,426	45,914	25
Sauchie and Coalsnaughton	435	27	16	57,955	38,823	7
Stirling: Allan Park South	164	26	-	69,996	25,483	80
Stirling: Church of The Holy Rude	140	19	-	-	29,898	3
Stirling: Viewfield Erskine	253	22	26	37,929	21,628	7
Stirling: North	335	23	22	68,125	51,888	46
Stirling: St Columba's	450	50	-	104,455	69,799	100
Stirling: St Mark's	179	11	-	31,886	16,897	36
Stirling: St Ninian's Old	613	66	-	-	58,141	51
Strathblane	183	18	45	75,338	44,754	74
Tillicoultry	570	64	35	101,575	60,190	100
Tullibody: St Serf's	345	19	25	57,937	34,948	10

24. Dunfermline

Congregation	Com	Eld	G	In 16	M&M	–18
Aberdour: St Fillan's	354	19	-	73,474	47,888	10
Beath and Cowdenbeath: North	205	22	19	59,339	40,121	28
Cairneyhill	103	18	-	28,290	16,087	10
Limekilns	239	42	-	76,249	43,275	10
Carnock and Oakley	166	21	24	57,059	35,398	14
Saline and Blairingone	146	13	16	38,125	28,562	16
Cowdenbeath: Trinity	290	20	10	69,927	44,028	16
Culross and Torryburn	59	18	-	51,144	33,864	24
Dalgety	505	45	20	133,459	74,162	94
Dunfermline: Abbey	637	64	-	126,240	84,412	160
Dunfermline: East	73	-	-	53,324	10,008	60
Dunfermline: Gillespie Memorial	153	26	14	39,599	40,580	17
Dunfermline: North	152	16	-	38,124	24,522	6
Dunfermline: St Andrew's Erskine	175	24	13	48,641	28,750	7
Dunfermline: St Leonard's	311	26	27	81,106	44,972	17
Dunfermline: St Margaret's	232	39	11	70,300	51,137	34
Dunfermline: St Ninian's	164	19	23	-	30,133	35
Dunfermline: Townhill and Kingseat	305	22	30	-	44,382	30
Inverkeithing	312	27	-	59,075	44,024	63
North Queensferry	50	7	-	19,333	9,794	4
Kelty	262	25	34	63,525	50,561	16
Lochgelly and Benarty: St Serf's	381	38	-	62,971	46,252	16
Rosyth	203	22	-	38,614	22,196	29
Tulliallan and Kincardine	279	22	34	65,218	35,798	70

25. Kirkcaldy

Congregation	Com	Eld	G	In 16	M&M	–18
Auchterderran Kinglassie	295	28	16	53,053	29,454	6
Auchtertool	64	-	-	9,715	6,089	-
Kirkcaldy: Linktown	234	31	27	56,959	38,653	36
Buckhaven and Wemyss	239	23	24	47,966	34,451	6
Burntisland	289	35	16	-	45,132	42
Dysart: St Clair	434	26	16	59,735	34,184	10
Glenrothes: Christ's Kirk	197	15	31	37,254	29,629	8
Glenrothes: St Columba's	439	38	-	60,652	38,564	88
Glenrothes: St Margaret's	266	26	31	60,172	38,594	70
Glenrothes: St Ninian's	222	34	18	72,840	43,739	27

Congregation	Com	Eld	G	In 16	M&M	–18
Kennoway, Windygates and Balgonie St Kenneth's	629	50	55	88,156	59,924	30
Kinghorn	297	19	-	84,194	46,944	15
Kirkcaldy: Abbotshall	471	41	-	78,799	40,015	8
Kirkcaldy: Bennochy	423	38	33	85,052	57,334	7
Kirkcaldy: Pathhead	344	38	42	77,862	48,645	140
Kirkcaldy: St Bryce Kirk	338	32	26	79,668	71,743	35
Kirkcaldy: Templehall	156	12	14	38,381	25,558	2
Kirkcaldy: Torbain	222	32	14	-	27,612	70
Leslie: Trinity	165	13	-	24,544	19,559	3
Leven	471	-	31	109,323	68,644	-
Markinch and Thornton	583	40	-	93,746	53,196	9
Methil: Wellesley	303	25	18	60,658	24,985	142
Methilhill and Denbeath	188	19	34	30,241	22,789	8

26. St Andrews

Congregation	Com	Eld	G	In 16	M&M	–18
Abdie and Dunbog	149	18	-	22,508	15,470	6
Newburgh	195	11	-	19,191	16,375	-
Anstruther and Cellardyke: St Ayle	389	37	38	90,444	57,077	30
Kilrenny	107	11	-	30,989	20,508	2
Auchtermuchty	268	-	15	37,863	24,677	-
Edenshead and Strathmiglo	139	13	-	-	13,583	-
Balmerino	119	18	-	-	15,183	-
Wormit	178	15	35	36,259	24,167	32
Boarhills and Dunino	141	8	-	18,662	16,730	-
St Andrews: Holy Trinity	331	30	37	-	85,370	15
Cameron	90	13	11	19,782	13,066	-
St Andrews: St Leonard's	538	46	21	132,097	78,643	28
Carnbee	89	15	20	15,888	11,817	1
Pittenweem	236	13	15	22,258	16,620	2
Ceres, Kemback and Springfield	350	33	24	61,451	69,798	5
Crail	334	22	40	-	31,864	9
Kingsbarns	65	10	-	17,460	10,415	-
Creich, Flisk and Kilmany	82	11	-	22,131	18,087	2
Cupar: Old and St Michael of Tarvit	498	30	22	147,102	83,584	-
Monimail	91	13	-	-	15,659	4
Cupar: St JoŸ's and Dairsie United	663	51	31	-	71,946	15
Elie Kilconquhar and Colinsburgh	324	27	58	87,429	57,723	20
Falkland	131	20	-	41,640	19,259	3
Freuchie	135	18	17	24,517	12,987	-
Howe of Fife	294	21	-	59,700	38,148	12
Largo and Newburn	261	17	-	48,809	36,092	1
Largo: St David's	105	15	29	-	22,938	5
Largoward	46	6	-	7,802	5,743	4
St Monans	249	12	27	57,489	42,052	20
Leuchars: St Athernase	291	22	23	-	39,951	13
Newport-on-Tay	363	38	-	72,292	49,393	43
St Andrews: Hope Park and Martyrs'	544	48	26	173,016	84,382	123
StratŸinness	92	14	-	19,056	11,108	-
Tayport	240	16	17	36,970	39,969	8

Congregation	Com	Eld	G	In 16	M&M	–18
27. Dunkeld and Meigle						
Aberfeldy	172	13	-	-	26,383	137
Dull and Weem	114	12	11	-	16,598	5
Grantully, Logierait and Strathtay	132	9	6	30,219	28,225	2
Alyth	651	34	26	78,837	50,826	20
Ardler, Kettins and Meigle	382	20	30	47,018	34,221	21
Bendochy	81	13	-	23,697	16,381	2
Coupar Angus: Abbey	285	15	-	-	26,121	56
Blair Atholl and Struan	114	14	-	17,544	19,590	-
Braes of Rannoch	16	4	-	11,286	8,596	-
Foss and Rannoch	85	8	-	14,393	11,816	10
Blairgowrie	846	50	36	119,825	72,937	109
Caputh and Clunie	146	17	10	19,844	18,900	-
Kinclaven	134	12	16	20,633	14,028	-
Dunkeld	333	27	-	98,842	67,931	55
Fortingall and Glenlyon	48	10	-	17,183	12,916	4
Kenmore and Lawers	58	6	20	18,524	22,465	6
Kirkmichael, Straloch and Glenshee	99	5	-	14,207	12,788	7
Rattray	331	16	-	37,576	20,767	11
Pitlochry	347	31	21	90,370	58,103	25
Tenandry	51	7	-	20,541	17,308	-
28. Perth						
Aberdalgie and Forteviot	176	10	-	29,615	9,135	15
Aberuthven and Dunning	196	18	-	45,597	26,721	38
Abernethy & Dron & Arngask	285	25	21	34,993	36,220	18
Almondbank Tibbermore	263	14	23	-	26,517	9
Methven and Logiealmond	247	16	-	-	20,764	9
Ardoch	168	17	30	38,938	17,790	-
Blackford	108	19	-	28,578	13,807	20
Auchterarder	503	29	47	122,628	73,696	51
Auchtergaven and Moneydie	497	-	28	46,596	45,550	-
Redgorton and Stanley	324	15	34	44,008	28,038	20
Cargill Burrelton	255	22	22	30,788	22,113	8
Collace	110	9	15	14,812	9,826	8
Cleish	207	13	11	42,191	28,519	15
Fossoway St Serf's and Devonside	217	17	-	45,292	34,241	12
Comrie	404	28	20	86,831	67,245	18
Dundurn	54	8	-	18,743	10,429	-
Crieff	637	38	29	-	67,588	15
Dunbarney and Forgandenny	542	30	20	92,002	52,616	36
Errol	253	22	22	-	30,648	30
Kilspindie and Rait	64	6	-	12,084	8,031	-
Fowlis Wester, Madderty & Monzie	277	19	13	43,724	32,432	23
Gask	82	9	12	17,040	19,951	-
Kinross	658	41	49	143,985	66,462	157
Muthill	247	21	14	42,502	28,761	21
Trinity Gask and Kinkell	46	4	-	7,820	5,815	-
Orwell and Portmoak	433	35	31	86,112	51,264	34
Perth: Craigie and Moncrieffe	606	36	40	-	57,082	85

Congregation	Com	Eld	G	In 16	M&M	–18
Perth: Kinnoull	384	34	20	157,547	50,803	25
Perth: Letham St Mark's	481	9	20	115,738	70,972	70
Perth: North	973	51	35	210,319	125,702	72
Perth: Riverside	63	7	-	47,910	19,554	41
Perth: St JoŸ's Kirk of Perth	452	28	-	97,159	64,768	-
Perth: St Leonard's-in-the-Fields	428	38	-	-	54,809	4
Perth: St Matthew's	765	38	18	89,292	64,181	132
St Madoes and Kinfauns	282	29	-	47,699	40,872	52
Scone and St Martins	-	-	50	118,650	74,820	-

29. Dundee

Congregation	Com	Eld	G	In 16	M&M	–18
Abernyte	86	11	-	17,856	12,887	10
Inchture and Kinnaird	159	25	-	36,188	25,665	8
Longforgan	175	20	20	-	29,906	11
Auchterhouse	142	14	15	26,733	15,746	10
Monikie & Newbigging and Murroes & Tealing	454	25	13	51,395	32,899	7
Dundee: Balgay	340	27	23	73,832	42,783	20
Dundee: Barnhill St Margaret's	713	51	74	-	94,896	31
Dundee: Broughty Ferry New Kirk	690	46	38	108,031	63,452	98
Dundee: Broughty Ferry St James'	133	10	14	-	29,196	76
Dundee: Broughty Ferry St Luke's and Queen Street	389	50	17	74,349	47,445	13
Dundee: Broughty Ferry St Stephen's and West	304	24	-	-	29,316	-
Dundee: Camperdown	130	9	4	-	18,070	-
Dundee: Chalmers Ardler	178	20	-	82,846	50,690	70
Dundee: Coldside	253	18	-	57,301	35,368	87
Dundee: Craigiebank	156	12	-	30,974	19,831	30
Dundee: Douglas and Mid Craigie	119	11	16	25,960	17,627	48
Dundee: Downfield Mains	365	26	18	86,486	50,928	107
Dundee: Dundee (St Mary's)	528	41	14	86,187	60,600	-
Dundee: Fintry Parish Church	92	-	-	50,676	31,596	-
Dundee: Lochee	487	33	30	85,671	43,900	232
Dundee: Logie and St JoŸ's Cross	190	11	22	-	56,889	14
Dundee: Meadowside St Paul's	468	28	20	73,489	32,609	26
Dundee: Menzieshill	250	15	-	-	23,864	141
Dundee: St Andrew's	448	44	28	116,504	70,009	21
Dundee: St David's High Kirk	217	47	24	50,889	36,516	42
Dundee: Steeple	201	29	-	123,934	71,206	14
Dundee: Stobswell	407	39	-	69,734	43,911	-
Dundee: Strathmartine	238	21	22	44,557	30,700	-
Dundee: Trinity	431	33	26	-	32,417	65
Dundee: West	273	29	21	72,767	49,830	-
Dundee: Whitfield	41	7	-	-	6,727	58
Fowlis and Liff	139	13	8	27,480	26,000	43
Lundie and Muirhead	279	29	-	48,405	25,830	48
Invergowrie	384	54	37	61,332	40,712	-
Monifieth	1,028	58	48	-	82,307	107

30. Angus

Congregation	Com	Eld	G	In 16	M&M	–18
Aberlemno	195	11	-	26,973	12,680	12
Guthrie and Rescobie	217	8	12	27,264	13,617	12

Congregation	Com	Eld	G	In 16	M&M	−18
Arbirlot	138	10	-	-	18,428	1
Carmyllie	100	12	-	23,428	22,108	10
Arbroath: Knox's	277	18	26	42,776	25,540	40
Arbroath: St Vigeans	490	36	16	63,637	44,008	90
Arbroath: Old and Abbey	455	29	-	89,436	69,271	35
Arbroath: St Andrew's	567	45	37	156,335	98,410	80
Arbroath: West Kirk	714	75	39	91,281	64,286	31
Barry	189	7	14	26,081	16,939	2
Carnoustie	308	21	16	-	47,470	15
Brechin: Cathedral	472	33	15	-	52,288	-
Brechin: Gardner Memorial	459	20	-	55,102	39,208	20
Farnell	110	12	-	-	10,214	10
Carnoustie: Panbride	643	33	-	75,307	46,225	30
Colliston	168	5	12	17,942	11,382	1
Friockheim Kinnell	136	15	21	20,993	12,189	1
Inverkeilor and Lunan	113	6	17	18,835	16,993	4
Dun and Hillside	395	44	32	-	40,564	200
Dunnichen, Letham and Kirkden	247	15	20	41,470	24,636	-
Eassie, Nevay and Newtyle	200	15	20	23,685	21,050	30
Edzell Letˠot Glenesk	337	-	22	35,094	33,758	-
Fern Careston Menmuir	101	11	-	14,324	13,155	14
Forfar: East and Old	775	48	46	120,472	53,369	35
Forfar: Lowson Memorial	873	-	28	110,329	49,763	-
Forfar: St Margaret's	474	26	19	88,975	49,194	91
Glamis, Inverarity and Kinettles	354	26	-	55,207	45,478	16
Kirriemuir: St Andrew's	267	17	27	42,667	32,043	25
Oathlaw Tannadice	124	8	-	18,365	18,548	3
Montrose: Old and St Andrew's	641	44	19	78,822	59,804	38
Montrose: South and Ferryden	425	17	-	39,088	44,988	15
The Glens and Kirriemuir Old	938	69	42	-	75,068	100
The Isla Parishes	133	19	11	-	30,246	10

31. Aberdeen

Congregation	Com	Eld	G	In 16	M&M	−18
Aberdeen: Bridge of Don Oldmachar	183	8	-	51,849	35,987	9
Aberdeen: Cove	55	-	-	-	8,000	-
Aberdeen: Craigiebuckler	747	71	29	-	70,935	110
Aberdeen: Ferryhill	335	49	20	80,880	54,563	95
Aberdeen: Garthdee	178	15	-	-	20,662	30
Aberdeen: Ruthrieston West	317	34	16	70,800	44,627	4
Aberdeen: High Hilton	314	28	23	51,603	33,260	80
Aberdeen: Holburn West	403	43	28	104,259	67,202	18
Aberdeen: Mannofield	988	95	45	-	97,723	15
Aberdeen: Mastrick	225	14	-	38,993	32,399	15
Aberdeen: Middlefield	102	5	-	7,961	2,770	-
Aberdeen: Midstocket	460	44	38	95,583	69,562	20
Aberdeen: Northfield	150	12	18	27,030	15,872	2
Aberdeen: Queen Street	357	34	26	82,975	65,409	46
Aberdeen: Queen's Cross	417	39	18	-	93,659	15
Aberdeen: Rubislaw	439	60	30	142,377	88,106	22
Aberdeen: St Columba's Bridge of Don	248	18	-	-	54,486	100

Congregation	Com	Eld	G	In 16	M&M	–18
Aberdeen: St George's Tillydrone	94	-	-	15,139	3,000	-
Aberdeen: St JoŸ's Church for Deaf People	89	1	-	-	-	-
Aberdeen: St Machar's Cathedral	513	33	-	-	77,428	10
Aberdeen: St Mark's	309	36	26	104,337	64,307	19
Aberdeen: St Mary's	305	37	-	70,476	44,009	50
Aberdeen: St Nicholas Kincorth, South of	311	25	23	76,114	44,490	80
Aberdeen: St Nicholas Uniting, Kirk of	339	30	14	88,335	12,806	7
Aberdeen: St Stephen's	160	21	13	-	45,646	44
Aberdeen: South Holburn	470	49	62	100,924	65,401	13
Aberdeen: Stockethill	92	6	-	38,502	7,025	48
Aberdeen: Summerhill	123	17	-	28,276	19,193	4
Aberdeen: Torry St Fittick's	320	17	19	71,763	43,357	1
Aberdeen: Woodside	259	-	25	43,780	34,507	-
Bucksburn: Stoneywood	392	12	6	33,473	27,347	-
Cults	738	70	37	181,988	97,417	102
Dyce	946	54	30	-	57,016	140
Kingswells	323	23	20	53,663	32,943	8
Newhills	399	36	37	-	74,993	12
Peterculter	560	47	-	243,819	67,428	252

32. Kincardine and Deeside

Congregation	Com	Eld	G	In 16	M&M	–18
AberlutŸott	177	8	11	13,123	11,915	-
Laurencekirk	372	8	24	29,467	19,693	-
Aboyne and Dinnet	296	7	22	42,362	33,579	45
Cromar	210	12	-	27,510	27,491	-
ArbutŸott, Bervie and Kinneff	465	31	28	75,158	51,552	16
Banchory-Ternan East	546	30	33	98,448	60,849	165
Banchory-Ternan West	576	27	30	-	65,505	60
Birse and Feughside	213	16	9	33,595	33,172	30
Braemar and Crathie	195	29	6	-	41,994	22
Drumoak - Durris	378	18	-	55,564	41,567	36
Glenmuick (Ballater)	257	20	-	41,613	26,802	14
Maryculter Trinity	143	14	9	39,748	29,110	60
Mearns Coastal	222	10	-	22,437	19,642	15
Mid Deeside	594	40	24	58,284	39,594	60
Newtonhill	236	11	13	26,370	20,449	124
Portlethen	292	17	-	54,286	48,059	5
Stonehaven: Dunnottar	563	23	19	-	49,119	12
Stonehaven: South	237	11	-	-	24,873	9
Stonehaven: Fetteresso	552	36	27	-	100,935	133
West Mearns	461	21	28	-	38,325	8

33. Gordon

Congregation	Com	Eld	G	In 16	M&M	–18
Barthol Chapel	78	10	8	-	5,402	16
Tarves	258	15	30	-	15,055	88
Belhelvie	358	34	18	90,296	57,695	62
Blairdaff and Chapel of Garioch	321	27	8	-	24,321	14
Cluny	185	10	-	27,367	16,413	18
Monymusk	99	5	-	23,088	10,211	26
Culsalmond and Rayne	161	9	-	11,352	10,064	-

Congregation	Com	Eld	G	In 16	M&M	–18
Daviot	141	-	-	12,478	9,036	-
CusŸie and Tough	247	11	-	26,451	16,261	1
Echt	163	9	-	25,228	17,779	3
Midmar	119	7	-	15,450	8,883	3
Ellon	1,392	76	-	169,129	99,958	107
Fintray Kinellar Keithhall	164	15	12	-	25,764	10
Foveran	296	10	-	48,758	36,139	18
Howe Trinity	495	24	35	80,132	47,902	75
Huntly: Cairnie Glass	603	10	14	-	38,311	2
Insch-Leslie-Premnay-Oyne	325	24	17	49,402	25,654	7
Inverurie: St Andrew's	811	34	-	-	67,042	33
Inverurie: West	632	44	22	87,838	56,969	11
Kemnay	471	35	-	67,865	51,381	137
Kintore	670	37	-	65,253	58,774	8
Meldrum and Bourtie	401	28	32	75,054	48,349	28
Methlick	340	24	20	75,161	33,873	36
New Machar	412	19	14	61,744	51,353	37
Noth	235	8	-	28,413	19,511	1
Skene	1,158	69	47	153,736	90,909	169
Strathbogie Drumblade	429	35	30	62,186	45,950	15
Udny and Pitmedden	251	-	12	72,816	44,086	88
Upper Donside	350	22	-	36,400	27,841	28

34. Buchan

Congregation	Com	Eld	G	In 16	M&M	–18
Aberdour	107	-	11	11,992	8,916	-
Pitsligo	80	-	-	-	14,460	-
Auchaber United	145	-	9	14,564	13,980	-
Auchterless	183	-	10	23,374	16,492	-
Banff	576	-	-	69,216	49,558	-
King Edward	140	-	9	-	12,491	-
Crimond	163	12	-	25,522	16,116	10
Lonmay	108	-	13	18,570	10,729	-
Cruden	386	-	21	49,209	35,474	-
Deer	686	-	21	52,636	47,706	-
Fraserburgh: Old	517	-	54	-	79,270	-
Fraserburgh: South	268	-	-	-	33,983	-
Inverallochy and Rathen: East	81	-	-	18,170	9,558	-
Fraserburgh: West	481	-	-	70,039	50,550	-
Rathen: West	96	8	-	12,284	7,129	7
Fyvie	221	-	15	41,616	27,735	-
Rothienorman	119	8	-	15,322	8,826	21
Longside	423	25	-	73,973	41,489	53
Macduff	619	-	30	98,021	56,614	-
Marnoch	381	-	12	31,203	25,246	-
Maud and Savoch	176	12	-	26,465	20,225	8
New Deer: St Kane's	335	11	14	47,617	38,969	28
Monquhitter and New Byth	284	18	12	23,041	22,120	2
Turriff: St Andrew's	542	-	15	-	30,867	-
New Pitsligo	262	-	-	-	17,773	-
Strichen and Tyrie	449	-	21	51,968	35,042	-

Congregation	Com	Eld	G	In 16	M&M	–18
Ordiquihill and Cornhill	137	10	12	11,933	7,512	32
Whitehills	273	-	19	36,411	28,156	-
Peterhead: New	633	-	35	25,152	103,537	-
Peterhead: St Andrew's	447	-	20	50,106	37,673	-
Portsoy	305	-	20	47,472	23,439	-
St Fergus	164	10	9	-	8,604	3
Sandhaven	67	6	-	-	3,248	36
Turriff: St Ninian's and Forglen	742	-	20	71,930	51,411	-

35. Moray

Aberlour	288	-	22	47,661	31,569	-
Alves and Burghead	145	-	27	-	21,502	-
Kinloss and Findhorn	94	19	12	33,536	20,736	-
Bellie and Speymouth	347	-	29	57,255	50,310	-
Birnie and Pluscarden	251	-	21	-	30,904	-
Elgin: High	442	-	-	72,382	40,998	-
Buckie: North	380	-	44	61,136	38,408	-
Rathven	78	15	17	-	12,210	5
Buckie: South and West	215	-	34	46,073	24,456	-
Enzie	69	5	-	9,431	9,782	-
Cullen and Deskford	286	-	21	-	37,427	-
Dallas	47	-	9	15,055	8,762	-
Forres: St Leonard's	175	-	32	-	29,610	-
Rafford	58	-	-	13,919	9,834	-
Duffus, Spynie and Hopeman	223	31	12	67,723	31,188	44
Dyke	115	-	10	26,985	19,722	-
Edinkillie	77	-	-	16,287	14,235	-
Elgin: St Giles' & St Columba's South	435	-	43	115,184	75,817	-
Findochty	41	8	12	20,454	10,068	16
Portknockie	60	9	14	21,968	10,698	45
Forres: St Laurence	372	-	23	79,871	49,792	-
Keith: North, Newmill, Boharm and Rothiemay	503	-	16	42,527	70,601	-
Keith: St Rufus, BotripŸie and Grange	901	-	35	-	62,249	-
Knockando, Elchies and Archiestown	230	-	9	37,728	26,176	-
Rothes	295	-	15	40,313	26,342	-
Lossiemouth: St Gerardine's High	254	-	27	52,396	34,583	-
Lossiemouth: St James'	293	-	34	52,236	33,865	-
Mortlach and Cabrach	303	12	12	32,393	24,054	2
St Andrew's-Lhanbryd and Urquhart	356	35	23	61,096	47,321	25

36. Abernethy

Abernethy	138	12	-	52,903	27,635	70
Boat of Garten, Duthil and Kincardine	137	17	27	45,887	20,465	19
Alvie and Insh	70	6	-	33,954	20,051	25
Rothiemurchus and Aviemore	67	6	-	14,084	9,537	8
Cromdale and Advie	62	2	-	16,613	14,576	-
Dulnain Bridge	31	6	-	12,782	8,799	-
Grantown-on-Spey	185	17	-	50,140	24,964	26
Kingussie	91	20	-	31,178	17,818	19
Laggan	37	7	-	23,002	9,821	7

Congregation	Com	Eld	G	In 16	M&M	–18
Newtonmore	71	12	-	30,917	18,421	20
Tomintoul, Glenlivet and Inveraven	125	11	-	24,538	16,886	-

37. Inverness

Congregation	Com	Eld	G	In 16	M&M	–18
Ardersier	52	7	-	21,390	8,398	14
Petty	45	7	8	-	8,303	-
Auldearn and Dalmore	56	-	-	11,519	7,834	-
Nairn: St Ninian's	175	12	27	57,711	29,467	5
Cawdor	153	12	-	26,028	17,453	5
Croy and Dalcross	57	8	13	18,225	8,108	3
Culloden: The Barn	233	18	-	98,580	58,428	115
Daviot and Dunlichity	55	5	8	14,497	9,714	8
Moy, Dalarossie and Tomatin	28	5	10	8,586	6,682	8
Dores and Boleskine	70	7	-	15,484	8,454	-
Inverness: Crown	528	52	35	-	78,191	103
Inverness: Dalneigh and Bona	162	14	15	55,064	45,811	56
Inverness: East	228	25	-	101,920	83,168	44
Inverness: Hilton	237	9	-	82,211	53,462	44
Inverness: Inshes	243	17	-	171,225	81,198	210
Inverness: Kinmylies	75	10	-	45,396	35,547	55
Inverness: Ness Bank	545	62	28	149,057	92,421	173
Inverness: Old High St Stephen's	413	-	-	106,920	78,784	-
Inverness: St Columba	54	4	-	60,421	5,000	37
Inverness: Trinity	203	27	16	-	45,612	37
Kilmorack and Erchless	98	9	17	50,860	34,912	21
Kiltarlity	56	5	-	26,738	12,375	12
Kirkhill	69	7	15	30,387	11,899	5
Nairn: Old	415	40	21	113,566	63,490	86
Urquhart and Glenmoriston	106	9	-	59,347	33,837	10

38. Lochaber

Congregation	Com	Eld	G	In 16	M&M	–18
Acharacle	36	5	-	22,722	10,560	15
Ardnamurchan	15	5	-	9,296	4,889	7
Ardgour and Kingairloch	47	5	16	13,752	8,055	2
Morvern	39	5	8	10,331	7,043	18
Strontian	26	4	-	5,951	4,663	3
Duror	31	6	13	14,413	6,841	-
Glencoe: St Munda's	39	8	-	14,711	8,337	-
Fort Augustus	70	10	6	21,370	14,094	15
Glengarry	28	5	10	-	7,867	10
Fort William: Duncansburgh MacIntosh	339	24	16	83,616	55,380	36
Kilmonivaig	61	6	14	21,419	17,336	12
Kilmallie	102	14	19	30,695	25,201	15
Kinlochleven	48	7	13	23,144	11,491	3
Nether Lochaber	45	9	-	15,935	12,017	-
North West Lochaber	86	14	11	31,735	19,360	15

39. Ross

Congregation	Com	Eld	G	In 16	M&M	–18
Alness	71	10	-	36,133	18,355	17
Avoch	17	5	-	16,127	9,516	5

Congregation	Com	Eld	G	In 16	M&M	–18
Fortrose and Rosemarkie	72	6	-	25,986	27,549	4
Contin	47	12	-	15,672	14,656	-
Fodderty and Strathpeffer	92	18	-	30,159	17,487	21
Cromarty	47	6	-	13,027	4,609	-
Resolis and Urquhart	74	7	-	34,600	26,057	8
Dingwall: Castle Street	145	17	22	53,709	29,202	50
Dingwall: St Clement's	180	31	17	71,155	33,755	20
Fearn Abbey and Nigg	47	7	-	21,827	17,228	-
Tarbat	34	5	-	-	8,901	-
Ferintosh	131	22	18	51,597	32,822	14
Invergordon	138	9	-	56,414	37,561	56
Killearnan	110	17	-	29,002	35,424	-
Knockbain	43	8	-	-	13,909	-
Kilmuir and Logie Easter	63	9	17	39,910	22,707	3
Kiltearn	58	8	-	30,570	17,697	7
Lochbroom and Ullapool	38	7	-	-	19,330	4
Rosskeen	114	14	12	54,625	37,525	58
Tain	98	7	17	49,626	29,470	6
Urray and Kilchrist	79	14	-	55,817	30,557	52

40. Sutherland

	Com	Eld	G	In 16	M&M	–18
Altnaharra and Farr	24	1	-	-	6,660	-
Assynt and Stoer	11	2	-	18,190	6,699	4
Clyne	58	13	-	-	18,685	2
Kildonan and Loth Helmsdale	30	6	-	11,254	8,204	6
Creich	16	4	-	11,701	14,564	2
Kincardine Croick and Edderton	42	10	-	16,595	15,310	10
Rosehall	18	3	-	9,689	6,785	4
Dornoch: Cathedral	308	35	42	-	69,724	64
Durness and Kinlochbervie	16	3	-	16,154	12,591	4
Eddrachillis	8	2	-	13,432	8,221	1
Golspie	57	12	3	-	27,663	35
Lairg	29	3	12	20,921	14,813	-
Rogart	12	4	-	-	9,764	-
Melness and Tongue	39	6	-	-	14,461	6

41. CaitŸess

	Com	Eld	G	In 16	M&M	–18
Bower	28	3	-	-	7,721	-
Halkirk Westerdale	45	6	9	10,826	11,041	-
Watten	22	3	-	9,791	8,002	-
Canisbay	34	4	11	-	9,946	18
Dunnet	18	3	5	6,746	5,035	12
Keiss	27	1	-	-	4,608	-
Olrig	45	3	5	8,669	5,124	-
The North Coast Parish	44	11	22	20,065	13,677	-
The Parish of Latheron	62	13	9	24,778	17,999	16
Thurso: St Peter's and St Andrew's	129	11	19	-	32,093	20
Thurso: West	185	20	22	55,359	32,317	9
Wick: Pultneytown and Thrumster	238	13	25	51,468	39,004	18
Wick: St Fergus	202	30	23	48,517	39,162	3

Congregation	Com	Eld	G	In 16	M&M	–18
42. Lochcarron-Skye						
Applecross, Lochcarron and Torridon	54	6	13	33,908	36,376	6
Bracadale and Duirinish	54	-	9	29,314	21,574	-
Gairloch and Dundonnell	73	3	-	66,889	41,594	20
Glenelg Kintail and Lochalsh	84	10	10	33,382	39,638	3
Kilmuir and Stenscholl	47	5	-	36,189	21,385	12
Portree	93	-	-	67,855	39,949	-
Snizort	29	3	-	30,971	22,167	2
Strath and Sleat	127	-	10	97,151	59,631	-
43. Uist						
Benbecula	60	-	11	32,446	25,422	-
Carinish	78	-	15	48,170	27,543	-
Berneray and Lochmaddy	49	3	10	23,806	17,333	1
Kilmuir and Paible	28	4	-	30,286	18,668	10
Manish-Scarista	29	3	-	36,637	23,817	10
Tarbert	61	7	-	70,265	40,780	25
44. Lewis						
Barvas	72	9	-	61,488	52,856	23
Carloway	44	2	-	23,075	15,192	27
Cross Ness	59	4	-	43,808	34,413	60
Kinloch	34	5	-	35,809	27,638	24
Knock	28	4	-	-	19,555	8
Lochs-Crossbost	10	1	-	18,460	15,421	7
Lochs-in-Bernera	24	3	-	-	13,037	14
Uig	21	3	-	-	16,942	2
Stornoway: High	83	3	-	-	62,462	20
Stornoway: Martin's Memorial	300	11	-	145,727	70,547	80
Stornoway: St Columba	135	9	44	91,960	60,068	160
45. Orkney						
Birsay, Harray and Sandwick	300	27	36	36,811	26,196	35
East Mainland	224	20	13	22,045	18,028	19
Eday	8	-	-	-	1,989	-
Stronsay: Moncur Memorial	51	7	-	11,659	9,694	9
Evie	23	-	-	5,472	8,241	-
Firth	89	4	-	39,373	15,639	25
Rendall	44	5	-	15,097	6,689	20
Rousay	14	-	-	2,281	3,291	-
Flotta	24	7	-	-	2,978	-
Hoy and Walls	53	7	12	7,241	3,722	3
Orphir and Stenness	145	12	16	24,350	16,673	7
Kirkwall: East	347	21	25	79,247	43,587	17
Shapinsay	39	7	-	8,779	5,610	9
Kirkwall: St Magnus Cathedral	521	39	27	84,665	42,417	-
North Ronaldsay	7	2	-	-	1,391	-
Papa Westray	8	4	-	11,011	3,974	2
Westray	83	17	24	25,716	18,907	40
Sanday	50	4	8	7,863	7,134	-

Congregation	Com	Eld	G	In 16	M&M	–18
South Ronaldsay and Burray	135	11	17	17,326	10,845	8
Stromness	287	30	19	-	27,002	3
46. Shetland						
Burra Isle	33	6	11	12,687	5,611	12
Tingwall	48	11	12	30,399	20,883	35
Delting	68	-	14	14,079	12,427	-
Northmavine	60	6	-	7,927	7,604	-
Dunrossness and St Ninian's	39	-	-	-	11,667	-
Sandwick, Cunningsburgh & Quarff	61	8	12	23,471	14,492	17
Lerwick and Bressay	324	24	6	75,885	48,254	35
Nesting and Lunnasting	29	6	3	5,854	5,209	-
Whalsay and Skerries	172	14	15	-	14,026	20
Sandsting and Aithsting	35	7	-	7,817	4,950	16
Walls and Sandness	31	-	-	6,940	5,124	-
Unst and Fetlar	78	9	19	18,909	11,987	-
Yell	44	-	12	11,771	7,645	-
47. England						
Corby: St Andrew's	234	12	-	37,477	32,363	2
Corby: St Ninian's	293	14	-	44,263	30,425	10
Guernsey: St Andrew's in the Grange	181	20	-	70,547	43,600	21
Jersey: St Columba's	106	15	-	51,022	40,960	1
Liverpool: St Andrew's	24	-	-	-	12,206	-
London: Crown Court	218	31	3	-	58,768	14
London: St Columba's	870	55	-	-	188,015	25
Newcastle: St Andrew's	102	16	-	-	8,162	6

INDEX OF ADVERTISERS

INDEX OF MINISTERS

NOTE: Ministers who are members of a Presbytery are designated 'A' if holding a parochial appointment in that Presbytery, or 'B' if otherwise qualifying for membership. 'A-1, A-2' etc. indicate the numerical order of congregations in the Presbyteries of Edinburgh, Glasgow, and Hamilton.

Also included are ministers listed in Section 6:

(1) Ministers who have resigned their seat in Presbytery and hold a Practising Certificate (List 6-D)

(2) Ministers who have resigned their seat in Presbytery but who do not hold a Practising Certificate (List 6-E)

(3) Ministers serving overseas (List 6-J) – see also Presbyteries 48 and 49

(4) Ordained Local Ministers and Auxiliary Ministers, who are listed both in Presbyteries and in List 6-A and List 6-B respectively

(5) Ministers who have died since the publication of the last *Year Book* (List 6-R) NB *For a list of the Diaconate, see List 6-C.*

INDEX OF PARISHES AND PLACES

NOTE: Numbers on the right of the column refer to the Presbytery in which the district lies. Names in brackets are given for ease of identification. They may refer to the name of the parish, which may be different from that of the district, or they distinguish places with the same name, or they indicate the first named charge in a union.

INDEX OF SUBJECTS